The Whisperers

ORLANDO FIGES

The Whisperers

Private Life in Stalin's Russia

ALLEN LANE
an imprint of
PENGUIN BOOKS

ALLEN LANE

Published by the Penguin Group
Penguin Books Ltd, 80 Strand, London WC2R ORL, England
Penguin Group (USA) Inc., 375 Hudson Street, New York, New York 10014, USA
Penguin Group (Canada), 90 Eglinton Avenue East, Suite 700, Toronto, Ontario, Canada M4P 2Y3
(a division of Pearson Penguin Canada Inc.)
Penguin Ireland, 25 St Stephen's Green, Dublin 2, Ireland
(a division of Penguin Books Ltd)
Penguin Group (Australia), 250 Camberwell Road, Camberwell, Victoria 3124, Australia
(a division of Pearson Australia Group Pty Ltd)
Penguin Books India Pvt Ltd, 11 Community Centre, Panchsheel Park, New Delhi – 110 017, India
Penguin Group (NZ), 67 Apollo Drive, Rosedale, North Shore 0632, New Zealand
(a division of Pearson New Zealand Ltd)
Penguin Books (South Africa) (Pty) Ltd, 24 Sturdee Avenue, Rosebank, Johannesburg 2196, South Africa

Penguin Books Ltd, Registered Offices: 80 Strand, London WC2R ORL, England

www.penguin.com

First published 2007
1

Set in PostScript Adobe Sabon
Typeset by Rowland Phototypesetting Ltd, Bury St Edmunds, Suffolk
Printed in Great Britain by Clays Ltd, St Ives plc

A CIP catalogue record for this book is available from the British Library

ISBN: 978-0-713-99702-6

www.greenpenguin.co.uk

For my mother, Eva Figes (née Unger, Berlin 1932)
and to the memory of the family we lost

Contents

List of Illustrations

Note on Proper Names

Russian names are spelled in this book according to the standard (Library of Congress) system of transliteration, but some Russian spellings are slightly altered. To accommodate common English spellings of well-known Russian names I have changed the Russian 'ii' ending to a 'y' in surnames (for example, Trotskii becomes Trotsky) but not in all first names (for example, Georgii) or place names. To aid pronunciation I have opted for Pyotr instead of Petr, Semyon instead of Semen, Andreyev instead of Andreev, Yevgeniia instead of Evgeniia, and so on. In other cases I have chosen simple and familiar spellings that help the reader to identify with Russian names that feature prominently in the text (for example, Julia instead of Iuliia and Lydia instead of Lidiia). For the sake of clarity I have also dropped the Russian soft sign from all personal and place names (so that Iaroslavl' becomes Iaroslavl and Noril'sk becomes Norilsk). However, bibliographical references in the notes preserve the Library of Congress transliteration to aid those readers who wish to consult the published sources cited.

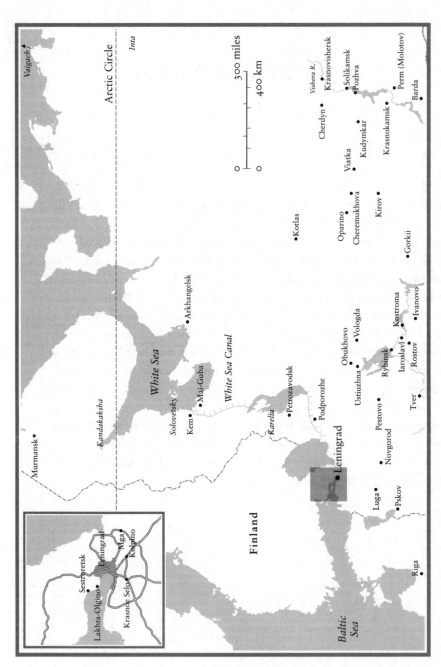

Northern European USSR

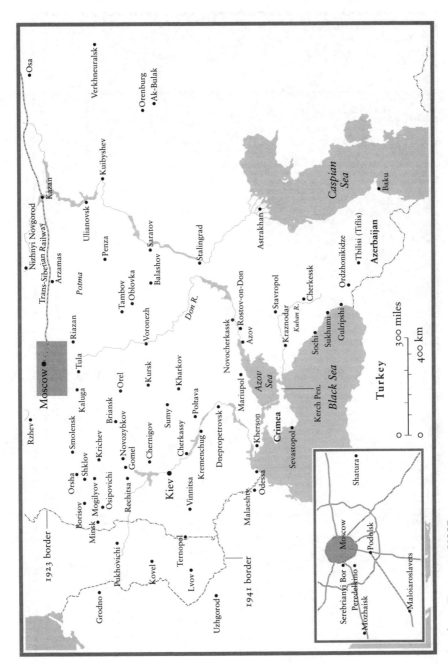

Southern European USSR

500 miles
1000 km

Severnaia
Zemlia

ARCTIC OCEAN

Kara Sea

Vaigach

Dudinka
Norilsk

Vorkuta

Arctic Circle

Inta

T h e U r a l s

Ob R.

Enisei R.

Lialia R.
Chermoz
Nizhnii Tagil
Chusovoe
Baraba
Tiumen
Szerdlovsk
Cheliabinsk
Magnitogorsk

Narym
Gerasimovka
Ilinka
Krivosheino

Omsk
Trans-Siberian Railway
Tomsk
Uiar
Kansk
Taishet
Marinsk
Krasnoiarsk
Abakan
Cheremukhova
Lake
Baikal
Irkutsk

Ekaterinoslav
Borovoe
Stolpovo
Barnaul
Tashtagol
Tashtyp
Akmolinsk
Semipalatinsk

Alzhir

Karaganda

Chelkar

Kazalinsk

Alma-Ata

Chimkent
Dzhambul
Tashkent

Mongolia

Western and Central Siberia

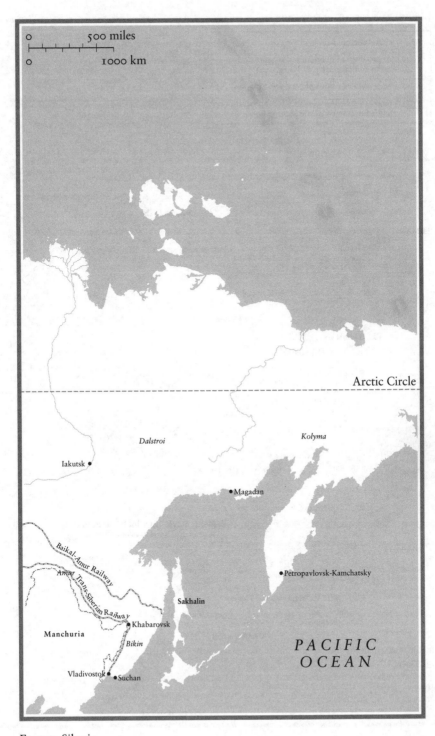

Eastern Siberia

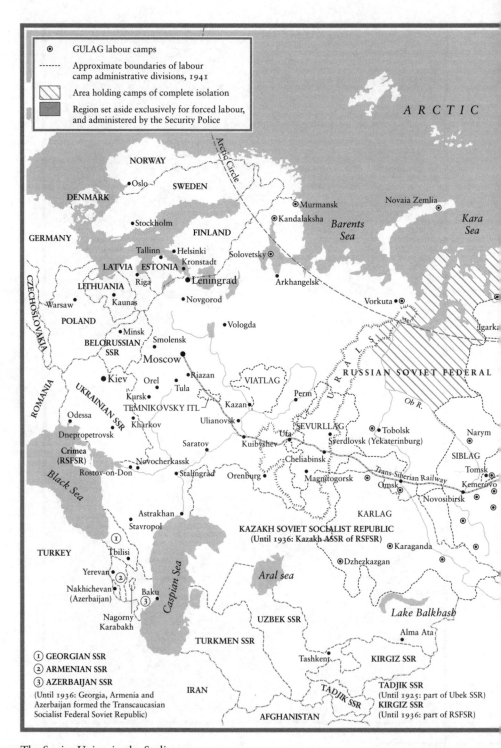

The Soviet Union in the Stalin era

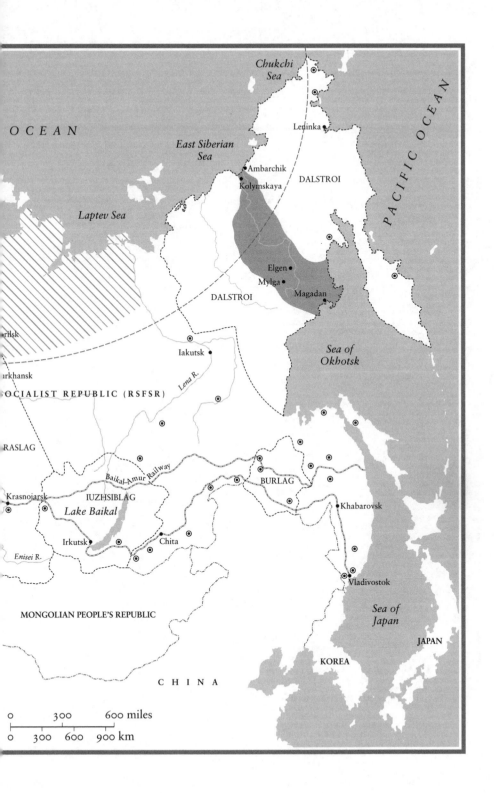

OCEAN

Chukchi Sea

Leninka

East Siberian Sea

Ambarchik

Kolymskaya

DALSTROI

Laptev Sea

Elgen

Mylga

Magadan

DALSTROI

rilsk

Iakutsk

rkhansk

Lena R.

OCIALIST REPUBLIC (RSFSR)

Sea of Okhotsk

RASLAG

Baikal-Amur Railway

BURLAG

Krasnojarsk

IUZHSIBLAG

Lake Baikal

Khabarovsk

Irkutsk

Chita

Enisei R.

Vladivostok

MONGOLIAN PEOPLE'S REPUBLIC

Sea of Japan

JAPAN

KOREA

C H I N A

PACIFIC OCEAN

| 0 | 300 | 600 miles |
| 0 | 300 | 600 | 900 km |

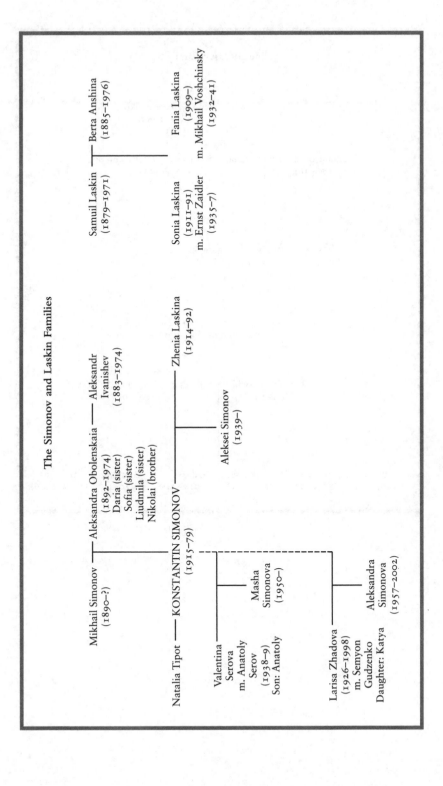

The Simonov and Laskin Families

Mikhail Simonov ——— Aleksandra Obolenskaia ——— Aleksandr
(1890–?)   (1892–1974)   Ivanishev
                        Daria (sister)   (1883–1974)
                        Sofia (sister)
                        Liudmila (sister)
                        Nikolai (brother)

Samuil Laskin ——— Berta Anshina
(1879–1971)   (1885–1976)

Natalia Tipot ——— KONSTANTIN SIMONOV
                     (1915–79)

Zhenia Laskina
(1914–92)

Aleksei Simonov
(1939–)

Sonia Laskina
(1911–91)
m. Ernst Zaidler
(1935–7)

Fania Laskina
(1909–)
m. Mikhail Voshchinsky
(1932–41)

Valentina
Serova
m. Anatoly
Serov
(1938–9)
Son: Anatoly

Masha
Simonova
(1950–)

Larisa Zhadova
(1926–1998)
m. Semyon
Gudzenko
Daughter: Katya

Aleksandra
Simonova
(1957–2002)

The Bushuev Family

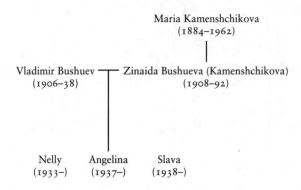

Maria Kamenshchikova
(1884–1962)

Vladimir Bushuev ⎯⊤⎯ Zinaida Bushueva (Kamenshchikova)
(1906–38)   (1908–92)

Nelly   Angelina   Slava
(1933–)   (1937–)   (1938–)

The Golovin Family

Nikolai Golovin ⎯⊤⎯ Yevdokiia Golovina (Soboleva)
(1882–1958)   (1886–1955)

Ivan   Maria   Nikolai   Aleksei   Anatoly   Antonina
(1907–41)   (1910–85)   (1912–41)   (1915–74)   (1920–41)   (1923–2006)

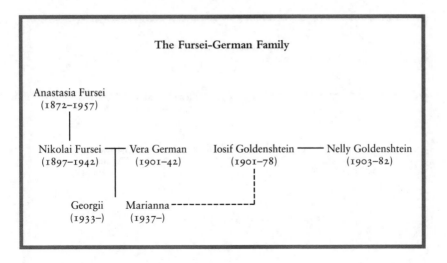

The Fursei–German Family

Anastasia Fursei
(1872–1957)

Nikolai Fursei ── Vera German   Iosif Goldenshtein ── Nelly Goldenshtein
(1897–1942)   (1901–42)   (1901–78)   (1903–82)

Georgii   Marianna
(1933–)   (1937–)

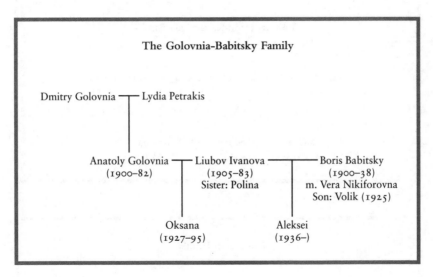

The Golovnia–Babitsky Family

Dmitry Golovnia ── Lydia Petrakis

Anatoly Golovnia ── Liubov Ivanova ── Boris Babitsky
(1900–82)   (1905–83)   (1900–38)
                     Sister: Polina   m. Vera Nikiforovna
                                       Son: Volik (1925)

Oksana   Aleksei
(1927–95)   (1936–)

The Konstantinov Family

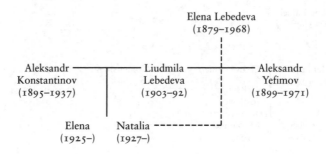

Elena Lebedeva
(1879–1968)

Aleksandr —————— Liudmila —————— Aleksandr
Konstantinov   Lebedeva   Yefimov
(1895–1937)   (1903–92)   (1899–1971)

Elena   Natalia ------------
(1925–)   (1927–)

The Nizovtsev-Karpitskaia Family

Pyotr Nizovtsev —— Anna Karpitskaia —— Mikhail Sizov
(1893–1937)   (1900–37)   (1898–1981)

Aleksei   Vladimir   Marksena
(1927–)   (1932–?)   (1923–)

The Slavin Family

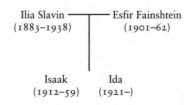

Ilia Slavin —————— Esfir Fainshtein
(1883–1938)   (1901–62)

Isaak   Ida
(1912–59)   (1921–)

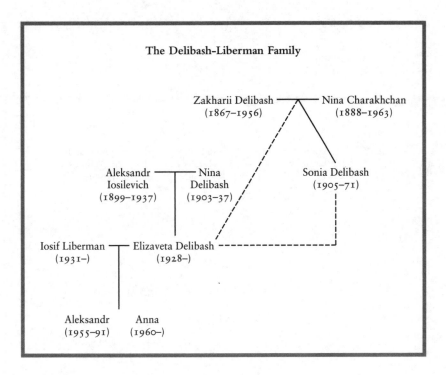

The Delibash-Liberman Family

Zakharii Delibash   Nina Charakhchan
(1867–1956)   (1888–1963)

Aleksandr   Nina
Iosilevich   Delibash   Sonia Delibash
(1899–1937)   (1903–37)   (1905–71)

Iosif Liberman   Elizaveta Delibash
(1931–)   (1928–)

Aleksandr   Anna
(1955–91)   (1960–)

Introduction

Antonina Golovina was eight years old when she was exiled with her mother and two younger brothers to the remote Altai region of Siberia. Her father had been arrested and sentenced to three years in a labour camp as a 'kulak' or 'rich' peasant during the collectivization of their northern Russian village, and the family had lost its household property, farming tools and livestock to the collective farm. Antonina's mother was given just an hour to pack a few clothes for the long journey. The house where the Golovins had lived for generations was then destroyed, and the rest of the family dispersed: Antonina's older brothers and sister, her grandparents, uncles, aunts and cousins fled in all directions to avoid arrest, but most were caught by the police and exiled to Siberia, or sent to work in the labour camps of the Gulag, many of them never to be seen again.

Antonina spent three years in a 'special settlement', a logging camp with five wooden barracks along a river bank where a thousand 'kulaks' and their families were housed. After two of the barracks were destroyed by heavy snow in the first winter, some of the exiles had to live in holes dug in the frozen ground. There were no food deliveries, because the settlement was cut off by the snow, so people had to live from the supplies they had brought from home. So many of them died from hunger, cold and typhus that they could not all be buried; their bodies were left to freeze in piles until the spring, when they were dumped in the river.

Antonina and her family returned from exile in December 1934, and, rejoined by her father, moved into a one-room house in Pestovo, a town full of former 'kulaks' and their families. But the trauma she had suffered left a deep scar on her consciousness, and the deepest wound of all was the stigma of her 'kulak' origins. In a society where social class was everything, Antonina was branded a 'class enemy', excluded from higher schools and many jobs and always vulnerable to persecution and arrest in the waves of terror that swept across the country during Stalin's reign. Her sense of social inferiority bred in Antonina what she herself describes as a 'kind of fear', that 'because we were kulaks the regime might do anything to us, we had no rights, we had to suffer in silence'. She was too afraid to defend herself against the children who bullied her at school. On one occasion, Antonina was singled out for punishment by one of her teachers, who said in front of the whole class that 'her sort' were 'enemies of the people, wretched kulaks! You certainly deserved to be deported, I hope you're all exterminated here!' Antonina felt a deep injustice and anger that made her want to shout out in protest. But she was silenced by an even deeper fear.[1]

This fear stayed with Antonina all her life. The only way that she could conquer it was to immerse herself in Soviet society. Antonina was an intelligent young woman with a strong sense of individuality. Determined to overcome the stigma of her birth, she studied hard at school so that one day she could gain acceptance as a social equal. Despite discrimination, she did well in her studies and gradually grew in confidence. She even joined the Komsomol, the Communist Youth League, whose leaders turned a blind eye to her 'kulak' origins because they valued her initiative and energy. At the age of eighteen Antonina made a bold decision that set her destiny: she concealed her background from the authorities – a high-risk strategy – and even forged her papers so that she could go to medical school. She never spoke about her family to any of her friends or colleagues at the Institute of Physiology in Leningrad, where she worked for forty years. She became a member of the Communist Party (and remained one until its abolition in 1991), not because she believed in its ideology, or so she now claims, but because she wanted to divert suspicion from herself and protect her family. Perhaps she also felt that joining the Party would help her career and bring her professional recognition.

Antonina concealed the truth about her past from both her husbands, each of whom she lived with for over twenty years. She and her first husband, Georgii Znamensky, were life-long friends, but they rarely spoke to one another about their families' pasts. In 1987, Antonina received a visit from one of Georgii's aunts, who let slip that he was the son of a tsarist naval officer executed by the Bolsheviks. All those years,

Antonina Golovina, 1943

without knowing it, Antonina had been married to a man who, like her, had spent his youth in labour camps and 'special settlements'.

Antonina's second husband, an Estonian called Boris Ioganson, also came from a family of 'enemies of the people'. His father and grandfather had both been arrested in 1937, although she did not discover this or tell him about her own hidden past until the early 1990s, when, encouraged by the policies of glasnost introduced by Mikhail Gorbachev and by the open criticisms of the Stalinist repressions in the media, they began to talk at last. Antonina and Georgii also took this opportunity to reveal their secret histories, which they had concealed from each other for over forty years. But they did not speak about such things to their daughter Olga, a schoolteacher, because they feared a Communist backlash and thought that ignorance would protect her if the Stalinists returned. It was only very gradually in the mid-1990s that Antonina at last overcame her fear and summoned up the courage to tell her daughter about her 'kulak' origins.

The Whisperers reveals the hidden histories of many families like the Golovins, and together they illuminate, as never before, the inner world of ordinary Soviet citizens living under Stalin's tyranny. Many books describe the externals of the Terror – the arrests and trials, enslavements and killings of the Gulag – but *The Whisperers* is the first to explore in depth its influence on personal and family life. How did Soviet people live their private lives in the years of Stalin's rule? What did they really think and feel? What sort of private life was possible in the cramped communal apartments, where the vast majority of the urban population lived, where rooms were shared by a whole family and often more than one, and every conversation could be overheard in the next room? What did private life mean when the state touched almost every aspect of it through legislation, surveillance and ideological control?

Millions of people lived like Antonina in a constant state of fear because their relatives had been repressed. How did they cope with that insecurity? What sort of balance could they strike between their natural feelings of injustice and alienation from the Soviet system and their need to find a place in it? What adjustments did they have to make to overcome the stigma of their 'spoilt biography' and become accepted as equal members of society? Reflecting on her life, Antonina says that she never really believed in the Party and its ideology, although clearly she took pride in her status as a Soviet professional, which entailed her acceptance of the system's basic goals and principles in her activities as a doctor. Perhaps she led a double life, conforming to Soviet norms in her public life whilst continuing to feel the counter-pull of her family's peasant-Christian values in her private life. Many Soviet people lived by such dualities. But equally there were 'kulak' children, not to mention those born to families of noble or bourgeois origin, who broke completely with their past and immersed themselves in the Soviet system ideologically and emotionally.

The moral sphere of the family is the main arena of *The Whisperers*. The book explores how families reacted to the various pressures of the Soviet regime. How did they preserve their traditions and beliefs, and pass them down to their children, if their values were in conflict with the public goals and morals of the Soviet system inculcated in the younger generation through schools and institutions like the Komsomol? How did living in a system ruled by terror affect intimate relationhips? What did people think when a husband or a wife, a father or a mother was suddenly arrested as an 'enemy of the people'? As loyal Soviet citizens how did they resolve the conflict in their minds between trusting the people they loved and believing in the government they feared? How could human feelings and emotions retain any force in the moral vacuum of the Stalinist regime? What were the strategies for survival, the silences, the lies, the friendships and betrayals, the moral compromises and accommodations that shaped millions of lives?

For few families were unaffected by the Stalinist Terror. By conservative estimates, approximately 25 million people were repressed by the Soviet regime between 1928, when Stalin seized control of the Party leadership, and 1953, when the dictator died, and his reign of terror, if not the system he had developed over the past quarter of a century, was at last brought to an end. These 25 million – people shot by execution squads, Gulag prisoners, 'kulaks' sent to 'special settlements', slave labourers of various kinds and members of deported nationalities – represent about one-eighth of the Soviet population, approximately 200 million people in 1941, or, on average, one person for every 1.5 families in the Soviet Union. These figures do not include famine victims or war dead.[2] In addition to the millions who died, or were enslaved, there were tens of millions, the relatives of Stalin's victims, whose lives were damaged in disturbing ways, with profound social consequences that are still felt today. After years of separation by the Gulag, families could not be reunited easily; relationships were lost; and there was no longer any 'normal life' to which people could return.

A silent and conformist population is one lasting consequence of Stalin's reign. Families like the Golovins learned not to talk about their past – some like Antonina even hiding it from their closest friends and relatives. Children were taught to hold their tongues, not to speak about their families to anyone, not to judge or criticize anything they saw outside the home. 'There were certain rules of listening and talking that we children had to learn,' recalls the daughter of a middle-ranking Bolshevik official who grew up in the 1930s:

What we overheard the adults say in a whisper, or what we heard them say behind our backs, we knew we could not repeat to anyone. We would be in trouble if we even let them know that we had heard what they had said. Sometimes the adults would say something and then would tell us, 'The walls have ears,' or 'Watch your tongue,' or some other expression, which we understood to mean that what they had just said was not meant for us to hear.[3]

Another woman, whose father was arrested in 1936, remembers:

We were brought up to keep our mouths shut. 'You'll get into trouble for your tongue' – that's what people said to us children all the time. We went through life afraid to talk. Mama used to say that every other person was an informer. We were afraid of our neighbours, and especially of the police . . . Even today, if I see a policeman, I begin to shake with fear.[4]

In a society where it was thought that people were arrested for loose tongues, families survived by keeping to themselves. They learned to live double lives, concealing from the eyes and ears of dangerous neighbours, and sometimes even from their own children, information and opinions, religious beliefs, family values and traditions, and modes of private existence that clashed with Soviet public norms. They learned to whisper.

The Russian language has two words for a 'whisperer' – one for somebody who whispers out of fear of being overheard (*shepchushchii*), another for the person who informs or whispers behind people's backs to the authorities (*sheptun*). The distinction has its origins in the idiom of the Stalin years, when the whole of Soviet society was made up of whisperers of one sort or another.

The Whisperers is not about Stalin, although his presence is felt on every page, or directly about the politics of his regime; it is about the way that Stalinism entered people's minds and emotions, affecting all their values and relationships. The book does not attempt to solve the riddle of the Terror's origins, or to chart the rise and fall of the Gulag; but it does set out to explain how the police state was able to take root in Soviet society and involve millions of ordinary people as silent bystanders and collaborators in its system of terror. The real power and lasting legacy of the Stalinist system were neither in the structures of the state, nor in the cult of the leader, but, as the Russian historian Mikhail Gefter once remarked, 'in the Stalinism that entered into all of us'.[5]

Historians have been slow to enter the inner world of Stalin's Russia. Until recently, their research was concerned mostly with the public sphere, with politics and ideology, and with the collective experience of the 'Soviet masses'. The individual – in so far as he appeared at all – featured mainly as a letter-writer to the authorities (i.e. as a public actor rather than as a private person or family member). The private sphere of ordinary people was largely hidden from view. Sources were the obvious problem. Most of the personal collections (*lichnye fondy*) in the former Soviet and Party archives belonged to well-known figures in the world of politics, science and culture. The documents in these collections were carefully selected by their owners for donation to the state and relate mainly to these figures' public lives. Of the several thousand personal collections surveyed in the early stages of the research for this book, not more than a handful revealed anything of family or personal life.*

The memoirs published in the Soviet Union, or accessible in Soviet archives before 1991, are also generally unrevealing about the private experience of the people who wrote them, although there are some exceptions, particularly among those published in the glasnost period after 1985.[6] The memoirs by intellectual émigrés from the Soviet Union and Soviet survivors of the Stalinist repressions published in the West are hardly less problematic, although they were widely greeted as the 'authentic voice' of 'the silenced', which told us what it had 'been like' to live through the Stalin Terror as an ordinary citizen.[7] By the height of the Cold War, in the early 1980s, the Western image of the Stalinist regime was dominated by these intelligentsia narratives of survival, particularly those by Yevgeniia Ginzburg and Nadezhda Mandelshtam, which provided first-hand evidence for the liberal idea of the individual human spirit as a force of internal opposition to Soviet tyranny.[8] This moral vision – fulfilled and symbolized by the victory of 'democracy' in 1991 – had a powerful influence on the memoirs that were written in enormous numbers after the collapse of the Soviet regime.[9] It also had an impact on historians, who after 1991 were more inclined than they had been before to emphasize the forces of popular resistance to the Stalinist dictatorship.[10] But while these memoirs speak a truth for many people who survived the Terror, particularly for the intelligentsia strongly committed to ideals of freedom and individualism, they do not speak for the millions of ordinary people, including many victims of the Stalinist regime, who did not share this inner freedom or feeling of dissent, but, on the contrary, silently accepted and internalized the system's basic values, conformed to its public rules and perhaps collaborated in the perpetration of its crimes.

The diaries that emerged from the archives seemed at first more promising. They are of all kinds (writers' diaries, working diaries, literary almanacs, scrapbooks, daily chronicles, and so on) but relatively few from the Stalin period reveal anything reliably – without intrusive

---

*The personal collections held in the archives of science, literature and art (e.g. SPbF ARAN, RGALI, IRL RAN) are sometimes more revealing, although most of these have closed sections in which the most private documents are contained. After 1991, some of the former Soviet archives took in personal collections donated by ordinary families – for example, TsMAMLS, which has a wide range of private papers belonging to Muscovites.

interpretative frameworks – about their writer's feelings and opinions. Not many people ran the risk of writing private diaries in the 1930s and 1940s. When a person was arrested – and almost anyone could be at almost any time – the first thing to be confiscated was his diary, which was likely to be used as incriminating evidence if it contained thoughts or sentiments that could be interpreted as 'anti-Soviet' (the writer Mikhail Prishvin wrote his diary in a tiny scrawl, barely legible with a magnifying glass, to conceal his thoughts from the police in the event of his arrest and the seizure of the diary). On the whole the diaries published in the Soviet period were written by intellectuals who were very careful with their words.[11] After 1991, more diaries – including some by people from the middling and lower echelons of Soviet society – began to appear from the former Soviet archives or came to light through voluntary initiatives like the People's Archive in Moscow (TsDNA).[12] But overall the corpus of Stalin-era diaries remains small (though more may yet be found in the archives of the former KGB), far too small for broad conclusions to be drawn from them about the inner world of ordinary citizens. An additional problem for the historian of private life is the 'Soviet-speak' in which many of these diaries are written and the con-formist ideas they express; without knowledge of the motives people had (fear, belief or fashion) to write their diaries in this way, they are difficult to interpret.[13]

In recent years a number of historians have focused their attention on 'Soviet subjectivity', emphasizing from their reading of literary and private texts (above all diaries) the degree to which the interior life of the individual citizen was dominated by the regime's ideology.[14] Accord-ing to some, it was practically impossible for the individual to think or feel outside the terms defined by the public discourse of Soviet politics, and any other thoughts or emotions were likely to be felt as a 'crisis of the self' demanding to be purged from the personality.[15] The internaliz-ation of Soviet values and ideas was indeed characteristic of many of the subjects in The Whisperers, although few of them identified with the Stalinist system in the self-improving fashion which these historians have suggested was representative of 'Soviet subjectivity'. The Soviet mentalities reflected in this book in most cases occupied a region of the consciousness where older values and beliefs had been suspended or suppressed; they were adopted by people, not so much from a burning desire to 'become Soviet', as from a sense of shame and fear. This was the sense in which Antonina resolved to do well at school and become an equal in society – so that she could overcome her feelings of inferiority (which she experienced as a 'kind of fear') as the child of a 'kulak'. Immersion in the Soviet system was a means of survival for most people, including many victims of the Stalinist regime, a necessary way of silencing their doubts and fears, which, if voiced, could make their lives impossible. Believing and collaborating in the Soviet project was a way to make sense of their suffering, which without this higher purpose might reduce them to despair. In the words of another 'kulak' child, a man exiled for many years as an 'enemy of the people' who nonetheless remained a convinced Stalinist throughout his life, 'believing in the justice of Stalin . . . made it easier for us to accept our punishments, and it took away our fear'.[16]

Such mentalities are less often reflected in Stalin-era diaries and letters – whose content was generally dictated by Soviet rules of writing and propriety that did not allow the acknowledgement of fear – than they are in oral history.[17] Historians of the Stalinist regime have turned increasingly to the techniques of oral history.[18] Like any other discipline that is hostage to the tricks of memory, oral history has its methodological difficulties, and in Russia, a nation taught to whisper, where the memory of Soviet history is overlaid with myths and ideologies, these problems are especially acute. Having lived in a society where millions were arrested for speaking inadvertently to informers, many older people are extremely wary of talking to researchers wielding microphones (devices associated with the KGB). From fear or shame or stoicism, these survivors have suppressed their painful memories. Many are unable to reflect about their lives, because they have grown so accustomed to avoiding awkward questions about anything, not least their own moral choices at defining moments of their personal advancement in the Soviet system. Others are reluctant to admit to actions of which they are ashamed, often justifying their behaviour by citing motives and beliefs that they have imposed on their pasts. Despite these challenges, and in many ways because of them, oral history has enormous benefits for the historian of private life, provided it is handled properly. This means rigorously cross-examining the evidence of interviews and checking it, wherever possible, against the written records in family and public archives.

The Whisperers draws on hundreds of family archives (letters, diaries, personal papers, memoirs, photographs and artefacts) concealed by survivors of the Stalin Terror in secret drawers and under mattresses in private homes across Russia until only recently. In each family extensive interviews were carried out with the oldest relatives, who were able to explain the context of these private documents and place them within the family's largely unspoken history. The oral history project connected with the research for this book, which focuses on the interior world of families and individuals, differs markedly from previous oral histories of the Soviet period, which were mainly sociological, or concerned with the external details of the Terror and the experience of the Gulag.[19] These materials have been assembled in a special archive, which represents one of the biggest collections of documents about private life in the Stalin period.*

The families whose stories are related in *The Whisperers* represent a broad cross-section of Soviet society. They come from diverse social backgrounds, from cities, towns and villages throughout Russia; they include families that were repressed and families whose members were involved in the system of repression as NKVD agents or administrators of the Gulag. There are also families that were untouched by Stalin's Terror, although statistically there were very few of these.

From these materials, *The Whisperers* charts the story of a generation born in the first years of the Revolution, mostly between 1917 and 1925, whose lives thus followed the trajectory of the Soviet system. In its later chapters the book gives voice to their descendants as well. A multi-generational approach is important to understanding the legacies of the regime. For three-quarters of a century the Soviet system exerted its influence on the moral sphere of the family; no other totalitarian system had such a profound impact on the private lives of its subjects – not even Communist China (the Nazi dictatorship, which is frequently compared to the Stalinist regime, lasted just twelve years). The attempt to understand the Stalinist phenomenon in the *longue durée* also sets this

---

*Most of the archives were collected by the author in collaboration with the Memorial Society, a human rights and historical association organized in the late 1980s to represent and commemorate the victims of Soviet repression. Housed in the archives of the Memorial Society in St Petersburg (MSP), Moscow (MM) and Perm (MP), most of them are also available on line (http://www.orlandofiges.com) together with the transcripts and sound extracts of the interviews. Some of the materials are available in English. For more details on the research project connected with this book see the Afterword and Acknowledgements below.

book apart. Previous histories of the subject have focused mainly on the 1930s – as if an explanation of the Great Terror of 1937–38 were all one needs to grasp the essence of the Stalinist regime. The Great Terror was by far the most murderous episode in Stalin's reign (it accounted for 85 per cent of political executions between 1917 and 1955). But it was only one of many series of repressive waves (1918–21, 1928–31, 1934–5, 1937–8, 1943–6, 1948–53), each one drowning many lives; the population of the Gulag's labour camps and 'special settlements' peaked not in 1938 but in 1953; and the impact of this long reign of terror continued to be felt by millions of people for many decades after Stalin's death.

The family histories interwoven through the public narrative of *The Whisperers* are probably too numerous to be followed by the reader as individual narratives, although the index can be used to connect them in this way. They are rather to be read as variations of a common history – of the Stalinism that marked the life of every family. But there are several families, including the Golovins, whose stories run throughout the narrative, and there is a family tree for each of these. At the heart of *The Whisperers* stand the Laskins and the Simonovs, families connected through marriage, whose contrasting fortunes in the Stalin Terror became tragically intertwined.

Konstantin Simonov (1915–79) is the central figure and perhaps (depending on your view) the tragic hero of *The Whisperers*. Born into a noble family that suffered from repression by the Soviet regime, Simonov remade himself as a 'proletarian writer' during the 1930s. Although he is largely forgotten today, he was a major figure in the Soviet literary establishment – the recipient of six Stalin Prizes, a Lenin Prize and a Hero of Socialist Labour. He was a talented lyric poet; his novels dealing with the war were immensely popular; his plays may have been weak and propagandistic, but he was a first-rate journalist, one of Russia's finest in the war; and in later life he was a superb memoirist, who honestly examined his own sins and moral compromises with the Stalinist regime. In 1939, Simonov married Yevgeniia Laskina, the youngest of three daughters in a Jewish family that had come to Moscow from the Pale of Settlement, but he soon abandoned her and their baby son to pursue the beautiful actress Valentina Serova – a romance that inspired his most famous poem, 'Wait For Me' (1941), which was known by heart by almost every soldier fighting to return to a girlfriend or a wife. Simonov became an important figure in the Writers' Union between 1945 and 1953, a time when the leaders of Soviet literature were called upon by Stalin's ideologues to take part in the persecution of their fellow writers who were deemed too liberal, and to add their voice to the campaign against the Jews in the arts and sciences. One of the victims of this official anti-Semitism was the Laskin family, yet by this time Simonov was too involved in the Stalinist regime to help them; perhaps in any case there was nothing he could do.

Simonov was a complex character. From his parents he inherited the public-service values of the aristocracy and, in particular, its ethos of military duty and obedience which in his mind became assimilated to the Soviet virtues of public activism and patriotic sacrifice, enabling him to take his place in the Stalinist hierarchy of command. Simonov had many admirable human qualities. If it was possible to be a 'good Stalinist', he might be counted in that category. He was honest and sincere, orderly and strictly disciplined, though not without considerable warmth and charm. An activist by education and by temperament, he lost himself in the Soviet system at an early age and lacked the means to liberate himself from its moral pressures and demands. In this sense Simonov embodied all the moral conflicts and dilemmas of his generation – those whose lives were overshadowed by the Stalinist regime – and to understand his thoughts and actions is perhaps to understand his times.

I

Children of 1917

(1917–28)

I

Elizaveta Drabkina did not recognize her father when she saw him at the Smolny Institute, the Bolshevik headquarters, in October 1917. She had last seen him when she was only five years old, just before he had disappeared into the revolutionary underground. Now, twelve years later, she had forgotten what he looked like. She knew him only by his Party pseudonym. As a secretary at the Smolny Institute, Elizaveta was familiar with the name 'Sergei Gusev' from dozens of decrees which he had signed as Chairman of the Military Revolutionary Committee of the Petrograd Soviet, the body placed in charge of law and order in the capital. Hurrying along the Smolny's endless vaulted corridors, where resting soldiers and Red Guards jeered and whistled as she passed, she had distributed these decrees to the makeshift offices of the new Soviet government, housed in the barrack-like classrooms of this former school for noblewomen. But when she told the other secretaries that the signature belonged to her long-lost father, none of them saw anything remarkable in that fact. There was never any suggestion that she should contact him. In these circles, where every Bolshevik was expected to subordinate his personal interests to the common cause, it was considered 'philistine' to think about one's private life at a time when the Party was engaged in the decisive struggle for the liberation of humanity.[1]

In the end, hunger drove Elizaveta to approach her father. She had just finished lunch in the smoke-filled basement dining hall when a small but muscular and handsome man in military dress and a pince-nez came in, trailed by a retinue of Party workers and Red Guards, and sat down at the long central table, where two soldiers were serving cabbage soup and porridge to the eager proletarians. Elizaveta was still hungry. From

The four secretaries of Iakov Sverdlov, chief Party organizer of the
Bolsheviks, the Smolny Institute, October 1917: Drabkina second from right

a smaller table in the corner, she watched the new arrival as he ate his
soup with a spoon in one hand and, with a pencil in the other, signed
the papers his followers placed in front of him.

Suddenly I heard someone call him 'Comrade Gusev'.

So this must be my father, I realized. Without thinking, I stood up and squeezed
my way around the crowded tables towards him.

'Comrade Gusev, I need you,' I said. He turned to me. He looked very tired.
His eyes were red from lack of sleep.

'I am listening, comrade!'

'Comrade Gusev, I am your daughter. Give me three roubles for a meal.'

Perhaps he was so exhausted that all he heard was my request for three
roubles.

'Of course, comrade,' Gusev said, reaching into his pocket and pulling out a
green three-rouble note. I took the money, thanked him, and bought another
lunch.[2]

Lenin loved this story. He often called on Drabkina to retell it in the
years before his death, in 1924, when she became close to him. The tale
took on legendary status in Party circles, illustrating the Bolshevik ideal
of personal sacrifice and selfless dedication to the revolutionary cause.
As Stalin was to say, 'A true Bolshevik shouldn't and couldn't have a
family, because he should give himself wholly to the Party.'[3]

The Drabkins were a good example of this revolutionary principle. Elizaveta's father (whose real name was Iakov Drabkin) had joined Lenin's Social Democrats as a schoolboy in 1895. Her mother, Feodosia, was an important agent ('Natasha') in the Party's underground who took her daughter along as a foil on the frequent trips she made to Helsingfors (Helsinki) to purchase ammunition for the revolutionaries in St Petersburg (the dynamite and cartridges were smuggled back in a bag containing Elizaveta's toys). After the abortive Revolution of 1905 Elizaveta's parents were driven into hiding by the tsar's police. The five-year-old girl went to live with her grandfather in Rostov, where she remained until the February Revolution of 1917, when all the revolutionaries were released by the newly installed Provisional Government.* Elizaveta was reunited with her mother in Petrograd (as St Petersburg was then called). She joined the Bolshevik Party, became a machine-gunner in the Red Guards, took part in the storming of the Winter Palace during the Bolshevik seizure of power on 25 October and was hired as a secretary to Iakov Sverdlov, chief Party organizer of the Bolsheviks. The job brought her to the Smolny, where her father, Gusev, worked.[4]

The Bolsheviks in power urged their rank and file to follow the example of the revolutionaries in tsarist Russia who had 'sacrificed their personal happiness and renounced their families to serve the working class'.† They made a cult of the 'selfless revolutionary', constructing a new morality in which all the old commandments were superseded by the single principle of service to the Party and its cause. In their utopian vision the revolutionary activist was the prototype of a new kind of

---

*The Provisional Government was formed by liberals and moderate socialists to steer the country through to the end of the First World War and the democratic election of a Constituent Assembly. Its political authority soon collapsed, however, as workers, peasants and soldiers formed their own local revolutionary committees, the Soviets in particular, to carry out a radical social revolution. It was in the name of the Soviets that Lenin's Bolsheviks seized power in October 1917. The Bolsheviks, who numbered about 350,000 members on the eve of their insurrection, represented the revolutionary arm of the Social Democratic (Marxist) Party, whose moderate wing, the Mensheviks, supported the Provisional Government. In March 1918, the Bolsheviks renamed themselves the Russian Communist Party.

†There were plenty of examples to choose from, such as Aleksandr Fadeyev (the father of the future writer), who left his wife and three children to dedicate himself to the 'people's cause' in 1905, or Liuba Radchenko, who left her husband and their two young daughters because, as she put it in her diary, 'it was the duty of the true revolutionary not to be tied down by a family' (RGAE, f. 9455, op. 3, d. 14, l. 56).

human being – a 'collective personality' living only for the common good – who would populate the future Communist society. Many socialists saw the creation of this human type as the fundamental goal of the Revolution. 'The new structure of political life demands from us a new structure of the soul,' wrote Maksim Gorky in the spring of 1917.[5]

For the Bolsheviks, the radical realization of the 'collective personality' involved 'blowing up the shell of private life'. To allow a 'distinction between private life and public life', maintained Lenin's wife, Nadezhda Krupskaia, 'will lead sooner or later to the betrayal of Communism'.[6] According to the Bolsheviks, the idea of 'private life' as separate from the realm of politics was nonsensical, for politics affected everything; there was nothing in a person's so-called 'private life' that was not political. The personal sphere should thus be subject to public supervision and control. Private spaces beyond the state's control were regarded by the Bolsheviks as dangerous breeding grounds for counter-revolutionaries, who had to be exposed and rooted out.

Elizaveta rarely saw her father after their encounter. They were both preoccupied with revolutionary activities. After 1917, Elizaveta continued to work in Sverdlov's office; during the Civil War (1918–20), she served in the Red Army, first as a medical assistant and later as a machine-gunner, fighting the White, or counter-revolutionary, armies and the Western powers that supported them in Siberia, the Baltic lands and south Russia. During the campaign against Admiral Kolchak's White Army on the Eastern Front she even fought under the command of her father, who by that time held a senior position in the Revolutionary Military Council, the central command organ of the Soviet forces, headed by Leon Trotsky. Elizaveta frequently heard her father address the soldiers, but she never approached him, because, as she later put it, she did not think that Bolsheviks should 'concern themselves with personal affairs'. They met only twice during the Civil War, once at Sverdlov's funeral in March 1919 and then, later that year, at an official meeting in the Kremlin. In the 1920s, when both father and daughter were actively involved in Party work in Moscow, they met more frequently, and even lived together for a while, but they never became close. They had spent so long apart that they could not form a familial relationship. 'My father never talked about himself to me,' Elizaveta recalled, 'and I realize now that I got to know him only after he died [in 1933], when people told me stories about him.'⁷

The Civil War was not just a military struggle against the White armies: it was a revolutionary war against the private interests of the old society. To fight the Whites the Bolsheviks developed their first version of the planned economy (War Communism), which would become a model for Stalin's Five Year Plans. They tried to stamp out private trade and property (there were even plans to replace money with universal rationing); seized the peasants' grain to feed the cities and the troops; conscripted millions of people into labour armies, which were used on the 'economic front' to cut down trees for fuel, build roads and repair railways; imposed experimental forms of collective labour and living in dormitories and barracks attached to factories; waged a war against religion, persecuting priests and believers and closing hundreds of churches; and silenced all dissent and opposition to the Dictatorship of the Proletariat. On the 'internal front' of the Civil War, the Bolsheviks unleashed a campaign of terror (the 'Red Terror') against 'the bourgeoisie' – former tsarist officials, landowners, merchants, 'kulak' peasants, petty traders and the old intelligentsia – whose individualistic values made them potential supporters of the Whites and other 'counter-revolutionaries'. This violent purging of society, the Bolsheviks believed, offered a short-cut to the Communist utopia.

By the spring of 1921, the policies of War Communism had ruined the Soviet economy and brought much of peasant Russia to the brink of famine. One-quarter of the peasantry in Soviet Russia was starving. Throughout the country the peasants rose up against the Bolshevik regime and its grain requisitionings in a series of rebellions which Lenin himself said were 'far more dangerous than all the Whites put together'. In much of rural Russia Soviet power had virtually ceased to exist, as the peasants took control of the villages and cut off grain supplies to the cities. Hungry workers went on strike. The sailors of the Kronstadt naval base, who had helped the Bolsheviks seize power in nearby Petrograd in October 1917, now turned against them in a mutiny whose Anarchist-inspired banners of revolt called for free elections to the Soviets, 'freedom of speech, press and assembly for all who labour', and 'freedom for the peasants to toil the land as they see fit'. It was clear that the Bolsheviks were facing a revolutionary situation. 'We are barely holding on,' Lenin acknowledged at the start of March. Trotsky, who had called the Kronstadt sailors the 'pride and joy of the Revolution', led the assault against the naval base. Military might and ruthless terror were used in equal measure against the peasant uprisings. An estimated 100,000 people were imprisoned or deported and 15,000 people shot during the suppression of the revolts. But Lenin also realized that to stem the tide of popular revolt and get the peasants to resume food deliveries to the cities, the Bolsheviks would have to abandon the detested policies of War Communism and bring back free trade. Having defeated the White armies, the Bolsheviks surrendered to the peasantry.[8]

The New Economic Policy (NEP), which Lenin introduced at the Tenth Party Congress in March 1921, replaced food requisitioning with a relatively lenient tax in kind and legalized the return of small-scale private trade and manufacturing. It favoured agriculture and the production of consumer goods over the development of heavy industry. As Lenin saw it, the NEP was a temporary but necessary concession to the smallholding peasantry – wedded to the principles of private family production – to save the Revolution and get the country on its feet again. He talked about it lasting 'not less than a decade and probably more'. The restoration of the market brought back life to the Soviet economy. Private trade responded quickly to the chronic shortages that had built up in the years of Revolution and the Civil War. By 1921, the Soviet population was living in patched-up clothes and shoes, cooking with broken utensils, drinking from cracked cups. Everybody needed something new. Traders set up booths and stalls, flea-markets boomed, and peasant traders brought foodstuffs to the towns. Licensed by new laws, private cafés, shops and restaurants, night clubs and brothels, hospitals and clinics, credit and saving associations, even small-scale manufacturers sprang up like mushrooms after the rain. Moscow and Petrograd, graveyard cities in the Civil War, suddenly burst into life, with noisy traders, busy cabbies and bright shops lighting up the streets just as they had done before 1917.

To many Bolsheviks the return to the market seemed like a betrayal of the Revolution. The introduction of the NEP was met with deep suspicion by the Party's rank and file (even Lenin's 'favourite', Nikolai Bukharin, who later became the main defender of the NEP, warmed to it only slowly during the course of 1921–3), and Lenin had to use all his powers of persuasion and authority to force it through at the congress. Among the urban workers, in particular, there was a widespread feeling that the NEP was sacrificing their class interests to the peasantry, which was growing rich at their expense, because of higher food prices. It seemed to them that the boom in private trade would inevitably lead to a widening gap between rich and poor and to the restoration of capitalism. They dubbed the NEP the 'New Exploitation of the Proletariat'. Much of their anger was focused on the 'NEPmen', the private traders who thrived in the 1920s. In the popular imagination, formed by Soviet propaganda and cartoons, the 'NEPmen' dressed their wives and mistresses in diamonds and furs, drove around in huge imported cars, snored at the opera, sang in restaurants and boasted loudly in expensive hotel bars of the dollar fortunes they had wasted at the newly opened race-tracks and casinos. The legendary spending of this newly wealthy class, set against the backdrop of mass unemployment and urban poverty in the 1920s, gave rise to a bitter feeling of resentment among those who thought that the Revolution should end inequality.

On the 'internal front' the NEP entailed a reprieve for the vestiges of 'bourgeois culture' which Communism had promised to eliminate but could not yet do without. It brought a halt to the war against the old middle class and the professional intelligentsia, whose expertise was needed by the Soviet economy. Between 1924 and 1928 there was also a temporary relaxation in the war against religion: churches were no longer closed or the clergy persecuted at the rate that they had been before (or would be afterwards); although the propaganda war against the Church continued apace, people were allowed to observe their faith much as they had always done. Finally, the NEP allowed a breathing space for the old domestic habits and family traditions of private life, a source of real concern among many Bolsheviks, who feared that the customs and mentalities of Russia's 'petty bourgeoisie' – the millions of small-scale traders and producers whose numbers were swollen by the NEP – would hold back and even undermine their revolutionary campaign. 'Imprisoning the minds of millions of toilers,' Stalin declared in 1924, 'the attitudes and habits which we inherited from the old society are the most dangerous enemy of socialism.'[9]

The Bolsheviks envisaged the building of their Communist utopia as a constant battle against custom and habit. With the end of the Civil

War they prepared for a new and longer struggle on the 'internal front': a revolutionary war for the liberation of the communistic personality through the eradication of individualistic ('bourgeois') behaviour and deviant habits (prostitution, alcoholism, hooliganism and religion) inherited from the old society. There was little dispute among the Bolsheviks that this battle to transform human nature would take decades. There was only disagreement about when the battle should begin. Marx had taught that the alteration of consciousness was dependent on changes to the material base, and Lenin, when he introduced the NEP, affirmed that until the material conditions of a Communist society had been created – a process that would take an entire historical epoch – there was no point trying to engineer a Communist system of morality in private life. But most Bolsheviks did not accept that the NEP required a retreat from the private sphere. On the contrary, as they were increasingly inclined to think, active engagement was essential at every moment and in every battlefield of everyday life – in the family, the home and the inner world of the individual, where the persistence of old mentalities was a major threat to the Party's basic ideological goals. And as they watched the individualistic instincts of the 'petty-bourgeois' masses become stronger in the culture of the NEP, they redoubled their efforts. As Anatoly Lunacharsky wrote in 1927: 'The so-called sphere of private life cannot slip away from us, because it is precisely here that the final goal of the Revolution is to be reached.'[10]

The family was the first arena in which the Bolsheviks engaged the struggle. In the 1920s, they took it as an article of faith that the 'bourgeois family' was socially harmful: it was inward-looking and conservative, a stronghold of religion, superstition, ignorance and prejudice; it fostered egotism and material acquisitiveness, and oppressed women and children. The Bolsheviks expected that the family would disappear as Soviet Russia developed into a fully socialist system, in which the state took responsibility for all the basic household functions, providing nurseries, laundries and canteens in public centres and apartment blocks. Liberated from labour in the home, women would be free to enter the workforce on an equal footing with men. The patriarchal marriage, with its attendant sexual morals, would die out – to be replaced, the radicals believed, by 'free unions of love'.

As the Bolsheviks saw it, the family was the biggest obstacle to the socialization of children. 'By loving a child, the family turns him into an egotistical being, encouraging him to see himself as the centre of the universe,' wrote the Soviet educational thinker Zlata Lilina.[11] Bolshevik theorists agreed on the need to replace this 'egotistic love' with the 'rational love' of a broader 'social family'. *The ABC of Communism* (1919) envisaged a future society in which parents would no longer use the word 'my' to refer to their children, but would care for all the children in their community. Among the Bolsheviks there were different views about how long this change would take. Radicals argued that the Party should take direct action to undermine the family immediately, but most accepted the arguments of Bukharin and NEP theorists that in a peasant country such as Soviet Russia the family would remain for some time the primary unit of production and consumption and that it would weaken gradually as the country made the transition to an urban socialist society.

Meanwhile the Bolsheviks adopted various strategies – such as the transformation of domestic space – intended to accelerate the disintegration of the family. To tackle the housing shortages in the overcrowded cities the Bolsheviks compelled wealthy families to share their apartments with the urban poor – a policy known as 'condensation' (*uplotnenie*). During the 1920s the most common type of communal apartment (*kommunalka*) was one in which the original owners occupied the main rooms on the 'parade side' while the back rooms were filled by other families. At that time it was still possible for the former owners to select their co-inhabitants, provided they fulfilled the 'sanitary norm' (a per capita allowance of living space which fell from 13.5 square metres in 1926 to just 9 square metres in 1931). Many families brought in servants or acquaintances to prevent strangers being moved in to fill up the surplus living space. The policy had a strong ideological appeal, not just as a war on privilege, which is how it was presented in the propaganda of the new regime ('War against the Palaces!'), but also as part of a crusade to engineer a more collective way of life. By forcing people to share communal apartments, the Bolsheviks believed that they could make them communistic in their basic thinking and behaviour. Private space and property would disappear, the individual ('bourgeois') family would be replaced by communistic fraternity and organization, and the life of the individual would become immersed in the community. From the middle of the 1920s, new types of housing were designed with this transformation in mind. The most radical Soviet architects, like the

Constructivists in the Union of Contemporary Architects, proposed the complete obliteration of the private sphere by building 'commune houses' (*doma kommuny*) where all the property, including even clothes and underwear, would be shared by the inhabitants, where domestic tasks like cooking and childcare would be assigned to teams on a rotating basis, and where everybody would sleep in one big dormitory, divided by gender, with private rooms for sexual liaisons. Few houses of this sort were ever built, although they loomed large in the utopian imagination and futuristic novels such as Yevgeny Zamiatin's *We* (1920). Most of the projects which did materialize, like the Narkomfin (Ministry of Finance) house in Moscow (1930) designed by the Constructivist Moisei Ginzburg, tended to stop short of the full communal form and included both private living spaces and communalized blocks for laundries, baths, dining rooms and kitchens, nurseries and schools. Yet the goal remained to marshal architecture in a way that would induce the individual to move away from private ('bourgeois') forms of domesticity to a more collective way of life.[12]

The Bolsheviks also intervened more directly in domestic life. The new Code on Marriage and the Family (1918) established a legislative framework that clearly aimed to facilitate the breakdown of the traditional family. It removed the influence of the Church from marriage and divorce, making both a process of simple registration with the state. It granted the same legal rights to de facto marriages (couples living together) as it gave to legal marriages. The Code turned divorce from a luxury for the rich to something that was easy and affordable for all. The result was a huge increase in casual marriages and the highest rate of divorce in the world – three times higher than in France or Germany and twenty-six times higher than in England by 1926 – as the collapse of the Christian-patriarchal order and the chaos of the revolutionary years loosened sexual morals along with family and communal ties.[13]

In the early years of Soviet power, family breakdown was so common among revolutionary activists that it almost constituted an occupational hazard. Casual relationships were practically the norm in Bolshevik circles during the Civil War, when any comrade could be sent at a moment's notice to some distant sector of the front. Such relaxed attitudes remained common throughout the 1920s, as Party activists and their young emulators in the Komsomol (Communist Youth League) were taught to put their commitment to the proletariat before romantic love or family. Sexual promiscuity was more pronounced in the Party's youthful ranks than among Soviet youth in general. Many Bolsheviks regarded sexual licence as a form of liberation from bourgeois moral conventions and as a sign of 'Soviet modernity'. Some even advocated promiscuity as a way to counteract the formation of coupling relationships that separated lovers from the collective and detracted from their loyalty to the Party.[14]

It was a commonplace that the Bolshevik made a bad husband and father because the demands of the Party took him away from the home. 'We Communists don't know our own families,' remarked one Moscow Bolshevik. 'You leave early and come home late. You seldom see your wife and almost never see your children.' At Party congresses, where the issue was discussed throughout the 1920s, it was recognized that Bolsheviks were far more likely than non-Party husbands to abandon wives and families, and that this had much to do with the primacy of Party loyalties over sexual fidelity. But in fact the problem of absent wives and mothers was almost as acute in Party circles, as indeed it was in the broader circles of the Soviet intelligentsia, where most women were involved in the public sphere.[15]

Trotsky argued that the Bolsheviks were more affected than others by domestic breakdown because they were 'most exposed to the influence of new conditions'. As pioneers of a modern way of life, Trotsky wrote in 1923, the 'Communist vanguard merely passes sooner and more violently through what is inevitable' for the population as a whole.[16] In many Party households there was certainly a sense of pioneering a new type of family – one that liberated both parents for public activities – albeit at the cost of intimate involvement with their children.

Anna Karpitskaia and her husband Pyotr Nizovtsev were high-ranking Party activists in Leningrad (as Petrograd was called after Lenin's death). They lived in a private apartment near the Smolny Institute with their three children, including Marksena,* Anna's daughter from her first marriage, who was born in 1923. Marksena rarely saw her parents, who left for work before she awoke in the morning and returned very late at night. 'I felt the lack of a mother's attention,' recalls Marksena, 'and

---

*After Marx and Engels – one of many Soviet names made up from the annals of the Revolution after 1917. Other common 'Soviet' names included: Vladlen (Vladimir Lenin), Engelina, Ninel, Marlen (for Marx and Lenin) and Melor (for Marx, Engels, Lenin and October Revolution).

was always jealous of children whose mothers did not work.' In the absence of their parents the children were placed in the care of two servants, a housekeeper and a cook, both peasant women who had recently arrived from the countryside. However, as the eldest child, from the age of four, as far as she recalls, Marksena had 'complete authority and responsibility for the household'. The cook would ask her what to make for dinner and ask her for the money to buy food from a special store reserved for Party officials. Marksena would report to her mother if the servants broke the household rules, 'or if they did something I didn't think was right', but more often, she recalls, 'I would tell them off myself if they did anything I did not like.' Marksena felt responsible – she understood that it suited her mother to leave her in charge – and accepted this as natural: 'My mother made it clear that what went on at home was no concern of hers, and I never questioned this.'

Brought up to reflect the values of the new society, Marksena was a child of 1917. She was regarded by her parents as a 'small comrade'. She had no toys, no space of her own where she could play freely as a child. 'My parents treated me as an equal and spoke to me as an adult,' recalls Marksena. 'I was taught from an early age to be independent and to do everything for myself.' On her first morning at primary school, when she was only seven, her mother walked her to the school and told her to memorize the route – a complex journey of nearly three kilometres – so that she could walk home on her own that afternoon. 'From that day on, I always walked to school,' recalls Marksena. 'It never crossed my mind that anyone should walk with me.' Marksena bought all her own books and stationery from a shop in the city centre which took her an hour to reach by foot. From the age of eight she was going to the theatre on her own, using the pass her parents had for Party officials which let her sit in one of the boxes by the side of the stalls. 'No one ever told me what to do,' recalls Marksena. 'I brought myself up on my own.'

Marksena's parents were distant figures in her life. Even during holidays, they would travel on their own to one of the resorts for Party officials in the Crimea, leaving the children in Leningrad. Her parents did, however, impose their ideological rigidities, which Marksena recalls as a source of annoyance. Her mother would reprimand her for reading Pushkin and Tolstoy instead of the didactic books for children favoured by the Party, such as Vladimir Obruchev's scientific adventure *Land of Sannikov* (1926) or *The Republic of Shkid* (1927) by Grigorii Belykh and Aleksei Panteleyev, a story about homeless orphans sent to school in Leningrad, both of which were brought home by Anna and dutifully read by Marksena but then put in a cupboard and forgotten. Marksena was forbidden by her mother to invite friends home from school, because, she said, it was better that they did not see how comfortably the Party's leaders lived – albeit modestly and in a Spartan style – compared with their families. She was very seldom praised or given compliments by her parents, and almost never kissed or held. Her only source of affection was her grandmother, who looked after her when she was ill. 'I liked going to her house,' remembers Marksena. 'She paid me lots of attention. She taught me how to sew, how to thread a bead necklace. She had toys for me and even bought me a little wooden toy kitchen, which she set up in the corner of her room, where I liked to play.'[17]

An absence of parental affection was described by many children born to Party families after 1917. In this respect the child-rearing customs of the Soviet elite were not that different from those of the nineteenth-century Russian aristocracy, which took little interest in the nursery and left the children, from their earliest days, in the care of nannies, maids and other household servants.[18]

Angelina Yevseyeva was born in 1922 to a family of Bolsheviks. Her parents had met when they were fighting for the Red Army in the Civil War. Returning to Petrograd in 1920, her father became a commander of one of the divisions involved in the suppression of the Kronstadt mutiny. In 1925, he enrolled in the Military-Medical Academy, where he spent his evenings studying. Angelina's mother was an official in the Commissariat of Trade. Shortly after Angelina's birth she began attending the Institute of Foreign Trade, also studying in the evenings. Angelina recalls a childhood spent largely in the care of a housekeeper:

My mother loved me, she was patient and attentive, but not affectionate, she never indulged me or played with me as a child. She expected me to behave like an adult, and treated me like one . . . My father was entirely preoccupied by his work. I felt that I got in his way. I must have been a nuisance to my parents. I didn't like being at home. I grew up in the courtyard and the street and was a naughty child. Once, when I was 8, my father brought a fish tank back from a work trip to Moscow. Because he would not let me go out and play, I tipped over the tank and let all the fish spill out on to the floor. He beat me with a hose, and I shouted back: 'You're not a father, you're a stepmother, a stepmother!'[19]

Maria Budkevich was born in Moscow in 1923 to the family of a Party functionary at Military Encyclopedia, the main publisher of the Soviet armed forces. Her father lived in a separate apartment from the rest of the family, not because he was separated from Maria's mother, a researcher on the Party's history of the Civil War, but because he found it more convenient for his work to live on his own. Maria saw her father so infrequently that, at the age of five or six, she began to doubt that she had one. 'I did not understand what a father was,' she recalls. 'I knew that other girls had someone they called "papa", but I hardly ever saw my own father. He would suddenly appear one day from a trip abroad. There would be a great fanfare, with presents for everyone, and then he would disappear again.'[20]

Elena Bonner's parents were Party activists in Leningrad. They worked from early in the morning until late at night and rarely saw their children, who were left in the care of their grandmother. Elena longed for her mother's affection. She 'played at being a crybaby' and frequently pretended to be sick in order to force her mother to stay at home. She was envious of other children whose mothers did not work and seemed 'always very cheerful' by comparison. Even when her parents were at home they were so preoccupied by their Party work that they paid little attention to the children. When she was nine or ten, Elena recalls, 'my parents spent their evenings and nights writing brochures, which they said were on "questions of Party construction". For a long while I thought the Party built houses.'[21]

The Bonners lived in a special hostel for Party workers in the former Astoriia Hotel in Leningrad. Everything in the sparsely furnished rooms was geared towards their work. Until the 1930s, when Stalin started to reward his loyal officials with luxury apartments and consumer goods, most Party members lived in a similarly minimalist style. Even senior officials lived quite modestly. The family of Nikolai Semashko, the Commissar for Health from 1923 to 1930, occupied a small and barely furnished flat in the Narkomfin house in Moscow. 'They were never interested in any sort of *byt* [bourgeois comfort] or décor,' recalls one of their neighbours.[22]

The Bolshevik idealists of the 1920s made a cult of this Spartan way of life. They inherited a strong element of asceticism from the revolutionary underground, the source of their values and their principles in the early years of the Soviet regime. The rejection of material possessions was central to the culture and ideology of the Russian socialist intelligentsia, which strove to sweep away all signs of 'petty-bourgeois' domesticity – the ornamental china on the mantelpiece, the singing canaries, all the plants, soft furniture, family portraits and other banal objects of the domestic hearth – and move towards a higher and more spiritual existence. The battle against 'philistine *byt*' was at the heart of the revolutionary urge to establish a more communistic way of life. As the poet Maiakovsky wrote in 1921:

> From the wall Marx watches and watches
> And suddenly
> Opening his mouth wide,
> He starts howling:
> The Revolution is tangled up in philistine threads
> More terrible than Wrangel* is philistine *byt*
> Better
> To tear off the canaries' heads –
> So Communism
> Won't be struck down by canaries.[23]

In the Bolshevik aesthetic it was philistine to lavish attention on the decoration of one's home. The ideal 'living space' (as the home was called by Soviet officials) was minimally decorated and furnished. It was purely functional, with space-efficient furniture, like divans that doubled as beds. In the Bolshevik imagination this simple way of living was a form of liberation from bourgeois society in which people were enslaved by the cult of possessions. In *Cement* (1925), Fyodor Gladkov's influential novel, a man and wife, both Party activists, sacrifice their personal happiness and leave their home and daughter to help rebuild a cement factory destroyed by the Civil War. When the husband Gleb begins to miss the old domestic comforts of their home, he is soon reminded of a higher purpose by his wife: 'Do you want pretty flowers to bloom on the windowsill and a bed piled with pillows? No, Gleb, in the winter I live in an unheated room, and I eat in the communal kitchen. You see, I am a free Soviet citizen.'[24]

Among the Bolsheviks there was a similarly austere attitude towards personal appearance – fashionable clothes, elaborate hairstyles, jewellery,

*Leader of the White Armies in south Russia during the Civil War.

perfume and cosmetics were all consigned to the realm of vulgar *byt*. The 'new people' of the Party vanguard dressed in plain and simple clothes – in pseudo-proletarian or quasi-military dress – without any hint of adornment. During the time of the NEP, when the Bolshevik leaders were anxious that the Party rank and file might be corrupted by the comforts and temptations of the 'bourgeois' culture that had suddenly become available to them, these Spartan attitudes were promoted as a symbol of ideological purity. In 1922, Aron Solts, the Party's leading spokesman on Communist ethics, warned that the NEP might seduce members into believing that 'there exists some sort of personal life in which they are completely free to follow their own tastes, and even to imitate what bourgeois society considers elegant'. Solts called upon the Bolsheviks to purge this bourgeois instinct from within themselves by changing their aesthetic attitudes. It was 'ugly for a person to have rings, bracelets, gold teeth', and in his view such behaviour 'must arouse asethetic indignation' within the Party's ranks.[25]

Valentina Tikhanova was born in Moscow in 1922. She grew up in the household of the Bolshevik leader Vladimir Antonov-Ovseyenko, the man who led the storming of the Winter Palace in October 1917. Her mother had met the famous Bolshevik in Prague, where Vladimir was the Soviet ambassador, and had left Valentina's father, an editor at a publisher, to marry him in 1927. Valentina recalls the small apartment where her family had lived in Moscow in the 1920s as 'simply furnished with the most ordinary furniture and wrought-iron beds'. The only thing of any value was a large malachite box which belonged to her mother. There were no ornaments or decorations in the apartment, and her parents had no interest in such things. Even when her mother became the wife of an ambassador, she did not wear jewellery. Asceticism ruled in the Antonov-Ovseyenko home as well. Their apartment in the Second House of Sovnarkom, a large apartment block for senior Party officials in Moscow, consisted of four small rooms. In Valentina's cell-like room the only furniture was a fold-up bed, a writing desk and a small bookcase. Recalling this austere atmosphere, Valentina describes it as a conscious element of her family's intelligentsia principles (*intelligentnost'*) and Soviet ideology. 'We were Soviet people (*sovki*),' she reflects. 'We lived for our beliefs in the future happiness of our society, not for the satisfaction of our own needs. There was a moral purity about the way we lived.'[26]

Liudmila Eliashova grew up in the family of a Latvian Bolshevik. Her father, Leonid, had run away from Riga and joined the Bolsheviks in Petrograd as a teenager in 1917. He was ashamed and resentful of his wealthy Jewish parents, who had been strict and cruel, and part of his attraction to the workers' movement was its Spartan way of life, which, as he acknowledged in a letter to his wife in 1920, he embraced as a 'renunciation of my bourgeois class'. According to his daughter Liudmila, Leonid attached personal significance to the words of the *Internationale*, 'We renounce the old world / We shake its dust from our feet!' 'He needed to renounce not just his class,' she says, 'but also his family, and the lifestyle to which he had grown accustomed, with its comfortable apartments and dachas, fine cuisine, fashionable clothes, games of tennis, and much more.' He brought up his daughters, Liudmila (born in 1921)

Leonid Eliashov, 1932

and Marksena (in 1923), to be ashamed of any wealth or comfort that set them higher than the working class. He would tell them that they should feel guilty eating a good breakfast, when there were other children, poorer than themselves, who had less to eat. At mealtimes he would say: 'It is shameful we are eating fish or sausage when everybody else eats bread and eggs. What makes us better than others?' He believed strongly in the 'Party Maximum' – a system of capping the salaries of Party members in the 1920s – and brought up his family to live within its means. The girls were not allowed to buy new shoes unless the old ones were literally falling apart. They were allowed sweets only on the major Soviet holidays. 'We lived very modestly,' recalls Liudmila.

Our furniture was cheap – it was all purchased from the government. We ate simply, our clothes were plain. I never saw my father wearing anything but his military uniform, a vest and boots. Mother had her 'special outfit' for the theatre and one or two other dresses, but that was all . . . Trips to the theatre were our only luxury – that and lots of books.

Like many children of 1917, Liudmila and her sister were brought up to believe that self-denial was synonymous with moral purity and with the revolutionary struggle for the future happiness of everyone. In 1936, she wrote on the cover of her diary: 'Suffering destroys the insignificant and hardens the strong.'[27]

For some families, the asceticism of the Party activist was too much of a strain. The Voitinskys are a case in point. Iosif Voitinsky was born in St Petersburg in 1884 to a liberal family of Russified Jews. His father was a professor of mathematics, his brother Nikolai an engineer, and, like his other brother, Vladimir, Iosif was a graduate of the Law Faculty at St Petersburg University. The family was broken up by the October Revolution. Iosif's parents fled to Finland. Vladimir, a former Menshevik and a leading figure in the Provisional Government of 1917, emigrated to Berlin, where he became a vocal critic of the Bolsheviks. Iosif and his sister Nadezhda were the only members of the family who remained in Petrograd. Like Vladimir, Iosif was a former Menshevik, but he hoped to make good by joining the Bolsheviks and fighting in the Civil War. To prove his loyalty he even wrote to his brother in Berlin – no doubt with an eye to the letter being read by his superiors – pleading with him to 're-evaluate his political principles and return to Soviet Russia for our common work'. Terrified of punishment for his brother's counter-revolutionary activity, Iosif gave himself entirely to the Party's cause. 'Because of my sins in a former life, they have only made me a pro-bationary member,' he wrote to Nikolai, 'but I am taking on a lot of Party duties, and like a good Communist, I am always ready to be sent to hell.'[28]

In fact he was sent to Yekaterinoslav, where he worked in the legal department of the local trade union organization. Iosif lived with his wife Aleksandra in a damp and barely furnished basement room. 'We cannot find anything better,' Aleksandra wrote to Nadezhda in 1922. 'Everywhere is very expensive and only the NEPmen can afford the rent. As for our domestic life, we are lacking the most basic things – linen,

Iosif and Aleksandra, Yekaterinoslav, 1924

clothes, needles, thread. In a word, we are lacking everything.' Iosif was too preoccupied to deal with such 'domestic details'. He was 'impractical and disorderly in everything except his work', according to his wife. The couple had no money, because the 'Party Maximum' left them with a small amount, most of which they sent to Iosif's mother in Finland. Aleksandra did her best to supplement their income by picking up casual jobs. But she resented having to work and blamed the Party for ruining her 'dreams of a family'. In 1922, Aleksandra had an abortion. As she explained in a letter to Nadezhda, she had wanted to have the child but had terminated her pregnancy because she was 'worn down by ill health' and did not want to 'add to Iosif's burdens' at a time when he was 'weighed down by his Party work'. The couple's marriage was suffering. There were constant arguments about money. Iosif had been having an affair with another woman, who gave birth to a son in 1924, and he was supporting them financially as well. Relations with Aleksandra were strained to breaking-point. Iosif would often go away on Party work, either to Moscow, where he taught a course on labour law, or to the Kuban, where he worked for the trade unions. 'I rarely see my Iosif,' Aleksandra wrote to Nadezhda in 1925. 'It makes me bitter that it has ended up this way, but such is our way of life these days. There is no place for private life, and we must bury romance as a relic of the past.'[29]

2

The Bolsheviks saw education as the key to the creation of a new society. Through the schools and the Communist leagues for children and youth (the Pioneers and the Komsomol) they aimed to indoctrinate the next generation in the new collective way of life. As one of the theorists of Soviet schooling declared in 1918:

We must make the young into a generation of Communists. Children, like soft wax, are very malleable and they should be moulded into good Communists . . . We must rescue children from the harmful influence of the family . . . We must nationalise them. From the earliest days of their little lives, they must find themselves under the beneficent influence of Communist schools . . . To oblige the mother to give her child to the Soviet state – that is our task.[30]

The primary mission of the Soviet school was to remove children from the 'petty-bourgeois' family, where the old mentalities of private life undermined the cultivation of social instincts, and to inculcate in them the public values of a Communist society. 'The young person should be taught to think in terms of "we",' wrote Anatoly Lunacharsky, the Commissar for Education, in 1918, 'and all private interests should be left behind.'[31]

The dissemination of Communist values was the guiding principle of the Soviet school curriculum. In this sense, as Soviet educational thinkers acknowledged, the role of Marxism in Soviet schools was similar to the role of religion in tsarist schools. In the more experimental schools there was a strong emphasis on learning through practical activities rather than theory. Even in the United Labour Schools, which were meant to provide a national framework for all Soviet schoolchildren from the primary level to university, the programme was usually organized around a series of workshops (instead of classrooms) where children were taught technical and craft skills as an introduction to the mainstream academic subjects, particularly science and economy.[32]

Political indoctrination was geared towards producing activists. The propaganda image of the ideal child was a precocious political orator mouthing agitprop. Communism could not be taught from books, educational thinkers maintained. It had to be instilled through the whole life of the school, which was in turn to be connected to the broader world of politics through extra-curricular activities, such as celebrating Soviet holidays, joining public marches, reading newspapers and organizing school debates and trials. The idea was to initiate the children into the practices, cults and rituals of the Soviet system so that they would grow up to become loyal and active Communists.

Children were indoctrinated in the cult of 'Uncle Lenin' from an early age. At kindergartens they were called 'October children' (*oktiabriata*) from the moment they were able to point towards the picture of the Soviet leader. After Lenin's death, when it was feared that a generation of children would grow up without knowing who he was, schools were instructed to establish 'Lenin Corners', political shrines for the display of propaganda about the god-like founder of the Soviet state. Legendary tales about Lenin and the other heroes of the Revolution were an impor-

A Lenin Corner, 1920s

tant means of political education. Most children did not understand the ideology of the Soviet state – they saw the Revolution as a simple struggle between 'good' and 'evil' – but they could identify with the heroic deeds of the revolutionaries.

Progressive schools were organized as miniature versions of the Soviet state: work plans and achievements were displayed in graphs and pie-charts on the walls; classes were organized like regiments; and the daily running of the school was regulated by a bureaucratic structure of councils and committees, which introduced the children to the adult world of Soviet politics. There were schools where the children were encouraged to organize their own police; where they were invited to write denunciations against pupils who had broken the school rules; and where they even held classroom trials. To instil an ethos of collective obedience some schools introduced a system of politicized drilling, with marches, songs and oaths of allegiance to the Soviet leadership. 'We marched as a class on public holidays,' recalls Ida Slavina of her school-days in Leningrad. 'We were proud to march as the representatives of our school. When we passed a building with people watching from the windows, we would slow down and chant in unison: "Home-sitters, window-watchers – shame on you!" '[33]

Aleksei Radchenko was born in 1910 to a family of famous revolution-aries. His uncle Stepan was a veteran of the Marxist underground move-ment from its pre-Lenin days, while his father Ivan was a founding member of the Bolshevik Party, charged with developing the Soviet peat industry (seen as a vital source of energy) after 1917. The family lived in Shatura, a small town to the east of Moscow, in a large and comfort-able house near the power plant, which turned peat into electricity for the Soviet capital. Aleksei's mother Alisia came from a petty-bourgeois German-Swedish family in Tallinn, and there were traces of that middle-class upbringing in her personal tastes, in her aspirations to respectability and in her preoccupation with domestic happiness. But ideologically she was committed to the Communist ideal of sweeping away this old bourgeois culture and creating a new type of human being. A pioneer of Soviet pedagogical theories and a close associate of Krupskaia in her educational work, Alisia saw the schooling of her son as a laboratory for his communistic education. Her theories were derived largely from the ideas of Pyotr Lesgaft, the founder of Russian physical education, whose lectures she attended in St Petersburg in 1903–4, and from the writings of Maksim Gorky, in whose honour she had named her son (Gorky's real name was Aleksei Peshkov). She taught Aleksei languages, made him study the piano and the violin, set him chores around the house and the garden allotment to encourage his respect for manual labour and arranged visits to the houses of the poor to develop his social conscience. The head of Shatura's United Labour School from October

1917, Alisia organized the school as a commune, combining academic lessons with agricultural labour on a farm so the children would understand from the beginning what it was to live a communist life.[34]

Aleksei was brought up to venerate his father and other revolutionaries. A sickly boy who suffered from a spine disease that made it hard for him to walk, Aleksei lived in a world of bookish fantasies. He idolized Lenin and took to heart his father's words of encouragement that he 'should become like him'. Hearing about Lenin's mortal illness in December 1923, he confessed to his diary: 'I would run away from home and give Lenin all my blood, if that would help save his life.' After the Soviet leader died, Aleksei set up a Lenin Corner in his room,

Aleksei and Ivan Radchenko, 1927

covering the walls with pictures of the Soviet leader and texts of speeches which he learned by heart. Alisia kept a journal of Aleksei's political development, which she filled with entries from his diaries, examples of his school-work and drawings, supplemented by her own commentaries on the education of her son. As she herself described it, her journal was a 'scientific log' that might serve as a 'guide to the question of Communist education in families and schools'. Alisia encouraged her son to mix with the other children in Shatura – who came from the families of the mainly peasant workers at the power plant – and tried to make him feel that he was a leader of these less privileged friends by arranging games and activities for them at their large house. 'Follow the example of your father,' Alisia wrote in the margins of her son's diary.

'Learn to be a leader to your little friends, just as he is a leader to the working class.' Encouraged by his mother, Aleksei established a 'secret' organization with some of his school comrades: the Central Bureau of the Russian Committee of the Association of Children of the World. They had their own insignia, their own revolutonary song ('The Beginning') written for the children by Alisia and their own home-made red banners, with which they marched through Shatura on public holidays.[35]

The children of 1917 were encouraged to play at being revolutionaries. Soviet educational thinkers were influenced by the ideas of 'learning through play' promoted by European pedagogues such as Friedrich Froebel and Maria Montessori. They saw structured play as an educational experience though which children would assimilate the Soviet values of collectivity, social activism and responsibility. The whole purpose of the Soviet school, with its wall newspapers, Lenin Corners, councils and committees, was to instil in children the idea that they too were potential revolutionaries and should be ready to rise up in revolt – if necessary, against their own parents – if called upon to do so by the Party leadership. Raisa Berg, who grew up in an intelligentsia family in Leningrad during the 1920s, recalls her schoolfriends' comradeship and readiness for battle:

The students of our class were united by a great spirit of friendship, trust and solidarity. Between ourselves and our wonderful teachers, whom we all loved, without exception, there was nevertheless a ceaseless battle, a real class war. We had no need for calculated strategies or conspiracies, we lived according to an unwritten code: the only thing that mattered was loyalty to our comrades. We could not tell our parents anything: they might betray us to the teachers.[36]

One of the most popular courtyard games of the 1920s was Reds and Whites, a Soviet Cowboys and Indians in which the events of the Civil War were played out by the children, often using air-guns (*pugachi*) marketed especially for the game. Reds and Whites often ended up in actual fights, for all the boys wanted to be Lenin, as one of them recalls:

We would fight for the right to play the role of the leader. Everybody wanted to be the Reds, the Bolsheviks, and no one wanted to be the Whites, the Mensheviks. Only the grown-ups could end these quarrels – by suggesting that we fight without assigning names, and whoever won would be the Bolsheviks.

Another game was Search and Requisition, in which one group (usually the boys) would play the role of a Red Army requisitioning brigade and another group (the girls) would act as 'bourgeois speculators' or 'kulak' peasants hiding grain.[37]

Games like Reds and Whites and Search and Requisition encouraged children to accept the Soviet division of the world into 'good' and 'bad'. Studies carried out in Soviet schools in the 1920s showed that children, on the whole, were ignorant about the basic facts of recent history (many pupils did not know what a tsar was) but that they had been influenced by the dark and threatening images of the supporters of the old regime in Soviet propaganda, books and films. These images encouraged many children to believe that 'hidden enemies' continued to exist, a belief that was likely to produce irrational fears, hysteria and aggression against any sign of the old regime. One young schoolgirl asked her teacher: 'Do the bourgeois eat children?' Another, who had seen a classmate wearing an old shirt with a crown embossed on the starched cuff, suddenly shouted out in class: 'Look, he is a supporter of the tsar!'[38]

Many of the children of 1917 had their first experience of politics in the Pioneers. Established in 1922, the Pioneer organization was modelled on the Scout movement, one of the last independent public bodies in Communist Russia which had been outlawed by the Soviet government in 1920. The ethos of the Scouts, which had sought to foster in its youthful members a sense of public duty through practical activities, continued to prevail in many of the Pioneer organizations (as it did in some elite Soviet schools) during the 1920s. About one-fifth of Soviet children between the ages of ten and fourteen were enrolled in the Pioneers by 1925, and the fraction increased in subsequent years. Like the Scouts, the Pioneers had their own moral codes and rituals. They had an oath which every Pioneer was meant to learn by heart (many can recall it after three-quarters of a century): 'I, a Young Pioneer of the Soviet Union, before my comrades do solemnly swear to be true to the precepts of Lenin, to stand firmly for the cause of our Communist Party and for the cause of Communism.' The Pioneers did a lot of marching and singing, gymnastics and sport. They had a responsive chant ('Pioneers, be prepared!' Answer: 'Always prepared!') which was borrowed from the Red Army. They were organized in brigades. They had their own banners, flags and songs, and their own uniform (a white shirt and a red scarf), which was a source of immense pride and, it seems, for many the main attraction of the Pioneers. 'I did not understand the obligations of the movement. Like everybody else, I just wanted the red scarf,' recalls one Pioneer. Vera Minusova, who joined the Pioneers in

Vera Minusova, early 1930s

Perm in 1928, remembers: 'I liked the uniform, especially the scarf, which I ironed every day and wore to school. These were the only smart and neat clothes I had. I was proud and felt grown-up when I wore them.' Valerii Frid, a schoolboy in Moscow in the 1920s, was so proud of his red scarf that he slept with it on for several nights after he joined the Pioneers.[39]

Through the Pioneers Soviet children experienced a strong sense of social inclusion. Every child wanted to become a Pioneer. It was glamorous and exciting to be a Pioneer, and the red scarf was an important mark of social acceptance and equality. Children excluded from the Pioneers – as many of them were, because of their social background – experienced intense feelings of shame and inferiority. Maria Drozdova was expelled from the Pioneers because she came from a 'kulak' family. So intense was her desire to be reinstated that she wore the scarf concealed underneath her shirt for many years. Sofia Ozemblovskaia, the daughter of a Polish nobleman, was banned from the Pioneers after she was spotted in church. She still recalls her expulsion with emotion:

Suddenly they posted an announcement – a 'news flash' – on the wall-newspaper in the corridor at school: 'Form lines immediately!' Children came running out of all the classrooms and formed ranks in the playground. I was made to stand in front of the whole brigade to be shamed. The children shouted: 'See what shame she has brought to our brigade by going to the church!' 'She is not worthy of the scarf!' 'She has no right to wear the scarf!' They threw dirt at me. Then they tried to tear the scarf from me. I began to cry. I shouted: 'I won't give you the scarf! I won't give you the scarf!' I fell down on my knees and begged them not to take the scarf from me. But they took it all the same. From that day on, I was no longer a Pioneer.[40]

The purpose of the Pioneer organization was to indoctrinate Soviet children in Communist values and discipline. The were subject to the same regime of 'work plans' and 'reviews' used in the Komsomol and the Party. According to the psychologist and educational theorist A. B. Zalkind, the Party's leading spokesman on the social conditioning of the personality, the aim of the Pioneer movement was to train 'revolutionary-Communist fighters fully freed from the class poisons of bourgeois ideology'. Krupskaia believed that the Pioneers would replace the family as the main influence on Soviet children. Pioneers were taught to be hard-working and obedient, pure in thought and deed. 'Through the Pioneers I learned to be smart and tidy, to finish all my tasks on time, and to be disciplined in everything I did,' reflects Minusova. 'These became my principles for life.'[41]

Pioneers were activists. There was a wide range of club activities – organizing demonstrations, editing wall-newspapers, voluntary work (*subbotniki*),* plays and concerts – designed to instil social activism and a sense of leadership in the Pioneers. Vasily Romashkin was born in 1914 to a peasant family in Moscow province. Looking back on his school career and his involvement in the Pioneers during the 1920s, he recalls this emphasis on public activity:

What did being a 'Soviet person' mean? It meant loving the Soviet motherland, working hard and setting an example, as we were taught at school and in the

---

Subbotniki, Saturday labour campaigns, were introduced in the Civil War. Students, workers and other citizens were dragooned as 'volunteers' into manual labour tasks such as clearing rubbish from the streets. It soon became a permanent feature of the Soviet way of life: not only days but whole weeks were set aside when the population would be called upon to work without pay.

Pioneers. I took these words to heart. In my third school year [in 1924] I was already the chairman of the school committee. Later I became the chairman of the school court, a prosecutor in school trials, and deputy chairman of the school's trade union. I was an active Pioneer. Through the Pioneers I learned to love my school and country more than my own family. I loved the head-teacher of our village school as if she were my own mother.[42]

Not all Pioneers were as active as Romashkin. For many children, the activities of the Pioneers were really just a form of play. Ida Slavina, the daughter of a prominent Soviet jurist, recalls forming her own club in the apartment block where she grew up in Leningrad:

I liked to read the children's journal *Murzilka*, which had on its cover the slogan: 'Mama! Papa! We shall overthrow your power!' The journal called on children to establish a new way of life by pooling all their toys and organizing themselves as a club, similar to the Pioneers. I was the leader of the children on our staircase. I read aloud from the journal and explained the meaning of the articles to the members of my club. The building administration allowed us to use a basement room for our meetings. We covered the walls with pictures of our revolutionary heroes, and stored all our toys there.[43]

Other Pioneers were more serious about their political activities. Encouraged by their seniors, they would imitate the practices of adult Communists and perform the roles of bureaucrats and policemen. These precocious enthusiasts would bring briefcases to 'executive meetings', where they would speak in Party slogans, recording formal minutes, and denounce those teachers they suspected of holding counter-revolutionary views. There were even Pioneers who helped the police hunt out 'spies' and 'enemies' by acting as informers on the street.[44]

At the age of fifteen, Soviet children progressed from the Pioneers to the Komsomol. Not all children made the transition. In 1925, the Komsomol had a million members – about 4 per cent of the Komsomol-age young (from the age of fifteen to twenty-three) – a fraction five times smaller than the percentage of children in the Pioneers.[45] To join the Komsomol was to enter on a career path towards Party membership. There were many jobs and college courses that were open only to members of the Komsomol, or which selected such members over candidates who were better qualified. Nina Vishniakova recalls joining the Komsomol as a 'huge event':

To this day [she wrote in 1990] I can remember every word of the rule book – it stirred so many feelings in me: I recall thinking that I was now suddenly a responsible adult ... It seemed to me that I could do far more than I had been able to do before I joined. It had always been my dream to belong to the Soviet elite, to achieve something important, and now that dream was coming true.[46]

The poet Yevgeny Dolmatovsky, who was born in 1915 to a family of Moscow lawyers, recalls his graduation from the Pioneers to the Komsomol in 1930. Arriving late at the admission meeting, Dolmatovsky was reprimanded by the secretary of the Komsomol, who said that he was 'evidently not mature enough to join the Komsomol' and was 'only joining as a careerist'. When Dolmatovsky told his father about the incident, he was criticized for making light of it. 'They are watching you,' his father warned, 'and you must prove that you are ready to give yourself to them.' At the next meeting Dolmatovsky was questioned by a girl, who asked him if he was 'ready to sacrifice his life for Soviet power'.[47]

Belonging to the Komsomol entailed accepting the orders, rules and ethics of the Communist Party. Members of the Komsomol were supposed to put their loyalty to the Revolution above their loyalty to the family. They were no longer children, but young Communists, expected, like Party members, to live their lives in the public sphere. The Komsomol functioned as a reserve army of youthful activists and enthusiasts for the Party, providing volunteers for Party work as well as spies and informers ready to denounce corruption and abuse. Such tasks held a broad appeal for Soviet youth in the 1920s and 1930s, shaped as they were by the ideals of the Revolution and the Civil War, when action and energy had carried the day. Many young people joined the Komsomol not because they were Communists, but because they were activists: they wanted to do something, and there was no other channel for their social energy.[48] Members were charged with exposing 'class enemies' among parents and teachers and, as if in training for the job, took part in mock trials of 'counter-revolutionaries' in schools and colleges.

Born too late (between 1905 and 1915) to be raised in the values of the old society, and too young to have taken part in the bloody fighting of the Civil War, these young activists had a highly romantic view of the Revolution's 'heroic period'. 'We yearned to be associated with the revolutionaries, our older brothers and fathers,' recalls Romashkin. 'We identified ourselves with their struggle. We dressed like them, in a military style, and spoke a type of army jargon, which we copied from the older village boys who had brought this language home from the Red Army.' The activists embraced the Spartan culture of the Bolsheviks with a vengeance. Having grown up in the barren economic landscape of the First World War, the Revolution and the Civil War, they were no strangers to austerity. Even so, they were especially militant in their ascetic rejection of all personal ('bourgeois') wealth and pleasure that detracted from the revolutionary struggle. Some formed communes and pooled all their money and possessions to 'abolish individualism'. In moral terms, too, they were absolutists, struggling to break free of the old conventions.[49]

The Komsomol idealists of the 1920s were a special group – one that would play a major role in the Stalinist regime. Their guiding ethos was described by Mikhail Baitalsky, a Komsomol activist in the Odessa region, who formed a club together with his friends. 'Everyone was pure, ready to give his life if need be to defend Communism,' Baitalsky writes in his memoirs. 'Those who showed off or complained were called rotten intellectuals. "Rotten intellectual" was one of the most insulting labels. Only "self-seeker" was worse.' In these circles there was total commitment to the Party's cause. Nobody was shocked, for example, when it was reported that an agent of the Cheka (the political police) had confiscated his own father's hardware shop for the Revolution's needs. Thoughts of personal happiness were considered shameful, and should be banished. The Revolution demanded the sacrifice of today's pleasures for a better life in the future. As Baitalsky put it:

With hopes fixed on the future, a feeling of personal participation in the world revolution, which was imminent, and a readiness to share full responsibility for it, we felt uplifted and fortified in all matters, even in very ordinary ones. It was like waiting for a train that was to take us somewhere to accomplish something wonderful and happily straining to hear its whistle in the distance . . .[50]

Intimate relations between young men and women were seen as a distraction from the collective passion for Revolution. Marriage was dismissed as a 'bourgeois' convention. 'It is inadmissable to have thoughts of personal relationships,' declared a Komsomol activist in the Red Putilov Factory in Leningrad in 1926. 'Such ideas belong to an era – before the October Revolution – that has long passed.'[51] Baitalsky had a long courtship with a Jewish girl called Yeva, the secretary of the local Komsomol cell. But there was little opportunity for romance because Yeva was zealously devoted to her work, and all he could hope for was to hold her hand and steal a kiss when he walked her home from Komsomol meetings. Eventually they married, and Yeva had a son, whom they named Vi, in honour of Lenin (the letters of Lenin's first two names). In 1927, Baitalsky was expelled as a 'Trotskyist counter-revolutionary', following the expulsion of Trotsky from the Party. Yeva put her loyalty to the Party first. Assuming that her husband had been guilty of counter-revolutionary activity, she renounced him and made him leave their home. Baitalsky was arrested in 1929.

Looking back on these events from the perspective of the 1970s, Baitalsky thought that Yeva was a good person, but that her goodness had retreated before a sense of duty to the Party, whose articles of faith had predefined her response to 'good' and 'evil' in the world. She had subordinated her own personality and powers of reason to the collective and 'unapproachable authority' of the Party. There were 'tens of thousands' of Yevas among the Bolsheviks, and their unquestioned acceptance of the Party's judgement persisted even as the Revolution gave way to the Stalinist dictatorship:

These people did not degenerate. On the contrary, they changed too little. Their internal world remained as before, preventing them from seeing what had begun to change in the outside world. Their misfortune was their conservatism (I would call it 'revolutionary conservatism'), expressed in their unchanging devotion . . . to the standards and definitions acquired during the first years of the Revolution. It was even possible to convince such people that for the good of the Revolution they needed to confess to being spies. And many were convinced, and they died believing in the revolutionary necessity for doing so.[52]

3

'We Communists are people of a special brand,' Stalin said in 1924. 'We are made of better stuff . . . There is nothing higher than the honour of belonging to this army.' The Bolsheviks saw themselves as the bearers of virtues and responsibilities that distinguished them from the rest of society. In his influential book on *Party Ethics* (1925), Aron Solts compared the Bolsheviks to the aristocracy in tsarist times. 'Today,' he wrote, 'it is we who form the ruling class . . . It is according to how we live, dress, value this or that relationship, according to how we behave that customs will be established in our country.' As a ruling proletarian caste, it was unacceptable for the Bolsheviks to mix closely with people from a different social class. It was 'bad taste', for example, argued Solts, for a Bolshevik to take a wife from a class outside the proletariat, and such marriages were to be condemned in the same way as 'the marriage of a count to a housemaid would have been condemned in the last century'.[53]

The ethos of the Party rapidly came to dominate every aspect of public life in Soviet Russia, just as the ethos of the aristocracy had dominated public life in tsarist Russia. Lenin himself compared the Bolsheviks to the nobility, and indeed, joining the Party after 1917 was like moving up a class. It brought preferment to bureaucratic posts, an elite status and privileges, and a personal share in the Party-state. By the end of the Civil War, the Bolsheviks had entrenched themselves in all the leading positions of the government, whose bureaucracy ballooned as almost every aspect of life in Soviet Russia was brought under state control. By 1921, the Soviet bureaucracy was ten times bigger than the tsarist state had ever been. There were 2.4 million state officials, more than twice the number of industrial workers in Russia. They formed the main social base of the regime.

Elite attitudes took root very quickly in the families of Bolsheviks, and they were passed down to their children. The majority of Soviet schoolchildren took it for granted that Party members had a higher status than other members of society, according to a study using controlled games in various schools in 1925. Left to themselves to decide a dispute between two boys, the other children usually decided in favour of the boy who claimed priority on the grounds that his parents were Bolsheviks. The study suggested that Soviet schools had engineered an important change in children's values, replacing the old sense of fairness and equality that had once ruled within the working class with a new hierarchical system. The children of Party members had a well-developed sense of entitlement. In one controlled game a group of children were playing trains. The boys wanted the train to go and would not wait for a little girl to get aboard, but the girl said: 'The train will wait. My husband works in the GPU [the political police] and I do as well.' She then boarded the train and demanded to be given a free ticket.[54]

The defining qualification of this self-proclaimed elite was 'Communist morality'. The Bolshevik Party identified itself as a moral as well as political vanguard, whose messianic sense of leadership demanded that its members prove their worthiness to belong to that elite. As one of the elect, every member was obliged to demonstrate that his private conduct and convictions conformed to the Party's interests. He had to show himself to be a true believer in Communism; to demonstrate that he possessed a higher moral and political consciousness than the mass of the population; that he was honest, disciplined, hard-working and selflessly devoted to the cause. This was not a moral system in the conventional sense. The Bolsheviks rejected the idea of abstract or Christian morality as a form of 'bourgeois oppression'. Rather, it was a system in which all moral questions were subordinated to the Revolution's needs. 'Morality,' wrote one Party theorist in 1924, 'is what helps the proletariat in the class struggle. Immorality is everything that hinders it.'[55]

Belief was the crucial moral quality of every 'conscious' Bolshevik. It distinguished the true Communist from the 'careerist' who joined the Party for personal ends. And belief was synonymous with a clear conscience. The Party purges and show trials were conceived as an inquisition into the soul of the accused to expose the truth of his or her beliefs (hence the importance attached to confessions, which were regarded as the revelation of the hidden self). Belief, moreover, was a public matter rather than a private one. Perhaps it was connected with the Orthodox tradition of public confession and penance, which was so different from the private nature of confession in the Christian West. Whatever the case, Communist morality left no room for the Western notion of the conscience as a private dialogue with the inner self. The Russian word for 'conscience' in this sense (sovest') almost disappeared from official use after 1917. It was replaced by the word soznatel'nost', which carries the idea of consciousness or the capacity to reach a higher moral judgement and understanding of the world. In Bolshevik discourse soznatel'nost' signified the attainment of a higher moral-revolutionary logic, that is, Marxist-Leninist ideology.[56]

Not all Bolsheviks were expected to possess a detailed knowledge of the Party's ideology, of course. Among the rank and file it was enough to be involved in the daily practice of its rituals – its oaths and songs, ceremonies, cults and codes of conduct – just as the believers of an organized religion performed their belief when they attended church. But the Party's doctrines were to be taken as articles of faith by all its followers. Its collective judgement was to be accepted as Justice. Accused of crimes by the leadership, the Party member was expected to repent, to go down on his knees before the Party and welcome its verdict against him. To defend oneself was to add another crime: dissent from the will of the Party. This explains why so many Bolsheviks surrendered to their fate in the purges, even when they were innocent of the crimes of which they stood accused. Their attitude was revealed in a conversation reported by a friend of the Bolshevik leader Iurii Piatakov not long after Piatakov's expulsion from the Party as a Trotskyist in 1927. To earn his readmission Piatakov had recanted many of his oldest political beliefs, but this did not make him a coward, as his friend had charged. Rather, as Piatakov explained, it showed that

a true Bolshevik will readily cast out from his mind ideas in which he has believed for years. A true Bolshevik has submerged his personality in the collectivity, 'the Party', to such an extent that he can make the necessary effort to break away from his own opinions and convictions ... He would be ready to believe that black was white and white was black, if the Party required it.[57]

Nevertheless, because he had changed his views so radically, Piatakov, like other 'renegades', was never fully trusted or believed by Stalin, who ordered his arrest in 1936.

The purges began long before Stalin's rise to power. They had their origins in the Civil War, when the Party's ranks grew rapidly and its leaders were afraid of being swamped by careerists and 'self-seekers'. The targets of the early purges were entire social groups: 'regenerate bourgeois elements', 'kulaks', and so on. Bolsheviks from a working-class background were exempt from scrutiny, unless a specific denunci-ation had been made against them at a purge meeting. But during the 1920s there was a gradual shift in the practice of the purge, with a growing emphasis on the private conduct and convictions of individual Bolsheviks.

The shift was accompanied by an ever more elaborate system for the inspection and control of Party members' private lives. Applicants to join the Party had to demonstrate belief in its ideology. Great stress was placed on when they were converted to the cause, and only those who had fought with the Red Army in the Civil War were taken to have proved their commitment. At regular intervals throughout their lives, Party members were required to write a short autobiography or to complete a questionnaire (*anketa*), giving details about their social background, their education and career, and the evolution of their political consciousness. These documents were essentially a form of public confession in which the Party members reaffirmed their worthiness to be of the elect. The key thing was to show that the formation of their political consciousness owed everything to the Revolution and the Party's tutelage.[58]

A tragic incident at the Leningrad Mining Academy served to buttress the Party's insistence on supervising its members' private life. In 1926, a student committed suicide at the academy hostel. It turned out that she had been driven to it by the cruel behaviour of her common-law husband. Konstantin Korenkov was not brought to trial, though he was excluded from the Komsomol on the grounds of 'moral responsibility for the suicide of a comrade'. The Control Commission of the regional Party organization – a sort of regional Party court – overruled this decision, which it considered harsh, and replaced it with a 'severe reprimand and warning'. A few weeks later Korenkov and his younger brother robbed the cashier's office at the Mining Academy, stabbing the cashier to death and wounding his wife. The case was seized upon by Sofia Smidovich, a senior member of the Central Control Commission, the body placed in charge of Party ethics and legality, who portrayed 'Korenkovism' as an 'illness' whose main symptom was indifference to the morals and behaviour of one's comrades:

The private life of my comrade is not of my concern. The students' collective watches how Korenkov locks up his sick, literally bleeding wife – well, that is his private life. He addresses her with curse words and humiliating remarks – nobody interferes. What's more: in Korenkov's room a shot resounds, and a student whose room is one floor beneath does not even think it necessary to check out what is going on. He considers it a private affair.

Smidovich argued that it was the task of the collective to enforce moral standards among its members through mutual surveillance and intervention in their private lives. Only this, she argued, would foster real collectivism and a 'Communist conscience'.[59]

The system of mutual surveillance and denunciation which Smidovich envisaged was not entirely an invention of the Revolution of 1917. Denunciations had been a part of Russian governance for centuries. Petitions to the tsar against officials who abused their power had played a vital role in the tsarist system, reinforcing the popular myth of a 'just tsar' who (in the absence of any courts or other public institutions) protected the people from 'evil servitors'. In Russian dictionaries the act of 'denunciation' (*donos*) was defined as a civic virtue ('the revelation of illegal acts') rather than a selfish or malicious act, and this definition was retained throughout the 1920s and 1930s.[60] But under the Soviet regime, the culture of denunciation took on a new meaning and intensity. Soviet citizens were encouraged to report on neighbours, colleagues, friends and even relatives. Vigilance was the first duty of every Bolshevik. 'Lenin taught us that every Party member should become an agent of the Cheka, that is, he should watch and write reports,' argued Sergei Gusev, who had risen to become a senior member of the Central Control Commission.[61] Party members were instructed to inform on their comrades, if they believed that their private thoughts or conduct threatened Party unity. In factories and barracks a list of candidates for membership was posted outside the office of the Party cell. Members of the collective were then invited to write denunciations against the candidates, pointing out their personal shortcomings (e.g. heavy drinking or rudeness), which would then be discussed at a Party meeting. Reports of private conversations became an increasingly common feature of this denunciatory practice, although some Party leaders expressed reservations about the morality of such actions. At the Fourteenth Party Congress in 1925 it had been decided that reporting on a private conversation was generally to be frowned upon, but not if such conversation was deemed 'a threat to Party unity'.[62]

Invitations to denunciation were central to the culture of the purge that developed during the 1920s. In Party and Soviet organizations there were regular purge meetings where Party members and officials were made to answer criticisms solicited from the rank and file in the form of written and oral denunciations. These meetings could get very personal, as the young Elena Bonner discovered, when she observed one in the Comintern hostel:

They asked about people's wives and sometimes about their children. It turned out that some people beat their wives and drank a lot of vodka. Batanya [Bonner's grandmother] would have said that decent people don't ask such questions. Sometimes the one being purged said that he wouldn't beat his wife anymore or drink anymore. And a lot of them said about their work that they 'wouldn't do it anymore' and that 'they understood everything'. Then it resembled being called into the teacher's room: the teacher sits, you stand, he scolds you, the other teachers smile nastily, and you quickly say, 'I understand,' 'I won't,' 'of course, I was wrong,' but you don't mean it, or just want to get out of there to join the other kids at recess. But these people were more nervous than you were with the teacher. Some of them were practically crying. It was unpleasant watching them. Each purge took a long time; some evenings they did three people, sometimes only one.[63]

Increasingly, there was nothing in the private life of the Bolshevik that was not subject to the gaze and censure of the Party leadership. This public culture, where every member was expected to reveal his inner self to the collective, was unique to the Bolsheviks – there was nothing like it in the Nazi or the Fascist movement, where the individual Nazi or Fascist was allowed to have a private life, so long as he adhered to the Party's rules and ideology – until the Cultural Revolution in China. Any distinction between private and public life was explicitly rejected by the Bolsheviks. 'When a comrade says: "What I am doing now concerns my private life and not society," we say that cannot be correct,' wrote one Bolshevik in 1924.[64] Everything in the Party member's private life was social and political; everything he did had a direct impact on the Party's interests. This was the meaning of 'Party unity' – the complete fusion of the individual with the public life of the Party.

In his book on *Party Ethics*, Solts conceived of the Party as a self-policing collective, where every Bolshevik would scrutinize and criticize his comrades' private motives and behaviour. In this way, he imagined, the individual Bolshevik would come to know himself through the eyes of the Party. Yet in reality this mutual surveillance did just the opposite: it encouraged people to present themselves as conforming to Soviet ideals whilst concealing their true selves in a secret private sphere. Such dissimulation would become widespread in the Soviet system, which demanded the *display* of loyalty and punished the *expression* of dissent. During the terror of the 1930s, when secrecy and deception became necessary survival strategies for almost everyone in the Soviet Union, a whole new type of personality and society arose. But this double-life was already a reality for large sections of the population in the 1920s, especially for Party families, who lived in the public eye, and for those whose social background or beliefs made them vulnerable to repression. People learned to wear a mask and act the role of loyal Soviet citizens, even if they lived by other principles in the privacy of their own home.

Talk was dangerous in this society. Family conversations repeated outside the home could lead to arrest and imprisonment. Children were the main source of danger. Naturally talkative, they were too young to understand the political significance of what they overheard. The playground, especially, was a breeding ground of informers. 'We were taught to hold our tongues and not to speak to anyone about our family,' recalls the daughter of a middle-ranking Bolshevik official in Saratov:

There were certain rules of listening and talking that we children had to learn. What we overheard the adults say in a whisper, or what we heard them say behind our backs, we knew we could not repeat to anyone. We would be in trouble if we even let them know that we had heard what they had said. Sometimes the adults would say something and then would tell us, 'The walls have ears,' or 'Watch your tongue,' or some other expression . . . But mostly, we learned these rules instinctively. No one explained to us that what was spoken might be dangerous politically, but somehow we understood.[65]

Nina Iakovleva grew up in an atmosphere of silent opposition to the Soviet regime. Her mother came from a noble family in Kostroma that had fled the Bolsheviks in the Civil War; her father was a Socialist Revolutionary* who had been imprisoned after taking part in the large-scale peasant uprising against the Bolsheviks in Tambov province in 1921 (he escaped from jail and ran away to Leningrad, where he was rearrested in 1926 and sentenced to five years in the Suzdal special isolation prison camp). Growing up in the 1920s, Nina knew instinctively that she was not allowed to speak about her father to her friends at school. 'My mother was demonstratively silent about politics,' recalls Nina. 'She made a declaration of her lack of interest in political affairs.' From this silence Nina learned to hold her tongue. 'No one laid down specific rules about what could be spoken, but there was a general feeling, an atmosphere within the family, that made it clear to us that we were not to speak about father.' Nina also learned to mistrust everyone outside her immediate family. 'I love no one, I love only Mama,

*The Socialist Revolutionaries (SRs) were the largest party in Russia in 1917. Drawing their support from the peasantry, they held a majority in the Constituent Assembly, which was closed down by the Bolsheviks in January 1918.

Papa and aunt Liuba,' she wrote to her father in 1926. 'I only love our family. I love no one else.'[66]

Galina Adasinskaia was born in 1921 to a family of active oppositionists. Her father was a Socialist Revolutionary; her mother and grandmother Mensheviks (all three were arrested in 1929). In the 1920s, when it was still possible for former SRs and Mensheviks to work in the Soviet government, Galina's parents lived a double life. Her father worked in the administration of cooperatives, an economic organization promoted by the NEP, and her mother in the Ministry of Trade, yet in private both retained their old political opinions. Galina was protected and excluded from this secret sphere of politics. She was brought up to become a 'Soviet child' (she joined the Pioneers and the Komsomol). 'Politics was something that my parents did at work, or wrote about. But at home they never spoke about such things . . . They thought of politics as a dirty business.'[67]

The households Nina and Galina were brought up in may have been extreme, but the rules of silence which they learned instinctively were observed by many families. Sofia Ozemblovskaia, the daughter of the Polish nobleman who was banned from the Pioneers after being spotted at church, lived with her family in the front half of a wooden house in a village near Minsk. 'At home we never talked about politics or anything like that,' she remembers. 'Father always said, "The walls have ears." Once he even showed us how to hear our neighbours' conversation by listening through a glass against the wall. Then we understood. From then on we too were afraid of our neighbours.'[68]

Liubov (Liuba) Tetiueva was born in 1923 in Cherdyn, a small town in the Urals. Her father, Aleksandr, an Orthodox priest, was arrested in 1922 and held in prison for the best part of a year. After his release he was put under pressure by OGPU (the political police) to become an informer and write reports on his own parishioners, but he refused. The Cherdyn soviet deprived the Tetiuevs of civil rights and a rationing card when rationing was introduced in 1929.* Aleksandr's church was taken over by the 'renovationists' (obnovlentsy), church reformers who sought to simplify the Orthodox liturgy and who had the backing of the Soviet

---

*They were lishentsy (literally meaning the 'disenfranchised') – a category of people, mainly from the old intelligentsia, the petty bourgeoisie and the clergy, deprived of civil and electoral rights. During the 1920s the lishentsy were subjected to a growing level of discrimination by the Bolsheviks, with many families denied access to Soviet schools and state housing or deprived of ration cards.

The Tetiuev family (Liubov, aged four, seated centre), Cherdyn, 1927

regime. Shortly afterwards, Aleksandr was arrested for a second time, following a denunciation by the *obnovlentsy*, who accused him of sowing 'discord among believers' (by refusing to join them). Liubov's mother was dismissed from her job in the Cherdyn Museum, where she worked on the library catalogue, while the elder of her two brothers was expelled from his school and the Komsomol. The family depended on the earnings of Liubov's older sister, who worked as a schoolteacher. Liubov recalls her childhood in the 1920s:

If my parents needed to talk about something important, they would always go outside the house and speak to one another in whispers. Sometimes they would talk with my grandmother in the yard. They never held such conversations in front of the children – never ... Not once did they have an argument or talk critically about Soviet power – though they had much to criticize – not once in any case that we could hear. The one thing my mother always said to us was: 'Don't you lot go chattering, don't go chattering. The less you hear the better.' We grew up in a house of whisperers.[69]

4

Many families experienced a growing generation split during the 1920s: the customs and habits of the old society remained dominant in the private spaces of the home, where seniority ruled, but young people were increasingly exposed to the influence of Soviet propaganda through school, the Pioneers and the Komsomol. For the older generation the situation posed a moral dilemma: on the one hand, they wanted to pass down family traditions and beliefs to their children; on the other, they had to bring them up as Soviet citizens.

Grandparents were the main transmitters of traditional values in most families. The grandmother, in particular, played a special role, taking prime responsibility for the upbringing of the children and the running of the household, if both the parents worked, or playing an important auxiliary role, if the mother worked part-time. In the words of the poet Vladimir Kornilov, 'It seemed that in our years there were no mothers. / There were only grandmothers.'[70] The influence of the grandmother was felt in a variety of ways. By running the household, the grandmother had a direct effect on children's manners and habits. She told the children stories of 'the old days' (before 1917), which in time could serve as a reference-point or counterweight to Soviet history, enabling them to question the propaganda they were fed in school. She kept alive the cultural values of the nineteenth century by reading to the children from pre-revolutionary Russian literature, little read in Soviet schools, or by taking them to the theatre, galleries or concert halls.[71]

Elena Bonner was brought up by her grandmother. 'Batania, not Mama, was the centre of my life,' she later wrote. As Party activists, Elena's mother and father were often absent from the Bonner home. In her relationship with her grandmother Elena found the love and affection she longed for but did not receive from her parents. Batania provided a moral counterbalance to the Soviet influence of Elena's mother and father. As a child, Elena was aware that her grandmother – a plump but 'astonishingly beautiful' woman with a 'calm and imperious manner' – inhabited a different world from the Soviet one in which her parents lived.

Batania's friends and acquaintances rarely came to our building, where only she and the children were not Party members. But I often went with her to call on them. I saw that they lived differently – they had different dishes, different furniture. (At our house Batania was the only one with normal furniture and a few nice things . . .) They talked about everything differently. I felt (this impression definitely came from Papa and Mama) that they were a different sort of people – what I couldn't tell was whether they were worse or better.

Batania Bonner with her grandchildren (from left: Zoria,
Elena, Yegorka), Moscow, 1929

Batania's conservative moral outlook was rooted in the world of the
Russian-Jewish bourgeoisie. She was hard-working, strict but caring,
entirely dedicated to the family. During the 1920s Batania worked as a
'specialist' (*spets*) – a much-derided but still necessary class of 'bourgeois'
experts and technicians – in the Leningrad customs office, where she
was an accountant. She earned more than Bonner's parents on the 'Party
Maximum'. Batania had old-fashioned frugal attitudes about money
and housekeeping that were a source of constant friction with the 'Soviet
regime' Elena's parents imposed on the household. She read a lot but
'stubbornly refused to read contemporary literature' and did not go, 'on
principle', to the cinema, such was her disdain for the modern world.
She had 'nothing but scorn for the new order', talked disaparagingly of
the Party leaders and scolded her own daughter for the excesses of the
Bolshevik dictatorship. When she was really angry she would say things
starting with the phrase: 'Let me remind you that before that Revolution
of yours . . .' After the Soviet government banned the Shrovetide holiday,
the most colourful in the Orthodox calendar, Batania, who sympathized
with all old customs, told her granddaughter: 'Well, you can thank your
mummy and daddy for this.' Not surprisingly, Elena was confused by
the clash of values in her family. 'There was a colossal conflict over our
education,' she recalls in interview.

Grandmother would bring home books for me from the Children's Golden
Library, various stupidities, and Mama disapprovingly would purse her lips,

though she never dared say anything to grandmother. Mama brought home different books, Pavel Korchagin,* for example, which she brought home for me in manuscript, and I read that too. I didn't know which type of book I liked better.

Elena loved her grandmother and respected her 'more than anyone else in the world', but, not surprisingly, she wanted to identify with her parents and their world: 'I always perceived Papa's and Mama's friends as my own kind and Batania's as strangers. In essence, I already belonged to the Party.'[72]

In the Moscow home of Anatoly Golovnia, the cameraman for most of Vsevolod Pudovkin's films in the 1920s and 1930s, Anatoly's mother Lydia Ivanovna was a domineering influence. Born into a Greek merchant family from Odessa, she had been educated at the Smolny Institute, where she acquired the refined attitudes and habits of the Russian aristocracy. Lydia passed on these customs to the Golovnia household, which she ran with iron discipline in the 'Russian Victorian' manner. Lydia was contemptuous of the 'vulgar' manners of Anatoly's wife, a film actress of extraordinary beauty called Liuba, who had come to Moscow from a poor peasant family in Cheliabinsk. She thought her taste for expensive clothes and furniture reflected the material acquisitiveness of the 'new Soviet bourgeoisie', the class of peasants and workers rising through the ranks of the bureaucracy. In a heated argument, after Liuba came home from a shopping spree, she told her that she represented 'the Revolution's ugly side'. Lydia herself had simple tastes. She always dressed in the same black full-length dress with deep pockets in which she kept a powder case and a lorgnette. A survivor of the famine that swept through south-east Russia and Ukraine at the end of the Civil War, she lived in fear of starvation, although Anatoly's earnings were more than adequate to provide for the household, which also included Liuba's sister and her daughter Oksana. Lydia planned out every meal in a small notebook, with exact quantities of the necessary items that needed to be bought. She had her favourite shops, the elite Filippovsky bakery and the Yeliseyev store on Tverskaia Street, where

---

*How the Steel Was Tempered (1932–4), Nikolai Ostrovsky's novel about the establishment of Soviet power and the heroic life of a Komsomol activist, Pavel Korchagin, which inspired many Soviet children in the 1930s and 1940s.

'she would allow herself the luxury of drinking an iced glass of tomato juice'. Looking back on her childhood, Oksana wrote in 1985:

Grandmother was a very modest and disciplined person. She was something of a moralist, a pedagogue perhaps. She always tried to do the 'correct thing'. I remember how she liked to say to her son, who was a convinced Bolshevik: 'If you did things as I do them, you would have built your Communism long ago.' She was fearless about what she said, and concealed nothing of what she thought or did. She believed strongly that ideas should be spoken clearly and aloud, without pretence, deceit or fear. She often said to me: 'Do not whisper, it is rude!'* Now I realize that she behaved this way to set a moral example to her granddaughter – to show me the correct way to behave. Thank you, Grandmother![73]

Grandmothers were also the main practitioners and guardians of religious faith. It was nearly always the grandmother who organized the christening of a Soviet child, sometimes without its parents' knowledge or consent, who took the children to church and passed down religious customs and beliefs. Even if they retained their religious faith, the parents of Soviet children were less likely to communicate it to them, partly out of fear that the exposure of such beliefs, say in school, could have disastrous consequences for the family. 'My grandmother took me to be christened, although my father and mother were violently opposed,' recalls Vladimir Fomin, who was born into a family of factory workers in Kolpino, near Leningrad. 'It was all done in secret in a country church. My parents were afraid that they would lose their jobs at the factory if people found out that I had been christened.'[74]

A grandmother's religious beliefs could set the child on a collision course with the ideological system in Soviet schools. Born in 1918 to a family of wealthy Tiflis engineers, Yevgeniia Yevangulova spent much of her childhood with her grandparents in Rybinsk, because her father, Pavel, who was Chief of Mines in the Soviet Mining Council, was frequently on work trips in Siberia, while her mother, Nina, who was studying in Moscow, could not cope with the child care. A devout merchant's wife of the old school, Yevgeniia's grandmother was a major

---

*Growing up in Rome, where she was born in 1924, Elena Volkonskaia recalls her mother using the same phrase. Born in 1893, Elena's mother was the daughter of Pyotr Stolypin, Prime Minister of Russia 1906–11, and another graduate of the Smolny Institute (interview with Elena Volkonskaia, Cetona, July 2006).

influence on her upbringing. She gave her a little cross to wear beneath her blouse on her first day at school. But a group of boys discovered it and made fun of her. 'She believes in God!' they pointed and shouted. Yevgeniia was traumatized by the incident. She turned inward. When she was invited to join the Pioneers, she refused, a rare act of protest among children of her age, and later on refused to join the Komsomol.[75]

Boris Gavrilov was born in 1921. His father was a factory manager and senior Party member in one of the industrial suburbs of Leningrad. His mother was a schoolteacher. Boris was brought up by his maternal grandmother, the widow of a wealthy ivory merchant, whose religious faith had a lasting influence on him:

Grandmother had her own room – we had five rooms altogether – where the walls were covered with religious images and large icons with their votive lamps. It was the only room in the house where icons were allowed by my father. My grandmother went to church and took me along with her, without telling my father. I loved the Easter service, although it was very long . . . This church was her only joy – she didn't go to the theatre or the cinema – and all she read were religious books, which were also the first books I learned to read. My mother was religious too, but she didn't go to church. She didn't have the time, and my father wouldn't have allowed it in any case. At school I was taught to be an atheist. But I was more attached to the beauty of the church. When my grandmother died, and my parents were divorced [in 1934], my mother encouraged me to keep going to church. Sometimes I even received communion and went to confession. I have always worn a cross, although I don't consider myself to be especially religious. Naturally, I never said a word about my religion at school, or when I joined the army [in 1941]. Things like that had to be concealed.[76]

The division between home and school created conflicts in many families. Children were often confused by the contradiction between what their parents said and what they were taught by their teachers. 'At home you hear one thing, and at school another. I don't know which is best,' a schoolboy wrote in 1926. The issue of religion was particularly confusing. One schoolgirl noted feeling 'torn between two forces': at school she was taught that 'there is no God, but at home my grandmother says that God exists'. The question of religion divided young and old, especially in the countryside, where teachers encouraged children to challenge the beliefs and authority of their elders. 'Over tea, I argued with my mother about the existence of a God,' wrote one rural schoolboy in 1926. 'She said that Soviet power was wrong to fight religion and crack down on the priests. But I assured her: "No, Mama, you are wrong. Soviet power is correct. The priest is a liar."' Once they joined the Pioneers, children grew in confidence. They became conscious of themselves as members of a movement dedicated to sweeping away the backward customs of the past. 'One day during Lent, when I came home from school, my grandmother gave me just potatoes for my tea,' wrote one Pioneer. 'I complained, and my grandmother said, "Don't be angry, the Lenten fast has not yet passed." But I replied: "For you that may be so, because you are old. But we are Pioneers, and we are not obliged to recognize these rituals."' This assertiveness was even more pronounced in the Komsomol, where militant atheism was considered a sign of a 'progressive' political consciousness, and almost a prerequisite of membership.[77]

Parents had to choose very carefully what to tell their children about God, often making a conscious decision not to give their children a religious upbringing, even if they themselves had religious leanings. They recognized that their children needed to adapt to Soviet culture if they were to succeed in their adult lives. This compromise was particularly common in professional families, who understood that the fulfilment of a child's ambitions was dependent on accreditation from the state. One engineer, the son of an architect, recalls that his parents were brought up before the Revolution to believe in God and to follow the principles which they had been taught by his grandparents. But he was brought up to honour different principles, 'to be decent', as he put it, 'and to respond to all the social demands made of him'. A similar situation prevailed in the Moscow household of Pyotr and Maria Skachkova, both librarians. Although they were religious and always went to church, they did not educate their three daughters to believe in God. As one of them recalls:

My parents thought this way: once religion was prohibited, they would not talk about it with their children, because we would have to live in a different society from the one in which they had grown up. They did not want to make us lead a double life, should we join the Pioneers, or the Komsomol.[78]

Many families did lead a double life. They celebrated Soviet public holidays like 1 May and 7 November (Revolution Day) and conformed to the regime's atheist ideology, yet still observed their religious faith in the privacy of their own home. Yekaterina Olitskaia was a member of the Socialist Revolutionary Party. In the 1920s she was exiled to Riazan, where she moved in with an old woman, the widow of a former railway worker, and her daughter, a Komsomol member who worked in a paper factory. The old woman was devoutly religious but, on her daughter's insistence, she kept her icons in a secret cupboard concealed by a curtain in the back room of the house. Her daughter was afraid that she would be fired if the Komsomol discovered that there were icons in her home. 'On Sundays and big holidays they would draw the curtains in the evening and light the votive lamps,' writes Olitskaia. 'They would usually make sure to lock the doors.' Antonina Kostikova grew up in a similarly secretive household. Her father was the peasant chairman of a village Soviet in Saratov province from 1922 to 1928, but he privately maintained his Orthodox faith. 'Our parents were very religious,' recalls Antonina. 'They knew all the prayers. Father was especially devout, but he rarely spoke about religion, only when at home at night. He never let us [his three children] see him pray. He told us that we had to learn what they told us about God at school.' Antonina's mother, a simple peasant woman, kept an icon hidden in a compartment inside a table drawer which Antonina only found on her mother's death in the 1970s.[79]

The secret observance of religious rituals occurred even in Party families. Indeed it was quite common, judging from a report by the Central Control Commission which revealed that almost half the members expelled from the Party in 1925 had been purged because of religious observance. There were numerous Party households where Christ rubbed shoulders with the Communist ideal, and Lenin's portrait was displayed together with the family icons in the 'red' or 'holy' corner of the living room.[80]

The nanny, another carrier of traditional Russian values within the Soviet family, was a natural ally of the grandmother. Nannies were employed by many urban families, especially in households where both parents worked. There was an almost limitless supply of nannies from the countryside, particularly after 1928, when millions of peasants fled into the cities to escape collectivization, and they brought with them the customs and beliefs of the peasantry.

Virtually all the Bolsheviks employed nannies to take care of their children. It was a practical necessity for most Party women, at least until the state provided universal nursery care, because they went out to work. In many Party families the nanny acted as a moral counterweight to the

Peasant nanny, Fursei family (Leningrad)

household's ruling Soviet attitudes. Ironically the most senior Bolsheviks tended to employ the most expensive nannies, who generally held reactionary opinions. The Bonners, for example, had a series of nannies, including one who had worked in Count Sheremetev's household in St Petersburg, a Baltic German (an acquaintance of Batania's old landowner friends) who taught the children 'good manners', and even one who had once worked for the Imperial family.[81]

Nannies could exert a profound influence on family life. In the Leningrad household of the Party activists Anna Karpitskaia and Pyotr Nizovtsev, for example, there was a peasant nanny called Masha, a devout Old Believer,* who observed her religious rituals in their home. She ate separately using her own plates and cutlery, prayed every morning and evening in her room and involved the children in the elaborate rites of her belief. Masha also practised as a healer, as she had done in her native village in the northern Russian countryside, making herbal remedies to cure the children of various illnesses. A kind and caring person, Masha earned the respect of her employers, who protected her from the Soviet authorities' pursuit of religious activists. Her presence contributed to the rare liberal atmosphere that prevailed in this household. 'We did not think it strange to have an Old Believer in the family,'

*The Old Believers were adherents of the Russian Orthodox rituals observed before the Church reforms of the 1650s had brought them closer into line with those of the Greek Orthodox liturgy.

recalls Anna's daughter Marksena. 'There was no trace in our household of the militant atheism found in other Party households at that time. We were brought up to be tolerant of all religions and beliefs, although we ourselves were atheists.'[82]

Inna Gaister was another child of Bolsheviks who was deeply affected by the counter-values of her nanny. Inna's father, Aron Gaister, was a senior economist in Gosplan (the State Planning Commission); her mother, Rakhil Kaplan, an economist in the People's Commissariat of Heavy Industry. Both her parents came from labouring families in the Pale of Settlement, the south-west corner of the Russian Empire, where the tsar's Jews had been forced to live. The couple met in Gomel, a town in Belarus; they joined the Party in the Civil War and in 1920 moved to Moscow, to a communal apartment. Aron studied at the Institute of Red Professors, while Rakhil worked in the Textile Workers' Union. Like many Soviet Jews, the Gaisters invested their hopes in the programme of industrialization, which they believed would end all backwardness, inequality and exploitation in the Soviet Union. Two months after the birth of their first child, Inna, in 1925, they hired a nanny called Natasha, who moved into their new home. Natasha Ovchinnikova

Natasha Ovchinnikova

came from a peasant family in Riazan province, south of Moscow, whose small farm had been ruined by the Bolshevik grain requisitionings of the Civil War. During the famine of 1921 Natasha fled to the capital.

She rarely spoke about her family in the Gaister home. But even at the age of eight or nine, Inna was aware that the world her nanny grew up in was very different from the one in which her parents lived. Inna noticed how Natasha prayed in church; she heard her crying in her room. She saw the poverty of her relatives from Riazan – who had also made their way to the capital and were living as illegal immigrants in a crowded barracks – when she went with her to visit them. Natasha's niece, a girl with whom Inna liked to play, had no shoes, so Inna brought her a pair of her own and then lied that she had lost them when her parents asked about the missing shoes. Although still too young to question anything politically, Inna had already formed a tacit alliance with Natasha and her family.[83]

The peasant world from which these nannies came was largely dominated by the traditions of the patriarchal family. In 1926, the peasantry represented 82 per cent of the Soviet population – 120 million people (in a total population of 147 million people) dispersed in 613,000 villages and remote settlements across the Soviet Union.[84] The peasantry's attachment to individual family labour on the private household farm made it the last major bastion of individualism in Soviet Russia and, in the view of the Bolsheviks, the main social obstacle to their Communist utopia.

In some areas, especially in central Russia, urban ways were filtering down to the countryside, and literate peasant sons were displacing fathers at the head of family farms, or breaking free from extended families to set up households of their own. But elsewhere the traditions of the patriarchal peasant family remained dominant.

Antonina Golovina was born to a peasant family in 1923, the youngest of six children. Their village, Obukhovo, 800 kilometres north-east of Moscow, was an ancient settlement of wooden houses in the middle of a forest; there was a pond in the middle of the village and a large wooden church, built in the eighteenth century. The Golovins had always lived in Obukhovo (twenty of the fifty-nine households in the village were occupied by Golovins in 1929).[85] Antonina's father, Nikolai, was born in the village in 1882, and apart from the three years he had spent in the army in the First World War, he lived his whole life there. Like many villages, Obukhovo was a tightly knit community where family and kin relations played a crucial role. The peasants thought of themselves as a single 'family' and taught their children to address other adults in familial terms ('aunty', 'uncle', and so on). Bolshevik attempts to divide the peasantry into separate and warring social classes – the 'kulaks' (or the 'rural bourgeoisie') and the poor peasants (the so-called 'rural proletariat') – failed miserably in Obukhovo, as they did in much of Soviet Russia during the Civil War.

As a hard-working, sober and successful peasant from the largest village clan, Nikolai was a well-respected figure in Obukhovo. 'He was a quiet man – he did not talk to pass the day – but worked honestly and got things done, and the peasants valued that,' one of the villagers recalls. After his return from the First World War, Nikolai became a leader of the peasant commune in Obukhovo. Governed by an assembly of its leading farmers, the peasant commune was an ancient institution, set up under serfdom, which regulated virtually every aspect of village and agrarian life. Its powers of self-government had been considerably broadened by the Emancipation of the serfs in 1861, when it took over most of the administrative, police and judicial functions of the landlords and became the basic unit of rural administration. The commune controlled the peasants' land, which in most parts of Russia was owned communally but farmed individually; set the common patterns of cultivation and grazing necessitated by the open-field system of strip-farming (where there were no hedges between the strips or fields); and periodically redivided the arable land among the peasant farms according to their household size – an egalitarian principle that also helped the commune pay its taxes to the state by ensuring that the land was fully worked by families with labourers. In 1917, the commune became the organizing kernel of the peasant revolution on the land. After the collapse of the old rural order and the flight of most of its leaders, the gentry and the clergy, from the countryside, the peasants throughout Russia seized control of all the land and – without waiting for any direction from the central government or the revolutionary parties in the towns – redistributed it through the peasant commune and the various village councils (soviets) and committees which they had set up to rule their own affairs during 1917.[86]

Before the Revolution, Nikolai had rented arable from the village priest. Like most peasants in Russia, where overpopulation and inefficient farming resulted in shortages of land, he had depended on this rented arable to feed his family. In 1917, the commune seized control of the Church's land and divided it with the communal land among the peasants. Nikolai was given four hectares of ploughland and pasture, a norm set in proportion to the number of 'eaters' in his family (i.e. household size). He now had almost twice as much land as he had farmed before 1917, and none of it was rented any more. But four hectares were not enough to live on in Obukhovo, or anywhere in northern Russia, where the soil was poor and the land broken up by woodland into disparate plots and then (to make sure that every peasant received an equal share of these small plots) broken up again by the commune into narrow strips, each one no more than a few feet wide and unsuitable for modern ploughs. The Golovins' arable land consisted of about 80 separate strips in eighteen different locations – numbers not unusual for peasants in the Vologda region. To supplement their income the peasants worked in trades and crafts, which had always played a vital role, almost as important as agriculture, in the economy of the northern villages, and which now flourished in the NEP, when the government encouraged rural trades and even subsidized them through cooperatives. Nikolai had a leather workshop in the backyard of his farm. 'In our household,' recalls Antonina,

we had enough to live on, but only as a result of our own hard work and thrift. All six children laboured on the land, even the youngest, and Father worked long hours making shoes and other leather goods in his workshop. When he bought a cow from the market, he made sure to get everything from it. He slaughtered the cow, sold the meat, dressed the hide himself (every peasant in our region knew this craft), manufactured boots from the leather and then sold them at the market too.[87]

This work ethic was 'the main philosophy of our education as children,' she recalls. It was typical of the most industrious peasant families that children were brought up to work on the farm from an early age. These peasants took pride in their labour, as Antonina remembers:

Father liked to say that everything we did should be done well – as if it was done by a master. That is what he called the 'Golovin way' – his highest words of praise . . . When we went to school he told us all to study hard and learn a good profession. In his eyes the good professions were medicine, teaching, agronomy and engineering. He did not want his children to learn shoe-making, which he considered a hard life, though he was an artist in his craft, and we children and anybody else who came to our house were inspired by the beauty of his work.[88]

Nikolai built his own house, a long, whitewashed single-storeyed building near the millstone in the middle of Obukhovo. The only brick house in the whole village, it had a dining room as well as a bedroom sparsely furnished with factory furniture bought in Vologda and two iron beds, one for Nikolai and his wife, Yevdokiia, the other for their two daughters (the boys slept on the floor of the dining room). Outside the kitchen, the only entrance to the house, there was a sheltered yard for animals, with a cowshed, a pigsty, a stable and two barns. The yard also contained a bath-house, a toilet, a tool store and a workshop, and, beyond the yard, there was a garden full of apple trees.

Nikolai was a strict father. 'All the children were afraid of him,' recalls his daughter Antonina, 'but it was a fear based on respect. As our mother liked to say, "God is in the sky and father in the house." Whatever father said we took as law. Even the four boys.' In this type of patriarchal household there was little tenderness or intimacy between adults and children. 'We never kissed or hugged our parents,' Antonina says. 'We did not love them in that way. We were brought up to respect and revere them. We always obeyed them.' But that did not mean there was no love. Nikolai adored his youngest daughter, who recalls a tender moment from her childhood, when she was only four. Dressed in his best cotton shirt for a holiday, her father carried her in his strong arms to the village church.

Suddenly, he took my hands and held them tightly to his lips. He closed his eyes and kissed my hands with real feeling. I remember that. Now I understand how much I meant to him, how much he needed to express his love. He was so clean, so sweet-smelling, in that new shirt laced with brown embroidery.[89]

5

For the elites of the old society the passing-down of family traditions and values to the next generation was particularly complicated; if they wanted to succeed in the new society, they could not simply stick to their customary ways, but had to adjust to Soviet conditions. To maintain a balance between old and new, families could adopt various strategies. They could, for example, lead a double life, retreating to a private world ('internal emigration') where they secretly held on to their old beliefs, perhaps concealing them from their own children, who were brought up in a Soviet way.

The Preobrazhenskys are a good example of a formerly elite family that secretly maintained some aspects of their old life even as they largely adapted to Soviet conditions. Before 1917, Pyotr Preobrazhensky had worked as a priest at the Priazhka Psychiatric Hospital in St Petersburg. He was one of the 'spiritualists' to whom the Empress Aleksandra had turned for help to cure the tsarevich from haemophilia before the arrival of Rasputin at the court. Pyotr's wife was a graduate of the Smolny Institute and a confidante of the Dowager Empress Mariia Fyodorovna. After 1917, Pyotr and his oldest son worked as porters at the hospital. His younger son, who had been a choir master at the Aleksandr Nevsky Monastery, joined the Red Army and died fighting in the Civil War. Pyotr's eldest daughter became a secretary in the Petrograd Soviet, while his younger daughter, Maria, gave up her career as a concert pianist to become inspector of collective farms in the Luga area. Maria's husband, a singer, became a sanitary worker in the Priazhka Hospital. Throughout the 1920s, the family lived together in an office at the back of the hospital. They never grumbled about their desperate poverty, but lived quietly, accepting the tasks set them by the new regime – with one exception. Every evening the icons were brought out of their secret hiding place, the votive lamps lit, and prayers held. The family went to church, celebrated Easter and always had a Christmas tree, even after Christmas trees were banned as a 'relic of the bourgeois way of life' in 1929. Maria and her husband made their daughter Tatiana wear a gold cross on a necklace, which they told her to keep concealed. 'I was brought up to believe in God and at the same time to learn from Soviet school and life,' recalls Tatiana. The Preobrazhenskys inhabited the margin between these two worlds. Pyotr secretly continued to work as an unofficial priest for people who still preferred to bury relatives with Christian rites – the silent majority of the Soviet population.* 'We never earned enough to make ends meet,' explains Tatiana, 'so my grandfather went around the cemeteries of Leningrad performing sacraments for a small fee.'[90]

---

*The government encouraged people to cremate their dead in secular Soviet ceremonies by providing free state cremations, but according to one morgue official in the early 1920s, 'the Russians are still either too religious or too superstitious to part from the Orthodox burial traditions' (GARF, f. 4390, op. 12, d. 40, l. 24).

For the old professional elites there was another way to adapt to Soviet society whilst maintaining their traditional family way of life. Doctors, lawyers, teachers, scientists, engineers and economists could put their skills at the disposal of the new regime, thereby hoping to safeguard some parts of their privileged existence. They could even live quite well, at least in the 1920s, when the expertise of these 'bourgeois specialists' was badly needed by the new regime.

Pavel Vittenburg was a leading figure in the world of Soviet geology and played an important role in the development of the Arctic Gulags, or forced labour camps, at Kolyma and Vaigach. He was born in 1884, the eighth of nine children in a family of Baltic Germans in Vladivostok in Siberia. Pavel's father came from Riga, but he was exiled to Siberia after taking part in the Polish uprising against tsarist rule in 1862–4. After his release he worked for the Vladivostok Telegraph. Pavel studied in Vladivostok, Odessa and Riga, and then went to Tübingen, in Germany, before moving to St Petersburg, a young and serious-minded Doctor of Science, in 1908. He married Zina Razumikhina, the daughter of a railway engineer and a distant relative, who was then studying medicine in St Petersburg. The couple bought a large and comfortable wooden house in the elite dacha resort of Olgino on the Gulf of Finland near St Petersburg. Three daughters were born: Veronika in 1912, Valentina in 1915 and Yevgeniia in 1922. It was a close and intimate family. As a father, Yevgeniia recalls, Pavel was 'attentive, patient and loving', and at Olgino they 'lived a happy life, with music, painting and evenings of reading as a family'. There were long summer walks, and lazy meals that were beautifully prepared by the nanny Annushka, who had nursed Zina as a child. The Vittenburgs were often joined by artists and writers, like the famous children's writer Kornei Chukovsky, who spent several summers at their house. This Chekhovian existence continued throughout the 1920s.

The Vittenburgs were driven by a strong ethos of public service, which was almost the defining feature of the nineteenth-century intelligentsia. After 1917, Zina used her medical training to set up a hospital in the neighbouring town of Lakhta, where she treated patients free of charge. Pavel, elected chairman of the Lakhta Council in 1917, organized a school to teach technology to children of the labouring poor. 'He was always working,' Yevgeniia recalls. 'If he was not writing, he was planning explorations for the Polar Commission or organizing papers for

The Vittenburg family at Olgino, 1925

the Geological Museum. He was always doing something and rarely could relax.' Pavel was committed to the cause of polar exploration and geology, then still in its infancy, in which the Soviet Union led the world. Polar explorers were portrayed as heroes in Soviet books and films, and during the 1920s, the Soviet government invested a large share of its scientific budget in geological surveys of potential mining operations in the Arctic zone. Pavel was not interested in politics but he welcomed the attention from the Soviet regime and the opportunity it gave him to pursue his science in an organized and disciplined environment. 'The past ten years have been a heroic period of polar exploration,' Pavel wrote in 1927, shortly before leaving Olgino to carry out a survey of the gold-fields at Kolyma. 'The future promises even greater achievements.'[91]

Another elite couple who adapted to Soviet conditions in this way were the parents of the writer Konstantin Simonov, who stands at the centre of this book. Simonov was another child of 1917. His mother Aleksandra descended from the Obolenskys, a grand and ancient clan of princely bureaucrats and landowners, who occupied a prominent position in the Imperial system, although her father Leonid, like many noblemen, had entered commerce in the 1870s. Born in 1890, and a graduate of the Smolny Institute, Aleksandra was a woman of the 'old order', whose aristocratic attitudes were frequently at odds with Soviet ways. Tall and imposing, 'Alinka', as she was known within the family, had old-fashioned notions of 'correct behaviour' – rules of conduct she passed down to her son, who was well known for his gentlemanly manners throughout his life (even at the height of his career in the Stalinist establishment). Alinka expected people to be courteous, especially to women, loyal to their friends and constant in their principles. She was 'a pedagogue', recalls her grandson, and 'never tired of telling other people how they should behave'.[92]

In 1914, Aleksandra married Mikhail Simonov, a colonel of the General Staff who was almost twice her age, and a year later Konstantin was born.* An expert on military fortifications, Mikhail fought in Poland in the First World War, rising to become a general-major in the Fifth Army and the chief of staff of the 4th Army Corps. In 1917, he disappeared. For the next four years, Aleksandra did not hear from Mikhail, who was, it seems, in Poland on some secret mission that prevented him from making contact with his family in Soviet Russia. Perhaps he joined the Polish Army, or possibly the Whites, with whom the Poles were allied in the Russian Civil War. In any case he was reluctant to return to Russia, where his status as a tsarist general, if not as a counter-revolutionary, might well lead, at the very least, to his arrest by the Bolsheviks. It is unclear how much Aleksandra knew about the activities of her husband. Whatever she knew, she concealed it from her son, no doubt to protect his interests. In 1921, Mikhail wrote to Aleksandra from Poland. He begged her to come with their son and live with him in Warsaw, where he had become a Polish citizen. Aleksandra could not make up her mind what to do. She took seriously her marriage vows, and Mikhail was gravely ill. But in the end she was too much of a patriot to leave Russia. 'My mother reacted with sad incomprehension to the Russian post-revolutionary emigration, even though she had friends and relatives who had fled abroad,' recalled Simonov in later years. 'She simply could not understand how it was possible to leave Russia.'[93]

Aleksandra joined the army of young women from noble and bourgeois families who worked as typists, accountants and translators in the offices of the new Soviet government. In the autumn of 1918, she was evicted from her apartment in Petrograd. It was the height of the Red

---

*They christened him Kirill and called him that throughout his life, but when he embarked on his literary career, in the 1930s, he changed his name to Konstantin, because he found it awkward to pronounce his r's. For the sake of clarity we shall call him Konstantin throughout the text.

Terror, the Bolshevik campaign against the old elites, when 'former people' like the Obolenskys, ruined nobles and members of the 'bourgeoisie' were kicked out of their homes and stripped of all their property, put to work in labour teams, or arrested and imprisoned by the Cheka as 'hostages' in the Civil War against the Whites. After many months of unsuccessful petitioning to the Soviet, Aleksandra and the boy Konstantin left Petrograd for Riazan, 200 kilometres south-east of the Soviet capital, where they lived with Aleksandra's older sister Liudmila, the widow of an artillery captain killed during the First World War, whose regiment was based in the Riazan garrison. They were among the millions of urban-dwellers who fled the hungry cities in the Civil War to be closer to supplies of food.[94]

Riazan was a town of about 40,000 residents in the early 1920s. One of its main institutions was the Military School, established by the Bolsheviks to train commanders for the Red Army in the Civil War. Among its staff was Aleksandr Ivanishev, a colonel in the tsarist army, wounded twice (and three times the victim of a poison-gas attack) in the First World War, who had been enrolled by Trotsky in the Red Army as a commander. Aleksandra married Ivanishev in 1921. For a daughter of the elite Obolensky clan, it was no doubt a case of marrying down: Aleksandr was the son of a humble railway worker. But Aleksandra had fallen on hard times and in her husband's military ethos she found a reflection of the principles of her own noble class, not least its ideals of public service, from which, it seems, she took some comfort in these uncertain circumstances.[95]

Aleksandr was a consummate 'military man' – punctual, conscientious, orderly and strictly disciplined – although kind and gentle-hearted in nature. He ran the household in Riazan like a regiment, recalls Konstantin:

Our family lived in the officers' barracks. We were surrounded by military personnel, and the military way of life ruled our every step. The morning and evening parades took place on the square in front of our house. Mother was involved in various army committees with the other wives of officers. When guests came to our house the talk was always about the army. In the evenings my stepfather drew up plans for military exercises. Sometimes I helped him. Discipline in the family was strict, purely military. Everything was planned by the hour, with orders given to the .00. You could not be late. You could not refuse a task. You had to learn to hold your tongue. Even the smallest lie was strictly frowned upon. In accordance with their service ethic, my mother and father introduced a strict division of labour in our home. From the age of six or seven, I was burdened with more and more responsibilities. I dusted, washed the floor, helped wash the dishes, cleaned the potatoes, took care of the kerosene and fetched the bread and milk.[96]

This upbringing had a crucial influence on Simonov. The military values which he assimilated as a child ('obedience and conscientiousness, a readiness to overcome all obstacles, the imperative to say "yes" or "no", to love strongly, and to hate as well', as he himself defined these qualities) prepared him to embrace the quasi-military Soviet system of political command in the 1930s and 1940s.

> At thirteen years I knew:
> That what is said is meant.
> Yes is yes. No is no.
> To argue is in vain.
> I knew the meaning of duty.
> I knew what sacrifices were.
> I knew what courage could achieve,
> There is no mercy for cowardice!
>   (From 'Father', 1956)[97]

Simonov revered his stepfather ('a man I never saw in anything but military uniform') and from an early age considered him to be his real father. The military principles of duty and obedience he assimilated from Aleksandr were combined in him with the ideas of public service he received from his mother and her aristocratic milieu. These principles were reinforced by the books he read as a boy, which were infused with the Soviet cult of the military. He was inspired by legendary stories of the Civil War, like Dmitry Furmanov's *Chapaev* (1925), a 'Soviet classic' read by every schoolchild. His boyhood heroes were all military men. His schoolbooks were filled with doodles of the soldier he wanted to become.[98] Just as early, Simonov was conscious of the need to take his place in a hierarchy of command. He was brought up to think of himself not just as a soldier, but as an officer, with responsibility for lesser men. At the same time, his hypertrophied sense of public duty and obedience also required subordination to his superiors. As he himself would write,

Konstantin (far left), Aleksandra and Aleksandr Ivanishev
(right), Riazan, 1927

his idea of 'being good' was synonymous with 'honesty' and 'conscientiousness' (*poriadochnost*') – a concept that would later form
the basis of his support for the Stalinist regime. All his formative
relationships involved figures of authority. As an only child, he spent
most of his time in the company of adults, and he was quite adept at
winning their approval. Without close friends at school, he never really
learned the moral lessons of friendship, or loyalty to peers, which
might have worked against his growing tendency to please superiors,
although comradeship was a dominating theme of his poetry (a sphere
for his yearnings) in the 1930s and 1940s. Simonov was clever and
precocious. He read a lot and studied hard. He joined lots of clubs,
took part in plays and was a Pioneer. Aside from his doodles, his
schoolbooks reveal a serious boy who spent long hours drawing maps
and graphs, making lists and charts and organizing tasks like a
bureaucrat.[99]

In his memoirs, written in the last year of his life, Simonov maintained
that his parents had accepted the Soviet regime. He could not remember
any conversations in which they had voiced their disapproval of the
government, or regretted not having emigrated after 1917. In his pre-

Page from Simonov's school notebook (1923)

sentation, his parents took the view that, as members of the intelligentsia, it was their duty to stay and work for Soviet Russia and, even if their own values were not 'Soviet', it was their obligation to bring up Konstantin as a 'Soviet' child. But this is only half the truth. Behind her appearance of political loyalty, Aleksandra concealed a critical opinion of the Soviet regime, which had, after all, brought disaster to her family. Aleksandra's brother Nikolai was forced to flee to Paris after 1917 (as a former governor of Kharkov province, he would have been arrested by the Bolsheviks). She never saw him again. The rest of the family – Aleksandra, her mother and three sisters – lived in fear and poverty, first in Petrograd and then in Riazan. After the Civil War, Aleksandra's sisters Sonia and Daria returned to Petrograd; and when their mother died in 1923, Liudmila went back to Petrograd as well. Left on her own in Riazan, Aleksandra struggled to adapt to the Soviet environment ('I was born in another world,' she wrote to her son in 1944. 'The first twenty-five years of my life were spent in conditions of comfort . . . Then my life was suddenly destroyed . . . I washed and cooked and went to the shops and worked all day'). In addition to passing on the values of the aristocracy, Aleksandra also strove to keep religious practices alive. She took her son to church until he was twelve (in his later letters to his aunts he continues to greet them in religious terms on Orthodox holidays). Yet she also taught him that his noble origins were dangerous and that they needed to be hidden if he was to advance.[100] Despite the relatively liberal climate of the NEP, the class war unleashed by the Revolution had only come to a temporary halt, and, beneath the peaceful surface, pressures were growing for a renewed purge of the old elites which threatened families like the Simonovs.

In 1927, Simonov was taken by his mother to stay with relatives of his stepfather in the countryside near Kremenchug. 'Aunt Zhenia' lived with her husband, Yevgeny Lebedev, an old general who had long ago retired from the tsarist army on account of his wounded leg, which left him paralysed and dependent on his younger wife. The general was a liberal type, good-natured and optimistic, and he did not grumble or complain about the Soviet government. Konstantin enjoyed his company, because he was interesting and told stories well. One day, after walking in the woods, Konstantin came back to his aunt's house. The door was opened by a stranger, who turned out to be one of several OGPU men, who had come to search the house for incriminating evidence of counter-revolutionary activity prior to the arrest of the general. In his memoirs Simonov recalls the incident:

At the moment I entered one of the OGPU men was lifting up the mattress, on which the old man was resting, and searching underneath ... 'Sit down, boy, and wait,' he said to me, pointing to a stool. He was not exactly rude, more imperious, and I understood that I had to sit and obey him ... The search was being conducted by two men in uniform, but they had not produced a search warrant, and the old general was cursing them, getting very angry, and threatening to complain about their unlawful behaviour. Aunt Zhenia, it seemed to me, was relatively calm, fearing most of all that her husband might have a heart attack, and tried to calm him down without success. The men carried on with the search, leafing through the pages of every book in turn, looking under oilcloths and embroideries that were stacked on shelves. The old man, propped up against the wall and half-lying on the bed, continued cursing ... Finally, the search came to an end, and, without taking anything, the men left. They behaved with restraint, they did not swear or scold, because they were dealing with an old man who was paralysed ... In my consciousness this event did not appear as something frightening, tragic or disturbing; it seemed more or less normal.

The interesting thing about this episode is the way it was perceived by Simonov. He had witnessed an illegal act of state repression against his family, but he was not frightened by it, or so he later claimed; somehow he even saw it as a routine ('normal') procedure. Simonov would respond in a similar manner to the arrest of other relatives, including his step-father and three aunts, during the 1930s, rationalizing the events as 'necessary' acts – mistakes, perhaps, because his relatives were surely innocent, but understandable in the broader context of the state's need to root out potential counter-revolutionaries.[101]

In 1928, Simonov moved with his parents to Saratov, a large industrial city on the Volga, where Aleksandr became an instructor in the military school. The family lived in the barracks, occupying two adjoining rooms, and shared a communal kitchen with several other families. Simonov began at a secondary school, but in 1929, at the age of just fourteen, he abandoned it, deciding not to complete the academic education planned for him by his parents, but to switch to a Factory Apprentice School (FZU), where general education was combined with technical training. Like many children of the old intelligentsia, Simonov was eager to fashion a new 'proletarian' identity for himself so as to break free of his social origins, which were certain to hold him back in Soviet society. The FZUs and higher technical institutions of the late 1920s were full of children from intelligentsia families who, refused entry to university (which now favoured applicants from the working class), had gone instead to factory or technical schools to qualify as 'proletarians', a qualification that would open doors to further jobs and education. Like Simonov, who registered his mother as an 'office worker', many children from the old elite concealed their social origins, or made selective use of their biographies, to gain admission to technical schools and colleges. Most went on to become engineers or technicians in the industrial revolution of the First Five Year Plan (1928–32), developing a new professional identity that liberated them from the great dilemma about social class – because all that mattered was their dedication to the cause of Soviet industry. Simonov's rejection of the academic education chosen for him by his parents was significant: it was the moment when he turned his back on the old civilization, into which he had been born, and adopted a 'Soviet' identity.

At the FZU Simonov learned to become a lathe-turner. In the evenings he worked as an apprentice at a munitions factory in Saratov. Simonov had 'no real talent for industrial work', as he later came to recognize, and only persevered 'from vanity'. In his letters to his aunt Sonia in

Leningrad, the teenage boy displayed his social activism and enthusiasm for the Soviet cause:

1929
Dear Auntie Sonia!
Forgive me for taking so long to reply to your nice letter. I have never been so busy. I am a member of four clubs: I'm on the governing committee of two of them, and the chairman of one (the young naturalists). Besides that, I'm a member of the commission of [socialist] competition, the reading group, the school's editorial board and the chemical brigade [against posion-gas attacks]. I'm also an instructor in collective assistance, a member of the management committee [reporting to the school administration on the political activities and opinions of the students at the FZU] and part of MOPR [the International Society of Workers' Aid]. At the moment, I'm also organizing anti-religious propaganda through the management sub-committee and running the class committee. Recently I was placed in charge of organizing a chess club in the school. I think that's all of it.[102]

It is hard to say what lay behind this frenzy of activity – the energies of a teenager brought up in the public-service ethos, the calculation that through these commitments he might hide his social origins and secure his position in Soviet society, or a passionate belief in the Communist ideal. But it was the start of Simonov's involvement in the Stalinist regime.

6

The mercantile class, too, found ways to adapt to the new regime, especially after the introduction of the NEP. In 1922, Samuil Laskin, his wife and their three daughters left the town of Orsha and settled in Moscow. The family moved into a basement room near the Sukharevka market, which was then a by-word for the private trade that flourished under the NEP. Samuil Laskin was a small tradesman, a dealer in herring and other salted fish. Like many Jews, he had come to Moscow to take advantage of the new opportunities for private traders. He had all sorts of dreams for his daughters, wanting them to benefit from Soviet schools and universities so that they could join the professions, from which, as a Jew, he had been barred before 1917.

Born in 1879, Samuil came from a large clan of traders in Orsha, a market town of single-storeyed wooden houses, without running water or sewers, in the Pale of Settlement. His father, Moisei, a wholesale merchant of salted fish, lived in a run-down wooden house between the Orthodox and Catholic churches on the busy road to Shklov. Orsha was a multi-cultural town where Russians, Poles, Belorussians, Latvians and Lithuanians lived together with the Jews (there was one small pogrom in 1905). The Laskins spoke Yiddish and Russian. They observed the Jewish rituals, went to synagogue and sent their children to the Jewish school, but they also placed a high value on their children's education and advancement in Russian society. Moisei had six children. The three oldest (Sima, Saul and Samuil) were all schooled at home; but the younger children (Fania, Iakov and Zhenia) went to university and qualified as doctors, somehow managing to circumvent the tsarist restrictions that barred Jews from Russian universities and professions.* It was an extraordinary achievement for those times, especially for the two girls, Fania and Zhenia.[103]

Samuil followed Moisei into trade. In 1907, he married Berta, the daughter of a Jewish trader in the neighbouring town of Shklov, where the couple lived with their three daughters, Fania (born in 1909), Sonia (1911) and Yevgeniia (1914), until the Revolution of 1917. A kind and gentle man, practical and wise, with a lively interest in literature and international politics, Samuil embraced the Revolution as the liberation of the Jews. He had always dreamed of educating his beloved daughters, and with the declaration of the NEP, which made it possible for him to make a living in Moscow, he thought his dream would at last come true.

The NEP turned Moscow into a vast market-place. The city's population doubled in the five years after 1921. After the hardships of the Civil War, when private trade had been outlawed, there was a huge demand for anything the market could provide. Great crowds flocked to the street markets, like the Sukharevka, where traders dealt in everything, from scrap-iron to clothes, pots and pans, and works of art. Samuil had a herring stall on Bolotnaia Square, a food market that catered to the city's busy restaurants and cafés, on the south side of the Moscow River, not far from the Kremlin. No one knew more than

---

*Fania and Iakov went to Iurev (Tartu) University in Estonia, one of the few universities in the Empire to admit Jews before 1917.

Samuil did about the herring trade. He could open a tin of the salted fish and tell at once where it had come from – the Volga River or the Aral Sea, near Astrakhan or Nizhny Novgorod.

Life was hard at first. The Laskins' basement room on First Meshchan-skaia Street was bare. They slept on mattresses on the floor and sus-pended a curtain from the ceiling to separate the children's sleeping area from the adults'. They shared a toilet and a kitchen with the other residents on the upper floor. But by 1923, Samuil's herring business was thriving, and the Laskins moved into a rented flat on the second floor of a once-grand house on Sretenskaia Street. It was a comfortable apart-ment with three spacious rooms, a large bathroom and its own private toilet and kitchen, a rare luxury in Moscow in those days. Samuil was doing so well that he was able to send money every month to his parents in Orsha, and to help his nephew Mark, who had also come to Moscow with his family. There were regular Laskin outings to the Bolshoi Theatre, where Samuil always bought a box.[104]

But then, in 1923–4, shortages of goods and price inflation inflamed proletarian resentment of the NEPmen and their new wealth, and to quash popular unrest the city Soviets closed down 300,000 private businesses.[105] The Laskins became victims of the backlash. Samuil's business survived, but he was forced to pay a special tax to the Moscow Soviet and, like many small tradesmen, he was relegated to the sub-class of *lishentsy* – people who were deprived of electoral and other civil rights. Samuil endured these punishments calmly. For several years he paid the excessive 'business rent' on his corrugated-iron stall – one of many special taxes imposed by the Moscow Soviet on private traders to appease the working class's resentment of the NEP. In 1925, Samuil turned down an invitation to move to Iran, where the fish industry was heavily dependent on Russian expertise. He wanted his three daughters to grow up in the Soviet Union, to take advantage of the many opportuni-ties he believed – mistakenly, as it turned out – had opened up. Fania was the eldest and most practical of the three girls. In 1926, she passed her school exams with distinction, but because of her father's status as a *lishenets*, she was rejected when she applied to a medical college, so she worked instead in a factory and studied economics at night school. Sonia was a serious-minded girl, articulate and bright with a striking beauty, who had suffered from polio as a child, which left her partly paralysed. Barred like her sister from higher education, Sonia studied statistics in evening classes at the Sokolniki Industrial School in Moscow, before enrolling at the Institute of Steel in 1928. Like many Jews, including her cousin Mark, who became an engineer, Sonia embraced the industrial programme of the First Five Year Plan, which promised

The Laskin family (from left to right): Berta, Sonia, Yevgeniia (Zhenia), Fania, Moscow, 1930. Samuil was in exile at this time

to modernize the backward peasant Russia, the Russia of pogroms, from which the Laskins had come to the city to escape. Yevgeniia (Zhenia), the youngest of the girls, was more artistic in her temperament and studied literature, a passion shared by all her family. The Laskin household was 'always in the middle of a literary debate', recalls Fania. When Sonia was rejected by the Komsomol, as a child of a *lishenets*, in 1927, the three girls formed a reading circle of their own with Mark and children of their parents' friends who lived nearby. They would discuss politics and hold 'show trials' of characters from literature. Once they held a trial of the Old Testament: they found a copy of the Bible and studied it together for a month.[106] Public trials of literary works, ideologies and religious customs were popular agitprop events in the 1920s and 1930s.

The Laskins were typical of the first generation of Soviet Jews. They identified with the Revolution's internationalism, which promised to eradicate all national prejudice and inequalities, and with its liberating vision of the modern city, which offered Jews unprecedented access to schools and universities, science and the arts, professions and trades. Within a generation of 1917, Russia's Jews had become an urban people, as the population of the rural shtetls in the former Pale of Settlement either emigrated or died out (by the start of the Second World War, 86 per cent of Soviet Jews lived in urban areas, half of them in the eleven largest cities of the USSR). Moscow's Jewish population grew from 15,000 in 1914 to a quarter of a million Jews (the city's second largest ethnic group) in 1937.[107] The Jews flourished in the Soviet Union. They made up a large proportion of the elite in the Party, the bureaucracy, the military command and the police. Judging from the memoirs of the period, there was relatively little anti-Semitism or discrimination, although there were many Jews, like Samuil Laskin, who were deprived of civil rights because of their social class and their connection with private trade. It is true that numerous synagogues were closed, but this was a result of the general Bolshevik campaign against religion in the 1920s and 1930s. The family continued as the real centre of Jewish religious life, with the older generation taking charge of the traditional prayers and rituals, which in most households coexisted with the observance of Soviet public holidays and the acceptance of Soviet beliefs by the younger in particular. There was a thriving secular Yiddish culture, actively promoted by the Soviet government, with Yiddish language schools, Yiddish cinema and Yiddish theatres, including the Moscow State Yiddish Theatre, under the direction of Solomon Mikhoels, which became a focal point for many Bolsheviks and left-wing Jewish intellectuals. In most Jewish families in the big cities the attachment to traditional Jewish culture lived side by side with an intellectual commitment to Russian-Soviet literature and art as a means of entry to the wider culture of the international world.[108]

This complex multiple identity (Jewish-Russian-Soviet) was retained by Samuil and Berta. Neither was religious. They never went to synagogue or observed Jewish rituals and holidays, though Berta always prepared Jewish food on Soviet holidays. Samuil and Berta knew Yiddish, but Russian was the language they spoke at home. Their daughters understood them when they spoke Yiddish, but did not speak it properly and made no effort to learn the language, which they regarded as an 'exotic relic' of the past. For the daughters, the question of identity was simpler. 'We did not want to think of ourselves as Jews,' recalls Fania. 'Nor did we want to be Russians, though we lived in Russia and were steeped in its culture. We thought of ourselves as Soviet citizens.' The family looked to education, industry and culture as the road to personal liberation and equality. Samuil took an active interest in Soviet politics and drew enormous pride from the achievements of prominent Jewish Bolsheviks like Trotsky. Although not an educated man, he filled his house with books and newspapers and loved to discuss political events, especially events abroad, on which he was extremely well informed. He held a 'kitchen parliament' with friends and relatives who came on Sundays for the famous 'Laskin suppers'; Berta's Jewish cooking was said to be unrivalled in Moscow.[109]

In some Jewish families the desire to be 'Soviet' was reflected in the suppression of any lingering identification with Jewish culture or religion. In the Gaister household, for example, Jewish customs were so minimal, consisting of little more than the odd Jewish dish, or phrase in Yiddish, or family legends about the pogroms in tsarist times, that even as a teenager Inna was not really conscious of herself as a Jew. Rebekka Kogan, born in 1923 to a Jewish family in the Gomel area, where Inna's parents met, recalls her own childhood in Leningrad as 'entirely Soviet'. Her parents observed the main Jewish customs and spoke Yiddish on occasion, especially when they did not want Rebekka to understand, but otherwise they brought her up 'in a modern way', she says, 'without religion, or the influence of my grandparents, who still clung to Jewish ways'.[110]

Ida Slavina had a similar childhood. She was born in Moscow in 1921 to the family of a prominent Soviet jurist, Ilia Slavin, who had played an important role in the emancipation of the Jews in Belorussia. Ilia had been born in a small town near Mogilyov in 1883, the eldest son in a large family of poor Jewish labourers. From the age of twelve, Ilia worked and studied in a local pharmacy. By qualifying as a pharmacist, he was legally entitled to live outside the Pale of Settlement.* In 1905, he enrolled as an external student at the Law Faculty of Kharkov University. Despite his lack of formal education beyond the age of twelve, Ilia came top in the first-year examinations, which allowed him to enrol officially, as one of the 3 per cent of Jewish students permitted by the government's quota. After he had graduated from the university, Ilia was offered a position in the faculty, provided he converted to Christianity. But he turned the offer down and returned to the Pale of Settlement, where

---

*Jews were allowed to live outside the Pale of Settlement if they were merchants of the first guild, exceptionally talented craftsmen, university students or qualified pharmacists.

he worked as an assistant to a barrister in Mogilyov. During the First World War, when the Germans occupied the western territories, Ilia moved to Petrograd, where he worked in the headquarters of the Union of Towns, helping Jews from the Pale of Settlement to resettle in Russia. After 1917, Ilia was elected as a judge and worked in the People's Courts of Mogilyov, Gomel and Vitebsk. He moved to Moscow in 1921 and continued to rise in the Soviet legal establishment. A handsome, brilliant man, kind and gentle-hearted, Ilia had high ideals, which he invested in the Soviet experiment, even to the point of denying his Jewishness.

From 1903, Ilia had been an active Zionist, a well-known member of the Proletarians of Zion Party, which aimed to establish a socialist society in Palestine. Ilia's Zionism was a product of his life in the Pale of Settlement, where the Proletarians of Zion were mainly based. But once in Petrograd, where he came into contact with Jews who were Europeanized and assimiliationist, Slavin began to move away from Zionism to Social Democracy. Having embraced the Revolution as an international cause, Slavin accepted the need to subordinate Jewish national interests to the class struggle. As the Chairman of the Vitebsk Court, he even defended the perpetrators of a working-class pogrom against the Jews in 1919, on the grounds that it was an expression of their class hatred of the Jewish factory managers.[111] In 1920, Ilia left the Zionist movement, briefly joining the Bundists (Jewish Marxists) before moving to the Bolsheviks in 1921. Slavin acknowledged his 'political mistakes' (Zionism and Jewish nationalism) in his autobiography, written when he joined the Bolsheviks, and from that moment on he banished Jewish culture from the Slavin home. He taught his wife Esfir to read and write in Russian, forbade her to speak Yiddish and brought up his two children, Isaak (born in 1912) and Ida, to be Soviet people without any Jewish traditions. Ida remembers:

Father tried so hard to be correct, to live the life of the ideal Bolshevik. We had no Jewish customs in our home, and we never spoke Yiddish – we children did not even know it. Once he had become a Bolshevik, my father made an effort to purge from our home everything that reminded him of the ghetto and the Pale of Settlement. As an internationalist, he believed in the equality of nations, in the Soviet Union, and filled our house with Soviet things. His prized possession was a marble miniature of Lenin's mausoleum that he kept on his desk.[112]

The Slavin family, 1927. Ida is with her father Ilia (centre), her mother Esfir to his right

Prospects for the new urban Jews, however, shone less brightly as the NEP came under further attack. In 1928, the Moscow Soviet again imposed a special business tax on small traders. For Samuil Laskin, the tax came at an awkward time. The NEP had re-established rights of private and cooperative ownership in housing, and earlier that year he had put money into a building project on Zubov Square: speculative builders were constructing a two-storeyed house in the courtyard of a large apartment block in this fashionable district of Moscow, and with his investment Samuil was set to own a three-room apartment on the upper floor. Samuil had dreams of private property – he wanted to provide for his three daughters while they were still studying – and so he refused to pay the tax in full. He was arrested, imprisoned briefly in Moscow and then sent into exile in Nizhny Novgorod.[113] The arrest was part of a nationwide assault on private trade, which began in 1927 and led eventually to the overturning of the NEP. This campaign against the NEP was inextricably linked to the rise of Stalin and the defeat of his two main rivals in the Party leadership, Trotsky and Bukharin, who continued to support the policies of a mixed economy introduced by Lenin in 1921.

The Bolsheviks had always been ambivalent about the NEP, but many of their proletarian supporters, who could not afford the prices charged by private shops, were firmly opposed to it. Their mistrust of the NEP was reinforced by the wild fluctuations of the market, which drove up prices whenever shortages of goods in the countryside led the peasants to withhold their foodstuffs from the towns. The first major breakdown of the market had occurred in 1923–4, when the Soviets had launched their initial attack on the NEPmen, largely to appease the grievances of the working class against the price inflation. In the middle of the 1920s the market stabilized, but a second major breakdown took place in 1927–8, when a poor harvest coincided with a shortage of consumer goods. As the price of manufactures rose, the peasantry reduced its grain deliveries to the state depots and cooperatives; the fixed procurement prices were far too low for them to buy the household goods they needed. Instead the peasants ate their grain, fed it to their cattle, stored it in their barns or sold it on the private market rather than release it to the state. Supporters of the NEP differed on the correct way to respond to the crisis. Bukharin favoured raising the procurement prices, mainly to preserve the market mechanism and the union with the peasants which Lenin had said was the basis of the NEP, although he acknowledged that the greater state expenditure would slow down the rate of investment in industry. Trotsky, Kamenev and Zinoviev (the United Opposition) were wary of making more concessions to the peasantry, which they feared would only postpone the Soviet goal of socialist industrialization. In their view, the state should resort to temporary requisitioning of the peasants' grain to secure the stocks of food and capital it needed to boost production of consumer goods, and only then restore the market mechanism with the peasantry. Stalin sided with Bukharin – but just until the defeat of Trotsky and Zinoviev at the Fifteenth Party Congress in December 1927 – after which he turned against Bukharin and the NEP. Denouncing the grain crisis as a 'kulak strike', Stalin called for a return to the requisitionings of the Civil War in order to support a Five Year Plan to industrialize the Soviet Union. He spoke in violent terms about rooting out the final remnants of the capitalist economy (petty trade and peasant farming), which, he claimed, had blocked the country's progress to socialist industrialization.

Stalin's violent rhetoric – his calls for a return to the class war of the Revolution and the Civil War – appealed to a broad section of the Party's proletarian base, among whom there was a growing sense that the bourgeoisie was returning in another form through the NEPmen, the 'bourgeois specialists' and the 'kulaks'. Many felt that the NEP was a retreat from the Bolshevik ideal of social justice and feared that it would lead to the restoration of a capitalist economy. 'We young Communists had all grown up in the belief that money was done away with once and for all,' recalls one Bolshevik. 'If money was reappearing, wouldn't rich people reappear too? Weren't we on the slippery slope that led back to capitalism? We put these questions to ourselves with feelings of anxiety.' Stalin's call for a return to the methods of the Civil War had a special appeal to younger Communists – those born in the 1900s and the 1910s – who were too young to have taken part in the revolutionary fighting of 1917–21 but who had been educated in the 'cult of struggle' based on stories of the Civil War. One Bolshevik (born in 1909) maintained in his memoirs that the militant world-view of his contemporaries had prepared them to accept Stalin's arguments about the need for 'renewed class war' against the 'bourgeois specialists', NEPmen, 'kulaks' and other 'hirelings of the bourgeoisie'. Young Communists had become disheartened, as one Stalinist explains:

The Komsomols of my generation – those who experienced the October Revolution at the age of ten or younger – chafed at our fate. In the Komsomol, in the factories, we lamented that there was nothing remaining for us to do: the Revolution was over, the harsh but romantic years of the Civil War would not come again, and the older generation had left us only a boring, prosaic life devoid of struggle and excitement.

Aleksei Radchenko wrote in his diary in 1927:

Progressive youth today has no real interest or focus for activity – these are not the years of the Civil War but just the NEP – a necessary stage of the Revolution but a boring one. People are distracted by personal affairs, by family matters . . . We need something to shake us up and clear the air (some people even dream of war).[114]

Stalin played on these romantic notions, of the Civil War as the 'heroic period' and the Soviet Union as a state engaged in a constant struggle with capitalist enemies at home and abroad. He manufactured the 'war scare' of 1927, filling the Soviet press with bogus stories about British 'spies' and 'invasion plans' against the Soviet Union, and used this fear to call for mass arrests of potential 'enemies' ('monarchists' and 'former people'). He also used the threat of war to support his arguments for a

Five Year Plan and building of the armed forces. The NEP, he argued, was too slow as a means of industrial armament, and not secure enough as a means of procuring grain in the event of war. Stalin's conception of the Five Year Plan was wholly predicated on ceaseless struggle with the enemy. In his political battles with Bukharin for the control of the Party in 1928–9, Stalin accused him of subscribing to the dangerous view that the class struggle would lessen over time and that 'capitalist elements' could be reconciled with a socialist system (in fact Bukharin argued that the struggle would continue in the economic sphere). This view, Stalin argued, would lead the Party to lower its defences against its capitalist enemies, allowing them to infiltrate the Soviet system and subvert it from within. In a precursor to the claims by which he rationalized the expanding waves of state repression in the Great Terror, Stalin insisted, on the contrary, that the resistance of the bourgeoisie was bound to intensify as the country moved towards socialism, so that renewed vigour was constantly required to 'root out and crush the opposition of the exploiters'.[115] This was the rationale that rallied Stalin's forces and secured his victory against Bukharin. Terror was the inspiration, not the effect, of the Five Year Plan.

The assault against the private traders was the opening battle of a renewed revolutionary war. Thousands of NEPmen were imprisoned or driven from their homes. By the end of 1928, more than half the 400,000 private businesses registered in 1926 had been taxed out of existence or closed down by the police; by the end of 1929, only one in ten remained. New restrictions on the *lishentsy* made life even harder for the families of the NEPmen. Rationing cards (introduced in 1928) were denied to the *lishentsy*, who were thus forced to buy their food from the few remaining private shops, where prices rose dramatically. More frequently than before, their families were expelled from state housing, and their children barred from Soviet schools and universities.[116]

Samuil Laskin returned to Moscow from exile in Nizhny Novgorod at the height of this class war. In the spring of 1929 the Laskins moved into their new home on Zubov Square. Samuil and Berta had one room, Sonia another, while Fania and Zhenia shared the living room. But Samuil's dreams of owning his own home were soon dashed by the abolition of private ownership, which followed the overturning of the NEP. The Laskin home was nationalized by the Moscow Soviet, which turned it into a communal apartment and moved in an old couple (both well known as police informers), who were given the two largest rooms, leaving all the Laskins to share just one rented room. In November 1929, Samuil's herring business was expropriated by the state. Samuil was arrested for a second time, held for several weeks in the Butyrki jail, and then exiled to Voronezh, from which he returned in 1930 to begin a new life as a Soviet employee in the fish trade.[117]

Samuil had lost everything. But he bore his reduced conditions, as he bore everything, without complaining once about the Soviet regime. Nadezhda Mandelshtam, a friend of Zhenia in the 1950s, wrote about this aspect of Samuil's character in her memoirs about the Stalin years:

Zhenia's father was a small, indeed, the smallest imaginable, tradesman, who brought up three daughters and dealt in salted herring. The Revolution made him blissfully happy: it proclaimed equal rights for Jews and enabled him to realize his dream of giving his three clever daughters a good education. When the NEP was launched, he took it at face value, and, to feed his daughters, started up his salted herring business – only to have it confiscated when he was unable to pay his taxes. No doubt he too did sums on his abacus to see how he could save his family. He was shipped off to Narym, or some such place. But he was broken neither by this nor by his previous stretch in prison – to which he went at a time when 'new methods', that is, tortures of a more refined kind than primitive beating, were being introduced in cases involving 'the confiscation of valuables'. From his first place of exile he sent a letter of such heartrending tenderness to his wife and three daughters that they decided to show it to no one outside the family. His whole life was spent in and out of exile, and later the same thing started with his daughters and their husbands, who also went into exile and camps. If it had not been for the father, who stood at the centre of it and never changed with the years, the fate of this family would have epitomized the typical Soviet life story. He was the quintessence of Jewish saintliness, possessing those qualities of mysterious spirituality and goodness which sanctified Job.[118]

2

The Great Break

(1928–32)

I

On 2 August 1930, the villagers of Obukhovo celebrated Ilin Day, an old religious holiday to mark the end of the high summer when Russian peasants held a feast and said their prayers for a good harvest. After a service in the church, the villagers assembled at the Golovins, the biggest family in Obukhovo, where they were given home-made pies and beer inside the house while their children played outside. As evening approached, the village dance (*gulian'e*) began. Led by a band of bala-laika players and accordionists, two separate rows of teenage boys and girls, dressed in festive cottons, set off from the house, singing as they danced down the village street.[1]

That year the holiday was overshadowed by violent arguments. The villagers were bitterly divided about whether they should form a collective farm (kolkhoz), as they had been ordered by the Soviet government. Most of the peasants were reluctant to give up their family farms, on which they had worked for generations, and to share their property, their horses, cows and agricultural equipment in a kolkhoz. In the collective farm all their land, their livestock and their tools would be collectivized; the peasants' individual plots of land would be grouped together in large fields suitable for tractors; and the peasants would become wage labourers, with only tiny kitchen gardens on which to keep their poultry and grow a few vegetables. The villagers of Obukhovo had a fierce attachment to the principles of family labour and property and they were frightened by the stories they had heard about collectiviz-ation in other northern villages. There were terrifying tales of soldiers forcing peasants into the kolkhoz, of mass arrests and deportations, of houses being burned and people killed, and of peasants fleeing from their villages and slaughtering their cattle to avoid collectivization. 'On our farms we can all work for ourselves,' Nikolai Golovin had warned a meeting of the commune in July, 'but on the kolkhoz we will become serfs again.'[2] Many of the older peasants in Obukhovo had been born before the abolition of serfdom in 1861.

In 1917, Nikolai had led the peasant revolution on the land. He organized the confiscation of the Church's land (there were no gentry estates in the area) and through the commune and the Soviet oversaw the redivision of the village land, allocating strips of arable land to the family farms according to their household size. Nikolai was well regarded by the other villagers, whose smallholding family farms, worked with their own labour on communal land, had increased in number as a result of the Revolution, and they often came to him for agricultural advice. They valued his intelligence and honesty, his industry, sobriety and quiet modesty, and trusted his opinions, because he understood and could explain in simple terms the policies of the Soviet government. The old millstone outside his house was an informal meeting place where villagers would gather in the summer evenings, and Nikolai would give his views on local incidents.[3]

The Golovins were defenders of peasant tradition. Their family farm was organized on patriarchal lines, where all the children worked under the command of their father and were brought up to obey him as an almost god-like figure of authority ('God is in the sky and father in the house'). Like all peasants, the Golovins believed in the rights of family labour on the land. This had been the guiding principle of the agrarian revolution of 1917–18. In the Civil War, when Nikolai had helped to organize the Red Army in the north, he had given his support to the Soviet regime on the understanding that it would defend these peasant rights (throughout the 1920s he kept a portrait of Kliment Voroshilov, the Soviet Commissar of Military Affairs, next to the icons in the main room of his house). But these rights were increasingly attacked by the Bolsheviks, whose militant young Komsomol activists led the campaign for collectivization in Obukhovo. The Komsomol held meetings in the village school, where violent speeches were made by agitators against the richest peasants in Obukhovo – most of all against the Golovins. The villagers had never heard such propaganda in the past and many were impressed by the long words used by the leaders of the Komsomol. At these meetings the villagers were told that they belonged to three

Yevdokiia and Nikolai with their son
Aleksei Golovin (1940s)

mutually hostile classes: the poor peasants, who were the allies of the proletariat, the middle peasants, who were neutral, and the rich or 'kulak' peasants, who were its enemies.* The names of all the peasants in these different classes were listed on a board outside the village school. These divisions were entirely generated by the Komsomol. The villagers had no previous conception of themselves in terms of social class. They had always thought of themselves as one 'peasant family', and the poorest peasants were normally respectful, and even deferential, to the most successful peasants like the Golovins. But at the meetings in the village school, when their tongues were loosened by alcohol, the poor would add their voice to the denunciations of the 'kulak Golovins'.[4]

The Komsomol in Obukhovo consisted of a dozen teenagers who

---

*The term 'kulak', derived from the word for a 'fist', was originally used by the peasants to distinguish exploitative elements (usurers, sub-renters of land, wheeler-dealers and so on) from the farming peasantry. An entrepreneurial peasant farmer, in their view, could not be a 'kulak', even if he hired labour. The Bolsheviks, by contrast, misused the term in a Marxist sense to describe any rich peasant. They equated the 'kulak' with a 'capitalist' on the false assumption that the use of hired labour in peasant farming (which was extremely rare in most of Russia) was a form of 'capitalism' (as opposed to a way of making up for shortages of labour on the farm). During the Civil War the Bolsheviks attempted to stir up class war in the countryside and requisition grain by organizing the landless peasants (mainly urban types) into Committees of the Poor (*kombedy*) against the 'kulaks', who were accused of hoarding grain. During collectivization the term 'kulak' was employed against any peasant – whether rich or poor – who was opposed to entering the collective farms.

went around the village in semi-military uniforms and carried guns. They were intimidating to the villagers. Their leader was Kolia Kuzmin, the eighteen-year-old son of a poor and alcoholic peasant whose squalid house with its broken roof was located at the far end of the village, where the poorest families in Obukhovo lived. As a boy, Kolia had been sent out by his family to beg from the other farms. He would often come to the Golovin household with a 'neighbourly request for matches, salt, kerosene or flour, which in the Kuzmin household never lasted until the New Year,' recalls Antonina, the daughter of Nikolai. Her father took pity on the teenager, giving him a job in his leather workshop in the courtyard of his farm; Kolia worked there for several years, until 1927, when he joined the Komsomol and turned against the Golovins.[5]

In many villages, especially remote ones like Obukhovo, the Bolsheviks depended on the Komsomol to do their agitation in the absence of a Party cell. For every rural Party member there were four rural Komsomol members in the mid-1920s. The nearest Party office to Obukhovo was seven kilometres away in the district town of Ustiuzhna. Since the village Soviet in Obukhovo was dominated by the Golovins, the restless young men of the village who joined the Komsomol were placed in charge of leading the campaign for the kolkhoz. From the autumn of 1928, when the Party leadership began to call for mass collectivization, Kuzmin and his comrades went around the village, inciting the poorest peasants to join them in a battle against the 'counter-revolutionary' influence of the 'kulaks' and the Church, and sending unsigned letters of denunciation to the district town. In the spring of 1929, Nikolai was expelled from the Obukhovo Soviet and deprived of his civil rights as 'the capitalist owner of a leather-working enterprise'. Then, in November, his house was searched by the village Komsomol, together with officials from the district town, who imposed a heavy tax of 800 roubles on his 'kulak' farm. This tax, part of a nationwide policy to 'squeeze out' the 'kulaks' and confiscate their property, resulted in the ruination of almost 4,000 peasant households in Vologda alone.[6]

To pay the tax Nikolai was forced to sell two milking cows, his shoe-making machinery, an iron bed and a trunk of clothes. With two of his four brothers, he even worked that winter on a building site in Leningrad to earn some extra cash. The three brothers were thinking of leaving Obukhovo, where the collectivization of agriculture now seemed unavoidable, and they wanted to find out what life was like in the city.

They slept on benches in a dormitory, ate their meals in cafeterias and saved up enough to send several hundred roubles home, but after a few months of living in this way, they decided to return to their village. 'It is no life for a human being,' Nikolai explained in a letter to his family, 'if one has to purchase everything, bread, potatoes and cabbage, from a shop.'[7]

Nikolai's return, in the spring of 1930, brought his relations with the Komsomol to a breaking point. One evening, he was having supper at his house with his brother Ivan Golovin, a peasant from the neighbouring village. They were sitting at the kitchen table by the window, and their silhouettes, illuminated by a kerosene lamp, were clearly visible to Kuzmin and his followers, who gathered outside in the dark. The young men were clearly drunk. They shouted at the 'kulaks' to 'come out', and then shot at the window. Ivan was hit in the head. He lay dead in a pool of blood.

A few weeks later, Kuzmin came again to Nikolai's house, this time with two Party officials from the district town. There was a gathering at Nikolai's house that night, and the main room was full of friends and relatives. Kuzmin accused them of holding an illegal assembly. 'Kulaks, open up, stop conspiring against Soviet power!' he shouted, banging on the door. He had a gun and shot into the air. Confronting the intruders on the porch, Nikolai refused to let them in. Kuzmin threatened to murder Nikolai ('I shall shoot you, just as I murdered your brother, and no one will punish me,' he was heard to say), whereupon a brawl ensued, and Nikolai pushed Kuzmin to the ground. Kuzmin and his comrades went away. A few days later he wrote to the chief of the Ustiuzhna political police (OGPU) denouncing Nikolai as a

kulak exploiter who is spreading anti-Soviet propaganda in our village together with a dozen other kulak elements. They are saying that the Soviet government is robbing the people. Their aim is to sabotage collectivization by turning the people against it.

Kuzmin must have known that this would be enough to get his former patron arrested, especially since his denunciation was supported by the two Bolsheviks, who added for good measure that Nikolai was 'always drunk' when he 'cursed the Soviets'.[8]

Sure enough, on 2 August, as their guests were readying to leave the Golovins at the end of the Ilin holiday, two officials came to arrest

Nikolai. Imprisoned in Ustiuzhna, Nikolai was convicted by a three-man OGPU tribunal of 'terrorist intent' (for striking Kuzmin to the ground) and sentenced to three years at the Solovetsky prison complex located on an island in the White Sea. The last time Antonina saw her father was through the bars of the Ustiuzhna jail. She had walked to the district centre with her mother, her brothers and sisters to catch a glimpse of Nikolai before he was dispatched to the Solovetsky camp. For the next three years the image of her father behind bars haunted Antonina's dreams.[9]

A few weeks after Nikolai's arrest, the peasants of Obukhovo were herded to a village meeting, at which they passed a resolution to close down their family farms and, handing over all their land, their tools and livestock, to establish a kolkhoz.

Collectivization was the great turning-point in Soviet history. It destroyed a way of life that had developed over many centuries – a life based on the family farm, the ancient peasant commune, the independent village and its church and the rural market, all of which were seen by the Bolsheviks as obstacles to socialist industrialization. Millions of people were uprooted from their homes and dispersed across the Soviet Union: runaways from the collective farms; victims of the famine that resulted from the over-requisitioning of kolkhoz grain; orphaned children; 'kulaks' and their families. This nomadic population became the main labour force of Stalin's industrial revolution, filling the cities and industrial building sites, the labour camps and 'special settlements' of the Gulag (Main Administration of Camps). The First Five Year Plan, which set this pattern of forced development, launched a new type of social revolution (a 'revolution from above') that consolidated the Stalinist regime: old ties and loyalties were broken down, morality dissolved, and new ('Soviet') values and identities imposed, as the whole population was subordinated to the state and forced to depend on it for almost everything – housing, schooling, jobs and food – controlled by the planned economy.

The eradication of the peasant family farm was the starting-point of this 'revolution from above'. The Bolsheviks had a fundamental mistrust of the peasantry. In 1917, without influence in the countryside, they had been forced to tolerate the peasant revolution on the land, which they had exploited to undermine the old regime; but they had always made it clear that their long-term goal was to sweep away the peasant smallholding system, replacing it with large-scale mechanized collective farms in which the peasants would be transformed into a 'rural proletariat'. Marxist ideology had taught the Bolsheviks to regard the peasantry as a 'petty-bourgeois' relic of the old society that was ultimately incompatible with the development of a Communist society. It was too closely tied to the patriarchal customs and traditions of Old Russia, too imbued in the principles and habits of free trade and private property and too given over to the 'egotism' of the family ever to be fully socialized.

The Bolsheviks believed that the peasants were a potential threat to the Revolution, as long as they controlled the main supply of food. As the Civil War had shown, the peasantry could bring the Soviet regime to the verge of collapse by keeping grain from the market. The grain crisis of 1927–8 renewed fears of a 'kulak strike' in Stalinist circles. In response, Stalin reinstituted requisitioning of food supplies and engineered an atmosphere of 'civil war' against the 'kulak threat' to justify the policy. In January 1928, Stalin travelled to Siberia, a key grain-producing area, and urged the local activists to show no mercy to 'kulaks' suspected of withholding grain. His battle-cry was backed up by a series of Emergency Measures instructing local organs to use the Criminal Code to arrest any peasants and confiscate their property if they refused to give their grain to the requisitioning brigades (a wild interpretation of the Code that met with some resistance in the government). Hundreds of thousands of 'malicious kulaks' (ordinary peasants like Nikolai Golovin) were arrested and sent to labour camps, their property destroyed or confiscated, as the regime sought to break the 'kulak strike' and transformed its overcrowded prisons into a network of labour camps (soon to become known as the Gulag).[10]

As the battle for grain intensified, Stalin and his supporters moved towards a policy of mass collectivization in order to strengthen the state's control of food production and remove the 'kulak threat' once and for all. 'We must devise a procedure whereby the collective farms will turn over their entire marketable production of grain to the state and co-operative organizations under the threat of withdrawal of state subsidies and credits,' Stalin said in 1928.[11] Stalin spoke with growing optimism about the potential of large-scale mechanized collective farms. Statistics showed that the few such farms already in existence had a much larger marketable surplus than the small agricultural surpluses produced by the vast majority of peasant family farms.

This enthusiasm for collective farms was relatively new. Previously, the Party had not placed much emphasis on collectivization. Under the NEP, the organization of collective farms was encouraged by the state through financial and agronomic aid, yet in Party circles it was generally agreed that collectivization was to be a gradual and voluntary process. During the NEP the peasants showed no sign of coming round to the collective principle, and the growth of the kolkhoz sector was pretty insignificant. After 1927, when the state exerted greater pressure through taxation policies – giving credits to collective farms and imposing heavy fees on 'kulak' farms – the kolkhoz sector grew more rapidly. But it was not the large *kommuny* (where all the land and property was pooled) but the smaller, more informal and 'peasant-like' associations called *TOZy* (where the land was farmed in common but the livestock and the tools were retained by the peasants as their private property) that attracted the most peasant interest. The Five Year Plan gave little indication that the Party was about to change its policies; it projected a moderate increase in the land sown by collective farms, and made no mention of departing from the voluntary principle.

The sudden change in policy was forced through by Stalin in 1929. The *volte face* was a decisive blow against Bukharin, who was desperately trying to retain the market mechanism of the NEP within the structure of the Five Year Plan, which in its original version (adopted in the spring of 1929 but dated retroactively to 1928) had envisaged optimistic but reasonable targets of socialist industrialization. Stalin pushed for even higher rates of industrial growth and, by the autumn of 1929, the target figures of the Five Year Plan had been raised dramatically. Investment was to triple; coal output was to double; and the production of pig-iron (which had been set to rise by 250 per cent in the original version of the Plan) was now set to quadruple by 1932. In a wave of frenzied optimism, which was widely shared by the Party rank and file, the Soviet press advanced the slogan 'The Five Year Plan in Four!'[12] It was these utopian rates of growth that forced the Party to accept the Stalinist policy of mass collectivization as, it seemed, the only way to obtain a cheap and guaranteed supply of foodstuffs for the rapidly expanding industrial labour force (and for sale abroad to bring in capital).

At the heart of all these policies was the Party's war against the peasantry. The collectivization of agriculture was a direct assault on the peasantry's attachment to the village and the Church, to the individual family farm, to private trade and property, which all rooted Russia in the past. On 7 November 1929, Stalin wrote an article in *Pravda*, 'The Year of the Great Break', in which he heralded the Five Year Plan as the start of the last great revolutionary struggle against 'capitalist elements' in the USSR, leading to the foundation of a Communist society built by socialist industry. What Stalin meant by the 'great break', as he explained to Gorky, was the 'total breaking up of the old society and the feverish building of the new'.[13]

From the summer of 1929, thousands of Party activists were sent into the countryside to agitate for the collective farms. Like the villagers of Obukhovo, most of the peasants were afraid to give up a centuries-old way of life to make a leap of faith into the unknown. There were precious few examples of good collective farms to persuade the peasantry. A German agricultural specialist working in Siberia in 1929 described the collective farms as 'candidates for death'. Very few had tractors or modern implements. They were badly run by people who knew little about agriculture and made 'crude mistakes', which 'discredited the whole process of collectivization'. According to OGPU, the perception of the peasants was that they would 'lose everything' – their land and cows, their horses and their tools, their homes and family – if they entered a kolkhoz. As one old peasant said: 'Lecturer after lecturer is coming and telling us that we ought to forget possessions and have everything in common. Why then is the desire for it in our blood?'[14]

Unable to persuade the peasantry, the activists began to use coercive measures. From December 1929, when Stalin called for the 'liquidation of the kulaks as a class', the campaign to drive the peasants into the collective farms took on the form of a war. The Party and the Komosomol were fully armed and mobilized, reinforced by local militia, special army and OGPU units, urban workers and student volunteers, and sent into the villages with strict instructions not to come back to the district centres without having organized a kolkhoz. 'It is better to overstep the mark than to fall short,' they were told by their instructors. 'Remember that we won't condemn you for an excess, but if you fall short – watch out!' One activist recalls a speech by the Bolshevik leader Mendel Khataevich, in which he told a meeting of eighty Party organizers in the Volga region:

You must assume your duties with a feeling of the strictest Party responsibility, without whimpering, without any rotten liberalism. Throw your bourgeois humanitarianism out of the window and act like Bolsheviks worthy of comrade Stalin. Beat down the kulak agent wherever he raises his head. It's war – it's them or us. The last decayed remnant of capitalist farming must be wiped out at any cost.[15]

During just the first two months of 1930, half the Soviet peasantry (about 60 million people in over 100,000 villages) was herded into the collective farms. The activists employed various tactics of intimidation at the village meetings where the decisive vote to join the kolkhoz took place. In one Siberian village, for example, the peasants were reluctant to accept the motion to join the collective farm. When the time came for the vote, the activists brought in armed soldiers and called on those opposed to the motion to speak out: no one dared to raise objections, so it was declared that the motion had been 'passed unanimously'. In another village, after the peasants had voted against joining the kolkhoz, the activists demanded to know which peasants were opposed to Soviet power, explaining that it was the command of the Soviet government that the peasants join collective farms. When nobody was willing to state their opposition to the government, it was recorded by the activists that the village had 'voted unanimously' for collectivization. In other villages only a small minority of the inhabitants (hand-picked by the activists) was allowed to attend the meeting, although the result of the vote was made binding on the population as a whole. In the village of Cheremukhova in the Komi region, for example, there were 437 households, but only 52 had representatives at the village assembly: 18 voted in favour of collectivization and 16 against, yet on this basis the entire village was enrolled in the kolkhoz.[16]

Peasants who spoke out against collectivization were beaten, tortured, threatened and harassed, until they agreed to join the collective farm. Many were expelled as 'kulaks' from their homes and driven out of the village. The herding of the peasants into the collective farms was accompanied by a violent assault against the Church, the focal point of the old way of life in the village, which was regarded by the Bolsheviks as a source of potential opposition to collectivization. Thousands of priests were arrested and churches were looted and destroyed, forcing millions of believers to maintain their faith in the secrecy of their own homes. Rural Communists and Soviet officials who opposed forcible collectivization were expelled from the Party and arrested.

In Stalin's view, the war against the 'kulaks' was inseparable from the collectivization campaign. As he saw it, there was nothing to be gained from trying to neutralize the 'kulaks', or from attempting to involve them as farm labourers in the kolkhoz, as some Bolsheviks proposed. 'When the head is cut off,' Stalin argued, 'you do not weep about the hair.'[17] To his mind, the persecution of the 'kulaks' had two purposes: to remove potential opposition to collectivization; and to serve as an example to the other villagers, encouraging them to join the collective farms in order not to suffer the same fate as the 'kulaks'.

For all the talk of 'kulaks', there was no such objective category. The term was so widely and randomly applied that virtually any peasant could be dispossessed as a 'kulak', yet this vagueness only added to the terror which the war against the 'kulaks' was intended to create. According to Leninist ideology, the 'kulaks' were capitalist farmers who employed hired labour, but this could not be said of more than a handful of the peasants who were actually repressed as 'kulaks' after 1929. The NEP had allowed the peasants to enrich themselves through their own labour, and some peasants, like the Golovins, had been able, through hard work, to build up a modest property on their family farms.* But the NEP had kept a tight control on the employment of hired labour, and in any case, after 1927, when taxes on the peasants were increased, most of the richest peasants, like the Golovins, lost much of their private wealth. The idea of a 'kulak class' of capitalist peasants was a fantasy. The vast majority of the so-called 'kulaks' were hard-working peasants like the Golovins – the most sober, thrifty and progressive farmers in the village – whose modest wealth was often the result of having larger families. The industry of the 'kulaks' was recognized by most of the peasantry. As one kolkhoz labourer said in 1931, the campaign against the 'kulaks' merely meant that all 'the best and hardest workers of the land' were pushed out of the collective farms.[18]

The destruction of the 'kulaks' was an economic catastrophe for the Soviet Union. It deprived the collective farms of the work ethic and

---

*The Golovins had two barns, several pieces of machinery, three horses, seven cows, a few dozen sheep and pigs, two carts, as well as household property, which included iron bedsteads and a samovar, both signs of wealth in the Soviet countryside.

expertise of the country's most industrious peasants, ultimately leading to the terminal decline of the Soviet agricultural sector. But Stalin's war against the 'kulaks' had little to do with economic considerations – and everything to do with the removal of potential opposition to the collectivization of the village. The 'kulaks' were peasant individualists, the strongest leaders and supporters of the old rural way of life. They had to disappear.

The 'liquidation of the kulaks' followed the same pattern nationwide. In January 1930, a Politburo commission drew up quotas of 60,000 'malicious kulaks' to be sent to labour camps and 150,000 other 'kulak' households to be exiled to the North, Siberia, the Urals and Kazakhstan. The figures were part of an overall plan for 1 million 'kulak' households (about 6 million people) to be stripped of all their property and sent to labour camps or 'special settlements'. The implementation of the quotas was assigned to OGPU (which raised the target to 3 to 5 per cent of all peasant households to be liquidated as 'kulak') and then handed down to the local OGPU and Party organizations (which in many regions deliberately exceeded the quotas in the belief that this demonstrated the vigilance expected by their superiors).[19] Every village had its own quota set by the district authorities. Komsomol and Party activists drew up lists of the 'kulaks' in each village to be arrested and exiled. They took inventories of the property to be confiscated from their homes when the 'kulaks' were expelled.

There was surprisingly little peasant opposition to the persecution of the 'kulaks' – especially in view of Russia's strong historical traditions of village solidarity (earlier campaigns against the 'kulaks', in the Civil War for example, had failed to split the peasantry). Certainly there were places where the villagers resisted the quota, insisting that there were no 'kulaks' among them and that all the peasants were similarly poor, and places where they refused to give up their 'kulaks', or even tried to defend them against the activists when they came to arrest them. But the majority of the peasantry reacted to the sudden disappearance of their fellow villagers with passive resignation born of fear. In some villages the peasants chose the 'kulaks' from their own number. They simply held a village meeting and decided who should go as a 'kulak' (isolated farmers, widows and old people were particularly vulnerable). Elsewhere, the 'kulaks' were chosen by drawing lots.[20]

Dmitry Streletsky was born in 1917 to a large peasant family in the

Kurgan region of Siberia. He recalls how his parents were selected for deportation from their village as 'kulaks':

There was no inspection or calculation. They simply came and said to us: 'You are going.' Serkov, the chairman of the village Soviet who deported us, explained: 'I have received an order [from the district Party committee] to find 17 kulak families for deportation. I formed a Committee of the Poor and we sat through the night to choose the families. There is no one in the village who is rich enough to qualify, and not many old people, so we simply chose the 17 families. You were chosen,' he explained to us. 'Please don't take it personally. What else could I do?'[21]

It is very difficult to give any accurate statistics for the number of people who were repressed as 'kulaks'. At the peaks of the 'anti-kulak campaign' (during the winter of 1929–30, the early months of 1931, and the autumn of 1932) the country roads were filled with long convoys of deportees, each one carrying the last of their possessions, pathetic bundles of clothes and bedding, or pulling them by cart. One eye-witness in the Sumy region of Ukraine saw lines 'stretching as far as the eye could see in both directions, with people from new villages continually joining' as the column marched towards the collecting points on the railway. There they were packed into cattle trucks and transported to 'special settlements'. Since the railways could not cope with the huge numbers of deportees, many of the 'kulaks' were held for months awaiting transportation in primitive detention camps, where children and the elderly died like flies in the appalling conditions. By 1932, there were 1.4 million 'kulaks' in the 'special settlements', mostly in the Urals and Siberia, and an even larger number in labour camps attached to Gulag factories and construction sites, or simply living on the run. Overall, at least 10 million 'kulaks' were expelled from their homes and villages between 1929 and 1932.[22]

Behind such statistics are countless human tragedies.

In January 1930, Dmitry Streletsky's family was expelled from the farm in Baraba in the Kurgan region, where they had lived for fifty years. His grandfather's house was destroyed – the farm tools and the carts, the horses and the cows transferred to the kolkhoz, while smaller items – such as clothes and linen, pots and pans – were distributed to the villagers. The family icons were all smashed and burned. Dmitry's grandparents, three of their four sons and their families (fourteen people

'Kulaks' exiled from the village of Udachne,
Khryshyne (Ukraine), early 1930s

in total) were rehoused in a cattle shed and barred from contact with
the other villagers, until the order for their deportation arrived from the
district town. Six weeks later, they were all exiled to a lumber camp in
the Urals (where the grandparents died within a year). Dmitry's father,
Nikolai, stayed with his family in Baraba. A Red Army veteran of the
Civil War, Nikolai had organized the first collective farm (a *TOZ*) in
the village, and his agricultural expertise was desperately needed by the
kolkhoz. Nikolai was allowed to keep his house, where he lived with his
wife Anna and their six children. But then, one day in the early spring
of 1931, they too were informed that they had been 'chosen' as 'kulaks'
for a second wave of deportations from Baraba. They were given just
one hour to pack their meagre belongings, before they were escorted
from the village under guard, left on their own on the open steppe and
told never to return. 'We lost everything,' recalls Dmitry.

What could we hope to pack up in an hour? Father wanted to take his walking-
sticks (one of them had a silver top), but the guards would not let him. They also
took my mother's gold chain and ring. It was daylight robbery. Everything was
left behind – our home, our barns, our cattle, our linen, clothes and chinaware.
All we had was a few scraps of clothing – and of course ourselves – our parents,
children, brothers and sisters – the true living wealth of our family.[23]

Valentina Kropotina was born in 1930 to a poor peasant family in
Belarus. They were repressed as 'kulaks' in 1932. Valentina's earliest

memory is of running with her parents from their home, which was burned on the orders of the village Communists. They set fire to it in the middle of the night, when the family was asleep inside. Valentina's parents barely had time to rescue their two daughters before escaping, with severe body burns, from their house engulfed in flames. Valentina's father was arrested that same night. He was imprisoned and later exiled to the Amur region of Siberia, where he spent the next six years in various labour camps. The family house and barn were burned to the

Valentina Kropotina (second from left) and her sister
(second from right) with three of their cousins, 1939

ground; the cow and pigs were confiscated for the collective farm; the fruit trees in their garden were cut down; their crops destroyed. All that was left was a sack of peas. Valentina's mother, an illiterate peasant woman called Yefimia, was barred from joining the kolkhoz. She was left to live with her two young daughters in the ruins of their house. Yefimia built a shack from the rubble of her former house on the edge of the village. She scraped a living from various cleaning jobs. Valentina and her sister did not go to school – as 'kulak daughters' they were banned for several years. They grew up on the streets, following their mother to her cleaning jobs. 'All my childhood memories are sad,' reflects Valentina. 'The main thing I remember is the feeling of hunger, which never went away.'[24]

Klavdiia Rublyova was born in 1913, the third of eleven children in a peasant family in the Irbei region of Krasnoiarsk in Siberia. Her mother died in 1924, while giving birth, leaving her father, Ilia, to bring up all the children on his own. An enterprising man, Ilia took advantage of the NEP to branch out from farming to market gardening. He grew poppy seeds and cucumbers, which could easily be tended by his young children. For this he was branded a 'kulak', arrested and imprisoned, and later sent to a labour camp, leaving his children in the care of Klavdiia, who was then aged just seventeen. The children were deprived of all their father's property: the house, which he had built, was taken over by the village Soviet, while the horses, cows and sheep and the farm tools were transferred to the kolkhoz. For several weeks, the children lived in the bath-house, until officials came to take them all away to an orphanage. Klavdiia ran off with the youngest child to Kansk, near Krasnoiarsk, where her grown-up sister Raisa lived. Before they went they sold their last possessions to the other villagers. 'We had nothing much to sell, we were just children,' Klavdiia recalls. 'There was a fur-lined blanket and an old sheepskin, a feather mattress, and a mirror, which somehow we had rescued from our house. That was all we had to sell.'[25]

What were the motives of the men and women who carried out this brutal war against the peasantry? Most of the collectivizers were conscripted soldiers and workers – people anxious to carry out orders from above (and in some cases, to line their pockets). Hatred of the 'kulaks' had been drummed into them by their commanders and by propaganda which portrayed the 'kulak parasites' and 'bloodsuckers' as dangerous 'enemies of the people'. 'We were trained to see the kulaks, not as human beings, but as vermin, lice, which had to be destroyed,' recalls one young activist, the leader of a Komsomol brigade in the Kuban. 'Without the kolkhoz,' wrote another collectivizer in the 1980s, 'the kulaks would have grabbed us by the throat and skinned us all alive!'[26]

Others were carried away by their Communist enthusiasm. Inspired by the romantic revolutionary passions stirred up by the propaganda of the Five Year Plan, they believed with the Bolsheviks that any miracle could be achieved by sheer human will. As one student in those years recalls: 'We were convinced that we were creating a Communist society, that it would be achieved by the Five Year Plans, and we were ready for any sacrifice.'[27] Today, it is easy to underestimate the emotional force of these messianic hopes and the fanaticism that it engendered, particularly in the younger generation, which had been brought up on the 'cult of struggle' and the romance of the Civil War. These young people wanted to believe that it was their calling to carry on the fight, in the words of the 'Internationale', for a 'new and better life'. In the words of one of the '25,000ers' – the urban army of enthusiasts sent into the countryside to help carry out the collectivization campaign: 'Constant struggle, struggle, and more struggle! This was how we had been taught to think – that nothing was achieved without struggle, which was a norm of social life.'[28]

According to this militant world-view, the creation of a new society would involve and indeed necessitate a bitter struggle with the forces of the old society (a logic reinforced by the propaganda of the Five Year Plan, with its constant talk of 'campaigns', 'battles' and 'offensives' on the social, economic, international and internal 'fronts'). In this way the Communist idealists reconciled the 'anti-kulak' terror with their own utopian beliefs. Some were appalled by the brutal violence. Some were even sickened by their own role in it. But they all knew what they were doing (they could not plead that they were ignorant or that they were simply 'following orders'). And they all believed that the end justified the means.

Lev Kopelev, a young Communist who took part in some of the worst atrocities against the Ukrainian peasants, explained how he rationalized his actions. Kopelev had volunteered for a Komsomol brigade which requisitioned grain from the 'kulaks' in 1932. They took everything, down to the last loaf of bread. Looking back on the experience in the 1970s, Kopelev recalled the children's screams and the appearance of the peasant men – 'frightened, pleading, hateful, dully impassive, exting-uished with despair or flaring up with half-mad daring ferocity':

It was excruciating to see and hear all this. And even worse to take part in it . . . And I persuaded myself, explained to myself. I mustn't give in to debilitating pity. We were realizing historical necessity. We were performing our revolu-tionary duty. We were obtaining grain for the socialist fatherland. For the Five Year Plan.[29]

There was widespread peasant resistance to collectivization, even though most villages acquiesced in the repression of 'kulaks'. In 1929–30, the police registered 44,779 'serious disturbances'. Commu-nists and rural activists were killed in their hundreds, and thousands more attacked. There were peasant demonstrations and riots, assaults against Soviet institutions, acts of arson and attacks on kolkhoz property, protests against closures of churches. It was almost a return to the situation at the end of the Civil War, when peasant wars throughout the land had forced the Bolsheviks to abandon requisitioning and introduce the NEP, only this time round the Soviet regime was strong enough to crush the peasant resistance (indeed, many of the peasant uprisings of 1929–30 were provoked by the police to flush out and suppress the 'kulak rebels'). Realizing their own impotence, the peasantry adopted the traditional 'weapons of the weak' to sabotage collectivization: they slaughtered their own livestock to prevent them being requisitioned by the collective farms. The number of cattle in the Soviet Union fell by 30 per cent in 1929–30, and by half from 1928 to 1933.[30]

Faced with the ruin of the Soviet countryside, Stalin called for a temporary halt to the collectivization campaign. In an article in *Pravda* ('Dizzy with Success') on 2 March 1930, he accused local officials of excessive zeal for using force against the peasantry and setting up kolkhozes by decree. Millions of peasants saw this as a licence to leave the collective farms, and they voted with their feet. Between March and June 1930 the proportion of Soviet peasant households enrolled in the collectives fell from 58 to 24 per cent (in the central Black Earth region it fell from 83 to just 18 per cent). But leaving the collective farm turned out to be no easy matter. It was almost impossible for the peasants to retrieve their private property, their tools and livestock. For six months there was an uneasy truce. Then, in September 1930, Stalin launched a second wave of collectivization, the stated aim of which was to collectivize at least 80 per cent of the peasant households – up from 50 per cent the first time around – and eliminate all 'kulaks' by the end of 1931. The Politburo instructed OGPU to prepare a thousand 'special settlements', each to receive up to 300 'kulak' families, in remote regions of the North, Siberia, the Urals and Kazakhstan. Two million people were exiled to these places in 1930–31.[31]

In September 1930, right at the start of this second wave, the kolkhoz in Obukhovo was established. 'New Life' (*Novyi byt*), the name of the kolkhoz, became the name of the village, which had been in existence as Obukhovo since 1522. Red flags were posted at the village gate to show that it had been collectivized. The old wooden church in the centre of the village was pulled down and broken up for wood, its bells removed and taken off to be melted down, while a group of peasant women watched and cried.

The peasants lost their plots of land, which were reorganized into large collective fields. The kolkhoz took away the work-horses and locked up all the cows in dairy sheds; but the promised new machinery did not arrive, so the cows were returned to their owners for milking, and a milk tax was imposed on every house. Kolia Kuzmin, the leader of the Komsomol, became the chairman of the kolkhoz. He took a bride from a nearby village and moved into the biggest house, which had been confiscated from the exiled 'kulak' Vasily Golovin. Kuzmin was responsible for the daily management of the kolkhoz, even though he was perhaps the least experienced farmer in the whole village. He was often drunk and violent. The first winter was a disaster. The kolkhoz delivered a large state quota of grain and milk, but half the horses died, and each kolkhoz worker was paid just 50 grams of bread a day.

Some of the villagers continued to resist. There were angry scenes when Kolia Kuzmin came to take away their property with an armed brigade. Many peasants ran away rather than be forced to join the kolkhoz. The Golovins were scattered as a clan. Of the 120 Golovins living in Obukhovo in 1929, only 71 remained by mid-1931 (20 had fled to various towns; 13 were exiled as 'kulaks'; and 16 were moved out to isolated homesteads, having been excluded from the collective farm).

As for Nikolai's immediate family, it was broken up entirely. Two of his brothers were exiled. His mother fled to the nearest town. His oldest son was arrested and sent to work as a Gulag labourer on the White Sea Canal (Belomorkanal). Two other children, Maria and Ivan, ran away to escape arrest. His wife Yevdokiia and their three youngest children tried to join the collective farm, but they were barred as 'kulak elements', and isolated from their fellow villagers. Only the Puzhinin family, their oldest friends, would talk to them. 'The atmosphere was terrible,' remembers Antonina. 'Mama often cried. We stopped playing outside; neighbours did not visit us any more. We grew up overnight.' Yevdokiia and her children were allowed to stay in their family house and keep a cow and a tiny plot of land, from which they managed to survive for a few months, partly because they were helped in secret by their relatives. But life became unbearable when Kuzmin took away their cow (milk was their main source of food). In January 1931, Kuzmin declared a policy of 'squeezing out the last of the kulak Golovins', and the village Soviet imposed a huge tax (1,000 kilograms of grain) on Yevdokiia. 'Kuzmin and his gang would not give up,' recalls Antonina: 'they kept on coming back, taking all we had and demanding more. When all the grain had gone, they confiscated the last household property, farming tools and wagons, furniture and pots and pans, leaving us just one iron bed, some old linen and some clothes.'

Then the order for their deportation came. On 4 May, a cold spring day, Yevdokiia and her children were expelled from their house and sent into exile in Siberia. They were given just an hour to pack their things for the long journey. The Puzhinins took the iron bed for safe-keeping. The bed was the last possession of the Golovins, the place where all their children had been born and the last trace of their roots in Obukhovo, where the family had lived for several hundred years. Antonina recalls their leaving:

Mama remained calm. She dressed us in our warmest clothes. There were four of us: Mama; Aleksei, who was then fifteen; Tolia was ten; and I was eight ... Mama wrapped me in a woollen shawl, but Kolia Kuzmin, who had come to supervise our expulsion, ordered the shawl removed, saying that it had been confiscated too. He would not listen to Mama's pleading about the cold weather and the long journey that awaited us. Tolia gave me one of his old caps with ear-flaps, which he had thrown away becaused it was torn, and I wore this on my head instead. I felt ashamed to be wearing a boy's cap instead of the shawl [traditionally worn by peasant girls]. Mama bowed and crossed herself before the family icons, and led us out the door ... I remember the grey wall of silent people who watched us walk towards the cart. No one moved or said anything ... No one hugged us, or said a parting word; they were afraid of the soldiers, who walked with us to the cart. It was forbidden to show sympathy towards the kulaks, so they just stood there and stared in silence ... Mama said farewell to the crowd. 'Forgive me, women, if I have offended you,' she said, bowing and making the sign of the cross. Then she turned and bowed and crossed herself again. She turned and bowed four times to say goodbye to everyone. Then, when she was seated in the cart, we set off. I recall the faces of the people standing there. They were our friends and neighbours – the people I had grown up with. No one approached us. No one said farewell. They stood there silently, like soldiers in a line. They were afraid.[32]

2

Returning to his native Belorussian village in June 1931, the writer Maurice Hindus, who had emigrated to the USA almost a quarter of a century before, remarked on what he saw as a 'fresh slovenliness that had come over the people' as a result of collectivization. 'Houses, yards, fences, were in sad need of repair.' Holy Trinity was approaching,

yet nowhere was there a sign of paint on windows or shutters or a roof with a fresh coating of thatch. Was this neglect a mere accident? That I could not believe. The uncertainties that the kolkhoz had spread abroad were no doubt holding people back from improving their households.[33]

Hindus might have made his observation in virtually any village that had been collectivized. Dispossessed of their land and livestock, the peasants lost the sense of attachment to their family farms that had been the source of their pride and independence; once reduced to labourers in the kolkhoz, they no longer had the means or even the incentive to keep up their homes.

The peasants worked in kolkhoz brigades, receiving payment in the form of a small food ration (which they were expected to supplement by growing vegetables and keeping pigs and chickens on their private garden plots) and a once- or twice-a-year cash sum (enough on average to buy a pair of shoes). The lion's share of kolkhoz production was purchased by the state through a system of compulsory 'contracts' which kept prices very low, so that kolkhoz managers were forced to squeeze the peasants to retain any funds for running costs. The peasants said that collectivization was a 'second serfdom'. They were tied down to the land and exploited by the state, just as their ancestors had been enserfed and exploited by the landowners.

Economically, the collective farms were a dismal failure. Few had tractors to replace the horses slaughtered by the peasantry (human draught was used to plough a good deal of their land in the early years). The collective farms were badly run. The managers were people, like Kuzmin, who had been chosen for their loyalty to the Party rather than their agricultural expertise. There was nothing to replace the initiative and energy of the so-called 'kulaks', the hardest-working peasants before collectivization. The newly created kolkhoz labourers had no real interest in their work. They focused their attention on their garden plots and pilfered kolkhoz property. Many kolkhoz peasants found it very hard to reconcile themselves to the loss of their private household property. They knew which horse or cow had once belonged to them, and tried to use their former horse to till the land, or to milk their former cow.[34]

Olga Zapregaeva was born in 1918, the fourth of six children in a peasant family in Krivosheino, a small village in the Tomsk region of Siberia. When Krivosheino was collectivized, in 1931, the kolkhoz took her family's household property (three cows and three horses, farm tools, carts and two barns full of hay), leaving them with just their chickens and their goats. 'We were not paid anything in the kolkhoz,' recalls Olga, who left school to work in the fields at the age of just thirteen. 'We had to live from what we grew in our garden, from our chickens and our goats.' There were no tractors on the kolkhoz, so the peasants ploughed the fields with their own horses, which were kept in a special stable near the kolkhoz offices, although Olga's mother, like many of the villagers, worried that her horses were unhappy there, and often brought them home to make sure that they were groomed and fed. In an effort to eradicate this connection between the peasants and their animals, the kolkhoz chairmen of the area embarked on a policy of sending people away from their villages. Olga's father was allowed to remain on the kolkhoz in Krivosheino, but Olga and her mother and the other children were sent off to a different kolkhoz, 8 kilometres away, near the village of Sokolovka, where they lived in a rented room. 'We worked there for two years,' recalls Olga. 'We saw our father only once or twice, because we had only one day free from work, and it was rarely the same day as his.' In 1935, the family was reunited in Tomsk, where Olga's father worked in the stables of a building site. Olga's mother got a job in a meat factory, and the family lived together in a dormitory with a dozen other families, all former peasants who had left the land.[35]

After a good harvest in 1930, the harvests of 1931 and 1932 were disastrously bad. Yet state procurements in 1932–3 were more than twice the level they had been in the bumper years of 1929 and 1930. The Party based its excessive grain levies on the good results of 1930 and on inflated 1931 and 1932 figures submitted by local officials, eager to demonstrate their political success. The actual harvest of 1932 was at least one-third smaller than official figures showed (it was in fact the poorest harvest since the famine year of 1921). The inevitable outcome was widespread famine, beginning in the spring of 1932 and culminating during the next year, when 70 million people (nearly half the Soviet population) were living in the famine area. The number of deaths is impossible to calculate, not least because so many of them were unregistered, but the best demographic estimates suggest that between 4.6 million and 8.5 million people died of starvation or disease between 1930 and 1933. The worst affected areas were in the Ukraine and Kazakhstan, where peasant resistance to collectivization was particularly strong, and the grain levies were excessively high. This conjunction has prompted some historians to argue, in the words of Robert Conquest, that the famine was 'deliberately inflicted', that it was a 'massacre of men, women and children' motivated by Communist ideology. This is not entirely accurate. The regime was undoubtedly to blame for the famine. But its policies did not amount to a campaign of 'terror-famine', let alone of genocide, as Conquest and others have implied.[36] The regime was taken by surprise by the scale of the famine, and had no reserves to offer its victims. It continued to requisition grain from the worst-affected areas and only reduced its procurements in the autumn of 1932, which was too little and too late. Once the famine raged, the regime tried to conceal the extent of it by stopping people fleeing from the devastated regions to the cities of the north.[37]

Nonetheless millions of people fled the land. For every thirty peasants who entered the kolkhoz, ten left agriculture altogether, mostly to become wage labourers in industry. By the early months of 1932, there were several million people on the move, crowding railway stations, desperately trying to escape the famine areas.[38] The cities could not cope with this human flood. Diseases spread. Pressure grew on housing, food and fuel supplies, which encouraged people to move from town to town in search of better conditions. Frightened that its industrial strongholds would be overrun by famine-stricken and rebellious peasants, the Politburo introduced a system of internal passports to limit immigration to the towns. The new law stated that adults were required to have a passport registered with the police to obtain the residence permit (propiska) necessary for employment in the towns. The system was introduced in seven major cities in November 1932, and then extended to other towns during the next year. It was used by the police, not just to control the movement of the population, but to purge the towns of 'socially dangerous elements' ('kulaks', traders, disgruntled peasants) who might become a source of opposition to the Soviet regime. As it turned out, the law merely forced millions of homeless peasants to keep moving from town to town, working illegally in factories and construction sites, until the passport system caught up with them.[39]

Families disintegrated, as younger peasants left their homes for the cities. Millions of children were abandoned in these years. Many peasants left their children when they ran away from the collective farms. 'Kulaks' gave their children to other families rather than take them on the long journey to the 'special settlements' and other places of exile, where it was said that many children died. 'Let them exile me,' explained one Siberian 'kulak', 'but I will not take my children. I don't want to destroy them.' Among famine victims, the abandonment of children was a mass phenomenon. Mothers left their children on doorsteps, delivered them to Soviet offices or abandoned them in the nearest town. Orphans lived on building sites. They roamed around the streets, rummaging through rubbish for unwanted food. They scraped a living from begging, petty theft and prostitution, many joining children's gangs which controlled these activities in railway stations, drinking places and busy shopping streets. Some of these children were rounded up by the police and taken to 'reception centres', from which they were then sent on to children's homes and camps. According to police figures, an astonishing 842,144 homeless children were brought to the reception centres during 1934–5. By the end of 1934, there were 329,663 children registered in orphanages in Russia, Ukraine and Belarus alone, and many more in special homes and labour camps ('labour-educational colonies') controlled by the police. From April 1935, when a law was passed lowering the age of criminal responsibility to twelve, the number of children in the Gulag system began to rise steadily, with over 100,000 children between the ages of twelve and sixteen convicted by the courts and tribunals for criminal offences in the next five years.[40]

When they left Obukhovo, Yevdokiia Golovina and her three young children were taken to the nearest railway station at Pestovo, 56 kilometres away, where they were held in a detention camp. Three days later, they were loaded into cattle trucks for the six-week journey to Kemerovo in Siberia. The trucks were full of families, with children, men and women of all ages. A bucket in each truck served as the toilet, which was emptied once a day, when the doors were opened and a piece of bread was given to each person by the guards. At Kemerovo the Golovins were taken to a distribution centre, where several hundred families were kept under guard in an open field, enclosed by a high barbed-wire fence, with nothing but their baggage to sleep on. A month later, they were transferred to Shaltyr, a 'special settlement' for 'kulaks' in the remote Altai region of Siberia.

The 'special settlements' were primitive and isolated camps. Most of them consisted of a few barracks, built by the exiles on their arrival, in which several hundred people slept on wooden planks, although in many 'special settlements' the 'kulaks' lived in dug-outs in the ground, or were housed in abandoned churches and buildings, cattle sheds and barns. The overcrowding was appalling. At the Prilutsky Monastery near Vologda there were 7,000 exiles living on the grounds, with just one kitchen, but no proper toilet or washing facilities. In Vologda itself 2,000 people were living in a church. An eye-witness described the living conditions of 25,000 exiles in Kotlas:

In the barracks, which are each meant to house 250 people, it is almost dark, with little window openings here and there that let in light only to the lower bunks. The inhabitants prepare food outside, on camp fires. The latrine – is just a fenced-off area. Water – there is a river below, but it is still frozen. The local residents lock the well ('You will infect us; your children are dying') and sell water in bottles.

The 'special settlements' were not technically a form of imprisonment (the mass deportations were carried out by administrative directives beyond the jurisdiction of the courts) but from the spring of 1931 they were controlled by the organs of OGPU, which was responsible for the exploitation of their slave labour. The exiles in the 'special settlements' had to report once a month to the police. Matvei Berman, the chief of the Gulag system, said that conditions in the settlements were worse than in the labour camps. The men were employed in back-breaking work in logging-camps and mines, the women and the children in lighter work. They were given very little food (a few loaves of bread for a whole month). When they succumbed to illness and disease, they were simply left to die, as they did in their hundreds of thousands during the winter of 1931–2.[41]

Shaltyr consisted of five two-storeyed wooden barracks built along a river bank. The population (about a thousand peasants) had been sent

Exiles in a 'special settlement' in western Siberia, 1933

there from all over the Soviet Union, though Russians, Ukrainians, Volga Germans and Siberians were the largest groups. The men were sent to fell timber at a nearby logging camp, returning on Sundays. Yevdokiia's son Aleksei Golovin was one of them, although he was just fifteen. On 1 September, her younger son Tolia and her daughter Antonina went to school – a single class for all the children of the settlement housed in one of the barracks. The girls were forced to cut their braids (tradition-ally worn by peasant girls before they were married) – as if to symbolize their renunciation of the peasant culture into which they had been born. To mark the start of the school year the Commandant of the settlement gave a speech in which he told the children that they should be grateful to Soviet power, which was 'so good and kind that it allowed even us, the children of the kulaks, to study and become good Soviet citizens'. The 'reforging' (*perekovka*) of human beings who did not fit the mould of the 'Soviet personality' was an important ideological feature of the Gulag system in its early years, even in remote and isolated settlements like Shaltyr.

The first winter at Shaltyr was very cold. The snowfall was so heavy that it destroyed two of the barracks, forcing many of the boys, including Tolia, then aged ten, to live in dug-outs in the ground. There were no able-bodied men – they spent the winter at the logging-camp – so the schoolchildren were mobilized to clear the snow in the mornings. For several weeks the settlement was stranded by the snow. There were no food deliveries, so people lived off the few supplies which they had brought from home. Several hundred people were struck down by typhus; they were isolated in one of the barracks and left to fend for themselves, since there were no medicines. Yevdokiia was one of the typhus victims. Antonina writes in her memoirs:

Every day we went to see Mama. We stood by the window, through which we could see her lying on her plank. Her head was shaved. Her eyes were wide open and wandering. She had lost her memory and did not recognize us. Tolia knocked on the window. He was in tears. He cried out: 'Mama, Mama, don't get ill, get up.'

Yevdokiia survived. But so many of the typhus victims died that winter that the Commandant decided that there was no time to bury all of them. Their corpses were frozen in the snow until the spring thaw, when they were thrown into the river.

The second winter was even worse than the first. The exiles were not given any food, part of a deliberate policy to reduce the population of the settlement by three-quarters, it appears. The exiles ate tree bark and the rotten roots of potato plants, which they mashed up into cakes. Their stomachs swelled, and many of them died. Everyone had dysentery by the spring. The Golovins were saved by a stroke of luck. One day, the Commandant was inspecting the barracks, when he noticed that Yevdokiia was reading the Gospel. He needed someone literate to deliver and collect the post from Tsentralnyi Rudnik, a Gulag mining settlement 12 kilometres away. He selected her. When she went to get the post, Yevdokiia would take a bucket of berries, collected by her children in the nearby woods, and sell them at the market in Tsentralnyi Rudnik to buy food and clothes. 'The Commandant knew everything, of course, but turned a blind eye,' recalls Antonina, 'because there was no one else to collect the post.' Once, a packet of potato seeds arrived in the mail. Yevdokiia was placed in charge of a work team to sow the seeds. Antonina recalls the joy of that occasion:

It was like a holiday! We were all so happy to be digging potatoes! Adults and children – we all worked so hard. We were true peasants, our ancestors had worked the land for centuries, and now we were allowed to work the land again. Mama was the brigade leader, and the Siberian, Snegirev, was the chairman of our collective. We were not allowed to form a kolkhoz, because we were kulaks. Mama was afraid that the potatoes would not grow without fertilizer – none of us had any experience of growing potatoes. But in the autumn we dug up a huge harvest, and no one died from hunger that winter. The potatoes had saved us.[42]

Dmitry Streletsky and his family walked in snow for several days to reach their first place of exile, a large abandoned cellar in Kurgan, where several hundred 'kulak' families, including many of their distant relatives, were simply left, without food or water, to fend for themselves. They would have starved without the help of relatives and other people in Kurgan who brought them food. They were held in the cellar for a week, people sleeping as best they could on their baggage or on the bare floor, and then loaded into cattle trucks for the long train journey to Usole, north of Perm, from where they were force-marched by armed guards to the factory town of Pozhva, 150 kilometres away. There they were housed in a workshop, everybody sleeping on a cement floor. 'Father was in agony,' recalls Dmitry. 'He aged overnight. He said that his life had been destroyed . . . Everybody felt the same. But even though they had no choice but to do as they were told, people tried to keep their dignity. They refused to be like slaves to the authorities.' Dmitry's father was sent to fell timber and build a 'special settlement' near Chermoz. The rest of the family was squeezed into a room above a joiner's workshop with three other families. Six months later, they joined Dmitry's father at the 'special settlement'. There were ten barracks in the settlement, each with space for 500 people to sleep on plank beds. Encircled by a high barbed-wire fence, the settlement was located in the middle of a large pine forest, where the men were sent to cut down trees, returning once a week. With a daily ration of just 200 grams of bread, the death rate in the settlement was very high. But the Streletskys managed to survive through their peasant industry: the children gathered mushrooms and sold them in Chermoz; their mother went at night to steal potatoes from the fields of a kolkhoz; while their father struck a deal with the workers of a nearby slaughter-house, helping them to build their wooden houses in exchange for cattle blood (which, unlike meat and bones, would not be missed by the authorities). In the famine year of 1933, when the daily ration was cut to 50 grams of bread, half the population in the 'special settlement' died from hunger and disease, but the Streletskys managed to survive by drinking blood.[43]

The Streletskys were fortunate in that they were able to remain together as a family. For many other people the experience of exile was synonymous with fragmentation. Klavdiia Rublyova lost touch with seven of her brothers and sisters after the arrest of her father in 1930. They were sent to various children's homes, and she never heard from them again. Klavdiia and her younger sister Natalia went to live with their grown-up sister Raisa in Kansk, near Krasnoiarsk in Siberia. Klavdiia worked as a nanny in a doctor's home, but then the passport system arrived in the Siberian town, and as a 'kulak' daughter she was forced to flee. Leaving Natalia with Raisa, Klavdiia went to stay with her uncle, a senior inspector of forest work in Cheremkhovo, near Irkutsk, where she was registered by the Soviet in her uncle's name. In November 1933, her uncle received a letter from Klavdiia's father, Ilia. Released from jail, Ilia was now living in a 'special settlement' somewhere in the region of Tashtyp, 2,000 kilometres away, not far from the border with China. Klavdiia travelled by train before hitching a lift to Tashtyp, which was deep in snow when she arrived in January 1934. For a long time she could not find any work. Without her father's name on her registration papers, nobody would employ her, but as a 'kulak' daughter she was too afraid to reveal her identity. In the end she was taken in by the chairman of the Tashtyp Soviet, who employed her as a nanny and set her up with casual work in a clothing factory. One day, while talking to the chairman's sister-in-law, Klavdiia showed two photographs, one of her two brothers, Leonid and Aleksandr, the other of herself with her two sisters.

She [the sister-in-law] said immediately: 'Lenka [Leonid], I know him!' I was astonished that she knew my brother. 'Where is he? Where is he?' I asked, trying to control myself ... At that time I was afraid of every word I said, in case I revealed that my father was in exile.

Klavdiia found her brother in Tashtyp. Through him, she discovered that her father was living in a 'special settlement' attached to the Kirov mine in Khakasin. He had begun a new life with a second wife, as Klavdiia recalls:

The photographs that Klavdiia showed. Left: Leonid (the older brother) with Aleksandr, 1930. Right: Klavdiia is standing on the right, Natalia in the middle, and Raisa on the left with her husband, Kansk, 1930

I went to visit them. When I arrived in the evening, they were just coming back from their work at the mine. They were bringing in their cow. They were not afraid or surprised to see me. My father greeted me as if he had just seen me the day before. I sat with them for a few minutes outside the barracks where they lived. Then I left.[44]

That was the last time Klavdiia saw her father. He was rearrested and then shot in August 1938.

Many 'kulak' families fled the 'special settlements' and took their chances living on the run. According to OGPU sources, by the summer of 1930, escapes from the 'special settlements' had become a 'mass phenomenon', with tens of thousands of 'kulak' runaways. The escapes reached their peak during the famine. In 1932–3, OGPU counted a staggering 422,866 'kulaks' who had fled from the 'special settlements', and only 92,189 who had subsequently been caught.[45]

The Ozemblovskys were a minor noble family of Polish origin. After 1917, they lost their land in Belarus, but remained in their village, Oreshkovichi in the Pukhovichi region of Minsk province, where they continued farming on a level with the peasantry. Aleksandr and Serafima had four children, two boys and two girls, the oldest born in 1917 and the youngest in 1928, the year when the kolkhoz in Oreshkovichi was organized. Aleksandr gave all his livestock and tools to the kolkhoz, keeping just one cow to feed his family, but he refused to enter the kolkhoz. He wanted to emigrate to the USA or France, as many other Poles in the area had done, but Serafima argued: 'Who will touch us? What have we done wrong? We gave away all our property!' Aleksandr was arrested in the spring of 1930. A few days later they came for the family. 'Get your things. You and the children are going into exile,' the OGPU soldier said. Serafima wrapped some clothes in blankets and managed to conceal some gold items, before she was bundled with her children into carts and taken to a church, where several hundred 'kulak' families were already held. A few days later, they were rejoined by their men and were loaded into wagons for the 3,000-kilometre journey to a remote settlement in the Komi region of the North. There they were told to 'make themselves a home' in an empty barn. 'There was nothing for us there – no planks for beds, no knives or spoons,' recalls Sofia. 'We made mattresses out of branches we collected in the woods.'

Gradually, the exiles built a settlement of wooden huts, one for every family, as they had once lived in their own villages. With the gold that they had brought with them, the Ozemblovskys bought a cow. Family life began again. But then came the famine, and their existence returned to being unbearable. The Ozemblovskys hatched an escape plan. Because their youngest son was already ill, they decided that the women should escape, leaving Aleksandr to look after the boys and run the risk of rearrest. Serafima and the two girls, Sofia, then aged nine, and Elena, five, walked by night and slept by day in the forest. They lived mainly from berries. Serafima had several gold teeth. She would pull one of them to buy a lift in a peasant cart or to bribe an official. Eventually, she and the girls made it back to Belarus. They hid for a week in the Pukhovichi house of Serafima's parents, who were so afraid of being arrested for hiding her that they advised their daughter to give herself up to the police. Serafima went to the police in Pukhovichi, who listened to her story of escape and felt so sorry for her that they told her to run away again and offered to give her twenty-four hours before coming after her. Serafima left Elena with her parents and went to the nearby town of Osipovichi, where she and Sofia rented a room from an old couple. She put Sofia into school. Then she returned to the Komi region to try to find her husband and her sons. 'Mama left without a word – no goodbye, no advice about how I might survive,' recalls Sofia.

For the next year, Sofia lived with the old couple, who turned out to be very cruel. 'They cursed me, called me the daughter of an enemy of the people and threatened to kick me out onto the street, if I did not do what they said. I cried all the time. I had no money of my own, and nowhere to go.' Sofia became so miserable that she ran away to her grandparents, who took her in with Elena, although they themselves had been evicted from their Pukhovichi home and were now living in an old bath-house.

The Ozemblovsky family. Left: Aleksandr and Serafima on their wedding day in 1914. Right: Serafima with Sasha (left) and Anton (right) on their return from exile in 1937

Meanwhile, Serafima had arrived at the Komi settlement, only to find that Aleksandr was no longer there: he had been arrested the day after her escape and sentenced to three years in the nearby Kotlas labour camps. Their elder son, Anton, had been recruited as an informer by the police (he was trained to eavesdrop and report on the conversations of the settlers and was paid in bread for each report). Their younger son, Sasha, still very sick, was being cared for by the schoolteacher. Within days of her arrival, Serafima was arrested and taken to Kotlas. But again she managed to escape, running from the convoy on the way back from work and disappearing deep into the woods. Again she made the 3,000-kilometre trek back to Pukhovichi, where she was reunited with her two daughters. They settled in a small house in Osipovichi, bought for them by relatives, and lived off what they grew in the small garden, where they kept a goat and pigs. In 1937, they were joined by Sasha and Anton (who continued to work for the police in Belarus). Two years later the family reunion was completed by the return of Aleksandr, recently released from the Kotlas camps. Sofia recalls the moment of return:

Mama ran out to meet him and threw herself into his arms. Papa said: 'Mother, where are the children?' Mama answered: 'Don't worry – the children are alive and well, all four of them.' Papa collapsed to his knees and began to kiss her hands and feet, thanking her for saving us.[46]

The story of the Okorokovs is even more remarkable. In May 1931, Aleksei Okorokov was deported as a 'kulak' from his village Ilinka in the Kuznetsk region of south-western Siberia. Exiled to the North, he escaped from his convoy, walking for a month to return to his village, 900 kilometres away. When he got there he found out that his wife Yevdokiia and their two daughters, Maria, then aged seven, and Tamara, nine, had been exiled with his parents to a 'special settlement' near Narym, 800 kilometres to the north-west. With forged papers, Aleksei travelled day and night to reach the settlement, from which a few days later the family departed with a whole brigade of 'kulak' runaways, including children and grandparents, which Aleksei organized. They walked by night – Maria on her mother's back and Tamara carried by her father – so that they would not be seen by the patrols that searched the taiga for 'kulak' runaways. For ten nights they walked, sometimes ending up in the same place from which they had started out, for it was difficult to navigate in this terrain, until they ran out of food and water and the old collapsed from exhaustion. On the eleventh night, they were surrounded by a patrol, which shot at them, wounding Aleksei in the stomach. The soldiers took them off in a large cart with other runaways to a nearby village, where they were held in a bath-house. The runaways were sent back to Narym, although the elderly were left behind, including Aleksei's parents, who did not see their family again.

Once again the Okorokovs managed to escape. While the convoy to Narym was preparing to depart, Yevdokiia bribed a villager to get the patrol drunk, allowing her to run away with Aleksei and their daughters. They headed towards Tomsk, hiding by day (when they could see the guards and their dogs in the distance on the road) and travelling by night (when bears and wolves were the main danger). After several nights of walking without bread or anything to eat, they came across a settlement of the Kerzhaki tribe that had been struck down by smallpox: all the children were already dead. The headman offered to trade some bread, a jar of honey and a boat in exchange for Tamara, who was old enough to work in the tribe. He threatened to inform the police if Aleksei did not agree. Reluctantly, Aleksei consented. Yevdokiia became hysterical, but he would not give in to her entreaties. 'We stayed with the Kerzhaki for a week to gather our strength,' recalls Maria.

Mama would not stop crying, and my sister began to understand that something was wrong. On the day of our departure, Papa took my sister into a separate room and locked her up in it. Then he led away Mama, who was half-dead with grief, and placed her with me and the provisions in the boat. Then we rowed away.

After they had gone a few kilometres, Aleksei moored the boat, hid his wife and daughter in the bushes and walked back to the Kerzhaki settlement to rescue Tamara. Four days later he returned, carrying Tamara on his back.

But their troubles were far from over. A patrol caught up with them, as they were making their way north. They were taken to another camp, a barrack surrounded by a high wire fence, 8 kilometres from Tomsk, where they spent the next six months. Aleksei transported vegetables by horse and cart to Tomsk, while Yevdokiia and the children were put to work with other prisoners in a kolkhoz. In Tomsk Aleksei got to know a town official, who took pity on his family and, as an act of conscience, agreed to help them escape. One day Aleksei covered his daughters with potato sacks and drove them in his cart to Tomsk, where they hid in the official's house. They were joined by Yevdokiia, who had jumped on to a train as it passed through the field where she was working. Dressed in new clothes bought for them by the official, the Okorokovs returned by train to Kuznetsk (which by this time had been renamed Stalinsk). Aleksei worked in a coal mine and Yevdokiia in a canteen. And family life began again. 'Father at once set to work building us a wooden house with one window and a clay oven. We lived in our little corner, without hurting anyone, and depending on no one.'

And then a few months later, the passport system arrived in Stalinsk. Aleksei decided to go back to Ilinka, his native village, in the hope of getting registered, but as soon as he arrived he was arrested and imprisoned in a labour camp. Yevdokiia, waiting in Stalinsk, finally received a letter from Aleksei. Because the letter would alert the police to her whereabouts, Yevdokiia fled with her daughters to the nearby town of Tashtagol, where the passport system had not yet been introduced. Aleksei joined them shortly afterwards, having somehow managed to escape from the prison camp. He built a shack in which they lived. Yevdokiia picked up casual jobs. When she realized that she was pregnant, she performed an abortion on herself, smashing her fists against her womb and pulling out the foetus. She nearly died. She lay in bed for several months. None of the doctors in the town would even look at her, because abortion had been declared illegal by the government. Yevdokiia cured herself by eating herbs.

In 1934, the passport system reached Tashtagol. Aleksei was re-arrested and sent to the Stalinsk metal works as a penal labourer. Yevdokiia and the girls were arrested too. By sheer coincidence, they were sent off to join him at the metal works. They lived together – one of several hundred families – in a dug-out which ran along the river bank against the outside of the factory wall. The 'roof' was made of branches and pine needles packed with mud; the 'walls' leaked in the rain. Aleksei made some rudimentary furniture. He carved wooden cups and spoons. Once again the Okorokovs began to piece together a domestic existence. Miraculously, they had survived and managed to remain together as a family, but the traumas of the past three years had left their mark, especially on the girls. Maria and Tamara both suffered from nightmares. They were frightened and withdrawn. 'After three years of living on the run,' reflects Maria, 'my sister and I had grown accustomed to not talking. We had learned to whisper rather than to talk.'[47]

3

The promise of the Five Year Plan was the creation of a modern industrial society. 'We are marching full steam ahead on the road to industrialization, to socialism, leaving behind our age-old Russian backwardness,' Stalin said in 1929. 'We are becoming a nation of metal, motors and tractors, and when we have placed the Soviet man in an automobile and the peasant on a tractor, then let the capitalists of the West, who so proudly vaunt their civilization, attempt to catch up with us.'[48]

The symbols of this progress were the huge construction projects of the First Five Year Plan: industrial cities like Magnitogorsk, a vast complex of steel and iron works built from scratch on the barren slopes of the Urals; railroads and canals, like the Moscow–Volga and the White Sea Canal, which opened up new areas to exploitation and supplied the booming cities with basic goods; and enormous dams like Dneprostroi, the largest hydro-electric installation in the world, whose turbines were turning by 1932. These 'successes' had an important propaganda value for the Stalinist regime at a time when there was still considerable opposition – inside and outside the Party – to the policies of forcible collectivization and the over-ambitious industrial targets of the Five Year Plan. They enabled it to foster the belief in 'socialist progress', in the imminent arrival of the Soviet utopia, which became the ideological justification for the sacrifices demanded from the people for the plan's fulfilment. In his memoirs, written in the 1980s, Anatoly Mesunov, a peasant son who became an OGPU guard at the White Sea Canal, sums up the effect of this propaganda on millions of 'ordinary Stalinists', as he describes himself:

I had my doubts about the Five Year Plan. I did not understand why we had to drive so many convicts to their deaths to finish the canal. Why did it have to be done so fast? At times it troubled me. But I justified it by the conviction that we were building something great, not just a canal, but a new society that could not have been built by voluntary means. Who would have volunteered to work on that canal? Today, I understand that it was very harsh and perhaps even cruel to build socialism in this way, but I still believe that it was justified.[49]

Stalin's industrial revolution was very different from the industrialization of Western societies. As Mesunov suggests, the rates of growth that Stalin had demanded in the Five Year Plan could not have been achieved without the use of forced labour, particularly in the cold and remote regions of the Far North and Siberia, where most of the country's minerals and fuel supplies were located. The supply of slave labour, beginning with the mass arrest and deportation of the 'kulaks' in 1929, was the economic rationale of the Gulag system. Although originally conceived as a prison for the regime's enemies, the Gulag system soon developed as a form of economic colonization – as a cheap and rapid way of settling the land and exploiting the industrial resources of the Soviet Union's remote regions, where nobody would want to live – and this rationale was openly acknowledged by Gulag officials among themselves.[50] Historians have different views of the Gulag's origins – some seeing it as a by-product of Stalin's consolidation of political power, others emphasizing its role as a means of isolating and punishing phantom 'classes' like the 'bourgeoisie' and the 'kulaks', or national and ethnic groups which were deemed dangerous to the state.[51] These factors all played their part, but the economic motive was key, growing in importance from the moment the regime began to look for ways to make its prisons pay for themselves.

In the 1920s, the labour camps were basically prisons in which the prisoners were expected to work for their keep. The most important was the Solovetsky Camp of Special Significance (SLON), established by OGPU in a former monastery on the White Sea island of that name in 1923, which was to become the prototype of the Gulag in its use of slave labour. Employed in tsarist times to incarcerate political dissidents, the monastery was turned by the Bolsheviks into a general prison for all its adversaries – members of the outlawed opposition parties, intellectuals, former Whites – as well as 'speculators' and common criminals. One of the prisoners was Naftaly Frenkel, a Jewish businessman from Palestine who had become involved in smuggling to Soviet Russia and was arrested by the Soviet police in 1923. Shocked by the prison's inefficiency, Frenkel wrote a letter setting out his ideas on how to run the camp and put it in the prisoners' 'complaints box'. Somehow the letter got to Genrikh Iagoda, the fast-rising OGPU boss. Frenkel was whisked off to Moscow, where he explained his plans for the use of prison labour to Stalin, who was keen on the idea of using prisoners for economic tasks. Frenkel was released in 1927 and placed in charge of turning SLON into a profit-making enterprise. The prison's population expanded rapidly, from 10,000 in 1927 to 71,000 in 1931, as SLON won contracts to fell timber and build roads and took over factories in Karelia, on the Finnish border. Most of the new arrivals were 'kulak' peasants, like Nikolai Golovin, who came to the Solovetsky camp in December 1930. The prisoners were organized according to their physical abilities and given rations according to how much work they did. The strong survived and the weak died.[52]

In 1928, as the mass arrests of 'kulaks', priests and traders, 'bourgeois specialists' and engineers, 'wreckers', 'saboteurs' and other 'enemies' of Stalin's forced industrialization threatened to overwhelm the Soviet prison system, the Politburo established a commission to study the possible use to which the growing prison population could be put. Headed by the Commissar of Justice, N. M. Ianson, the commission included Interior Commissar V. N. Tolmachyov as well as Iagoda, the OGPU chief. The three men were locked in battle for control of the prison population, but Stalin clearly favoured Iagoda, who proposed using it to colonize and exploit the industrial resources of the Far North and Siberia through a new network of labour camps. There was an almost inexhaustible supply of timber in these remote areas; and geologists, like Pavel Vittenburg, were charting rich reserves of gold, tin, nickel, coal, gas and oil, which could be cheaply mined by convict labourers. In April 1929, the commission proposed the creation of a new system of 'experimental' camps, each with 50,000 prisoners, controlled by OGPU. The commission underlined that, by concentrating larger numbers in the camps, the costs of maintaining this slave labour force could be reduced from 250 to just 100 roubles per capita per year. Two months later, the Politburo passed a resolution ('On the Use of Prison Labour') instructing OGPU to establish a network of 'correctional-labour camps' for the 'colonization of [remote] regions and the exploitation of their natural wealth through the work of prisoners'. From this point on, the political police became one of the main driving forces of Soviet industrialization. It controlled a rapidly expanding empire of penal labour camps, whose population grew from 20,000 prisoners in 1928 to 1 million by 1934, when OGPU merged with the NKVD (People's Commissariat of Internal Affairs); the new authority then took control of the political police and directed all these labour camps through the Gulag.[53]

The largest of the early penal labour camps, Belbaltlag, with more than 100,000 prisoners by 1932, was used to build the White Sea Canal, 227 kilometres of waterway connecting the Baltic with the White Sea. The idea of the canal had first been advanced in the eighteenth century, but it had proved beyond the technical capabilities of the old regime, so the idea of building it was a vital part of the propaganda mission of the Five Year Plan to demonstrate the superiority of the Soviet system. It was a fantastically ambitious project, given that the planners intended to construct the canal without machines or even proper surveys of the land. Critics of the project (who envisaged building it with free labour) had argued that the huge construction costs could not be justified because there was relatively little shipping on the White Sea. But Stalin was insistent that the canal could be built both cheaply and in record time – a symbol of the Party's will and power – as long as OGPU supplied sufficient prison labour. Frenkel was put in charge of construction. The methods he had used in SLON were re-employed on the canal, as were many of the prisoners, who were transferred from the Solovetsky camp to the canal. To save time and money, the depth of the canal was soon reduced from 22 feet to just 12, rendering it virtually useless for all but shallow barges and passenger vessels (in some of the southern sections, built in a rush at the end of the project in 1932–3, the canal was only 6 feet deep). Prisoners were given primitive hand tools – crudely fashioned axes, saws and hammers – instead of dynamite and machinery. Everything was done by hand – the digging of the earth, the dragging of the heavy stones, the carting of the earth in wheelbarrows, the construction of the wooden cranes and scaffolding, not to mention the camp sites, which were built by the prisoners themselves along the route of the canal. Worked to exhaustion in the freezing cold, an unknown number of prisoners, but somewhere in the region of 25,000, died in the first winter of 1931–2 alone, although among the survivors the number of dead was rumoured to be much higher. Dmitry Vitkovsky, a former prisoner of the Solovetsky labour camp who worked as a supervisor on the White Sea Canal, recalls the scene:

At the end of the workday there were corpses left on the work site. The snow powdered their faces. One of them was hunched over beneath an overturned wheelbarrow, he had hidden his hands in his sleeves and frozen to death in that position. Someone had frozen with his head bent down between his knees. Two were frozen back to back leaning against each other. They were peasant lads and the best workers one could possibly imagine. They were sent to the canal in tens of thousands at a time, and the authorities tried to work things out so no one got to the same sub-camp as his father; they tried to break up families. And right off they gave them norms of shingle and boulders that you'd be unable to fulfil even in summer. No one was able to teach them anything, to warn them; and in their village simplicity they gave all their strength to their work and weakened very swiftly and then froze to death, embracing in pairs. At night the sledges went out and collected them. The drivers threw the corpses onto the sledges with a dull clonk. And in the summer bones remained from the corpses which had not been removed in time, and together with the shingle they got into the concrete mixer. And in this way they got into the concrete of the last lock at the city of Belomorsk and will be preserved there for ever.[54]

Apart from the physical destruction of human life, the White Sea Canal brought untold suffering to many families.

Ignatii and Maria Maksimov were childhood sweethearts from the village of Dubrovo in the Valdai region of Novgorod province. They were married in 1924, when Maria turned sixteen, and worked on Ignatii's family farm until 1927, when they moved to Leningrad, where Ignatii found work as a carpenter. In October 1929, five months after the birth of their daughter Nadezhda, Ignatii was arrested (he had taken part in a peasant uprising against the Bolsheviks in 1919) and was sent first to the Solovetsky camp, and then to the northern sector of the White Sea Canal. Meanwhile, Maria was evicted from their room in Leningrad. She returned with Nadezhda to Dubrovo, only to discover that her parents' house, like the Maksimovs', had been destroyed, and both families sent into exile. No one from her family was left in Dubrovo. Maria was advised by an old neighbour to flee the village to avoid arrest herself. Carrying her baby, she walked across the border into the neighbouring province of Tver (hoping this would put her beyond the reach of the Novgorod police) and knocked on the door of the first house of the first village she came across. The door was opened by an old couple. Maria went down on her knees and begged them to take in her daughter, so that she could run away: nobody would give work to a woman with a child. The couple were kind people. They nursed Nadezhda for two years, while Maria got a job as a cook on the Leningrad to Murmansk railway. The railway ran along the northern sector of the White Sea Canal, where Ignatii was working, although

Maria did not know that at the time. She knew nothing about her husband until 1932, when she heard from an acquaintance that he was at a labour camp somewhere in the region of Belomorsk, where the canal ran into the White Sea. Maria tried to make contact with her husband by writing notes on little scraps of paper and throwing them from the kitchen-carriage window as the train passed the building works at Belomorsk. Finally, a miracle occurred: she received a letter from Ignatii, who was actually in a camp near Kem, 55 kilometres further north on the railway line towards Murmansk. At the end of 1932, Ignatii was released and sent into exile in Arkhangelsk, where he was reunited with Maria and Nadezhda.[55]

Maria, Nadezhda and Ignatii Maksimov with Ignatii's brother
Anton (standing), Arkhangelsk, 1934

The Gulag was more than a source of labour for building projects like the White Sea Canal. It was itself a form of industrialization. The first industrial complex of the Gulag system was the integrated pulp-and-paper mill at Vishlag, an OGPU complex of labour camps on the Vishera River in the Urals. The complex began life in 1926 as a vast network of logging camps administered by SLON, but it was not until the summer of 1929, when Eduard Berzin, the Latvian Bolshevik, was placed in charge of building works, that the camp developed its industrial activities. The purity of the Vishera's waters led the Politburo to choose it as the site for producing the high-quality paper that began to appear in the early 1930s, when prestigious publications like the *Large Soviet Encyclopedia* were printed on the paper of the Vishlag mill. By 1930, the Vishlag camps had a population of 20,000 prisoners (including the writer Varlam Shalamov): 12,000 were employed in the logging camps; 2,000 in the smaller factories (making bricks and cellulose); while the rest were used to build the pulp-and-paper mill, as well as the barracks settlements at Krasnovishersk and Gorod Sveta ('Town of Light'), which grew into civilian towns.[56] Berzin conceived of these Gulag settlements as an 'experimental form of industrial development' whose cultural institutions would re-educate the prisoners to become 'Soviet workers'. Gorod Sveta boasted film and radio clubs, libraries and canteens, health centres, gardens laid out with fountains, wildlife areas, open-air theatres, debating areas and the 'main camp club' in a colonnaded building, which reminded Shalamov of the Parthenon, 'only it was more frightening'.[57]

Vishlag was typical of the Gulag system in its early years, when the idea of using prison labour to 'reforge' human beings in a Soviet mould was not just propaganda but an article of faith for many Bolsheviks. For all that, the Vishlag camp with its paper-mill was primarily an economic venture. Berzin's operating principles were based entirely on the projected returns from his investments, which included moral and material incentives to stimulate the prisoners to meet production plans. In November 1931, Berzin moved on to become the first boss of Dalstroi (Far Northern Construction Trust), a vast conglomerate of labour camps (including the infamous Kolyma camps) in the north-east corner of Siberia – an area the size of Western Europe between the Pacific and the Arctic oceans – where the world's biggest gold reserve lay beneath the frozen ground. Berzin ran the Dalstroi camps on the same economic principles as he had run Vishlag: his job was to get his prisoners to dig as much gold as possible (by the mid-1930s the gold production of the Dalstroi camps exceeded the total gold production of the Soviet Union in 1928).[58] During Berzin's reign (1931–7) conditions in the Dalstroi camps were much better than they would become in later years, when many prisoners would look back with nostalgia to the Berzin period, as Shalamov did in his *Kolyma Tales*:

Berzin attempted – not without success – to solve the problem of colonizing this severe and isolated region and the allied problem of reforging the souls of the convicts. A man with a ten-year sentence could accumulate enough work credits to be released in two or three years. Under Berzin there was excellent food, a workday of four to six hours in the winter and ten in the summer, and colossal salaries for convicts, which permitted them to help their families and return to the mainland as well-to-do men when their sentences were up . . . The cemeteries dating back to those days are so few in number that the early residents of Kolyma seemed immortal to those who came later.[59]

Vishlag itself was dismantled in 1934, but by then the pulp-and-paper mill at Krasnovishersk had become an industrial centre, a major economic power in the northern Urals, drawing many peasants into industry.

The rise of industry required engineers and other technical specialists. Ivan Uglitskikh was born in 1920 to a peasant family in Fyodortsovo, in the Cherdyn region of the Urals. Banned as a 'kulak' from the kolkhoz in Fyodortsovo, Ivan's father fled to Cherdyn and worked on the river barges transporting timber down to the pulp-and-paper mill at Krasnovishersk, where his brother and uncle were both in the labour camp. Ivan grew up with a strong desire to get on in life. His father was always telling him to learn a profession. 'There was nothing where we lived, no industry at all,' recalls Ivan. 'My dream was to go to Perm, but that was far away, and I could not afford the fare . . . The main thing was to have a profession. Without that there was no future.' The only place where he could study beyond the age of fourteen was the Factory Apprentice School (FZU) attached to the pulp-and-paper mill. All the teachers were former Vishlag prisoners, as Ivan recalls:

They were engineers, specialists in their professions, brought from the camp to train us in paper production and electrical work. I trained as an electrician, and then worked at the paper mill. I could get work in any town and any factory, because in those years there was a huge demand for skilled workers like myself. I even went to Perm and worked there on the landings for the river-boats . . . I was proud of my success. My parents were proud of me as well.[60]

Millions of peasant sons were coming to the towns and forging a new identity for themselves. Between 1928 and 1932 the urban population grew at the extraordinary rate of 50,000 people every week. The popu-

The Uglitskikh family (Ivan standing
at the back), Cherdyn, 1938

lation of the cities grew too fast for the state to cope with the rising
demand for consumer goods, which were low on the list of Soviet
priorities for the Five Year Plan, so after 1928 rationing was introduced
for foodstuffs, fuel and various household items. With private trade
repressed, the streets turned grey, restaurants and cafés disappeared,
shop windows emptied, and people dressed more shabbily. Alexandre
Barmine, a Soviet diplomat who returned to Moscow in the summer of
1930, after four years abroad, recalled feeling shocked by the economic
hardship he discovered in the capital:

After the improvements of 1922–28, Moscow showed appalling changes. Every
face and every house front was eloquent of misery, exhaustion, and apathy. There
were scarcely any stores, and the rare display windows still existing had an air
of desolation. Nothing was to be seen in them but cardboard boxes and food
tins, upon which the shopkeepers, in a mood of despair rather than rashness,
had pasted stickers reading 'empty'. Everyone's clothes were worn out, and the
quality of the stuff was unspeakable. My Paris suit made me feel embarrassed.
There was a shortage of everything – especially of soap, boots, vegetables, meat,
butter and all fatty foodstuffs.[61]

The housing situation was desperate. In 1928, the Soviet city dweller had on average 5.8 square metres of living space, but many of the poorest workers had no more than a couple of square metres they could call their own. An American describes the conditions in which many Moscow workers lived:

Kuznetsov lived with about 550 others, men and women, in a wooden structure about 800 feet long and fifteen feet wide. The room contained approximately 500 narrow beds, covered with mattresses filled with straw or dried leaves. There were no pillows, or blankets . . . Some of the residents had no beds and slept on the floor or in wooden boxes. In some cases beds were used by one shift and by others at night. There were no screens or walls to give any privacy . . . There were no closets or wardrobes, because each one owned only the clothing on his back.[62]

Many workers from peasant families had little expectation of private space. Back in the village, families traditionally ate together from a common bowl and slept together on benches by the stove. Still, for many it must have been a shock to share their living space with other families when they moved into the towns.

Nadezhda Pukhova was born in 1912 to a large peasant family in Pskov province. In 1929, she ran away from the kolkhoz and came to Kolpino, a large industrial suburb of Leningrad, where she found a job at the Izhora machine-building plant. Nadezhda rented the corner of a ground-floor room in a wooden house, not far from the factory. It was a large and draughty room, heated by a primus stove, with a kitchen-toilet and its own side-entrance from the yard. Nadezhda met her husband Aleksandr at the house. He was the eldest son of a peasant family in the Rybinsk region of Iaroslavl province and had recently arrived in Kolpino to take up an apprenticeship as a garage mechanic. The owner of the house was a distant relative, who let Aleksandr rent a corner in the upstairs room. After they were married, Aleksandr moved downstairs to live with Nadezhda on the ground floor. The couple rigged up a curtain round their bed to give them some privacy from the other families. In all there were sixteen people living in the room, including a prostitute, who brought clients back at night, and a fireman, who got up at 4 a.m. to go to work. 'We slept badly,' recalls Nadezhda. 'The fireman, who slept in the next bed to us, would get up in the night and light a match to see what time it was. Men were always coming in and out with Olga [the prostitute]. She said that she would kill us if we reported her. People's nerves wore very thin.' During the winter Aleksandr's relatives from Iaroslavl would stay with them. They came in search of factory work, or to sell felt boots they made to supplement their income from the kolkhoz. 'They all came – aunts, uncles, sisters, brothers with their wives,' recalls Nadezhda.

I was shocked by the way they lived – it was so dirty and primitive. It was not like that in Pskov, where my parents' house was always very clean. Aleksandr's relatives slept on the floor – the women with blankets, the men with just their tunics to keep them warm. They made the room smell like horses.[63]

The Golovins also followed the route of migration to town. In February 1933, Nikolai was finally released from the Solovetsky labour camp. Warned not to join Yevdokiia and his children in Shaltyr, where he might be rearrested, he made his way to Pestovo, a small town near Vologda, where he managed to find work as a carpenter on a building site. Like many provincial towns in the early 1930s, Pestovo was full of 'kulak' runaways. Among them was Yevdokiia's brother, Ivan Sobolev, a former priest who had changed his name and begun working as an accountant in the logging industry, after the Bolsheviks closed down his village church. Nikolai became the leader of his work brigade on the construction site and moved into a tiny wooden cabin that had been abandoned by a forester. Gradually, the family was reunited. Nikolai, the son, came to Pestovo from the White Sea Canal – one of the 12,000 prisoners released as a reward for their hard work on the canal's completion in August 1933 – and joined his father's work brigade. The other son, Ivan, who had run away from Obukhovo when they came to arrest the Golovins, also came to Pestovo after years of wandering around Siberia. He too joined his father's work brigade. Maria, the daughter, who had also fled Obukhovo, arrived next, in 1934. She had been so frightened by her three years on the run as a 'kulak' daughter that she changed her name and married a Bolshevik worker, who beat her and renounced her when he found out her true identity. Finally, in December 1934, after several months of writing petitions to the NKVD in Ustiuzh, Nikolai was reunited with his wife Yevdokiia and their three other children, Antonina, Tolia and Aleksei, who returned safely from the 'special settlement'. The woodsman's cabin, which Nikolai had made into a home, was very small, but to

Antonina, who had spent three years in the barracks at Shaltyr, it seemed like a paradise:

There was just one little room. Inside it was an iron bed – the very one that our neighbour Puzhinin had saved for us when we were deported from our home – the bed in which our parents slept and where we, their children, had all been born. It was our bed, unmistakably, it had the same nickel-plated spheres on the bedposts, the same mattress. It was the one thing we had left from our old life.[64]

The bed from the Golovin household in Obukhovo (photographed
in Pestovo in 2005). It is more ordinary than the legendary bed Antonina
recalls from her childhood

4

On 3 September 1932, two boys were found dead in a forest near the village of Gerasimovka in western Siberia. They had been stabbed to death by their own relatives, it was reported in the press, because Pavlik, the older boy, who was fifteen and an active member of the Pioneers, had denounced his father, Trofim Morozov, as a 'kulak' to the Soviet police. The rest of the Morozovs had taken their revenge. The true facts of the case are hard to disentangle from the web of lies and political intrigue. From the start of the investigation, the murder was scripted by the Soviet press and the police as a political crime, with Pavlik in the role of a model Pioneer and his killers cast as 'kulak counter-revolutionaries'.

Gerasimovka was a remote village in the forest near Tavda, 350 kilometres north-east of Sverdlovsk in the Urals. It was surrounded by labour camps and 'special settlements'. At night the villagers could hear the barking of guard dogs. Gerasimovka was a miserable place. The poorest peasants had one cow, the richest two. Only nine had a samovar. There was just one teacher in a rudimentary school, established as late as 1931, which had only thirteen books. Like much of the peasantry in western Siberia, the villagers of Gerasimovka were fiercely independent. They had moved east from central Russia to win their land and freedom in the nineteenth century and were not about to give that up by joining the collective farms. None of the households in the village had signed up for the kolkhoz in August 1931; little wonder the Soviet press described the place as a 'kulak nest'.[65]

Trofim Morozov was a sober and hard-working peasant of average means who had been wounded twice whilst fighting for the Red Army in the Civil War. He commanded respect among his fellow villagers and was serving his third term as chairman of the village Soviet in the autumn of 1931, when it was brought to the attention of OGPU that he was selling false papers to the 'kulak' exiles in the 'special settlements'. His son may have been the informant. Contrary to the propaganda of the Soviet press, Pavlik was not in fact a Pioneer (there was no Pioneer organization in Gerasimovka) but he clearly wanted to be one, and after the opening of the school he became active in agitation work, which brought him close to the police. In Gerasimovka Pavlik had the reputation of someone who informed on neighbours when they did something wrong (years later the villagers recalled him as a 'rotten kid'). He bore a grudge against his father, who had abandoned the family home for another woman, leaving Pavlik, as the eldest son, to look after his mother Tatiana, an illiterate peasant woman who appears to have been mentally unbalanced by the departure of Trofim and may have encouraged Pavlik to report him in a fit of jealousy. According to the press reports of Trofim's trial in the village school in November 1931, Pavlik denounced his father's crimes, and when Trofim shouted out, 'It's me, your father,' the boy told the judge: 'Yes, he used to be my father, but I no longer consider him my father. I am not acting as a son, but as a Pioneer.' Trofim was sentenced to a labour camp in the Far North and later shot.[66]

Emboldened by his appearance in the trial, Pavlik began to inform on villagers who concealed grain or spoke out against the kolkhoz. He was helped by his younger brother Fyodor, who was then aged nine. The villagers were enraged by the boys' activities. Sergei Morozov, Pavlik's grandfather, barred them from his house, and other members of the family tried to stop them from reporting to the police. But there is no evidence that the family was involved in the murder of the boys, which was probably the work of teenagers, including Pavlik's cousin, Danila, following a squabble over a harness and a gun.[67]

Once the murder was reported in the local press, the investigation was immediately politicized. Danila was leaned upon to denounce Sergei, his own grandfather, as the murderer. The denunciation was supported by two other members of the family: Tatiana, who was ready to blame anyone for the murder of her sons; and Pavlik's cousin, Ivan Potupchik, an ardent Stalinist and police aide, who was rewarded for his role in the affair by promotion to the Party's ranks. In the end, five members of the Morozov 'kulak clan' were put on trial in November 1932: Pavlik's uncle and godfather, who were accused of plotting the murder; his grandfather and cousin Danila, who were said to have carried it out; and his grandmother, who was supposed to have lured the boys into the woods. Their guilt was taken as proven from the start of this show trial (the prosecutors cited Stalin's speeches on the intensification of the class struggle in the countryside to demonstrate the murderers' political motives). Four of the five – all except Pavlik's uncle for some incomprehensible reason – were sentenced to 'the highest measure of punishment' – execution by a firing squad.[68]

By this stage, the national press had drawn its own conclusions. In its version Gerasimovka was an emblem of backward peasant Russia, and the Morozovs an archetype of the patriarchal 'kulak' family, which collectivization would sweep away. Pavlik soon became the hero of a propaganda cult, launched in the autumn of 1933, when Gorky called for the building of a monument to the young martyr, who, the writer said, had 'understood that a relative by blood may also be an enemy of the spirit, and that such a person is not to be spared'.[69] The cult was everywhere. Stories, films, poems, plays, biographies and songs all portrayed Pavlik as a perfect Pioneer, a loyal vigilante of the Party in the home. His selfless courage, which he had displayed by sacrificing his own father, was promoted as an example for all Soviet schoolchildren.

The cult had a huge impact on the moral norms and sensibilities of a whole generation of children, who learned from Pavlik that loyalty to the state was a higher virtue than family love and other personal ties. Through the cult the idea was sown in millions of minds that snitching on one's friends and relatives was not shameful but public-spirited. It was indeed expected of the Soviet citizen.[70]

Who was most affected by this lesson of the Morozov tale? Few children in stable families where moral principles were clearly set by the parents, as far as one can tell from interviews, although on this awkward issue, which today is understood in the context of the Terror, memory is unreliable. But Pavlik was, it seems, a positive example for many people who had grown up in unstable or oppressive families, where the influence of the elders was too weak to counteract the ideas of the Soviet regime. The propagandists of the cult were typical in this respect. Pavel Solomein, for example, the Sverdlovsk journalist who first brought Pavlik's story to the attention of the Soviet public in the press, had run away from his brutal stepfather when he was a child and had grown up in a series of orphanages. Gorky was on his own from the age of nine, when he was expelled from his grandfather's house – a place of cruelty and backwardness where the men took to the bottle and the women found solace in God – to fend for himself in the industrial towns of the Volga. For many people from unhappy backgrounds such as this, Pavlik was a hero because he had freed himself from the 'darkness' of his family's way of life; by developing his own political consciousness and becoming active in the public sphere, he had found a higher form of 'family' in the Pioneers, who were marching with the Party and the Soviet people to a 'light and radiant future'. Pavlik's story had a strong appeal for orphans in particular. Untouched by the influence of family life, they could not understand what the boy had done wrong by denouncing his own father. Brought up by the state, they were indoctrinated to be loyal and grateful to it for saving them from destitution, which they were told awaited orphans who had not been lucky enough to have been born in the Soviet Union, the greatest country in the world.

Mikhail Nikolaev was three years old in 1932, when his parents were arrested and he was sent to an orphanage and given a new name. He never found out what his real name was, nor the names of his parents, nor who they were, why they were arrested, or what had happened to them after their arrest. It was a policy in children's homes to remould children like Mikhail as 'Soviet citizens' by erasing their original identity. As a boy, Mikhail was deeply influenced by the tale of Pavlik Morozov, which was drummed into orphans from an early age. He thought of Pavlik as a 'real hero', and dreamed of emulating his achievement by 'discovering a spy'. Looking back on his childhood, Mikhail suspected he would have thought differently about his boyhood hero, had he grown up in a family:

We orphans had an impoverished understanding of life compared with normal children. We were deprived of family events, of conversations around the kitchen table – of all that unofficial and, in my view, most important information that forms a person's understanding of life and his relation to the world. Our 'window on the world' was the classroom, the Pioneers, the radio in the red corner, and [the newspaper] 'Pioneer's Truth' (*Pionerskaia Pravda*). All the information from these sources was the same, and there was only one way to interpret it.[71]

The popularity of Pavlik's story, especially among the young, reinforced a profound cultural and generation gap – between the old world of the patriarchal village and the new urban world of the Soviet regime – which divided many families. The rural population was increasingly young and literate. According to the census of 1926, 39 per cent of the rural population was under fifteen years of age (and more than half aged less than twenty) while peasant sons in their early twenties were more than twice as likely to be literate than their fathers (peasant women of the same age were five times more likely to be literate than their mothers). Educated in Soviet schools, these younger peasants no longer shared the attitudes and beliefs of their parents. Through the Pioneers and the Komsomol many of them found the confidence to break away from their control. They would refuse to go to church, to wear a cross, or to observe religious rituals, often citing Soviet power as the new authority in such matters, which sometimes led to arguments with their parents. They looked increasingly towards the cities for their information and values, and as the popular culture of the towns spread to remote villages in the 1920s and 1930s, more and more rural youth came to prefer the towns to the countryside. Its effect was to encourage rural children to regard the towns as a better and more cultured way of life than the countryside. A survey of the Komsomol in one of the most agricultural districts of Voronezh province during the mid-1920s found that 85 per cent of its members came from peasant families: yet only 3 per cent said that they wanted to work in agriculture. Most rural children wanted to leave the countryside and go off to the city for a shop or office job, to study in colleges and enter the industrial professions, or to join the military.[72]

The Medvedev family was torn apart by this division between the young and old. Andrei Medvedev was born in 1880 in the village of Oblovka, on the railway line between Tambov and Balashov, 570 kilometres south-east of Moscow. A blacksmith by trade, he made a living in the winter from fixing metal roofs on the houses of the wealthier peasants, but in the summer he worked with his five brothers on the family farm of his father, Fyodor, in whose household all seventeen Medvedevs lived. Fyodor was a peasant patriarch, devoutly Orthodox, with long white hair down to his shoulders, who ruled his household in the old-fashioned way. 'We lived by the customs of ancient times,' recalls one of his granddaughters. 'Everybody ate from the same bowl, and my grandfather gave the sign for all of us to start by knocking with his spoon on the side of the bowl. No one said a word unless he spoke.'

In 1923, Andrei married Alyona, a young woman half his age, who had fled with her relatives from hungry Petrograd to the Tambov countryside in 1917. Alyona came from a poor family of labourers. Her father was a railway porter who was left with seven children when his wife died; in Tambov they had eked out a living doing jobs on peasant farms. Andrei brought his young wife into Fyodor's home, and in 1924, their daughter Nina was born. From the start Alyona found it hard to submit to the patriarchal customs of the household. Although she had just three years of schooling, Alyona became the village Soviet's secretary. She organized a school and taught the village children – and many of its adults – how to read. Andrei was not interested in books – there were none in the Medvedev home – so she brought home books and magazines from the local market town from which the children learned to read. In 1928, Alyona's school became a 'liquidation point' (*likpunkt*) in the Komsomol campaign for the liquidation of illiteracy (*likbez*), which was part of the Soviet campaign against religion and the patriarchal culture of the countryside. Alyona became an activist in Zhenotdel, the Women's Department of the Party, which often took her off to conferences in the district town. Appalled by Alyona's independence, Fyodor threatened to expel her from the house and often argued with his son, one of the leaders of the village Soviet, who supported his wife's activities, even though he was himself a jealous type and did not like her going on her own to town.

In September 1929, a kolkhoz was formed in Oblovka. Only twenty-nine of the sixty-seven households in the village had agreed to join it, but this was deemed enough to force it through. Andrei was elected the chairman of the kolkhoz. But Fyodor refused to join. His cow had given birth to a new calf, which he did not want to give up. Father and son argued violently. 'They would have killed each other, if my mother had not intervened,' recalls Nina. 'They cursed each other and vowed to go their separate ways.' The household farm was split. Andrei moved with his share of its property to the kolkhoz, while Fyodor, at the age of eighty-one, continued farming on his own. Four months later, the old man was arrested as a 'kulak' – one of twelve 'kulaks' arrested in Oblovka, all on the basis of a report by the village Soviet. Fyodor's house was smashed to bits, and he was exiled to Siberia. But the family drama did not end there. As the chairman of the kolkhoz, Andrei had tied his future to the countryside, but Alyona was drawn towards the towns, largely in the hope of finding a cure for her daughter Nina, who had been blinded by illness and needed special care. In April 1930, Alyona left Andrei and returned with Nina to her family in Leningrad, where they rented a tiny corner in a room owned by friends of relatives. 'We had only four square metres,' recalls Nina, 'just enough for a narrow bed with a bedside table and two little chairs, on which I slept, while Mama occupied the bed.' For two years the family was split, but then, in October 1932, Andrei, too, came to Leningrad. The pull of family had proved stronger than his commitment to the collective farm. The Medvedevs moved to a larger room in the city centre, Alyona taught at Nina's school, and Andrei worked as a roofer in the works department of OGPU.[73]

Many families succumbed to the twin pressures of collectivization and urbanization, as the Medvedevs did. Collectivization was only the last in a whole series of social cataclysms for the Russian peasantry – among them the Great War, the Revolution, the Civil War and the famine, which destroyed millions – but, in a way, it was the most traumatic because it divided families, setting sons against their fathers, over whether to embrace the Soviet way of life. How many sons actually denounced their own fathers is hard to say. There were certainly a few, if not quite as many as one might believe from the Soviet press, which gave the impression in the 1930s that the countryside was full of real-life Pavlik Morozovs. The press reported that a Pioneer called Sorokin had caught his father stealing kolkhoz grain and had him arrested by the police; that a schoolboy called Seryozha Fadeyev had told his headmaster where his father had concealed a store of potatoes; and that a thirteen-year-old boy called Pronia Kolibin had denounced his own mother for stealing grain from the kolkhoz fields (he was rewarded with a trip to Artek, the famous Pioneer holiday camp in the Crimea, while his mother was sent to a labour camp).[74]

The Pioneers encouraged children to emulate Pavlik Morozov by informing on their parents. Pioneer brigades were commonly employed to watch the kolkhoz fields and report on peasants stealing grain. *Pioner-skaia Pravda* printed names of young informers and listed their accomplishments. At the height of the Pavlik Morozov cult in the 1930s, the true Pioneer was almost expected to prove his worthiness by denouncing his own relatives. One provincial journal warned that Pioneers who failed to inform on their families should be treated with suspicion and, if found to be lacking vigilance, should be denounced themselves. In this climate it is not surprising that parents were afraid to speak in the presence of their own children. As one doctor recalled:

I never spoke against Stalin to my boy. After the story of Pavlik Morozov you were afraid to drop any kind of unguarded word, even in front of your own son, because he might inadvertently mention it in school, the directorate would report it, and they would ask the boy, 'Where did you hear that?' and the boy would answer, 'Papa says so and Papa is always right,' and before you knew it, you'd be in serious trouble.[75]

One man who got into serious trouble was the father of Aleksandr Marian. Aleksandr was a leader of the Komsomol in his native village of Malaeshty, near Tiraspol in south-west Ukraine. In 1932, when he was seventeen, he denounced his father Timofei in a letter to the police. Aleksandr was a fanatical supporter of collectivization, welcoming the war against the 'kulaks', whom he described in his diary on 8 June 1931 as 'the last but biggest class of exploiters in the USSR'. Timofei did not agree. He was critical of collectivization, and said so to his son, who promptly denounced him. Timofei was arrested and sent to a labour camp. In his diary, in October 1933, Aleksandr reported an exchange with a comrade in the Komsomol who claimed that he should be deprived of the leadership on account of his father's 'counter-revolutionary' views. Aleksandr wrote:

I had to explain to the comrade that my father was arrested on my demand. The reason for his falling into an anti-Soviet position was his experience in Austria as a prisoner of war [in the First World War] . . . He returned with a love of Austrian order, convinced that the bourgeois smallholdings which he had seen in Austria were the key to agricultural wealth . . . The mistakes of the first period of collectivization he saw simply as chaos, not as a temporary complication. If only he had known the laws of the dialectic, if only he had been politically literate, he would have recognized the error of his views and would have recanted them.[76]

Such fanatically ideological denunciations were probably quite rare. More commonly, young people behaved reactively, renouncing family members rather than denouncing them, and even then, only after their relatives had been exposed as 'enemies'. Indoctrinated by their schools and the Pioneers, they saw no point perhaps in harming their own prospects by not distancing themselves from family members who had, in any case, already been arrested. There were often complex pressures and considerations that affected such behaviour. People could be threatened with expulsion from the Pioneers and the Komsomol, or barred from colleges and professions, unless they proved their Soviet loyalty and vigilance by renouncing their arrested relatives. This accounts for the formulaic notices printed in their thousands in the Soviet press:

I, Nikolai Ivanov, renounce my father, an ex-priest, because for many years he deceived the people by telling them that God exists, and that is the reason I am severing all my relations with him.[77]

Some of these renunciations may have been encouraged by the parents themselves, who recognized the need for their children to break from them, if they were to advance in Soviet society. In 1932, for example, a sixteen-year-old boy from a traditional Jewish household near Kremenchug wrote to the local Yiddish-language newspaper renouncing his family's backward ways:

I refuse to be part of this family any longer. I feel that my real father is the Komsomol, who taught me the important things in life. My real mother is our motherland; the Union of Soviet Socialist Republics and the people of the USSR are my family now.

According to his younger sister, who was later interviewed, the boy had written this renunciation on his father's insistence. 'When I was fourteen,' the girl recalls,

my father called me and my brother into a room and explained that his way of life was not appropriate for modern times. He did not want us to repeat his mistakes, such as observing Jewish religious traditions. He said we had to go to the editor of a school wall-newspaper and announce there that we were now living a new life and that we did not want to have anything in common with the religious past of our father. My father made us do this. He said it meant nothing to him, but he thought this action would open up a brighter future for us.[78]

Other factors, too, not least ambition, led young people to renounce their relatives. Many of these public letters of renunciation were written on the eve of leaving home for universities or careers in the towns; they were a declaration of a new identity, a commitment to Soviet dreams and goals. The early 1930s were a period of enormous opportunity and social mobility: workers' sons and daughters aspired to become professionals; peasant children dreamed of coming to the towns. All these ambitions were purposefully fuelled by Soviet propaganda, which placed the cult of personal success at the centre of the Five Year Plan. Films, books and songs featured the exploits of 'ordinary heroes' from the proletariat – engineers and scientists, model workers, aviators and explorers, ballerinas, sportsmen and women – who were all bringing glory to the Soviet Union. Young people were encouraged to believe that they could emulate their achievements, provided they worked hard and proved themselves as worthy Soviet citizens.

Such ambitions were often held most dearly by the children of 'kulaks' and other 'enemies' of the Soviet regime – a paradox that stands at the centre of the conflict between 'kulak' fathers and their sons. Growing up with the stigma of their origins, they wanted to be recognized as equal members of society, which could only be achieved by breaking with the past. Some renounced their 'kulak' relatives; others erased them from their biography or claimed that they were 'dead', or had 'run away'. Such acts of denial were often necessary for survival. Yet the memory of them can still evoke feelings of remorse and shame, not because these young people had actually denounced anyone, but because they lived relatively 'normal' lives and pursued careers while their parents disappeared in the Gulag. They had reconciled themselves to the

Soviet system and had found their place in it, even though they knew that the system had destroyed their own family.

No one expressed these feelings of remorse more powerfully than the poet Aleksandr Tvardovsky. He was born in 1910 in the village of Zagore, in Smolensk province, where his father, Trifon, a blacksmith, made a comfortable but modest living for his wife and seven children. Aleksandr was a teenage Communist. He joined the Komsomol in 1924 and became an activist in the village. He often argued about politics with his father and twice ran away from home, unable to reconcile himself to his family's peasant way of life. In 1927, he joined the Russian Association of Proletarian Writers (RAPP), moved to Smolensk, and published his first poem, 'To a Father and Rich Man' ('Ottsu-bogateiu') in the Komsomol newspaper *Young Comrade*:

> In your home there is no shortage,
> You are rich – and I know this,
> Of all the five-walled peasant houses,
> The best is yours.[79]

In the spring of 1930, the authorities imposed a heavy tax on Trifon's family. Fearing arrest, Trifon ran away to the Donbass in search of work, followed in the autumn by his sons Ivan (then aged seventeen) and Konstantin (twenty-two), who reckoned they would ease their mother's burden by going off in search of their father. Ivan returned that winter, only to discover that he had been barred from the village school as a 'kulak' son. In March 1931, the Tvardovsky family – with the exception of Aleksandr – was deported from Zagore. Konstantin (who had been imprisoned in Smolensk) and Trifon (arrested on his return from the Donbass) joined their convoy on its way to the Urals. The family spent the next two years in and out of labour camps and 'special settlements', living on the run, picking up odd jobs in factories and mines wherever they could find a loophole in the passport system, splitting up and reuniting, until the autumn of 1932, when Trifon found work as a blacksmith in a factory in the Urals town of Nizhny Tagil.

All this time, Aleksandr was studying at the Pedagogical Institute in Smolensk, where he was making a name for himself as a young poet. In his first long poem, *The Road to Socialism* (1931), he gave a glowing picture of life on the collective farms. He spoke in favour of the campaign against the 'kulaks' at student meetings at the institute. But he clearly felt uneasy about the way in which his family had been treated, because in the spring of 1931, he went to see the regional Party secretary, I. P. Rumiantsev, in the hope that he might intervene to ease their lot. Rumiantsev said, recalled Tvardovsky in 1954, that 'in life there were moments when one had to choose between one's family and the Revolution'. After this meeting, Tvardovsky was singled out as a 'waverer'. His loyalty was tested by the Soviet authorities. At literary meetings he was attacked as a 'kulak' son. He only escaped expulsion after a courageous and vigorous defence by the local writer Adrian Makedonov (who was later arrested).[80]

Afraid for his career, Tvardovsky distanced himself from his family. In the spring of 1931, his parents wrote to him from the 'special settlement' at Lialia in the Urals. They did not expect him to help them with money – they knew that he had none, recalled Ivan in 1988: 'they simply hoped that he might want to keep in touch with his own mother and father, and with his brothers and sisters'. Ivan takes up the story:

Aleksandr wrote back twice. In the first letter he promised to do something. But a second letter soon arrived. It contained these lines, which I cannot forget: 'My dears! I am neither a barbarian nor an animal. I ask you to fortify yourselves, to be patient and to work. The liquidation of the kulaks as a class does not mean the liquidation of people, even less the liquidation of children . . .' Later on there was the phrase: '. . . I cannot write to you . . . do not write to me.'

When this letter was read to Ivan's mother, she

bowed her head and sat down on a bench, where she lost herself in thoughts, which she spoke out loud, although what she said was not for us, but for herself, to reassure herself of her son's love and devotion.

'I know, I feel, I believe . . . that it was hard for him,' she said. 'My son, surely, had no choice. Life is like a carousel. What can you do?'[81]

Two months later, in August 1931, Trifon took his youngest son Pavlik and ran away from Lialia, where the rest of the family remained. After a month they reached Smolensk and searched for Aleksandr at the House of Soviets, where they knew that he was working in the editorial offices. Trifon asked the guard to call his son:

I knew what he had written to us at Lialia, but I reasoned: he is my son! He might at least take care of Pavlushka [Pavlik]. What harm had the boy done him, his own brother? Aleksandr came out. God forbid, how can it be that a meeting with a son can be so frightening! I looked at him in a state of near panic: he was all grown up, slender and handsome! His father's son! He stood there and looked at us in silence. And then he said, not 'Hello, father', but 'How did you get here?'

'Shura [Aleksandr]! My son!' I said. 'We are dying there! From hunger, illness, arbitrary punishments!'

'So you ran away?' he asked abruptly, not, it seemed, in his own voice. And his look was different too, it fixed me to the ground.

I remained silent – what could I say? Let it be that way – I was only sorry for Pavlushka. He was just a boy who had come in hope of his brother's love, and it had turned out so differently!

'I can only help by sending you back, free of charge, to the place where you came from!' – those were Aleksandr's precise words.

I realized that there was no point in asking, begging, any more. I simply asked him to wait while I went to a friend in Stolpovo, who owed me money, and then, when I returned, he could do what he liked with me. He was visibly shaken.

'All right, go,' he said.

At Stolpovo Trifon went to see his friend. They drank together, while Pavlik slept. Then at midnight, the police arrived to arrest Trifon. Aleksandr had betrayed him.[82]

Four years passed before Aleksandr saw or heard from his family again. During this time, Ivan believes, Aleksandr poured his guilt feelings into his unpublished poetry:

> What are you, brother?
> How are you, brother?
> Where are you, brother?
> On what Belomorkanal?
> ('Brothers', 1933)

In 1935, Ivan went to visit Aleksandr in Smolensk. Having fled the 'special settlement', Ivan had spent the past three years living on the run, taking casual jobs in Moscow and other industrial towns, but he yearned to see his native town and he felt the time had come to let his brother know what had happened to his family. The brothers had two brief meetings, at which Aleksandr warned his brother to leave Smolensk: 'There is nothing for you here,' he told Ivan. 'You will find nothing but unpleasantness. For me, by contrast, it is important to live here, where people know me well!'[83]

At the time, Ivan was full of bitterness towards his brother. But in later years he came to understand the pressures on Aleksandr, his need to remain in a place where people knew and respected him, and where

Aleksandr Tvardovsky, 1940

his success offered some protection. Reflecting on his brother's choices, Ivan wrote with compassion:

I dare say that my visit stirred up guilt feelings and remorse in him. He couldn't have forgotten the letters he wrote to us in exile, nor his meeting with father at the House of Soviets. I felt sorry for my brother. Whether I liked it or not, I had to recognize that he was a sincere member of the Komsomol and had been so since the 1920s. I now think that Aleksandr saw the revolutionary violence that swept away our parents, brothers and sisters, although unjust and mistaken, as a kind of test, to see if he could prove himself as a true member of the Komsomol. Maybe there was nobody he had to prove this to – maybe he just had to prove it to himself. No doubt he rationalized it in this way: 'Every kulak is somebody's father, and his children someone's brothers and sisters. What makes my family any different? Be brave and strong, don't give in to abstract humanitarianism and other feelings outside class interests.' This was his logic: if you support collectivization, that means you support the liquidation of the kulaks as a class, and you do not have the moral right to ask for an exception for your own father. It is possible that in his heart Aleksandr mourned for his family, but it was just one of many kulak families.[84]

5

The 'great break' of 1928–32 destroyed old ties and loyalties uniting families and communities. It gave birth to a new kind of society in which people were defined by their relation to the state. In this system social class was everything; the state promoted 'proletarians' and repressed the 'bourgeoisie'. But class was not a fixed or rigid category. As millions of people left their homes, changed their jobs or moved around the country, it was relatively easy to change or reinvent one's social class. People learned to fashion for themselves a class identity that would help them advance. They became clever at concealing or disguising impure social origins, and at dressing up their own biographies to make them seem more 'proletarian'.

The notion of 'working on the self' was commonplace among the Bolsheviks. It was central to the Bolshevik idea of creating a higher type of human personality (the New Soviet Man) by purging from oneself the 'petty-bourgeois' and individualistic impulses inherited from the old society. As one Party leader wrote in 1929: 'We are all people of the past with all the drawbacks from the past, and a great deal of work should be done on all of us. We must all work on ourselves.'[85] At the same time, the ability of people to change and manipulate their class identity was a cause of great concern to the Party leadership.[86] It was widely feared that the 'proletariat' – the imagined social base of the dictatorship – would become 'diluted' by the mass influx of the ruined peasantry and other 'petty-bourgeois types' ('kulaks', traders, priests, etc.) into the towns; that the Party would be swamped by 'self-seekers' and adventurers who had managed to conceal their impure social origins.

There were lots of stories about such impostors in the Soviet press. The most famous was Vladimir Gromov, who in 1935 was sentenced to ten years of penal labour on the White Sea Canal for assuming the identity of a skilled engineer and prize-winning architect. Gromov had used forged papers to get high-paid jobs and a prestigious Moscow flat. He even managed to persuade the People's Commissar for Supply, Anastas Mikoian, to give him an advance of a million roubles.[87] The concern with impostors betrayed a profound anxiety within the Party leadership. It influenced the culture of the purge, whose violent rhetoric of denunication was based on the rationale of exposing the true identity of 'hidden enemies'. Throughout the 1930s the Party leadership encouraged the popular belief that colleagues, neighbours, even friends and relatives, might not be what they appeared to be – a belief that did much to poison personal relationships and fuel the mass terror of 1937–8. 'Look at what those enemies of the people are like,' Elena Bonner's younger brother said on the arrest of their father. 'Some of them even pretend to be fathers.'[88]

As with collectivization, the launching of the Five Year Plan was accompanied by a massive social purge of 'class enemies' and other 'alien elements' to remove all potential opposition and dissent. With the introduction of the passport system, the police was instructed to step up its campaign to exclude from the towns the 'socially impure' – 'kulaks', priests, merchants, criminals, 'parasites' and prostitutes, gypsies and other ethnic groups (Finns, Koreans, Volga Germans, and so on).[89] Fear of social exclusion drove millions of people to conceal their origins. For while the ideology theoretically allowed for self-transformation, the process could be long and uncertain. Concealment could seem the more reliable, certainly the shorter, path toward social acceptance. In the chaos of the early 1930s it was relatively easy to change one's identity by simply moving to another town, or by getting new papers. False papers could be easily obtained through bribery, or bought from forgers, who were found in every market town. But it was not even necessary to pay for a clean biography. Many people simply threw away their old papers and applied for new ones from a different Soviet, giving different information about their background and sometimes even changing their names and place of birth.[90] In the provinces Soviet officials and police were notoriously inefficient and corrupt.

For women, marriage was another way to cover up their social origins. Anna Dubova was born in 1916 to a large peasant family in Smolensk province. Her father was arrested as a 'kulak' in 1929 and later sent to work on a construction site in Podolsk, just south of Moscow, where his wife and children moved with him. Anna's mother got a job at a rabbit farm, while Anna enrolled at a factory school (FZU) attached to a bakery. Just when they thought that they were on their way to becoming 'normal' people once again, the family was denounced for concealing its 'kulak' origins by a friend of Anna's sister from the Komsomol. The Dubovs were deported. They lost all their possessions and rights of residence. Anna's parents went with their younger children to Rzhev, 200 kilometres east of Moscow, where they lived in 'some kind of shed' belonging to her father's relatives. Anna fled to Moscow, where another sister, who was married to a Muscovite, gave her a place to sleep on the floor of their tiny room. Without a residence permit, living illegally, Anna nevertheless pursued her ambitions. After graduating from the FZU, she became a pastry cook at the Bolshevik Cake Factory, where she specialized in decorating cakes. Her future began to seem bright. But there was always the danger that she would lose everything if her 'kulak' origins and illegal status were exposed. 'All this time,' she said in interviews in the 1990s:

I was afraid whenever I saw a policeman, because it seemed to me that he could tell that something about me wasn't right. And I got married just so that I could cover up my background ... My husband was from the *bednota* [the poor peasantry]. He was a member of the Komsomol and the secretary of a village Soviet not far from Moscow. As a member of the Komsomol it was his job to identify and dispossess kulaks ... My marriage was a kind of camouflage. I had no place to live, but once I was married we had a little room to ourselves. And when I went to bed, I would think to myself, Dear Lord, I'm in my very own bed.

Anna's husband was a kind man but he drank a lot. 'I kept dreaming, "Lord, if only I could marry a decent sort of fellow." I lived with him, but I dreamed about a decent husband, even though I had already given birth to our daughter.'[91]

People forced to live this double life were haunted by the threat of exposure. 'I was in a constant state of fear,' recalls a former secret police colonel, an exemplary Communist, who concealed his noble origins throughout his life. 'I thought all the time, "Suppose it is suddenly discovered who I really am." Then all I have worked for, all I have built for myself and my family, my life, my career will suddenly collapse.' But fear was only one of a number of contradictory impulses and emotions – passivity, the desire to withdraw, shame, inferiority – which could give rise in the same person to both a secret hatred of the Soviet regime and a will to overcome one's stigma by demonstrating devotion to the Soviet cause. People lost themselves in this duality. The inner self was swallowed up in the public personality. As one man recalled, 'I began to feel that I was the man I had pretended to be.'[92]

The young Simonov experienced something similar. Concealing his noble origins, he enrolled as a 'proletarian' in the factory school (FZU) in Saratov, where he studied to become a lathe-turner. Simonov had joined the factory school, against the wishes of his stepfather, who had wanted him to study at a higher institute or university – the educational trajectory typical of the old-world service class from which his parents came. But the teenage Simonov was excited by the vision of the new industrial society. He saw the proletariat as the new ruling class and wanted to join it. 'It was the beginning of the Five Year Plan,' recalls Simonov, 'and I was swept along by its romantic spirit. I joined a club to discuss the Plan and its variants, which interested me far more than my studies at the secondary school. My stepfather was so cross that he barely spoke to me during my first year at the factory school.'[93]

The atmosphere at the factory school was militantly proletarian. Half the students came from workers' families and the other half from children's homes. As the son of a princess, Simonov was dangerously out of place, but he did his best to look the part, giving up the shorts and sandals of his early teenage years and donning a worker's tunic and peaked cap in an effort to fit in. At the core of Simonov's attraction to the proletariat was the notion of the independence of the working man: 'The life of a fully grown man, as I saw it, only started on the day he began to work and bring money home. I wanted to be independent and earn my own living as soon as possible.'[94] Of course, by joining the army of industrial workers, Simonov would also become independent from his family, whose noble background was sure to hold him back.

To support his studies at the factory school in Saratov, Simonov worked as an apprentice at the Universal Factory in the evenings. He assembled cartridges for the assault rifles produced by the huge munitions plant. By the spring of 1931, he was earning 15 roubles, a modest monthly wage, but an important contribution to the household budget, particularly after April, when his stepfather Aleksandr was arrested and Simonov became, at the age of fifteen, the sole breadwinner in the family.

Simonov 'the proletarian', 1933

The arrest was an orderly affair. The knock on the door came at ten o'clock in the evening. The family had already gone to bed, because Aleksandra had been feeling ill. Aleksandr would not let the police come into their barracks apartment until he had dressed. Konstantin awoke to find his stepfather reading the search warrant with a magnifying glass:

The search went on for a long time; they conducted it properly, going methodically through everything in both rooms, even looking at my factory school notebook on the technology of metals, at my notebooks from the seventh class, and leafing through my mother's huge trove of letters – she loved to write a lot and liked all her relatives and friends to write a lot to her . . . When the men finished the search, tidied up the papers and letters and, it seems to me – though I may be mistaken – made some sort of list of the confiscated things, I thought that was the end of it. But then one of them took a paper from his pocket and handed it to Father. It was a warrant for his arrest. At that moment I did not think, though I later realized, that the arrest had been planned from the very start, regardless of the results of the search. It was hard to look at Mother. Although she had a strong character, it was clear that she was ill, she'd sat up all night with a high temperature and she was shaking all over. Father was calm. Having read the paper – again inspecting it with his magnifying glass, which he took out from the pocket of his vest – and having made quite sure that it really was an order for arrest, he briefly kissed mother, and told her that he would return when the misunderstanding had been sorted out. Without saying a word, he shook my hand firmly and left with the men who had arrested him.[95]

Like Aleksandr, Simonov believed that a misunderstanding had occurred. He must have known that many specialists had been arrested in Saratov, including several officers from the military school where his stepfather taught. But like most people who had lost a relative in the arrests, Simonov assumed that his stepfather had been arrested by mistake. 'I thought that the others must be guilty of something, that they were enemies, but I did not connect them with my stepfather.'[96] This distinction helped him to maintain his confidence in the Soviet system of justice, which was reinforced by the orderly behaviour of the OGPU officers, not just during the arrest of Aleksandr, but also during the arrest of his stepfather's relative, Yevgeny Lebedev in Kremenchug, which Simonov had witnessed four years earlier.

On Aleksandra's orders, Simonov informed his teachers at the factory school about the arrest. Not to report it would be cowardly, she said. Simonov was not expelled from the school, but he was advised to postpone his application to the Komsomol until his stepfather was released. Aleksandra and her son were evicted from their small apartment in the barracks. All their belongings were thrown on to the street – a table with some stools, two bookcases, a wardrobe, a bed and a trunk for officers from the First World War with a hammock in which Simonov had slept. It was pouring with rain. Neighbours took in Aleksandra, who was running a fever, while her son walked around the outskirts of Saratov, looking for a place for them to live. Having found a room to rent, he got a lorry-driver to help them move their things. All his life he would recall this day – when he took charge of his family – as the moment when he came of age.

I remember it without resentment, even with some measure of self-satisfaction, because I had proved that I could cope with anything. I had a sense of injury, but it was mainly for my mother . . . She could not forgive the people who were responsible for our eviction. No doubt it is because I felt her injury, when I was just a boy, that I still remember their names . . .[97]

Simonov's response to his stepfather's arrest was not to blame or question the Soviet regime, but to work even harder to support his family. Perhaps the arrest of his stepfather also reinforced his conviction that he needed to protect himself by strengthening his proletarian identity. Throughout that summer, Simonov continued to study in the day and to work by night at the factory. He was promoted to the second grade of apprentice workers and received a doubling of his wage, which was enough to support his mother and send two parcels every week to his stepfather in prison. Aleksandra earned some extra cash by teaching French and German at a secondary school. In the autumn Aleksandr was released from jail. 'He hugged and kissed my mother. He even kissed me too, which was unusual,' remembers Simonov. 'Something in him had altered. At first I did not notice. But then I understood: his face was cold and white, not his usual sunburnt look.'[98]

Aleksandr did not speak about the tortures he had suffered in the jail. The only thing he would say was that all the charges against him had been withdrawn, because he had refused to confess, even under 'severe pressure'. As Simonov recalls, the lesson that he learned from this affair was all about the need to remain firm:

Today [in 1978] I ask myself: did the events of that summer in Saratov leave any trace on my general approach to life, on my psychology as a fifteen–sixteen-year-old boy? Yes and no! With my stepfather things turned out as they should. He remained what he had always been – a model of clarity and conscientiousness – and the people who knew him were all convinced that he was innocent. And in those awful months, almost everybody with whom we had to deal was good to us – and that too was right, just what we would expect. Still, the story of my stepfather's interrogation, which had ended as it should, because he was a very strong and solid person, left me with a feeling of unease, the feeling that a weaker person would have come out differently from this situation, because he would not have been able to withstand what he did. This alarming thought stayed in my mind . . . But above all, I sensed, perhaps unconsciously, that I had grown up, for I too had proved that I could cope in a crisis.[99]

The children of 'kulaks', no less than those of bourgeois or noble families, felt the pressure to conceal their social origins. They were widely banned from Soviet schools and universities, from the Pioneers and the Komsomol, from the Red Army and from many jobs. Their fear of exclusion was frequently reflected in a desperate urge to prove themselves as 'Soviet citizens' by distancing themselves from their families. In 1942, Wolfgang Leonhard, the twenty-year-old son of a

German Communist who had come to Moscow in 1935, was deported to the Karaganda region of Kazakhstan. He studied at a teacher-training college, where most of the students were 'kulak' children, who had been exiled to this semi-desert region in the early 1930s. They had suffered terribly as young children but had since been allowed to go to school. They were now about to become teachers. As Leonhard notes, this brought about a complete change in their political identity:

Most of my fellow-students used to go home at the weekends. That is to say, they used to go to one of the [special] settlements which lay in the inner or outer environs of Karaganda. When they came back, they often spoke indignantly about their parents. 'They still don't understand anything at all!' I often heard them say. 'I've tried so often to explain to them why collectivization is justified, but the old people just never will understand it!'

These sons and daughters of the kulaks who had been exiled here as small children had in fact become Stalinists with the passage of time.[100]

Many 'kulak' children ended up as ardent Stalinists (and even made careers for themselves by joining the repressive organs of the state). For some the transformation involved a long and conscious process of 'working on themselves' that was not without its psychic costs. Stepan Podlubny is an example. Born in 1914 to a peasant family in the Vinnitsa region of western Ukraine, Stepan and his mother fled to Moscow in 1929, after his father had been exiled as a 'kulak' to Arkhangelsk. Stepan found a job as an apprentice in the factory school of the *Pravda* printing plant. He joined the Komsomol, headed a brigade of shock workers, edited a wall-newspaper (a form of agitprop), became a member of the factory board, and at some point it seems he was recruited as an informer by the police. All this time he carefully concealed his 'kulak' origins. He kept a diary which charted his own struggle to purge the 'sick psychology' of his peasant ancestors and reconstruct himself as a Soviet citizen. He tried to read the correct books, to adopt all the correct attitudes, to cultivate himself by dressing neatly and learning how to dance, and to develop in himself the Soviet public virtues of activity and vigilance. He drew up a 'balance sheet' of his 'cultural progress' at the end of every year (just as the state's own planning agencies drew up annual balances of economic progress in the Five Year Plan). His 'kulak' background was a constant source of self-loathing and self-doubt. He saw it as an explanation for his own shortcomings, and wondered whether he was capable of ever really becoming a fully equal member of society:

13.9.1932: Several times already I have thought about my production work. Why can't I cope with it painlessly? And in general, why is it so hard for me? . . . A thought that I can never seem to shake off, that saps my blood from me like sap from a birch tree – is the question of my psychology. Can it really be that I will be different from the others? This question makes my hair stand on end, and I break out in shivers. Right now, I am a person in the middle, not belonging to one side nor to the other, but who could easily slide to either.

Podlubny was constantly afraid that his origins would be exposed, that he would be denounced at work (a 'snake pit' filled with 'enemies'), leading to his sacking and possible arrest. Eventually his 'kulak' origins were indeed discovered by OGPU, which told him it would not take action, provided he 'continued to do good work for them'. It seems likely that Podlubny began to inform on his work colleagues. In his diary he confessed to feeling trapped – he was repulsed by his public persona and he clearly longed to 'be himself'.

8.12.1932: My daily secretiveness, the secret of my inside – they don't allow me to become a person with an independent character. I can't come out openly or sharply, with any free thoughts. Instead I have to say only what everyone [else] says. I have to walk on an uneven surface, along the path of least resistance. This is very bad. Unwittingly I'm acquiring the character of a lickspittle, of a cunning dog: soft, cowardly, and always giving in.

The news that a fellow student had not been punished after he had been exposed as the son of a 'kulak' was greeted by Podlubny as a 'historical moment', suggesting as it did that he no longer needed to feel so stigmatized by his social origins. He embraced this personal liberation with joy and gratitude towards the Soviet government.

2.3.1935: The thought that I too can be a citizen of the common family of the USSR obliges me to respond with love to those who have done this. I am no longer among enemies, whom I fear all the time, at every moment, wherever I am. I no longer fear my environment. I am just like everybody else, free to be interested in various things, a master interested in his lands, not a hireling kowtowing to his master.

Six months later, Podlubny was accepted as a student at Moscow's Second Medical Institute. He had always dreamed of studying at a higher institute, but knew his 'kulak' origins would be a stumbling block. The fact that the Komsomol at the *Pravda* plant had supported his application was for him the final affirmation of his new Soviet identity.[101]

For many 'kulak' children, the urge to be recognized as Soviet, to become a valued member of society, had less to do with politics or personal identity than with drive and industry.

Antonina Golovina was a bright girl, full of energy and initiative, with a strong sense of individuality which she took from her father, Nikolai. At Shaltyr, she was the leader of the school brigade. She taught the other children how to read. On her way back to Pestovo, where she joined her father in 1934, the eleven-year-old girl made a firm resolution to 'study hard and prove myself'.[102] At her new school she was taunted and abused by the older boys as a 'kulak daughter' (there were many 'kulak' children in the school in Pestovo) and picked on by the teachers. One day, when the children were told off for misbehaving, Antonina was called up to the front of the class for a special reprimand by one of the senior teachers, who shouted that she and 'her sort' were 'enemies of the people, wretched kulaks! You certainly deserved to be deported, I hope you're all exterminated here!' In her 'Memoirs' (2001) Antonina recalls the incident as the defining moment in her life. She felt a deep injustice and anger that made her want to shout back at the teacher in protest. Yet she was silenced by an even deeper fear about her 'kulak' origins.

Suddenly, I had this feeling in my gut that we [kulaks] were different from the rest, that we were criminals, and that many things were not allowed for us. Basically, as I now understand, I had an inferiority complex, which possessed me as a kind of fear that the regime might do anything to us, because we were kulaks, that we had no rights, and we had to suffer in silence.

After the incident with the teacher, a classmate called Maria, whose father had been arrested as a 'kulak', whispered to Antonina: 'Listen, let's write a letter of complaint about the old witch for calling us all these things!' Antonina was afraid, so Maria wrote the letter for them both. She wrote that as children they were not to blame that their parents had been kulaks, and pleaded for the chance to prove themselves by studying hard. The two girls decorated the letter by drawing a New

Year's tree.* Antonina hid the letter in a bundle of laundry (her mother did the cleaning and washing for the school) and delivered it to the headmaster's door. The headmaster sympathized with the two girls. He called them to his office and told them that 'in secret he agreed with us, but that we were not to say a word to anyone'. Evidently, the teacher who had been so harsh to them was spoken to by him, because she later softened her approach. She even gave the girls parts to play in the school drama, which was all about the suffering of a peasant nanny (played by Antonina) in the home of a 'kulak' (Maria). Antonina writes in her memoirs:

At the end of my final monologue I had to say the words: 'You have sucked the life from me, I now see, and I do not want to stay with you. I am leaving you to go to school!' – and with these words I left the stage. There was thunderous applause. I had stepped into the role to such an extent that my indignation appeared genuine.[103]

Antonina threw herself into her studies. She loved school and did very well, appearing several times in the list of outstanding students (*otlichniki*) displayed in the school hall. It meant that she was chosen to march in the school parades on Soviet holidays. Antonina loved these demonstrations – not because she was political (she thought it was demeaning to carry a banner) but because she was proud to represent her school. She yearned to join the Pioneers and was so heartbroken when she was excluded because of her 'kulak' origins that she wore a home-made version of their scarf and went to the club-house when they assembled in the desperate hope that they might include her in their games.[104] Gradually, she made a place for herself. In 1939, she was admitted to the Komsomol, despite her 'kulak' past (possibly the Komsomol Committee had turned a blind eye to her past, because it valued her initiative and energy). Emboldened by this success, Antonina summoned up the courage to travel incognito to her native village – by then known as the 'New Life' kolkhoz – in the summer of 1939. There she discovered that her old home had been turned into an office for the kolkhoz.[105]

---

*The Christmas tree was banned in the Soviet Union in 1929, but in 1935 it was reinstated as the New Year tree. The New Year holiday shared many of the attributes of the traditional Christmas (the family gathering, the exchange of presents, the Father Christmas figure of Uncle Frost, etc.).

The *otlichniki* (outstanding students) of Class B, Pestovo School, 1936.
The thirteen-year-old Antonina (the only child without the uniform of
the Pioneers) is standing on the left.

As she grew in confidence and ambition, Antonina decided to stop
trying to get accepted for who she was and simply make up a new
identity. She began to lie about her origins whenever she was asked to
fill out questionnaires. 'I knew what I was doing,' she recalls. 'I had
decided to write a new biography for myself.' From the end of her
teenage years, Antonina lived a secret life. She did not speak about her
family to any of her friends. She did not tell her first serious boyfriend,
whom she met in 1940, because she was afraid that he might leave her
if he found out about her past. For the next fifty years, she hid her
identity from her family, because she was afraid, for them and for herself.
Looking back, she remembers:

I had to be alert all the time, not to slip up and give myself away. When I spoke
I had to think: did I forget something? Did I say anything that might make people
suspicious? It was like that all the time ... I was afraid, and I would remain
silent. This fear lasted all my life. It never went away ... Mama always said,
'When you live with wolves, you must learn to live like wolves!'[106]

3

The Pursuit of Happiness

(1932–6)

I

In 1932, Fania Laskina married Mikhail Voshchinsky, a Party worker and chief administrator of building works at the Vesnin Brothers' architectural workshops, one of Moscow's leading construction companies. Fania left the Laskin home on Zubov Square and, after a few months in rented rooms, moved with her husband to a three-room apartment in the fashionable Arbat area. It was a tiny apartment, just 58 square metres in total area, but in comparison with the living conditions of the vast majority of Muscovites it was modern and luxurious, with its own kitchen, its own bathroom and toilet, and even its own private telephone.[1]

Fania Laskina and Mikhail Voshchinsky
(wedding photograph) Moscow, 1932

Moscow grew at a furious pace in the early 1930s. From 1928 to 1933 the population of the capital increased from 2 million to 3.4 million, mainly on account of the mass influx of peasants into industry. Their arrival put enormous pressure on the housing stock. After 1933, the growth of the city was controlled by the passport system and by mass expulsions of 'alien elements'.[2] To live in Moscow was the dream of millions. The city was the centre of power, wealth and progress in the Soviet Union. Propaganda portrayed it as living proof of the better life to come under socialism.

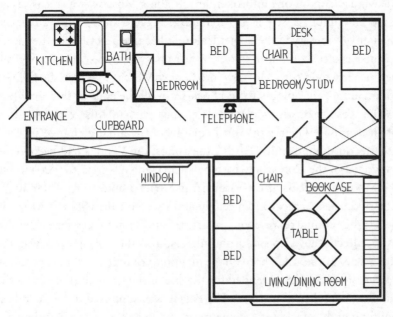

The Laskin household in the Arbat: Sivtsev Vrazhek 14, apt. 59

Stalin took a personal interest in the 'socialist construction' of his capital. In 1935, he signed an ambitious Master Plan for the Reconstruction of Moscow. The Vesnin Brothers, Leonid, Viktor and Aleksandr, were among the architects responsible for drawing up the plan under the direction of the Moscow Soviet. The plan envisaged a city of 5 million inhabitants, with vast new residential suburbs connected by highways, ring roads, parklands, sewage systems, communication networks and a Metro system that would be the most advanced in the industrial world. Everything was planned on a monumental scale. The medieval city centre, with its narrow streets and churches, was largely cleared to make room for wider streets and squares. A vast new parade route was constructed through the centre of the capital. Tverskaia (renamed Gorky) Street was broadened to a width of 40 metres by knocking down the old buildings (many architectural monuments, including the eighteenth-century chambers of the Moscow Soviet, were reassembled further back from the main road). Red Square was cleared of its market stalls to allow for the march of the massed ranks past the Lenin Mausoleum, the sacred altar of the Revolution, on 1 May and Revolution Day. There were even plans to blow up St Basil's Cathedral, so that the marchers could file past the Mausoleum in one unbroken line. Stalin's Moscow was recast as an imperial capital, a Soviet St Petersburg. Bigger, taller, more advanced than any other city in the Soviet Union, it became a symbol of the future socialist society (Bukharin said that the Master Plan was 'almost magical' because it would turn Moscow into 'a new Mecca, to which the fighters for mankind's happiness would flock from all the ends of the earth').[3]

The Vesnin Brothers played a leading part in this transfiguration of the capital. Their work on it involved a dramatic change in their architectural philosophy. During the 1920s, the Vesnins had been in the vanguard of the Constructivist movement, which sought to incorporate the Modernist ideals of Le Corbusier in Soviet architecture. Their adoption of the neoclassical and monumental style, in which Stalin's Moscow was to be rebuilt, represented an artistic and a moral compromise. But as architects they depended on patrons, and the only patron was the state. The brothers had been on the planning committee for the grandiose Palace of the Soviets, intended for the site of the Cathedral of Christ the Saviour, demolished in 1932. The Palace was supposed to be the tallest building in the world (at 416 metres it was to be 8 metres taller than the Empire State Building, which opened in New York in 1931) with a colossal statue of Lenin (three times the size of the Statue of Liberty) at its summit.[4] The Palace was never built,* but for years the site was a monument to the promise of Moscow.

The Vesnins also helped to oversee the construction of the Moscow

---

*The foundations leaked, even after they were blocked with tombstones from the city's cemeteries. Children jumped the fences to swim in the foundations or to fish for carp. Building was halted by the outbreak of the war in 1941. It was not resumed. But pictures of the Palace continued to appear on matchboxes, and the local Metro stop (today's Kropotkin Station) continued to be known as the Palace of the Soviets. The site was later turned into a swimming pool.

Metro, another icon of Communist progress. The tunnelling began in 1932. By the spring of 1934, the enterprise employed 75,000 workers and engineers, many of them peasant immigrants and Gulag prisoners. The digging was extremely dangerous work. There were frequent fires and cave-ins, because of the softness of the soil, and more than a hundred people died during the construction of the first line, 12 kilometres of track between Sokolniki and Gorky Park. Gulag labour was employed in all the city's major building projects during the 1930s (there were several labour camps in the vicinity of the capital). A quarter of a million prisoners took part in the construction of the Moscow–Volga Canal, which provided water for the growing population of the capital. Many of them died from exhaustion, their bodies buried in the foundations of the canal. Like Peter's capital, St Petersburg, which was in many ways its inspiration, Stalin's Moscow was a utopian civilization constructed on the bones of slaves.

When the first Metro line was opened, in 1935, Lazar Kaganovich, the Moscow Party boss, hailed it as a palace of the proletariat: 'When our worker takes the Metro, he should be cheerful and joyous. He should think of himself in a palace shining with the light of the advancing, all-victorious Socialism.'[5] The Metro stations were built as palaces, with chandeliers, stained-glass panels, brass and chrome fittings, walls of marble (there were twenty different kinds), porphyry, onyx and malachite. Maiakovsky Station (1938) matched the beauty of a church, with its oval ceiling cupolas, mosaic designs, marble patterned floors and stainless-steel arches, which created a bright and lofty atmosphere in the central hall. Drawing up their plans for the Stalin Factory (Avtozavod) Metro Station during the late 1930s, the Vesnins likened the effect they aimed to achieve to the atmosphere inside a cathedral. The finished station (1943), with its high, almost gothic marble columns, its simple use of space and light, and its white marble bas reliefs depicting the 'achievements' of the Five Year Plans (Magnitogorsk, the Stalin Factory, the Palace of the Soviets, the Moscow–Volga Canal), perfectly accomplished their ideal.[6] The splendour of these proletarian palaces, which stood in such stark contrast to the cramped and squalid private spaces in which the majority of people lived, played an important moral role (not unlike the role played by the Church in earlier states). By inspiring civic pride and reverence, the beauty of the Metro helped to foster popular belief in the public goals and values of the Soviet order.

Maiakovsky Station, 1940   Avtozavod Station, 1940s

The Vesnin brothers were also involved in building private homes. They were commissioned to design two- and three-room apartments, like the one Mikhail Voshchinsky and Fania Laskina occupied after their marriage. 'We were very happy there,' recalls Fania. 'It was the first time that either of us had ever lived in an apartment with a bathroom and kitchen. Misha [Mikhail] had his own study. And there was always room for visitors to stay.'[7]

This new emphasis on the construction of private apartments represented a fundamental change in Soviet housing policy. During the 1920s, when the utopian dream of building new collective forms dictated policy, the Bolsheviks had given priority to 'commune houses' (*doma kommuny*) – huge communal blocks with rows of rooms for several thousand workers and their families, shared kitchens and washing and laundry facilities, which would liberate women from domestic drudgery and teach the inhabitants to organize their lives collectively. The Constructivists in the Union of Contemporary Architects had been in the vanguard of this Soviet campaign to obliterate the private sphere by making people live in a communal way. But Moscow's housing priorities were turned around in 1931: despite the chronic shortages of accommodation in the Soviet capital – a situation exacerbated by more than a million new arrivals – it was decreed that the main type of housing to be built in Moscow was the luxury house with individual family flats.

The change in policy was obviously connected to the rise of a new political and industrial elite, whose loyalty to the Stalinist regime was secured by the handing down of material rewards. The Five Year Plan had produced a huge demand for new technicians, functionaries and managers in all branches of the economy. According to the chairman of Gosplan, the state planning agency, 435,000 engineers and specialists were needed for the new demands of industry in 1930. The old ('bourgeois') industrial elites were mistrusted by the Stalinist leadership (only 2 per cent of Soviet engineers were Party members in 1928). Many of these specialists had been opposed to the fantastically optimistic targets of the Five Year Plan in industry. They were massively purged (as 'saboteurs' and 'wreckers') in the industrial terror of 1928–32, when the chaos introduced by the Five Year Plan and the constant breakdown in the supply of fuel and raw materials led many workers to denounce their bosses when the factory shut down work and they lost pay. The hounding out of the 'bourgeois specialists' from senior positions of industrial management, the economic commissariats, the planning agencies, the academies and the teaching institutes created opportunities for the 'proletarian intelligentsia' to be promoted in their place. The first Five Year Plan was the heyday of the Factory Apprentice Schools (FZUs), which trained workers, many of them peasants who had recently arrived from the countryside, for the expanding ranks of the industrial professions and administrative posts in the economy. From 1928 to 1932, the number of students in the FZUs increased from 1.8 to 3.3 million (nearly half of them of peasant origin); 140,000 workers were promoted from the factory floor to management (many of them trained while on the job); and 1.5 million workers left the factory for administrative jobs or higher schools. Meanwhile, a million workers were enrolled in the Party. Controls were dropped to encourage recruitment (in many factories the entire workforce was enrolled en masse), as the Party leadership attempted to create a proletarian social base to support and implement its policies.[8]

Stalin needed reliable support. The Great Break had created social chaos and widespread discontent, which destabilized his leadership. The archives of the Party and the Soviets are filled with letters and petitions of complaint from angry workers and peasants about the hardships of the Five Year Plan. They wrote to the Soviet government, to Mikhail Kalinin, the Soviet President, or directly to Stalin, to complain about the injustices of collectivization and the over-requisitioning of peasant grain, about the problems they encountered in their factories, about the corruption of Soviet managers and officials, the lack of housing and foodstuffs in the shops.[9] This was not a people resigned to its fate. There were uprisings and strikes throughout the land.[10] Anti-Soviet graffiti was almost just as visible as Soviet propaganda in many city streets.[11] In rural areas there was widespread opposition to the Soviet regime which was voiced in rhyming songs (*chastushki*):

> The Five Year Plan, the Five Year Plan
> The Five Year Plan in Ten.
> I won't go to the kolkhoz:
> The kolkhoz has no bread![12]

Within the Party there was no formal opposition to the Stalin line, but there was a good deal of concealed dissent and discontent about the enormous human costs of 1928–32. In 1932, this began to coalesce around two informal groups. One was made up of Trotsky's former followers from the Left Opposition of the 1920s (I. N. Smirnov, V. N. Tolmachyov, N. B. Eismont), who held various meetings at which there was talk of removing Stalin from the leadership. The other consisted of remnants of the more moderate Right Opposition, led by supporters of the NEP such as Rykov and Bukharin, and in particular by N. N. Riutin, a former district secretary in the Moscow Party organization. Riutin held a small and secret meeting of old comrades in March 1932, the outcome of which was a 194-page typewritten document entitled 'Stalin and the Crisis of the Proletarian Dictatorship'. It was a detailed critique of Stalin's policies, methods of rule and personality, which was circulated in the Party's ranks, until OGPU intercepted it. All the leading members of the so-called Riutin Platform were arrested, expelled from the Party and imprisoned in the autumn of 1932. Most of them were later to be shot in the Great Purge of 1937, when many more Old Bolsheviks, veterans of 1917, were charged with some connection to the group.[13]

The exposure of the Riutin group increased Stalin's paranoia about opposition in his own Party. It coincided with the suicide of Stalin's wife, Nadezhda Allilueva, in November 1932, which seriously unhinged the leader, making him mistrustful of everybody in his entourage. In January 1933, the Politburo announced a thoroughgoing purge of the Party's ranks. The purge instructions did not mention members suspected of belonging to opposition groups, but their call for the expulsion of 'duplicitous elements who live by deceiving the Party, who conceal from it their real aspirations, and who, under the cover of a false oath of "loyalty" to the Party, seek in fact to undermine the Party's policy' made it clear that weeding out dissenters was an urgent task for the Party, which needed to close ranks behind the leadership.[14]

Through the purging of the old and the recruitment of the new, the nature of the Party was gradually evolving in the 1930s. While the Old Bolsheviks were losing ground, a new class of Party bureaucrats was emerging from the industrial rank and file, largely made up of workers promoted to administrative posts (*vydvizhentsy*). The *vydvizhentsy* were the sons (and very rarely, the daughters) of the peasantry and the proletariat, trained in the FZUs and other technical institutes during the First Five Year Plan. This cohort of functionaries became the mainstay of the Stalinist regime. By the end of Stalin's reign, they composed a large proportion of the senior Party leadership (57 of the top 115 ministers in the Soviet government of 1952, including Leonid Brezhnev, Andrei Gromyko and Aleksei Kosygin, were *vydvizhentsy* of the First Five Year Plan).[15] The emerging elite of the early 1930s was generally conformist and obedient to the leadership that had created it. With only seven years of education, on average, few of the new functionaries had much capacity for independent political thought. They took their ideas from the statements of the Party leaders in the press, and parroted their propaganda slogans and political jargon.* Their actual knowledge of

---

*Pavel Galitsky (b. 1911) remembers being questioned by his Party bosses at the Red Arsenal Factory in Leningrad during the purges of 1932. The son of a priest, Galitsky was the editor of the factory's wall-newspaper. He had recently joined the Party, but his family background made him vulnerable. The head of the purge committee, who was the chairman of the regional Party committee and the factory's director, put Galitsky on the spot by asking him to give a summary of 'Lenin's book *The Anti-Dühring*' (there was no such work by Lenin, but there was a famous book by Friedrich Engels with that name that had outlined in encyclopedic detail the Marxist conception of philosophy, natural science and political economy). Galitsky had no idea about the book but, as he recalls, 'I knew that anti meant against, so I said that Lenin wrote against this Dühring, and they said, "Correct! Well done, clever lad!"' (MSP, f. 3, op. 53, d. 2, l. 6).

Marxist-Leninist ideology was meagre and easily contained in the *The Short Course* (1938), Stalin's history of the Party, which they all knew by heart. They identified completely with the Stalinist regime; they linked their personal values to its interests, and all of them were eager to advance their own careers by implementing orders from above.

The character of this new elite was caustically portrayed by Arkadii Mankov, an accountant in the Red Triangle Factory in Leningrad. The son of a lawyer, Mankov was working at the factory so that he could qualify as a 'proletarian' and gain entry to the Institute of Librarians. In a 1933 diary entry, he described his boss – a young man of twenty-five, who started his career in the same way as tens of thousands of young men:

He appeared in Leningrad from nobody knows where, and through the labour exchange got a job at the factory. When he had worked there for a couple of months, he joined the Komsomol, became an activist – that is, did everything that he was asked to do – and spoke up at the meetings, showing off his knowledge of Stalin's and Molotov's articles, whereupon he was suddenly promoted to work in the administration as a labour economist . . . His entire achievement consists in having an important title, and in getting nicely paid (300 roubles a month). He gives the impression of a highly successful person who is pleased with himself and his position. He smiles sweetly, wears a spotlessly white English shirt and tie and a dark new jacket and has a confident and even arrogant manner. Although he holds a high post, he has no specific job. He does all the petty tasks: keeps tabs on people, checks the accounts, sets the work norms. He considers it his business to stick his nose into everything – to express 'the factory view' – to insist, shout, threaten. He collects information carefully and fills out pointless forms and cards which are never seen by anyone. He takes a particular interest in investigating the legality of all innovation in the workshop and is always checking the rulebook.[16]

Competing for material and political rewards, this type of functionary easily turned against his rivals in the Soviet hierarchy. In 1932, a manager at Transmashtekh, a vast industrial conglomerate, wrote to the Soviet President Mikhail Kalinin:

The problem with Soviet power is the fact that it gives rise to the vilest type of official – one that scrupulously carries out the general designs of the supreme authority . . . This official never tells the truth, because he doesn't want to distress the leadership. He gloats about famine and pestilence in the district or ward controlled by his rival. He won't lift a finger to help his neighbour . . . All I see around me is loathsome politicizing, dirty tricks and people being destroyed for slips of the tongue. There's no end to the denunciations. You can't spit without hitting some revolting denouncer or liar. What have we come to? It's impossible to breathe. The less gifted a bastard, the meaner his slander. Of course the purge of your Party is none of my business, but I think that as a result of it, decent elements still remaining will be cleaned out.[17]

In *The Revolution Betrayed* (1936), where he outlined his theory of the 'Soviet Thermidor', Trotsky pointed to the vast 'administrative pyramid' of bureaucrats, which he numbered at 5 or 6 million, on which Stalin's power depended.[18] This new ruling caste did not share the democratic instincts or the Spartan cult of the Old Bolsheviks, who had been so worried that the Party rank and file would be corrupted by the bourgeois influences of the NEP. On the contrary, they hoped to become a Soviet bourgeoisie. Their interests centred on the comforts of the home, on the acquisition of material possessions, on 'cultivated' pursuits and manners. They were socially reactionary, clinging to the customs of the patriarchal family, conservative in their cultural tastes, even if politically they believed in the Communist ideal. Their main aim was to defend the Soviet system, from which they derived their material well-being and position in society.

The system, in turn, made sure they were content. During the Second Five Year Plan (1933–7) the government increased its investment in consumer industries, which had been starved of capital in the rush to build new factories and towns. By the middle of the 1930s, the supply of foodstuffs, clothes and household goods had markedly improved (millions of children who grew up in these years would recall the mid-1930s as a time when they were given their first pair of shoes). From the autumn of 1935, rationing was gradually lifted, giving rise, in Soviet propaganda, to an optimistic mood among consumers as shop windows filled with goods. Cameras, gramophones and radios were mass-produced for the aspiring urban middle class. There was a steady rise in the production of luxury goods (perfumes, chocolate, cognac and champagne), which catered mainly to the new elite, although prices were reduced for Soviet holidays. It was important to the Soviet myth of the 'good life' to give the impression that luxury goods previously affordable only by the rich were now being made accessible to the masses, who could afford them too if they worked hard. New consumer magazines informed the Soviet shopper about the growing diversity of clothing fashions and furnishing designs. Huge publicity was given to the opening of department stores and luxury food shops, like the former Yeliseyev store, renamed Grocery No. 1, which reopened on Moscow's Gorky Street in October 1934. 'The new store will sell more than 1,200 food-stuffs,' announced the newspaper *Evening Moscow*:

In the grocery department there are 38 kinds of sausage, including 20 new kinds that have not been sold anywhere before. This department will also sell three kinds of cheese – Camembert, Brie and Limburger – made for the store by special order. In the confectionary department there are 200 kinds of sweets and pastries ... The bread department has up to 50 kinds of bread ...

The next day, the store was visited by 75,000 people (most, one suspects, just to look).[19]

The promotion of a Soviet consumer culture was a dramatic ideological retreat from the revolutionary asceticism of the Bolsheviks in the first decade of the Revolution, and even in the period of the First Five Year Plan, when Communists were called upon to sacrifice their happiness for the Party's cause. The Soviet leadership was now communicating the contrary message: that consumerism and Communism were compatible. Socialism, Stalin argued in 1934, 'means, not poverty and deprivation, but the elimination of poverty and deprivation, and the organization of a rich and cultured life for all members of society'. Stalin developed this idea at a conference of kolkhoz labourers in 1935. Reprimanding the collective farms for trying to eliminate all private household property, Stalin called for the kolkhoz workers to be allowed to keep their poultry and their cows, and to be given larger garden allotments, to stimulate their interest in the collective farms. 'A person is a person. He wants to own something for himself,' Stalin told the delegates. There was 'nothing criminal in this' – it was a natural human instinct to want private property, and it would 'take a long time yet to rework the psychology of the human being, to re-educate people to live collectively'.[20]

A further sign of this retreat from the ascetic culture of the Revolution was the new importance the Party now assigned to personal appearance and etiquette. The early Bolsheviks considered it anti-socialist to care about such petty things. But from the 1930s the Party declared that cultivated manners and good grooming were compulsory for the young Communist. 'We endorse beauty, smart clothes, chic coiffures, manicures,' announced *Pravda* in 1934. 'Girls should be attractive. Perfume and make-up belong to the "must" of a good Komsomol girl. Clean shaving is mandatory for a Komsomol boy.' Perfumes and cosmetics were sold in growing quantities and varieties during the 1930s. Conferences were held to debate fashion and personal hygiene.[21]

There was also a new emphasis on having fun. 'Life has become better, comrades. Life has become more joyous,' announced Stalin in 1935. 'And when life is joyous, work goes well.' Dancing, which had been condemned by the early Bolsheviks as a frivolous pursuit, was officially encouraged by the Stalinist regime. It soon became the rage, with dance schools opening everywhere. There were carnivals in Moscow's parks, and huge parades to celebrate the Soviet holidays. The Soviet cinema churned out happy musicals and romantic comedies. The people did not have much bread, but there were lots of circuses.

The consolidation of the Stalinist regime was closely connected to the creation of a social hierarchy structured by the granting of material rewards. For those at the top of the pyramid these rewards were immediately available for industry and loyalty; for those at the bottom they were promised in the future, when Communism had been reached. The regime was thus connected to the establishment of an aspirational society, at the heart of which was a new middle class made up of the Party and industrial elites, the technical intelligentsia and professionals, military and police officers, and loyal industrial workers who proved their worth by working hard (the Stakhanovites).* The defining principle of this new social hierarchy was service to the state. In every institution,

---

*In August 1935, the Donbass coalminer Aleksei Stakhanov dug a record amount of coal. Widely applauded in the national press, his achievement began a movement of rewarding skilled and devoted workers, efficiency being one of the stated aims of the Second Five Year Plan. Stakhanovism soon developed into another form of 'shock labour' in which workers who had exceeded the production quotas were rewarded with bonuses in pay, consumer goods, better housing and even promotion to administrative jobs (especially in the police). For the Stalinist regime, the movement was a means of raising the production norms and of lowering the basic rates of pay by making workers more dependent on piece rates. It placed enormous pressure on managers and officials, who took the blame (and were frequently denounced as 'saboteurs' and 'wreckers') when shortages of fuel or raw materials prevented the Stakhanovites from meeting their targets.

the slogan of the Second Five Year Plan ('Cadres Decide Everything!') served to uphold the state's loyal servitors; and their loyalty was handsomely rewarded with higher rates of pay, special access to consumer goods, Soviet titles and honours.

The emergence of a Soviet middle class was further supported by the regime's cultivation of traditional ('bourgeois') family values from the mid-1930s. This represented a dramatic reversal of the anti-family policies pursued by the Party since 1917. It was partly a reaction to the demographic impact of the Great Break: the birthrate had declined disastrously, posing a serious threat to the country's labour supply and military strength; the divorce rate had increased; and child abandonment had become a mass phenomenon, as families fragmented, leaving the regime to cope with the consequences. But the return to traditional family values was also a reflection of the conservatism of the new industrial and political elites, most of whom had risen only recently from the peasantry and the working class. As Trotsky wrote in 1936, the change in policy was a frank admission by the Soviet regime that its utopian attempt to 'take the old family by storm' – to root out the habits and customs of private life and implant collective instincts – had failed.[22]

From the middle of the 1930s, the Party adopted a more liberal approach towards the family and the private home. The notion of 'private life' (*chastnaia zhizn'*) – a closed and separate sphere beyond the state's control and scrutiny – was still rejected ideologically. But the idea of 'personal life' (*lichnaia zhizn'*) – an individual or family realm that remained open to public scrutiny – was actively promoted by the state. In this configuration of the private–public division, the private and the personal were defined in terms of individuality; but the domination of the public sphere demanded visibility of every aspect of the individual's life. The practical effect was to liberate a space within the four walls of the home for the free expression of domesticity (consumer taste, ways of living, domestic habits, and so on), while retaining political controls on the private conduct of the individual, especially the Communist. 'The Party does not interfere or create standards for the trifles of the everyday life of the Communist,' announced *Rabotnitsa*, the Party's main newspaper for women, in 1936; 'it does not insist on rules of behaviour for every Party member in every aspect of a member's life. But the Party does require that every member behave in their private life in a way that serves the interests of the Party and the working class.'[23]

The new emphasis on building private homes was one sign of this change in policy. All the major ministries had their own blocks of flats in Moscow, which they allocated to their leading officials. Bolshevik families who had led a relatively austere existence in the 1920s now enjoyed lives of relative luxury, as they were rewarded with new homes, privileged access to food shops, chauffered cars, dachas, holidays in special government resorts and sanitoria. For many of these families, the 1930s were a time when they first gained their own domestic space and autonomy. The granting of dachas to the Soviet elite – organized on a large scale from the 1930s on – was particularly important to the encouragement of private family life. At the dacha, safe from watchful eyes and listening ears, relatives could sit and talk in ways that were inconceivable in public places; moreover, the everyday routines of simple country life – swimming, hiking, mushroom-picking, reading, lounging in the yard – provided families some respite from the constraints of Soviet society.

Within the home the Stalinist regime promoted a return to traditional family relations. Marriage became glamorous. Registration offices were smartened up. Marriage certificates were issued on high-quality paper (from Vishlag) instead of on the wrapping paper used before. Wedding rings, which had been banned as Christian relics in 1928, reappeared in Soviet shops after 1936. A series of decrees aimed to strengthen the Soviet family: the divorce laws were tightened; fees for divorce were raised substantially, leading to a sudden fall in the divorce rate; child support was raised; homosexuality and abortion were outlawed. Among the Soviet elite there was a return to conventional and even rather prudish sexual attitudes. The good Stalinist was expected to be mono-gamous, and devoted to his family, as Stalin was himself, according to the propaganda of his cult.* The conduct of the Bolshevik in his intimate relations was closely scrutinized. It was not unusual for a Bolshevik to be expelled from the Party because he was judged to be a bad father or husband. The wives of Party members were expected to return to the traditional role of raising children in the home.

This ideological restoration of the family was closely tied to its

---

*In October 1935, Stalin made a well-publicized visit to his mother in Tbilisi. It began a press campaign to show the Party leader as a family man. Stalin was photographed in the Kremlin gardens with his children, something he had never permitted before (most Soviet people had never even known that Stalin had children).

promotion as the basic unit of the state. 'The family is the primary cell of our society,' wrote one educationalist in 1935, 'and its duties in child-rearing derive from its obligations to cultivate good citizens.' From the middle of the 1930s, the Stalinist regime increasingly portrayed itself through metaphors and symbols of the family – a value-system familiar to the population at a time when millions of people found themselves in a new and alien environment. The cult of Stalin, which took off in these years, portrayed the leader as the 'father of the Soviet people', just as Nicholas II had been the 'father-tsar' (*tsar-batiushka*) of the Russian people before 1917. Social institutions like the Red Army, the Party and the Komsomol, and even the 'Proletariat', were reconceived as 'big families', offering a higher form of belonging through comradeship. In this patriarchal Party-state the role of the parent was now strengthened as a figure of authority who reinforced the moral principles of the Soviet regime in the home. 'Young people should respect their elders, especially their parents,' declared *Komsomolskaia Pravda* in 1935. 'One must respect and love parents, even if they are old-fashioned and do not like the Komsomol.' It was a dramatic change from the moral lessons taught by the cult of Pavlik Morozov, which had encouraged Soviet children to denounce their parents if they were opposed to the policies of the government. As of 1935, the regime reinterpreted the Morozov cult, playing down the story of Pavlik's denunciation and emphasizing new motifs, such as Pavlik's hard work and obedience at school.[24]

Children of the Soviet elite who grew up in these years recall them with nostalgia, particularly for the experience of 'normal family life'. Marina Ivanova was born in 1928 to a family of senior Party officials. Her father was the Secretary of the Party in the town of Mga, 50 kilometres south-east of Leningrad, where the family had a spacious dacha, although they lived mostly in the Leningrad apartment of Marina's grandfather, a former nobleman. 'The apartment was luxurious,' recalls Marina,

with ten large rooms where I could run as a child. The rooms had high ceilings and enormous windows looking out onto the gardens . . . Oil paintings [copies] by Repin and Levitan hung on the walls. A grand piano and a billiard table stood in the two reception rooms . . . This apartment is the place of my happiest childhood memories. I remember crowded parties, with family friends and relatives, and all their children, gathered in our home for the New Year. The children had on masquerade costumes, and Papa would dress up as Uncle Frost and appear with chocolates and gifts for everyone, which he would put around the New Year tree.[25]

Inna Gaister's family moved to the prestigious block of flats reserved for senior Soviet officials (the 'House on the Embankment') opposite the Kremlin in Moscow after her father Aron became the head of the agricultural section of Gosplan in 1932. They had a large apartment with the latest Soviet furniture provided by the government, and a library with several thousand books. The family enjoyed a cultured Russian lifestyle, combining their Communist ideals with the privileges of the Soviet elite. They had a pass to the Imperial Box at the Bolshoi Theatre. There were frequent holidays to special Party resorts in the Crimea, and Astafevo, near Moscow. But Inna's fondest memories are of summers at their family dacha at Nikolina Gora:

The settlement was located in a beautiful pine forest, on a high hill above a bend in the Moscow River. It was a place of magnificent beauty, one of the finest in the Moscow area ... Our plot was right above the river, on a high bank. The dacha was a large two-storeyed house: my mother's brother, Veniamin, with barely hidden envy used to call it her 'villa'. There were three large rooms downstairs and three upstairs. And an enormous verandah. The rooms were usually full of people. There were always some of my parents' many relatives – mostly my cousins – staying there. On weekends my mother's and father's friends would come from Moscow ... and I had my own friends from the nearby dachas. We used to spend most of our time on the river. Papa had built a stairway from our dacha down to the river, to make it easier for my grandmother to get to the water. It was a winding stairway – the slope was very steep – with at least a hundred steps. Long after we left, people still called it Gaister's stairway. At the bottom there was a little wooden pier for swimming. Since the water around our pier was very deep, I was only allowed to swim there with my father. My friends and I preferred the pier below the Kerzhentsev dacha, where the water was shallow and good for swimming.[26]

But such happy memories were not everyone's lot. For many families, the 1930s were a time of growing strain. The restoration of traditional relations often created tensions between husbands and their wives. According to Trotsky, who wrote extensively on the Soviet family, the Stalinist regime had betrayed the commitment of the Bolshevik revolutionaries to liberate women from domestic slavery. His assertion is supported by statistics, which reveal how household tasks were divided within working-class families. In 1923–34, working women were spending three times longer than their husbands doing household chores, but by 1936 they were spending five times longer. For women nothing changed in the 1930s – they worked long hours at a factory and then did a second shift at home, cooking, cleaning, caring for the children on average for five hours every night – whereas men were liberated from most of their traditional domestic duties (chopping wood, carrying water, preparing the stove) by the modernization of workers' housing, which increased the provision of running water, gas and electricity, leaving them more time for cultural pursuits and politics.[27]

But Trotsky also had in mind the sexual politics of families:

One of the dramatic chapters in the great book of the Soviets will be the tale of the disintegration and breaking up of those Soviet families where the husband as a Party member, trade unionist, military commander or administrator, grew and developed and acquired new tastes in life, and the wife, crushed by the family, remained on the old level. The road of the two generations of the Soviet bureaucracy is sown thick with the tragedies of wives rejected and left behind. The same phenomenon is now to be observed in the new generation. The greatest of all crudities and cruelties are to be met perhaps in the very heights of the bureaucracy, where a very large percentage are parvenus of little culture, who consider that everything is permitted to them. Archives and memoirs will some day expose downright crimes in relation to wives, and to women in general, on the part of those evangelists of family morals and the compulsory 'joys of motherhood', who are, owing to their position, immune from prosecution.[28]

Vladimir Makhnach was born in 1903 to a poor peasant family in Uzda, 60 kilometres south of Minsk in Belarus. His mother died while giving birth to him, and his father emigrated to the USA in 1906, leaving Vladimir to be brought up by his aunt. At the age of fourteen, he ran away from home to join the Red Guards, taking part in the seizure of power in Minsk in October 1917. He spent the next four years in the Red Army and fought against the Poles, who invaded Soviet Russia in the Civil War. In 1921, Vladimir joined the Bolsheviks and began his studies at the Mogilyov Agricultural Academy, where he met and fell in love with Maria Chausova. Born in 1904, Maria was the daughter of a peasant trader in the small town of Krichev, 100 kilometres east of

Mogilyov. The youngest of six sisters, and the first to study beyond secondary school, Maria graduated from the Agricultural Academy with a distinction in agronomy and economics in 1925. The couple lived together as de facto man and wife in Mogilyov (like many Soviet youths in the 1920s, they refused to register their marriage as a sign of protest against bourgeois conventions). After graduating from the Agricultural Academy, Vladimir pursued a career in research. In 1928, he went to Moscow, where he joined the Institute of Peat (then regarded by the Bolsheviks as an important source of energy) and researched a dissertation under the direction of Ivan Radchenko, the veteran Bolshevik and friend of Lenin, who was the head of the institute. Vladimir's impeccable credentials, his proletarian origins and his enthusiasm for Stalin's industrialization plans soon attracted the attention of the Moscow Party organization, which called him up to work with Radchenko on the development of new energy supplies for Moscow in 1932. Vladimir became the first director of the Mosgaz Trust – a newly founded industrial complex entrusted with the task of providing gas to the rapidly expanding capital.[29]

Maria followed Vladimir to Moscow, where she worked in the Commissariat of Agriculture as an economist until 1933, when their son Leonid was born. On Vladimir's promotion to Mosgaz, they moved from a small room in a communal apartment to a large private flat on Sparrow Hills (renamed the Lenin Hills in 1935). They enjoyed all the privileges of Stalin's new elite: a chauffered government limousine; a private dacha in the exclusive settlement of Serebrianyi Bor; and access to the secret shops reserved for Party workers, where hard-to-get consumer goods were readily available. Leonid describes his earliest memories as

fragmentary recollections filled with a sense of abundance and the atmosphere of a magical fairy-tale: there I am on my father's strong shoulders looking round at a sea of lights and marble splendour (it must have been in the newly opened Metro in Moscow) . . . There we are by the Lenin Mausoleum on Red Square on 1 May.[30]

Maria employed a nanny, who lived in the pantry of the Makhnach apartment. Maria's aim was to go back to work at the Commissariat. But Vladimir was violently opposed to the idea (he told Maria that 'a senior Party leader should have a wife who stays at home') and lost his temper when she tried to change his mind. Like many Party men, Vladimir believed that his family life should be subordinated to his Party obligations: because his work was more important to the Party than his wife's, it was her duty to support him by organizing a 'well-ordered Communist home'. In November 1935, he wrote to Maria from a work trip to Leningrad:

My darling! I shall be away for several weeks. I shall write to you with my news and instructions. For the moment all I need is a few books [a list follows] . . . It would be a good idea to decorate the hall, it's a little dark. That is all. Make sure our little one is safe and sound. And take care of yourself. Wrap up warm when you go out . . . Forget your illusions of going back to work. Your place now is in the home.[31]

Vladimir Makhnach, 1934   Maria and Leonid, 1940s

The return to 'bourgeois' material values was sometimes yet another source of tension within families. Anatoly Golovnia was a leading figure in the Soviet cinema, the cameraman and close collaborator of Vsevolod Pudovkin, who directed several classic Soviet films, *Mother* (1926), *Storm over Asia* (1930) and *The Deserter* (1933), and won the Stalin Prize no less than five times. Golovnia was born in 1900 in the Crimean town of Simferopol. His father, a minor nobleman, died when he was two, leaving his mother to raise Anatoly and his brother Pyotr on a small pension. The family moved to Kherson, where the boys received a grant from the Noble Assembly to study at the First Gymnasium, a type of grammar school. After the October Revolution, Anatoly joined the Cheka, while Pyotr joined the Whites. In 1920, Anatoly was put in charge of a small Cheka unit with the task of ambushing a White brigade encamped nearby. The brigade was led by his closest friend at school, the son of the chairman of the Kherson Noble Assembly. Anatoly could not bring himself to carry out the order, so he plied his men with vodka and crossed over to the Whites to warn them to escape. This whole episode of Anatoly's life – which is documented in his diaries – was erased from his biography. For the next three years, Anatoly lived on the run from the Reds. First he settled in Tashkent, where he tried to become an agronomist, but after he was rejected from the agricultural school, he fled to Moscow, where he enrolled at the State Technical-Institute of Cinematography (GTK), the newly opened film school in the Soviet capital, to study camera-work in September 1923. It was there that he met and fell in love with Liuba Ivanova, a young actress of extraordinary beauty, who had just arrived in Moscow from Cheliabinsk in the Urals, where she had been born in 1905, the youngest of fourteen children in a peasant family. The couple were soon married, but they spent a lot of time apart, working on location for their films. Their daughter Oksana was often sent by train to stay with aunts in Kherson, or to Cheliabinsk, where she would stay with her grandmother.

In 1933, Anatoly and Liuba received their first apartment – two small rooms in a communal flat located in the courtyard annexe of a large housing block in the centre of Moscow. Their daughter Oksana, who was then aged seven, recalls the apartment in her memoirs (1981):

The floorboards were painted red [because there was no carpet] ... Today's young people, who live for material possessions, would think that they were visiting a store of discarded furniture, or even a rubbish dump. The most valuable thing in our flat was the 'Slavonic' chest of drawers. All our kitchen goods were stored in a home-made cupboard painted white. There were two spring mattresses, Papa's writing table, and three Finnish bookcases with glass fronts – my favourite piece of furniture, because they contained our books ... I slept on a fold-up camp-bed behind the china cupboard in a corner of the living room. The camp-bed was the only thing that 'belonged' to me. I would talk to it at night. I used to think it told me dreams.[32]

These were modest living quarters for two important figures of the Soviet cinema. By this time Liuba was a leading actress at the Mezhrabpomfilm studios and had starred in several silent films. Anatoly attached little significance to personal property. He was 'opposed to it on principle', as he often said, and strongly disapproved of luxury and abundance. 'White shirts and ties were the only things he owned in excessive quantities,' recalls Oksana. Anatoly's austerity was rooted in the values of his class (the impoverished nobility from which so many of Russia's leading writers, artists, thinkers and revolutionaries had emerged) and the frugal habits of his mother, who had raised her sons on a small widow's pension, making sacrifices so that they could go to school. It was precisely this ethos of hard work and discipline that had attracted Anatoly to the Bolsheviks in 1917. According to his granddaughter, there was 'always something of the Chekist in his character. He was severe and strict as a grandfather and never once indulged me as a child.'[33]

Liuba was different. Warm and affectionate, excessive in her passions, she was used to being spoilt, as she had always been as the youngest and most pretty in her family, and eager to enjoy the high life of Moscow. She dressed expensively and had a lot of jewellery. In 1934, Liuba fell in love with the glamorous and handsome boss of Mezhrabpomfilm, Boris Babitsky. She left Anatoly and went to live with Babitsky at his dacha in Kratovo, just outside the capital, where he was living with his

From left: Anatoly Golovnia as Chekist, 1919;
Liuba Golovnia, 1925; Boris Babitsky, 1932

son (Volik) from a previous marriage. In the autumn, Liuba and Boris returned to Moscow. They moved into a spacious apartment (just beneath the offices of Mezhrabpomfilm) in the Comintern hotel (Hotel

Lux), in the centre. The apartment was luxurious, four large rooms off a corridor with parquet floors, and a large kitchen where a housekeeper and a nanny slept. 'It was a palace, a museum, a fairy-tale,' recalls Oksana, who went to live there in 1935. The interior was designed and built by a French worker from the Comintern. The furniture – valuable antiques, bronze vases, leather chairs and Persian carpets – was purchased at heavily discounted prices from the NKVD warehouses in Leningrad. The furniture had been confiscated from families of the old nobility and bourgeoisie who had been arrested and expelled from their homes, on Stalin's orders, following the murder of Sergei Kirov, the Party boss of Leningrad, in December 1934. 'Mama was very proud of her acquisitions,' recalls Oksana, 'and liked to tell us stories about every piece.'[34]

Anatoly's mother, the domineering Lydia Ivanovna, who took her values from the old nobility, thought that Liuba had 'bourgeois pretensions'. She ridiculed her 'vulgar tastes' in clothes and furniture because they reflected the 'material acquisitiveness of the new Soviet elite'. She thought her son had married beneath him and once even said in a heated argument that Oksana was 'the biggest mistake of the Revolution', because she was the child of their mismarriage. Convinced that Liuba left her son for Babitsky because he could better satisfy her expensive tastes, Lydia tried to persuade Anatoly, who was distraught by Liuba's departure, that he might lure her back with a more spacious apartment. But Anatoly would not compromise his principles. Looking back on these events in her memoirs, Oksana reflected on the three conflicting views on property that agitated her family: those of the nobility; the Spartan attitudes of the revolutionary Bolsheviks; and the materialistic attitudes of the new Soviet elite. Oksana sympathized with her mother's position. She felt that her attachment to her country home was not so much a desire for property as a yearning for the sort of family life she had known as a child:

Mama always used to say that we were going to 'our dacha' – as if it belonged to us. I remember this because Papa often said that he was opposed to the idea of things belonging to anyone. At that age, I had no idea about property and did not think about my mother's aspirations to have something of her own. Today, as I try to understand her better, I think that it was not just about property. Mama was not simply building a dacha – she was building a family. She made her family out of real things, just as her peasant ancestors had done for centuries. She loved Boris, she loved me and she loved Volik, and that love was the focus of her home.[35]

Volik Babitsky and Liuba and Oksana at the Kratovo dacha, 1935

2

Few people enjoyed the lifestyle of Liuba Golovnia. For most of the Soviet population the 1930s were years of material shortage, and even for the new bureaucracy, with access to special shops, the supply of goods was hardly plentiful. According to one estimate, during the first half of the 1930s the number of families receiving special provisions (a good estimate of the Soviet nomenklatura) was 55,500, of which 45,000 lived in Moscow. The goods they received allowed these families to live in greater comfort than the vast majority, but by Western standards they still lived very modestly. Here is a list of the goods received by the families of government workers in the centre of Moscow for one month in 1932:

    4 kg of meat
    4 kg of sausage
    1.5 kg of butter
    2 litres of oil
    6 kg of fresh fish

2 kg of herring
3 kg of sugar
3 kg of flour
3 kg of grains
8 cans of food
20 eggs
2 kg of cheese
1 kg of black caviar
50 g of tea
1,200 cigarettes
2 pieces of soap

These families could also purchase clothes and shoes from special shops with coupons given to them by the government, and they had first access to any luxury foods or consumer goods when they became available. But their privileged position was relatively marginal, and the majority of Stalin's ordinary functionaries lived a modest existence, with no more than a few extra clothes or a slightly larger living space than the average citizen. As Mankov noted with sarcasm in his diary: 'The most that anyone can dream to own: two or three different sets of clothes, one of which is imported, an imported bicycle (or motorcycle) and an unlimited opportunity to buy grapes at 11 rbs a kilogram (when they are on sale).'[36]

There was a direct correlation between the allocation of material goods and power or position in the socio-political hierarchy. Below the Soviet elite nobody had many possessions – most people lived in a single pair of clothes – and there was barely enough food for everyone. But in the distribution of even these few goods there was a strict ranking system with infinite gradations between the various categories of employee based on status in the workplace, skill level and experience, and to some extent on geographical location, for rates of pay were better in Moscow and other major cities than they were in the provincial towns and rural areas. Despite its egalitarian image and ideals, this was in fact a highly stratified society. There was a rigid hierarchy of poverty.

Private trade partly compensated for the frequent shortages of the planned economy. People sold and exchanged their household goods at flea markets. If they could afford it, they could buy the produce grown by kolkhoz peasants on their garden allotments and sold at the few remaining urban markets tolerated by the government. People were allowed to sell their furniture and other precious items at the state commission stores, or exchange their jewellery and foreign currency for luxury foodstuffs and consumer goods at the Torgsin shops developed by the regime in the early 1930s to draw out the savings of the population and raise capital for the Five Year Plan. The black market flourished on the margins of the planned economy. Goods unavailable in the state stores were sold at higher prices under the counter, or siphoned off to private traders (bribe-paying friends of the manager) for resale on the black market. To cope with the problems of supply an 'economy of favours' came into operation through small informal networks of patrons and clients (a system known as '*blat*'). In many ways the Soviet economy could not have functioned without these private connections. To get anything (a rented room, household goods, a railway ticket, a passport or official papers) required personal contacts – family and kin, colleagues, friends, or friends of friends. The same black-market principles were known to operate in Soviet factories and institutions, where many goods and services were supplied and exchanged on the basis of personal contacts and favours. Soviet propaganda portrayed *blat* as a form of corruption (the aim of rooting out these private networks of patron–client relations assumed an important role in the purges), and this view was shared by many workers, in particular. But most people were ambivalent in their attitude to *blat*: they recognized that it was not right morally, and certainly not legal, but relied on it, as everybody did, to fulfil their needs and get around a system they knew to be unfair. Without *blat* it was impossible to live with any comfort in the Soviet Union. As the proverb said: 'One must have, not a hundred roubles, but a hundred friends.'[37]

Housing shortages were so acute in the overcrowded towns that people would do almost anything to increase their living space. The mass influx of peasants into industry had put enormous pressure on the housing stock in the cities. In Moscow the average person had just 5.5 square metres of living space in 1930, falling to just over 4 square metres in 1940. In the new industrial towns, where house-building lagged far behind the growth of the population, the situation was even worse.[38] In Magnitogorsk, for example, the average living space for working-class families was just 3.2 square metres per capita in 1935. Most of the workers lived in factory barracks, where families were broken up, or in dormitories, where a curtain around their plank-beds provided the only privacy. One female worker in Magnitogorsk drew a vivid picture of life in her barracks:

Dormitories without separate rooms, divided into four sections, tiny kitchen areas where it was impossible to turn around, stoves thoroughly overrun with pots and pans, people in greasy work clothes (there were no showers at the steel plant), children in the hallways, queuing for water, wretched 'furniture' – metal cots, bedside tables, home-made desks and shelves.

Many barracks were deliberately built without kitchens or washrooms in order to force their inhabitants to use the public dining halls, public baths and laundries. But most of the workers in Magnitogorsk proved resistant to this collectivization of their private life and preferred to live in dug-outs in the ground (*zemlianki*), where, despite the primitive conditions, there was at least a modicum of privacy. In 1935, about a quarter of the population of Magnitogorsk lived in these dug-outs. There were entire shanty towns of *zemlianki* on wasteland near the factories and mines. Workers demonstrated fierce resistance to the Soviet's attempts to wipe out this last zone of private property.[39]

In Stalin's Russia human relations revolved around the struggle over living space. According to Nadezhda Mandelshtam:

Future generations will never understand what 'living space' means to us. Innumerable crimes have been committed for its sake, and people are so tied to it that to leave it would never occur to them. Who could ever leave this wonderful, precious twelve and a half square metres of living space? No one would be so mad, and it is passed on to one's descendants like a family castle, a villa or an estate. Husbands and wives who loathe the sight of each other, mothers-in-law and sons-in-law, grown sons and daughters, former domestic servants who have managed to hang onto a cubby hole next to the kitchen – all are wedded forever to their living space and would never part with it. In marriage and divorce the first thing that arises is the question of living space. I have heard men described as perfect gentlemen for throwing over their wives but leaving them the living space.[40]

There are endless tales of bogus marriages to obtain a place to live, of divorced couples sharing rooms together rather than give up their living space, of neighbours denouncing one another in the hope of getting extra space.[41]

In 1932, Nadezhda Skachkova, the nineteen-year-old daughter of a peasant widow in Tver province, was studying at the Railway Institute in Leningrad. She was living in a student hostel, sharing one small room with several other girls. Like many recent arrivals from the countryside, Nadezhda was not registered to live in Leningrad. With the introduction of the passport system, she stood to be evicted from her room. Through acquaintances Nadezhda got in contact with a young Ukrainian soldier who had a room (8 square metres) in a communal apartment. The soldier was about to join his unit in the Donbass. Nadezhda paid him 500 roubles to marry her, money which her mother raised by selling her last cow and household property, and then moved into his room, where she was joined by her mother. Nadezhda met her husband only once:

We went to see him the evening before he left for the army. We settled the payment. Then we went to the registry office to marry and after that to the house administration so that they could register us [Nadezhda and her mother] as residents. And that was that. The people in the house administration smiled, of course – they knew that we were getting round the rules. They checked that all the details were correct. My husband left the next morning. And Mama and I had eight square metres to ourselves . . . Of course I never thought to live with him. He was a simple country lad, barely literate. He sent us one or two letters – 'How are you?' and that sort of thing. He wrote not 'Donbass' but 'Dobas'. Good Lord! Even that he could not spell.[42]

The most common type of living space in the Soviet cities was the communal apartment (*kommunalka*), in which several families co-inhabited a single apartment, sharing a kitchen, a toilet and a bathroom, if they were lucky (many urban residents relied on public baths and laundries).[43] In Moscow and Leningrad three-quarters of the population lived in communal apartments in the middle of the 1930s, and that way of living remained the norm for most people in those cities throughout the Stalin period.[44] Along with everything else, the *kommunalka*, too, changed in nature in the 1930s. Whereas its purpose in the 1920s was to address the housing crisis and at the same time strike a blow against private life, it now became primarily a means of extending the state's powers of surveillance into the private spaces of the family home. After 1928, the Soviets increasingly tightened their control of the 'condensation' policy, deliberately moving Party activists and loyal workers into the homes of the former bourgeoisie so that they could keep an eye on them.[45]

The Khaneyevskys experienced every phase of *kommunalka* living. Aleksei Khaneyevsky came from a wealthy clan of merchants in Voronezh. He arrived in Moscow to study medicine in 1901. Aleksei became a military doctor, serving with distinction in the First World War, when he was promoted to the rank of lieutenant-colonel, a rank that gave him the status of a nobleman. In 1915, Aleksei rented a comfortable and spacious apartment on Prechistenka Street near the centre of Moscow. He lived there with his wife, Nadezhda, their two young daughters, Irina (born in 1917) and Elena (1921), together with a nanny, until 1926, when the Moscow Soviet imposed its 'condensation' policy on the family. A factory worker, Marfa Filina, moved into a room in the apartment, followed by the family of a tailor, Vasily Kariakin, and then the family of Nikolai Sazonov, a Red Army veteran of proletarian origins who had risen to become a professor at the Communist Academy. Where three adults and two children had been living in the 1920s, there were fourteen people cramped in the apartment by 1936, when Nikolai Sazonov's second wife moved into the flat with her mother. They shared the hallway, the kitchen (where two houseworkers slept), a toilet and a bathroom, which had no water (it was used as a store) so the only place to wash was at the cold-water tap in the kitchen. The Khaneyevskys attempted to isolate themselves from their new neighbours by putting up a door to close off the back of the apartment, where they lived. Their neighbours liked the door because it added to their privacy as well. In 1931, the district Soviet ordered that a bathroom be installed – it was part of the Soviet campaign for personal hygiene at that time – so the door was taken down. But life without the door proved very difficult, with constant arguments between the Khaneyevskys and the Sazonovs, so Aleksei paid a bribe to the Soviet to let them take away the bath. The bathroom was again turned into a store and the private door returned. The Khaneyevskys' relations with the Sazonovs remained problematic, however. Nikolai's mother-in-law was mentally unstable and often threw a fit in the corridor, accusing somebody of stealing food, which she hid beneath her bed. Class differences played a part in these conflicts. Nadezhda worried that the Sazonovs would steal her silver. She took offence when they appeared semi-naked in the corridor. She said they smelled and told them they should wash more frequently.[46]

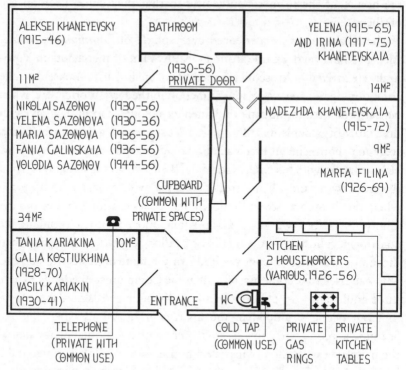

| ALEKSEI KHANEYEVSKY (1915-46) 11M² | BATHROOM (1930-56) PRIVATE DOOR | YELENA (1915-65) AND IRINA (1917-75) KHANEYEVSKAIA 14M² |

The Khaneyevsky household (communal apartment), Prechistenka
(Kropotkin) Street, 33/19, Flat 25

Many of the old apartment owners felt that they were picked on by the new inhabitants because they were seen by them as members of the 'bourgeoisie'. Vera Orlova, a countess before 1917, lived in a communal apartment that had once been a part of her family's house. She and her husband moved into a single room with their daughter, who describes the poisonous atmosphere in the apartment during the 1930s.

Communal life was terrifying. The inhabitants measured every square centimetre of the corridor and every patch of common space and protested because mother left some valuable pieces of furniture there. They claimed they took up too much space, that she had to keep them in her room, that the corridor did not belong to her. The 'neighbours' timed how long we spent in the bathroom. In some communal apartments the inhabitants installed timers [on the lights] in the toilet, so that no one consumed more than their fair share of electricity.[47]

The Khaneyevsky household was not overcrowded by comparison with the majority of communal apartments in Moscow and Leningrad. Yevgeny Mamlin grew up in a *kommunalka* with sixteen families (fifty-four people), each one living in a single room, and all sharing one kitchen. There were two toilets, and two basins with cold water, but no bathroom.[48] Minora Novikova grew up in a communal apartment in Moscow. There were thirty-six rooms – each with at least one family – on a corridor that ran round three sides of the house. In her room there were ten people living in a space of only 12.5 square metres. 'How we slept is hard to say,' recalls Minora.

There was a table in the room, on which my grandmother slept. My brother, who was six, slept in a cot underneath the table. My parents slept in the bed by the door. My other grandmother slept on the divan. My aunt slept on a large feather mattress on the floor with her cousin on one side, while my sister (who was then aged sixteen), my cousin (ten), and I (eleven) somehow squeezed in between them – I don't remember how. We children loved sleeping on the floor: we could slide our bodies underneath our parents' bed and have a lot of fun. I don't imagine that it was much fun for the adults.[49]

Nina Paramonova lived in a similar 'corridor system' in Leningrad. The apartment occupied the whole floor of a house that had been requisitioned from a German baron by the Institute of Trade in 1925, and Nina moved there in 1931 with her husband, a ship designer, when she took a job as an accountant in the Leningrad railway administration. The apartment had seventeen rooms, with at least one family in each. Altogether there were over sixty people, who all shared a kitchen, a toilet and a shower room (with cold water).[50]

At the other end of the social spectrum, the Third House of Soviets, a communal apartment for government workers in the centre of Moscow, also had a 'corridor system'. The brother of Stalin's wife, Fyodor Alliluev, lived with his mother in a room on the second floor. Ninel Reifshneider, the daughter of a veteran Bolshevik and political writer, lived with her parents, her grandparents, her brother and her sister in one of the nine rooms on the floor below, a living space of 38 square metres for six people, not counting her father, who usually slept in the Metropol Hotel, where he also kept a room. There were thirty-seven people living in the nine rooms of the corridor. They shared a large kitchen, where there was a shower and a bath behind a screen on one

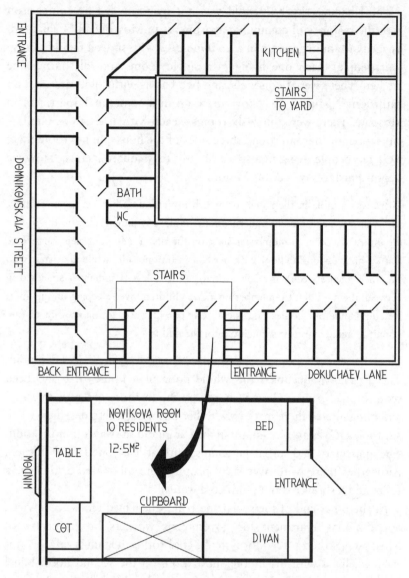

Communal apartment ('corridor system'), Dokuchaev Lane,
Moscow, 1930–64

side and a toilet cubicle on the other side. There were two other toilet
cubicles at the end of the corridor. In the yard there was a communal
woodshed, with wood for heating the cookers and the stoves. The house
was conceived as an experiment in collective living but it had the services

expected by the Soviet elite. There was a playground for the children, a club-house and a cinema in the basement. On each corridor there was a cleaner, a housekeeper and a nanny, paid for by the residents collectively.[51]

The communal apartment was a microcosm of the Communist society. By forcing people to share their living space, the Bolsheviks believed that they could make them more communistic in their basic thinking and behaviour. Private space and property would disappear, family life would be replaced by Communist fraternity and organization, and the private life of the individual would be subjected to the mutual surveillance and control of the community. In every communal apartment there were shared responsibilities, which the inhabitants would organize between themselves. Bills for common services, such as gas and electricity, or the telephone, were distributed equally, either on the basis of usage (e.g. the number of telephone calls, or how many light bulbs there were in each room) or on the basis of room or family size. Repair costs were also paid collectively, although there were often arguments about individual responsibility that usually had to be resolved by a meeting of the residents. The cleaning of the common spaces (the hall, the entrance, the toilet, bathroom and kitchen) was organized by rota (usually displayed in the hall). Everybody had 'their day' for washing clothes. In the mornings there were queues for the bathroom, also organized by a list of names. In this mini-state, equality and fairness were to be the ruling principles. 'We divided everything as equally as possible,' recalls Mamlin. 'My father, who was the elder of our household, worked out everything to the last kopeck, and everybody knew how much they had to pay.'[52]

The post of elder (*otvetstvennyi kvartoupolnomochennyi*) was established in 1929, when the communal apartment was legally defined as a social institution with specific rules and responsibilities to the state: the enforcement of sanitary regulations; tax collection; law enforcement; and informing the police about the private life of the inhabitants.[53] The elders were supposed to be elected by the residents, but in fact it was more common for them to elect themselves and to be accepted by the residents, either through the force of their personality or else their standing in society. Nina Paramonova remembers that their elder 'ran the household like a dictatorship. We all respected her because she was so strict. We were afraid of her. Only she had the authority to make people do the cleaning when it was their turn.'[54] A new law of 1933 placed the elders in sole charge of the communal apartment; their links to the police were reinforced; and they were given the command of the yardmen (*dvorniki*), notorious informers, who cleaned the staircase and the yard, patrolled the household territory, locked the courtyard gates at night and kept an eye on everyone who came and went. Through the elders and yardmen, the household management became the basic operational unit of the police system of surveillance and control.

By the middle of the 1930s the NKVD had built up a huge network of secret informers. In every factory, office, school, there were people who informed to the police.[55] The idea of mutual surveillance was fundamental to the Soviet system. In a country that was too big to police, the Bolshevik regime (not unlike the tsarist one before it) relied on the self-policing of the population. Historically, Russia had strong collective norms and institutions that lent themselves to such a policy. While the totalitarian regimes of the twentieth century sought to mobilize the population in the work of the police, and one or two, like the Stasi state in the GDR, managed for a while to infiltrate to almost every level of society, none succeeded, as the Soviet regime did for sixty years, in controlling a population through collective scrutiny.

The *kommunalka* played a vital role in this collective system of control. Its inhabitants knew almost everything about their neighbours: the timetable of their normal day; their personal habits; their visitors and friends; what they purchased; what they ate; what they said on the telephone (which was normally located in the corridor); even what they said in their own room, for the walls were very thin (in many rooms the walls did not extend to the ceiling). Eavesdropping, spying and informing were all rampant in the communal apartment of the 1930s, when people were encouraged to be vigilant. Neighbours opened doors to check on visitors in the corridor, or to listen to a conversation on the telephone. They entered rooms to 'act as witnesses' if there was an argument between man and wife, or to intervene if there was too much noise, drunken behaviour or violence. The assumption was that nothing could be 'private' in a communal apartment, where it was often said that 'what one person does can bring misfortune to us all'. Mikhail Baitalsky recalls the communal apartment of a relative in Astrakhan where there was a particularly vigilant neighbour living in the room next door: 'Hearing the sound of a door being unlocked, she would thrust her pointed little nose into the corridor and pierce you with a photographic glance. Our relative assured us that she kept a card index of his vistors.'[56]

In the cramped conditions of the communal apartment there were frequent arguments over personal property – foodstuffs that went missing from the shared kitchen, thefts from rooms, noise or music played at night. 'The atmosphere was poisonous,' recalls one inhabitant. 'Everyone suspected someone else of stealing, but there was never any evidence, just a lot of whispered accusations behind people's backs.'[57] With everybody in a state of nervous tension, it did not take a lot for fights to turn into denunciations to the NKVD. Many of these squabbles had their origins in some petty jealousy. The communal apartment was the domestic centre of the Soviet culture of envy, which naturally arose in a system of material shortages. In a social system based on the principle of equality in poverty, if one person had more of some item than the other residents, it was assumed that it was at the expense of everybody else. Any sign of material advantage – a new piece of clothing, a better piece of kitchenware, or some special food – could provoke aggression from the other residents, who naturally suspected that these goods had been obtained through *blat*. Neighbours formed alliances and continued feuds on the basis of these perceived inequalities. One woman, who still lives in the communal apartment in Moscow where she grew up in the 1930s,* recalls a long-running feud between her mother, who worked in a bakery, and the yardman's wife, who was well known as an informer. Whenever cakes or buns appeared in the kitchen, the yardman's wife would accuse her mother of theft or sabotage and threaten to denounce her to the authorities.[58] Mitrofan Moiseyenko was a factory worker who supplemented his income by repairing furniture and windows and doing odd jobs for the residents of his communal block in Leningrad. In the spring of 1935, he was involved in an argument with his neighbours, who accused him of charging them too much for his repairs. His neighbours denounced him to the police, absurdly claiming that he had been hiding Trotsky in his workshop in the basement of the block. Mitrofan was arrested and sentenced to three years in a labour camp near Magadan.[59]

The kitchen was the scene of many arguments. In the evenings, when it was bustling with people, it was always prone to overheat. The kitchen

*For this reason she wishes to remain anonymous.

was a common space, but within it, in most communal flats, each family had its own ring for cooking on the stove, its own private kitchen table, where meals were normally eaten and its own place for storing food in the kitchen cupboards, on the open shelves, or between the inner and the outer windows, where winter temperatures were as cold as in a fridge. This confusion between private and common space was a constant source of friction; using someone else's cooking ring, their utensils or their supplies was enough to stoke a scandal. 'They were not malicious arguments,' recalls Minora Novikova. 'We were all poor, and nobody had anything worth stealing. But there was never enough room, everyone was tense in the kitchen, and petty squabbles were unavoidable. Imagine thirty women cooking at one time.'[60]

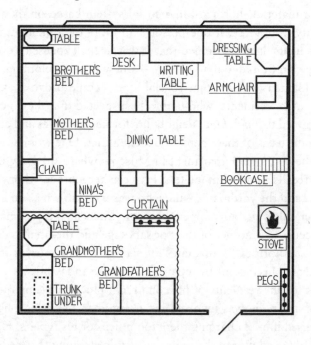

The Reifshneiders' room (38 square metres) in the Third House of Soviets, Sadovaia Karetnaia, Moscow

The lack of privacy was the greatest source of tension. Even in the family's own room, there was no space to call one's own. The room had many functions – bedroom, dining room, a place to receive guests, a study for the children to do their schoolwork, sometimes even a kitchen. 'In our room,' recalls Ninel Reifshneider, there were no private things or bits of furniture, no special shelf or chair or table that belonged to anyone as property. Even my grandparents, who had their beds behind a curtain screen to give them some privacy, had nothing they could really call their own. My grandmother kept some special items in a trunk beneath her bed, but the table by her bed, for example, was used by all of us.

In many family rooms the younger children slept behind a makeshift screen, a bookcase or a wardrobe, to give them some quiet apart from the adults and their evening guests (and to stop them watching the adults when they got undressed and went to bed). Parents had to make love quietly in the middle of the night.[61]

In such close quarters, little was left to the imagination. Neighbours grew accustomed to seeing one another semi-naked in the corridor. They saw each other at their worst – in drunken or unguarded moments – without the mask that people wore to protect themselves in public areas. They knew when their neighbours had a visitor from the doorbell system (in which every room had its own set number or sequence of rings on the front-door bell). Rooms used for the most intimate functions (the bathroom, kitchen and toilet) were shared by everyone; inferences could easily be drawn from bits of evidence that were left behind. The clothes line in the kitchen, the personal items in the bathroom, the night-time trips to the toilet – these told neighbours everything. In this form of 'public privacy', private life was constantly exposed to collective scrutiny.[62]

People felt the lack of privacy in many different ways. Some resented the constant intrusions – neighbours entering the room, knocking on the bathroom door or spying on visitors. Others reacted to the constant noise, the lack of cleanliness or the sexual attentions of older men towards the girls. The toilet and the bathroom were a source of constant friction and anxiety. In the communal apartment where Elena Baigulova lived in Leningrad in the 1930s there was just one toilet for forty-eight people. People brought their own soap and toilet paper, which they kept in their room. In 1936, one of the inhabitants married a black man. 'There was a scandal when he first appeared,' recalls Elena. 'People would not share a toilet or a bathroom with the man. They thought that he was dirty because he was black.'[63]

Private conversations were a particular problem. Talk was clearly audible between adjoining rooms, so families adapted by whispering among themselves. People were extremely careful not to talk to neighbours about politics (in some communal apartments the men would not talk at all).[64] Families from a bourgeois or noble background were careful to conceal their origins. Alina Dobriakova, the granddaughter of a tsarist officer, grew up in a *kommunalka* in Moscow where all the other residents were factory workers and their families, 'a conglomeration of unfriendly people', as she recalls. Alina was forbidden to say a word to anyone about the photographs of her grandfather which were kept hidden in their room. Her mother joined the Party and took a job as an official to conceal their past. 'If our neighbours knew who my mother's father was,' recalls Alina, 'there would have been much unpleasantness . . . so we lived in a grave-like silence.'[65] Talking in a communal apartment could be very dangerous. In the Khaneyevsky household, Nadezhda was practically deaf, but outspoken in her anti-Soviet views. She would explain to her daughters how life had been better under the tsar and would start to shout. Her husband Aleksei, who was terrified of the Sazonovs in the next room, would remind her not to shout: 'Whisper, or we shall be arrested.'[66]

People battled for a modicum of privacy. They kept their towels and toiletries, their kitchen pots and pans, their dishes, cutlery, even salt and pepper in their rooms. They did their washing, cooking, eating, drying clothes in the privacy of their own room. Areas of common space were partly privatized: families might claim a place on the shelf; a patch of corridor; a section of the kitchen table; a peg or space for shoes by the front door in the hallway. All these arrangements were well known to the inhabitants, but a stranger coming into the apartment would not be aware of them. People dreamed of a private space where they might get away from their neighbours. Yevgeny Mamlin 'yearned for a kitchen with a serving hatch connected to his room so that he could cook and take his meals without using the communal kitchen, but that was just a dream,' recalls his daughter. The escape to the dacha in the summer months was a relief from the pressures of the communal apartment, for those who could afford to rent a country house.[67]

At its best the communal apartment fostered a sense of comradeship and collectivity among its inhabitants. Many people look back with nostalgia to their years in a communal apartment as a time when they shared everything with their neighbours. 'Before the war we lived in harmony,' recalls one inhabitant:

Everybody helped one another, and there were no arguments. No one was stingy with their money – they spent their wages as soon as they were paid. It was fun to live then. Not like after the war, when people kept their money to themselves, and closed their doors.

Part of this nostalgia is connected to recollections of childhood happiness, of a time when, despite material hardships, the yard was clean and safe for children's games, and the communal apartment retained the atmosphere of an extended 'family'. In the *kommunalka* children mixed with other families far more than their parents did: they played together and were always in each other's rooms, so they experienced this togetherness more than anyone. 'We lived as one big family,' recalls Galina Markelova, who grew up in a communal apartment in Leningrad during the 1930s:

In those days everybody lived with their doors open, and we children had the run of the whole house. We would play in the corridor and run from room to room while the adults played at cards or dominoes. They didn't play for money, just for fun. And there was always lots of laughter. There were too many adults for them all to play, so they would take turns, with some watching while the others played. We celebrated Soviet holidays together, like a family, with everybody bringing something nice to eat or drink. It was very jolly on birthdays, with lots of games and songs.[68]

But the closeness could be stifling. The film director Rolan Bykov, who grew up in a communal apartment in the 1930s, recalls the way of life as repressive, as an effort to stamp out any sign of individuality. The 'law of the collective' ruled in the household, recalls Bykov, and there was no use trying to kick against it – that 'would unite everybody' against those who refused to conform. Elizaveta Chechik had similar feelings about the communal apartment she grew up in:

To some extent we were brought up together by all the adults on the corridor. Some of the children I played with had very strict parents, Bolsheviks. I was afraid of them and felt uncomfortable in their presence. Looking back now, I realize that I grew up with the feeling that I was not free, that I could not be myself, in case someone observed me and disapproved. It was only when I was in the apartment and no one else was there that I felt release from this fear.[69]

The communal apartment had a profound psychological impact on those who lived in them for many years. During interviews many long-term residents confessed to an intense fear of being on their own.* The communal apartment practically gave birth to a new type of Soviet personality. Children, in particular, were influenced by collective values and habits. Families lost control of their own children's upbringing in a communal apartment: their cultural traditions and habits tended to be swamped by the common principles of the household as a whole. Looking back on her childhood, Minora Novikova believes that the *kommunalka* made her more inclined to think in terms of 'we' rather than in terms of 'I'.

Everything was held in common. There were no secrets. We were all equal, we were all the same. That is what I was accustomed to, and in later life it seemed strange to me when I encountered different ways. I remember on my first trip [as a geologist] I bought some sweets and shared them all around. The group leader said to me: 'You should write down how much you spent, so that you can get reimbursed.' That struck me as a monstrous idea, because from my childhood I was used to sharing anything I had.

Others who grew up in a *kommunalka* credit communal life with teaching them the public values of the Soviet regime – love of work, modesty, obedience and conformity. But a sense of wariness, of self-consciousness, was never far behind. 'It was a constant effort to control oneself and make oneself fit in,' recalls one inhabitant.

It was a different feeling of repression from arrest, imprisonment and exile, which I've also experienced, but in some ways it was worse. In exile one preserved a sense of one's self, but the repression I felt in the communal apartment was the repression of my inner freedom and individuality. I felt this repression, this need for self-control, every time I went into the kitchen, where I was always scrutinized by the little crowd that gathered there. It was impossible to be oneself.[70]

---

*Psychiatrists have also found a high proportion of people suffering from paranoia and schizophrenic delusions among long-term residents.

3

Soviet citizens were quick to protest against material shortages and inequalities. They wrote in their thousands to the government to complain about corruption and inefficiencies, which they linked to the privileges of the new bureaucracy. Yet at the same time there were many citizens who perservered in the expectation that they would live to see the Communist utopia. The Soviet regime was sustained by this idea in the 1930s. Millions of people were persuaded to believe that the hardships of their daily lives were a necessary sacrifice for the building of a Communist society. Hard work today would be rewarded tomorrow, when the Soviet 'good life' would be enjoyed by all.

In *Ideology and Utopia* (1929) the German sociologist Karl Mannheim discussed the tendency of revolutionary Marxists to experience time as a 'series of strategical points' along a path to a future paradise, which they perceive as real and tangible. Because this future is a factor in the present and defines the course of history, it gives meaning to everyday realities. In the Soviet Union this idea of time had its origins in the utopian projections of the 1917 Revolution. For the Bolsheviks, October 1917 was the beginning of Year One in a new history of humanity (just as 1789 marked the start of the new world created by the Jacobins). Projecting the present into the future, Soviet propaganda portrayed the Revolution moving forwards (on the 'march of history') towards the Communist utopia; it hailed the achievements of the Five Year Plans as proof that this utopia was just over the horizon.[71]

The Five Year Plans played a crucial role in this utopian projection. The conception of the Plan was to accelerate the arrival of the socialist future by speeding up the tempo of the whole economy (hence the slogan 'The Five Year Plan in Four!'). Indeed the Plan was to conquer time itself by subordinating it to the proletarian will. In the capitalist economies of the West work was organized according to a strictly rational division of time. But in the Soviet Union work was structured according to the goals set by the Five Year Plans. Because the achievement of this goal was always imminent, it made sense to 'storm' production, to work for a brief but frenzied spell to reach that goal, when it would be possible to rest. The Stalinist economy was based on this 'storming' of production to meet the Five Year Plans, just as the system as a whole was based on the idea that present hardship would be rewarded in the Communist utopia. Nikolai Patolichev, a *vydvizhenets* of the First Five Year Plan who later rose to the Party's senior ranks, remembers: 'We Soviet people consciously denied ourselves a lot.'

We said to ourselves: 'Today we don't have things that we really need. Well, so what? We shall have them tomorrow.' That was the power of our belief in the Party's cause! Young people of my generation were happy in this belief.[72]

Looking back on the 1930s, many people recall a sense of living for the future rather than for the present. The feeling was particularly strong in the generation that had grown up since 1917 – young people, like Patolichev, who were totally immersed in the values and ideals of the Soviet regime. For this generation the Communist utopia was not a distant dream but a tangible reality, just around the corner and soon to arrive. Soviet schoolchildren in the 1920s and 1930s imagined Communism as a transformation of their own immediate reality (cows full of milk, busy factories) rather than in far-off science-fiction terms.[73] That was how they had been brought up to regard the Soviet future by Soviet propaganda and by Socialist Realist literature and art. Socialist Realism, as officially defined at the First Congress of the Writers' Union in 1934, entailed the 'truthful, historically concrete representation of reality in its revolutionary development'. The artist's role was to portray the world not as it was in the present but as it would become (and was becoming) in the Communist future.

According to Liudmila Eliashova (born in 1921) and her sister Marksena (1923), this conception of the Communist utopia was widely shared by their friends at school in Leningrad:

We were all educated in the expectation of a happy future. I remember when my sister broke our favourite porcelain doll. We did not have the money to buy another doll but we went to the department store, where there were dolls on display, and Marksena said: 'When there is Communism we shall have that doll.' We pictured Communism as a time, which we would live to see, when everything would be free, and everyone would have the happiest life imaginable. We were glad to be waiting for this beautiful future.[74]

Raisa Orlova, who grew up in Moscow in the 1930s, recalls the sense of 'hurtling towards the future'. It made the present seem unreal:

I had an unshakeable conviction that my existence between these old walls [the apartment on Tverskaia Street in Moscow where she grew up] was merely a preparation for the real life to come. That life would start in a new and sparkling white house; there I would do exercises in the morning, there the ideal order would reign, there all my heroic achievements would commence. The majority of my contemporaries – whether they lived in tents, dug-outs, communal flats or what were then considered luxurious private apartments – shared the same kind of provisional, rough and ready approach to life. Faster, faster towards the great goal, towards the new life. Everything could and should be changed: the streets, the houses, the cities, the social order, human souls. And it didn't seem all that difficult. First the enthusiasts would outline the plan on paper. Then they would tear down the old ('You can't make an omelette without breaking eggs'). Then they would clear the rubble, and in the space that had been cleared they would erect the edifice of the socialist dream. That's how Russia was being reconstructed. We thought it was possible to do the same with people.[75]

Moscow was the building site of this utopia. In the imagination of the Communists, where 'soon' and 'now' were all confused, Moscow had a legendary status and significance as a symbol of the socialist utopia that was under construction. In this city of fantastic dreams and illusions, a foundation pit was a future housing block, the demolition of a church signalled the appearance of a Palace of Culture. The German Communist Wolfgang Leonhard, who arrived in Moscow with his parents in 1935, describes their confusion when they sought to replace their outdated 1924 map: the new map showed all the improvements which, according to the Master Plan, were destined for completion by 1945. 'We used to take both town plans with us on our walks,' Leonhard writes: 'one showing what Moscow had looked like ten years before, the other showing what it would look like ten years hence.'[76]

The speed of change in the Soviet Union in the early 1930s was intoxicating. The illusion that a new world was being created led many people – including a large number of socialist intellectuals in the West – to delude themselves about the Stalinist regime. Nina Kaminskaia, a young law student, continued to believe in the new world even after her father was sacked from his job in a Soviet bank and evidence of a darker reality was mounting. In her memoirs she remembers a song she and her friends would sing, a song of joy at the happy life to come, which symbolized the optimism of their generation and their blindness to the tragedy which their parents were already going through:

> Believing in our country is so easy,
> Breathing in our country is so free:
> Our glorious, beloved Soviet land . . .
> Our Soviet life is so good and bright
> That children in ages to come
> Will probably cry in their beds at night
> Because they were not born in our lifetime.[77]

Members of the Soviet intelligentsia were so swept up by this optimistic atmosphere that they closed their eyes to the horrors perpetrated by the Stalinist regime in the name of progress. Boris Pasternak wrote to Olga Freidenberg, in April 1935:

The fact is, the longer I live the more firmly I believe in what is being done, despite everything. Much of it strikes one as being savage [yet] the people have never before looked so far ahead, and with such a sense of self-esteem, and with such fine motives, and for such vital and clear-headed reasons.

Nadezhda Mandelshtam recalls how she and her husband, the poet Osip Mandelshtam, were also sometimes drawn to think this way, fearing momentarily that the Revolution would pass them by if they 'failed to notice all the great things happening before our eyes'. Osip was arrested in 1934, after he had read out to his friends his seditious poem about Stalin ('the murderer and peasant-slayer'). As Nadezhda Mandelshtam observed, it was easier to believe in what was being done for the Communist utopia than to insist, as her husband had, on confronting reality: 'A man who knew that you cannot build the present out of the bricks of the future was bound to resign himself beforehand to his inevitable doom and the prospect of the firing squad.'[78]

To accept this vision of the future entailed adopting certain attitudes that smoothed the way to collusion with the regime. It meant the acceptance of the Party as the source of Truth. For many people this belief involved a constant struggle between the observed truth of existing reality and the higher Revolutionary Truth of the Party. They were forced to live in the margins between these two truths – to acknowledge the failures of the Soviet system while still believing in the promise of a better life to come – something they could only accomplish through a conscious act of political faith. Lev Kopelev, a young Communist who took part in some of the worst excesses against the 'kulaks' in 1932–3, recalls his efforts to subordinate his moral judgement (what he called 'subjective truth') to the higher moral goals ('objective truth') of the Party. Kopelev and his comrades were horrified by what they were doing to the peasantry, but they deferred to the Party: the prospect of retreating from this position, on the basis of what they had been brought up to dismiss as the 'bourgeois' ideals of 'conscience, honour [and] humanitarianism', filled them with dread. 'What we feared most,' recalls Kopelev, 'was to lose our heads, to fall into doubt or heresy and forfeit our unbounded faith.'[79]

Wolfgang Leonhard was similarly conscious of a dual reality. By the time he joined the Komsomol, he had 'long since realized that reality in the Soviet Union was completely different from the picture presented in *Pravda*'. His mother had been arrested in 1937; his friends and teachers had all been taken away; and he had been living in an orphanage. But, as he explains to his Western readers, who 'might find it strange' to read about his joy on being admitted to the Komsomol,

Somehow I dissociated these things, and even my personal impressions and experiences, from my fundamental political conviction. It was almost as if there were two separate levels – one of everyday events and experiences, which I found myself criticising; the other that of the great Party line which at this time, despite my hesitations, I still regarded as correct, from the standpoint of general principle.[80]

Even at the height of the Great Terror of 1937–8 there were many believers who managed to keep their faith. They explained away the mass arrests according to the abstract formula *'les rubiat – shchepki letiat'* ('When the forest is cut down the chips will fly', or 'You can't make an omelette without breaking eggs').

Believing in the 'march towards Communism' required an acceptance of its human costs. The Party told its followers that they were involved in a life-or-death struggle against 'capitalist elements' at home and abroad which would end in the final victory of the Communist utopia. Hitler's rise to power, in 1933, was a crucial turning-point in this struggle. It was taken as a vindication of Stalin's theory that the further the Soviet Union advanced towards Communism, the greater its enemies' resistance would be. The Party hardened its position, forcing sceptics to put aside their doubts and join the struggle against Fascism (or run the risk of being denounced as 'Fascist hirelings'). From 1933, the purging of the Party was intensified, with closer scrutiny of individual deeds to root out passive members and 'hidden enemies'. Whole sections of society were targeted as 'enemies' and 'alien elements', beginning with the remnants of the old nobility and the bourgeoisie in Leningrad, who were arrested and exiled in their thousands following the murder of the city's Party boss, Sergei Kirov, in December 1934. Any group that was deemed to be a 'relic of the capitalist past' (former 'kulaks', petty traders, gypsies, prostitutes, criminals, vagrants, beggars and so on) was likely to be purged as an obstacle to the building of a Communist society. Between 1932 and 1936, tens of thousands of these 'socially harmful elements' were rounded up by the police and expelled from the towns.[81] Most of them were sent to the Gulag.

4

In August 1933, a 'brigade' of 120 leading Soviet writers went on a boat tour of the White Sea Canal organized by Semyon Firin, the OGPU commander of the labour camps at the canal. The idea of the trip had its origins in a meeting that took place in Maksim Gorky's Moscow house in October 1932, at which a number of the country's leading writers discussed the tasks of literature with several Politburo members, including Stalin, and other Party functionaries. In one of the earliest statements of the Socialist Realist doctrine, Gorky called for a heroic literature to match the 'grand achievements' of the Five Year Plans, and Stalin, who compared the Soviet writers to 'engineers of the human soul', proposed a tour of the canal to inspire them. Everything was organized by OGPU. 'From the minute we became the guests of the Chekists, complete Communism began for us,' the writer Aleksandr Avdeyenko later commented ironically. 'We were given food and drink on demand. We paid nothing. Smoked sausage, cheeses, caviar, fruit, chocolate, wines and cognac – all was in plentiful supply. And this was a year of famine.'[82]

After staying at the luxury Astoriia Hotel in Leningrad, the writers went by train to the White Sea Canal, where they inspected dams and locks and visited the cultural centre to watch a theatrical performance put on by the prisoners. From the safety of their ship, they saw convicts working, but were not allowed to talk to them. To many of the writers it was obvious that they were being presented with a sanitized version of camp life. 'It was evident to me that they were showing us "Potemkin Villages",' recalled Tamara Ivanova in 1989. But if the writers had their doubts, few were brave enough to voice them at the time. During the trip the writers had the chance to question Firin, who acted as their guide. According to Avdeyenko, the only writer who asked about the use of forced labour was Dmitry Mirsky – a former prince (Prince Dmitry Sviatopolk-Mirsky) who had fought with the White Army in the Civil War, emigrated to Britain, joined the Communists and returned to the Soviet Union in 1932 because he believed that Stalin's Russia was 'going to play an enormous role in world history', and he wanted to be part of it. Mirsky's questioning made the other writers uncomfortable. He clearly had his suspicions about the reasons for the secrecy surrounding the construction of the canal. 'Here at every step there are hidden secrets. Under every dam. Under every lock,' Mirsky told Avdeyenko, seemingly referring to the corpses buried there. But even Mirsky did not let such doubts interfere with his participation in the publication of a book commissioned by OGPU to celebrate the completion of the canal. Edited by Firin and Gorky, *The White Sea Canal* was compiled at shock-work speed by thirty-six leading Soviet writers (including Mikhail Zoshchenko, Viktor Shklovsky, Aleksei Tolstoy and Valentin Kataev) together with the artist Aleksandr Rodchenko (who took the photographs). The book was presented 'as a token of the readiness of Soviet writers to serve the cause of Bolshevism' to the delegates of the Seventeenth Party Congress in January 1934. Though it was presented as a history of the canal's construction, the book's chief theme and propaganda message was the redemptive and liberating influence of physical labour. By taking part in the great collective work of building the canal, criminals and 'kulaks', it was claimed, 'began to feel useful to society'. Through penal labour, they were remade as socialists.[83]

The writers had different reasons for colluding in this legitimation of the Gulag. No doubt there were some who believed in the Stalinist ideal of *perekovka*, the remoulding of the human soul through penal labour. Zoshchenko, for one, wrote a story for *The White Sea Canal* about a petty thief called Rottenberg who, having lost his way in life, returns to the correct path through penal labour on the canal. As he explained in an article for *Literary Leningrad*, Zoshchenko believed the factual basis of his tale:

I was interested in people who had built their lives on idleness, deceit, theft and murder, and I gave all my attention to the theme of their re-education. In truth, I was quite sceptical at first, supposing that this famous reforging was simply the cynical expression of the prisoners' desire to receive freedom or bonuses. But I must say that I was mistaken on that score. I saw authentic reforging [on the trip to the White Sea Canal]. I saw real pride in the construction workers and noticed a real change in the psychology of many of these comrades (as they may now be called).[84]

Gorky was also a believer. He never visited the White Sea Canal. But this was no obstacle to his glowing praise of it in the book commissioned by OGPU (just as ignorance was no obstacle to foreign socialists, like Sidney and Beatrice Webb, who also praised the canal as 'a great engineering feat . . . a triumph in human regeneration' in 1935). Having spent the 1920s in the West, Gorky had returned to the Soviet Union on the first of several summer trips in 1928 and had settled there for good in 1931. The 'great Soviet writer' was showered with honours; he was given as his residence the famous Riabushinsky mansion in Moscow; two large dachas; private servants (who turned out to be OGPU spies); and supplies of special foods from the same police department that catered for Stalin. So perhaps it is not surprising that Gorky failed to see the immense human suffering that lay behind the 'grand achievements' of the Five Year Plan. In the summer of 1929, Gorky had visited the Solovetsky labour camp. The writer was so impressed by what he was shown by his OGPU guides that he wrote an article in which he claimed that many of the prisoners had been reformed by their labour in the camp and loved their work so much that they wanted to remain on the island after the completion of their sentences. 'The conclusion is obvious to me,' Gorky wrote: 'we need more camps like Solovetsky.'[85]

Other writers went on the trip from curiosity, as Mirsky no doubt did. Or because they were afraid of the consequences if, like the writer Mikhail Bulgakov, they refused to have anything to do with the project. Viktor Shklovsky, the literary theorist and novelist whose brother was imprisoned in a labour camp, did not join the writers' brigade, but he made a separate trip to the White Sea Canal and promoted the idea of *perekovka*, not just in the OGPU volume but in several other works.

He even wrote the screenplay for a propaganda film about the White Sea Canal. It seems unlikely that Shklovsky wrote out of conviction (during his trip to the White Sea Canal he responded to an OGPU officer's question about how he felt to be at the canal with the quip: 'Like a live silver fox in a fur store'). In the words of his daughter, it was just 'the price he had to pay for his brother's life'. Shklovsky's brother was released in 1933. But in 1937 he was rearrested and disappeared for ever in the Gulag.[86]

Careerist motives also played a role. They were certainly a factor for Avdeyenko, an unknown writer of proletarian origins when he joined the trip to the White Sea Canal, although only two years later, in 1935, his first novel was critically acclaimed in the Soviet press. 'The trip is how I got to the top and my life took off,' Avdeyenko later acknowledged. 'A shock worker called to literature! In one action I joined the ranks of writers worthy of high honour in the Soviet pantheon.' Avdeyenko became a regular contributor to *Perekovka* – the in-house OGPU (NKVD) journal of the labour camps at the White Sea Canal – where he wrote in praise of penal labour as a form of human reforging.[87]

Konstantin Simonov was another 'proletarian writer' to make his name through the White Sea Canal. In 1933, he was working as a mechanic – one of the hundreds of technicians under the command of Boris Babitsky – at the Mezhrabpomfilm studios. Simonov and the other mechanics would spend their lunch-breaks watching Pudovkin and Golovnia at work on the film set of *The Deserter* (an experience which, he claimed, awoke his interest in the arts). 'In those years,' recalls Simonov, 'I had no proper education, but I read a lot of books, history books in particular, and for the first time in my life I tried to write.' Inspired by the propaganda of the White Sea Canal, Simonov 'filled a notebook with bad poems' about the reforging of the penal labourers which somehow came to the attention of Goslitizdat (the State Publishing House) and OGPU. Extracts from one of these poems, 'The White Sea Canal', were published in a collection of poetry by young Soviet writers in 1933. On the back of this success, in April 1934 Simonov applied to Goslitizdat for permission to visit the canal and collect materials about the reforging of its convict labourers for a collection of poetry in praise of the labour camps. Goslitizdat approved the trip and paid for Simonov to spend a month at the Medvezhegorsk labour camp on the White Sea Canal, where he was employed as a journalist by *Perekovka*. He lived in the barracks with a team of prisoners, who did not take the nineteen-year-old poet very seriously ('they laughed at me when I told them I was writing a poem about the White Sea Canal'). For this reason, it seemed to Simonov, the prisoners 'were relatively natural with me'.[88]

By the early summer of 1934, the construction of the White Sea Canal had been largely completed. The labourers observed by Simonov were engaged in building roads and installations – relatively easy tasks compared with the heavy manual digging of the main canal in 1931–3, when tens of thousands died. As the project came to an end, the camp administration rewarded labourers with bonuses, honours and medals. It also granted early release orders to some of the petty criminals who made up the workforce on the part of the canal visited by Simonov. The main aim of these rewards was to fulfil the myth of *perekovka*. They gave the prisoners an incentive to work hard and reform themselves (or give the impression that they were reformed) in order to gain their freedom or material advantages. Simonov was taken in. He was young and innocent. As he recalled in his memoirs, he returned from the White Sea Canal 'ready to write new poetry about the reforging of people through labour':

Even though I had not been there long, I was convinced that I had seen with my own eyes how that reforging was actually taking place – as I believed it should – for what else but labour can redeem a person's sins in a society such as ours?

Simonov was particularly impressed by a story he had been told about an engineer, a close associate of the Provisional Government ('practically the last commandant of the Winter Palace'),

who was sentenced to eight if not ten years under Article 58 and worked so well in his capacity as an engineer on the White Sea Canal that he was released after just three years; he then worked voluntarily as the chief engineer on a construction site connected to the Moscow–Volga Canal. That kind of story was reinforced by my own impressions from my journey.*

*It is possible that Simonov was thinking here of Pyotr Palchinsky (1875–1929), the mining engineer whom Kerensky placed in command of the Winter Palace in October 1917. Imprisoned by the Bolsheviks, Palchinsky was released and subsequently allowed to resume his work at the Russian Technical Institute during the 1920s. He was rearrested in 1928 and executed the next year. There were many camp legends about famous prisoners like Palchinsky, and it seems that Simonov was taken in by one of them.

In reality, the willingness of certain specialists to go on working in the Gulag system after their release was seldom the result of reforging. But Simonov believed that what he saw at the White Sea Canal matched the stories he had heard or had read in the Soviet press. 'In my perception,' Simonov recalled in his memoirs, 'the White Sea Canal was not just about the construction of a canal, but a humanitarian school for the reconstruction of bad people into good, of common criminals into builders of the Five Year Plan.'[89]

For Simonov – a nobleman involved in the reconstruction of his own identity as a 'proletarian writer' – the idea of *perekovka* had a special resonance. In his memoirs Simonov recounts how he perceived the reforging of the 'kulaks' and 'bourgeois saboteurs' as 'highly promising for society', and as an inspiration for himself, because it showed 'the possibility of burying the past and moving on to a new path'. The reforging of the former oppositionists at the Seventeenth Party Congress (the 'congress of victors') in 1934 was another inspiration to the young writer, as he strove to make a career for himself in an artistic sphere that was so tightly supervised by the Party. At that congress several Party leaders who had been opposed to Stalin's extreme policies (Bukharin, Kamenev, Zinoviev, Rykov, Tomsky, Piatakov and others) were allowed to speak. They recanted their old positions and heaped praise on Stalin in the name of Party unity, and they were received in a manner that suggested that the Party leadership had rehabilitated them. Simonov took comfort from their example. As he saw it, the reception of the repentant oppositionists proved that the Party was a place where people like himself might receive forgiveness for their past. Simonov understood that his own reforging would depend on the reconstruction of his political personality. Like the former oppositionists, he had to show that he was a worthy Communist by renouncing his own past. His writings on the White Sea Canal were the means to that end. After he returned from the canal Simonov applied for a second time to join the Komsomol. On the previous occasion, following the arrest of his stepfather in 1931, he had been advised to withdraw his application. But this time he was invited to join. This acceptance was a 'huge relief' for Simonov. In his memoirs he remembers 1934 as the high-point of his hopes in the future:

I cannot speak for other people of my age, but for me 1934 was the year of brightest hope in all my youth. There was a sense that the country had come through a difficult period and that, although problems still remained, life was becoming easier, in both spiritual and material terms. I was happy to be taking part in the building of this new life ... The correctness of Stalin, who was leading the industrialization of the country and achieving great success, seemed indisputable to me. As I saw it, he was right to argue with his opponents and to show that they were wrong.[90]

In the summer of 1934, shortly after his return, Simonov wrote a poem, 'Horizon', about the reforging of a criminal in the labour camps. The poem was heavily edited – and in places censored – by the Cultural-Educational Department of OGPU, which concluded that the poem was very badly written ('pretentious', 'clumsy', 'cacophonous', 'mechanical' and 'sentimentalized') but worthy of publication for its propaganda value nonetheless.[91] 'Horizon' was reworked by Simonov and eventually published as 'Pavel Chyorny' in 1938. In later years Simonov would look back at this poem 'with feelings of horror'. He insisted on excluding it from all collections of his published works.[92] But the poem was the making of Simonov's career. It demonstrated his ability to turn out poetry that could be used by the Stalinist regime. Simonov was encouraged to apply to the Gorky Literary Institute. He was even given a recommendation by his political patrons in Goslitizdat and the Cultural-Educational Department of OGPU.[93]

Located in the former Herzen palace on the Tver Boulevard, the Literary Institute was opened in 1933 to encourage writers from the working class (until 1936 it was called the Workers' Evening Literary University). Classes took place in the evening, which allowed Simonov to continue with his job at Mezhrabpomfilm and supplement his 200-rouble grant. Most of the students at the Literary Institute were not from the working class at all. They had been born to noble or bourgeois families and, like Simonov, had qualified for entry to the institute by going through a factory school or by working in a factory. Half the students were members of the Komsomol or the Party. The institute was a cosmopolitan place, with writers from twenty-seven different nationalities.[94] Among the many Jewish students were two young women who would become Simonov's first wives: Natalia Tipot, the daughter of a well-known variety theatre-man, who married Simonov in 1935; and Zhenia Laskina, the youngest daughter of the ruined NEPman Samuil Laskin, who joined the institute in 1936 and married Simonov in 1939.

By his own admission Simonov had no special affinity for literature. It was a career he pursued because of his spoilt biography. 'If it were not for my noble origins,' he had told Natalia, 'I would not have been interested in literature at all, only in politics and history.'[95] Nor was Simonov considered to be among the most talented students at the Literary Institute (in 1936 he was ranked seventh in a list of excellence headed by the poet Margarita Aliger). But he was known as a conscientious student who was well organized (he carefully planned out the time he spent on working, reading, even socializing) and always punctual in completing his tasks. His fellow students nicknamed Simonov the 'iron bottom' because he worked so hard. 'He just sat down and wrote and wrote,' recalls the poet Yevgeny Dolmatovsky (who came in second on the list of excellence). Aliger remembers Simonov as someone who stood out as a leader from the start. Usually dressed in a leather jacket, like the Bolsheviks in the Civil War, or in a jacket, shirt and tie, Simonov distanced himself from the bohemian culture of the other students at the institute, spending his spare time in Komsomol activities or writing book reviews rather than in playing billiards. Not surprisingly, he was held in

Simonov in 1936

high regard by the administration of the institute, which saw him as a Party loyalist and entrusted him with many tasks (in 1937 he would play a leading role in the denunciation of 'anti-Soviet elements' within the institute). Simonov was serious and censorious, more like a literary bureaucrat than a young poet. 'Not having written my own book,' he recalled in 1945,

I wrote many critical reviews of books written by others. I was very strict and impatient, which just goes to show that the most crudely negative reviews of a book are always written by reviewers who have not succeeded or could not succeed in writing such a book themselves.[96]

As a poet at the institute, Simonov was learning how to write for his political superiors. The theme of *perekovka*, which became a commonplace of the Socialist Realist tradition in the 1930s, reappeared in several of his early poems, which returned to the subject of the White Sea Canal. But increasingly his poetry was shaped by the hopes of the Five Year Plans and by the heroic theme of struggle epitomized by the Spanish Civil War. Here Simonov was deeply influenced by his poetry teacher, Vladimir Lugovskoi (1901–57), a charismatic figure to the young poets at the institute, whose room was filled with swords and guns, memorabilia from his fighting days in the Russian Civil War and the last campaign against the Basmachi Muslim rebels in Central Asia in 1931. Simonov explored the theme of masculinity and heroic courage in poems like 'The General', which was inspired by the death of the Hungarian Communist Mate Zalka (also known as General Lukach) in the Spanish Civil War. For Simonov, who took his basic values from the military ethos of his stepfather, the bravery and self-sacrifice of fighters such as Zalka were not just 'wonderful human qualities' but 'virtues of the first necessity' in a world engulfed by the struggle between socialism and Fascism. As Simonov explained to a foreign journalist in 1960, 'we young Communists of the 1930s hated with a passion anyone who showed signs of complacency by imagining that our future victory would be easy and bloodless'. This was a generation immersed in the notion of struggle – a generation that lived in readiness for war. Recalling his student years, Simonov was speaking for a whole epoch when he wrote in 1973:

The Literary Institute opened the same year the Nazis came to power. All our years of study were overshadowed by the sense of an impending war with Fascism. These were years when it was impossible to think of literature and one's path in it without thinking how, sooner or later, we too would be forced to play a part – whether with a pen or a rifle in our hands was not yet clear – in this looming struggle with Fascism.

On 1 January 1936, Simonov had his first poem published in *Izvestiia*, 'New Year's Toast'. It was an early sign of the favour with which the young poet – then just twenty years of age – would come to be regarded by the Party leadership. In the poem, Simonov conjured up the idea of a final struggle between light and dark:

> Friends, today we stand on high alert!
> Wolves encircle our Republic!
> So we raises our glasses,
> And drink in silence
> To those who stand by the machine-gun,
> To those whose only friend is the rifle,
> To everyone who knows the verb 'to fight',
> A sad verb that we need to know.
> To those who can leave a silent room
> And walk into the unknown fire . . .[97]

At the same time as Simonov was making his career, his three Obolensky aunts were languishing in exile in Orenburg, a city on the eastern Volga steppes 1,500 kilometres south-east of Moscow, having been expelled from Leningrad in the repressions that followed the murder of Kirov. Simonov was fond of his three aunts. He had written to them regularly since he was a child. Liudmila, the eldest of his mother's three sisters, had married an artillery captain from a family of Russified Germans, Maximilian Tideman. His death in the First World War had left Liudmila and her three children stranded in Riazan, where Maximilian's regiment had been based. After returning to Petrograd in 1922, Liudmila worked as a teacher in a school for handicapped children. By the time of her arrest, in 1935, her three children had grown up. Two went with her to Orenburg, but her eldest son remained in Leningrad, where he was highly valued as a manager at the Red Triangle Factory, which helped to protect him from arrest. Daria, or 'Dolly', the middle sister, was severely handicapped, the left side of her body deformed and paralysed, which made it hard for her to move. Personal misfortune had turned her into a cantankerous old maid. Dogmatically religious, she made no secret of her hatred of the Soviet regime and clung to the traditions of the aristocracy. In 1927, Dolly came to visit Aleksandra in Riazan. There were constant arguments about religion which, claims Simonov, led him to become an atheist (although in his later letters to his aunts Simonov continued to express religious sentiments). Simonov visited Dolly in Leningrad on several occasions, but he thought of it as a duty call. He much preferred Sonia, his third and youngest aunt, with whom he often stayed in Leningrad. Sonia was a plump woman with a 'round face and a kind smile' which reflected, as Simonov recalls, 'her simple good nature and openness'. Unlike Dolly, Sonia adapted to the Soviet system, although her manners, values and beliefs retained traces of the nineteenth-century culture of the aristocracy. Trained as a teacher, she worked as a librarian and lived alone in a large room in a communal apartment. But she was not bitter or unhappy with her lot. On the contrary, Simonov recalls her as the liveliest and most fun of all his aunts. Not having children of her own, she loved to have her nephews and her nieces stay with her. She had a soft spot for Konstantin, her youngest nephew, whose interest in books she helped to stimulate. 'My dear, darling Kiriushonchik,' she wrote to Simonov, 'I hope that you grow up to become useful and a comfort to us all, who love you so dearly. I hope that you will always have enough to eat, as we had in olden times.'[98]

The last time Simonov saw Sonia was in the autumn of 1933, when he stayed with her in Leningrad. He wrote his first poems in her room. In February 1935, Sonia was exiled with Liudmila and Dolly to Orenburg. Simonov recalls his mother's reaction when she found out, in Moscow, that her 'three sisters had been sent into exile, along with many other people she had known since her childhood in St Petersburg'.

She sat there in tears with the letters [she had just received from Orenburg], and suddenly she said: 'If I had returned then with Liulia [Liudmila] from Riazan to Petrograd, I would be together with them now, of course.' I remember being shocked by the way she said these words. She spoke with some sort of guilt that she was not with them, that she had somehow managed to escape the ordeal that afflicted her sisters. Then she asked my stepfather: 'Maybe, we will be exiled from here?' When she said 'we' she was not talking about the family; she meant herself, her origins, the Obolensky clan.[99]

Simonov does not explain why he was so shocked. Perhaps he was surprised by his mother's expression of guilt. But there was something else besides. Simonov had been brought up to think of himself as a 'Soviet person'. Even the arrest of his stepfather had failed to shake him from this view. On the contrary, it had reinforced his striving to fashion for himself a proletarian identity. All his efforts to recast himself, first as an engineer and then as a 'proletarian writer', had strengthened his identification with the Soviet system. But his mother's response to the arrest of his aunts – which was, it seems, the first time that he had heard her identify herself as a 'social alien' in Soviet terms – forced him to confront reality.

Simonov's mother and stepfather sent monthly packages of food and clothes to Orenburg, and he himself put aside a part of his own earnings to help with these parcels. In 1936, Aleksandra visited her three sisters. As Simonov recalls, she was afraid that she might not return (many people feared that they would be arrested if they visited their exiled relatives). Simonov's stepfather, always practical, thought it would be better if she did not go, because if she was arrested it would be even harder to help her three sisters. But Aleksandra insisted on going, because, as she said, 'if she did not, she would cease to be herself'. On her return from Orenburg, Aleksandra was 'exhausted, sad, worn out from the long journey and the terrible conditions there', recalls Simonov, 'but she was not without hope for the future ... because she thought that nothing worse could happen to them now'.[100]

But worse was to come. In 1937, Sonia and Dolly were arrested and imprisoned in Orenburg. Sonia was shot, and Dolly later died in a labour camp. Only Liudmila survived. Looking back on these events in the last year of his life, Simonov recalled his reaction to the death of his favourite aunt:

When I found out that she had been imprisoned, and then we ceased to hear from her, and then they told us that she had died – although not where or how – I remember experiencing this strong and painful feeling of injustice that was related entirely to her [Sonia], or most of all to her. The feeling would not leave my soul – I am not afraid to say this – and it stayed forever in my memory as the main injustice committed by the state, by Soviet power, against myself, personally. The feeling is particularly bitter because I know that, had Sonia been alive, she would have been the first person I would have helped when I was in a position to do so.

Simonov's regret was based on the awareness he gained in later years – the awareness that he had colluded in the system of repression that destroyed his aunts. Yet as he admits in his memoirs, at the time of their arrest his reaction had been different. He felt sorry for his aunts, but he found a way to rationalize and perhaps even justify their fates:

I cannot remember what I thought about it then [in 1937], how I judged and explained to myself what had happened ... I know that I could not have been unaffected, if only because I loved one of my aunts [Sonia] very much ... But perhaps I thought: 'You can't make an omelette without breaking eggs.' This acceptance seems much more cynical today than it felt then, when the Revolution, the breaking up of the old society, was still not so distant in people's memories, and when it was rare to have a conversation without recourse to that phrase.[101]

If Simonov's encounter with the White Sea Canal brought him closer to the regime, for others it had the opposite effect. In 1929, Ilia Slavin, the former Zionist and a leading jurist at the Institute of Soviet Law in Moscow, was transferred to Leningrad to bolster the legal department of the Communist Academy. During the purges of that year the Law Department of Leningrad University had been closed down and its 'bourgeois' academics expelled. The legal department of the Communist Academy, which replaced it, was deemed in need of trusted Bolsheviks like Slavin to strengthen its resolve against the 'bourgeois Rightists' of the Soviet legal world whose presence was still felt in Leningrad.[102] Slavin had become a major figure in the field of Soviet law. An adviser to the Commissariat of Justice, he was also a member of the commission that had written the Soviet Criminal Code of 1926, the first major overhaul of criminal law since 1917. In Leningrad the Slavins had two rooms in a large apartment which they shared with another family (in Moscow they had lived in a communal apartment shared by fifteen families). Eventually, they moved to a three-room flat in the House of the Leningrad Soviet, where many government workers, scientists and artists lived. 'We were relatively privileged,' recalls Ilia's daughter Ida Slavina.

My brother and his wife had their own room, my parents had another, where my father also worked, and I slept in the dining room. When there were guests I went to sleep in my parents' room and then was moved to the divan in the dining room when my parents went to bed ... But there was no hint of luxury – it was a Spartan, almost puritanical, way of life, entirely dedicated to the socialist ideals of my father . . . We shared our extra rations – of which father was ashamed – with our poorer friends and relatives . . . Books were our only luxury.[103]

Slavin served his political patrons with a violent attack on the 'bourgeois tendencies' of a number of leading Soviet jurists in a book commissioned by the Communist Academy as part of the regime's purge of the legal academic establishment in 1931. In this short but poisonous text, *Sabotage on the Front of Soviet Criminal Law*, Slavin compared the writings of several leading academic laywers in the 1920s with their writings before 1917 in order to expose what he claimed were their real but concealed 'bourgeois' views. Writing from political conviction, in the belief that the old legal thinking needed to be rooted out, Slavin denounced these jurists for attempting to subvert the basic ideological tenets of the Soviet legal system. He singled out for criticism the former Law Department at Leningrad University, which, he maintained, had been training 'yesterday's priests and White Guardists' to pose as 'the Marxists of today and the Communists of tomorrow'. Several of the jurists Slavin attacked were subsequently removed from their posts in the universities of Leningrad and Moscow, and forced to look for work in the provinces.[104]

In the Slavin family archive there is a photograph of Ilia Slavin with his fellow teachers and some students at the Communist Academy in 1931. On the back it is inscribed: 'To Comrade Slavin! In fond memory of you as a firm Communist of the Bolshevik guard, as our teacher, as a steadfast fighter on the ideological front, an iron broom purging vermin from the academic heights.' For Ida Slavina it is hard to reconcile this description with her memory of her father as a soft and tender man. Perhaps Slavin was sucked into the system of repression because he was too weak to resist the demands of the Party. Maybe he felt vulnerable because of his previous involvement in the Zionist movement and wrote the book to prove his worthiness as a member of the 'Bolshevik guard'. Or perhaps, as Ida thinks, he 'lost his way' because he was misled by his beliefs.

Slavin believed in *perekovka*. Before 1917, he had carried out experiments in reforging by setting up a workshop and a cultural centre for the prisoners of a local jail in Mogilyov, where he worked as a legal assistant and was acquainted with the prison governor. The idea of reforging surfaced in many of his legal writings in the 1920s and 1930s,

Teachers and students of the Law Department of the Communist Academy in Leningrad, 1931 (the white-haired Slavin is seated on the far left of the front, seated row)

particularly in his articles on the idea of Comrade Courts (*tovarishcheskie sudy*), tribunals at the workplace, in which he argued for the use of penal labour as a form of community service to reform the prisoner.[105]

In 1933, Slavin was given a new task by the leadership of the Communist Academy – to write a book provisionally entitled 'The Reforging of Penal Labourers as Exemplified by the White Sea Canal'.[106] In essence, he was asked to come up with a legal and philosophical justification for the Gulag labour camps. Perhaps Slavin's previous writings on reforging played a role in earning him this dreadful commission. But the main reason why he had been chosen was because he had already shown, through *Sabotage on the Front of Soviet Criminal Law*, that he was prepared to construct legal arguments for the regime's system of repression.

To believe in *perekovka* was one thing, to see it in action another. In 1932–3, Slavin made several trips to the White Sea Canal and to other sites of penal labour, including the Moscow–Volga Canal and the Kolyma labour camps in north-east Siberia. What he saw there destroyed his belief in the Soviet ideal of reforging. Ida recalls how her father returned from these trips 'exhausted and depressed' – how 'he would not talk to anyone for several days, as if he was living in a state of shock'. Slavin was particularly shaken by his visit to a children's labour colony, where he was alarmed by the brutal discipline that was used by the guards to 'reforge the children in the Soviet spirit'. Slavin could not bring himself to write the book on the White Sea Canal. For several years he postponed its completion. A number of draft chapters were torn up (one of them entitled 'Fascist Distortions in the Policy of Reforging'), as he came to realize that there was no *perekovka* in the camps.

Slavin knew he was trapped. After the murder of Kirov, when half the staff was purged from the Communist Academy, Slavin feared that he would be arrested too. Ida recalls her parents locking themselves in their room: 'They sat up talking, whispering, all night.' The Party archives confirm that in December 1934 Slavin's name was added to a list of political suspects ('to be arrested at a future date') who had left other parties to join the Bolsheviks.[107]

Under growing pressure from the leaders of the Communist Academy, Slavin submitted some draft chapters of the book on the White Sea Canal. In these chapters Slavin offered a number of criticisms of the daily workings of the Gulag system, but made no reference to the policy of reforging, of which he had seen no evidence. The chapter he had once called 'Fascist Distortions' now appeared as 'Distortions in the Policy of Reforging'. It was a courageous act, for which Slavin was sharply criticized by the editorial commission of the Communist Academy in May 1935. That event was a moral turning-point. Sensing that he could no longer hold to his Bolshevik beliefs, he renewed his old contacts with the Zionists – a desperate attempt, in Ida's words, 'to put the clock back and make up for his political mistakes'. But Slavin must have known that it was too late. He was in a hopeless situation. Completing the book on *perekovka* might have saved him, but he could not do this morally, so he kept putting it off, surely aware that the longer he delayed the closer he was moving to his own arrest. 'I am finished,' Slavin told a meeting of his Party comrades at the Communist Academy in March 1937, 'I am a political bankrupt.'[108]

5

In the middle of the 1930s, the Gulag population swelled to huge proportions, as the victims of collectivization and the famine were rounded up and sent to labour camps, now considered an integral component of the Soviet industrial economy. Between 1932 and 1936, the population of the labour camps, labour colonies and 'special settlements' reached 2.4 million people (the prison population would add another half a million).[109] This slave labour force played an especially vital role in the timber, construction and mining industries in the remote regions of the Arctic North, where free labour would not go. Consequently, even inside the Gulag it was possible for people to advance their careers. Opportunities were available, not only to prison guards and administrators, whose service in the Gulag often brought promotion in the NKVD, but also to a select number of prisoners, provided they had skills required by the Gulag system and the commitment – or willingness to adapt – to the Party line.

Pavel Vittenburg, the geologist who had played such a leading role in the Soviet exploration of mining areas in the Arctic zone, was arrested in April 1930. He was one of several hundred scientists expelled in a purge of the Academy of Sciences. Imprisoned in Leningrad, he was gradually broken down by interrogations and by threats against his family, until he finally confessed to belonging to a monarchist organization that had helped to organize the Iakutsk rebellion in 1927 (when Vittenburg had been involved in the exploration of the Kolyma goldfields in north-east Siberia). The breaking point had come when his interrogator had got up in his presence and made a call to order the arrest of Pavel's wife, Zina (Zinaida). While Pavel was in jail, Zina lived in constant expectation of arrest. The family was forced to move into one room of their spacious country house in Olgino, while an OGPU informer occupied the other rooms and organized the confiscation of their property. Pavel's daughter Yevgeniia recalls accompanying her mother on weekly trips to Leningrad to enquire about Pavel at the OGPU offices on Gorokhovaia Street:

She would leave me, an eight-year-old girl, by the fountains (which were not working then) in the Admiralty gardens, telling me that I should wait for her return. If she did not come, it would mean that she had been arrested, and I was to go to an address she had written on a piece of paper, which I kept in my pocket. Tatiana Lvovna lived there, and she would take me in.

In February 1931, Pavel was sentenced to be shot. At the last moment he was given a reprieve and sentenced to ten years in a labour camp instead. His house at Olgino was confiscated (it became the dacha of an OGPU official). Pavel was sent to the Mai-Guba logging camp to fell timber for the White Sea Canal and then transferred as a sewage engineer to the labour camp near Kem, on the northern sector of the canal where it ran into the sea. Zina meanwhile moved with two of her daughters, Yevgeniia and Valentina, into a single room in a communal apartment in Leningrad (her eldest daughter Veronika had moved to Dagestan). There were sixteen people living in the communal apartment, including its original owners, an elderly couple who occupied the front room and their former servant, a woman full of 'class hatred', who lived behind a curtain in the corridor. During the summer Zina sent her two daughters to stay with relatives in Kiev, while she worked as a volunteer doctor in the labour camp at Kem so as to be close to her husband.[110]

Shortly after Zina's return to Leningrad, in August 1931, Pavel was sent as a geologist to the island of Vaigach as part of a special OGPU expedition to explore the possibility of mining its precious minerals.

Zina and Pavel Vittenburg at the
Kem labour camp (White Sea Canal), 1931

Pavel was lucky. He was saved by his expertise as a geologist. Although still a prisoner, he was allowed to work in his own field and demonstrated his talents in the service of the Gulag. The Vaigach expedition was led by Fyodor Eikhmans, the OGPU head of the whole Gulag, who left his post in Moscow to set up the first camp on the remote Arctic island in the Kara Sea in June 1930. Nearly half of the 1,500 prisoners were geologists, topographers and engineers, who surveyed the island's rich deposits of zinc and lead and searched in vain for gold and platinum, Eikhmans's real reasons for getting involved in the project. The Nenets people (Samoyeds), who lived on the island and provided transport for the expedition, told of ancient legends about the 'golden woman', a totem doll of solid gold. Conditions in the camp were very difficult, especially in the first months before the barracks had been built, when everybody had to live in tents. The zinc and lead mines were all dug by hand, discipline was harsh – people were shot for the slightest infraction – and many died from the extreme cold, which regularly reached temperatures of −40°C during the winter.[111]

By the time Vittenburg arrived the hunt for gold had become desperate, which probably explains why he was called up to reinforce the number of geologists already there. Pavel was quickly made the chief geologist. He completed the survey of Vaigach, which led to the opening of the Gulag mining complex, the first mines within the Arctic Circle, in 1934. He published several articles about the expedition in OGPU periodicals and even kept a scrapbook on the island's natural history. For a prisoner, Pavel enjoyed a privileged existence. He received special rations, lived in a separate house for specialists and even had his own office. In March 1932, he was allowed a visit by his family, who returned in the summer to accompany him on a major expedition around Vaigach. Leaving Valentina with a friend in Leningrad, Zina came with Yevgeniia to live with Pavel in the summer of 1933, when the new commander of the camp, Aleksei Ditsklan, who replaced Eikhmans in October 1932, allowed specialists to be joined by their families. Her letters home describe the conditions:

Vaigach Is.

26 Aug. 1933

My dear little daughters, Veronichka and Liusenka [Valentina]. Late in the evening on the 24th we finally arrived at Papa's. It took 6 days, 3 of them in cold force-five winds, to get here. Gulenka [Yevgeniia] was very brave considering that most of the passengers around us were sea-sick all the time . . . Papochka met us on the ship, loaded everything onto his motorboat, and by 11 o'clock we were home. Papochka looks very well, he has put on weight, his face is an excellent colour, without a single wrinkle. His mood is good, he is full of energy and, as always, he is happy in his work . . . We are living very well in a house for specialists, remarkably in fact, if you stop to think that this is the 70th parallel. We have two delightful rooms, each with three windows, so they are very light, even though they face towards the north-east and north-west. There is an enormous stove with an oven, so I shall have to improve my housekeeping skills, which I have completely lost. I shall send you a photograph of Papa with the next ship, and you will see for yourselves how good it is here and how much weight Papa has put on . . . Yesterday evening we were at a reception to bid farewell to those [prisoners] returning to the mainland, and to welcome the new arrivals. We liked the speeches very much, and the Heroes of Labour were very well received. The Vaigach expedition, it appears, came in first in the All-Union Socialist Competition. There is a wonderful reforging (*perekovka*) of people happening here: all the prisoners return to the mainland as qualified, literate and conscious workers. If only we could reforge more like that . . . The evening ended with a 'living newspaper' [a form of agitprop] and an excellent concert. That's all my news from the first one and a half days . . .[112]

Gradually, within the confines of the labour camp, the Vittenburgs returned to the routines of family life. Zina worked as a doctor in the camp clinic. Yevgeniia attended the school for children of the specialists and administrators. 'Our life revolved around the work of Mama and Papa,' recalls Yevgeniia.

Every morning, in whatever temperature, Papa filled a pan with cold water and washed himself in our room, ate some breakfast and then went to work in the geological section. When he returned we would eat our dinner, and then he would sit down at his desk. Mama was always tired from her work. In the evening she had barely strength to read. I did all the housework after school, because I had the most time. I fetched our dinners (two for voluntary workers and one for a prisoner) from the canteen. The cooks were all Chinese. They were excellent, they taught me how to bake. In general the food seemed royal to us compared with what we had in Leningrad.[113]

Pavel Vittenburg in his office, Vaigach labour camp, 1934

What lies behind this rosy view of the Gulag? According to Yevgeniia, Zina's optimism, even her belief in *perekovka*, was genuinely held, not just written in her letters for the benefit of the censors.[114] No doubt the happiness of being reunited as a family must have played a part. But equally important were the relatively privileged conditions of specialists like the Vittenburgs which sheltered them from the worst aspects of life inside the camp. Possibly, too, they were so wrapped up in their work that they willingly accepted any view that allowed them to continue with it and sleep easily at night.

In 1934, there was a revolt on the island of Vaigach. A gang of prisoners working on the far side of the island rebelled and killed their guards. There was nowhere for the rebels to escape, and eventually they were shot or captured and brought back to the camp. As one of the camp doctors, Zina had to inspect their wounds and decide which prisoners were fit to return to work. She saw evidence of terrible beatings, but nothing shook her faith in *perekovka*, nor her readiness, as she had agreed in her contract of employment, to enforce the camp's regime of labour discipline by reducing the time spent by prisoners on sick leave. For her work in the aftermath of the uprising, Zina was rewarded with the honourable title of 'shock worker' (*udarnitsa*) and listed in the 'Red Book' of the camp. She helped to teach the prisoners to read and to learn a craft in the belief that this would help reforge their personality and rehabilitate them to society. She even joined the

Party school and wrote to tell her daughters that she loved her studies there.[115]

Pavel was equally prepared to go along with the official view of the Gulag, according to Yevgeniia. In her view, he 'lived entirely for his science' and 'took little interest in politics'. He was 'grateful to the Soviet regime for giving him the opportunity to continue working in his field, and grateful too that his family had been allowed to join him at Vaigach'. If he believed the propaganda about *perekovka*, it was because, according to his daughter, 'he was sincere, naive perhaps, and romantic by nature'. Much of this is perhaps true. But it is the viewpoint of a loving daughter who cherishes the memory of her father. Seen from a different perspective, Pavel's actions could be described as a profound moral compromise. His work was clearly flourishing in the environment of the labour camp, where everything he needed was provided for. 'How pleasant to be a commander at Vaigach,' Pavel wrote in his diary. 'There is a semi-military discipline and complete obedience among the workers here.' In July 1935, Pavel was given early release, six years before the end of his sentence, in recognition of his valuable work. But he wanted to complete his geological research on Vaigach, so he signed a contract with the administration to continue working voluntarily. This, it seems, was a crucial turning-point, the moment when he ceased to be a prisoner, working for the Gulag by compulsion, and became a collaborator in the Gulag system to advance his own research.

After finishing his work on Vaigach, Pavel went to the Dmitrov labour camp, where he was employed as a geologist in the construction of the Moscow–Volga Canal. Meanwhile, Zina and Yevgeniia, having returned to Leningrad, found that 'life became more comfortable'. They went back to the communal apartment where they had lived before – and Valentina and Veronika joined then. They soon received an extra room, after the old owners of the apartment were arrested in the Leningrad terror following the murder of Kirov. Because they were not allowed to recover their old furniture from Olgino, which was still used as a dacha by the NKVD, the Vittenburgs were invited to the NKVD warehouse and allowed to help themselves to furniture confiscated from the victims of the Leningrad arrests. Valentina and Veronika picked out a pair of antique armchairs, a divan, a mirror, a bookcase and a grand piano.[116]

Pavel returned to Leningrad in 1936. For the next two years, he worked for the Gulag administration of the Arctic Ocean, leading several expeditions to Severnaia Zemlia. 'How to get more living space so that we can live together comfortably – as one united close-knit family – that is the task I cannot seem to solve,' Pavel wrote to Yevgeniia in 1936. Although he had managed to secure a privileged position through his work in the Gulag, he still felt insecure politically, and he worried about his family.

It is hard to accept that I am so powerless to arrange a comfortable life for all of you, as you deserve after all your suffering with me. The one thing I could do is build a little house, but Mama will not hear of it. Powerful people, who might help me, have turned their backs on me. When will I regain even a tenth of the influence I had before 1930?

Pavel made a conscious effort to Sovietize himself. He took lessons in the Party's history, and embraced the Truth that it taught him. By the end of 1936, he was ready to accept its teachings on the 'Trotskyists' and other 'enemies' of the Soviet regime. 'What a shame that I never knew anything about this,' Pavel wrote in his diary. 'If only I had known how reading history broadens the horizon and enables one to reach a proper understanding of the Party's general line. Maybe my life would not have been forced on to the stony path of exile and imprisonment. For what was my life destroyed? That bastard Trotsky is to blame for thousands of lost lives!'[117]

Pavel's story reminds us that the Gulag was far more than a prison camp. As one of the driving forces of the Soviet industrial economy, it employed a vast army of specialists and technicians – engineers, geologists, architects, research scientists, even aircraft designers – and gave them unique opportunities to develop their careers.

Pavel Drozdov was born in 1906 to a peasant family in Chernigov. His father was actively involved in the Marxist movement before 1917. After both his parents were killed in the Civil War, Pavel went to Moscow, joined the Economics Faculty of Moscow University and then trained as an electrician. (He later worked for Moscow Energy, the power station responsible for the electrification of much of the capital.) In 1925, Pavel was arrested for his participation in a student organization at Moscow University. He was exiled for three years to the Krasnovishersk region, where he worked in a logging camp attached to Vishlag, then still in its early days. On his release, in 1927, a year before the end of his sentence, Pavel chose to remain at the camp, where he was employed as an accountant. He married Aleksandra, a young peasant girl from a village near the camp, and had two children, who lived with him in the hostel for administrators in the camp complex. In 1929, when Eduard Berzin, the 'enlightened' Gulag chief, arrived at Vishlag, Pavel's fortunes changed dramatically. Berzin championed the reforging of prisoners, and in Drozdov he believed that he had found a living example of his ideal. Berzin recognized the talents of Pavel, in particular his photographic memory (Berzin liked to say that Pavel had a 'built-in calculator in his head'). He rapidly promoted Pavel in the camp administration, and often drew attention to the former prisoner as an example of reforging in his talks to senior officials at Vishlag. In 1929, Pavel was appointed chief accountant of the logging camp and, in 1930, chief accountant of the entire Vishlag complex. As one of Berzin's close associates, Pavel followed Berzin when he left Vishlag to organize the Dalstroi network of labour camps in north-east Siberia. In Magadan, the capital of this Gulag empire, Pavel became the chief accountant in the Planning Section of the Dalstroi Trust and an inspector of the Dalstroi labour camps. Promoted to the rank of lieutenant-general in the NKVD, Pavel was rewarded with a four-room flat, which was big enough to house not just his family, but the family of his sister too. He was also given an apartment in Moscow, where Aleksandra and the children would spend the winter months. The family lived a privileged existence, with access to the special shops and sanatoria exclusively reserved for the Stalinist elite, and manufactured gifts from the Dalstroi factories on the Soviet holidays.[118] Not bad for a man who, only a few years before, had been a common prisoner in the Gulag.

Mikhail Stroikov was born in 1901 to a family of Old Believers near Ivanovo, 300 kilometres north-east of Moscow. In 1925, he enrolled as a student at the Moscow Architectural Institute and married Elena, a young artist at a *rabfak* school (which prepared students from working-class backgrounds to study at an institute). Their daughter Julia was born in 1927. Just before her birth, Mikhail was arrested and exiled to Siberia: he had belonged to a student group opposed to the agrarian policies of the Bolsheviks. Elena was expelled from the *rabfak* school and went to work in a textile factory. In 1930, Mikhail returned to Moscow and rejoined the Architectural Institute, but two years later he was rearrested and imprisoned for two years in the Butyrki jail. Mikhail was considered a brilliant student. He had not been able to complete his dissertation before his arrest, but thanks to the intervention of his professor, he was allowed to do so in the Butyrki, and even to defend it at the institute. It is inconceivable that Mikhail could have done this without the support of the political police. He had two uncles in OGPU, and one of his oldest friends was Filipp Bazanov, Elena's first husband, who was also a senior official in OGPU. Bazanov helped Elena (and tried to persuade her to return to him) while Mikhail was in jail. In 1934, Mikhail was exiled to Arkhangelsk. Although he had relatives in Arkhangelsk, among them the family of the former vice-governor of Murmansk, Mikhail did not visit them, because he did not want to endanger them.

Mikhail was saved by his architectural expertise. He was employed by the NKVD as a planner-architect on several major building projects – factories and bridges – using Gulag labour from the nearby camps. He soon became one of the chief architects of Arkhangelsk. Even as a prisoner in exile, Mikhail enjoyed better living conditions than Elena and Julia in Moscow. Mikhail was earning good money. He ate in the NKVD cafeteria for engineers and technicians, where meat was served every day, whereas Julia and Elena were living in Moscow on a diet of porridge and bread. Mikhail sent them money to buy meat. Julia was often ill and desperately needed better food. At the end of 1934, Elena sent her to live with her father in Arkhangelsk, in the hope that she would benefit from Mikhail's relatively comfortable position. The last time Julia had seen her father (the only recollection she had of him) was two years earlier, in the Butyrki prison, a visit which had left her in such a state that, at the age of only six, she had tried to commit suicide. Mikhail rented the corner of a room from an old woman, Elena Petrovna, who prepared their meals. Julia recalls these meals – pork cutlets with macaroni, pancakes with mincemeat, chicken legs, ice cream – with nostalgia.

In the evenings, when Papa returned from work, he would ask me: 'What shall we order from Elena Petrovna? What do you want to eat?' I couldn't get enough of her delicious food and I would always say [the first dish she had cooked for us], 'Macaroni and cutlets! Macaroni and cutlets!' One day Papa had enough. He implored me: 'Liusenka, think of something else, I can't eat any more.' But I could not think of any other food.

For Julia the years she spent in Arkhangelsk, from 1934 to 1937, were the happiest in her life. She thrived at school. She loved the ballet. Her father took her to the theatre and bought a gramophone so she could dance to ballet music in their tiny living space. 'Papa's Corner', as Elena called this living space, was just seven square metres, with a plywood partition and door constructed by Mikhail to divide it from the rest of the room, where Elena Petrovna lived. Mikhail was very proud of his construction, which created the illusion of a separate room. 'Papa's Corner' was just big enough for a single bed, a table, a chair and a bookcase on the wall. But it was a home of sorts, and Julia was happy to be living there with her father.

'Papa's Corner'. Drawing by Mikhail Stroikov, 1935

In January 1937, Elena came to Arkhangelsk. The end of Mikhail's sentence was approaching, and she wanted to return to Moscow as a family. But the authorities would not let her stay in Arkhangelsk until the end of Mikhail's exile, and so Elena went back to Moscow with Julia. A few weeks later, in March, Mikhail was arrested and sentenced to five years in a labour camp for 'counter-revolutionary agitation' (he was shot in 1938). Elena knew nothing about his arrest. There were no more letters from her husband. She only learned what had happened the next summer when she went back to Arkhangelsk and spoke to Elena Petrovna.[119]

The Vittenburgs, the Drozdovs and the Stroikovs were exceptional, of course. The vast majority of the Gulag population was used as slave labour, or left to languish in prison camps and remote settlements, with little access to the comforts of normal life, or even prospect of reprieve. The cost in human lives was enormous. NKVD statistics show that over 150,000 people died in Soviet labour camps between 1932 and 1936.[120] These figures cast a different light on the mid-1930s, a period which has often been regarded as the calm before the storm of 1937–8 (the poet Anna Akhmatova called the middle thirties the 'vegetarian years'). For those whose lives were devastated by the Great Terror, that view of the mid-thirties may be true. But for millions of people whose families were scattered in the Gulag's labour camps and colonies, these years were as bad as any other.

Reading the letters of these prisoners to their relatives at home (letters that were written with censorship in mind), it is striking how the Gulag changed the values and priorities of so many of these prisoners – particularly the 'politicals', who had sacrificed so much for their ideals. Where before they might have looked for happiness in their career, or in the promise of a Communist utopia, years of living in a prison camp or exile forced them to rethink and place greater value on the family.

Tatiana Poloz (née Miagkova) was born in 1898 to the family of a barrister in the Borisoglebsk region of Tambov province. Her mother, Feoktista, the daughter of a priest, was a member of the Social Democratic Party who sided with the Bolsheviks when they split with the Mensheviks in 1903; she encouraged Tatiana to enter politics. In 1919, Tatiana joined the Bolshevik Party and took part in propaganda work behind the lines of Denikin's White Army on the Southern Front in the Civil War. It was there that she met her husband, Mikhail Poloz, a leading member of the Borotbists (Socialist Revolutionaries), the only Ukrainian party with a mass peasant following, who at that time was serving in the Military Council of the Ukrainian independent government. At the end of the Civil War, the Borotbists merged with the Bolsheviks, the Ukraine was brought under Soviet rule, and Poloz became the Ukraine's political representative (*polpred*) in Moscow. Tatiana joined the Higher Party School, attending lectures by Trotsky. In 1923, Mikhail was named Commissar of Finance in the Soviet Ukrainian government. He and Tatiana settled in Kharkov (the capital of Soviet Ukraine until 1934), where their daughter Rada was born in 1924.

Three years later, Tatiana was exiled to Astrakhan, and then, in

1929, to Chelkar in Kazakhstan. She was accused of being an active oppositionist, with links to the Smirnov group, an important faction of the Left Opposition led by Trotsky until the expulsion of its leaders from the Party in 1927. In the autumn of 1929, Mikhail visited Tatiana in Kazakhstan. He pleaded with her to renounce her opposition politics for the sake of their daughter, who was then living with her grandmother. At one point, according to a fellow oppositionist who was also exiled in Chelkar, Mikhail whispered something in her ear: 'It was some sort of secret information that left her utterly despondent and defeated.' Perhaps Mikhail had told her that Smirnov and his group had been negotiating a capitulation with the Stalinist authorities in the hope of being reinstated in the Party. On 3 November 1929, an article by Smirnov appeared in *Pravda* in which he declared his full support for the Five Year Plan and the 'general line of the Party', renounced his Trotskyist position and called on all his followers 'to overcome their hesitations and return to the Party'. Four hundred members of the Smirnov group subsequently signed a declaration of submission to the Party's general line, including Tatiana, who was then released from exile and allowed to return to her family.[121]

In 1930, the family moved from Kharkov to Moscow, where Poloz became Deputy Chairman of the All-Union Soviet Budget Commission, while Tatiana worked as an economist in the automobile industry. They lived with Tatiana's mother, Feoktista, and a housekeeper, in a large apartment in the House on the Embankment, the prestigious block of flats for government workers opposite the Kremlin, although, as romantic revolutionaries who had always lived for their ideas, the family did not attach much importance to their privileged lifestyle. Tatiana kept to her Trotskyist position, against the wishes of both her husband, who insisted that opposition to Stalin was futile, and her mother, who was a convinced Stalinist. In 1933, Tatiana was rearrested, along with the rest of the Smirnov group, and sentenced to three years in a special isolation prison camp in Verkhneuralsk in the Urals. Mikhail was arrested a few months later, in 1934, convicted of attempting to establish a Ukrainian bourgeois government and sentenced to ten years at the Solovetsky labour camp. Evicted from the House on the Embankment, Rada and her grandmother moved to a furnished apartment in the outskirts of Moscow, where they were joined by Rada's aunt Olga, whose husband had been arrested three years earlier, and their son

Volodia. Feoktista 'tried to teach me to respect and love my parents,' recalls Rada.

But at the same time she expected me to love and respect Soviet power. It was not an easy task, but somehow she managed it. Grandmother sincerely believed that Stalin did not know about the scale of the arrests . . . She thought that there were so many enemies of Soviet power that it was hard for the authorities to work out which ones were guilty. In our house one often heard the expression, 'You cannot make an omelette without breaking eggs.'[122]

The Poloz family, 1934: Rada is standing between her aunt
Olga and her grandmother, Feoktista. The boy is Olga's son Volodia

Between 1933 and June 1936, Tatiana wrote 136 letters to Feoktista and Rada, an average of one letter every week. This is one of the largest surviving collections of private letters from the Gulag.[123] The early letters reflect Tatiana's political preoccupations. She asks for Marx's writings to be sent. She comments in detail on the latest political events. In June 1934, for example, Tatiana's letters were full of praise for the crew of the *Cheliuskin*, which had just completed a pioneering voyage across the Arctic Ocean from Leningrad to the Bering Straits. The journey had ended in disaster when the steamship was crushed by ice and sank beneath the Chukchi Sea in February 1934. But the crew, which camped on an iceberg, was finally rescued by Soviet planes and flown back to Moscow, where propaganda turned their story into one of heroic survival. The *Cheliuskin* crew had 'shown the world what Bolsheviks are!' Tatania wrote on 24 June, adding four days later, on the same subject:

Pride in being a Soviet citizen was probably never as all-embracing and intense as it is today. Pride in the 'good qualities' of the Soviet people, in the fine Soviet aeroplanes, in the good Soviet scientists and sailors and all the rest, pride in Bolshevism, which showed the supreme power of its ideas and organization on those icebergs. And what power that must have for the education of children!

Rada's political education was a constant concern in these letters. 'Mama was always writing about how Communism should be built,' recalls Rada.

She wanted me to become an engineer and a writer . . . And her letters had an influence on me. Although I was brought up by my grandmother, I liked to think that, through these letters, I was being brought up by my mother too.[124]

Tatiana wanted Rada to grow up as a Communist. She spilled a sea of ink on commentaries about her behaviour at home (which she said she had read about 'in the newspapers' to avoid revealing Feoktista as her source).

12 June 1935
And how are our household duties going, my little monkey? In the newspapers they write that you do your household chores without much pleasure and often forget what has to be done. But they also write other things. I read this telegram in *Izvestiia*: 'Moscow (TASS) – the shockworker and model student Rada, 11, today was asked to clean the dishes and the kitchen. The task was fulfilled very well. The dishes were cleaned and everything tidied. Rada surveyed the results of her labour with great satisfaction and told our correspondent that from now on she will fulfil all her chores to the same standards of excellence.' The correspondent approved, of course, and so do I. Study, little monkey, cook, wash, clean, as you are asked: the main thing is to do as you are asked.

The longer Tatiana remained in prison, the more her letters were preoccupied by family relationships. Mikhail was not allowed to write to Moscow, but he was allowed to correspond with Tatiana, whose letters thus became the only means of information for Rada about her father, and for Mikhail about his daughter. Reflecting on her mother's letters, Rada believes that they allowed Tatiana to maintain the family connections she needed to survive. They were 'full of optimism', Rada

Letter (extract) from Tatiana to Rada, 12 June 1935

writes in her memoirs; 'she was always reminding us that time was passing, and was always looking forward to the happy time when the family would be together once again'. Many of Tatiana's prison letters came with little gifts – rag dolls, toy animals and even clothes – which she had made for Rada in the prison camp.[125]

On her release from the Verkhneuralsk prison in 1936, Tatiana was exiled to Uralsk and then to Alma-Ata. Feoktista spent two weeks with Tatiana in Uralsk in March 1936. These were precious weeks for Tatiana, who later wrote of a new intimacy she experienced with her mother when they sat together, 'my head resting on your shoulder', and talked about the past.[126] Shortly after Feoktista's return to Moscow, Tatiana wrote: 'Mamusenka! I came home but this is not a home. You are not here, there is no *home* [written in English] – no cosy warmth.' In April, when Tatiana moved to Alma-Ata, she began to pin her hopes on the possibility of Rada coming to be with her. She invested all her energies in organizing the move. Her letters from this time were filled with hopes and excitement, as Rada writes: 'Her stubborn strength and persistence were completely focused on the tasks of finding work and a little room where she could live with her daughter.' The trip did not materialize. In June 1936, just as Rada was about to leave Moscow to join her mother in Alma-Ata, Tatiana was rearrested and sent to an unknown labour camp. 'We bought the train tickets to Alma-Ata,' recalls Rada,

we found some people to look after me on the journey, packed all my things and sent a telegram with details about my arrival. The answer came: 'The addressee does not live here.' We returned the ticket. I stayed in Moscow and never saw my mother again.

Tatiana was sent to Kolyma, one of the worst of Stalin's Gulag colonies. In November 1937, she was shot. Mikhail was executed in Karelia during the same month. His correspondence with his wife (a 'Trotskyist') was recorded in his NKVD file as sufficient proof of guilt to sentence him to death.[127]

Rada did not know about her parents' death. She tried not to think about them, because she did not know if they were alive or not. But once she saw her mother in a dream:

To start with I was on the deck of a ship in the middle of the sea. In my hands I held two schoolbooks covered in glued-on brown paper. I opened one of them and recognized my mother's handwriting. The first sentence was very strange: 'When you read these lines, I will already be at the bottom of the sea . . .' I read a few more lines, which I can't recall. Then I became gripped with fear. There were enormous pipes with water gushing out. My fear increased, seizing hold of me, until I awoke.[128]

Rada believed the 'message' of her dream – that her mother had been drowned – and began to think about her all the time. Later, when she heard tales from Kolyma survivors about a ship of prisoners that had gone down, she was even more convinced of her mother's fate. She continued to believe her dream for many years and, even after she received a death certificate from the authorities stating that her mother had been shot, Rada went on thinking that she had been drowned.

Tatiana Poloz was not the only fervent socialist who felt the pull of family after imprisonment. Nikolai Kondratiev was born in 1892 to a peasant family in Kostroma province, 400 kilometres north-east of Moscow. He studied economics at St Petersburg University, joined the

Socialist Revolutionary Party and played a leading role in formulating the agrarian reforms of 1917. In the 1920s, Kondratiev was a prominent economist advising the Soviet government. He was a firm supporter of the NEP, favouring the primacy of agriculture and the manufacturing of consumer goods over the development of heavy industry. It was at this time that he advanced his theory of long-term cycles in the capitalist economy ('Kondratiev waves') which made him famous throughout the world. But with the overturning of the NEP Kondratiev was removed from all his posts. In July 1930, he was arrested on charges of belonging to an illegal (and probably non-existent) 'Peasant Labour Party'. Stalin wrote to Molotov: 'Kondratiev and a few other scoundrels must definitely be shot.'[129] But in fact Kondratiev was sentenced to eight years in the special isolation prison camp housed in the fourteenth-century Spaso-Yefimeyev Monastery in Suzdal, where he was imprisoned from February 1932.

Kondratiev's health deteriorated rapidly. He was in and out of the prison hospital with complaints of severe headaches, dizziness and intermittent deafness, chronic rheumatism in the legs, diarrhoea, vomiting, insomnia and depression. By 1936, he was practically blind. Yet Kondratiev carried on with his research and prepared five new books. He wrote over 100 letters to his wife, Yevgeniia,[130] nearly all of them with little notes attached for his daughter Elena ('Alyona'), who was born in 1925. The pain of separation which Kondratiev felt is almost palpable in these letters. It is his daughter that he misses most. The situation was all the more poignant because Kondratiev was obviously such a loving father. He desperately wanted to play an active role in his daughter's upbringing, and the worst part of his suffering in jail was not being able to do this. 'How terrible that she is growing up in my absence,' he wrote to Yevgeniia in March 1932. 'This torments me more than anything.'[131] As a father, Nikolai poured all his love into his letters to Elena. When she did not write to him, he reproached her for not loving him enough. Nikolai would constantly remind her of little incidents from their life together before his arrest. He drew pictures in his letters and told her stories about the wildlife around the monastery – birds that came to visit him, foxes he had seen. In many of his letters Nikolai included pressed flowers, or grasses from the meadows near the monastery. Above all, he focused his attention on his daughter's intellectual development. He set her riddles and puzzles. He recommended books for her to read, asking her to write with her impressions about them. He encouraged her to keep a diary, corrected the mistakes in her letters and nagged her to 'write neatly and always try to do things well'.[132] On the bottom of many of his letters a young child has written the word: 'Papa'. They were all Elena had of him. She grew up to become a botanist, a professor of Moscow University. Perhaps her father's letters influenced her interest in botany.

Nikolai and Elena ('Alyona') Kondratiev, 1926

In 1935, Nikolai sent Elena a fairy-tale which he had written and illustrated to mark her name day.[133] 'The Unusual Adventures of Shammi' tells the story of a kitten who goes in search of the ideal land, where 'people, animals and plants live in happiness and harmony'. Shammi sets off with his friend, the tomcat Vasia, who is very cowardly and reluctant to go. On the way they encounter many animals who try to dissuade them from going on, promising them happiness if they give up the search, but Shammi pushes ahead, attracting various animals – a goat, a donkey, a horse and a hen – who 'all work hard and want a better life'. But soon the travellers lose their way. They begin to argue among themselves. Some get eaten by a crocodile. Others are shot by hunters in the wood.

On 31 August 1938 Kondratiev wrote to his daughter:

'The Unusual Adventures of Shammi' (detail)

My sweet darling Alyonushka.

Probably your holidays are over now and you are back at school. How did you spend the summer? Did you get stronger, put on weight, get tanned? I very much want to know. And I would like very, very much to see you and kiss you many, many times. I still do not feel well, I am still ill. My sweet, Alyonushka, I want you not to get sick this winter. I also want you to study hard, as you did before. Read good books. Be a clever and a good little girl. Listen to your mother and never disappoint her. I would also be happy if you managed not to forget about me, your papa, altogether. Well, be healthy! Be happy! I kiss you without end. Your papa.[134]

This was the last letter. Shortly afterwards, on 17 September, Nikolai was executed by a firing squad.

4
The Great Fear
(1937–8)

I

Julia Piatnitskaia did not know what to think when her husband was arrested on the night of 7 July 1937. Osip Piatnitsky was a veteran Bolshevik, a member of the Party from its foundation and one of Lenin's most trusted comrades. In an article in *Pravda* to mark Piatnitsky's fiftieth birthday, in January 1932, Lenin's widow Krupskaia had described him as a 'typical revolutionary-professional who gave himself entirely to the Party, and lived only for its interests'. It was hard for Julia to understand how Osip could have become an 'enemy of the people'. She was a committed Bolshevik, but she did not know whether to believe the Soviet press, which had named Piatnitsky as a 'traitor' and a 'spy', or the man she had loved for nearly twenty years. Osip was the father of her two children, but after his arrest she was no longer certain if she really knew her husband. 'Who is Piatnitsky?' Julia wrote in her diary. 'A true revolutionary or a scoundrel? . . . Either could be true. I do not know. That is the most agonizing thing.'[1]

Julia had met Osip in 1920, when she was twenty-one and he was thirty-nine. Julia was born into a Russian-Polish family in Vladimir. Her mother was a Polish noblewoman who had broken all the customs of her caste and religion by marrying a Russian Orthodox priest without her parents' permission. Julia, who was six when her mother died, inherited her romantic and rebellious temperament. Passionate and beautiful, at the age of just sixteen Julia ran away from her father's home to enrol as an nurse in the Russian army during the First World War. She married a young general, who disappeared in action in 1917. During the Civil War, Julia joined the Bolsheviks. She worked for the Red Army as a spy, infiltrating the military headquarters of Admiral

Kolchak, the White Army leader on the Eastern Front. Eventually, her cover was blown. Narrowly escaping with her life, she fled to Moscow, had a nervous breakdown, and while recovering in a hospital met Osip, who was visiting a friend. Julia was highly strung and volatile, emotional and poetic. She had a strong sense of justice, rooted in her strict religious upbringing, which profoundly influenced her politics. She was kind and warm, adored by everyone who met her, according to the daughter of one of Osip's comrades. 'We children were always calm in her presence. When she was there, we forgot our worries . . . She was always full of life.'[2]

Osip, by contrast, was stern and taciturn. A stocky man, with soft, attractive features, he was a model of the professional revolutionary. Modest to the point of selflessness, he rarely talked about his private life (many of his oldest Party comrades had no idea he had a family). Osip had been one of the most important activists in the Marxist underground before 1917. He was in charge of smuggling illegal literature between Russia and Europe. He spent a great deal of time abroad, especially in Germany, where he was known by the pseudonym 'Freitag' (Friday), or 'Piatnitsa' in Russian, from which the name Piatnitsky was derived (his real Jewish surname was Tarshis). When he married Julia, Osip was the Secretary of the Moscow Party's Central Committee. But he was soon transferred to the Comintern, the international organization of the Communist Party, where he ran the crucial Organization Department and effectively became the leader of the entire Comintern. Piatnitsky oversaw a huge expansion in the Comintern's activities, as it tried to spread the Revolution to all corners of the world. His *Memoirs of a Bolshevik* (1926), a handbook of the Party's organizational and ethical principles, was translated into more than twenty languages. Piatnitsky was exhausted by his work. 'I was in the Comintern from morning until night,' he recalled.[3] In the middle of the 1920s – when he was still in his early forties – his hair went white and then fell out.

Osip's work also placed a heavy burden on his family life. The Piatnitsky apartment in the House on the Embankment was always full of foreign visitors. Osip missed out on the childhood of his two young sons, Igor (born in 1921) and Vladimir (in 1925). His constant absence was a source of many arguments with Julia, who also became increasingly disillusioned with the bourgeoisification of the Party and Stalin's dictatorship during the 1930s. Igor recalls an argument between his parents – it must have been in 1934 – when she began to recite in a loud

and angry voice the seditious verses of the early nineteenth-century poet
Dmitry Venivitinov:

> The dirt, the stench, the cockroach and the flea
> And everywhere the presence of his lordly hand
> And all those Russians who babble constantly –
> All this we must call our holy fatherland.

Osip and Julia (seated on the right of the front step) with their sons Igor
(next to Osip) and Vladimir Piatnitsky (on Julia's knee) and neighbours'
children at their dacha near Moscow, late 1920s

Terrified of their neighbours overhearing, Osip pleaded with his wife:
'Keep your voice down, Julia!'[4]

By 1935, Piatnitsky's standing in the Comintern had made him known
to Communists throughout the world (Harry Pollitt, the British Communist, said that Piatnitsky *was* the Comintern). At this time, Stalin's
foreign policy was geared towards the containment of Nazi Germany by
strengthening relations with the Western democratic states ('collective
security'). In 1934, the Soviet Union had even joined the League of
Nations, which it had denounced only two years previously as an
'imperialist conspiracy'. The Comintern was subordinated to this foreign
policy. Led by its new General Secretary, the Bulgarian Communist
Georgi Dimitrov, the Comintern's task was now to build alliances with

the European socialists and steer them into coalition governments ('Popular Fronts') with the centre parties to counteract the Fascist threat. The policy had some success in France and Spain, where Popular Front governments were elected in 1936. But there were critics of this strategy within the Comintern, among them Piatnitsky. Many Communists, including former members of the Left Opposition led by Trotsky in the 1920s, saw it as a betrayal of the international revolutionary cause, which in their view could only be advanced by 'United Fronts' of Communists and socialists, excluding the centre parties of the bourgeoisie; they found common cause with former members of the more moderate Right Opposition, led by Rykov and Bukharin, who were increasingly opposed to Stalin's abuse of power. Both these groups regarded Stalin as a 'counter-revolutionary'. By 1936, the Comintern was full of whispered discontent with Stalin's foreign policies. Leftists linked the Stalinist rapprochement with the Western powers to the bourgeoisification of the Soviet elite. Deeply committed to the ideal of world revolution, they were afraid that the Soviet Union, under Stalin's leadership, was becoming not an inspiration to the proletarians of the West, but a guardian of order and security. They were particularly disillusioned by Stalin's failure to give adequate support to the various left-wing defenders of the Republic in the Spanish Civil War, when, in the autumn of 1936, General Franco's Nationalists – with massive aid from Fascist Italy and Nazi Germany – advanced to the outskirts of Madrid. Even some of Stalin's loyal supporters sometimes found it hard to go along with what they saw as the betrayal of their ideological commitment to revolutionary internationalism. As one Old Bolshevik explained to William Bullitt, the US Ambassador to the Soviet Union, in 1935: 'You must understand that world revolution is our religion and there is not one of us who would not in the final analysis oppose even Stalin himself if we should feel that he was abandoning the cause of world revolution.'[5]

Stalin grew increasingly mistrustful of the Comintern, which he feared was slipping out of his control. At its Seventh Congress, in August 1935, he engineered a radical reshuffle of its leadership. Piatnitsky was dismissed from the executive and placed in charge of a new department in the Central Committee to supervise the work of the Party bureaucracy. The show trial of the former oppositionists, Kamenev and Zinoviev, in August 1936, was a clear warning from Stalin to his critics that all policies would be decided at the top. Nowhere was this more the case than in the Comintern, where the opposition was identified by Stalin with the work of 'foreign spies'. 'All of you there in the Comintern are playing right into the enemy's hands,' Stalin wrote to Dimitrov in February 1937. Several thousand Comintern officials and foreign Communists were arrested in 1937–8. The German, Polish, Yugoslav and Baltic Communist parties were practically wiped out. At Comintern headquarters and the Hotel Lux in Moscow, where many of the Comintern's officials lived, there was so much panic that, in the words of one official, 'many are half mad and incapable of working as a result of constant fear'.[6]

Piatnitsky was denounced by Stalin as a Trotskyist. He was later implicated in a 'Fascist Spy Organization of Trotskyists and Rightists in the Comintern'. But according to the version of events related by his sons, the real cause of his arrest was a brave speech they believe he made at the Plenum of the Central Committee in June 1937.* Apparently, Piatnitsky had been shocked by what he had discovered in his work at the Central Committee. He was particularly troubled by the enormous personal power of Stalin and his unbridled use of the NKVD to eliminate his enemies. At the June plenum, it is believed, Piatnitsky accused the NKVD of fabricating evidence against 'enemies of the people' and called for the establishment of a special Party commission to oversee the work of the NKVD. It was a suicidal speech, as Piatnitsky must have realized. When he finished speaking there was silence in the hall. The tension was palpable. A recess was called. On instructions from Stalin, several Party leaders, including Kaganovich, Molotov and Voroshilov, attempted to

---

*There is no record of Piatnitsky's speech, and no surviving stenographic record of the June plenum, although there is evidence which suggests that whatever Piatnitsky had said was erased from the corrected stenogram (a common practice in the archives of the Central Committee) where it might encourage other dissidents. Before closing the last plenum session on 29 June, Stalin announced: 'As far as Piatnitsky is concerned, the investigation is ongoing. It should be completed in the next few days.' At the bottom of the page there is a handwritten note by one of Stalin's secretaries: 'This communication was crossed out by comrade Stalin because it should not go into the stenogram' (RGASPI, f. 17, op. 2, d. 622, l. 220). There may be other records of the alleged incident in closed archives (such as the Presidential Archive in the Kremlin). Until that evidence becomes available, the only record of Piatnitsky's stand against the mass arrests of the Old Bolsheviks comes from his son Vladimir, who claims to have reconstructed the events of the June plenum from his father's personal file in the FSB archive, fragmentary evidence in other archives and the alleged reminiscences of Kaganovich, as related to him by Samuil Guberman, the head of Kaganovich's secretariat (*Zagovor*, pp. 59–70; interviews with Vladimir Piatnitsky, St Petersburg, September 2005. See also, in support of the Piatnitsky version of events, B. Starkov, 'Ar'ergardnye boi staroi partiinoi gvardii', in *Oni ne molchali* (Moscow, 1991), pp. 215–25).

Osip Piatnitsky at the Seventh Congress of the Comintern, Moscow, 1935

persuade Piatnitsky to withdraw his statement and thus save his life. Molotov begged him to think about the consequences for his wife and children. But Piatnitsky would not back down; he claimed that he knew what his destiny would be, but that his 'conscience as a Communist' would not allow him to retract his words. According to Kaganovich, Piatnitsky told him that his protest had been a conscious and premeditated act. 'He said that for the unity and moral purity of the Party he was ready to sacrifice his life and, if necessary, to trample on the corpses of his children and his wife.' When this was reported to Stalin, the leadership resolved to adjourn the plenum for the day. The next morning the plenum opened with a speech by Nikolai Yezhov, the NKVD chief, denouncing Piatnitsky as a tsarist spy who had been sent by the capitalist powers to infiltrate the Comintern. Yezhov called for a vote of censure against Piatnitsky. It was passed with three abstentions, one of them by Krupskaia, who refused to believe the NKVD charges against Piatnitsky ('He is the most honest of men. Lenin greatly loved and respected him') right up until his arrest.[7] Piatnitsky returned from the plenum 'exhausted and depressed', Julia noted in her diary. When she asked him what was wrong, Piatnitsky 'talked of all the children, of all the innocents, who were forced to live under constant psychological stress'.[8]

For the next two weeks, Piatnitsky stayed at home, locked away in his office. He ate very little, and spent all day on the telephone trying to make contact with Yezhov. Julia could not bear the tension and went off to the dacha for a few days – a decision which she later regretted. 'I should have been by his side,' she wrote in her diary in March 1938. 'I did not understand what he was going through. I was not intelligent enough, or strong enough. To be the wife of such a person means to serve him, to be always at one's post.'[9] During this fortnight, Osip prepared for his arrest. He transferred his savings book and valuables to Julia and destroyed his private notebooks and letters. A seasoned revolutionary, who had been arrested many times before, he knew how to prepare. On 5 July he was expelled from the Party. He felt so despondent, Julia noted on her return from the dacha, that he thought of suicide. He could not imagine living without the Party. But the next day, when they paid a visit to old friends, Osip told them he had changed his mind. He said that he would submit to his punishment for the sake of Party unity: 'If a sacrifice has to be made for the Party, then however burdensome that sacrifice might be, I will bear it joyously.' Osip warned his sons to expect his arrest. He explained to them that he had argued with his comrades in the Party leadership and that they had denounced him; he denied his guilt and said that he would fight to prove his innocence as long as that was possible, but that, if he was arrested, they should not expect to see their father again. 'He warned me not to fight against Stalin. That was the main thing he told me,' remembered Igor.[10]

The NKVD came for Osip shortly after 11 p.m. on 7 July. Yezhov made the arrest in person. Bursting into the apartment, the NKVD men threw a dressing gown at Julia and told her to put it on. She began to shout and swear at them, whereupon Yezhov told her that 'Soviet citizens do not talk that way to representatives of the authorities'. Osip apologized for his wife's behaviour. He left with the NKVD men, carrying a small suitcase which contained his dressing gown and a toothbrush. Julia fainted as they left. When she came to, they had gone. 'I had just one thought,' she noted in her diary – 'the overwhelming thought that I will never see him again – that and a feeling of terrible powerlessness.' The next day, while Julia was at work, the NKVD broke into the apartment. They searched through Osip's papers and took away the family's valuables: cash and savings books, a radio, a bicycle, coats, sheets, linen, even little things like teacups disappeared. The door to Osip's office was then sealed with wax. No one dared to break the seal, but if they had, they would have found a library which the Piatnitskys could have sold to help them through the next few months, when, like all the families of 'enemies of the people', they were suddenly reduced to poverty.[11]

Osip's fate was probably decided long before his protest to the June plenum. In the Great Terror of 1937–8 – when at least 1.3 million people were arrested for crimes against the state – the Comintern was one of Stalin's main targets. The reasons for this are worth examining, because they are a key to the riddle of the Terror's origins.

Extraordinary even by the standards of the Stalinist regime, the Great Terror was not a routine wave of mass arrests, such as those that swept across the country throughout Stalin's reign, but a calculated policy of mass murder. No longer satisfied with imprisoning his real or imagined 'political enemies', Stalin now ordered the police to take people out of the prisons and labour camps and murder them. In the two years of 1937 and 1938, according to incomplete statistics, a staggering total of at least 681,692 people, and probably far more, were shot for 'crimes against the state' (91 per cent of all death sentences for political crimes between 1921 and 1940, if NKVD figures are to be believed). The population of the Gulag labour camps and colonies grew in these same years from 1,196,369 to 1,881,570 people (a figure which excludes at least 140,000 deaths within the camps themselves and an unknown number of deaths during transport to the camps). Other periods of Soviet history had also seen mass arrests of 'enemies', but never had so many of the victims been killed. More than half the people arrested during the Great Terror were later shot, compared to less than 10 per cent of arrests in 1930, the second highest peak of executions in the Stalin period, when 20,201 death sentences were carried out. During the 'anti-kulak operation' of 1929–32, the number of arrests was also very high (586,904), but of these victims only 6 per cent (35,689 people) were subsequently shot.[12]

The origins of the Great Terror are not easy to explain. Nor is it immediately clear why it was so concentrated in these two years. To begin to understand it, we must look at the Great Terror not as an uncontrolled or accidental happening, a product of the chaos of the Stalinist regime that could have erupted at almost any time – a view occasionally put forward[13] – but as an operation masterminded and controlled by Stalin in response to the specific circumstances he perceived in 1937.

Some historians have traced the origins of the Great Terror to the assassination of the Leningrad Party boss Sergei Kirov in December

1934 – an act, it is said, that set the regime on its murderous hunt for hidden enemies. But this theory raises the question of why the mass arrests and killings did not start in 1934–5. Why was there a two-year lull before the storm of 1937–8? After Kirov's murder there were mass arrests in Leningrad, but otherwise the years of 1935 and 1936 were relatively terror-free for the political classes in the rest of the Soviet Union. In fact, under the direction of Aleksandr Vyshinsky, the Procurator of the USSR, the regime made a conscious effort to return to a more stable and traditional legal order following the chaos of 1928–34.[14] Other historians have connected the Great Terror to Stalin's fears of an internal threat, particularly in the countryside, where, they argue, mass discontent could have turned political, if Soviet elections had been allowed to go ahead, as they had been promised by the 'Stalin Constitution' of 1936.[15] But the NKVD reports of domestic discontent were unreliable ('anti-Soviet sentiment' and 'threats of unrest' were often fabricated by the NKVD to justify increases in its budget and its staff) and it is far from clear whether Stalin or anybody else in the ruling circle took them at all seriously. In any case, these reports contain no suggestion that the internal threat was any greater in 1937 than it had been at any other time. There were just as many reports of discontent and opposition during 1928–32, but nothing in those years to match the intensity of state killing in 1937–8.

Yet other historians have suggested that the Great Terror is best understood 'as a number of related but discrete phenomena', each one capable of being explained on its own but not as part of a single event.[16] And indeed the Great Terror was a complex amalgam of different elements: the great 'show trials' against the Old Bolsheviks; the purging of the political elites; the mass arrests in the cities; the 'kulak operation'; and 'national operations' against minorities. But while it may be helpful to analyse the various components of the Terror separately, the fact remains that they all began and ended simultaneously, which does suggest that they were part of a unified campaign that needs to be explained.

The key to understanding the Great Terror as a whole lies perhaps in Stalin's fear of an approaching war and his perception of an international threat to the Soviet Union.[17] The military aggression of Hitler's Germany, signalled by its occupation of the Rhineland in 1936, and the occupation of Manchuria by the Japanese, convinced Stalin that the USSR was endangered by the Axis powers on two fronts. Stalin's fears were reinforced in November 1936, when Berlin and Tokyo united in a pact (later joined by Fascist Italy) against the Comintern. Despite his continuing support of 'collective security', Stalin did not place much hope in the Soviet alliance with the Western powers to contain the Axis threat: the Western states had failed to intervene in Spain; they appeared committed to the appeasement of Nazi Germany; and they reportedly gave Stalin the impression that it was their hidden aim to divert Hitler's forces to the East and engage them in a war with the USSR rather than confront them in the West. By 1937, Stalin was convinced that the Soviet Union was on the brink of war with the Fascist states in Europe and with Japan in the East. The Soviet press typically portrayed the country as threatened on all sides and undermined by Fascist infiltrators – 'spies' and 'hidden enemies' – in every corner of society.

'Our enemies from the capitalist circles are tireless. They infiltrate everywhere,' Stalin told the writer Romain Rolland in 1935. Stalin's view of politics – like many Bolsheviks' – had been profoundly shaped by the lessons of the First World War, when the tsarist regime was brought down by social revolution in the rear. He feared a similar reaction against the Soviet regime in the event of war with Nazi Germany. The Spanish Civil War reinforced his fears on this account. Stalin took a close interest in the Spanish conflict, seeing it (as did most of his advisers) as a 'valid scenario for a future European war' between Communism and Fascism.[18] Stalin put the military defeats of the Republicans in 1936 down to the factional infighting between the Spanish Communists, the Trotskyists, the Anarchists and other left-wing groups. It led him to conclude that in the Soviet Union political repression was urgently required to crush not just a 'fifth column' of 'Fascist spies and enemies' but all potential opposition before the outbreak of a war with the Fascists.

A paranoic fear of 'enemies' was, it seems, in Stalin's character. It had been reinforced by the suicide of his wife Nadezhda in 1932 and by the murder of Kirov, a man Stalin claimed to love like a brother. 'Maybe Stalin never trusted people very much,' wrote his daughter Svetlana, 'but after their deaths he stopped trusting them at all.'* Stalin blamed

---

*It is possible that Stalin had a hand in the murder of Kirov. The Leningrad Party boss was a very popular and more moderate leader than Stalin, who had good reason to be afraid that Kirov might emerge as a serious rival to his leadership. No hard evidence has ever come to light of Stalin's role in his murder. But Stalin used the murder to pursue his obsession with an internal threat and to persecute his 'enemies'.

the Kirov assassination on the 'Zinovievites' (the 'Leningrad Opposition') and issued orders for the supporters of Zinoviev, the former boss
of Leningrad, to be arrested, even though there was no evidence to
connect them with the murder. Many of them were ultimately convicted
of 'moral complicity' in Kirov's killing on the grounds that they had
created a climate of opposition which encouraged the assassination of
Soviet leaders. In the two and a half months following the murder,
when Stalin took charge of the investigation in Leningrad, nearly a
thousand 'Zinovievites' were arrested. Most of them were exiled to
remote settlements. Zinoviev and Kamenev, allies with Trotsky in the
United Opposition against Stalin in the 1920s, were arrested: Zinoviev
was sentenced to ten years' imprisonment, Kamenev to five. When the
NKVD officials proved reluctant to arrest so many Party loyalists, Stalin
called in Iagoda, the NKVD boss, and warned him to be more vigilant,
or else 'we will slap you down'. Iagoda's position was further undermined in 1935, when Yezhov, who was placed in charge of the Party
purge, claimed to have uncovered a large network of 'foreign spies' and
'terrorists' organized by Trotsky and Zinoviev and undetected by the
NKVD in the heart of the Kremlin. Stalin finally lost patience with
Iagoda and replaced him with Yezhov, a brutal executioner without
any moral conscience who was prepared to indulge Stalin's paranoic
fantasies by fabricating evidence of 'counter-revolutionary conspiracies'
and 'spy rings' everywhere. For several years, Yezhov had promoted the
theory that Kamenev and Zinoviev had been plotting on Trotsky's orders
from abroad to murder Kirov, Stalin and other members of the Party
leadership. On this basis, Stalin now reopened the Kirov investigation.
In August 1936, Zinoviev, Kamenev and fourteen other Party leaders
were put on trial for treason. All of them were sentenced to death, along
with 160 other people arrested in connection with the trial.[19]

This was the first of several 'show trials' in Moscow. Their aim was
to reveal and root out a coordinated ring of 'spies' and 'terrorists'
organized by former oppositionists. A second show trial, in January
1937, witnessed the conviction of Georgii Piatakov, Deputy Commissar
of Heavy Industry, Karl Radek and fifteen other former supporters of
Trotsky for industrial sabotage and espionage. In April–May 1937,
eight of the country's senior military commanders, including Marshal
Tukhachevsky (Deputy Commissar of Defence), General Uborevich
(Commander of the Belorussian Military District) and General Iakir

(Commander of the Kiev Military District), were arrested, tortured brutally and tried *in camera* for treason and espionage. It was said that they were financed by the Germans and the Japanese. All of them were shot on the same day. In the last and biggest of the show trials, in March 1938, Bukharin, Iagoda and Rykov, along with thirteen other senior officials, were sentenced to be shot for conspiring with the Zinovievites and Trotskyists to assassinate the Soviet leaders, sabotage the economy and spy at the behest of the Fascist powers. Iagoda's involvement in the plot supposedly explained why it had taken so long to uncover it.

When a Party leader was arrested, everybody in his social orbit came under suspicion. The typical provincial town was ruled by a clique of senior officials – the district Party boss, the police chief, the heads of the local factories, collective farms and prisons, the local Soviet leader – who each had their own patron–client networks in the town's institutions. These officials protected one another as long as their power circle was maintained. But the arrest of one would inevitably lead to the arrest of all the other members of his circle, as well as their hangers-on, once the NKVD got to work revealing the connections between them. In 1937, for example, the NKVD arrested the Party Secretary of Nikopol, in the eastern Ukraine. It also arrested his

assistants, his friends, the men and women he had put into jobs anywhere in Nikopol. The Commandant of the Nikopol garrison went into the hunters' bag, then the local Prosecutor and all his legal staff, finally the Chairman of the Nikopol Soviet ... the local bank, the newspaper, all commercial institutions were 'cleansed' ... the manager of the Communal Administration, the Chief of the Fire Brigades, the head of the Savings Institution ...[20]

The terror in the leadership thus spread down through the Party ranks, Soviet institutions and society. According to one estimate, 116,885 Party members were executed or imprisoned in 1937–8. The more senior a Party member was, the more likely he was to be arrested, for juniors in the ranks were always ready to denounce their superiors in order to replace them in their posts. Of the 139 Central Committee members elected at the Seventeenth Party Congress in 1934, 102 were arrested and shot, and five more killed themselves in 1937–8; in addition, 56 per cent of the congress delegates were imprisoned in these years. The decimation of the Red Army was even more complete: of the 767 members of the high command (brigade commanders and above),

412 were executed, 29 died in prison, 3 committed suicide, and 59 remained in jail.[21]

Stalin must have known that the vast majority of these victims were entirely innocent. But since it only took a small handful of 'hidden enemies' to make a Revolution while the country was at war, it was fully justified, in his view, to arrest millions to root these out. As Stalin said in June 1937, if just 5 per cent of the people who had been arrested turned out to be actual enemies, 'that would be a good result'. Evidence was a minor consideration. According to Nikita Khrushchev, then the head of the Moscow Party Committee, Stalin 'used to say that if a report [denunciation] was ten per cent true, we should regard the entire report as fact'. Everybody in the NKVD knew that Stalin was prepared to arrest thousands to catch just one spy. They knew that holding back from their quota of arrests would only get them into trouble for lack of vigilance. 'Better too much than not enough,' Yezhov warned his NKVD operatives. If 'an extra thousand people are shot [in an operation], that is not such a big deal'.[22]

For Stalin and his supporters, the Great Terror was a preparation for the coming war. Molotov and Kaganovich continued to defend this rationale until their deaths. 'Stalin played it safe' (*perestrakhoval*), explained Molotov in 1986. The 'great purge' was an 'insurance policy' – a necessary means for the leadership to ferret out the 'waverers', 'careerists' and 'hidden enemies' in the Party who might have proved troublesome in time of war. There were mistakes, Molotov admitted, many people were arrested unjustly, but 'we would have suffered greater losses in the war – and perhaps defeat – if the leadership had flinched and allowed internal strife'.

We were obligated to ensure that in time of war there would be no fifth column. It is doubtful that all of these people were spies, but . . . the main thing is that in the decisive moment there was no relying on them . . . If Tukhachevsky and Iakir and Rykov and Zinoviev joined the opposition during war, there would have been a cruel struggle and colossal losses . . . Everyone would have been destroyed!

In the 1980s, Kaganovich similarly justified the Great Terror: the leadership had realized that a war was approaching, and that the country needed to protect itself by 'draining the swamp (*boloto*)' – that is by 'destroying unreliables and waverers'. This was not just a post facto rationalization by Kaganovich. In June 1938, he had told the Donbass

Party that the mass repressions were necessitated by the threat of war and that the country 'would be at war already', if its 'internal enemies and spies' had not been destroyed in the 'great purge'.[23]

Coordinated in the Kremlin and carried out by the NKVD in the localities, the Great Terror spread throughout society as a series of mass campaigns to purge the country of 'anti-social' and potentially 'anti-Soviet' elements in the event of war. By far the biggest of these mass campaigns was the 'kulak operation' instituted by the infamous Directive 00447: it accounted for half of all arrests (669,929) and more than half the executions (376,202) in 1937–8. Nearly all the victims were former 'kulaks' and their families who had recently returned from 'special settlements' and Gulag labour camps after completing the standard eight-year sentence for 'counter-revolutionary agitation and propaganda' imposed during the collectivization campaign in 1929–30. Stalin was afraid that the country would be swamped by disgruntled and embittered 'kulaks' who might pose a threat in time of war. He was particularly concerned by NKVD reports about a White monarchist organization, the Russian General Military Union (ROVS), which was said to be preparing a 'kulak uprising' to coincide with a Japanese invasion of Siberia. Tens of thousands of alleged ROVS members were shot in the course of the 'kulak operation', although they were seldom counted in official statistics (the Altai NKVD, for example, made a separate report on the 22,108 ROVS members it had shot in 1937). The 'kulak operation' was connected to a wholesale purge of the local Soviets. It was particularly brutal in border areas, like the western provinces, and in regions, like the Donbass and western Siberia, where the regime feared the population most.[24]

There were also large-scale 'national operations', wholesale deportations and executions of Soviet minorities who were deemed potential 'spies' in the event of war: Germans, Poles, Finns and Latvians, Armenians and Greeks, Koreans, Chinese, even Kharbin Russians, who had returned to the Soviet Union from Manchuria following the 1935 sale of the Eastern China Railway to Manchukuo, the puppet Manchurian state set up by the Japanese in 1932. Stalin's distrust of the Poles in the western Soviet regions was particularly strong. It dated from the Russian Civil War, when Poland had invaded the Ukraine and then defeated the Red Army when it counter-attacked against Warsaw – a military defeat in which Stalin had been personally humiliated because of his tactical mistakes as a front-line commissar. Stalin saw the Soviet Poles (and many Belorussians and Ukrainians, whom he considered to be really 'Poles') as a fifth column of the 'semi-Fascist' Polish state of Marshal Jozef Pilsudski, which the Soviet leader feared would unite with Nazi Germany to attack the Soviet Union again. As a result of the 'national operation' against the Poles, launched by Directive 00485 in August 1937, almost 140,000 people were shot or sent to labour camps by November 1938.[25]

So many people disappeared in 1937–8, particularly in the Party and intelligentsia circles of the major capitals, that the arrests appeared random, as if anyone could be picked up by the Black Marias that roamed the streets at night. The prison population was a broad cross-section of the population. Most prisoners had no idea for what crime they were in jail. By the autumn of 1938, virtually every family had lost a relative, or knew of someone with imprisoned relatives. People lived in fearful expectation of the knock on the door in the middle of the night. They slept badly and awoke when they heard a car pull up outside. They would lie there waiting for the sound of footsteps to pass by on the staircase or in the corridor, before going back to sleep, relieved that the visitors were not for them. Liubov Shaporina, the founder of the Puppet Theatre in Leningrad, wrote in her diary on 22 November 1937:

The joys of everyday life. I wake up in the morning and automatically think: thank God I was not arrested last night, they don't arrest people during the day, but what will happen tonight, no one knows. It's like Lafontaine's lamb – every single person has enough against him to justify arrest and exile to parts unknown. I'm lucky, I am completely calm; I simply don't care. But the majority of people are living in complete terror.[26]

Vladimir Piatnitsky, Osip's son, recalls the atmosphere in the House on the Embankment before the arrest of his father:

There were more than 500 flats for elite Party workers in that gloomy building, and arrests were a regular occurence. Because I was always playing in the yard and corridors, I saw several arrests. In the evenings, as it grew dark, the house became deserted and silent. It was as if the inhabitants had gone into hiding in the expectation of catastrophe. Suddenly, several cars would drive into the yard, men in uniform and plain clothes would jump out and walk towards staircase entrances – each one knew the way to 'his' address. Then one saw the lights go on in several apartments. Since I knew where everybody lived, I could work out who was being arrested. If all the lights in the apartment went on, it meant there was a search. In those days many people expected to be arrested, but they did not know when their turn would come.[27]

People waited for their turn. Many packed a bag and kept it by their bed in order to be ready when the NKVD knocked on the door. This passivity is one of the most striking features of the Great Terror. There were many ways to avoid arrest – moving out of town and taking on a new identity by buying papers on the black market being the most simple and effective, for the NKVD was not good at tracking down people on the move.[28] The Russian people had a long tradition of fleeing persecution by the state – from the Old Believers to runaways from serfdom – and this tactic was adopted by millions of peasants who ran away from the collective farms and 'special settlements'. But the urban population by and large remained in place, without any sign of resistance, and waited for the Terror to take them.

Looking back, the film writer Valerii Frid (1922–98), who was arrested in 1943, thought that most people were paralysed by fear. They were so hypnotized by the power of the NKVD, which they believed was everywhere, that they could not contemplate resistance or escape.

I can think of no analogy in human history. So I'll have to make do with an example from zoology: the rabbit hypnotized by the boa constrictor . . . We were all like rabbits who recognized the right of the boa constrictor to swallow us; whoever fell under the power of its gaze would walk quite calmly and with a sense of doom into its mouth.[29]

Viacheslav Kolobkov recalls the panic of his father, a factory worker in Leningrad, when a car stopped outside their house at night.

Every night he would stay awake – waiting for the sound of a car engine. When it came he would sit up rigid in his bed. He was terrified. I could smell his fear, his nervous sweating, and feel his body shaking, though I could barely see him in the dark. 'They have come for me!' he would always say when he heard a car. He was convinced that he would be arrested for something he had said – sometimes, at home, he used to curse the Bolsheviks. When he heard an engine stop and the car door slam, he would get up and start fumbling in panic for the things he thought he would need most. He always kept these items near his bed in order to be ready when 'they' came for him. I remember the husks of bread lying there – his biggest fear was going without bread. There were many nights when my father barely slept – waiting for a car that never came.[30]

Faced with arrest, the Bolshevik elite were particularly passive. Most of them were so indoctrinated by their Party's ideology that any thought of trying to resist was easily outweighed by a deeper need to prove their innocence before the Party. Yevgeniia Ginzburg was the wife of a senior Party leader in Kazan and herself a Party activist. After her husband was taken, she lost her job and feared that her own arrest was imminent. Her mother-in-law was 'a simple, illiterate peasant woman born in the days of serfdom', recalls Ginzburg; she 'was of a deeply philosophical cast of mind and had a remarkable power of hitting the nail on the head when she talked about the problems of life'. This old peasant woman advised her to run away:

' "Out of sight, out of mind," they say. The farther away you are the better. Why not go to our old village, to Pokrovskoye?' . . .

'But how can I, Grandmother? How can I leave everything, the children, my work?' [Ginzburg replied].

'Well, they've taken your job away anyhow. And the children won't come to any harm with us.'

'But I must prove my innocence to the Party. How can I, a Communist, hide from the Party?'[31]

The belief in their own innocence disabled many Bolsheviks. Somehow they managed to convince themselves that only the guilty were arrested, and that they would be protected by their innocence. Elena Bonner recalls overhearing a late-night conversation between her parents, life-long Party loyalists, following the arrest of a close friend. Elena had woken up in the middle of the night, anxious because this arrest had made her realize 'that our turn was coming, inexorably and soon'.

It was dark in the dining room, but there were voices in my parents' room. I went to the door. And I could hear my mother blow her nose. Then she spoke, crying. I had never seen her cry. She kept repeating 'all my life' and sobbing . . . Papa replied softly, but I couldn't make out his words. Suddenly she shouted, 'I've known Styopa all my life. Do you know what that means? I've known him three times longer than you. Understand? Do you understand?' Then only sobs. And a creak and slippers shuffling on the floor – Papa had gotten out of bed. I jumped away from the door, afraid he was coming out. But he began pacing the room – five steps to the window, five to the bed, like a pendulum. He struck a match. Mama began speaking again, 'Tell me do you believe it? Do you believe this nightmare?' She had stopped crying. 'Do you believe that Agasi ... Do you believe that Pavel, that Shurka ... Do you believe that they ... ?' She didn't complete her sentences, but it was clear. Then she spoke calmly and softly and said, 'I know that you can't believe it.' Papa replied in a strange, pleading voice, 'But Rufa-*djan* [his name for Elena's mother Ruth], how can I not believe?' After a pause he went on. 'They're not arresting you and me, after all.'[32]

There were other Bolsheviks, among them Piatnitsky, who were so committed to their Communist beliefs that they were ready to confess to the charges against them, even if they knew that they were innocent, if that was what the Party demanded.* According to Communist morality, a Bolshevik accused of crimes against the Party was expected to repent, to go down on his knees before the Party and accept its judgement against him. This is what Piatnitsky must have meant when he said on the eve of his arrest that if a sacrifice was needed for the Party he would 'bear it joyously'.

Many Bolsheviks attempted to prepare their family for the likelihood of their arrest and, as best they could, to protect them. Pyotr Potapov, a transport official on the Kama River, sent his family to visit relatives in Nizhny Novgorod a few days before his arrest in August 1937. 'We had not been on holiday for more than five years,' recalls his daughter. 'He sensed what lay ahead and was afraid for us. He wanted us to be out of the way when the NKVD came for him.' Lev Ilin, a senior official on the Murmansk railway, moved his family out of their spacious flat in Leningrad and put them in a small cooperative apartment, so that they would not be forced to share their living space with another family in the event of his arrest. He made sure that his wife, who had never worked, took a job in a textile factory, so that someone in the family would be able to support their daughter. He begged his wife to divorce him, in the hope that she would be protected from arrest herself, but she refused, on the grounds that it would be a 'shameful act of betrayal'.

---

*They are epitomized by Rubashov, the old revolutionary in Arthur Koestler's novel *Darkness at Noon* (1940), who confesses to the treason charges made against him at his trial – even though he knows that he is innocent – because he wants to serve the state.

There were bitter arguments between the couple on this point, right up to the day of Lev's arrest.[33]

Stanislav and Varvara Budkevich, who were both arrested in 1937, tried to prepare their fourteen-year-old daughter Maria to cope on her own. They trained her to go shopping by herself, taught her not to say a word about her parents if they were arrested and forced her to read about the show trials in the newspapers, so that she might understand the nature of the threat that might take them both away. 'I understood everything,' recalls Maria. 'My father was close to Tukhachevsky, he worked with him in the General Staff, and our house was full of military personnel, so I understood what was happening when people were arrested, one by one.' Maria's father was arrested on 8 July; her mother on 14 July.

Mama sensed that they would come for her that night. For a long time that evening we sat together on our own, without Andrei [Maria's younger brother], although Mama knew that I had exams the next morning. It was midnight when at last she said to me, 'It is getting late, off you go to bed.'

The next morning Maria awoke to find her mother gone – she had been arrested during the night – and the NKVD men searching through her room. By her bed her mother had left Maria a goodbye note with some money.[34]

The jurist Ilia Slavin was arrested on the night of 5 November 1937. He had not written the book commissioned by the NKVD about the reforging of Gulag labourers on the White Sea Canal. On the day of his arrest, Ilia was called into the Party's offices in Leningrad and offered the position of Director of the Institute of Law; the previous director had just been arrested. Slavin was relieved. He had been expecting the worst, but now it seemed he had been saved. He returned home in a cheerful mood. That evening the Slavin family was celebrating Ida's sixteenth birthday. As Ida recalls:

Mama laid out a delicious spread. My brother made a special 'birthday edition' of our wall-newspaper 'Hallelujah' [an agitational billboard maintained at home by the Slavin family] and became the pianist for the evening. I put on a smart new dress to receive my schoolfriends . . . Papa was in his best form: he played with us, fooled around just like a child, danced with all the girls, drank a lot and even sang his favourite song, 'The Nightingale'.

When the guests had gone, Ilia began to talk about his plans for the next summer holiday. 'He wanted us to spend it all together as a family and spoke of going to the Caucasus and the Black Sea.'

The NKVD came at 1 a.m. Ida remembers:

I was suddenly awoken by a bright light and a strange voice, telling me to get dressed quickly. An NKVD officer was standing at the door. He made half an effort to look away as I struggled to get dressed and then led me into Papa's office. There was Papa, sitting on a stool in the middle of the room, looking suddenly much older. Mama, my brother and his pregnant wife sat with me on the divan. The yardman stood in the doorway while the NKVD officer made himself at home . . .

I remember only certain moments from that night:

Looking around my father's office, the NKVD officer (I shall always remember his name: Beigel) would sigh from time to time: 'What a lot of books you have. I am a student, and I don't have this many books.' Leafing through the books, he would stop whenever he found one with an inscription to my father, pound his fist on the table and demand in a loud voice, 'Who is this author?'

Then in an almost tragi-comic scene Beigel told me to bring my German textbook. Theatrically (he had evidently played this scene in many households with children of my age) he turned to an article by Karl Radek at the end of the textbook. At that time Karl Radek had been arrested but had not yet been sentenced or listed in the press as an 'enemy of the people'. With a grand gesture Beigel tore the pages out of the textbook, lit them with a match, and said, as if he was a noble hero: 'Be thankful that this thing has been destroyed and that I won't have to take you away with your daddy.' I was too frightened to say anything. But then my father broke the silence, and said 'Thank you.' . . .

Aside from this officious Beigel the main thing engraved in my memory is the motionless figure of my father. I had never seen him like that before – so totally dejected, his spirit somehow gone, almost indifferent to the humiliation he was suffering. He was unlike himself . . . When I looked at him, there was no expression on his face, he did not see or feel my gaze. He just sat there in the middle of the room – motionless and silent. It was him – and yet not him.

The house-search went on all night. From the office they went into the dining room and then into my brother's room. The floor was covered with pages ripped from books and manuscripts which had been pulled out of the cupboards and glass-fronted cabinets, photographs from family albums, which had been carefully stored in a special trunk. Many of these things they took away. They also took a camera, a pair of binoculars (evidence of 'espionage') and a typewriter – our old Underwood on which my father had typed all his articles . . .

What was he thinking during that long night, as they leafed through the pages of his life? Did it destroy his faith? What terror did he feel when Beigel (that insignificant worm!) recorded the details of his Party membership as evidence of his crime?

It was morning when the search came to an end; everything was registered for confiscation, and father was led into the corridor. We followed him. The door to my parents' room was sealed. They told Papa to get dressed. Mama had his things all ready in a little case [it contained a pair of spectacles, toiletries, a handkerchief and 100 roubles cash].

Then my father broke his silence and said: 'Goodbye.' Mama clung to him and cried, while he stroked her head, saying over and over, 'Don't worry, it will be sorted out.'

That night destroyed something inside me. It shattered my belief in harmony and meaning in the world. In our family there had been a cult of our father. He stood on such a pedestal for us that, when he fell, it felt as if the whole world was ending. I was terrified to look him in the eye, in case he saw my fear. The NKVD men led Papa towards the door. I followed him. Suddenly he turned around to look at me once more. He could see the chaos of emotions inside me. Choked by tears, I threw myself at him. He whispered in my ear: 'Little one, my beloved daughter, there are mistakes in history, but remember – we started something great. Be a good Young Communist.'

'Quiet!' shouted Beigel. Then someone pulled me away from Papa.

'Farewell, my loved ones. Believe in justice . . .' – he wanted to say something else but they took him out and down the stairs.[35]

The idea that Ida might be arrested was not an idle threat by the NKVD officer. At sixteen years of age, she could be arrested and

Ida Slavina (left) and her parents, 1937

imprisoned, and even executed, for the same crimes as any adult. In 1935, the Soviet government had lowered the age of criminal responsibility to just twelve – partly with the aim of threatening those in prison with the arrest of their children if they refused to confess to their crimes (a second decree that year allowed the arrest and imprisonment of relatives of anyone who was in prison for crimes against the state). In effect a hostage system was declared. Many Bolsheviks were threatened with the arrest of their relatives during the interrogations that preceded the show trials. Kamenev, for example, was threatened with the execution of his son: he agreed to sign his confession on Stalin's personal assurances that his family would not be touched. Zinoviev did the same. Ivan Smirnov gave in during his interrogation when he saw his daughter being roughly treated by the guards. Stanislav Kosior withstood brutal tortures but cracked when his sixteen-year-old daughter was brought into the room and raped in front of him.[36]

Whatever Stalin promised these Bolsheviks before their trial, once they had been shot, he ordered the arrest of many of their relatives. Kamenev's son was shot in 1939 (a younger son was sent to an orphanage and had his name changed to Glebov). Kamenev's wife, who had been sent into penal exile in 1935, was retried in 1938 and shot in 1941. Zinoviev's son was shot in 1937. His sister was sent to the Vorkuta camps and later shot. Three other sisters, two nephews, a niece, a cousin and a brother-in-law were sent to labour camps. Three of Zinoviev's brothers and a nephew were also shot. Smirnov's daughter was imprisoned. His wife was shot in one of the Kotlas labour camps in 1938. Virtually all the Trotsky clan was murdered by the NKVD between 1936 and 1938: Trotsky's brother Aleksandr; his sister Olga; his first wife Aleksandra Sokolovskaia; his sons Lev and Sergei; and both husbands of his daughter Zinaida (who had committed suicide in 1933).[37]

Stalin's obsession with punishing the kin of his enemies was perhaps something he had picked up from Georgia: vendettas between clans were part of politics in the Caucasus. In the Bolshevik elite, family and clans intersected with political allegiances; alliances were made through marriages; careers were broken through ties of blood to oppositionists and enemies. As Stalin saw it, the family was collectively responsible for the behaviour of its individual members. If a man had been arrested as an 'enemy of the people', his wife was guilty automatically, because unless she had denounced him, it was assumed that she had shared her husband's views or had tried to protect him. At the very least she was guilty of lack of vigilance. Stalin considered the repression of these relatives as a necessary measure to remove disgruntled people from society. Asked why the families of Stalin's 'enemies' had been repressed, Molotov explained in 1986: 'They had to be isolated. Otherwise, they would have spread all kinds of complaints, and society would have been infected by a certain amount of demoralization.'[38]

Julia Piatnitskaia lived in expectation of her own arrest. She confessed her worries to the diary she started keeping in the days leading up to the arrest of Osip on 7 July. Her fears floated on a sea of daily problems and anxieties. Vladimir, her younger son, had to be brought back from the Crimea, where he had been at the Artek camp for Pioneers since the start of June. Julia was afraid that he might be taken to an orphanage by the NKVD, if she was arrested before she could arrange for relatives and friends to take him in. Her older son Igor had just turned sixteen. Before the arrest of his father he had been eager to make a name for himself in the Komsomol, but everything was different now, and he too was in danger of arrest. Julia tried to deal with Igor's mixed emotions – anger at his father, grief at his loss, despondency and shame – while struggling to contain her own, equally confused feelings. 'Igor spends the whole day reading on his bed,' Julia noted in her diary on 11 July.

He says nothing about Papa, nor about the actions of his former 'comrades'. Sometimes I express my foul and poisonous thoughts, but he, like the Young Communist he is, forbids me to speak like that. Sometimes he says: 'Mama, I can't stand you when you're like this, I could murder you.'[39]

Julia's immediate concern was to make ends meet. Like many wives deprived of their husbands in the Great Terror, she was so preoccupied by the daily struggle to survive, so traumatized by her sudden fall in status, that she barely stopped to think about the danger she was in.[40] During the house search Julia lost her savings book and any valuables she might have been able to sell. All she had was a tiny salary from her office job, which hardly sufficed to feed the five dependants who were living in her flat (her sons, her aged father and stepmother and their daughter Liudmila, who did not have a job). They also had a boxer dog. The family lived on soup and kasha. Accustomed to a life of privilege as the wife of a senior Bolshevik, Julia found it hard to adapt to her poverty. She felt bitter and sorry for herself. She even went to the Party offices and complained to an official, who told her to toughen up and get used to the lifestyle of the proletariat. She spent much of her spare time wandering round the city in a fruitless search for a better job. The steel construction trust (TsKMash) had no room for 'specialists' ('We are not Fascist Germany,' the official said to Julia). Even the factory at the Butyrki prison had no need for workers of 'her sort' (i.e. wives of 'enemies'). 'The factory official didn't even look at my papers,' Julia wrote in her diary, 'he didn't want to ask me anything: he just looked at me and said "no".' Work colleagues refused to help. 'Everyone avoids me,' Julia wrote. 'Yet I so much need support, even just the slightest attention or advice.' At home, meanwhile, tensions grew as the situation steadily worsened. Julia's half-sister and stepmother frequently complained about the lack of food and blamed Osip for their troubles. They even tried to get Julia evicted from the apartment. After a few weeks, Liudmila got a job and moved out with her parents to another flat rather than 'be dragged down' with the Piatnitskys. 'If all of us can't be saved,' Liudmila said, 'then let those who are able save themselves.' Julia wondered if Liudmila and her parents felt ashamed of their behaviour. She doubted it:

It is only shameful that for seven years they were fed by Piatnitsky, Liuba [Liudmila] got to go to a good school, and they lived in a good apartment. As soon as we get into trouble, they think only about how to run as fast as possible from me and my children – from the unfortunates.[41]

Not long after they moved out, Julia and her sons were evicted from their home and placed in a smaller apartment on a lower floor of the House on the Embankment. They shared the apartment with the family of an Armenian Bolshevik who had been arrested in the spring. Julia was desperate, she felt as if her life was collapsing and she thought of suicide. In her desperation she went to see a neighbour, the only person in the House on the Embankment who was not afraid to speak to her, and talked about her woes. The old lady told her not to feel so sorry for herself: there were many officials who lived in smaller rooms. Besides, the woman said, Julia was better off without Piatnitsky, because, she explained, 'you were not getting along so well'. Now she only had to think about herself and her two sons, not about her husband any more. Reflecting on the conversation, Julia wrote in her diary that night: 'It is true that he did not spend much time with us. He was always working.

And it was obvious to everyone who came to scrounge from us – that is almost everyone – that we were not getting along.'[42] It was not the only doubt that Julia would have about her husband over the next year.

2

The diary of the writer Mikhail Prishvin, 29 November 1937:

Our Russian people, like snow-covered trees, are so overburdened with the problems of survival, and want so much to talk to one another about it, that they simply lack the strength to hold out any more. But as soon as someone gives in, he is overheard by someone else – and he disappears! People know they can get into trouble for a single conversation; and so they enter into a conspiracy of silence with their friends. My dear friend N . . . was delighted to spot me in a crowded [train] compartment, and when at last a seat was free, he sat down next to me. He wanted to say something but was unable to say it in such a crowd. He became so tense that every time he prepared himself to speak he looked around at the people on one side of us, and then at the people on the other side, and all he could bring himself to say was: 'Yes . . .' And I said the same in return to him, and in this way, for two hours, we travelled together from Moscow to Zagorsk:

  'Yes, Mikhail Mikhailovich.'

  'Yes, Georgii Eduardovich.'[43]

Talking could be dangerous at the best of Soviet times, but during the Great Terror a few careless words were all it took for somebody to vanish for ever. Informers were everywhere. 'Today a man talks freely only with his wife – at night, with the blankets pulled over his head,' the writer Isaak Babel once remarked. Prishvin wrote in his diary that among his friends there were 'only two or three old men' to whom he could talk freely, without fear of giving rise to malicious rumours or denunciations.[44]

  The Great Terror effectively silenced the Soviet people. 'We were brought up to keep our mouths shut,' recalls Rezeda Taisina, whose father was arrested in 1936.

'You'll get into trouble for your tongue' – that's what people said to us children all the time. We went through life afraid to talk. Mama used to say that every other person was an informer. We were afraid of our neighbours, and especially of the police. I am still afraid to talk. I cannot stand up for myself, or speak out in public, I always give in without saying a word. That's in my character, because of the way I was brought up when I was a child. Even today, if I see a policeman, I begin to shake with fear.[45]

Maria Drozdova grew up in a strictly religious peasant family in Tver province. In 1930, the Drozdovs fled the countryside to escape the collectivization of their village. With false documents they moved to Krasnoe Selo near Leningrad, where Maria's father worked in a furniture factory and her mother Anna in a hospital. Anna was an illiterate peasant woman. Convinced that the Bolsheviks were the Antichrist, whose agents heard and saw everything she did, she was afraid to go out in public or to talk outside the family's room in the communal apartment where they lived. When her father, a church warden, was arrested in 1937, Anna became paralysed with fear. She would not leave the house. She became afraid of talking in the room, in case the neighbours over-heard. In the evenings she was terrified of switching on the lamp, in case it drew the attention of the police. She was even afraid to go to the toilet, in case she wiped herself with a piece of newspaper which contained an article with Stalin's name.[46]

Among acquaintances there was a tacit agreement not to talk about political events. Anyone could be arrested and forced by the police to incriminate his friends by reporting such conversations as evidence of their 'counter-revolutionary' activities. In this climate, to initiate politi-cal discussions with anyone except one's closest friends was to invite suspicion of being an informer or provocateur.

Vera Turkina recalls the silence with which her friends and neighbours responded to the arrest of her father, the chairman of the provincial court in Perm:

There were three girls in the house opposite ours whose father had also been arrested . . . We all tried to avoid the subject. 'He is not here, he has gone away, somewhere', is all that we would say . . . My father was a victim of his 'loose tongue' – that's what we understood in our family – he was too direct and outspoken, and somewhere he had said more than he should have done. The belief that talk had been the cause of his arrest reinforced our own silence.[47]

Silent stoicism was a common reaction to the loss of friends and relatives. As Emma Gershtein wrote about the poet Mandelshtam in 1937: 'He did not speak of departed and now dead friends. No-one then did . . . Anything but tears! Such was the character of those years.'[48]

Silence reigned in many families. People did not talk about arrested relatives. They destroyed their letters, or hid them from their children, hoping it would protect them. Even in the home it was dangerous to talk about such relatives, because, as it was said, 'the walls have ears'. After the arrest of her husband, Sergei Kruglov, in 1937, Anastasia and her two children were moved into a communal apartment, where a thin partition wall separated them from the family of an NKVD operative in the neighbouring room. 'Everything was audible, they could hear us sneeze, even hear us talk in the quietest whisper. Mama was always telling us to be silent,' recalls Tatiana Kruglova. For thirty years, they lived in fear of talking, because they were convinced that their NKVD neighbour was reporting what they said (in fact he kept them in this state of fear because he wanted quiet and obedient neighbours).[49]

After the arrest of her father, Natalia Danilova was taken by her mother to live with her family, the Osorgins, where all talk about her father was prohibited. The Osorgins were a noble family, and several of its members had been arrested by the Bolsheviks, including the husband of Natalia's aunt Mania, who ruled the household with her forceful personality. 'She was hostile to my father, perhaps because he was a peasant and a socialist,' Natalia recalls. 'She seemed to think he was guilty, that he had merited his own arrest, and that through his actions he had brought trouble to the family. She forced this version of events upon the rest of us. She alone had the right to speak about such things; the rest of us could only whisper in dissent.'[50]

Families developed special rules of conversation. They learned to speak elliptically, to allude to ideas and opinions in a manner that concealed their meaning from strangers, neighbours and servants. Emma Gershtein recalls a cousin's wife, Margarita Gershtein, a veteran oppositionist, who was living with her family in Moscow for a while. One day Margarita was talking about the pointlessness of opposing Stalin and was in the middle of a sentence ('Of course, we could rub out Stalin, but . . .') when

the door opened and into the dining-room came Polya, our housemaid. I shuddered and was terrified, but Margarita, without altering her lazy pose, rounded off the phrase in exactly the same intonation, in the same clear voice: 'so,

Emmochka, go ahead and buy the silk, don't hesitate. You deserve a new dress after all you've done.' When the housemaid had left, Margarita explained that one should never give the impression of having been caught unawares. 'And don't creep about furtively or look uneasily around you.'[51]

Children, talkative by nature, were particularly dangerous. Many parents took the view that the less their children knew the safer everyone would be. Antonina Moiseyeva was born in 1927 to a peasant family in Saratov province. The Moiseyevs were categorized as 'kulaks' and exiled to a 'special settlement' in the Urals in 1929. After their return to Chusovoe, a town near Perm, in 1936, Antonina's mother made a point of telling her children:

'You must not judge anything, or you will be arrested,' she always said. We would stand all night in a queue for bread, and she would say to us, 'You must not judge! It's none of your business if the government doesn't have bread.' Mama told us that it was a sin to pass judgement. 'Hold your tongue!' she would always say when we left the house.[52]

Vilgelm Tell grew up in a Hungarian family in Moscow. His father was arrested in one of the 'national operations' in 1938, when Vilgelm was nine years old. As far as he recalls, there were no specific warnings or instructions from his mother or his grandparents about how he should behave, but he sensed the atmosphere of fear:

I knew subconsciously that I had to keep quiet, that I could not speak, or say what I thought. For example, when we travelled in a crowded tram, I knew I had to remain silent, that I could not mention anything, not even things I saw out the window . . . I also sensed that everybody felt the same way. It was always quiet in public places like a tram. If people spoke, it was only about something trivial, like where they had been shopping. They never spoke about their work or serious things.[53]

Oksana Golovnia remembers travelling on a crowded Moscow bus with her father, Anatoly, the film-maker, and mentioning her 'uncle Lodia' (the film director Pudovkin):

Papa whispered in my ear: 'Never say anybody's name when you are in a public place.' To my inquiring and frightened look, he then said aloud: 'Don't those little dumplings look just like little ears!' I knew what he meant to say – that someone sitting near by was listening. Papa's lesson stood me in good stead for life.[54]

In his diary of 1937 Prishvin wrote that people were becoming so adept at concealing meaning in their speech that they were in danger of losing the capacity to speak the truth altogether.

10 July:
Behaviour in Moscow: one cannot speak of anything or with anyone. The whole secret of behaviour is to sense what something means, and who means it, without saying anything. You have to eliminate completely in yourself any remnant of the need to 'speak from the heart'.[55]

Arkadii Mankov noted a similar phenomenon in his diary:

It is pointless to talk about the public mood. There is silence, as if nothing has happened. People talk only in secret, behind the scenes and privately. The only people who express their views in public are the drunks.[56]

As people drew into themselves, the social realm inevitably diminished. 'People have completely ceased to confide in each other,' Prishvin wrote in his diary on 9 October. It was becoming a society of whisperers:

The huge mass of the lower class simply goes about its work and whispers quietly. Some have nothing to whisper about: for them 'everything is as it ought to be'. Others whisper to themselves in solitude, retreating quietly into their work. Many have learned to keep completely silent . . . – as if lying in a grave.[57]

With the end of genuine communication, mistrust spread throughout society. People concealed their true selves behind public masks. Outwardly they conformed to the public modes of correct Soviet behaviour; inwardly they lived in a realm of private thought, inscrutable to public view. In this atmosphere fear and terror grew. Since no one knew what was concealed behind the mask, it was assumed that people who seemed to be normal Soviet citizens could in fact be spies or enemies. On the basis of this assumption denunciations and reports of 'hidden enemies' became credible, not just to the general public but to colleagues, neighbours and friends.

People sought refuge in a private world of truth. Some people took to diary-writing during the Great Terror. In spite of all the risks, keeping a diary was a way to carve out a private realm free of dissembling, to voice one's doubts and fears at a time when it was dangerous to speak.[58] The writer Prishvin confessed his greatest fears to his diary. In 1936, he had been attacked by literary bureaucrats in the Writers' Union for a bitter comment he had made at a New Year's party, a comment he now feared would cost him his freedom. 'I am very frightened,' he wrote, 'that these words will drop into the file of an informer reporting on the characteristics of Prishvin the writer.' Prishvin withdrew from the public sphere and retreated to his diary. He filled its pages with a microscopic scrawl, barely legible with a magnifying glass, to conceal his thoughts from the police in the event of his arrest and the seizure of the diary. For Prishvin, his diary was an 'affirmation of individuality' – a place to exercise his inner freedom and speak in his own true voice. 'One either writes a diary for oneself,' Prishvin mused, 'to dig down to one's inner self and converse with oneself, or one writes to become involved in society and secretly express one's views on it.'[59] For Prishvin, it was both. He filled his diaries with dissident reflections on Stalin, on the destructive influence of Soviet mass culture, and on the indestructibility of the individual human spirit.

The playwright Aleksandr Afinogenov began keeping a diary in 1926. He filled it with self-criticisms and thoughts on how he could improve himself as a Communist. Then, in the middle of the 1930s, he ran foul of the regime: the psychological perspective of his proletarian plays fell out of favour with the literary authorities, now committed to the doctrines of Socialist Realism. His play *The Lie* (1933) was attacked by Stalin, who said it lacked a positive Communist hero dedicated to the workers' cause. The literary group he belonged to – led by the former head of RAPP (Russian Association of Proletarian Writers) Leopold Averbakh – was said to be a 'Trotskyist agency in literature' plotting the downfall of the Soviet regime. In the spring of 1937, Afinogenov was expelled from the Party and evicted from his Moscow apartment by the NKVD. He moved to his dacha in Peredelkino, where he lived with his wife and daughter in almost total seclusion, not speaking to anyone. Old friends turned their back on him. One day, on a train, he overheard a conversation between two army officers who expressed their satisfaction that 'the Japanese spy Averbakh' had finally been caught and that his 'henchman Afinogenov' was in jail awaiting trial. As Afinogenov retreated to his inner world, his diary changed in character. There were still moments when he criticized himself, when he accepted the charges against him and tried to purge himself as a Communist, but there was more introspection, more pyschological immediacy, and more use of the 'I' rather than the 'he' which he had used before to refer to himself. The diary became a secret refuge for his private thoughts and reflections:

2 November 1937
Coming home, I sit down with my diary and think only of my private corner of the world, which remains untouched by politics, and I write about that. Now that I have been excluded from the general flow of life, I suddenly feel the need to talk with people about everything that's going on . . . but now that yearning for communication can only be fulfilled in these pages, because nobody will speak with me.[60]

Yevgeniia (Zhenia) Yevangulova started keeping a diary in December 1937, the year both her parents were arrested. The diary became a place for her to pour her emotions and keep up what she called an 'internal conversation' with her parents, who had disappeared in the Gulag. 'The burning hope will not leave me that one day my loved ones will read this diary, so I must try to make it true,' she wrote in the opening entry. For Yevangulova, a student at the Leningrad Institute of Technology, the diary was increasingly important as a connection to her individual self, which she feared was being submerged in the institute's collective way of life. She wrote on 8 March 1938: 'Maybe I have not expressed this correctly: my inner self has not gone away – whatever is inside a personality can never disappear – but it is deeply hidden, and I no longer feel its presence within me.' She felt that her personality could only be expressed through genuine connection with others – but there was no one. Her fellow students mistrusted her as the daughter of 'enemies of the people'; all she had was her diary. As she wrote in December 1939: 'Sometimes I feel a desperate yearning to find a true friend, someone who could understand me, somebody with whom I could share all my agonizing thoughts, apart from this silent diary.'[61]

Arkadii Mankov, like Yevangulova, yearned for human connection. He decided to show his diaries to a fellow student on the course he attended at the Public Library in Leningrad. Mankov's diary was filled with anti-Soviet thoughts, so it was an act of immense trust, even foolishness, to reveal it to a man he hardly knew, but as he confessed to his diary, he had acted out of 'loneliness, the daily, endless loneliness in which I lead my aimless life'.[62]

Prishvin too succumbed to the temptation for human connection. In December 1938, he asked a friend to help him find a secretary who could assist him with editing his diaries. He realized how dangerous it could be to let a 'stranger into my laboratory and understand the whole of me'. That night he had a nightmare. He was crossing a big open square and lost his hat. He felt that he had been laid bare. Asking a policeman where his hat had gone, he suddenly recalled, as he analysed it in his diary, that he had 'asked a stranger to get involved in the most intimate details of my life. The loss of my hat of secrecy had exposed me.' The woman who arrived at Prishvin's house a few days later for an interview was also apprehensive about the idea of working on the diaries of a man she did not know. She suggested that the two of them should get to know each other before they started on the work. They talked without a break for eight hours. They fell in love and within a year they were married.[63]

3

Informers were everywhere – in factories and schools and offices, in public places and communal apartments. By any estimate, at the height of the Great Terror millions of people were reporting on their colleagues, friends and neighbours, although it is hard to be precise because there are only scattered data and anecdotal evidence. According to one senior police official, every fifth Soviet office worker was an informer for the NKVD. Another claimed that regular informers numbered 5 per cent of the adult population in the major urban areas (in popular belief the number was higher still). The level of surveillance varied widely between cities. In Moscow, which was heavily policed, there was at least one informer for every six or seven families, according to a former NKVD official. In Kharkov, by contrast, there were only fifty informers in a city of 840,000 people (that is one informer for every 16,800 people), according to a former NKVD man, who claimed to have controlled all the city's informers. Between these two extremes the city of Kuibyshev may be more representative of the Soviet Union as a whole: in 1938, the police claimed to have about a thousand informers in a population of 400,000 people.[64] These figures represent only the registered informers, regularly used by the police and usually rewarded in some form (with money, jobs, housing, special rations, or protection from arrest). They do not include the millions of paid 'reliables' (factory and office workers, student activists, watchmen, janitors, etc.) who acted as the eyes and ears of the police in every nook and cranny of society.[65] Nor do they count the everyday reporting and denunciation – unsolicited by the NKVD – which made the police state so powerful. Everybody knew that 'loyal Soviet citizens' were expected to report suspicious conversations they had overheard: fear of punishment for 'lack of vigilance' compelled many people to collaborate.

There were two broad categories: voluntary informers, who were usually motivated by material rewards, political beliefs or malice towards their victims; and involuntary informers, who were entrapped by police threats or promises to help arrested relatives. It is difficult to condemn the informers in the second category: many found themselves in almost impossible situations where anybody might have given in to pressure from the NKVD.

In 1943, the writer Simonov was visited by 'X', a former classmate at the Literary Institute. After the arrest of his father, 'X' had been threatened with expulsion from the institute, unless he agreed to write reports about the conversations he overheard among his fellow students. From 1937 on, 'X' had worked as an informer for the NKVD. Moved by guilt and feelings of remorse, he sought out Simonov to warn him that he had reported their conversations. 'X' was 'overcome with shame,' he said. He was perhaps a little frightened too, for by 1943 Simonov had become a famous writer, with good connections to the Kremlin; it was even possible that he already knew about the reports of his former friend. 'X' told Simonov that he would kill himself if he discovered that anyone had suffered as a consequence of his informing. He explained that he had tried to keep his reports free of incriminating evidence, but he still felt that by his actions 'he had made his life unbearable'.[66]

Wolfgang Leonhard recalls an encounter with a fellow student in 1939, a girl with whom he had always felt that he could speak quite openly. They would go for walks in the parks of Moscow and discuss the grand political issues of the moment. One day she confessed that she had given in to pressure from the NKVD to write reports on what her fellow students were saying. Sad and burdened by her conscience, she wanted to warn Leonhard that, although she had not yet been required to report on him, they should not meet and have their conversations any more.[67]

Valerii Frid recalls how he was recruited as an informer in 1941. He was in the Komsomol and studying at the All-Union State Film Institute (VGIK), which had been evacuated from Moscow to Alma-Ata in Kazakhstan. The food situation was desperate. Frid was involved in a petty scam involving forged ration cards. One day he was called in to the offices of the NKVD. His interrogators knew all about the ration cards and warned that he would be expelled from the Komsomol and the institute unless he agreed to their demands and proved himself to be a 'Soviet person' by reporting on his fellow students. Interrogated through the night, he was threatened with violence and told that he would be put on trial. Frid gave in and signed an agreement to write the reports. As soon as he had signed, his interrogators shook his hand and became kind and friendly towards him. They said that he would not get into trouble with his ration cards – in fact he was free to continue dealing – and gave him a special number to call should he have any problems with the police. On his return to the hostel Frid broke down in tears. For three days he could not sleep or eat. In the end he wrote reports on only three students. He made sure the reports were very general and contained no incriminating facts. The NKVD officer, a small man with a complete set of gold teeth, to whom Frid gave these reports, was not pleased. But Frid was saved from any punishment by VGIK's return to Moscow in 1943.[68]

Sofia Ozemblovskaia became an informer when she was just seventeen. She was born into a Polish noble family in Osipovichi near Minsk in Belarus. After the Revolution of 1917, her parents turned themselves into peasant farmers, but during the collectivization of agriculture they were exiled as 'kulaks' to the Komi region of the North. In 1937, the family returned to Osipovichi, but they were later rearrested in one of the 'national operations' against the Poles and sent to a 'special settlement' near Perm. Sofia decided to escape. 'I had to get away to give myself a chance in life,' she explains. Sofia enrolled at a factory school – the quickest means of getting some 'proletarian origins' – and then entered the medical college in Kudymkar, a town near Perm in the Urals. No one asked her any questions about her 'kulak' origins. They did not even ask for her passport, which she did not have. Six months later, she was called in to the offices of the NKVD. 'I thought they were going to put me into jail because I had run away,' recalls Sofia. Indeed she was told that she would have to work for the NKVD if she did not want to be expelled from the college for hiding her social origins. Her task was to start up conversations with her fellow students about political events and write reports on everything they said. Sofia was given a passport. With the protection of the NKVD, she graduated from medical college and had a successful career in the ambulance service in Perm. Looking back, she feels no remorse for her actions, even though she knows that many students were arrested as a direct consequence of her reports. She believes that her actions were the necessary price of survival for a 'kulak' daughter in the Stalin years. Sofia married the son of a senior NKVD officer. When her children were growing up, she told them nothing about her police activities. But in the 1990s, 'when there was freedom and nothing left to fear', she decided to come clean:

I decided to tell my children and grandchildren everything. They were very glad. My grandson said: 'Oh, Granny, you are very clever to remember everything. We will remember this all our lives – how you were repressed, how our parents were repressed.'[69]

In her memoirs Olga Adamova-Sliuzberg tells the story of a young informer, the son of a Bolshevik executed in the Great Terror, whose task was to become acquainted with other children whose parents had been arrested. He reported every word of dissatisfaction they said, every doubt and question they raised. Many of his friends were arrested as a result of his reports. Olga met some of them in the Butyrki prison after her own arrest in 1949. She asked them what they thought about the boy. They were strangely understanding. The general opinion was that he was a 'good boy, but naive, who believed every slogan he heard and every word he read in the newspapers'. The boy's mother, 'a wonderful and honest woman', insisted to Olga that her son had not acted out of any malice but from the highest convictions. 'She talked a lot about his exceptional kindness, his brilliance and honesty.' Perhaps the boy felt he was acting patriotically by denouncing his own friends for the cause of Soviet power – just as the boy hero Pavlik Morozov had done in denouncing his father.[70]

Undoubtedly, during the Great Terror, many people wrote denunciations in the sincere conviction that they were performing their patriotic duty as Soviet citizens. They believed the propaganda about 'spies' and 'enemies' and set out to expose them, even among their friends. But above all, they were afraid of getting into trouble if somebody they knew was arrested and they had failed to denounce them: it was a crime to conceal one's contacts with the enemy and 'lack of vigilance' was itself the cause of thousands of arrests. In the climate of universal fear people rushed to denounce others before they were denounced by them. This mad scramble of denunciations may not explain the enormous numbers of arrests in the Great Terror – most of the NKVD's victims were arrested en masse in the 'national' and 'kulak operations' which did not depend on denunciations but on a prepared list of names – but it does explain why so many people were sucked into the police system as informers. Hysterical citizens would appear at the NKVD and Party offices with the names of relatives and friends who might be 'enemies of the people'. They would write with details about their colleagues and acquaintances, listing even a single meeting with people who had been connected with these 'enemies'. One old woman wrote to the Party office of her factory to inform them that her sister had once worked as a temporary cleaner in the Kremlin and had cleaned the office of a man who was later arrested.[71]

Fear drove people to try to purge themselves – to put themselves on the side of the pure – by removing the stain of contact with potential 'enemies'. Many of the most fanatical informers were people with a 'spoilt biography' (the children of 'kulaks' and 'class enemies' or former oppositionists) who had more reason than most to fear arrest. Informing on their friends became a way to prove their worthiness as 'Soviet citizens'. The NKVD had a deliberate policy of recruiting informers from vulnerable groups. They often picked on the relatives of the arrested who feared arrest themselves. Aleksandr Karpetnin, a former NKVD operative who was himself arrested in 1938, recalls his training in the recruitment of informers:

You would look for people who had something suspicious in their background. Let's say a woman whose husband had been arrested. The conversation would go like this:

'Are you a true Soviet citizen?'

'Yes, I am.'

'Are you ready to prove it? Everyone says they're good citizens.'

'Yes of course I'm ready.'

'Then help us. We won't ask much. If you notice any anti-Soviet acts or conversations, let us know. We can meet once a week. Beforehand you should write down what you noticed, who said what, who was present when they spoke.

That's all. Then we'll know that you really are a good Soviet citizen. We'll help you if you have any problems at work. If you're sacked or demoted, we'll help you.'

That was it. After that the person would agree.[72]

Olga Adamova-Sliuzberg tells the story of a young woman named Zina, a mathematics teacher from Gorkii, whom she met in the Lubianka jail. Zina had been arrested for failing to denounce one of her teachers, a lecturer in dialectical materialism who came to Gorkii from Moscow once a week. In conversations with Zina the lecturer had openly expressed his criticisms of the Stalinist regime. Because he stayed in Gorkii in a dormitory, he had used Zina's apartment to entertain his friends and had kept a trunk of his books there. When the NKVD carried out their search, it turned out the books were Trotskyist. Zina acknowledged her guilt. She decided to expiate her sin and 'clean all the stains from [her] conscience' by informing on other 'enemies' to the NKVD. She told her interrogators about a certain professor who had given lectures at her institute. One day there had been a power cut while the professor was performing an experiment. There were no candles, so, as she explained, Zina

split a ruler and lit a splinter from it, as the peasants do, to provide light. The professor finished his experiment by the light of the splinter and at the end remarked [poking fun at Stalin's famous phrase], 'Life has become better, life has become more joyous. God be praised, we have reached the age of the splinter!'

The professor was arrested. Zina did not feel that she had acted wrongly in denouncing him – just a little awkward when she had to confront him during his interrogation. Asked by Olga what she thought about having 'ruined someone's life' for such a petty thing, Zina replied: 'There are no petty things in politics. Like you, I failed to understand at first the criminal significance of his remark, but later I realized.'[73]

Many denunciations were motivated by malice. The quickest way to remove a rival was to denounce him as an 'enemy'. Lower-class resentments of the Bolshevik elite fuelled the Great Terror. Workers denounced bosses, peasants denounced kolkhoz chairmen, if they were too strict in their demands. Servants were frequently employed by the NKVD to inform against their employers. Markoosha Fischer, the Russian wife of an American journalist, employed a nanny who believed in 'enemies'.

She 'truly represented the mentality of the woman and man on the street', Markoosha wrote. 'She was not bothered by political doubts and accepted every official utterance as gospel.'[74] There were families that lived in constant fear of their servants.

In 1935, the NKVD placed new servants in the homes of many Party workers in Leningrad, as part of the campaign to increase surveillance following the assassination of Kirov. Anna Karpitskaia and Pyotr Nizovtsev, senior Party officials in Leningrad, were forced to sack their old housekeeper Masha, the devout Old Believer who had made herbal remedies. The new housekeeper, Grusha, was a 'stern, unpleasant woman', recalls Anna's daughter Marksena, who was then aged twelve. 'She had been sent to us by the police so that she could keep an eye on us.' Marksena and her younger half-brothers realized instinctively that they were not to talk in Grusha's presence. 'We barely ever said a word to her,' Marksena recalls. Grusha slept in the kitchen, apart from the family rooms, where Milia, the nanny who had been with the family for many years, was allowed to live. Grusha was also treated as a servant, unlike Milia or their old housekeeper, who had been considered part of the family. Anna and Pyotr were hostile to Stalin. Marksena remembers whispered conversations in which her parents shared their suspicions that Stalin was responsible for Kirov's death. They could have spoken openly in the presence of Masha – her religious background as an Old Believer had been a guarantee of her silence – but it was dangerous to voice such sentiments when Grusha was around. In July 1937, Marksena's parents were arrested (they were both shot in the autumn of that year). Her younger brothers were taken to an orphanage. Marksena moved to a communal apartment with her nanny Milia. Grusha disappeared.[75]

In this atmosphere of mistrust, hatred and malice it did not take a lot for petty arguments and jealousies to turn into denunciations. In 1937, Boris Molotkov, a country doctor from the Gorkii region, was approached by the district NKVD officer, an old friend of the family, who asked him to perform an abortion for his mistress. When Molotkov refused (abortions were illegal at that time), the NKVD officer arranged a series of informers to denounce the doctor as a 'counter-revolutionary'. Boris was arrested and imprisoned in the district jail. His wife was also arrested on trumped-up charges for the murder of a worker in the local hospital.[76]

Sexual and romantic interests often played a part in these deadly arguments. Unwanted lovers, wives and husbands – they were all denounced in large numbers in the Great Terror. Nikolai Sakharov was an engineer. His father was a priest who had been executed in 1937, but Nikolai was valued for his expertise in industry, and thought this would protect him from arrest. But then one day someone took an interest in his wife and denounced him as an 'enemy of the people'. Lipa Kaplan got into trouble with her factory boss when she refused his sexual demands. The boss arranged for an informer to denounce Lipa on the basis of some comment she had made after Kirov's murder three years earlier. At that time she had not been arrested (the denunciation was considered too absurd) but in 1937 it was sufficient to send her to Kolyma for ten years.[77]

Career motives and material rewards provided incentives for nearly all informers, although these motives were often mixed with political beliefs and fears in complex ways. Thousands of lower-ranking officials made their way up the Soviet hierarchy by reporting on their bosses (as the regime had encouraged them to do). One man, Ivan Miachin, promoted his career by denouncing no less than fourteen Party and Soviet leaders in Azerbaijan between February and November 1937. Justifying his activities, Miachin later said, 'We thought this was what we had to do ... Everybody was writing.' Perhaps Miachin thought that he was displaying vigilance. Perhaps he derived malicious pleasure from ruining the lives of his superiors, or pride from helping the police. There were informers of that type: busy-body letter-writers who carefully numbered their reports and signed them 'One of us' (*svoi*) or 'Partisan' to demonstrate their loyalty. But personal promotion, better pay and rations, or the promise of more living space, certainly played their part. When an apartment was vacated by the arrest of its inhabitants, it was often taken over by the NKVD officers, or divided up and occupied by other servitors of the Stalinist regime, such as office workers and chauffeurs, some of whom had no doubt been rewarded for giving information on the previous occupants.[78]

Ivan Malygin was an engineer in Sestroretsk, north of Leningrad. He was highly skilled and respected by the workers in his factory, who called him the 'tsar-engineer' and even helped his family when he was arrested by the NKVD. Malygin was something of a local celebrity. He wrote textbooks, popular pamphlets, and articles for the Soviet press.

He lived with his wife and their two children on the outskirts of the town in a large wooden house, which he had built himself. But, as often happens, his wealth and fame attracted jealousy. Malygin was arrested on the basis of a denunciation by a colleague at the factory, who was envious of his success. He claimed that Malygin used his house to maintain secret contacts with the Finns. It turned out that the denunci-

The Malygin house in Sestroretsk, 1930s

ation had been organized by a small group of NKVD officers, who forced Malygin to sell them his house for 7,000 roubles (it had recently been valued at nearly half a million). The officers threatened to arrest his wife if he refused to sell. Malygin was shot. His wife and children were evicted from the house, which was taken over by the NKVD officers and their families.[79] Their descendants live there to this day.

To make a career in the years of the Great Terror necessarily involved moral compromise, if not by outright informing, then by silent collusion with the Stalinist regime. Simonov, whose own career took off in these years, wrote with extraordinary candour and remorse about what he saw as the collaboration of the silent Soviet majority in the Great Terror. In his memoirs, dictated on his death-bed in 1979, Simonov accused himself:

To be honest about those times, it is not only Stalin that you cannot forgive, but you yourself. It is not that you did something bad – maybe you did nothing wrong, at least on the face of it – but that you became accustomed to evil. The events that took place in 1937–8 now appear extraordinary, diabolical, but to you, then a young man of 22 or 24, they became a kind of norm, almost ordinary. You lived in the midst of these events, blind and deaf to everything, you saw and heard nothing when people all around you were shot and killed, when people all around you disappeared.

Seeking to explain this detachment, Simonov recalled his own reaction to the arrest in 1939 of Mikhail Koltsov, a hugely influential writer, whose reports from the Spanish Civil War were an inspiration to the young literary circles in which Simonov moved. Deep down Simonov had never believed that Koltsov was a spy (as he confessed to the writer Fadeyev in 1949), yet somehow at the time he had managed to suppress his doubts. Whether out of fear and cowardice, or the desire to believe the state, or simply from an instinct to avoid subversive thoughts, he had made a small interior accommodation in order to conform to the necessities of the Stalinist regime. He had realigned his moral compass so as to navigate his way through the moral morass of the Great Terror with his own career and beliefs intact.[80]

Simonov was not an informer, but he was pressured by the Soviet authorities, which perhaps wanted him to become one. In the spring of 1937, Simonov was invited by Vladimir Stavsky, the Secretary of the Writers' Union, to join three other young prose writers from the Literary Institute on a working holiday in the Caucasus. They were to write about the life of Sergo Ordzhonikidze, the former Commissar for Heavy Industry, a famous Georgian and comrade of Stalin in the Civil War, who had just committed suicide. Shortly before they were due to leave, Simonov was summoned to Stavsky's office. Stavsky demanded that Simonov tell him 'all about the anti-Soviet conversations [he had been conducting] at the institute'. He wanted him to confess and repent, to put him in a position where it would be difficult to refuse the demands of the authorities. When Simonov denied that he had held such conversations, Stavsky claimed to 'have information' about him. He told him it was 'best to tell the truth'. Stavsky 'was clearly irritated by my apparent inability to be sincere and speak the truth', recalled Simonov. After several rounds of accusations by Stavsky and denials by Simonov, there was a stalemate, with Simonov refusing to cooperate. Stavsky accused him of spreading 'counter-revolutionary poetry' and banned him from the trip. Gradually it dawned on Simonov where Stavsky's 'information' had come from. Among the students at the institute there was a craze for Kipling's poetry. One day Simonov was drawn into a conversation about Kipling with a young teacher who then asked him what he thought about the poetry of Nikolai Gumilyov (who had been shot as a 'counter-revolutionary' in 1921). Simonov replied that he liked some of Gumilyov's poetry, though not as much as Kipling's. Encouraged by the teacher, he recited some of Gumilyov's verse. As he recalled the scene, Simonov felt terrified for the first time in his life. He knew he was in danger of arrest, not just for his views on Gumilyov, but also on account of his noble origins, which were, it seems, connected by the teacher to Simonov's indulgence of Gumilyov in his report to Stavsky. For the rest of the academic term Simonov avoided the teacher, who was himself arrested later that year (he had turned informer in a last desperate effort to save himself and had tried to entrap Simonov).[81]

By the spring of 1937, the Literary Institute was in a state of high anxiety. Like other Soviet institutions, the institute had been caught unawares by the sudden launching of the Great Terror; and inside it there was a sense of panic that this surprise attested to a 'lack of vigilance'. At a series of purge meetings, students and teachers called hysterically for greater 'Bolshevik vigilance and real self-criticism' to rid the institute of all 'formalists' and 'Averbakhians [Trotskyists]'. Several students were arrested, some for liberal or religious motifs in their poetry, others for defending Boris Pasternak (who had been criticized in the Soviet press for his individualistic style). About a dozen students were 'worked over' by the Komsomol (i.e. forced to recant their work at a student meeting where they were severely criticized). One of these students was expelled from the institute and handed over to the NKVD after she refused to renounce her father, a poet then out of favour, and bravely told her massed accusers: 'My father is the most honourable person in the Soviet Union.' For this she did ten years in Kolyma.[82]

Two of Simonov's good friends at the institute suffered persecution in the Great Terror: the poet Valentin Portugalov was arrested in February 1937, after a fellow student reported to the police something he had said; and in April of that year, Vladimir Lugovskoi, the charismatic teacher, was denounced by the Presidium of the Writers' Union for having allowed the republication (in 1935) of some poems from the 1920s (romantic verses about Russian nature), which had since come to be considered 'politically harmful'. Forced to recant his poems, Lugovskoi wrote 'On My Mistakes', a ten-page exercise in self-abasement, in which he pledged to purge himself of 'all the outmoded thoughts' that had prevented him from 'keeping up with the march of history'.[83] Lugovskoi was terrified. For the next few years he published no poetry, except for a 'Song About Stalin', which was set to music in 1939.[84] A soft-spoken and mild-mannered man, Lugovskoi also made a series of rabid political speeches in which he called for the blood of enemies. 'It is time,' he told a group of Moscow writers in October, 'to purge our country of all those bastard-enemies, the Trotskyists, to sweep away with an iron broom all those people who betrayed our Motherland, and to purge those elements within ourselves.'[85]

Simonov, too, reacted out of fear. Until the incident in Stavsky's office, he had been regarded as a model student and Soviet loyalist, but now this reputation was in doubt. Looking back at the Stavsky incident, Simonov recalled that he was 'stunned and shocked, not so much by a sense of sudden danger ... but more by the realization that they no longer believed or trusted me'. He set out to prove his worth in a series of attacks against the 'formalists' and other 'enemies' at the purge meetings in the institute.[86] The most extraordinary of these speeches, which he gave at an open meeting of the institute on 16 May, included a vitriolic condemnation of his friend Yevgeny Dolmatovsky:

Often there are conversations [in the institute] where people only speak about themselves. In particular, I recall having to listen to a disgusting speech by Comrade Dolmatovsky at a meeting of the fourth class. He did not say, 'the institute' and 'we', but rather, 'I and my institute.' His position was: 'The institute does not pay enough attention to individuals like me. The institute was founded to educate two or three talents, like me, Dolmatovsky, and only that justifies its existence. For talents like me – Dolmatovsky – the institute should lay on the best of everything, even at the expense of the rest of the students.'[87]

Perhaps Simonov had spoken in the spirit of self-criticism (which included criticism of one's closest friends) that had always been a part of the Komsomol ethos. Students were expected to demonstrate that they were loyal and vigilant. Perhaps he had meant no harm to his friend, although he was clearly jealous of the high regard for Dolmatovsky's talent, which was frequently expressed by the institute's Director (who placed Simonov in a lower category that was 'only good enough for teaching, journalism, or editorial work').[88] In the event, Simonov's denunciation had relatively minor consequences for Dolmatovsky. After graduating from the institute in 1938, he was sent to work as a journalist in the Far East – a posting well below his literary worth and one which he described as the hardest in his life. It could have been much worse. The two men remained on amicable terms and often wrote in praise of each other, but among Simonov's friends there was always the suspicion that Dolmatovsky harboured a grudge against him.[89]

As for Simonov, the years of the Great Terror, which were so catastrophic for many of his friends, catapulted him to prominence as a poet favoured by the Stalinist regime. In 1937, he contributed several poems to the cult of Stalin, including one, 'Parade', which was written for an orchestra and chorus:

> This is a song about Him,
> About his true friends,
> His true friends and comrades.
> The whole people
> Are His friends:
> You cannot count them,
> They are like drops of water in the sea.[90]

In 'Ice Battle' (1938) Simonov counterposed the nationalistic story of the thirteenth-century Russian prince Aleksandr Nevsky and his military defeat of the Teutonic Knights with the Soviet struggle against foreign and domestic enemies (a theme also handled in the epic film by Sergei Eisenstein, *Aleksandr Nevsky*, which was made in the same year). The poem, which was part of the propaganda effort to prepare the country for the likelihood of war with Germany, was the first real literary success for Simonov. It brought him 'fame and popularity', in the words of Lugovskoi, who cited it in recommending him for membership to the Writers' Union in September 1938.[91] Whatever damage had been done to Simonov's career by his refusal to become an informer was rectified, it seems, by the patriotic verses he had written since, for he was accepted as the youngest member of the Union with the full approval of Stavsky.

Simonov's betrayal of Dolmatovsky was not unusual in the frenzied atmosphere of the Great Terror. One informer recalled how he struggled with his conscience when approached by the NKVD to report on his friends (who had turned their back on him after the arrest of his father). He asked himself: 'Who are my friends? I have no friends. I owe loyalty to no one but those who can extract it from me – and to myself.'[92] Fear tore apart the bonds of friendship, love and trust. It tore apart the moral ties that hold together a society, as people turned against each other in the chaotic scramble to survive.

After her arrest, in 1937, Yevgeniia Ginzburg was betrayed by many of her friends. They were forced to denounce her to her face during her interrogation in the Kazan jail (such 'confrontations' were frequently arranged by the NKVD). One of them was Volodia Diakonov, a writer on the editorial staff at the newspaper where she had worked. 'We were old friends,' Ginzburg recalls.

Our fathers had been schoolmates, I had helped him to get his job, and had gladly, almost lovingly, taught him his trade as a journalist. He was five years my junior. He had often said he was as fond of me as of a sister.

During their confrontation the interrogating officer (who spoke Russian poorly) read out the statement that Diakonov had made, denouncing Ginzburg as a member of a 'counter-revolutionary terrorist group' at the newspaper. Diakonov attempted to deny this, claiming he had only said that she had held an important post on the editorial staff, but the officer insisted that he sign a statement confirming the existence of such a group.

'Volodya,' I said mildly, 'you know it's a trick. You never said anything of the kind. By signing this you'll be causing the death of hundreds of your comrades, people who have always been decent to you.'

[The interrogator's] eyes nearly popped out of his head.

'How dare you exert pressure on witness! I send you straight away to the lowest punishment cell. And you, Dyakonov, you signed all this yesterday when you were alone here. Now you refuse! I have you arrested at once for giving false evidence.'

He made a show of reaching for the bell – and Volodya, looking like a rabbit in front of a boa constrictor, slowly wrote his name in a hand as shaky as though he had had a stroke and quite unlike the bold sweep of the pen with which he signed his articles on the moral code of the new age. Then he whispered almost inaudibly:

'Forgive me, Zhenya. We've just had a daughter. I have to stay alive.'[93]

4

How did people respond to the sudden disappearance of colleagues, friends and neighbours in the Great Terror? Did they believe that they were really 'spies' and 'enemies', as claimed by the Soviet press? Surely they could not think that of people they had known for many years?

For true Communists there could be no doubting what they were told by the Party leadership. It was not a matter of whether they believed that Tukhachevsky or Bukharin was a spy, but whether they accepted the judgement of the Party in which they placed their faith. There were all sorts of ways to resolve the questions which arose when a trusted friend and comrade suddenly became an 'enemy'. Anatoly Gorbatov, a Red Army officer in Kiev, recalls the adjustment which he, like many in the army, had to make when Tukhachevsky and other senior military leaders were denounced as spies.

How can it be that men who took such a part in routing foreign interventionists and internal reactionaries . . . have suddenly become enemies of the people? . . . Finally, after mulling over a host of possible explanations, I accepted the answer most common in those days . . . 'Obviously,' many people said at the time . . . 'they fell into the nets of foreign intelligence organizations while abroad . . .'

When General Iakir was arrested it was a 'terrible blow'.

I knew Yakir well and respected him. Deep down, I nursed a hope that it was only a mistake – 'It will be sorted out and he will go free' – but this was the sort of thing that only the closest friends risked saying among themselves.[94]

Apparently, Iakir himself was prepared to accept the Party's decision, judging from his final words before the firing squad: 'Long live the Party! Long live Stalin!'[95]

Stalin's jails were full of Bolsheviks who continued to believe in the Party as the source of all justice. Some confessed to the charges against them just in order to preserve that faith. Although torture was frequently employed to extract confessions from the Bolsheviks, the 'decisive factor' in their surrender was not violence, according to a former prisoner (who was not a Communist), but the fact that the majority of convinced Communists had to at all costs preserve their faith in the Soviet Union. To renounce it would have been beyond their powers. Great moral strength is required in certain circumstances to renounce one's long-standing, deep-rooted convictions, even when these turn out to be untenable.[96]

Nadezhda Grankina encountered many Party members in the Kazan prison in 1938. They all continued to believe in the Party line. When she told them of the famine in 1932, they said 'it was a lie, that I was exaggerating so that I could slander our Soviet way of life'. When she told them how she had been kicked out of her home for no reason, or how the passport system had destroyed families, they would say, 'True, but that was the best way to deal with people like you.'

They thought I had got what I deserved because I was critical of the excesses. Yet when the same happened to them, they thought it was a mistake that would be fixed – because they had never had any doubts whatsoever, and whatever instructions had come down from the top, they had always cheered and carried them out ... And when they were being expelled from the Party, none of them stood up for each other; they all kept quiet or raised their hands in support of the expulsion. It was some kind of universal psychosis.[97]

For the mass of the population there were always two realities: Party Truth and truth based on experience. But in the years of the Great Terror, when the Soviet press was full of the show trials and the nefarious deeds of 'spies' and 'enemies', few were able to see through the propaganda version of the world. It took extraordinary will-power, usually connected to a different value-system, for a person to discount the press reports and question the basic assumptions of the Terror. For some people it was religion or their nationality that allowed them to take a critical view; for others a different Party creed or ideology; and for others still it was perhaps a function of their age (they had seen too much in Russia ever to believe that innocence protected anybody from arrest). But for anyone below the age of thirty, who had only ever known the Soviet world, or had inherited no other values from his family, it was almost impossible to step outside the propaganda system and question its political principles.

The young were particularly credulous – they had been indoctrinated in this propaganda through Soviet schools. Riab Bindel remembers:

At school they said: 'Look how they won't let us live under Communism – look how they blow up factories, derail trams, and kill people – all this is done by enemies of the people.' They beat this into our heads so often that we stopped thinking for ourselves. We saw 'enemies' everywhere. We were told that if we saw a suspicious character on the street, we should follow and report him – he might be a spy. The authorities, the Party, our teachers – everybody said the same thing. What else could we think?

After leaving school, in 1937, Bindel found a job in a factory, where the workers regularly cursed the 'enemies of the people'.

When the factory had a breakdown, they would say: 'Comrades, there is sabotage and treachery!' They would look for someone who had a blemish on his record and call him an enemy. They would put him in prison, beat him up until he confessed that he had done it. At his trial they would say: 'Look at the bastard who was working secretly among us!'[98]

Many workers believed in the existence of 'enemies of the people' and called for their arrest because they associated them with the 'bosses' (Party leaders, managers and specialists) whom they already blamed for their economic difficulties. Indeed, this mistrust of the elites helps to explain the broad appeal of the purges among certain sections of the population, which perceived the Great Terror as a 'quarrel among the masters' that did not affect them. This perception is neatly illustrated by a joke that circulated widely in the years of the Terror. The NKVD bangs on the door of an apartment in the middle of the night. 'Who's there?' the man inside asks. 'The NKVD, open up!' The man is relieved: 'No, no,' he tells them, 'you've got the wrong apartment – the Communists live upstairs!'[99]

The arrest of a close relative was not enough to shake most people from their belief in 'enemies'. Indeed, in many cases it reinforced it. Ida Slavina, whose father was arrested in 1937, held firm to her Komsomol convictions until 1953:

I didn't believe that my father was an enemy of the people. Of course I thought that he was innocent. Yet at the same time I believed that there were undoubtedly enemies of the people. I was utterly convinced that it was through their sabotage that good people like my father were being wrongly put in jail. The existence of these enemies was obvious to me ... I read about them in the press and hated them as much as anyone. With the Komsomol I went on demonstrations to protest against the enemies of the people. We cried: 'Death to the enemies of the people!' The newspapers gave us these slogans. They filled our heads with the show trials. We read the terrible confessions by Bukharin and other Party leaders. We were horrified. If such people were spies, then the enemies were everywhere.[100]

Roza Novoseltseva, whose parents were arrested in 1937, never thought that they were really 'enemies', but she was prepared to believe that senior Party leaders like Bukharin might be, because, as she put it at the time, 'someone has to be responsible for the tragic circumstances of our family'. Vladimir Ianin, who grew up in a family of Soviet diplomats, believed all the charges against the 'enemies of the people' – he thought that Yezhov was a 'great man' – even though his father, his older sister, six of his uncles and an aunt were all arrested in the Great Terror. It was only after the arrest of his mother, in 1944, that he began to question his belief. He wrote to Stalin to tell him that his mother was entirely innocent and to warn him that her arrest had proved that the NKVD had been taken over by the 'enemies of the people'.[101]

Even Stalin's victims continued to believe in the existence of 'enemies of the people'. They blamed them for their own arrest (which they put down to 'counter-revolutionary sabotage') or presumed that they themselves had been mistaken for real 'enemies of the people'. Dmitry Streletsky was the son of a 'kulak' family exiled as 'enemies of the people'. He continued to believe in all the propaganda of the Stalinist regime, becoming an ardent Stalinist until 1953. Looking back on his life, Streletsky believes that 'it was easier for us [the repressed] to survive our punishments if we continued to believe in Stalin, to think that Stalin was deceived by enemies of the people, rather than to give up hope in him.'

We never thought that Stalin was to blame for our suffering. We only wondered how it was that he did not know that he was being duped . . . My father himself said: 'Stalin does not know, which means that sooner or later we are bound to be released [from exile]' . . . Perhaps it was a form of self-deception, but psychologically it made life much easier to bear, believing in the justice of Stalin. It took away our fear.[102]

Pavel Vittenburg, the geologist who spent many years in labour camps, supported the Great Terror against 'enemies of the people'. As he ex-

plained in a letter to his wife from an expedition to Severnaia Zemlia in
February 1937:

You asked if I heard about the trial of Piatakov on the radio. I heard it all –
and now I understand that my own downfall is entirely due to those scoundrels
the Trotskyists – they tried to destroy our [Soviet] Union. So many innocent
non-party people have been sent into exile as a consequence of their dark
ways.[103]

For those who were less certain about the existence of all these
'enemies of the people', it was not so much the show trials that gave rise
to doubts (few people questioned the veracity of the prosecution case)
as the sudden disappearance of colleagues, friends and neighbours,
whose guilt did not seem plausible.

A common way to deal with such troubling thoughts was not to think
– to shun all politics and withdraw entirely into private life. Many
people managed to live through the Great Terror oblivious to political
events, even the political elite, who must have shut their eyes to the
disappearances in their circle. Mikhail Isaev was a leading Soviet jurist,
a member of the Supreme Court of the Soviet Union, who lived in
Moscow in some style with his wife and their four children. Throughout
the years of the Great Terror there was never any talk of politics at
home, judging from the recollections of his wife Maria, even though the
mass arrests affected many friends. Isaev seemed astonishingly unaware
of what was going on, even in his own house. In a letter to his daughter,
written in December 1937, he complained about the disappearance of
the housekeeper, an elderly spinster, who had not come to work for
several days. The house was in disorder, and Isaev was obviously
annoyed that she had 'gone away without any warning whatsoever'. He
had 'no idea' why the housekeeper had disappeared and wondered
whether he should fire her. It never crossed his mind that the housekeeper
had been arrested – as indeed she had – and that she had nobody to pass
a message to her employers.[104]

Many of the children of these elite families were sheltered from political events. Nina Kaminskaia, the daughter of a lawyer and former Kadet
(liberal) activist, never thought about politics – the subject was avoided
in her parents' home. Even when her father lost his job in a Soviet bank,
Nina went on living her 'carefree student life' at the law school where
she had enrolled in 1937. Years later, she discussed this with a friend.

Both of them agreed that they had lived quite happily through the Great Terror, without fear or even much awareness of what was going on: 'We had simply failed to perceive the horror and despair that gripped our parents' generation.' Nina's friend recalled an incident from 1937. She had come home from a party late at night and had lost her key:

There was nothing for it but to ring the bell and wake up her parents. For a long time there was no response, so she rang a second time. Soon she heard footsteps and the door was opened. There stood her father, dressed as though he had not been to bed at all but had just come in or was on the point of going out again. He was wearing a dark suit, a clean shirt, a neatly tied necktie. On seeing his daughter he stared at her in silence and then, still without a word, slapped her across the face.

Nina knew her friend's father. He was a cultivated man, without any violence in him. His reaction to the late-night knock was obviously sparked by his fear that 'they' had come for him. At first her friend was shocked by the assault:

Overcome by self-pity, she burst into tears and reproached her father, but after a while she completely forgot about the incident. Years passed before she recalled her father's pale face, his silence, and that blow – no doubt the only time in his life he ever hit anyone. She told me this story with great pain, racked by guilt at her own incomprehension and that of our whole generation.[105]

People dealt with their doubts by suppressing them, or by finding ways to rationalize them so as to preserve the basic structures of their Communist belief. They did not do this consciously and generally only became aware of their behaviour years later. Maia Rodak's father was denounced as an 'enemy of the people' in 1937 because he had inadvertently uttered a phrase once used by Trotsky in a letter to the Soviet authorities. After his arrest, Maia tried, as she now understands, to reconcile her doubts about the Terror with her Communist beliefs.

I was troubled by so many questions. In reaction, I made myself become a conformist. That's what happened, although I use the word 'conformist' only now ... It was not a game but a strategy of survival. For example, my friend Alla and I did not like the cult of Stalin, but the idea that it might be wrong was simply inadmissible, even to ourselves. I was aware of the constant need to correct myself, to purge myself of doubts.[106]

In his memoirs Simonov reflects on his reaction to the arrest of a relative (the brother of his mother's aunt), a senior army officer, in connection with the trial of Tukhachevsky and other senior military commanders in 1937. Simonov recalls that he had his doubts about the guilt of the accused. As a boy he had worshipped Tukhachevsky (whom he had often seen at his uncle's Moscow flat). Simonov's mother was irate about the arrest and certain of their relative's innocence. Consequently, Simonov weighed up the evidence with special care, but in the end he decided to accept what he had read in the Soviet press. Like most people at that time, Simonov assumed that nobody would dare to execute such senior commanders without conclusive evidence of treason against them:

It was impossible to doubt the existence of a dreadful conspiracy. Any doubts on that score were inconceivable – there was no alternative. I am talking of the spirit of those times: either they were guilty or it was impossible to understand.

By the same reasoning Simonov was ready to accept that his relative was guilty of some crime. Because his relative had been arrested once before (in 1931) and then released for lack of evidence, it seemed to Simonov that his rearrest must mean that firmer proof about his guilt had now come to light (a conclusion reinforced by the fact that his stepfather, who had also been arrested in 1931, was now left untroubled by the police).[107] In other words, Simonov interpreted the indicators in a way to reinforce his system of Communist belief, because disbelief was 'inconceivable'.

Another way for people to reconcile the sudden disappearance of friends and relatives with their belief in Soviet justice was to tell themselves that some good people were arrested 'by mistake'. According to this rationale, there were bound to be errors in identifying the true 'enemies of the people', because there were so many 'enemies', and they were so well hidden. In this way of thinking, the real enemy was always someone else – the sons and husbands of all the other women in the queue to hand in parcels at the prison gates – and never one's own friends and relatives.

Recalling the arrest of her husband in 1936, Olga Adamova-Sliuzberg summarized her reaction:

No, it was impossible; it couldn't happen to me, to him! Of course there had been rumours (just rumours – it was only the beginning of 1936) that something was going on, that there were arrests. But surely all this happened to other people; surely it couldn't happen to us.[108]

Olga's husband thought that there had been some 'misunderstanding' when he was arrested by the NKVD. Like millions of others, he left saying to his wife that it would all soon be sorted out ('It must be a mistake'). Sure that he would soon return, he took only an overnight bag. Slavin and Piatnitsky did the same.

Convinced that an error had been made, many people wrote to Stalin to appeal for the release of relatives. Anna Semyonova, who was brought up as a Communist, recalls writing to Stalin after the arrest of her father in June 1937. 'I imagined that after a few days Stalin would receive my letter, read it and say, "What is going on? Why has an honest man been arrested? Release him immediately and apologize to him." ' Three months later, when Anna's mother was taken away, she told herself again that 'it must be a mistake'.[109]

The downfall of Yezhov, the NKVD chief behind the Great Terror, reinforced this system of belief. Yezhov was brought down amidst a host of scandals (not all of them entirely false) about his private life in the autumn of 1938. There were homosexual affairs, bisexual orgies, bouts of heavy drinking and fantastic stories of his wife as an 'English spy'. But the real reason for Yezhov's fall was Stalin's growing sense that mass arrests were no longer a workable strategy. At the rate the arrests were going, it would not be long before the entire Soviet population was in jail. Stalin made it clear that the NKVD could not carry on incarcerating people, solely on the basis of denunciations, without checking their veracity. He warned against careerists who made denunciations to promote their position in society. After Yezhov's dismissal in December 1938, his replacement, Lavrenty Beria, immediately announced a full review of the arrests in Yezhov's reign. By 1940, 1.5 million cases had been reviewed; 450,000 convictions had been quashed, 128,000 cases closed, 30,000 people released from jail, and 327,000 people let out of the Gulag's labour camps and colonies. These releases restored many people's faith in Soviet justice. They allowed waverers to put the 'Yezhov terror' (Yezhovshchina) down to a temporary aberration rather than to systemic abuse. The mass arrests had all been Yezhov's doing, it was said, but Stalin had corrected his mistakes and exposed Yezhov as an 'enemy of the people' who had been trying to undermine the Soviet government by arresting its officials and spreading discontent. On 2 February 1940, Yezhov was tried by the Military Collegium, convicted of a terrorist conspiracy and of spying for Poland, Germany, Britain and Japan and shot in a special building which he himself had built for shooting 'enemies' not far from the Lubianka.[110]

Beria's appointment was greeted with relief. 'We were overjoyed by the appearance of this pure and ideal figure, as Beria appeared to us,' remembers Mark Laskin, who hoped, like many people, that 'all the innocents would now be released, leaving only the real spies and enemies in jail'.[111] Simonov recalls that Beria's review was enough to restore his belief in Soviet justice and dispel any doubts he may have had over the arrest of relatives. Indeed, its effect on Simonov was to reinforce his conviction that anybody who was not released, or who was arrested subsequently, must be guilty of some crime. Recalling his reaction to the arrest in 1939 of the writer Isaak Babel and the theatre director Vsevolod Meyerhold, Simonov confessed:

Despite the importance of these men in literature and the theatre, and the huge shockwaves which their sudden disappearance caused – already at that time – the fact that these arrests were so sudden and, in general, in those circles, so unusual, and because they took place under Beria, who was correcting Yezhov's mistakes – all this made me think: maybe these men are indeed guilty of something. Many of the people arrested during Yezhov's reign were perhaps innocent, but these people had been left untouched by Yezhov and were suddenly arrested when the old mistakes were being corrected. So it seemed likely that there were good reasons for their arrest.[112]

One of the people to have serious doubts about the charges against Meyerhold and Babel was Vladimir Stavsky, the former General Secretary of the Writers' Union, who had attempted to recruit Simonov as an informer. Born into a working-class family in the provincial town of Penza, Stavsky could not have risen to the summit of the Soviet literary establishment without learning how to compromise his moral principles. As Stalin's 'executioner of Soviet literature', he had authorized the arrests of numerous writers and personally wrote the denunciation which led to the arrest of Mandelshtam in the spring of 1938.[113] But all this time Stavsky was tormented by doubts and fears. He confessed his despair to his diary, which, like Prishvin, he wrote in a tiny scrawl, barely legible to anybody else. Stavsky was particularly troubled by a story he had heard about a Party official who used his chauffeured car as a brothel. 'I don't understand how it happened,' the chauffeur had said of the official. 'He was just an ordinary boy, one of us, but then he crossed some dividing line and turned into a pig with his whole mug covered in filth. A regular worker doesn't get that dirty in a whole lifetime.'[114] Perhaps as a response to his loss of faith, Stavsky began drinking heavily, put on weight and became ill, often not appearing at work for days on end, as he recovered from his latest alcoholic binge. He avoided meetings where writers were denounced, or only spoke against them in the mildest terms. For this he himself was finally denounced by the Party Committee of the Writers' Union in November 1937:

As the leader of the Writers' Union, comrade Stavsky makes a lot of noise about the need for vigilance in literature, he calls for a campaign for the revelation of enemies. But in reality he has helped to conceal the Averbakhians, he does not really speak out to disarm the enemies of the people and alien elements of the Party and he remains silent about his own mistakes in habouring connections with the enemy.[115]

Stavsky came under growing pressure from his political masters and was ultimately dismissed from the leadership of the Writers' Union in the spring of 1938.

There were many people, like Stavsky, who had doubts about the mass arrests, but few who spoke out against them. The possibilities for effective opposition were extremely limited in any case, as Piatnitsky's protest at the Party plenum clearly showed. Groups and individuals wrote to Party leaders to express their outrage at the mass arrests but nearly always did so anonymously. 'Hundreds of thousands of innocent people are languishing in jails, and no one knows what for . . . Everything is based on lies,' wrote one unnamed group to Molotov in June 1938 ('Excuse us if we do not sign our names, it is forbidden to complain').[116] There were some protests by Party members in the localities, particularly by the older Bolsheviks, whose political morals had been formed before the rise of Stalin.

Olga Adamova-Sliuzberg tells the story of one Old Bolshevik called Altunin she came across in Kolyma in 1939. He came from somewhere in Voronezh province and had worked as a tanner before joining the Party. A handsome middle-aged man with a reddish beard, he had once been very strong, but working in the mines had weakened him. By the time Olga met him he had been transferred to a women's construction brigade in Magadan, where he worked as a toolmaker. He told Olga his story:

When it all started in 1937, first this comrade was an enemy, then that one, and we expelled them from the Party, we all raised our hands; and then we killed them all, our own comrades.

At first I pretended to be ill. That way I didn't have to go to the Party meetings and raise my hand. But then I saw that something needed to be done: we could not go on like this, we were destroying the Party, killing good and honest people. I did not believe that they were all traitors, I knew these people well.

One evening I sat down and wrote a letter. I sent one copy to my local Party organization, one to Stalin, and one to the [Party's] Central Control Commission. I wrote that we were killing the Revolution . . . I poured my whole heart into this letter. I showed it to my wife. She said: 'This is suicide. The day after you send that letter they will put you in prison.' But I said: 'Let them put me in prison. Better to be behind bars than to raise my hand and kill a comrade.'

Well, she was right. I sent my letter and three days later I was in jail. They worked me over – and I got ten years in Kolyma.

Asked if he ever regretted what he had done, Altunin replied that there had been one occasion, when he was thrown into an isolation cell after his labour team had failed to clear the tree-roots of a forest in a very heavy frost:

Suddenly I felt really sorry for myself: other people had been sentenced for nothing, but I had put myself away. And what was the point of writing what I wrote? Nothing would change. Maybe Solts [head of the Central Control Commission] felt a bit ashamed, but the old Moustache [Stalin] – what did he care? There was no getting through to him. And right now, I thought, I could be sitting at home with my wife and children around the samovar in a warm room. As soon as I thought that, I began beating my head against the wall to stop such thoughts from entering my mind. All night long I ran around my cell cursing myself for such regrets.[117]

The only source of opposition capable of having any real influence was within the system of repression itself. Judges in the local courts were often quite effective in softening sentences, sometimes even throwing cases out on the grounds of lack of evidence, though after the summer of 1937, almost all the people swept up in the mass arrests were summarily tried and sentenced by the troikas, the special three-man tribunals (usually made up by the NKVD, the Procuracy and the Party) set up to circumvent the courts.[118] Within the NKVD, too, there were some brave officials willing to speak out against the mass arrests, particularly during the 'kulak operations', which reminded many local NKVD agents of the bloody chaos in 1928–33. Eduard Salyn, the NKVD chief in Omsk province, spoke out at a conference convened by Stalin and Yezhov to discuss the 'kulak operation' in July 1937. Salyn said that in his region there were

insufficient numbers of enemies of the people and Trotskyists to warrant a campaign of repression, and in general I consider it to be completely wrong to decide beforehand how many people to arrest and shoot.

Shortly after the conference Salyn was arrested, tried and shot.[119]

Mikhail Shreider was another NKVD officer who voiced his opposition to the mass arrests. In his memoirs, written in the 1970s, he describes himself as a 'pure Chekist', inspired by the Leninist ideals of Feliks Dzerzhinsky, the founder of the Cheka in 1917. Shreider wrote his memoirs to justify his work in the Cheka and portray himself as a victim of the Great Terror. According to his version of events, he became disillusioned with the Stalinist regime as he observed the corruption of his fellow NKVD officers during the 1930s. Comrades he had known as decent and honest men were now prepared to use any form of torture against 'enemies of the people', if it meant advancing their careers. Shreider was also troubled by the scale of the arrests. He could not believe in the existence of so many 'enemies of the people'. But he was afraid to express his doubts in case he was denounced. He soon discovered that many of his colleagues shared his fear, but no one would break the conspiracy of silence. Even when a trusted colleague disappeared, the most that any of his comrades dared to say was that he might be an 'honest man'. Nobody suggested that he might be innocent, because this would expose them to the risk of denunciation for questioning the purge. 'No one understood why all these arrests were happening,' recalled Shreider, 'but people were afraid to speak out, because that might raise suspicion that they were aiding or communicating with the "enemies of the people".'[120]

For several months, Shreider watched in silence as old friends and colleagues were arrested and sentenced to death. Unable to oppose the Terror, he became a sort of conscientious objector by not attending the executions of NKVD colleagues in the Lubianka yard. Then, in the spring of 1938, Shreider was transferred to Alma-Ata, where he became the second-in-command to Stanislav Redens, the NKVD chief of Kazakhstan (and the brother-in-law of Stalin). Shreider and Redens became close friends. They lived next door to each other, and their families were always in each other's homes. Shreider noticed Redens' growing disgust with the torture methods of his operatives. He thought that Redens was a man of humane sensibilities. Redens, for his part, had marked out Shreider as somebody who shared his doubts about the methods used in the Great Terror. Late one night he drove him out of town and stopped the car. The two men got out and began to walk. When they were out of earshot of the chauffeur, Redens said to Shreider. 'If Feliks Eduardovich [Dzerzhinsky] were still alive, he would have the lot of us shot for the way we're working now.' Shreider made out that he did not understand: to show complicity in such a thought was enough to warrant his immediate arrest, and he could not be sure that what his boss had said was not a provocation. Redens continued talking. It became clear to Shreider that he had meant what he had said. Shreider opened up his troubled soul as well. Once this trust had been established, the two men confided in each other. Redens regretted that all the decent Communists had been destroyed, while the likes of Yezhov remained untouched. Yet there were still subjects that were too dangerous for him to talk about. Looking back on these whispered conversations, Shreider thought that Redens knew far more about the Terror than he had let on: 'His situation and the circumstances of the times obliged him, like all of us, not to call things by their name, and not to talk about such things, even with his friends.'[121]

Shreider was emboldened by his conversations with Redens. They made him feel remorseful and angry. He wrote to Yezhov to protest against the arrest of an old colleague in the NKVD, and against the arrest of his wife's cousin, a student in Moscow, vouchsafing the innocence of both these men. A few days later, in June 1938, Redens received a telegram from Yezhov ordering the arrest of Shreider. Presented with this news in Redens' office, Shreider begged Redens to appeal to Stalin: 'Stanislav Frantsevich, you know me well, and you, after all, are his brother-in-law. It must be a mistake.' Redens replied: 'Mikhail Pavlovich, I shall put in a word for you, but I fear it is hopeless. Today it is you, no doubt tomorrow it will be my turn.' Shreider was imprisoned in the Butyrki prison in Moscow. In July 1940, he was sentenced to ten years in a labour camp followed by three years in exile. Redens was arrested in November 1938. He was shot in January 1940.[122]

5

On the night of her father's arrest, in May 1937, Elena Bonner was sent by her mother to stay with her aunt Anya and her uncle Lyova so that she would be out of the way during the NKVD search of the Bonner apartment. The fourteen-year-old Elena walked through Leningrad and knocked on the door of her relatives. 'The door opened immediately, as if they were expecting me,' recalls Elena, who then explained to her aunt and uncle what had happened. Her uncle was frightened and angry. He started asking questions about her father's work:

I didn't understand what he was getting at and tried to enter the apartment. Anya said something. Lyova practically shouted at her, 'Anya, damn it, you're always . . .' And he barred my way with his right arm across the doorway. Then he spoke in a loud whisper, very fast, 'We can't let you in; we can't. What's the matter? Don't you understand that?' He repeated it several times, spraying me with his spittle. Anya said something. I could see her mouth moving, but I heard nothing except Lyova's whisper as loud as a shout. I retreated from the door until my back was pressed against the bannister. The door slammed. I stood there, unable to comprehend what had happened to me. Then I wiped my face with my hand and started down the stairs. I hadn't reached the bottom of the flight when I heard the door opening. When I turned, Lyova was in the doorway. I was afraid he would call me back. But he said nothing and then started to close the door slowly. I shouted, 'Scoundrel!' and I saw him turn white.[123]

There are countless such stories of abandonment by friends and neighbours and even by kin following the arrest of a close relative. People were afraid of making contact with the families of 'enemies of the people'. They crossed the street to avoid them, did not talk to them in the corridors of communal blocks and forbade their children to play with theirs in the courtyard. People removed the photographs of friends and relatives who had disappeared, sometimes even tearing out or scribbling over faces in family portraits.

According to Solzhenitsyn:

The mildest and at the same time the most widespread form of betrayal was not to do anything bad directly, but just not to notice the doomed person next to one, not to help him, to turn away one's face, to shrink back. They had arrested a neighbour, your comrade at work, or even your close friend. You kept silence. You acted as if you had not noticed.[124]

Olga Adamova-Sliuzberg recalls that when her husband was arrested,

People spoke to me in a special tone of voice; they were afraid of me. Some would cross the road when they saw me coming towards them. Others paid me special attention, but this was heroic on their part, and I and they were both aware of it.[125]

After the arrest of her parents, in June 1937, Inna Gaister and her sister were evicted from their family dacha at Nikolina Gora. On the instructions of their parents they were taken by their nanny to the house of the poet Aleksandr Bezymensky, an old friend of their father, who they hoped would take them in. The poet drove them to the nearest station and put them on the first train to Moscow. 'He was too afraid to get involved,' recalls Inna. 'He often used to stay in my grandmother's house, but he and his wife had a new baby, and fear must have got the better of his decency.'[126]

When Stanislav and Varvara Budkevich were arrested, in July 1937, their daughter Maria and her younger brother were evicted from the family's two rooms in the communal apartment where they had lived in Leningrad. The rooms were then occupied by one of their neighbours, a wife and husband with three small children, who had been on friendly terms with the Budkeviches until 1937, when the wife had denounced them to the NKVD as counter-revolutionaries and spies (Stanislav was of Polish origin). The woman had even claimed that Varvara, a historical researcher, was a prostitute who brought her clients to the apartment. Maria's brother was taken to an orphanage, but she was left entirely by herself; she was then just fourteen. For the first few days Maria stayed with a schoolfriend. Then she found a room where she lived on her own. An old friend of the family, the wife of a Bolshevik official, advised Maria to ask her former neighbours if they knew anything about the whereabouts of her parents. When Maria went back to the communal apartment, she received a hostile reception:

My God, they were so afraid of me, they would not even let me in. Can you imagine? The woman who had taken over our rooms was annoyed and angry to see me. Whether her husband had already been arrested or was afraid that they would come for him, I don't recall. Maybe the family was in trouble. Anyway they would not help. The woman simply said: 'I don't know anything. Nothing. Understand? And please don't come here again!'[127]

Neighbours became strangers overnight. For nearly thirty years the Turkins had lived next to the Nikitins. They shared the ground floor of a three-storeyed wooden house on the corner of Soviet and Sverdlov Streets in Perm – the seven Turkins (Aleksandr, Vera and their two daughters, Vera's mother and her brother and sister) occupying three rooms on the right side of the house, and the Nikitins, a family of four, occupying three rooms on the left. Aleksandr Turkin was a veteran Bolshevik, one of Sverdlov's comrades from the revolutionary under-ground in Perm. Like all his family, Aleksandr was employed at the Motovilikha steelworks. He was also a journalist for the local newspaper and a judge in the regional court. In 1936, he was arrested as a Trot-skyist. His guilt was accepted as a 'proven fact' by his wife Vera, a factory worker who took no interest in politics. Vera's mother, a domineering woman who ran the Turkin household, also thought that Aleksandr was guilty. She cut his face out of the family portrait in the living room. 'If we have an enemy among us, we must clear him out,' she said. Vera was dismissed from her job at the Motovilikha plant after being injured in an accident (as the wife of an 'enemy of the people' she did not qualify for sickness benefit). The only job that she could find was selling news-papers in a street kiosk. Vera's brother and her sister Valia were also sacked from jobs at the plant. Valia, who was pregnant, was immediately renounced by her husband, who was granted a divorce on political grounds. The family struggled to make ends meet. There was never much to eat. But the hardest thing to bear, according to Vera's daughter, was their ostracism by friends and neighbours:

Everybody was afraid of us. They were afraid to talk to us, or even come near us, as if we had the plague and would infect them . . . Our neighbours avoided us, they forbade their children to play with us . . . In 1936 [when Aleksandr was arrested], nobody said anything about 'enemies of the people' – they just remained silent. But by 1937 everybody called us 'enemies of the people'.

The Nikitins, too, turned their backs on their neighbours. Anatoly Nikitin was a senior accountant at the Motovilikha works. Perhaps it was his fear of being sacked that made him cut all links with the Turkins. The two families used to eat together in a shared kitchen; their children used to play together in the yard outside. But now they kept apart and did not talk. The Nikitins even wrote to the Soviet to renounce their old neighbours and were rewarded with an extra room at the expense of the Turkins. Valia and her young baby were moved out of their room. They joined Valia's brother and mother in the room next door. Anatoly's sister then took over Valia's room, which was joined with the Nikitin side by reopening a connecting door.[128]

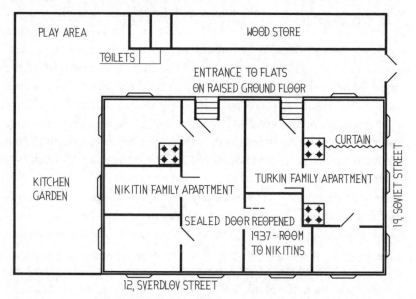

The Nikitin and Turkin apartments, Perm

The Piatnitskys were similarly ostracized after Osip's arrest in July 1937. Evicted from their apartment, with barely enough money to feed her sons, Julia turned for help to old friends in the Party. First she went to Aron Solts, a close friend of Osip for nearly thirty years. When she knocked on his door, Julia was told by his housekeeper: 'He is afraid. He will throw me out if he sees you here. He told me to tell you that he does not know you.' Julia then turned to Tsetsiliia Bobrovskaia, an Old Bolshevik whom she had known since 1917. At first she, too, refused to see Julia, but then she agreed to let her come in 'for a few minutes' before she went to work. She did not want to listen to Julia's story but told her tearfully: 'Go directly to the authorities, to Yezhov. Don't ask anything of your comrades. Nobody will help and nobody can help.' A few days later, Julia was on the Metro when she came across the widow of the Bolshevik leader Viktor Nogin: 'She looked at me but said nothing ... Then Lapev – a railwayman who knew Piatnitsky well – came into the carriage: he saw me and then for the whole journey turned to face the other way.' Julia's sons, Igor and Vladimir, were similarly abandoned by their friends. Vladimir's best friend, Yevgeny Loginov, the son of one of Stalin's secretaries, stopped coming to visit them. No one called on them any more. Vladimir was the target of a bullying campaign at school. 'They taunted me, calling me an enemy of the people,' he recalls, 'and they stole things from me, books and clothes, just because they knew that I couldn't defend myself.' Isolated and betrayed by all her friends, Julia reflected on the tenuous nature of human connection. She wrote in her diary on 20 July:

How awful people are to one another these days! I am convinced that if someone is friendly, or even just acts in a friendly or 'comradely' way, it's not from any human interest or feelings of goodwill, but simply because of some sort of material interest, or other kind of advantage. Everybody knows we've lost everything, that we have nothing to live on, that we have nothing to eat, and yet no one lifts a finger to help us. We are dying, and nobody is interested.[129]

As Elena Bonner discovered, even relatives turned their backs on the families of 'enemies of the people'. Aleksei Yevseyev and his wife Natalia were active Communists. Aleksei was a doctor, a senior consultant to the Red Army on venereal disease, Natalia an economist in the Far Eastern Timber Trust. They lived with their daughter Angelina in Khabarovsk in the Far East. In 1937, Aleksei and Natalia were both expelled from the Party (Aleksei was connected to Marshal V. K. Bliukher, whose Far Eastern Army was the target of a major purge). Angelina, who was then fifteen, recalls her father coming home after his expulsion from the Party:

He was terror-struck. He came home and said in horror: 'They're going to arrest me!' I was just a stupid girl, fifteen years of age, and I said: 'If you are arrested, it means it is necessary.' My father had always said to me, 'If they are arrested, it means it is necessary.' All my life I have lived with the echo of my words: 'It means it is necessary.' I didn't understand what it was all about.

Aleksei was arrested on 1 June. He was convicted of participating in a 'Fascist plot against the Soviet government' (he was shot in Khabarovsk in March 1938). After his arrest, Natalia and Angelina were evicted from their flat. Fearful of her own arrest, Natalia fled with Angelina to Moscow, where her family lived, hoping to leave her daughter in the care of relatives. At fifteen years of age, there was a danger that Angelina would be taken to an orphanage in the event of Natalia's arrest. None of Natalia's relatives, all ardent Communists, would help. Her younger sister, a Komsomol activist, when asked to take in Angelina, replied: 'Let Soviet power bring her up, we do not need her.' Natalia's mother was even more hostile. She told her granddaughter to her face: 'I hate your father, he is an enemy of the people, and I hate you as well.' For several days, Natalia and her daughter slept on a bench in the park, until at last they were taken in by Andrei Grigorev and his wife, old friends of Aleksei from his student days at Moscow University's Faculty of Medicine. At enormous personal risk, the Grigorevs concealed Angelina in the communal apartment where they lived, a stone's throw from the Kremlin. Angelina had no legal papers allowing her to remain in the Soviet capital, but the Grigorevs' neighbours in the communal apartment (among them Molotov's sister-in-law) turned a blind eye to the hideaway: it suited them to keep the doctors in the house. Leaving her daughter in Moscow, Natalia returned to Khabarovsk, where she was arrested a few weeks later.[130]

Shamsuvali and Gulchira Tagirov were schoolteachers in the Tatar region of Barda, 140 kilometres south-west of Perm. Shamsuvali was a revolutionary activist who had played a leading role in the establishment of the kolkhoz in their village of Akbash. In 1936, Shamsuvali was arrested as a 'Muslim nationalist' along with thirty-four other Tatar teachers and religious leaders in the Barda area (he was shot in 1938). Gulchira was left on her own with six children, the eldest aged eleven and the youngest just a few weeks old. As one of the people in the village who could read (in Tatar and in Russian), Gulchira was respected by the villagers, who made sure that she had enough food to feed her family. Even the arresting officer, who was filled with remorse for having to arrest a good man like Tagirov, helped Gulchira and her family. He brought them milk or fed them at his house. Once a week he passed letters between Gulchira and Shamsuvali, who was imprisoned in Barda. 'Forgive me,' he wrote to Shamsuvali in a letter of his own, 'I had no choice. They forced me to arrest you, even though I knew that you were innocent. Now I shall redeem my guilt and help your family.' Gulchira stayed on as a teacher in the Akbash village school, although her lessons were often monitored by NKVD operatives; they checked for signs of Muslim nationalism in everything she said.

In 1937, Gulchira and her six children were evicted from their house, following a denunciation by the chairman of the village Soviet. With their possessions on a horse and cart, they walked 20 kilometres to the village of Yekshur, where Shamsuvali's mother lived with her eldest son in a large two-storeyed house with room to spare. Shamsuvali's mother was an educated and religious woman: her house was full of books. But she refused to take them in. She blamed Gulchira for the arrest of her son. Having heard the rumours of her daughter-in-law's growing friendship with the arresting officer, perhaps she suspected that Gulchira had played an active part in Shamsuvali's arrest. Gulchira's

Gulchira Tagirova and her children (Rezeda centre), 1937.
The photograph was taken in a studio in Sarapul
and sent to Shamsuvali in prison

daughter, Rezeda, believes that her father's relatives were motivated by the fear that Gulchira was an 'enemy of the people' who had been responsible for the arrest of her husband and who might endanger them as well. Shamsuvali's mother told Gulchira that her house was full. She would not let her in, or even give her food for the children after their long walk. That night the family of Shamsuvali's younger brother moved into the spare rooms on the second floor (he sold his own house in Akbash, where he was a trader, to consolidate the move). Turned away by her husband's family, Gulchira and her children found a room to rent from a kolkhoz worker on the edge of the village. Shamsuvali's mother came to visit them on one occasion but complained about the noise made by the children and did not come again. Gulchira and her children lived in Yekshur for fifteen years, but only rarely did they see the Tagirov family, who refused to talk to them. 'The most painful thing,' recalls Gulchira, 'was to see them pass us on the street – surely there was no one to hear them there – but they still wouldn't speak to us, not even say hello.' Gulchira's children grew up in the same village as their cousins but rarely mixed with them. 'We went to school with them, but we never played with them, or went to their house,' recalls Rezeda. 'They were always cold towards us, and we were cold towards them.'[131]

Fear brought out the worst in people. Yet there were also acts of extraordinary kindness by colleagues, friends and neighbours, some-times even strangers, who took enormous risks to help the families of 'enemies of the people'. They took their children in, gave them food and money or put them up when they were evicted from their homes. There were Bolshevik officials and NKVD men who took pity on their victims' families and tried their best to assist them by warning them of danger or tracking down arrested relatives.[132]

In March 1937, the architect Mikhail Stroikov was rearrested in exile in Arkhangelsk. His wife Elena and their ten-year-old daughter Julia were taken in by an old friend of the family, Konstantin Artseulov, who was also living in exile in the town of Mozhaisk, 100 kilometres south-west of Moscow, with his wife Tatiana and their son Oleg, who was Julia's age. Konstantin was unemployed. An artist by training, he had been dismissed from his job as a pilot in the Soviet air force shortly before his arrest and as an exile could not find work in Mozhaisk. The whole burden of supporting the two families fell on Tatiana, who worked as a teacher in Mozhaisk. 'They sold everything they could in order to ensure that we were fed,' recalls Julia. 'They risked their own necks to take us in.' Julia remained with the Artseulovs while her mother went in search of work. In November 1937, Konstantin was denounced by a neighbour for harbouring the daughter of an 'enemy of the people'. He was rearrested, imprisoned and later shot. Still his wife Tatiana continued to shelter Julia, carefully concealing her from their malicious neighbours. Eventually, in 1938, Tatiana smuggled Julia to Moscow, where friends of Konstantin agreed to take her in until her mother found a job. Elena came for her that summer and took her to Pushkino, a small town north of Moscow, where Konstantin's connections helped her find a job in the Moscow City Committee of Artists, an organization responsible for producing portraits of the Soviet leaders. Elena became one of the leading portraitists of the Soviet leadership – an ironic ending for the wife of an 'enemy of the people'.[133]

Oleg Liubchenko's father, a Ukrainian journalist, was arrested in 1934 and shot in 1937. Exiled from Kiev, Oleg and his mother Vera ended up in Maloiaroslavets, a small town south-west of Moscow. They did not have a passport for Moscow, but they often went to stay there in a communal apartment on the Arbat, where Vera's family, once well-known landowners in Riazan, had lived for several years in the 1920s. Vera's sister still lived in the apartment. From 1936 to 1941 Oleg and his mother stayed in the flat illegally. All the inhabitants of the apartment were very welcoming, risking eviction and perhaps arrest for harbouring illegal immigrants. The elder of the apartment, an old Chekist called Klavdiia Kolchina, was particularly supportive. It was she who had originally invited Vera's family to live in the apartment at the end of the Civil War, when she had come to Moscow from Riazan and had met them on the street. Klavdiia had known of Oleg's father in Riazan, and was certain that he was innocent of the crimes for which he had been shot. Having been part of the Cheka, and knowing how they worked, she would often say: 'We have laws but no legality.' The head of the house committee was also well disposed, even though she was an active Communist. She was well aware that illegals were living in the flat but, recalls Oleg, on the rare occasions when he or his mother ventured into the courtyard, or when the head of the house committee saw them entering through a side door, she would 'look right past us with a stern expression, as if trying not to notice us'.[134] There were lots of illegals in the housing blocks of the Arbat, a prestige area of the capital that was hit hard by the Great Terror.

After Ilia Slavin was arrested in November 1937, his wife Esfir and their daughter Ida were ejected from their three-room apartment in the

House of the Leningrad Soviet. They were moved to a tiny room, 8 metres square, in a communal apartment, without running water or electricity, in the distant outskirts of Leningrad. Five months later, Esfir was arrested too. She was imprisoned in the Kresty jail and then sentenced to eight years in the Akmolinsk Labour Camp for the Wives of Traitors to the Motherland (ALZhIR) in Kazakhstan. Suddenly, the sixteen-year-old Ida, who had lived the sheltered life of a professor's daughter, was left on her own. 'I was completely unprepared for the daily chores of existence,' she recalls. 'I did not even know the price of bread, or how to wash my clothes.' Without any other relatives in Leningrad, Ida was unable to support herself; she could not even pay the rent on her small room. But she was saved by her classmates and their parents, who took turns to put her up for a few days (if they kept her any longer they would run the risk of being denounced by their neighbours for harbouring the daughter of an 'enemy of the people'). For many of these families, housing and feeding an extra child was a real burden. For Ida the importance of their help was inestimable: 'They not only gave me food and shelter, but the spiritual support I needed to survive.'

Ida studied hard at school for the exams she had to pass to graduate to the tenth and final class, from which she could apply to a higher institute. With help from friends, she found a cleaning job, which enabled her to pay the rent for her small room. Every day, she would travel for three hours between home and school, and then another hour to get to her cleaning job. Two nights a week, she would stand in prison queues trying to find out where her parents had been taken, and if they were still alive.

The other person to help Ida was the director of her school, Klavdiia Alekseyeva. An old and respected Party member, Alekseyeva had always been opposed to the Party culture of purging in her school and she had done her best to resist it by quietly protecting those children whose parents had been named as 'enemies of the people'. She had, for example, organized the lodging system that had rescued not just Ida but many other orphaned children in the school. On one occasion Alekseyeva had bravely overruled the Komsomol when it had tried to expel a fifteen-year-old girl for 'failing to denounce' her own mother, who had been arrested as an 'enemy of the people'. Ida recalls that Klavdiia opted for a relatively simple tactic. She was deliberately 'naive' and 'literal-minded' in her fulfilment of Stalin's famous 'directive': 'Sons do not answer for fathers.'*

In our school there were many children whose parents had been arrested. Thanks to Klavdiia, no one was expelled. There were none of those frightful meetings – which took place in other schools – where such children were obliged to renounce their parents ... The day after my mother's arrest, when I appeared at school, Klavdiia called me to her office and told me that until the end of the academic year my school meals would be paid for by the parents' committee. She suggested that I write a letter asking to be exempted from the school exams on health grounds [thus allowing Ida to advance automatically to the tenth class]. 'But Klavdiia Aleksandrovna,' I replied, 'I am perfectly healthy.' She shrugged her shoulders, smiled and winked at me.

Ida was exempted from the exams. But life continued to be very hard, and she came close to giving up her studies many times:

When I spoke of leaving school in order to find work, Klavdiia took me to her office and told me: 'Your parents will return – you must believe that. They will not forgive you, if you fail to finish your studies and make something of yourself.' That inspired me to continue.[135]

Ida became a teacher.

Ida Slavina was not the only child to be supported by the director of her school. Elena Bonner, a classmate of Ida's, was also helped by Klavdiia Alekseyeva. After the arrest of her parents, in the summer of 1937, Elena worked as a cleaner in the evenings, but that was not enough to pay the school fees (introduced in middle-level schools from 1938). She decided to leave school and get a full-time job, continuing her studies at night school, where she would not have to pay. Elena took the application form to Alekseyeva for her approval.

Klavdiia Alexandrovna took the piece of paper from me, read it, got up from her desk, shut the door to her office and said quietly, 'Do you really think I'd take money from you for your education? Go!'

---

*At a meeting of Party workers and combine-operators in December 1935, one young combine-operator said that he would fight for the victory of socialism even though he was the son of a 'kulak', to which Stalin replied: 'A son does not answer for his father.' The press seized on this mendacious slogan and built it up into the 'directive' of Stalin.

To get an exemption from the school fees Elena had to apply to a party official, the Komsorg, or Komsomol organizer, who 'kept an eye on the political and moral state of the students and teachers' and 'terrified everyone in the school – as the obvious representative of the NKVD'. Bonner was too frightened to apply. Her school fees ended up being paid by somebody anonymously – she believes by Klavdiia herself. Looking back on these events, Elena recalls that in their class of twenty-four there were eleven children whose parents had been arrested.

We all knew who we were but we did not talk, we did not want to draw attention to ourselves, but just carried on as normal kids . . . I am almost certain that every one of those eleven children finished the tenth class at the same time as me – they were all saved by the director of our school.[136]

Of all the professions, teachers feature the most frequently as the protectors and even saviours of children such as Ida Slavina. Many teachers had been schooled in the humanitarian values of the old intelligentsia, especially in elite schools like Slavina's. 'Most of our teachers were highly educated, humane and liberal people,' recalls Ida.

Our physical culture teacher had been an officer in the tsarist army and had fought in the Red Cavalry in the Civil War. He was fluent in three European languages . . . We had a drama group and a poetry club, both encouraged by our teachers, I now realize, as a way of exposing us to nineteenth-century literature, which had no place in the 'Soviet classroom'. Our history teacher, Manus Nudelman, was a brilliant story-teller and popularizer of history. He was a nonconformist, both in his ideas and in the way he dressed, which was eccentric and bohemian. In his lessons he carefully avoided the cult of Stalin which was mandatory for all history lessons in those times. He was arrested in 1939.[137]

Svetlana Cherkesova was only eight when her parents were arrested in 1937. She lived with her uncle and went to school in Leningrad, where her teacher, Vera Yeliseyeva, taught the children to be kind to Svetlana because she was 'an unfortunate' (a word from the lexicon of nineteenth-century charity). Svetlana remembers:

In our class there were no enemies of the people – that was what our teacher said. She made a point of taking in the children of people who had disappeared. There were lots of them. There was one boy, for example, who was living on the streets, he was always dirty, without shoes or clothes, for there was nobody to care for him. She bought him a coat out of her own money and took him home to clean him up.[138]

Vera Yeliseyeva was arrested in 1938.

Dmitry Streletsky was also treated kindly by his schoolteachers in Chermoz, where his family lived in exile from 1933. His physics teacher gave him money for his lunch, which his family could not afford. Dmitry wanted to thank his teacher, but when she put the money in his hand she would put her finger to her mouth to signal that he should not speak. The teacher was afraid of getting into trouble if it became known that she had been helping the son of an 'enemy of the people'. Dmitry recalls:

There were never any words: I never got the chance to say thank you. She would wait for me outside the dining hall and, as I passed, would slip three roubles in my hand. Perhaps she whispered something as I passed – something to encourage me – but that was all. I never spoke to her, and she did not really speak to me, but I felt enormous gratitude, and she understood.[139]

Inna Gaister's school (School No. 19) was in the centre of Moscow, close to the House on the Embankment where many of the Soviet leaders lived, and it had lots of children who had lost their parents in the Great Terror. At the nearby Moscow Experimental School (MOPSh), favoured by many of the Bolshevik elite, such children would have been expelled or forced to renounce their parents after their arrest. But at Gaister's school the atmosphere was different; the teachers had a liberal and protective attitude towards their students. After the arrest of both her parents, in June 1937, Inna went back to her school at the start of the academic year. For a long time she was frightened to tell her teachers what had happened. 'We were brought up on the story of Pavlik Morozov,' explains Inna, who feared that she would be expected to renounce her parents like the boy hero. But when at last she summoned up the courage and told her teacher everything, the teacher merely said: 'Well, so what? Now let's go to class.' Inna's father was one of the accused in the high-profile Bukharin trial, but none of her teachers drew attention to this fact. When school fees were introduced, her teacher paid them out of her salary (Vladimir Piatnitsky, Osip's youngest son, a student at the same school, was also supported by a teacher). Through the influence of these courageous teachers, School No. 19 became a place of safety for children of 'enemies of the people'. The other children were encouraged to feel protective towards them. Inna recalls an occasion involving one of the roughest boys in her class (he had been adopted by his parents from an orphanage and had severe behavioural problems). The boy had compiled a list of twenty-five 'Trotskyists' in the class (i.e. children of 'enemies of the people') and put it up on the classroom wall. He was attacked by all the other children in the class. Inna also remembers an incident connected with the Tukhachevsky trial, when Soviet schools were instructed to erase the image of this 'enemy of the people' from textbooks. At Gaister's school there was a different policy:

Some of the boys were defacing Tukhachevsky's picture in their books, adding a moustache or a pair of horns. One of our teachers, Rakhil Grigorevna, said to them: 'I have already said this to the girls and now I will say it to you: I am going to give each of you a piece of paper, and I want you to paste it neatly into your books to cover Tukhachevsky's face. But do it carefully, because today he may be a bad person, an enemy of the people, but tomorrow he and the others may return, and we may come to think of them all as good people once again. And then you will be able to take away the piece of paper without disfiguring his face.'[140]

6

When Sofia Antonov-Ovseyenko was arrested in the Black Sea resort of Sukhumi, on 14 October 1937, she did not realize that her husband Vladimir had been arrested three days earlier in Moscow. Vladimir was Sofia's second husband, and Sofia his second wife. The couple had met in Prague in 1927, when Vladimir, a veteran Bolshevik who had led the storming of the Winter Palace in October 1917, was the Soviet ambassador to Czechoslovakia (he was later the ambassador to Poland and to Spain). In 1937, when Vladimir was recalled to Moscow to take up the post of Commissar of Justice, they were still very much in love, but Sofia's arrest threw all that into doubt. After her arrest she was brought back to Moscow. From her prison cell, she wrote to Vladimir, begging him to believe that she was innocent. Sofia did not know that he would read the letter in another Moscow prison cell.

M[oscow]. 16/X. Prison.
My darling. I do not know if you will receive this, but somehow I sense that I

am writing to you for the last time. Do you recall how we always said that if someone in our country was arrested then it must be for good reason, for some crime – that is for something? No doubt there is something in my case as well, but what it is I do not know. Everything I know, you know as well, because our

Vladimir Antonov-Ovseyenko with his wife Sofia (right) and stepdaughter Valentina (Valichka), 1936

lives have been inseparable and harmonious. Whatever happens to me now, I shall always be thankful for the day we met. I lived in the reflection of your glory and was proud of it. For the past three days I have been thinking through my life, preparing for death. I cannot think of anything (apart from the usual shortcomings that differentiate a human being from an 'angel') that could be considered criminal, either in relation to other human beings or in relation to our state and government . . . I thought exactly as you thought – and is there anybody more dedicated than you are to our Party and country? You know what is in my heart, you know the truth of my actions, of my thoughts and words. But the fact that I am here must mean that I have committed some wrong – what I do not know . . . I cannot bear the thought that you might not believe me . . . It has been oppressing me for three days now. It burns inside my brain. I know your intolerance of all dishonesty, but even you can be mistaken. Lenin was mistaken too, it seems. So please believe me when I say that I did nothing wrong.

Believe me, my loved one . . . One more thing: it is time for Valichka [Sofia's daughter from her first marriage] to join the Komsomol. This will no doubt stand in her way. My heart is full of sorrow at the thought that she will think that her mother is a scoundrel. The full horror of my situation is that people do not believe me, I cannot live like that . . . I beg forgiveness from everyone I love for bringing them such misfortune . . . Forgive me, my loved one. If only I knew that you believed me and forgave me! Your Sofia.[141]

The Great Terror undermined the trust that held together families. Wives doubted husbands; husbands doubted wives. The bond between parent and child was usually the first of these family ties to unravel. The children of the 1930s, brought up on the cult of Pavlik Morozov, had been taught to put their faith in Stalin and the Soviet government, to believe every word they read in the Soviet press, even when it named their parents as 'enemies of the people'. Children were put under pressure by their schools, by the Pioneers and the Komsomol, to renounce arrested relatives, or suffer the consequences for their education and career.

Lev Tselmerovsky was eighteen years old when his father – a shock-worker and military engineer – was arrested in Leningrad in 1938. Lev had been a member of the Komsomol, a trainee pilot, who dreamed of joining the Red Army, but after the arrest of his father he was exiled without trial as a 'socially alien element' to Chimkent in Kazakhstan, where he worked in a factory. His mother and two sisters lived in Kazalinsk, 500 kilometres away. In September 1938, Lev wrote to Kalinin, the Soviet President, to renounce his father and appeal against the principle of being punished for his crimes:

A few words about my father. My mother told me that he was banished to the Northern camps for being a malcontent. I personally never believed it, because I myself heard him tell his sisters how he fought against the Whites in the North. He told us about his exploits. When S. M. Kirov was assassinated, he cried . . . But maybe this was all a clever disguise. He did tell me a few times that he had been in Warsaw . . . I think that my father should be allowed to answer for himself, but I do not want to suffer the disgrace that he has caused. I want to serve in the Red Army. I want to be a Soviet citizen with equal rights because I feel that I am worthy of that title. I was educated in a Soviet school in the Soviet spirit and therefore my views are obviously completely different from his. It is heartbreaking for me to carry the papers of an alien person.[142]

Anna Krivko was eighteen in 1937, when her father and her uncle – both factory workers in Kharkov – were arrested. Anna was expelled from Kharkov University and kicked out of the Komsomol as an 'alien element'. She went in search of a job to support her mother, her grandmother and her sister, who was then just a baby. She worked for a while on a pig farm but was sacked when they found out about the arrest of her father. She could not find any other employment. In January 1938, Anna wrote to her Soviet deputy, the Politburo member Vlas Chubar. She renounced her father and begged Chubar to help her family. Anna threatened to kill herself and her baby sister, if she couldn't grow up to live a decent life in the Soviet Union. Anna's letter of renunciation was extreme; she was desperate to prove that she was worthy of salvation as a loyal Stalinist. But it may also be that she genuinely hated her father for bringing such disaster to her family:

I do not know what my father and his brother are accused of, or how long they have been sentenced for. I feel ashamed and I do not want to know. I believe profoundly that the proletarian court is just, and if they have been sentenced, then it means they deserved it. I have no feelings of a daughter towards my father, only the higher feeling of duty as a Soviet citizen to the Fatherland, the Komsomol, which educated me, and the Communist Party. With all my heart I support the decision of the court, the voice of 170 million proletarians, and rejoice in that judgement. By my father's own admission, he was mobilized into Denikin's army, where he served as a White Guard for three months in 1919, and for this he was sentenced to two and a half years [in a labour camp] in 1929; that is all I know about his activities . . . If I had noticed any other sign of his anti-Soviet views – even though he is my father – I would not have hesitated for a moment to denounce him to the NKVD. Comrade Chubar! Believe me: I feel ashamed to call him my father. An enemy of the people cannot be my father. Only the people, who have taught me to hate all scoundrels, all enemies, without exception or mercy, can have that role. I hold on to the hope that the proletariat, Lenin's Komsomol and the Party of Lenin and Stalin will take the place of my father, that they will care for me as their true daughter and that they will help me on my path through life.[143]

Some parents, after their arrest, encouraged their children to renounce them, concerned not to jeopardize their social or career prospects. Olga Adamova-Sliuzberg met a woman called Liza in the Kazan jail in 1937. Liza had grown up in St Petersburg before the Revolution. She had spent her childhood on the streets because her mother was a beggar. After 1917, Liza worked in a factory. She joined the Party and married a Bolshevik official on the factory management committee. They lived well and brought up their two daughters, the eldest Zoia and the younger Lialia, to be model Pioneers. 'Sometimes we would have a children's morning at the factory,' Liza told Olga,

and our little girl Zoia would stand up and sing in her silk dress with her Pioneer's tie, and my husband would say to me, 'There's not a girl in the world who is better than our Zoia. She's going to be an Artist of the People when she grows up.' Then I would remember how I had tramped from door to door as a child . . . and I loved our Soviet government so much that I would have given up my life for it.

Liza's husband was arrested as a supporter of Zinoviev ('If I had known that he had betrayed Lenin, I would have throttled him with my own hands,' Liza said). Then she was arrested too. One day Liza got a letter from Zoia. It arrived late, on a Saturday, the day allotted for the prisoners to write, just as Liza was writing to Zoia:

Dear Mama, I'm fifteen years old now and I'm planning to join the Komsomol. I have to know whether you are guilty or not. I keep thinking, how could you have betrayed our Soviet power? After all, we were doing so well, and you and Papa were both workers. I remember how well we lived. You used to make us silk dresses and buy us sweets. Did you really get money from 'them' ['enemies of the people']? You'd have done better to let us go around in cotton frocks. But maybe you are not guilty after all? In that case I won't join the Komsomol and I'll never forgive them on your account. But if you're guilty, then I won't write to you any more, because I love our Soviet government and I hate its enemies and I will hate you if you are one of them. Mama, tell me the truth. I'd rather you weren't guilty, I wouldn't join the Komsomol. Your unhappy daughter, Zoia.

Liza had already used up three of the four allotted pages of her letter to Zoia. She thought for a moment and then wrote on the final page in big capital letters:

ZOIA, YOU ARE RIGHT. I AM GUILTY. JOIN THE KOMSOMOL. THIS IS THE LAST TIME I AM GOING TO WRITE TO YOU. BE HAPPY, YOU AND LIALIA. MOTHER.

Liza showed the correspondence to Olga, and then banged her head on the table. Choking on her tears, she said: 'It is better she hates me. How would she live without the Komsomol – an alien? She would hate Soviet power. It is better she hates me.' From that day, recalls Olga, Liza 'never said a word about her daughters and did not receive any more letters'.[144]

For many children the arrest of a close relative raised all sorts of doubts. All the principles they had believed as 'Soviet children' were suddenly in conflict with what they knew of the people they loved.

When her father was arrested as a 'Trotskyist', Vera Turkina did not know what to believe. Her mother and grandmother both accepted Aleksandr's guilt. There were reports in the Soviet press about the criminal activities of her father, who was a well-known Bolshevik in Perm. Wherever Vera went, she heard people whispering about her, the daughter of an 'enemy of the people', behind her back. 'My father became a source of shame,' Vera remembers.

People said to me that if he had been arrested, then he must be guilty of something. 'There is no smoke without fire,' everybody said. When my mother went to ask about my father at the NKVD offices, they told her: 'Wait and see, he will confess to everything.' I too assumed that he must be guilty. What else was I to believe?[145]

Elga Torchinskaia was a model Soviet schoolgirl. She loved Stalin, venerated Pavlik Morozov and believed in the propaganda about 'spies' and 'enemies'. She still thought this way when her father was arrested in October 1937. A veteran Bolshevik increasingly opposed to Stalin's policies, he had never talked to her about his political opinions. In the Torchinsky household in Leningrad, as in many families, politics was not a subject for discussion in the presence of children. Elga thus had no perspective on the mass arrests beyond the one she had learned in school – she had no other way to understand the reasons for the arrest of her father, no way of her own to question why it had happened. In 1938, two of Elga's uncles were arrested. One of them returned from the labour camps in 1939 and told Elga awful stories about his torture by the NKVD. Even this could not shake Elga from her conviction that if someone was arrested, it 'must have been for something he had done'. In 1939, when she turned sixteen, Elga applied to join the Komsomol. In her application she declared that her father was an 'enemy of the people', and falsely claimed that he was divorced from her mother. Her declaration was a renunciation of sorts, but, as Elga now admits, she was confused at the time, she was afraid to question anything and it was from ignorance that she rejected him. 'We were all zombies – that is what I think. My God, we were just young girls. We had been educated by the Komsomol. We believed everything we were told.'[146]

The silence, the lack of any news or information, exacerbated a family's uncertainty. Without word from the arrested person or anything to prove his innocence, relatives had nothing to cling to, nothing to oppose the public assumption of guilt.

Nina Kosterina was the daughter of a long-time Bolshevik. She had a model Soviet childhood, joining the Komsomol at the end of 1936, just as the first tremors of the Terror began to register on her political consciousness. When her uncle was arrested, Nina struggled to make sense of the event. She wrote in her diary on 25 March 1937:

Something frightful and incomprehensible has happened. They say that Uncle Misha was involved with some counter-revolutionary organization. What is going on? Uncle Misha – a member of the Party from the very first days of the Revolution – and suddenly an enemy of the people!

When their landlord was arrested, Nina wondered how she would react if the arrests came closer to home:

Something strange is happening. I thought and thought, and came to the conclusion: if my father also turns out to be a Trotskyist and an enemy of his country, I shall not feel sorry for him! I write this, but (I confess) there is a gnawing worm of doubt.

In December 1937, Nina's father was expelled from the Party and dismissed from his official position. Anticipating his arrest, he wrote to Nina to warn her: 'you must be sure that your father was never a scoundrel ... and has never blemished his name by anything dirty or base'. The letter played a crucial role: although confused and in despair, Nina was able to cling to the belief in her father's innocence when he was finally arrested, in September 1938. As she noted in her diary:

September 7
What an ominous darkness has shrouded my whole life. Father's arrest is such a blow ... Until now I have always carried my head high and with honour, but now ... Now Akhmetev [a classmate] can say to me, 'We're comrades in misfortune!' And just to think how I despised him and despised his father, a

Trotskyist. The nightmare thought oppresses me day and night: is my father also an enemy? No, it cannot be, I don't believe it! It's all a terrible mistake!

Nina's father spent two years in prison waiting for his 'trial' by a troika, which sentenced him to five years in a labour camp as a 'socially dangerous element'. In November 1940, he wrote his first letter home. Nina was touched by the beauty of the letter, in which she felt the spirit of her father, his 'strength and freshness', despite the hardships of the camp. But her mother was annoyed and merely asked: 'Is he guilty, or is he not guilty? If he's innocent, why doesn't he appeal against the sentence?' The next letter effectively answered her mother's question. 'There is nothing more to be said about my case,' Nina's father wrote. 'There is no case, only a soap bubble in the shape of an elephant. I cannot refute what is not, was not, and could never have been.'[147]

The disappearance of a father and a husband placed enormous strain on families. Wives renounced husbands who had been arrested, not necessarily because they thought their spouses might be 'enemies of the people', although they may have had that thought, but because it made survival easier and gave protection to their families (many husbands for this reason advised wives to renounce them). The state put pressure on the wives of 'enemies' to renounce their husbands publicly. Failure to do so could have serious consequences. Some women were arrested as the 'wives of enemies' and sent to labour camps, with or without their children. Others were evicted from their homes, dismissed from jobs, deprived of rations and civil rights. Financial pressures were applied as well: salaries were docked, savings frozen and rents raised. To encourage women to renounce their husbands, the cost of a divorce, which normally would set a couple back 500 roubles, was reduced to just 3 roubles (the price of a canteen meal) in cases of divorce from a prisoner.[148]

It took extraordinary resilience, and not a little bravery, for women to resist these pressures and stand by their husbands. Irina and Vasily Dudarev had been married for nearly fifteen years when Vasily was arrested in 1937. They had met in Smolensk in the early 1920s, when both of them were training to become teachers. A Bolshevik from the Civil War, Vasily became a senior Party figure in Orel. In 1933, he was sent to Azov, a town near Rostov at the mouth of the River Don, where he became the Party boss. Irina worked in a hosiery factory. She was not a political person, but out of love for Vasily she joined the Party and became a 'Party wife'. When he was arrested, Irina went in search of him – not just at the jails but also at the railway depots of Rostov and Bataisk, 30 kilometres away, where on Sunday evenings the trains containing prisoners were prepared for their departure to the labour camps:

I would walk along the tracks beside the trains in the hope of finding my husband so that I could give him some things for the journey. I saw many convoys. The ice-coated goods wagons were nailed shut; even the windows at the top were blocked with metal strips, leaving just a little crack. From the wagons I could hear the muffled hum of voices. As I passed along the train, I would call out: 'Is Dudarev there?' The hum would die away, and sometimes a voice would answer, 'No.' . . . But then one day a voice answered, 'Dudarev? Yes.' It was the train guard . . . I took out the clean clothes I had prepared and handed them in a little bag to the guard. He let me write a note, 'on business affairs'. I was so happy that Vasily would know that I was looking for him, and that I was thinking about him. I had been so afraid that, without news from me, he would think I had renounced him . . . In my note I wrote a list of the things I had handed to the guard and signed off: 'All are well. I kiss you.' A few minutes later the guard returned my bag with the note. On the other side was written in Vasily's hand: 'Got all. Thank you.'

Irina never doubted her husband's innocence. She was summoned repeatedly by the NKVD, presented with the 'evidence' of his criminal activities and threatened with arrest if she failed to denounce him, but she refused every time. Irina recalls a Party meeting at her factory where she was called upon to disclose her husband's crimes against the state. In similar circumstances most wives claimed that they had never known about their husband's crimes, but Irina courageously denied that hers had committed any crime:

I sat alone at one end of the table, while everybody else sat as close as they could to the committee leaders at the other end. No one would talk to me. One of the Party secretaries informed the meeting that Dudarev had been arrested as an enemy of the people, and that now they had to decide about me. The Party members spoke in turn. They did not have much to say except slogans. About me they said nothing, except that I had deceived the Party. They demanded that I tell them about my husband's crimes and explain why I had concealed them. No one looked at me. Trying to stay calm, I answered briefly, thinking very carefully about every word. I said that I had lived with my husband for fifteen years, that I knew him to be a good Communist, that through his influence I had joined the Party and that I did not believe for a moment that he had been involved in anything wrong. This gave rise to a lot of muttering. Someone shouted: 'But he has been arrested!' As if that were proof of guilt. One by one they tried to convince me that it was my Party duty to disclose Dudarev's crimes. But no one dared to state the charges against him ... Again and again they asked me to denounce Dudarev as an enemy of the people. Each time I refused.

Irina was expelled from the Party. She lost her position on the management committee of her factory and was demoted to a poorly paid job in the accounts department. A few days later, the town Soviet levied a large back-tax on her apartment, explaining that it was to pay for the 'surplus living space' she and her husband had occupied for several years. In July 1938, Irina was arrested 'for failing to denounce the enemy activities of her husband'. She was released the following December and returned to Smolensk.[149] Dudarev was shot in 1937.*

Julia Piatnitskaia did not know what to believe about her husband after his arrest. She wanted to think the best of him, but the desperate position in which Osip had left her made it hard not to bear him a grudge – as her sons did – for bringing such misfortune on the family. Sixteen-year-old Igor felt let down by his father, whose arrest had isolated him from his friends in the Komsomol. Twelve-year-old Vladimir blamed his father for ruining his dreams of a career in the Red Army. 'Vova [Vladimir] hates his father bitterly and feels sorry for Igor,' Julia wrote in her diary. Bullied by his former friends and frequently in trouble at school, Vladimir was shaken by an incident in the Pioneers: the leader had questioned him about his father, and when Vladimir refused to answer, declared, for everyone to hear: 'Your father is an enemy of the people. It is now your duty to decide your relation towards him.'

Julia and Vladimir had constant fights. On one occasion, when Vladimir was angry because his mother had refused to write to Yezhov for the return of his toy gun and some military books, which had been confiscated by the NKVD during the house search, he said to her in

---

*Irina never found out about his death. She continued to look for him, writing hundreds of letters to the Soviet authorities until her own death in 1974. After 1956, Irina was invited to rejoin the Party, but she refused.

anger: 'It is a shame they have not shot Papa, since he is an enemy of the people.' On another, when he came home with a poor mark from school, Julia lost her temper and swore at Vladimir. She told him, as she put it in her diary, 'that his bad behaviour showed he was the son of an enemy of the people.' Bursting into tears, Vladimir replied: 'Is it my fault that I was born the son of an enemy? I don't want you as my mother any more, I am going to an orphanage.' Julia threatened to send him off to bed with just a crust of bread. Vladimir said he would 'cut her throat'. Then she hit him twice across the face.[150]

Julia was at the end of her rope. Evicted from their flat and struggling to find a proper job, she began to question her husband even more intensely. 'There is only one thought in my head – who is Piatnitsky?' Julia asked herself.

20 July 1937
... Yesterday evening I thought about Piatnitsky and I was full of bitterness: how could he have let us fall into such a shameful mess? How can it be that he worked with those people and knew their methods, and yet could not foresee that they would condemn us to a life of torment and hunger? ... One could bear a bitter grudge against Piatnitsky. He let his children be destroyed; he lost all our money, and it wasn't much to begin with. But who exactly are these men who have stolen all our things? Authority now is nothing but arbitrary terror – and everybody is afraid. I am going mad. What am I thinking? What am I thinking?[151]

For six months Julia carried on this self-interrogation in her diary, trying to work out who her husband really was. Informed that he had been charged with espionage and counter-revolutionary activities on 7 February 1938, Julia wrote in her diary:

Who is he? If he is a professional revolutionary, as he claimed to be, this man I knew for seventeen years, then he was unfortunate: he was surrounded by spies and enemies, who sabotaged his work, and that of many others, and he just didn't see it ... But evidently Piatnitsky never was a professional revolutionary, but a professional scoundrel and a spy, which explains why he was so closed and severe as a man. Evidently, he was not the man we thought he was ... And all of us – I, his wife, the children – had no real significance for him.[152]

Igor was arrested on 9 February 1938. He was in his classroom at school when two soldiers came for him. Igor was imprisoned in the Butyrki jail. Consumed by worry for her son, Julia fell into complete despair. According to Vladimir, she had a nervous breakdown – she spent whole days in bed and often thought of suicide.[153] The only thing that kept her going was the idea of living for her sons, which she repeated like a mantra in her diary. 'It would be best to die,' she wrote on 9 March. 'But that would leave my Vovka and Igor without a human being in the world. I'm all they have, and that means that I must fight to stay alive.' Yet there were moments when Julia felt so despondent that the only salvation she could imagine was to break all human ties, even with her sons:

17 February 1938
Last night I thought I had found the solution: not death, though that is the easiest and most appealing solution, given my weak will and deep despair . . . but this idea: the children are not necessary: give Vovka to the state and live just for work – work ceaselessly, take time only for reading, live close to nature . . . have no feelings for any human being. It seemed such a good solution – to spend oneself in work, and not to have anybody close for them to take away. Why do I have Vovka and what good am I to him? I am buried by a mountain much too big to enjoy the life of a normal human being, to live for Vovka. He just wants to live, to have friends, the sun, a cosy home, a meaningful existence, but I – I am the wife of a counter-revolutionary.[154]

Julia tried to figure out the reasons for the arrest of Osip and Igor. Unlike Vladimir, she could not bring herself to hate Osip as an 'enemy of the people'. She noted in her diary: 'Vovka torments me because I am unable to hate Piatnitsky; at first I thought that I would surely end up hating him, but in the end I have too many doubts.' She tried to reason with Vladimir, arguing that his father 'could be innocent and they made a mistake, or maybe he was deceived by the enemies'.[155] Julia believed in the existence of 'enemies of the people'. She often pointed out 'suspicious' people in her diary, and she had no doubts about the justice of the Soviet courts. During the Bukharin trial, she was convinced that the 'evil-doers' had been rightly sentenced to be shot. Politically, she was naive, slow to understand the reality that engulfed her. She was more than willing to make Bukharin a scapegoat for the catastrophe that had destroyed her family. Commenting on the execution of Bukharin and his co-defendants in March 1938, Julia thought that 'the spilling of their evil blood' was 'too small a price for them to pay for the suffering the Party has endured'.

Today they are going to erase them from this earth, but that won't do much to reduce my hatred. I would give them an awful death: build a special cage for them in a museum for counter-revolutionaries, and let us come and gawk at them ... That would be unbearable for them: citizens coming to stare at them as if they were animals. Our hatred for them would never cease. Let them see how we go on working to build a better life, how we are all united, how we love our leaders, leaders who are not traitors. Let them see how we struggle against Fascism while they do nothing but feed themselves like animals, for they are not worthy to be called people.

Picturing the 'better life' of the future, when 'only honest people will be allowed to live and work', Julia saw some hope for her own family:

Maybe Igor will return, and Piatnitsky as well – if, that is, he is honest and, of course, innocent of the crimes which were committed by so many enemies, or of failing to detect all these reptiles; if his intentions were honest, then of course he will return. How I'd like to know! Piatnitsky – are you guilty in any way? Did you disagree with the Party line? Were you opposed to even one of our leaders? How much easier my life would be, if I knew the truth. And as far as Igor is concerned, I think of the words of F—. 'Everything that is well made will withstand the fire. And that which doesn't, we don't need.'[156]

Julia resolved to place her faith in the fire: if Osip was innocent, he too would survive the Terror.

Piatnitsky was imprisoned in the Butyrki jail, the same prison where his son was held. Lev Razgon encountered him in a crowded cell (built for twenty-five but housing sixty-seven) at the start of April 1938. Razgon saw a 'thin and crooked old man [Piatnitsky was then fifty-six] who bore the marks of battle in his face'.

[Piatnitsky] explained, when he saw me looking at his face, that these were the marks left by the metal buckle of his interrogator's belt. I had seen Piatnitsky in the early months of 1937 ... The man who stood before me now was totally unrecognizable as the man I had seen before. Only the eyes were the same bright, lively eyes, though now much more sad. They betrayed an immense spiritual suffering.

Piatnitsky asked about Razgon's case, about how he had been incriminated, and then Razgon asked him about his:

He went silent. Then he said that he had no illusions about his fate, that his case was moving to a close and he was prepared. He told me how they questioned him without a break, how they tortured him, beating out of him exactly what they needed, and threatening to beat him to death. He hadn't finished talking when they came for him again.[157]

On 10 April, Piatnitsky was transferred to the Lefortovo prison, where he was systematically tortured and interrogated every night from 12 April until his trial at the end of July. According to his main interrogator, who denied using physical measures of coercion, Piatnitsky behaved 'calmly and with restraint, but once, when he was in a state of agitation for some reason, he asked me for permission to have a drink, and going up to the water carafe, struck himself on the head with it'.[158] Osip was tried by the Military Tribunal of the Supreme Soviet, along with 137 other prisoners, on 27 July. He was charged with being one of the leaders of a Fascist spy-ring of Trotskyists and Rightists in the Comintern. A list of names of the convicted was sent by Yezhov to Stalin. At the top of the list, preserved in the Presidential Archives in the Kremlin, there is a brief handwritten order: 'Shoot all 138. I. St[alin]. V. Molotov.'[159]

None of this was known to Julia. She did not even know that Piatnitsky was being held in the Butyrki when she joined the queues outside its gates to hand in a parcel for her son. The longer she heard nothing from Osip, the harder it became for her to hold on to the hope that he was innocent. Everybody told her to forget Osip, to think about herself and her two sons. On 12 April, the night Osip's torture recommenced in the Lefortovo prison, Julia had a nightmare. She dreamed that she was being tormented by a cat. She thought the dream was significant and wondered if it meant that her son Igor was being tortured in the Butyrki (she had heard rumours about such things from the women in the prison queues). The thought of Igor's suffering altered Julia's feelings towards Osip, as she recorded in her diary:

My life has become an endless downward spiral. I talk with myself, in a whisper, and feel complete despair – for Piatnitsa [Piatnitsky] and Igor, but especially for my poor boy. He is spending his seventeeth spring in a miserable, dark and dirty prison, in a cell with strangers. The main thing is that he is innocent. Piatnitsky has lived his life – he failed to recognize the enemies who surrounded him, or became degenerate, which is not so astonishing, because he gave himself to politics, but Igor . . .[160]

The idea that it was too late to do anything for Osip reinforced Julia's determination to do whatever necessary to help Igor, whose life was still ahead of him. She had accepted the possibility of her husband's guilt. But she was not prepared to accept that her sixteen-year-old son could have been involved in any crime. Julia decided to renounce her husband in the hope that it would help save her son.

She went to the procurator's office in Moscow. Informed that Piatnitsky had committed a serious crime against the state, Julia replied: 'If that is the case, he means nothing to me any more.' The procurator advised Julia to begin a new life. She told him she would like to work for the NKVD, and he encouraged her to make a formal application, promising to support it. Julia saw the procurator as a sympathetic man:

I shook his hand warmly, though perhaps this was to display too much sentiment, something which I have never been able to control – but I felt close to this man, whose task is difficult but necessary, and I wanted to express my respect for him as a comrade, to show my moral support for those comrades who are rooting out the swine from our Party. Again I emphasize: despite my own suffering, and despite the possibility that innocents are being sacrificed (let one of these not be my Igor!), I must be true to principles, I must stay disciplined and patient, and I must, I absolutely must, find a way to make an active contribution, or else there will be no place for me among people.

Once she had adandoned her husband, Julia was prepared to think the worst of him. She wrote in her diary on 16 April:

Oh, I just can't understand it! But if it is so, then how I despise him, how I hate his base and cowardly, yet to me incomprehensible, soul! . . . Oh, what a good act he put on! Now I understand why he surrounded himself with the 'warm companionship' of all those spies, provocateurs and bureaucrats. But surely he had no real friends. He was essentially a gloomy man who never opened himself to me . . . Maybe he never loved the Party, maybe he never had its interests at heart? But what about us, me and the children, what was he thinking?[161]

Three weeks later, Igor was hauled before a three-man tribunal and charged with organizing a counter-revolutionary student group – a charge so absurd that even the tribunal threw it out, though it sentenced

Igor to five years in a labour camp on the lesser and much vaguer charge of anti-Soviet agitation.* Julia was told of her son's conviction on 27 May. She became hysterical and demanded that the procurator arrest her as well: 'If he is guilty, so am I.' Reflecting on events that evening, Julia groped towards an understanding of the Terror:

Perhaps Piatnitsky really was bad, and we must all perish on his account. But it is hard to die when I do not know who Piatnitsky really is, nor what crime Igor committed. He could not have done anything wrong. But then why did they take him? Maybe as someone who might become a criminal, because he is the son of an enemy . . . Maybe it's a way of forcefully mobilizing that part of the population which is not trusted by the state but whose labour can be used? I don't know, but it is logical. Of course if that is the case then Igor, and all the other people like him, will never come back. They serve a useful purpose to the state, but they depart from life. Anyway it is terrifying to have to remain behind – to have to wait and not to know.[162]

Julia herself was arrested on 27 October 1938. She was thirty-nine years old. Her diary was seized at the time of her arrest and used as evidence to convict her of conspiring with her husband against the government. She was sent to the Kandalaksha labour camp in the far northern region of Murmansk. Vladimir was sent with her, although he was very ill, having just recovered from an operation, and had to be taken from his bed. At Kandalaksha Vladimir was kept in the barracks and fed twice a day by an NKVD guard while Julia went to work on the construction of Niva-GES, a hydro-electric station near the camp. Shortly after their arrival Vladimir escaped and made his way back to Moscow, where he stayed with various schoolfriends, including the family of Yevgeny Loginov, whose father worked in Stalin's personal secretariat. Earlier the Loginovs had turned their back on the Piatnitskys, but now something made them change their minds. Common decency perhaps. Vladimir stayed with the Loginovs for three months. Then, one evening, he overheard a conversation between the Loginovs: Yevgeny's father had got into trouble for taking in Piatnitsky's son. To save them

*In 1941, Igor was charged again with organizing a 'counter-revolutionary conspiracy', this time involving children of 'enemies of the people', and five more years were added to his sentence. He returned to Leningrad in 1948, but was soon rearrested for 'counter-revolutionary agitation' and sentenced to five years (he served eight) in the Norilsk labour camp.

from any more trouble, Vladimir turned himself in to the Moscow Soviet. The official to whom he spoke was an old comrade of Piatnitsky from October 1917. He ordered sandwiches for Vladimir and then called the police. Vladimir was taken to the NKVD detention centre in the old Danilov Monastery, from which the children of 'enemies of the people' were sent on to orphanages across the Soviet Union.[163]

In March 1939, Julia was denounced by three co-workers at Niva-GES. They claimed that she had said that her husband had been wrongly arrested, that he was innocent, and that he had considered Stalin to be unfit as a leader of the proletariat. Convicted of anti-Soviet agitation, Julia was sentenced to five years in the Karaganda labour camp in Kazakhstan. Igor was a prisoner in the industrial section of the camp, and somehow Julia arranged a meeting with him there. 'We spent a remarkable and very sad day together,' recalls Igor, 'and then she went back [to the women's section of the camp].' Physically frail and mentally unbalanced, Julia was in no condition to withstand the hardships of camp life. She was still beautiful and attracted the attention of the camp commandant (which may explain why she had been allowed to visit Igor); but she refused his sexual demands, for which he punished her by sending her to work as a manual labourer in the construction of a dam. For sixteen hours every day she stood waist-high in freezing water, digging earth. She became ill and died on an unrecorded date in the winter of 1940.

In 1958, after his release from the labour camps, Igor was visited by an old acquaintance of the family, a woman called Zina, who had seen his mother in the Karaganda camp, where she too was a prisoner. Zina told Igor that Julia had died in the camp hospital and that she was buried in a mass grave. In 1986, Igor received another visit from Zina, by this time a woman of eighty. She told him that on the previous occasion she had lied about his mother, because Julia, before she died, had made her promise to spare Igor the awful details of her death (and because, as Zina now admitted, she had been afraid to speak the truth). But recently Zina had seen Julia in her dreams – Julia had asked her about her son – and she saw this as a sign that she should tell Igor about his mother's final days. Julia had not died in hospital. In December 1940, Zina had gone to look for Julia in the Karaganda camp. No one wanted to tell her where she was, but then one woman pointed to a sheep-pen on the steppe and said that she could be found there. Zina walked into the pen. Amongst the sheep, lying on the freezing ground, was Julia:

She was dying, her whole body was blown up with fever, she was burning hot and shaking. The sheep stood guard around her but offered no protection from the wind and snow, which lay around in mounds. I crouched beside her, she tried to raise herself but did not have the strength. I took her hand and tried to warm it with my breath.

'Who are you?' she asked. I told her my name and said only that I came from you, that you had asked me to find her . . .

How she stirred: 'Igor – my boy,' she whispered from her frozen lips. 'My little boy, help him, I beseech you, help him to survive.' I calmed her down and promised to look after you, as if that depended on me. 'Give me your word,' Julia whispered. 'Do not tell him how his mother died. Give me your word . . .'

She was half-delirious. I crouched down beside her and promised her.

Then from behind me a guard shouted: 'Where did you come from? How did you get here?' The guard grabbed me and frog-marched me out of the sheep-pen. 'Who are you?'

I explained that I had come as the section leader of a tool workshop and had found the woman accidentally. But I was detained. They told me that I should not breathe a word about what I had seen: 'Shut your mouth, and say nothing!'

Julia died in the sheep-pen. She had been left there when she fell ill, and no one was allowed to visit her. She was buried where she died.[164]

5

Remnants of Terror

(1938–41)

I

It was a warm summer evening, 28 July 1938, and Nelly's grandmother had gone to pick the raspberries in the garden, leaving her in charge of her sister Angelina while her mother, Zinaida Bushueva, nursed her baby brother and prepared the meal. Since the arrest of her father, nine months earlier, Nelly had grown used to helping in the house, although she was only four years old. Zinaida was breast-feeding Slava when the front door opened and two NKVD soldiers appeared. They told her to get dressed, and took her with the children to the NKVD headquarters in the centre of Perm. A few minutes later, Nelly's grandmother returned with the raspberries: the house was empty, her family had gone.

At the NKVD building the interrogator arranged for the two girls to be sent to children's homes. 'Your mama is going away on a long work trip,' he explained to Nelly. 'You will not see her again.' Zinaida became hysterical. When two guards came to take away the girls she began to scream and bite the other guards who held her down. As Nelly was led away, she looked back to see her mother being hit across the face. The two sisters were sent to different homes – Nelly to a Jewish orphanage (on account of her darker looks), Angelina to a nearby children's home. It was NKVD policy to break up the families of 'enemies of the people' and to give the children a new identity.

Zinaida was allowed to keep Slava – he had pneumonia and needed to be nursed by her. For three weeks, the mother and her baby son were held in a crowded prison cell. Zinaida was charged with failing to denounce her husband and sentenced to eight years in the Akmolinsk Labour Camp for Wives of Traitors to the Motherland (ALZhIR), part of the Karaganda camp complex in Kazakhstan. She was in a large

Angelina and Nelly Bushueva, 1937

convoy of female prisoners transferred from Perm to Akmolinsk in September 1938. On the day of their departure, they were made to kneel for several hours in one of the city's squares while they awaited transportation in small groups by horse and cart to the station. The residents of Perm stood around and watched the spectacle, but no one tried to help the prisoners, though Zinaida's mother, who had spotted her with Slava in the middle of the square, tried to get one of the guards to take a pullover for her. 'Get away, old woman,' the guard said, pushing her away with the point of his gun. At the station the convoy was loaded into cattle trucks. It took ten days for the train to get to Akmolinsk, a journey of 1,500 kilometres. Zinaida was in a truck with common criminals. At first they harassed her and tried to take her baby, believing it would get them released early from the camp, but after a few days, as Slava became sicker, they took pity on the mother and shouted for the guards to bring milk for her baby. On their arrival at the camp, Zinaida was forced to give up Slava to the orphanage at Dolinka, the administrative centre of the Karaganda camps. She did not see him for the next five years. A qualified accountant, Zinaida was offered work in the camp offices, a privileged position for a prisoner, but she begged to be employed in the heaviest agricultural work instead. 'I will lose my mind if I have time to think,' Zinaida explained to the camp commandant. 'I have lost my three children. Let me forget myself in manual labour.'

After she had seen her daughter kneeling with Slava in the square, Zinaida's mother went in search of Angelina and Nelly. With the help of her two sons, she found Nelly after a few weeks. But it was not until the spring of 1940 that she found Angelina, who by then, at the age of four, was old enough to recall something of the incident:

My cousin Gera, the son of uncle Vitia, lived near the orphanage. One day the orphanage children were out walking by the river, we walked in pairs in a long column, and I was at the very end. Gera and his parents were also out by the river. He recognized me immediately. He shouted, 'Look, there's our Aka!' Everybody stopped. There was quite a scene. The women from the orphanage would not let my relatives come near me, but uncle Vitia spoke to one of them, who said that I was called Alei, or Angelina, they were not sure . . .

Granny began to write appeals to the orphanage and then one day she came to get me . . . I remember the day. She brought a pair of red shoes with sparkly buckles and put them on my feet. I lifted up my feet and looked at the soles of the shoes – they were so smooth and clean and red. I would brush the dust from them. I wanted to take off the shoes and lick their soles, because they were such a bright colour, but Granny said: 'Enough, leave your shoes alone, let's go and find your sister Nelly.' I still recall my confusion – what was a sister? Who was Nelly? I had no idea. When we left the orphanage there was a girl waiting by the entrance. Granny said, 'This is Nelly, your sister.' I said, 'So?' The only thing I understood was that she was called Nelly, but not what a sister was. The girl came up to me. She had short black hair. She wore a grey raincoat. She was chewing the end of the collar. And I said: 'Why is she eating the collar?' And Granny scolded her: 'Again chewing your collar!'[1]

Angelina's childhood memories are dominated by the feeling of hunger. The daily fare in the orphanage had been so poor (dry brown bread and a thin grey gruel) that Angelina's first reaction to her bright red shoes was to try to eat them like a tomato. Things were not much better when she went to live with Nelly and her grandmother, who was too old and sick to work and lived in desperate poverty in a small room in a communal apartment, having been evicted from the family home following the arrest of Zinaida in 1938. By 1941 there were near-famine conditions in Perm (from 1940 known as Molotov). Many of the central avenues had been converted into vegetable allotments for selected residents, but Angelina's grandmother was not one of these. 'We learned to eat all sorts of things,' recalls Angelina: 'the spring leaves of linden trees; grass and moss; potato peelings which we collected at night from the rubbish bins of people who were better off than us.' Angelina was conscious of her hunger as a source of shame and degradation. It was hunger that defined her as a lower class of human being rather than the arrest of her parents as 'enemies of the people' – a concept which in any case she was too young to understand. Angelina was bullied by a gang of boys from the house across the street where factory workers lived. The boys knew that Angelina took the peelings from their bins, and they always mocked her about it when she passed them on the street. Angelina learned to hold her tongue and not answer back. But one day the leader of the gang, the biggest of the boys who came from a family of factory officials, gave a piece of buttered bread to a beggar on the street. 'He did it just for me to see,' recalls Angelina, 'he wanted to humiliate me, and I could not help myself; the sight of buttered bread was just too much, I would have given anything to have it for myself and could not bear to see it go to a beggar. I shouted at the boys: "What are you doing? There is butter on that bread!" They all laughed at me.'[2]

Like many children who had lost their parents in the Great Terror, Angelina was not fully aware of her loss. She could not remember her parents – she was only two when they were arrested – so unlike Nelly, who was old enough to recall them, she had no sense of having suffered when they disappeared. Once she learned to read, Angelina made up fantasies about her parents' death which she derived from books, especially from her favourite stories about Napoleon and the fire of Moscow. She recalls a conversation from the post-war years, when she was about ten:

A friend of my grandmother's came to visit us. She talked about my mother and father. My grandmother had pictures of all her children on the walls of our room. The woman pointed to each photograph and asked me who it was.

'Who is that?'

'Auntie Nina,' I replied.

'And that?'

'Uncle Sanya'

'And that?'

I said: 'That is Nelly's mother.'

'What do you mean Nelly's mother? She is your mother too.'

And I said: 'No, that is not my mother, but Nelly's mother.'

'So where is your mother?'

'My mother died in the fire of Moscow.'[3]

The real maternal figure in Angelina's life was her grandmother. It was she who rescued Angelina and Nelly from children's homes and eventually reunited them with their mother. Tales of children being saved by their grandmothers are commonplace from that time. From the beginning of the Great Terror, it often fell to grandmothers to try to keep together the scattered remnants of repressed families. Their untold acts of heroism deserve to be counted among the finest deeds in Soviet history.

Natalia Konstantinova and her sister Elena lost their parents in the Great Terror. Their father was arrested in October 1936 and executed in May 1937. Their mother, Liudmila, was arrested the following September and sentenced to eight years in a labour camp near Magadan as the wife of an 'enemy of the people'. Natalia, who was ten, and her sister, twelve, were both sent to an orphanage. They were rescued by their grandmother, a kind and gentle woman with nerves of steel, who struck a deal with the NKVD. Elena Lebedeva was born in Moscow in 1879 to a family of prominent merchants. She had four years of schooling before getting married, at the age of seventeen, and gave birth to seven children, the fourth of them Liudmila in 1903. When she appealed to the NKVD headquarters for the release of her granddaughters, Elena was told that she could only take the girls if she went to live with them in exile, but that she could stay in Leningrad if she left them in the orphanage. Elena did not hesitate. She took the girls, sold off her property and bought train tickets for the three of them to go to Ak-Bulak, a remote town on the steppeland between Orenburg and Kazakhstan (it was only after they arrived that she discovered that the NKVD paid the outbound fares of all exiles).

Ak-Bulak was a small dusty railway stop on the main line connecting Russia with Central Asia. The railway employed many of the 7,000 people who lived there, mainly Russians and Kazakhs, although there was also a sizeable community of political exiles who were unemployed. There was certainly no work for a fifty-eight-year-old grandmother. But relatives in Leningrad regularly sent Elena small amounts of cash and goods to sell at the market or trade with local women, whose friendship she worked hard to cultivate. Elena could not find a room to rent, so she lived with her granddaughters in a shack she bought and then divided with another exiled family. It was one of the oldest buildings in the town, dating back to the nineteenth century, and made from bricks of camel dung with a clay roof. They heated it in winter by burning dung

The house in Ak-Bulak where Elena lived with
her granddaughters, 1940s

in a clay oven. During the first year, in 1938–9, when there was famine in the area, it was a real struggle to survive. The girls had no shoes to wear. They went barefoot to the tin-shed school for exiled children, separated from the brick-made school for the children of the railway workers. But the girls did well at school and in the second year they were allowed to transfer to the other school. They even joined the Pioneers. Relations between the exiles and the railwaymen were good. 'No one called us exiles,' Natalia recalls. It was not until 1942, when both girls applied to join the Komsomol, that anybody pointed to the fact that their father was an 'enemy of the people', and even then, it was not one of the local children, but an evacuee from Moscow, who brought this up as an obstacle to their inclusion in the Komsomol.[4]

Looking back on the years she spent in Ak-Bulak, from 1938 to 1945, Natalia believes that she and her sister had a happy childhood, despite

Elena Lebedeva with her granddaughters, Natalia (left)
and Elena Konstantinova, Ak-Bulak, 1940

all the hardships they endured. 'We were very lucky to grow up in our
grandmothers' little world. We never had enough to eat, we barely had
a thing to call our own, but we were happy because we were loved by
our grandmother. No one could steal that from us.' Friends at school
would often ask Natalia where her parents were. She tried to avoid their
questions. She never talked about her parents, afraid that people would
assume that 'they must have been guilty of something if they had been
arrested'. Their arrest was a source of shame and confusion for Natalia.
She did not understand what they had done or why they had disappeared. But never for a moment did she doubt their innocence. Natalia
believes that her grandmother played a crucial role in sustaining this
belief: without her she would have given in to the pressures she encountered later on from the Pioneers and the Komsomol to renounce her
parents as 'enemies of the people'. 'My grandmother had seen it all,'
Natalia recalls. 'She understood what Soviet power was about, and
was not taken in by anything: she was nearly forty when the Revolution
came.'

Elena's values had been formed in a different century and social
milieu, but she understood that her granddaughters needed to survive
in the Soviet world, and did not try to impose on them her own anti-
Soviet views. She told them that their parents were good people who
had been arrested by mistake, and that one day they would both return.
She told them stories about their mother when she had been their age:

about how she was so beautiful; how she loved to play tennis; how she had so many handsome young admirers; how she met their father; and how they were so happy as a family. She told the girls that their mother had been just like them. Through these stories the two girls came to know their mother, and to feel her presence in their lives. According to Elena, 'Our grandmother was the most important person in our lives, even more important than our mother ... She took the place of our mother, even after we returned to Leningrad [in 1946] and were reunited with our real mother [in 1951].'[5]

Caring for grandchildren could be a heavy burden for grandparents, who were frequently deprived of housing, jobs, savings, pensions and rations after the arrest of their own children as 'enemies of the people'. And not all grandchildren could be saved. Veronika Nevskaia's father was arrested in August 1936, three years after the death of her mother in 1933, and sent to the Vorkuta labour camps. The six-year-old Veronika and her younger brother Valentin were sent to an orphanage. Veronika was adopted by her father's aunt Maria, who took her in the knowledge, as she had been warned by the NKVD, that, if she did, they would all be sent to live in exile in the Kirov region, 1,200 kilometres east of Maria's native Leningrad. A devoutly religious woman in her early seventies, Maria saw it as her Christian duty to care for all the children in her family: she lived on her own, her husband having died

Veronika and Maria,
Slobodskoi, Kirov region, 1939

many years before, and she had no children of her own. Maria found her nephew's children in the orphanage. She had always had a soft spot for Veronika. She bought her gifts and liked to read to her from the classics. But she was too old and weak to cope with Valentin, a difficult, unruly boy, who needed special care (he had been born with a malformed bladder that left him incontinent). Maria took Veronika but left her younger brother in the orphanage. They never heard from him again. In 1941 they received a telegram telling them that Valentin had died – he was then only seven – in the hospital of the orphanage. Looking back on these events, Veronika believes that her grandmother (as she calls her father's aunt) could not have coped with Valentin. But she also thinks that she was filled with feelings of remorse. A few days after they received the telegram, Maria died. Veronika was taken in by distant relatives, but she was soon passed by them to other relatives, and by them to others: no one was interested in an extra mouth to feed. Thus she lived for the next five years, an unwanted guest in the homes of distant family, until 1946, when she travelled to Vorkuta to be reunited with her father.[6]

The arrest of a parent turned many children into adults overnight. The eldest child, in particular, was suddenly expected to perform an adult role, helping with the household chores and caring for the younger children.[7] Inna Gaister was twelve years old when her parents were arrested in the summer of 1937. Together with her younger sisters, Natalia (seven) and Valeriia (one), and her cousin Igor (nine), Inna lived with her grandmother in the family apartment in the House on the Embankment in Moscow. Inna was charged with a large number of new responsibilities that cast her in the role of an auxiliary, if not the main, parent in the household. Inna wrote to the NKVD to ask for the return of their property sealed up in the family flat. She organized the parcels for her parents, and queued all night to hand them in at the Butyrki jail. When she discovered that her mother had been sent to the Akmolinsk labour camp (ALZhIR), Inna took an evening job, teaching younger children after school, so that she could save some money for the monthly parcels they were allowed to send to Akmolinsk from the summer of 1939. Shortly after the arrest of their parents, the Gaister children were evicted from their apartment. With their grandmother the four children moved into a rented room shared with eight other Gaister relatives – all children who had lost their parents in the Great Terror. There were thirteen people (twelve children and one grandmother) living in a room of 20 square metres. As the eldest child, Inna had to do the washing and help with the cleaning and cooking. It took at least an hour for Inna to travel by tram from her new home to her school; returning in the evening, she struggled to get the washing done and have it dried for the next day. She was physically exhausted (in photographs she appears with large dark rings around her eyes). Looking back on this period of her life, Inna thinks that it helped her to develop necessary survival skills:

It was a life that trained me for struggle. I was always fighting to survive – not just for myself but for the sake of Valiushka [Valeriia] and Natalka [Natalia]. I was only twelve when my parents were arrested. But with their arrest I grew up overnight. I understood that my childhood had come to an end. The first thing that happened is that our nanny left – she could not get on with granny. It was my job to look after Valeriia, who was still only a baby. I remember the last thing our nanny said before she left: 'You must wash her every evening!' I was horrified. 'Her nappy will be very soiled,' she said . . . I found myself in a completely new situation. I had to do the washing for the whole family, which was very large. And I had to study hard if my life was not to be ruined completely. I had Igor to support and Natalka too. Natalka would ask why everybody had a mother and a father except us. I told her that we had a grandmother who loved us very much.

Inna Gaister (aged thirteen) with her sisters Valeriia (three) and Natalia (eight), Moscow, 1939. The photograph was taken to send to their mother in the Akmolinsk labour camp (ALZhIR)

In many ways I was like a mother to Natalka and Valiushka, even though, in other ways, I was still a child myself.[8]

Inna's grandmother, like Elena Lebedeva, often spoke to the children about their parents. She wanted them to know that their parents had not abandoned them, that they loved them and would return to them. But other grandmothers took a different view.

The parents of Iraida Faivisovich were hairdressers in Osa, a small town in the Urals, south of Perm. They were arrested in the spring of 1939, supposedly for organizing a political conspiracy against the Soviet government, following reports by clients from their salon that they had heard the Faivisoviches complain about shortages. The four-year-old Iraida was taken in by neighbours and then passed around to various relatives, none of whom was keen to take her in, until at last she was rescued by her maternal grandmother, Marfa Briukhova. A simple peasant woman, devoutly Orthodox, Marfa had brought up sixteen children, including five who were not her own. Blaming her son-in-law for his arrest, and for the arrest of her daughter, she said that he had talked too much and told Iraida that she should learn to hold her tongue. Iraida grew up in an 'atmosphere of enforced silence' in which she was forbidden to talk or ask about her mother and father. Her feelings of inferiority, rooted in her status as an orphan child at school, were strengthened by this silence, which forced her to internalize her fears and longings for her parents. She heard their voices in her dreams. Imprisoned in a labour camp near Arkhangelsk, Iraida's mother wrote to her in Osa once a week, but Marfa burned the letters without even opening them. Marfa hid the photographs of Iraida's parents so that she would forget them. 'We will survive, the two of us, together,' she said to her granddaughter.[9]

Grandmothers played a crucial role as correspondents between the home and the labour camp. As writers and readers they sustained that crucial link between a parent and a child by which millions of families survived the separation of the Gulag.

When their parents were arrested, in 1936 and 1937, Oleg Vorobyov and his sister Natasha were rescued by their grandmother. Nadezhda Mikhailovna was a brave, intelligent woman, one of the first to qualify as a doctor in Tbilisi before the Revolution of 1905. Warned that the NKVD would take the children to an orphanage, she hurried them away to the Tula countryside, where she concealed them with their godparents for several months, before returning to Moscow, where she lived with the children and their grandfather in a series of rented rooms in a working-class suburb of the city. She believed that it would be safer there than in the centre of the capital where they had lived previously. It was generally the case that workers were less interested in the political background of their neighbours (they were more likely to be hostile towards them on class or ethnic grounds).[10] To protect her grandchildren Nadezhda adopted them and changed their names. Every week she wrote long letters to their father (in the Solovetsky labour camp) and their mother (in the Temnikovsky camps) with details of their everyday routines:

25 January 1939.
... Oleg is eager to go to school. Grandpa gets him up at half past seven in the morning – he only has to say it's time and he gets up. We put on the electric kettle and make fresh sandwiches with egg, fish, salami, and he washes it all down with a hot chocolate, coffee, tea or milk before he goes to school. He is very fussy with his food and does not eat a lot: half a roll and a glass of milk and he's full. He wants only half a roll to take to school.[11]

Few of the details were actually true (there was no egg, fish or salami, as far as Oleg can recall, only bread and sometimes butter) but the letters gave his parents the comforting idea that family life was continuing as normal in their absence and would be there for them when they returned.

Oleg's father Mikhail was a senior engineer. Before his arrest he had worked in the Ministry of Defence in Moscow. In 1940, he was transferred from Solovetsky to the Norilsk labour camp in the Arctic Circle, where expertise like his was badly needed for the building of the huge industrial complex, which would soon become the country's main producer of nickel and platinum. As a specialist, Mikhail was allowed to receive parcels and write home once a week. By corresponding with Nadezhda, Mikhail had a good idea of Oleg's state of mind, so that he could write to him with advice on his studies, reading, hobbies and his friends. 'His letters were a profound influence on me,' Oleg recalls.

I was guided by these letters perhaps even more than I would have been guided by my father if he had actually been there while I was growing up. Because

I longed for a father, I tried to behave in a way that I imagined he would have approved of, at least as I knew him from his letters.

Oleg was fortunate to have this connection with his father. Letters were written proof of a parent's love, something in which children could believe and which they could read as a sign of their parents' innocence. Sometimes they contained a drawing or a line of poetry, a dried flower or even fragments of embroidery, which expressed feelings and emotions that could not be conveyed by censored words. Relationships were built on these fragments.[12]

In all his letters Mikhail pressed upon Oleg the need to be a 'little man'.

25 August 1940.
My dear son, why have you not written to me for so long? I understand that you are on holiday . . . but I urge you to write at least one letter every five days . . . Put your drawings in with the letter and let Natasha write a little too . . . Never forget you are her protector. She is still very little and sometimes capricious, but you should talk sense to her. I have written many times that it is your duty as a man to protect Natasha, Granny and Grandpa, to make sure that they are safe, until my return. You are my second-in-command. You are the head of our little family. All my hopes depend on you.

Oleg and Natasha, 1940.
The photograph was taken to
send to Mikhail in Norilsk

Although only ten, Oleg felt that he became an adult when he received this letter. He felt responsible for Natasha, which made him view the world no longer as a child. In his own words, 'I grew up overnight.'[13]

2

The Bushuevs, the Gaisters and the Vorobyovs were the lucky ones – they were rescued by their relatives. But the arrest of their parents left millions of other children on their own. Many ended up in orphanages – intended for those under the age of sixteen – but others roamed the streets begging or joined the children's gangs, which controlled much of the petty crime and prostitution at railway stations, markets and other busy places in the big cities. It was largely to combat the mounting problem of child criminality that a law was passed in 1935 to lower the age of criminal responsibility to twelve. Between 1935 and 1940, the Soviet courts convicted of petty crimes 102,000 children between the ages of twelve and sixteen. Many ended up in the children's labour colonies administered by the NKVD.[14]

Some children slipped through the system and were left to fend for themselves. Mikhail Mironov was ten years old when his parents were arrested in 1936. They were both factory workers from the Ukraine, Red partisans in the Civil War, who had risen through the ranks of the Party, first in Moscow and then in Leningrad, before their arrests. Mikhail's sister Lilia had already left the family home in Leningrad to study medicine in Moscow. So Mikhail was alone. For a while, he lived with various relatives, but he was a burden to them all, factory workers struggling to survive with large families of their own. In September 1937, Mikhail was accepted as a student at the drawing school established by the House of Pioneers in Leningrad. His aunt Bela, who had taken care of Mikhail in the previous months, saw it as an opportunity to be rid of him, and sent him off to live in the student dormitory attached to the House of Pioneers. Mikhail lost all track of his father (who was shot in 1938) and never heard from his sister, who was afraid that she would be expelled from medical school if she revealed her spoilt biography by writing to her relatives. His only contact was with his mother, and he wrote to her often in the labour camps of Vorkuta. He was isolated and lonely, without friends or family, and in desperate need of a mother's love (his letters often end with such sentiments as 'I kiss you 100000000 times'). In the spring of 1941, Mikhail was excluded from the drawing school – for lack of talent – and enrolled instead in a factory school. Expelled from the dormitory in the House of Pioneers, he found a room in a barracks. 'It is very boring for me,' the fifteen-year-old boy wrote to his mother in July. 'There is no one here. Everyone has gone, and I am on my own.' In September, as the German troops encircled Leningrad, Mikhail escaped to Moscow, but by the time he arrived there, his sister had already been evacuated to Central Asia with her medical institute. None of his other Moscow relatives would take him in, so Mikhail ended up by living on the street. He was killed in the battle for Moscow in October 1941.[15]

Mikhail Mironov and his drawings (extract from a letter to his mother)

Maia Norkina was thirteen when her father was arrested in June 1937. A year later, when the NKVD took her mother too, Maia was expelled from her school in Leningrad. Maia had a number of aunts and uncles in Leningrad, but none would take her in. 'They were all afraid to lose their jobs,' Maia explains. 'Some were Party members – they were the most afraid and refused outright.' Everyone expected that Maia would be taken to an orphanage. But no one came for her. So she continued living in the three rooms that belonged to her family in a communal apartment conveniently situated in the centre of the city. Her relatives, eager to hang on to the precious living space, moved in one of her uncles and registered him as a resident, although in fact he was never there, because he lived with his wife and children in another part of the city. 'I was living on my own, completely independently,' recalls Maia. The fourteen-year-old girl would borrow books from her old school-friends. She'd travel for an hour to her aunt's for meals, or buy food with pocket money from her relatives; neighbours in the communal apartment sometimes gave her scraps of food. Every day she would stand in queues at the NKVD headquarters in Leningrad, hoping to hand in a parcel for her father; the officials took the parcels for a while and then told her that her father had been sentenced to 'ten years without rights of correspondence' (meaning – though she did not find this out for years – that he had been shot). To get a parcel to her mother, in the Potma labour camps, was even more onerous: it required her to stand in queues for two whole days and nights. Maia went on living this way until August 1941, when she turned eighteen and joined the People's Volunteers for the defence of Leningrad. She had no formal schooling and had little other choice.[16]

Zoia Arsenteva was born in 1923 in Vladivostok. Her father, the captain of a steamship, was arrested on a trip to Petropavlovsk-Kamchatsky on 25 November 1937; her mother was arrested in her home in Vladivostok on the same day. Zoia was not taken to an orphan-age: although only fourteen, she looked older than her years. She was left to fend for herself in the communal apartment where her family had lived since 1926. She had no other relatives to whom she could turn. Her mother's sister lived in Khabarovsk, but only came to Vladivostok, where she had a dacha, in the summertime; her father's family was in Leningrad. Zoia had enjoyed a sheltered childhood. Her mother did not work and had devoted herself to her only child. But now Zoia was forced to do everything for herself. She went to school. She cooked her meals on the little primus stove in the corridor of the communal apart-ment. With the help of her neighbours she sold off bits of the family inheritance (a gold watch, her mother's silver ring, her father's old binoculars and a camera, books and sculptures) to buy food and canteen meals in the factory near her house. Much of the money she raised this way was used to launch the appeal for the release of her father (accused of belonging to a 'Trans-Pacific Counter-revolutionary Organization'), who sent her weekly letters from his jail in Petropavlovsk-Kamchatsky with complex instructions about obscure points of law and the recovery of bank accounts. Once a week she wrote back to her father with a report on his case; once a week she queued up overnight outside the jail in Vladivostok to hand in a parcel for her mother. Her father was impressed with the way she had grown up and responded to the family crisis. In May 1940, he wrote to his wife, who was by then in a labour camp near Iaia in Siberia:

I have received two letters from Zizika [Zoia]. I feel so bad for her but rejoice too over her success; she is flourishing and healthy – soon she will be seventeen, and she is completely independent. She is a clever girl and deserves praise for her bravery – she was not afraid to live entirely on her own at the age of fourteen. She has even come to enjoy it. I imagine her as a little mistress of the house, fully in command of her domestic and school affairs.[17]

Zoia Arsenteva, Khabarovsk, 1941

From Zoia's perspective, coping on her own was not at all enjoyable. As she said years later, 'One day Mama was arrested, the next day I began my adult life.' In her letters to her parents she did not trouble them with the problems she faced. People posing as her parents' friends tried to take advantage of her, offering to help her sell her precious items and keeping half the profits for themselves. In the spring of 1939, a genuine acquaintance of her mother, a secretary in the city Soviet, moved her things into Zoia's room. She claimed that she was trying to protect her from having to share her living space with another family. But in fact, a few weeks later, the woman called for the police to arrest Zoia and take her to an orphanage, thus getting the room for herself. In the orphanage Zoia went on a hunger strike to protest against having been sent there. Eventually, through one of the workers in the orphanage, she made contact with her aunt from Khabarovsk, who had recently arrived to spend the summer at her dacha. Zoia stayed in the orphanage for three months, until her aunt managed to reclaim her room in the communal apartment and, on her sixteenth birthday, Zoia was allowed to return to it. She worked her way through the last year at school, studying at evening classes, and then attended the Railway Institute in Khabarovsk. In the winter of 1940, her father was sentenced to five years in a labour camp in Siberia, where he died in 1942. Her mother was released in 1944.[18]

Marksena Karpitskaia was thirteen when her parents, senior Party officials in Leningrad, were arrested on 5 July 1937. Marksena's younger brothers were sent to different orphanages – the older Aleksei (who was ten) to a children's home near Kirov, the younger Vladimir (who was five) to one in the Tatar Republic. Marksena was not taken to an orphanage because, like Zoia, she looked older than she was. Instead, she moved into a room in a communal apartment with her nanny, Milia, a simple peasant woman, who helped her and exploited her in equal measure. Like many children raised in Communist households in the 1920s, Marksena was brought up to be responsible from an early age. Her parents treated her as a 'small comrade' and put her in charge of her younger brothers. Now this training stood her in good stead:

Milia was with me, but I was in charge of everything, including the money. I paid Milia her salary, but then she began to steal from me, so I told her that I did not need her services any more. Still, I let her go on sleeping in my room, because she had nowhere else to stay.[19]

For a thirteen-year-old, Marksena was amazingly resourceful. She managed to survive by salvaging her parents' personal possessions, which were sealed up in their flat on their arrest, and selling them through Milia in a commission shop, the last official remnant of the private market, where Soviet citizens could buy and sell their household goods. The key to this complex operation was the assistance of senior party official and family friend Boris Pozern ('Uncle Boria'), at that time the Prosecutor for Leningrad Oblast, who had known Marksena since she was a little girl. Pozern sent a soldier to open up the flat so that Marksena could retrieve some money and take out things to sell: her father's suit and shoes; her mother's dress and a fur jacket; towels and sheets. 'Uncle Boria', who had risked his life to help the orphan girl, was arrested and shot in 1939.

Marksena, Leningrad, 1941

Marksena stored these items in her room in the communal apartment. Piece by piece, if not sold off, they were gradually stolen by the neighbours in the other rooms. Then Milia moved her boyfriend into the room, until Marksena found the courage to kick the couple out and put a lock on the door. For the next three years, Marksena lived in the communal apartment on her own. She sold her last possessions through an aunt, who had barely dared to talk to her after the arrest of her parents, but who now jumped at the opportunity to help Marksena sell her property. The communal apartment where Marksena lived was situated in a deeply proletarian area of Leningrad; all her neighbours were factory workers. They knew that she was living on her own – an illegal situation for a minor to be in – but none reported her to the police (apparently, they were more interested in keeping her near so they could steal from her). Bullied at school by one of the teachers as the daughter of an 'enemy of the people', Marksena transferred to a different school, where the headteacher was more sympathetic and helped her to conceal her spoilt biography. In 1941, at the age of seventeen, Marksena graduated with top marks in all subjects. She enrolled as a student in the Faculty of Languages at Leningrad University. When the university was evacuated, in February 1942, she remained in Leningrad, working in the Public Library. Until the city was cut off by the German troops, she kept writing to her brother Aleksei in his orphanage. Aleksei returned to Leningrad, deeply damaged by the orphanage, in 1946. Her younger brother Vladimir disappeared without a trace.[20]

The Great Terror swelled the orphan population. From 1935 to 1941 the number of children living in the children's homes of Russia, Belarus and Ukraine alone grew from 329,000 to approximately 610,000 (a number which excludes the children 'lent out' by the orphanages to Soviet farms and factories).[21] Most children's homes were little more than detention centres for homeless juveniles and runaways, young 'hooligans' and petty criminals, and the 'strange orphans' (as the writer Ilia Ehrenburg described them), who had lost their parents in the mass arrests of 1937–8. Conditions in these homes were so appalling that dozens of officials were moved to write to the authorities to express their personal distress at the overcrowding and the dirt, the cold and hunger, the cruelty and neglect, to which the children were systematically subjected. Children of 'enemies of the people' were singled out for harsh treatment. Like Marksena's younger brothers, they were often sent to different children's homes as part of a policy of breaking up the families of 'enemies'. They were told to forget their parents and, if young enough, were given different names to forge a new identity. They often suffered bullying and exclusion, sometimes at the hands of the teachers and caretakers, who were afraid to show them tenderness, in case they were accused of sympathizing with 'enemies'.[22]

After the arrest of their parents, Inessa Bulat and her sister Mella were sent to different children's homes. Inessa, who was three, was taken to a home in Leningrad, while Mella, eleven, was sent to one near Smolensk. Both girls were constantly reminded that they were the daughters of 'enemies of the people' – their parents having been arrested in connection with the trial of Piatakov and other 'Trotskyists' in January 1937.* Inessa has no recollection of her childhood prior to the orphanage. But what she recalls from the two years she spent there left a deep scar on her consciousness:

Conditions there were terrible – I could not even go into the toilet: the floors were covered ankle-deep in liquid shit . . . The building faced a big red-brick

---

*Their father, Pavel Bulat, was a political economist at the Military-Political Academy in Leningrad; their mother, Nina, an engineer and geologist.

wall. It felt like being trapped in a kind of hell . . . The head of the home would always say to me: 'Just remember who your parents are. Don't make any trouble: just sit quietly and don't stick your spy's nose into anything.' . . . I became withdrawn. I shut myself away. Later, I found it very difficult to lead a normal life. I had spent too long in the orphanage, where I had learned to feel nothing.

In Mella's orphanage there were 'several dozen' children of politicals. As she recalls:

None of us whose parents had been arrested ever dared to speak about our families. They called us 'Trotskyists' and always lumped us together, so we formed a sort of group. There was no particular friendship between us, but we tried to stick together . . . The other children would throw stones at us and call us names, so we kept together to protect ourselves.

Mella wrote to her grandmother in Leningrad. When her parents were arrested, her grandmother had refused to look after her and Inessa. Recently divorced from an alcoholic husband who had beaten her, she was living in terrible conditions in a basement room and working as an inspector at the Leningrad Tobacco Factory. She was afraid that she might lose her job if she gave shelter to children of 'enemies of the people'. She also thought that her grandchildren would be better off in a children's home. But Mella's letters shocked her. She had no idea of the appalling conditions in which her granddaughters had been living. In 1939, she rescued both girls from the children's homes and brought them back to live with her in her basement room in Leningrad.[23]

When Vladimir Antonov-Ovseyenko and his wife Sofia were arrested, in October 1937, their daughter Valentina was aged fifteen. Sofia and Vladimir were both shot on the same day, 8 February 1938. Vladimir was Valentina's stepfather. Her real father was Aleksandr Tikhanov, a printer from a large working-class family in Moscow who became an editor at the Young Guard publishing house in Moscow and then moved to International Books in Prague, where Sofia had met Vladimir, the Soviet ambassador. Valentina had seen her father before 1934, but then they lost contact. 'He did not come to see us when we returned to Moscow. I did not ask my mother why,' Valentina says, 'and she did not explain it. No doubt my father did not want to intrude on our life.' When Sofia and Vladimir were arrested, Valentina was taken to the NKVD detention centre in the grounds of the old Danilov Monastery, from which the children of the 'enemies of the people' were sent to orphanages across the Soviet Union. Immediately on her arrival Valentina became ill. Her father, Aleksandr, knew where she was but did not try to rescue her. Recently remarried, perhaps he was afraid of endangering relations with his new wife, who was herself arrested in 1938. From the Danilov Monastery, Valentina was transferred to a children's home in Dnepropetrovsk, where she remained until 1941, when she returned to Moscow. Reflecting on her life in this period, Valentina says:

The orphanage was a trauma that I never overcame. This is the first time I have spoken about it to anyone. These were the years when I was growing up, I needed a mother, a mother and a father, and when I began to understand that they were dead, a sense of loss cut into everything. At the orphanage they used to give us sweets for the New Year, sometimes the teachers made a fuss of us. But the only thing I felt was this awful sense of loss, of being on my own, without anyone. I was the only girl who had no mother to contact, who had no letters. I was all alone. The only one in the whole group whose mother had been shot [*long silence*]. And I felt that bitterly.[24]

Girls from Orphanage No. 1, Dnepropetrovsk, 1940.
Valentina is in the centre of the second row from the top

The one redeeming feature of the orphanage – it saved her from despair – was the strength of the friendships she formed there with the other orphan girls.

There are countless horror stories about growing up in orphanages. But there also examples of children finding love and 'family' there.

Galina Kosheleva was nine years old when she was taken to an orphanage, following the arrest and execution of her father, a peasant from the Podporozhe region, north-east of Leningrad, during the 'kulak operation' of 1937. The family dispersed. Galina and her brother were taken to Kirov, from where he was sent to an orphanage in the nearby town of Zuevka, and she northwards to Oparino, between Kirov and Kotlas. As soon as she arrived, Galina caught pneumonia. 'I had travelled all the way from Leningrad in a summer dress, with a white pelerine, nothing else, and just a pair of light sandals; it was summer when we left but November by the time we reached Kirov.' Throughout that winter Galina was very sick. She was nursed by the director of the orphanage, a young Siberian woman called Elizaveta Ivanova, who gave Galina her own winter coat and bought her milk with her own money from the neighbouring collective farm. The relationship between Elizaveta and Galina resembled one between mother and child. Without children of her own, Elizaveta doted on the nine-year-old girl: she read to her at night and helped her with her studies when she could not go to school. She wanted to adopt her but did not have the living space to qualify for adoption rights. Then, in 1945, Galina's mother suddenly appeared. In 1937, she had fled the NKVD and lived in hiding with a new-born baby. She had worked as an ice-breaker on the Murmansk Railway, until her capture by the German army, when she was sent to a Finnish concentration camp in Petrozavodsk. Liberated by Soviet troops in 1944, she went in search of her children. Galina was very sad to leave Elizaveta and the orphanage. She moved to Podporozhe with her mother and brother, and then to Leningrad in 1952. Throughout these years she kept on writing to Elizaveta at the orphanage. 'I loved her so much that it made my mother envious,' she recalls. 'I did not love my mother half as much, and relations between us in any case were not so good.'[25]

Nikolai Kovach was born in 1936 in the Solovetsky labour camp. Both his parents had been sentenced to ten years in the White Sea island prison in 1933. Because his mother was then pregnant with his older sister Elena, they were allowed to live together as a family within the prison. But then, in January 1937, the NKVD prohibited cohabitation in all labour camps. Nikolai's mother was sent to a camp in Karelia (where she was shot in November 1937); his father was dispatched to Magadan (where he was shot in 1938). Elena was sick with TB at the time, so she was sent to an orphanage in Tolmachyovo, south of Leningrad, where medical provision was part of the regime; but Nikolai was taken north to Olgino, the resort on the Gulf of Finland favoured by the Petersburg elite before 1917, where the NKVD had set up an orphanage for children of 'enemies of the people' in a wing of the old white palace of Prince Oldenburg.

Like Nikolai, many of the children in the orphanage had no recollection of their family. But they forged a special bond with the kitchen workers, who gave them love and affection, and perhaps the feeling of a family. 'There was a back staircase down to the kitchen area,' recalls Nikolai.

I would go that way and the cooks would say: 'Here comes Kolia!' They would stroke my hair and give me a piece of bread. I would sit there at the bottom of the stairs and eat the piece of bread, so that no one else saw me with it. Everyone was hungry then – I was afraid to lose my piece of bread . . . The cooks, ordinary women from the local area, felt sorry for us orphans and tried to help us.

The children also visited the old people in the area and helped them on their allotments. 'That was very good for us,' Nikolai recalls:

If we helped an old grandpa he would be pleased and would do something nice for us. He might be affectionate and stroke our hair. We needed warmth and affection, we needed all the things a family would have given us – although we didn't know what those things were. It didn't bother us that we didn't have a family, because we didn't know what a family was, or that there was such a thing. We simply needed love.

Often, they found it in their relationships with animals and pets. 'We had dogs, rabbits, horses,' Nikolai recalls.

Behind the fence at the orphanage there was a horse farm. We loved it there, we felt free. Sometimes in the summer the stable workers let us take the horses to the river. We rode bareback, swam in the river with the horses and rode back with squeals and cries of joy. On the meadow by the town there were horse races in the summertime. We were always there. No one knew the horses better than we did. We were in love with them.

Among the orphans, small informal groups of mutual support performed many of the basic functions of a family: boys of the same age would join together to protect themselves from the boys who called them 'enemies of the people' and tried to beat them up; older children would protect the younger ones, help them with their lessons and their chores and comfort them when they cried at night or wet their bed. All the children were united in their opposition to the teachers at the orphanage, who were strict and often cruel.[26]

Nikolai had no idea what his parents looked like. He did not even know that they were dead. But he saw his mother in his dreams:

I often dreamed of Mama. I think it was Mama. I did not see her face, or even her figure. They were very happy dreams. I was flying in the sky with Mama. She was hugging me and helping me to fly. But I could not see her – somehow she had her back to me, or we were side by side. We weren't flying high – just over the meadows and marshes near the orphanage. It was summertime. She would speak to me: 'Don't be afraid, we won't fly too high or too far away.' And we were smiling, we were always smiling in my dreams. I felt happiness – the physical sensation of happiness – only in those dreams. Still, today, when I think of happiness, I recall those dreams, that feeling of pure happiness.

Nikolai built up an imaginary picture of his parents, as did many other orphans. He never dreamed of his father but he pictured him as a pilot – a hero-figure in the Soviet Union in the late 1930s and 1940s. In his dreams he yearned for a family, even though, as Nikolai reflects, he had no idea what a family was. He did not see an actual family, not even a mother with her child, until he was thirteen.[27]

Without the influence of a family, Nikolai and his fellow orphans grew up with very particular ideas of right and wrong; their moral sense was shaped by what he calls the 'laws of the jungle' in the orphanage. These laws obliged every child to sacrifice himself for the collective interest. Nikolai explains:

If a person had done something wrong, for which we could all be punished, then that person was made to confess to the authorities. We would make him take the punishment rather than be punished as a group. If we could not persuade him verbally, we would use physical methods to make him own up to his crime. We would not denounce him – it was forbidden to betray one's own – but we made sure that he confessed.

But if it was forbidden to betray one's own, a different law applied to the relations between children and adults. The orphans all admired Pavlik Morozov. 'He was our hero,' Nikolai recalls.

Since we had no understanding of a family, and no idea what a father was, the fact that Pavlik had betrayed his father was of no significance to us. All that mattered was that he had caught a kulak, a member of the bourgeoisie, which made him a hero in our eyes. For us the story was all about the class struggle, not a family tragedy.[28]

The moral system of the orphanage – with its strong collective and weak familial links – made it one of the main recruiting grounds for the NKVD and the Red Army. There were millions of children from the 1930s who spent their lives in Soviet institutions – the orphanage, the army and the labour camp – without ever knowing family life. Orphan children were especially susceptible to the propaganda of the Soviet regime because they had no parents to guide them or give them any alternative system of values. Mikhail Nikolaev, who grew up in a series of children's homes in the 1930s, recalls that he and his fellow orphans were indoctrinated to believe that the Soviet Union was the best country in the world, and that they were the most fortunate children in the world, because everything had been given to them by the state, headed by the father of the country, Stalin, who cared for all children:

If we had lived in any other country, we would have died from hunger and from cold – that is what we were told . . . And of course we believed every word. We discovered life, we learned to think and feel – or rather learned not to think or feel but to accept everything that we were told – in the orphanage. All our ideas about the world we received from Soviet power.[29]

Mikhail, too, was very struck by the legend of Pavlik Morozov. He dreamed of emulating his achievement – of exposing someone as an enemy or spy – and was very proud when he became a Pioneer. Like many orphans, Mikhail saw his acceptance by the Pioneers as the moment he fully entered Soviet society. Until then, he had always been ashamed about his parentage. He had only fragmentary recollections of his mother and father: a memory of riding with his father on a horse; a mental picture of his mother sitting by a lamp and cleaning a pistol (which made him think that she must have been a Party official). He did not know who his parents were; nor did he know their names (Mikhail Nikolaev was the name he had been given when he first came to the orphanage). He recounted an incident from when he had been four or five years old: his former nanny had come to visit him in the children's home and had told him that his parents had been shot as 'enemies of the people'. Then she said: 'They should shoot you too, just as they shot your mother and father.' Throughout his childhood Mikhail felt ashamed on this account. But this shame was lifted when he joined the Pioneers: it was the first time he was recognized and valued by the Soviet system. As a Pioneer, Mikhail looked to Stalin as a figure of paternal authority and care. He believed all goodness came from him: 'The fact that we were fed and clothed, that we could study, that we could go to the Pioneers Camp, even that there was a New Year's tree – all of it was down to comrade Stalin,' in his view.[30]

The children at Mikhail's orphanage were put to work at an early age. They washed the dishes and cleared the yard from the age of four, worked in the fields of a collective farm from the age of seven, and, when they reached the age of eleven, they were sent to work in a textiles factory in the nearby town of Orekhovo-Zuevo, 50 kilometres east of Moscow. In the summer of 1941, Mikhail was assigned to a metal factory in one of the industrial suburbs of Orekhovo-Zuevo. Although he was only twelve, the doctors at the orphanage had declared him to be fifteen on the basis of a medical examination (Mikhail was big for his age) and had given him a new set of documents which stated – incorrectly – that he was born in 1926. There was a policy of declaring orphaned children to be older than their age so that they would become eligible for military service or industrial work. For the next two years Mikhail worked in the steel plant in a brigade of children from the orphanage. 'We worked in shifts – one week twelve hours every night, the next twelve hours every day. The working week was seven days.' The terrible conditions in the factory were a long way from the propaganda image of industrial work that Mikhail had received through books and films, and for the first time in his life he began to doubt what he had been taught. The children slept in their work clothes on the floor of the factory club and took their meals in the canteen. They were not paid. In the autumn of 1943, Mikhail ran away from the factory and

volunteered for the Red Army – he did so out of hunger, not patriotism
– and became a tank driver. He was just fourteen.[31]

Like Mikhail, Nikolai Kovach was extremely proud when he joined
the Pioneers. It gave him a sense of inclusion in the world outside the
orphanage and put him on a par with other children his age. Kovach
went on to join the Komsomol and become a Party activist; *The History
of the CPSU* was his 'favourite book'. He joined the Red Army as a
teenager and served in the Far East. When he was demobilized he could
not settle into civilian life – he had lived too long in Soviet institutions
– so he went to work for the NKVD: it enabled him to study in the
evening at its elite military academy. Kovach served in a special unit of
the NKVD. Its main task was to catch the children who had run away
from children's homes.[32]

3

Maria Budkevich, the fourteen-year-old girl who had been trained by
her parents to survive on her own in the event of their arrest, was able
to do so for the better part of a year after they were taken by the NKVD
in July 1937. She lived by herself in the family's apartment in Moscow
until the summer of 1938, when the NKVD took her to the detention
centre in the Danilov Monastery. While she had been living on her
own, Maria had been helped by an old friend of her parents, Militsa
Yevgenevna, who felt sorry for the child. Militsa's husband, a Bolshevik
official, had been arrested shortly before Maria's parents, so Militsa
presumed that they had been arrested on account of him. She soon
became frightened of the consequences for herself if she continued to
assist the daughter of an 'enemy', and called the NKVD. When they
came for Maria, Militsa said to her: 'Don't be cross with me . . . It will
be better for you in a children's home. Afterwards it will be easier, you
will no longer be the child of an enemy of the people.'[33]

From the Danilov Monastery Maria was transferred to an orphanage
near Gorkii with twenty-five other children of 'enemies of the people'.
The director of the orphanage was a paternal type who encouraged
Maria to study hard and make a career for herself, despite her spoilt
biography. She joined the Komsomol, though she was warned that she
would be forced to renounce her parents before she was admitted, and

took part in its activities, which mainly involved shrill denunciations of 'enemies of the people' and singing songs of thanks to Stalin and the Party in mass meetings and marches. As she recalls, she joined the Komsomol in the belief that this was what her parents would have wanted her to do: 'How could I have not joined? Mama always said that I had to become a Pioneer and then a Young Communist. It would have been shameful not to join.' Yet at the same time – without quite grasping the political events that led to the arrest of her parents – she felt that it was somehow wrong to join. She remembers feeling a sense of guilt towards her parents, as if she had betrayed them, although, as it turned out, she was not called upon to renounce them. Still, she felt awkward about taking part in Komsomol propaganda, and, as she recounts, 'only made a show of singing in praise of Stalin, mouthing words I did not quite believe'. At the root of her discomfort was her instinctive sense that her parents had been wrongly arrested (she even wrote to Stalin to protest in 1939), a conviction that conflicted with the political identity she had to adopt to survive and advance. As a member of the Komsomol, Maria was able to enroll at the Polytechnic Institute of Leningrad, a leading science university seldom attended by children of the 'enemies of the people'.[34]

Millions of children grew up in the grey area between the Soviet system and its 'enemies', constantly torn by competing loyalties and contradictory impulses. On the one hand, the stigma of a tainted biography reinforced their need to prove themselves as fully equal members of society, which meant conforming to Soviet ideals, joining the Komsomol and perhaps the Party too. On the other, these children could not help but feel alienated from the system that had brought such suffering on their families.

Zhenia Yevangulova had mixed emotions following the arrest of her parents in the summer of 1937. She was nineteen years old, she had just finished school, and now her chance of going on to study in Moscow was dashed. Instead she went to live with her father's uncle, a retired professor of metallurgy in Leningrad, who helped her to get into the Workers' Faculty (rabfak), from which she hoped to transfer to the Polytechnic Institute. As the day of her application to the institute approached, Zhenia became more fearful, knowing she would have to reveal the arrest of her parents in the anketa. She felt like a 'leper' and feared that she would be disqualified from joining the institute, even though she had got top marks in the entrance examinations. In 1938, she was admitted, albeit to the Metallurgical Department, where competition for places was not as acute as in other departments. Throughout her first year there, Zhenia confessed in her diary to a feeling of depression, even to thoughts of suicide. Reflecting on this sadness, she explained it to herself as the 'shutting down' of her personality that followed her parents' disappearance. At the Workers' Faculty, their arrest had been a source of constant shame; her fellow students had bullied her mercilessly, calling her the daughter of a 'traitor to the motherland'. At the institute, Zhenia tried to overcome this stigma by proving herself a model student.

There were moments when she struggled to break free of her parents, to enjoy herself with the other students, to move on with her life. But these brief moments of happiness were always followed by feelings of guilt when she recalled her parents in the camps. Shortly after the arrest of her father, Zhenia had had a dream in which her father reappeared as an aggressor. It continued to haunt her:

My father appeared from the mist of an adjoining room, pressed his pistol to my heart and shot. There was no physical pain, only the sensation that I had failed to stop him . . . And then I noticed that my chest was soaked in blood.

While at the institute, she went skating with her friends one evening and felt happy for the first time in many months. But that night she again saw her father in the dream and the next morning she awoke with a 'heavy feeling of depression'.[35]

Looking back on their teenage years, many of these 'strange orphans' recall that there was a moment – a moment they had all hoped for – when the stigma of repression was at last lifted and they were recognized as 'Soviet citizens'. This desire for social acceptance was felt by nearly all the children of the 'enemies of the people'. There were few who turned their backs on the Soviet system or became opposed to it.

For Ida Slavina, that moment of acceptance came in the summer of 1938, shortly after the arrest of her mother (her father was taken in 1937). She was invited by her physical education teacher to take part in a school parade. Ida was an athlete, tall and fit. She had participated in school marches as an athlete and gymnast since the age of fourteen, but after the arrest of her father she had been excluded from the parade team. In her memoirs (1995) she recalls her joy on being readmitted to the parade team as a gymnast-parachutist for a demonstration on the theme 'On Land and Sea and in the Sky' to celebrate the achievements of Soviet sport:

'On Land and Sea and in the Sky'
gymnastic demonstration, 1938:
Ida is in the middle of the back row

I remember the surprise of my interviewers,* when they recognized me in a photograph among a group of athletes at the parade. How, they asked, could I bring myself to go on a parade when my mother had only just been sent to a labour camp? Thinking back, I recognize the egoism of youth, of course; I was sixteen, I couldn't stand to be unhappy, I longed for happiness and love. But there was more to it than that. Joining the parade was also an expression of my deep desire to feel whole again in my shattered world. To feel again the sensation of being part of an enormous 'We'. Marching in columns, with everybody else, singing the proud song, 'We Have No Borders', it seemed to me that I was indeed a fully equal representative of my Motherland. I was filled with the belief [in the words of the song] that we would 'carry our Soviet banner over worlds and centuries'. I was with everyone! My friends and teachers once again believed in

*Ida was interviewed for the BBC film *The Hand of Stalin* (1989).

me – and that meant, or so I thought, that they must also believe in my parents' innocence.[36]

For most teenagers it was their admission to the Komsomol that symbolized their transition from children of an 'enemy of the people' to 'Soviet citizens'. Galina Adasinskaia was seventeen when her father was arrested in February 1938. Galina's parents were active oppositionists and there was no expectation that she would become a member of the Communist youth organization. Exiled with her mother from her native Leningrad to Iaroslavl, Galina felt acutely the stigma of repression and tried to overcome it by applying to the Komsomol nonetheless. She wrote to the Komsomol committee at her school, asking them, as she put it, to 'look into my case' (i.e. to examine her appeal to join in the light of her father's arrest). There was in this, as she admits, a conscious element of self-purging, an open declaration of her 'spoilt biography' in the hope of forgiveness and salvation by the collective. At the Komsomol meeting to discuss her appeal, the leaders ruled that Galina 'should be disqualified from membership as an enemy of the people'. But one of her classmates protested, and threatened that all the students would leave if Adasinskaia was excluded. 'The Party instructor became red with rage,' recalls Galina:

He sat there on his stool and began to shout: 'What is this? A provocation! Lack of vigilance!' But I was allowed to join the Komsomol. I was even elected as the class organizer and our organization took first place [in the socialist competition] at school.

For Galina this was the moment she was brought back into the collective fold. When she herself was arrested in 1941, she recalls, 'my investigator's eyes practically fell out when he saw my Komsomol record'.[37]

The renunciation of family traditions and beliefs was usually the sacrifice required for entry into Soviet society. Liuba Tetiueva was born in 1923, the fourth child in the family of an Orthodox priest in the town of Cherdyn, in the northern Urals. Liuba's father, Aleksandr, was arrested in 1922 and held in prison for the best part of a year. After his release he was put under pressure by OGPU to become an informer and write reports on his own parishioners, but he refused. When his church was taken over by the *obnovlentsy*, church reformers supported by the regime, Aleksandr was arrested for a second time but released a few months later in the autumn of 1929. Liuba's mother, Klavdiia, was subsequently dismissed from her job in the Cherdyn Museum, and her brother Viktor was expelled from school as the son of a 'class enemy'. In 1930, Aleksandr, eager to protect his family by distancing himself, took his son and moved to the town of Chermoz. In the hope of improving the boy's prospects Aleksandr gave Viktor up for adoption to a family of workers active in the Church; as a 'workers' son' Viktor finished seventh class at school and qualified as a teacher. The rest of the family also left Cherdyn, where they faced ruination, and went to live with Klavdiia's mother in Solikamsk, a new industrial town 100 kilometres to the south.

Growing up in Solikamsk, Liuba was brought up to 'know her place'.

Mama constantly reminded me that I was the daughter of a priest, that I should be careful not to mix with people, not to trust them, or to speak with them about my family. My place was to be modest. She used to say: 'Others are allowed but you are not.'

The family was very poor. Klavdiia worked as an instructor in *likbez* (an organization established to end illiteracy among adults) but her pay was not enough to feed the family without a ration card. They managed to survive thanks to small sums from Aleksandr, who worked in Chermoz as a priest. Then, in August 1937, Aleksandr was arrested yet again. In October he was shot. Klavdiia and the children kept going by selling their last possessions and growing vegetables. Help finally came in the form of money sent by some of Aleksandr's old parishioners – peasants helped by the Church during collectivization.

Liuba had seen her father only once after he moved to Chermoz. She visited him there in June 1937, a few weeks before his arrest. 'Papa was upset by my ignorance of religion,' recalls Liuba. 'He tried to teach me Old Church Slavonic, and I resisted. It was the first and last religious lesson in my life.' Years of repression had made Liuba want to break away from her family background. During the first year at her new school in Solikamsk she had been the target of an anti-religious propaganda campaign: the teacher would point to Liuba and tell the other children that they would all turn out as badly as she had, if they were exposed to religion. Bullied by the other children, Liuba was reduced to 'such a state of fear and hysteria', as she herself recalls, that

I was afraid to go to school. Eventually my mother and grandmother decided not to take me to church any longer; they told me it was best to have one education, and that I was to believe everything I was told about religion at my school.

Liuba joined the Pioneers. She was proud to wear the scarf, a sign of her inclusion, and became an activist, even taking part in demonstrations against the Church in 1938, when banners called for 'Death to all the priests!' Liuba became a teacher – the chosen profession of three of Aleksandr's four children. For nearly fifty years she taught the Party line against the Church. Looking back, Liuba is filled with remorse for having turned her back on her family's traditions and beliefs.* 'I always thought: how much easier it would have been for me if my father had been a teacher rather than a priest, if I had had a father, just like every other girl.'[38] Compared with her brother Viktor, who formally renounced his father at a meeting of the Komsomol, it could be said that Liuba only did what was absolutely necessary to survive in Soviet society.

Becoming a Soviet activist was a common survival strategy among children of 'enemies of the people'. It both deflected political suspicions from their vulnerability and enabled them to overcome their fear.

Elizaveta Delibash was born in 1928 in Minusinsk, Siberia, where her parents were then living in exile. Her father, Aleksandr Iosilevich, was the son of a Leningrad printer, a veteran Bolshevik and Cheka official from the beginning of the Soviet regime and the partner of Elizaveta Drabkina (the teenager who had found her father in the Smolny Institute in October 1917), until he fell in love with Nina Delibash, the daughter of a minor Georgian official, and married her in 1925. Two years later, Aleksandr was arrested after falling out with his former OGPU employers (he had left the police to study economics in Moscow in 1926). Exiled to Siberia, he was followed there by Nina, who was pregnant with their daughter. In 1928, Nina and her baby went back to the Soviet capital, followed after his release by Aleksandr, who found a job in the Ministry of Foreign Trade. In 1930, Aleksandr was rearrested and sentenced to ten years in the labour camp at Sukhobezvodny, part of the Vetlag Gulag complex near Gorkii. Nina was arrested at the same time and sent to a series of 'special settlements' in Siberia, from which

---

*After the collapse of Communism, Liuba became an active member of her church and published her own book about the life of her father (L. Tetiueva, *Zhizn' pravoslavnogo sviashchennika*, Perm, 2004).

she returned to Moscow in 1932. Elizaveta stayed with her father's family in Leningrad, occasionally visiting her mother in exile or in Moscow, until 1935, when she and Nina rejoined Aleksandr in the Sukhobezvodny camp. Nina worked as a volunteer, and the family lived together in the barracks of the camp, where Elizaveta went to school. But then, in April 1936, Elizaveta's parents were both rearrested. Aleksandr was executed in May 1937; Nina was sentenced to ten years in the Solovetsky labour camp, where she was shot in November 1937.

After the arrest of her parents, Elizaveta was saved from being sent to an orphanage by one of the other prisoners at Sukhobezvodny who brought her back to Leningrad after her release in 1936. Elizaveta stayed with various relatives – first with an uncle Grigorii (who was arrested in April 1937); then with an aunt Margo (who was arrested in July); and then with an aunt Raia (who was arrested in August) – whereupon some distant relatives rescued her from Leningrad and took her off to their dacha near Moscow, where they concealed her from the NKVD, before sending her to her mother's family in Tbilisi. Passed between these relatives, unaware of their concern to get her out of the police's way, she began to feel like an unwanted child.

Elizaveta's grandparents were plain folk – her grandfather was of peasant origin and her grandmother the daughter of a trader – but they had both been educated and they had imbibed the liberal-Christian values of the intelligentsia in Tbilisi. Elizaveta did not go to school but was taught at home by her grandmother, who had been a teacher in the Tbilisi Gymnasium before 1917. Her grandparents had no illusions about the purges. They told her that her parents were innocent and decent people who had been punished unjustly. Nina wrote twice to her parents from the Solovetsky camp. She added a few words of comfort and encouragement for her daughter. Her last letter was written just before her execution on 2 November 1937 and passed to one of her executioners, who sent it on illegally. 'Papa, Mama, I am going to die. Save my daughter,' Nina wrote. She told Elizaveta that she could always find her by the Great Bear in the night sky. 'When you see that, think of me,' she wrote, 'because I will be up there.' Nina's letters and all her photographs were destroyed after the arrest of her brother in Tbilisi in December 1937.*

---

*Elizaveta had no photograph of her mother until the early 1990s, when she received her mother's file from the former KGB archives.

But the memory of that final letter, which her grandmother read to her a dozen times, remained close to Elizaveta's heart: 'I was always waiting, always waiting for my mother,' she recalls. 'Even as an adult, when I went out at night, I would always look for the Great Bear and think about my mother. Until 1958 [when she found out that her mother had been shot] I saw it as a sign that one day she would return.'

Elizaveta Delibash, 1949

The arrest of her uncle made it dangerous for Elizaveta to remain in Tbilisi, as mass arrests swept through the Georgian capital. Although she was nearly ten, Elizaveta had not been to school, but none in Tbilisi would accept the daughter of an 'enemy of the people'. In January 1938, her grandparents put her on a train for Leningrad, where she lived with her mother's sister Sonia. A trade-union official at the Kirov Factory, a senior Party activist and an ardent Stalinist, Sonia was the only one of all her aunts and uncles not to be arrested in the Great Terror. Looking back on these traumatic years, Elizaveta thinks she did not really feel or understand the impact of the Terror on her life. Her relatives had not told her very much. By the time she was ten, she had already lived through such extraordinary things – growing up in exile and in labour camps, losing both her parents, finding salvation in a dozen different homes – that she had little sense of where 'normal' ended and 'abnormal' began. What she felt, she now recalls, was a rather vague and general feeling of disorientation and despondency rooted in the sense that she was 'unwanted and unloved'. This sense was exacerbated by the atmosphere in her aunt's apartment which, by comparison with the friendly cheer of her grandparents' house, was cold, severe and tense after the arrest of Sonia's husband in January 1938. Expelled from the Party shortly afterwards, Sonia kept a bag packed with some clothes and a few bits of dried bread in readiness for her own arrest, which she expected every night. Elizaveta became increasingly withdrawn. She developed a 'fear of people', she recalls. 'I was afraid of everyone.' She recounts an incident when her aunt had sent her out to buy some things from the local store. The shop assistant had mistakenly given her an extra 5 kopeks in change. When she returned home, her aunt told her to return the money to the shop and apologize. Elizaveta was terrified, not because of any shame that might have been attached to taking the extra change, but because she was afraid to approach the shop assistant (a stranger) and speak to her in a personal way.

Despite the arrest of her husband, the repression of virtually all her other relatives, and her own expulsion from the Party, Sonia remained a firm supporter of Stalin. She taught her niece to believe everything in the Soviet press and to accept the possibility that her parents had been guilty of some crime. She told her that her father had belonged to an opposition group and had therefore been arrested as an 'enemy of the people', although she also said that Nina had probably been innocent. 'Sonia rarely mentioned my parents,' recalls Elizaveta. 'I was afraid to ask her about them in case she said something disapproving about them. I understood that conversations on this theme were forbidden.' Perhaps Sonia thought her niece would be held back or become alienated from the Soviet system if she thought too much about her family's fate. Encouraged by her aunt, Elizaveta enrolled in the Pioneers and then the Komsomol. On each occasion she disguised the truth about her parents, as Sonia had advised her, by claiming that they had been arrested in 1935 (before the general purge of 'enemies of the people'). Elizaveta recalls entering the Komsomol:

I was overwhelmed with fear – it went back to the arrest of my parents when I was left all alone – fear of the outside world, fear of everything and everyone. I was afraid to make contact with anyone in case they asked about my family. Nothing was more frightening than a meeting of the Komsomol, where questions about origins were always asked.

Gradually she overcame her fears. Having been accepted by the Komsomol, Elizaveta gained confidence. 'For the first time in my life, I no longer felt like a black sheep,' she recalls. She excelled in her studies, which gave her genuine authority among her schoolmates. She became an activist – the elected secretary of her Komsomol at school and then the secretary of the Komsomol in the district where she lived in Leningrad. Looking back, Elizaveta thinks that her activism saved her, granting her some measure of control:

When I joined the Komsomol and became one of 'us', when I mixed with my contemporaries and became their leader, I was no longer so afraid. I could go and fight their cause, negotiate for them with the authorities. Of course, I was also fighting for myself, because, by appearing strong, I could keep my own fear in check.[39]

For 'kulak' children, who grew up in 'special settlements' and other places of exile, embracing the Soviet cause was the only way to overcome the stigma of their birth. By the late 1930s, many of the children exiled with their 'kulak' parents had reached the age of adulthood. The NKVD was inundated with petitions from these teenagers asking to be released from exile and rehabilitated into Soviet society. Some wrote official statements renouncing their families. During the early 1930s, only a very few appeals were successful: some 'kulak' daughters were allowed to leave their places of exile to marry men with the full rights of a Soviet citizen, but otherwise the view of the government was that the return of 'kulak' children would contaminate and demoralize society. However, from the end of 1938 there was a change of policy, with a new emphasis on the reforging and rehabilitation of 'kulak' children. At the age of sixteen they were now allowed to leave their places of exile and regain their civil rights – provided they renounced their family.[40]

Dmitry Streletsky was one such 'kulak' child. Born in 1917, in the Kurgan region, he was exiled with his family to a 'special settlement' near Chermoz in the northern Urals during collectivization. Growing up in the settlement, Dmitry felt the stigma of his 'kulak' origins acutely. 'I felt like an outcast,' he recalls. 'I felt that I was not a complete human being, that I was somehow blemished and made bad because my father was exiled . . . I did not feel guilty, like an enemy, but I did feel second-rate.' Education was his way out: ' "Study, study, children!", Father always said. "Education is the one good thing that Soviet power can give you." ' And Dmitry studied. He was the first boy from the settlement to complete the tenth class at the school and was rewarded for his industry by being admitted to the Komsomol in 1937. 'Proud and happy' to be recognized at last as an equal, he soon became an activist. Dmitry identified his own progress with the ideals of the Party. He saw the Party as a higher form of community, a 'comradeship of fair-minded, first-rate people', in which he could find his salvation. On his father's advice, Dmitry paid a visit to the NKVD commandant of the 'special settlement' and asked for help to continue his studies at a university. Commandant Nevolin was a decent type. He felt sorry for the bright young man, whose success at school was already known to him, and he clearly saw him as someone worth helping. Nevolin gave Dmitry a passport and 100 roubles, more than twice the monthly wage in the 'special settlement', and sent him to Perm with a letter of recommendation from the NKVD, which enabled him to enrol as a physics student at the university.

Dmitry never tried to hide his 'kulak' origins. He declared them in the questionnaire he filled out on entering the university and as a result he was bullied by the other students. He finally left, thinking that the farther he ran the more likely he was to find a place where he could study without being held back by his past. First he enrolled at the Sverdlovsk Mining Institute; then he moved even further east to Omsk, where he became a student at the Agricultural Institute. But here too his origins came back to haunt him. Six weeks into the first term, Dmitry was called in by the dean and told he had to leave the institute: they had received orders to expel the children of 'kulaks', priests and other 'alien social elements'. Despondently, he resolved to return to the Kurgan region, where he still had some relatives. Other than returning to the 'special settlement', he had nowhere else to go. Dmitry went to see his old teacher in the village school where he had studied as a boy, before being sent into exile. The teacher remembered him and invited him to work as a physics tutor in the school. Dmitry had no degree from a higher institute, but in truth the only qualification he really required was a sound knowledge of Stalin's history of the Party, the *Short Course*, and that was Dmitry's favourite book. He taught in the school for a year. In the summer of 1939, he went to visit his parents in Chermoz, who had written to tell him that conditions had improved in the 'special settlement'. In fact, when he arrived, the new commandant of the settlement, a less forgiving type than Nevolin, arrested him, confiscated his passport and threatened to send him to a labour camp. Once again, Dmitry was saved by his outstanding record as a student. The director of the Chermoz school, who recalled his star pupil, appealed to the NKVD, claiming that he desperately needed teaching staff. And so Dmitry was allowed to stay. He taught at the settlement's school for the next two years, until the outbreak of the war, when he was conscripted by the Labour Army and sent to a lumber camp ('kulak' sons were banned from front-line service in the army until April 1942).

Physics teacher Dmitry Streletsky (seated far right) with schoolboys of the seventh class in the Chermoz 'special settlement', September 1939. The director of the school, Viktor Bezgodov, is standing on the right

Despite all his suffering at the hands of the Soviet regime, Dmitry was a Soviet patriot, he believed fervently in the justice of the Party's cause, and wanted desperately to become a part of it. 'I dreamed of joining the Party,' he explains.

I wanted to be recognized as an equal human being, that is all I wanted from the Party. I did not want to join for my career. For me the Party was a symbol of honesty and dedication. There were honest, decent people who were Communists, and I thought I deserved to be counted among them.

It was a huge disappointment when he was turned down for Party membership in 1945 (recounting the episode sixty years later, his hands shake and he finds it hard to speak from emotion). But after 1956, when the Party tried to attract members from the groups which Stalin had repressed, he was at last admitted to the comradeship of equals he had yearned to join for over twenty years.[41]

4

Zinaida Bushueva was sentenced to eight years in the ALZhIR Labour Camp for Wives of Traitors to the Motherland near Akmolinsk in Kazakhstan. After five years in the camp she was transferred from the inner prison zone to the surrounding settlement, where conditions were better, and families could sometimes join the prisoners. Zinaida wrote to her mother in Molotov. Although she was desperate to be reunited with her two daughters, Angelina and Nelly, Zinaida did not want to 'spoil their lives' by subjecting them to the hardships of camp life. In Molotov, however, there were chronic shortages of food. It was a city overcrowded by evacuees from the war-torn Soviet territories, and families like the Bushuevs, 'enemies of the people' who had no food ration or allotment, were in dire straits. Zinaida's mother decided it was best to reunite the girls with their mother. She could not imagine that conditions in the camp could be any worse than they were in Molotov.

To get the children to ALZhIR they first had to be given to an orphanage: once they had been made wards of the state, Zinaida could appeal for their transfer to the labour camp. After three months at the orphanage, Angelina and Nelly were collected by their grandmother and taken on the train journey from Molotov to Kazakhstan, arriving in Akmolinsk late one January evening. Zinaida came to meet them at the station, where she found them sitting on the platform sheltering themselves from a snowstorm. She was dressed in a quilted jacket, trousers and felt boots, the standard winter clothes of a prisoner. When Nelly, who was nine, saw her mother, she ran up to her and flung her arms around her neck. But Angelina, who was only two when she had last seen her mother, was too young to remember her. She recoiled in fear. 'That's not my mama,' Angelina said. 'That's just a peasant uncle (*diaden'ka muzhik*) in his winter clothes.' After five years of hard labour, Zinaida had lost her feminine appearance; she no longer looked like the ideal image of a mother Angelina had seen in family photographs and built up in her mind.[42]

Left: Zinaida with her brothers, 1936. Right: Zinaida (centre) in ALZhIR, 1942. A rare private photograph of Gulag prisoners, it was taken to send to relatives. The three women were photographed together to reduce the costs

ALZhIR was the largest of the three labour camps in the Gulag system exclusively for female prisoners (the others being the Tomsk labour camp and the Temnikovsky camp in the Republic of Mordovia). Built in a hurry to meet the regime's urgent demand for prisons for the wives of 'enemies of the people', it received its first convoys of female convicts in January 1938. Most of them were housed in the barracks of a former colony for orphan children under the control of the NKVD. By 1941, there were an estimated 10,000 women in the camp, most of them employed in agriculture, like Bushueva, or in the textiles factory, which made uniforms for the Red Army. Conditions in the camps of Kazakhstan were relatively good compared to those in the Far North or Siberia. But for the women of ALZhIR – especially for those who had grown accustomed to the comfortable lifestyle of the Soviet elite – camp life was very difficult, particularly during the first years. Initially categorized as a high-security penal institution, ALZhIR imposed an extremely punitive 'special regime' (*spets-rezhim*) on its prisoners, as part of the campaign of repression against the 'wives of traitors'. The inner prison zone, distinct from the barracks settlement, was enclosed by a wire fence with observation towers and patrolled by guards with dogs. The women were awoken at 4 a.m. for work; the last roll-call before they were allowed to sleep was at midnight, although, as many prisoners recall, the guards were so innumerate that they often had to get the women up again to recheck their numbers. Food rations were given in accordance with the prisoner's fulfilment of her working quota; anyone who failed to meet the quota for ten days in succession was transferred to the 'death barracks' and left to die. 'Every morning the dead were carted out and buried in the mass grave just outside the camp,' recalls a former guard. The hardest thing to bear for many prisoners was the prohibition on letters from relatives (a condition of the 'special regime'). After May 1939, the 'special regime' was lifted. ALZhIR was designated as a 'general labour camp' and conditions began to improve. The barracks settlement was gradually enlarged, as more women completed their sentences in the prison zone or were rewarded for their labour in the prison with an early release to the settlement.* Conditions there were much more bearable. There were no fences, the women were escorted by the guards to work and counted every evening on their return, but otherwise they were left largely to themselves. There was a vibrant cultural life in the club house of the settlement, which was encouraged by the camp commandant, Sergei Barinov, who was to be remembered as a relatively kind and decent man. Among the women in the camp were the wives and relatives of many senior Bolsheviks and Red Army commanders; they included writers, artists, actresses and singers, even soloists from the Bolshoi Theatre in Moscow. According to Mikhail Iusipenko, the deputy commandant of ALZhIR, there were 125 doctors, 400 qualified nurses, 40 actresses and 350 pianists in the first convoy of prisoners. Mikhail Shreider, the second-in-command to the NKVD chief of Kazakhstan, recalls his discomfort on visiting ALZhIR, where there were so many of his former colleagues' wives, 'for whom I could do nothing'. The camp administration assured Shreider that the prisoners enjoyed good conditions at ALZhIR, but it still seemed to him a 'frightful place', as bad as any of the Gulag camps, not because of the physical conditions, but because it contained such a concentration of mothers separated from their children.[43]

In this respect the Bushuevs were fortunate to be together. Zinaida's son Slava, who had been put into the orphanage on their arrival at ALZhIR, was reunited with his mother when she was transferred to the barracks settlement. Her transfer also meant that Nelly and Angelina

---

*After the outbreak of the war, in June 1941, prisoners who had served their sentences in the prison zone were forced to live and work in the barracks settlement. A prisoner sentenced to three years in 1938 would thus not be released from ALZhIR until 1945.

Children at ALZhIR, 1942. Slava Bushuev is standing far right

could join her. They all lived in one of the barracks, which had long rows of sleeping planks on two levels. As Angelina remembers:

The other women rearranged themselves so that we could live as a family in one corner, with two of us on top and two below, a bedside table and a little corner shelf, which was all our own, where we kept our bread and jam . . . We took our meals from the canteen and ate them sitting on our sleeping planks . . . No one ever stole our things . . . There were four families in our barracks. Each one had a corner, where they could enjoy some privacy. It was agreed that this was right.

Angelina and Nelly went to the school in the labour camp. They even joined the Pioneers, which operated in the camp, encouraged by the authorities to cultivate a Soviet ethos in the children of 'enemies of the people'. There were no red scarfs in the labour camp, so the Pioneers made their own by dyeing cotton strips with the blood of mosquitoes, which swarmed all around the camp.[44]

However, most of the women at ALZhIR had little connection to their families. Once ALZhIR became a general labour camp the inmates were permitted to write and receive letters according to the rules of correspondence stipulated by the Gulag code of 1939: prisoners were allowed one letter and one parcel every month, or once every three months if, like most of the women of ALZhIR, they had been convicted of 'counter-revolutionary crimes'. But in reality the number of letters the women received depended on the whim of the camp guards, on the regime inside the camp and on the location of the camp (some labour camps were too remote to be reached by any mail). Inna Gaister recounts the elaborate arrangements for sending parcels to her mother in ALZhIR. Normal post offices did not accept parcels for dispatch to labour camps. Special posting stations were designated for the purpose, but since there were no public announcements about their location (the existence of the camps was not acknowledged by the Soviet authorities), people had to rely for information on the rumours that circulated within the prison queues. In 1938, all dispatches from Moscow were stopped, so Inna had to travel to Mozhaisk, a town 100 kilometres south-west of Moscow, and battle with the crowds to hand in a parcel at a designated carriage on a special train taking prisoners to Kazakhstan.[45]

To be deprived of these letters was a form of torture for the women of ALZhIR, who were sometimes known to make their feelings heard. When Esfir Slavina, the wife of the jurist Ilia Slavin, arrived at ALZhIR in 1938, she was horrified to find a large number of teenage girls – many of them younger than her sixteen-year-old daughter Ida – who had somehow ended up in the labour camp. Esfir was afraid that Ida, too, was in a camp somewhere, but she had no rights of correspondence and had heard nothing from her daughter. In fact Ida was coping on her own, staying in the homes of various schoolfriends in Leningrad and sending parcels to her mother, which never reached her. Esfir went on a hunger strike. It was the first sign of protest at ALZhIR, where the prisoners – mostly Party members or the wives of Bolsheviks – had on the whole been loyal to the Soviet regime and done their work conscientiously and without complaint. Esfir was not involved in politics. She had never paid attention to her husband's legal affairs, and her only interest was in her family. When she refused to eat, Esfir was put into a punishment block, but after several weeks, as she neared the point of physical collapse, the camp administrators finally agreed to let her receive letters from her family. Perhaps Esfir's hunger strike was not the determining factor: it is hard to imagine that the camp authorities were concerned about an individual death, and they were in any case already preparing to transfer ALZhIR from a 'special regime' to a 'general labour camp', which would allow the prisoners to receive letters from their relatives. But the authorities may have been concerned by the possible reaction by the other prisoners in the event of Esfir's death, for feelings on this issue had been running very high, and there had been frequent complaints about the lack of mail. A few days after the capitulation of the camp authorities, Ida was summoned to the NKVD headquarters in Leningrad and informed that she could send a parcel to her mother. It arrived in the winter months of early 1940, a time when hardly anyone in ALZhIR was receiving letters, let alone parcels. Esfir's victory made her a celebrity. Hundreds of women gathered in her barracks to inspect the precious contents of her parcel. It encouraged some of the others to protest to the camp authorities.[46]

As the rules of correspondence were relaxed, the women of ALZhIR poured all their emotions into their letters, often making little gifts to enclose for their children as tokens of their love. 'We so wanted for our children to have something we had made for them,' recalls one of ALZhIR's prisoners.[47]

Dina Ielson-Grodzianskaia was sentenced to ALZhIR in 1938, following the arrest of her husband Yevgeny, the director of the Moscow Higher Technical School, in December 1937 (he was shot in 1938). Their daughter Gertrud (Gerta), who was then aged five, and her younger brother were adopted by their aunt. A trained agronomist, Dina played a senior role in the agricultural management of the labour camp – one of the many 'trusties' in the Gulag system who worked as specialists or collaborated with the camp authorities to earn those small advantages which in a labour camp could make the difference between life and death.[48] Compared to the other prisoners, Dina was allowed to send and receive letters relatively frequently. She often sent her daughter little presents she had made by hand – a piece of clothing or a toy, or on one occasion a beautiful embroidered towel with animals, which Gertrud was to treasure all her life. 'I always kept it on my bed, wherever I was, in student dormitories, in every place I lived,' she recalls. 'In my mind it was synonymous with the fairy-tale mother of my imagination. In her

Embroidered towel (detail) made by Dina for Gertrud

absence I had constructed an image of a mother who was good and beautiful, but who lived far away.'[49]

The yearning for a mother found its parallel in the yearning for a child, even in the conditions of a labour camp. A printer from Ukraine, Hava Volovich was twenty-one when she was arrested and sentenced to a labour camp in the Far North in 1937. Feeling isolated and lonely, she longed to have a child, to feel the joy of a child's love. It was a longing felt by many women in the camps, as she recalls in a memoir full of emotion:

Our need for love, tenderness, caresses, was so desperate that it reached the point of insanity, of beating one's head against a wall, of suicide. We all wanted a child – the dearest and closest of all people, someone for whom we would give up our own life. I held out for a relatively long time. But I did so need and yearn for a hand of my own to hold, something I could lean on in those long years of solitude, oppression, and humiliation.

Hava had an affair with an unnamed man ('I did not choose the best of them by any means') and had a little girl with golden curls whom she called Eleonora. The camp had no special facilities for mothers. In the barracks where Hava gave birth three mothers were confined in a tiny room.

Bedbugs poured down like sand from the ceiling and walls; we spent the whole night brushing them off the children. During the daytime we had to go out to work and leave the infants with any old woman we could find who had been excused from work; these women would calmly help themselves to the food we had left for the children.

Motherhood gave Hava a new purpose and belief in life:

I believed neither in God nor in the Devil. But while I had my child, I most passionately, most violently wanted there to be a God . . . I prayed that God would prolong my torment for a hundred years if it meant that I wouldn't be parted from my daughter. I prayed that I might be released with her, even if only as a beggar or a cripple. I prayed that I might be able to raise her to adulthood, even if I had to grovel at people's feet and beg for alms to do it. But God did not answer my prayer. My baby had barely started walking, I had hardly heard her first words, the wonderful heartwarming word 'Mama', when we were dressed in rags, despite the winter chill, bundled into a freight car, and transferred to the 'mothers' camp'. And here my pudgy little angel with the golden curls soon turned into a pale ghost with blue shadows under her eyes and sores all over her lips.

Hava was put to work in a brigade felling trees and then transferred to a sawmill. By bribing the nurses in the children's home, she was allowed to see her daughter outside the normal visiting hours, before the morning roll-call and during her lunch break. What she found was disturbing:

I saw the nurses getting the children up in the mornings. They would force them out of their cold beds with shoves and kicks . . . Pushing the children with their fists and swearing at them roughly, they took off their night clothes and washed them in ice-cold water. The babies didn't even dare to cry. They made little sniffing noises like old men and let out low hoots. This awful hooting noise would come from the cots for days at a time. Children already old enough to be sitting up or crawling would lie on their backs, their knees pressed to their stomachs, making these strange noises, like the muffled cooing of pigeons.

One nurse, responsible for seventeen infants, found ways to speed up her work:

The nurse brought a steaming bowl of porridge from the kitchen, and portioned it out into separate dishes. She grabbed the nearest baby, forced its arms back, tied them in place with a towel, and began cramming spoonful after spoonful of hot porridge down its throat, not leaving it enough time to swallow, exactly as if she were feeding a turkey chick.

It was only their own children that the nurses cared for properly, and these, claims Hava, 'were the only babies who lived to see freedom'. Eleonora became sick. Her little body was covered in bruises:

I shall never forget how she grabbed my neck with her tiny skinny hands and moaned, 'Mama, want home!' She hadn't forgotten the bug-ridden slum where she first saw the light of day, and where she'd been with her mother . . .

Little Eleonora . . . soon realized that her pleas for 'home' were in vain. She stopped reaching out for me when I visited her; she would turn away in silence. On the last day of her life, when I picked her up (they allowed me to breast-feed her) she stared wide-eyed somewhere off into the distance, then started to beat her weak little fists on my face, clawing at my breast, and biting it. Then she pointed down at her bed. In the evening, when I came back with my bundle of firewood, her cot was empty. I found her lying naked in the morgue among the corpses of the adult prisoners. She had spent one year and four months in this world, and died on 3 March 1944.[50]

Most labour camps that included female prisoners also had children's homes. The children's compound in ALZhIR had 400 infants under the age of four in 1944. Nearly all of them had been conceived in the camp. In other labour camps some women wanted to be pregnant so as to be released from hard work, to receive better food, or perhaps even to be amnestied, as women with small children sometimes were.[51] Amnesties did not apply to most of the women of ALZhIR, because they had been convicted of 'counter-revolutionary crimes', and the other motivations were equally irrelevant to most of the prisoners who gave birth in the camp. According to a number of former ALZhIR prisoners, most of these 400 babies were conceived through rape by guards, above all by Mikhail Iusipenko, the deputy commandant of the camp, who preyed on the women prisoners. In later life, he liked to boast that he had 'enjoyed power over several thousand beautiful women, the wives of fallen Party leaders, at ALZhIR'.[52]

Sexual relations between female prisoners and their jailers were not always based on rape or the desire to conceive. Some women sought the protection of a guard by giving in to his sexual demands: to have sex with one man was better than to be raped by many. In mixed labour camps (with male and female zones) women also entered into sexual relations with trusties, whose privileged position brought them food and clothes, or a prized job in the kitchens or the offices.[53] Other than the laws of the jungle, it is hard to judge what governed these relationships – the power of the trusties to protect, harass and threaten the women, or the sexual power of the women, who were vastly outnumbered by the trusties – but from the women's perspective they were usually motivated by the struggle to survive.

Ketevan Orakhelashvili was sentenced to five years of hard labour in ALZhIR following the arrest of her husband, Yevgeny Mikheladze, the director of the Tbilisi Opera, in 1937.* Ketevan knew nothing of her husband's fate (he was shot in 1937), nor anything about her two children, Tina and Vakhtang, who grew up in a series of orphanages

---

*Yevgeny was tortured and then shot by Beria himself, who at that time was the Party boss in the Georgian capital. Ketevan was the prototype of the character of Ketevan Barateli in Tengis Abuladze's film *Repentance* (1984).

(they were sent to labour camps when they reached the age of adult-hood). Ketevan was young and beautiful. In ALZhIR she attracted the attention of many of the guards and Gulag administrators, including Sergei Drozdov, whom she married on her release in 1942. With their son, Nikolai, born in 1944, they lived in Karaganda, where Drozdov worked as an official in the administration of the labour camps in Kazakhstan.[54]

Ketevan with Sergei and their son Nikolai, Karaganda

Liudmila Konstantinova, the mother of Natalia and Elena, was a graduate of the Smolny Institute for Noblewomen in St Petersburg. Her first husband, a seismologist at the Pulkovo Observatory in Leningrad, was arrested in 1936; Liudmila herself was sentenced to eight years in a camp near Magadan. In 1938, Liudmila met a fellow prisoner, Mikhail Yefimov, a mechanic of peasant origins, who had completed his three-year sentence for 'hooliganism' (he had been arrested after getting involved in a drunken brawl), but had decided to stay on as a voluntary worker at the camp, where he lived in his own house in the settlement for officials and guards. Mikhail took an interest in Liudmila. At first, she rejected his approaches, because she still looked forward to the day when she would rejoin her husband and their family (she did not know that he had been shot). But then Liudmila became ill with a kidney infection. Mikhail sent her love letters with gifts of money. He brought her food. Liudmila never fully recovered from her illness. As time passed, she gave up hope of seeing her husband, presuming he had died, and became increasingly dependent on Mikhail, who showered her with attention. Granted a divorce from her husband (it was easy to divorce an 'enemy of the people'), Liudmila married Mikhail, settling with him in Rostov-on-Don after her release in 1945.[55]

It was not just to Gulag officials that women in the camp looked for protection. The fate of female prisoners could sometimes be determined by powerful protectors outside the camps. One of the prisoners in ALZhIR was Liuba Golovnia, the ex-wife of the film-maker Anatoly Golovnia. Liuba was arrested and sentenced to five years in the labour camp in April 1938, four months after the arrest of her second husband, Boris Babitsky, the head of the Mezhrabpomfilm studios in Moscow, who was shot in 1939. Liuba later thought that she had been arrested because she had purchased furniture from the NKVD warehouses in Leningrad (she felt so guilty about the furniture, which had been confiscated from the victims of arrests, that she sold it all after her return from the labour camps). But in fact she was arrested just because she was Babitsky's wife. Babitsky had been caught up in a scandal that led to dozens of arrests in the Soviet film world. The hit songs from Grigorii Aleksandrov's film *Veselye rebiata* ('Jolly Fellows') had somehow found their way to the USA, where they were released as a phonogram, leading to charges of espionage in the Mezhrabpomfilm studios in 1937–8.

When Liuba was arrested, the couple's three children from three different marriages were taken by the NKVD from her apartment in the Comintern hotel: the two-year-old Alyosha, Liuba's son from her marriage to Babitsky, was sent to an orphanage in the centre of Moscow, while Volik, Babitsky's thirteen-year-old son from his first marriage, and Oksana, eleven, Liuba's daughter from her marriage to Anatoly, were taken to the NKVD detention centre at the old Danilov Monastery. Oksana was kept with twenty other girls in one of the monastery's many cells, all filled to bursting with children. Volik was taken to a special area for the over-twelves who, having reached the age of criminal responsibility, would be transferred to the special 'children's camps' and penal colonies administered by the NKVD. Volik's fingerprints and mug-shots were taken for his criminal record.

A few weeks later, Oksana's father, Anatoly Golovnia, appeared at the monastery. Oksana recalls the moment she first saw her father in the courtyard. Dressed in a leather coat, he had his back to her, but she recognized him, even at a distance, and began shouting 'Papa! Papa!' from her cell window as loud as she could. Anatoly walked towards the gates. He was about to leave, having been informed by the director that Oksana was not there. A Black Maria – one of the notorious NKVD vans used to pick up suspects from their homes – passed Anatoly and drove through the gates, the noise of its engine blocking out the cries of his child. Oksana became desperate. She realized that this was her last chance. She let out one more shout. This time Anatoly turned around. She yelled again and waved her hands through the iron bars on the window. Anatoly looked up at the building. There were so many windows and so many faces peering out that Golovnia had a hard time finding his daughter's face, but at last he picked her out with his cameraman's eyes. He hurried back to the director's office, to which Oksana was summoned. She told her father that Volik had been brought to the monastery as well. To get her out was relatively straightforward: legally she was still Anatoly's child. But to rescue Volik, who was considered an adult, and in any case was not Anatoly's son, required help from contacts in the NKVD. After hours of negotiations and several phone calls to the Lubianka, Volik was released. As for Alyosha, Anatoly could not find out what had happened to him. But Oksana remembered where the NKVD car had dropped him before taking her and Volik to the monastery. With her father, she retraced the route they had followed from the Babitsky flat in the Comintern hotel. Locating the orphanage, Anatoly 'went inside and half an hour later reappeared with Alyosha in his arms', recalls Oksana.[56]

All three children found a refuge in Anatoly's home, two small rooms in a communal apartment in the centre of Moscow that he shared with his mother, the haughty Lydia Ivanovna. A year later, in September 1939, Volik's mother came for him, and the two disappeared into the countryside. Liuba's older sister Polina took Alyosha to the Babitsky dacha at Kratovo, where they lived with Polina's sister Vera and her father in two small rooms; the third and largest room was occupied by another family. Polina worked in Moscow and sometimes stayed at Anatoly's apartment. Widowed twice, without children of her own, Polina stoically bore the suffering life brought her. After her sister's arrest she had been evicted from her home and sacked from her job as the Secretary of the Moscow Maly Theatre. She worked for a while as a room-attendant in the Moscow Theatre Museum, but was fired from that job as well, and ended up as a machine operator in a factory.[57]

Nothing was heard from Liuba for a year. The 'special regime' at

ALZhIR forbade prisoners to write to relatives. Then, in the spring of 1939, just as the 'special regime' was lifted, a telegram arrived. Polina wrote back to her sister, and a busy correspondence started up between the two, nearly all of it about domestic details and the bringing up of the children, although, according to Oksana, there was much else said as well, but in code to conceal it from the censors. A devoted sister, Polina wrote to Liuba almost every week. She sent money, books, clothes, typed-out articles from magazines and photographs of the children, especially of Alyosha.

Anatoly wrote to Liuba less often, and his letters had a different character. He sent her money, food parcels and a manual for film projectionists, so that she could learn a practical skill. During the first year, Liuba had worked on a building site but she fell and broke her hand while hauling logs and was transferred to lighter work by Barinov, the camp commandant, who, after receiving a request from Anatoly, allowed her to run the cinema in the club house. This was not the only privilege that Liuba received from Barinov. In 1942, Polina died in Dzhambul, Kazakhstan, where she had fled with Alyosha when she became afraid of her own arrest in January of that year. Alyosha was placed in an orphanage by distant relatives, who then sent a telegram to Liuba in ALZhIR. Liuba was allowed to travel to Dzhambul, several hundred kilometres to the south of Akmolinsk, retrieve Alyosha from the orphanage and bring him back to live with her in ALZhIR's outer zone. It was an extraordinary concession to make to a prisoner, and Barinov, who signed the release papers, did so at great personal risk. It is possible that Liuba's beauty played its part in winning these concessions, though this is not the view of her fellow prisoners, who stressed instead the influence of Anatoly Golovnia. In his letters to Liuba, Anatoly wrote without apparent fear of the censors (in many of his letters he criticized the Soviet film authorities). Anatoly wrote about his love for Liuba. He forgave her for leaving him, and pleaded with her to come back to him on her release ('which may not be so far away as you believe . . . I am sure I can get somewhere if I petition the authorities for you'). Liuba, unaware of Babitsky's fate, warded him off. But Anatoly perservered. He wrote about the success of his films, *Minin and Pozharsky* (1939) and *Suvorov* (1941); about the prizes he had won (the Order of Red Labour in 1940 and the Stalin Prize in 1941); about the affluent life he enjoyed and the parties he attended in the Kremlin. He played on Liuba's emotions, emphasizing how much their daughter needed her: 'I shall wait for you and pray for your return, if only for Oksana's sake. I am a bad parent, as you know, and have little time for it. And our daughter is now at an age when she needs a mother's influence. She is shy with me.'[58] Anatoly must have known that Babitsky would not return. He made this clear to Liuba and tried to make her see that she would now be better off with him. He also clearly thought, or wanted to give Liuba the impression, that he possessed the influence to speed up her release, if only she agreed to come back to him.

5

In January 1939, the writer Konstantin Simonov married Zhenia Laskina, the youngest of Samuil Laskin's three daughters, who had been a student with Simonov at the Literary Institute since 1936. They had started their romance the previous spring, when Simonov was still married to Natalia Tipot, another classmate, although in those days the civil marriages formed in the bohemian circles of the Moscow student world did not have much real significance. According to Zhenia, Simonov began to court her with a romantic poem ('Five Pages') that he had originally written for Natalia. It was typical perhaps of all young poets to recycle love poems for new sexual conquests, and certainly typical of Simonov's relations with women at that time. He was quick and clumsy, prone to fall head over heels in love and sexually inexperienced.[59]

Zhenia was a tiny woman, almost pocket-sized, with graceful features. But Simonov was also clearly drawn by her spiritual qualities: she was generous and patient, devoted to her friends and she had that rare capacity to get on with almost anyone (a talent she inherited from her father) and to affect them with her kindness. Zhenia was the Secretary of the Student Union at the Literary Institute. During the purge meetings at the institute in 1937, when Simonov had denounced Dolmatovsky, she had courageously defended two foreign students – too weak to defend themselves – whose work she felt had been unfairly criticized by members of the teaching staff.[60] What attracted Zhenia to Simonov is hard to tell. She fell in love with him and continued to love him throughout her life. No doubt she was attracted by his good looks, by his poetic talent and intelligence, by his masculinity, and by his qualities of leadership, which had always made him stand out at the institute.

Zhenia and Konstantin on their honeymoon in the Crimea, 1939

Eight months after their wedding, in August 1939, their son Aleksei was born. After a difficult delivery, Zhenia and Aleksei were both ill and kept in isolation in the hospital for several days. 'I love you very much my little darling, everything in our lives together will be fine, I am convinced of that,' Simonov wrote to Zhenia.

I talked with the doctor, he said all is well. And the baby will recover gradually. Write to me what you like most about our son . . . Today I began on a new poem. Now I shall write every day . . . My sweetie, I so want to hear your voice, to see your little face which is no doubt pale and thin . . . Ask if I can send you Jewish liver.[61]

Shortly after the birth of their son, Simonov received his first assignment as a military correspondent. The newspaper *Geroicheskaia Krasnoarmeiskaia* ('Heroic Red Army') sent him to Khalkin Gol to cover the conflict between the Soviet Union and Japanese-controlled Manchuria. From Mongolia, where the Soviet forces were massed, he wrote to Zhenia, sending her the poem 'A Photograph'.

> I did not bring your photographs on my travels,
> Without them, as long as we remember, we will see.
> On the fourth day, the Urals far behind,
> I did not show them to my curious neighbours.[62]

The battle of Khalkin Gol (known in Japan as the Nomonhan Incident) was the decisive engagement of a border war that had been brewing since the Japanese invasion of Manchuria and the establishment of the Manchukuo puppet state in 1932. Stalin was afraid of Japan's imperial ambitions in Siberia as well as Mongolia, which though nominally part of China had been under Soviet influence since 1921. When skirmishes broke out on the disputed border between the Mongolians and the Japanese, Stalin sent in his heavy troops: 57,000 infantry, massed artillery, 500 tanks, and the best planes of the Soviet Air Force, all under the command of the rising star of the Red Army, General Georgii Zhukov. The Soviet forces pushed the Kwantung Army back from the Khalkin Gol River, where the Japanese maintained the border was, to Nomonhan, 16 kilometres further east, the border according to the Russians. Surprised by the heavy concentration of Red Army tanks and artillery, the Japanese bid for a cease-fire on 16 September. The Soviets claimed a mighty victory. The Red Army's invincibility – proclaimed by Soviet propaganda – had been confirmed, it seemed. The reality, however, was significantly less inspiring. As Simonov knew from his own experience, the losses on the Soviet side were far greater than acknowledged by the government (the Red Army claimed 9,000 killed and wounded but the actual number was 24,000, of whom 7,000 men were killed).[63] And there was no end of dreadful sights. Frustrated by the censorship of the military press, Simonov tried to offer a truer picture in his poetry. 'Tank' tells the story of a platoon of Soviet soldiers who suffer heavy losses in their hard-won victory against the Japanese. The soldiers leave behind a burned-out tank, which the poet puts forward as a monument to their bravery and sacrifice. Simonov's political minder, who was no less than Vladimir Stavsky, the former leader of the Writers' Union who had reprimanded him for 'anti-Soviet' conversations in 1937, blocked the poem's publication. He warned Simonov to stick more closely to the propaganda mission of the writer, namely to present an upbeat vision of the war. To that end, Stavsky suggested he replace the burned-out tank in the poem's final image with a brand new one.[64]

The border conflict with Japan strengthened Stalin's fears of becoming embroiled in a two-front war against the Axis powers. In the spring of 1939, Hitler's armies had marched into Czechoslovakia, unopposed by the British or the French, who continued to appease Hitler and who, it seemed to Stalin, were encouraging the Nazis and the Japanese to direct their aggressions against the Soviet Union. Although France and Britain were engaged in negotiations with the Soviet government for an alliance to defend Eastern Europe and the Baltic states against Nazi aggression, the Czechoslovak crisis demonstrated to Stalin that the Western powers were not acting in good faith. Throughout the spring of 1939, the British and the French had been dragging out the negotiations with the Soviets, using the reluctance of the Poles to allow Soviet troops to cross their borders as a stumbling block; they wanted the Soviet Union on their side to deter the Nazis diplomatically but were not prepared to sign a military pact. Meanwhile, the Germans were making overtures to the Soviet government, whose neutrality was essential if they were to launch their planned invasion of Poland. They proposed to divide Eastern Europe into separate spheres of influence, with the Soviet Union gaining Eastern Poland and the Baltic lands. By August, Stalin could no longer wait for the British and the French. Convinced that a European war was imminent, he knew that the Soviet Union would not be able to resist Nazi Germany, especially with so many of its forces in Manchuria; as he saw it, he had little option but to come to an agreement with Hitler. It was these immediate events of 1939, rather than a long-term calcu-lation, as many have supposed, that persuaded Stalin to sign the notori-ous Pact of Non-Aggression with Hitler's Germany on 23 August 1939. As the Soviet leader saw it, the pact would provide the Soviet Union with the breathing space it needed to arm itself as well as create a useful buffer zone in Eastern Europe and the Baltic lands. By remaining neutral in a war between two forces he considered hostile to the Soviet Union – the capitalist powers of the West and the Fascist states – Stalin hoped to see them wipe each other out in a long and draining conflict that might spark revolutions in both camps (as the First World War had done in Russia in 1917). As he told the Comintern, 'We are not opposed [to war], if they have a good fight and weaken each other.'[65]

Assured of Soviet neutrality, Germany invaded western Poland on 1 September; two days later Britain and France declared war on Germany; and shortly afterwards the Red Army entered Poland from the east, in accordance with the secret protocols of the Nazi–Soviet Pact which had divided Eastern Europe into German and Soviet zones. After the occupation of Poland, the Soviet Union began to pressure the Baltic states and Finland to accept territorial changes and Soviet bases on their soil. Estonia, Latvia and Lithuania gave in to the Soviet demands, signing pacts of 'defence and mutual assistance', which allowed their occupation by the Red Army. The invading Soviet troops were accompanied by NKVD units to carry out arrests and executions: 15,000 Polish POWs and 7,000 other prisoners were shot by the NKVD in the Katyn Forest near Smolensk; and at least a million 'anti-Soviet elements' were deported from Poland and the Baltic lands. Finland proved less compliant, rejecting Soviet demands for army bases on its soil. The Soviets launched an invasion of Finland in November 1939, certain of victory after their military successes in Manchuria, Poland and the Baltic states. But the war in Finland went disastrously. The Soviet troops were unprepared for winter fighting and could not breach the solid Finnish defences. In four months, 126,000 Soviet troops were killed and nearly 300,000 injured, until Soviet reinforcements finally broke through the Finnish lines and forced the Finns to sue for peace.[66]

For Simonov, as for many Communists throughout the world, the Nazi–Soviet Pact was a huge ideological shock. The struggle against Fascism was a fundamental aspect of the Communist mentality and rationale. 'My generation – those of us who turned eighteen around the time when Hitler came to power in 1933 – lived in constant expectation of a war with Germany,' Simonov recalled in the 1970s. 'For us that war began, not in 1941, but in 1933.' The Spanish Civil War was of particular significance to this generation, not least because they had been too young to fight in the Russian Civil War, whose history had inspired their heroic dreams. But also because they fervently believed that the Spanish Civil War was the opening battle in the last great struggle between Communism and Fascism that would reach its climax in a fight to the death between the Soviet Union and Nazi Germany. 'At Khalkin Gol,' Simonov recalled, 'that fight was no longer imaginary, it was no longer something we anticipated in the future, but something we had seen with our own eyes.' Simonov was at Khalkin Gol when he heard the news of the Nazi–Soviet Pact. His mind full of the bloody struggle the Soviet forces were then waging against the Japanese, he initially understood the pact as a pragmatic measure to keep the Germans from 'delivering a fatal blow to our backs'. He even welcomed the Soviet invasion of Poland and the Baltic lands as a necessary defensive measure against German military expansion. But morally, he was troubled. He felt the pact was a betrayal of Europe, of the Communist promise to defend the weak against tyrants, and he was uncomfortable with the new ideological order in which it was suddenly not acceptable to criticize Nazi Germany. 'They were still the same Fascists,' Simonov recalled, 'but we could no longer write or say aloud what we thought of them.'[67]

This inner conflict surfaced in several of Simonov's works, especially in his first major play, *A Young Man from Our Town* (*Paren' iz nashego goroda*), which he wrote in the autumn of 1940 on his return from Khalkin Gol. The play tells the story of a brash young Red Army officer, a Komsomol enthusiast called Sergei, who returns to Russia from the Spanish Civil War and volunteers to fight at Khalkin Gol. As a call to arms against Fascism, *A Young Man from Our Town* at moments seems to invite its audience to feel hostility towards Nazi Germany, but, as Simonov recalled, he could not make these sentiments explicit because of the Hitler–Stalin Pact. When the play was first performed, by the Lenin Komsomol Theatre in March 1941, it was left to the actors to suggest their opposition to the pact by adding more emotion to any lines that had anti-German implications.[68]

Conflicts of a different, more intimate sort run through the play as well. Its hero was modelled on the poet Mikhail Lukonin (1918–76), a friend of Simonov's at the Literary Institute who had fought in the war against Finland. Lukonin was only three years younger than Simonov, but he was considered to belong to a different generation of Soviet poets, mainly because he had been born after 1917 and had come from a proletarian family without any trace of the pre-revolutionary intelligentsia culture that marked Simonov's peers. Simonov idealized Lukonin: the younger poet, who had worked in a tractor factory in Stalingrad before joining the Literary Institute in 1937, embodied for him the ideal of the 'Soviet' and 'proletarian writer' he had tried so hard to become. In 1939, Simonov gave the completed draft of *A Young Man from Our Town* to the playwright Afinogenov, who liked the play but thought that its hero should have a surname. Simonov was at a loss – he did not know what to call him. Afinogenov asked Simonov what surname he would have chosen for himself, given the choice. Perhaps he recognized that Simonov had given his fictional hero all the qualities that he would have wanted for himself. Without hesitation Simonov replied that he would have liked to be called Lukonin and on that basis he named the hero of his play. The real Lukonin was not pleased: 'How would you like it if I wrote a play about a football player and called him Simonov?'[69]

The heroine of *A Young Man from Our Town* also had personal resonances: Simonov had written the lead female part for Valentina Serova, a star of the Soviet screen and stage, with whom he had fallen hopelessly in love. Simonov had first seen Valentina in a play at the Lenin Komsomol shortly after his return from Khalkin Gol, and although he was a married man and must have known that he had little chance of winning her heart, he brought *A Young Man from Our Town* to that theatre so that he could get closer to the actress. In that play, the female character is a rendering of Valentina, not as she was in reality, but as Simonov wanted her to be (trusting, loving, patient and forgiving), just as the hero of the play, Sergei Lukonin, is a portrait of Simonov as he would have liked himself to be (more masculine, more courageous, more Soviet than he was in reality). These two literary prototypes, the ideal Valentina and the ideal Simonov, reappear in nearly all his poems, plays and novels during the 1940s.

Valentina Serova, 1940

Valentina was young and beautiful, a famous widow and film star, but she had a secret history that made her vulnerable. Her father, Vasily Polovyk, a hydro-engineer from the Kharkov region of eastern Ukraine, had been arrested in Moscow during the industrial purges of 1930, when Valentina was thirteen, and sent to a labour camp. Released in 1935, Vasily was rearrested in 1937 and sentenced to eight years in the Solovetsky labour camp. All these facts were carefully concealed by

Valentina's mother, a well-known actress at the Kamerny Theatre in Moscow, where Valentina spent much of her childhood, playing all the leading parts for girls. Valentina's mother changed her name from Polovyk, a Ukrainian name, to the Russian Polovikova, and worked hard to erase all trace of her Ukrainian past. Valentina was brought up to deny all knowledge of her father (in later years she claimed she had never seen him as a child). It was not until 1959 (fifteen years after his release from the Solovetsky labour camp) that she summoned up the courage to meet him, and then only after he had got in touch with her.[70]

In 1935, Valentina joined the Komsomol. She soon attracted the attention of Aleksandr Kosaryov, the leader of the organization, whose well-known fondness for young actresses was easily indulged through his control of the Lenin Komsomol Theatre in Moscow. Kosaryov promoted the career of his beautiful young protégée. But in November 1938 he was arrested (and later shot) in a general purge of the Komsomol leadership, which was accused by Stalin of failing to root out the 'counter-revolutionaries' in its ranks. At a banquet in the Kremlin shortly before Kosaryov's arrest, Stalin had approached him, clinked glasses, and whispered in his ear: 'Traitor! I'll kill you!' The arrest of her patron placed Valentina in serious danger, particularly when she was denounced as a 'counter-revolutionary' by a jealous former boyfriend, whom she had jilted for Kosaryov. Called to account for herself at a purge meeting in the theatre workers' union, she was questioned about the arrest of her father and made to renounce him to avoid expulsion.[71]

What saved Valentina in the end was the influence of her new husband, the famous aviator Anatoly Serov, whom she had met at a banquet thrown by Kosaryov. Pilots featured prominently in the pantheon of Soviet heroes. The air force, in particular, symbolized the Soviet Union's military power and progress, and it was the glamour of the aeroplane that inspired many young men to join the military. With his handsome, clean-cut, healthy 'Russian' looks and perfect proletarian origins, Serov was the ideal figure for this propaganda role. His exploits in the Spanish Civil War were legendary, and by the time he met Valentina he had become a national hero and celebrity, one of the most honoured pilots of them all, and a Kremlin favourite. Married ten days after their first meeting, Anatoly and Valentina moved into the sumptuously furnished apartment recently vacated by Marshal Yegorov, who had been arrested in connection with the Tukhachevsky trial. They enjoyed the decadent lifestyle of the Stalinist elite, with late-night parties and receptions at the Kremlin. Disaster struck on their first wedding anniversary. Anatoly was killed in an air crash. The circumstances of the accident remain unclear, but Serov and his fellow pilot Polina Osipenko were flying at low altitude in poor weather. Both pilots were buried in the Kremlin Wall with full state honours. Four months later, in September 1939, Valentina gave birth to Anatoly's son, whom she named after him. As the widow of a military hero, she enjoyed the protection of the Soviet leadership, which helped to launch her career in the cinema. Her first major part, the title role in the hit film *A Girl With Character* (1939), was tailor-made for her. Stalin himself became one of her admirers. At his sixtieth birthday banquet in the Kremlin he proposed a toast to the widows of two famous pilots, Anatoly Serov and Valerii Chkalov, who were sitting near the end of one of the far tables. Stalin then invited Valentina to come up to his table to drink the toast with him. Her hand shook so violently that she spilled her wine. According to Valentina, Stalin squeezed her hand and said quietly: 'Don't worry, it's nothing. Just hold on, comrade Serova, we'll stand by you.'[72]

By the summer of 1940, Simonov was head over heels in love with Valentina, but she remained cool towards him. She was still in mourning for her husband – she had his baby son – and she did not want to encourage Simonov, a married man with a baby son the same age as her own. Simonov, Zhenia and Aleksei were now living in the Laskin apartment on Zubov Square. And though Zhenia did not realize the full extent of her husband's growing passion for the beautiful actress, she could not fail to notice his frequent absences from the Laskin home.[73] For a year their marriage soldiered on, while Simonov pursued his new romantic interest with little effect. Simonov was not the sort of man that Valentina was usually attracted to. He was too arduous in his attentions, too serious and dry, and he lacked the poise and confidence of her previous suitors, who were more successful and more powerful than Simonov. At the first rehearsal of *A Young Man from Our Town*, Simonov asked Serova what she thought about the play. In front of everyone, she said she thought it was 'a shitty play'. But even this did not deter him. He showered her with gifts. He wrote plays with parts for her. But most of all he sent her poetry, some of it recycled:

> I did not bring any photographs on my travels.
> Instead I wrote poems about you.
> I wrote them from sorrow
> I missed you
> And carried you with me . . .

Gradually, by the power of his pen, he wore her down, but it was not until 1943, when his love poem 'Wait For Me' had made Simonov the country's favourite poet and a figure of real influence in the Kremlin, that Serova succumbed to his eager passions and agreed to marry him. Simonov and Serova would become celebrities through 'Wait For Me', a poem that inspired millions of people to go on fighting through the war. But no one knew about the politics their marriage would serve, nor about Simonov's previous wife, whom he had abandoned with their child.[74]

6

'Wait For Me'

1941–45

I

In June 1941, Leonid Makhnach was staying at his grandparents' house in the small town of Krichev in Belorussia, 600 kilometres from the Soviet border with Poland. He had been sent there for a holiday by his parents, who were unable to leave Moscow, but wanted him to get out of the capital, where the heat that summer had been stifling. Leonid's father, Vladimir, was the director of the Mosgaz Trust, the main supplier of gas to the Soviet capital, and had to stay in Moscow to write a major report for the Party leadership on plans for energy in the event of war. The grandparents' house stood at the edge of Krichev, where the town gave way to thick oak woods and pasturelands. It was a modest wooden house of the sort inhabited by smallholders, labourers and traders throughout the western regions of the Soviet Union, with a little yard for pigs and a garden full of apple trees.

Although it was located in the western borderlands, Krichev had no defence plan to put into operation when the Germans launched their huge invasion force against the Soviet Union at first light on Sunday 22 June. The Soviet leadership was not prepared for war, and towns like Krichev had no inkling of the imminent invasion until noon that day, when Molotov, in a faltering voice, announced the beginning of hostilities on the radio. For the next three days the radio was Krichev's only source of news about the war. Then, on 26 June, without any warning from the Soviet authorities, Krichev was bombed by German planes. There was havoc in the town. People fled into the woods. Cows and pigs were left to run wild. Dead bodies lay in the street.

In the middle of this chaos Leonid's mother, Maria, arrived in Krichev. She had left Moscow on the first day of the invasion in the hope of rescuing her family before they were cut off by the German troops. Vladimir just then had left on a brief work trip to the Leningrad region and was not due to return to Moscow until the end of June. So Maria set off on her own. She managed to travel as far as Smolensk, which was under heavy aerial bombardment, but there were no trains to take her further west, towards the Soviet front. Maria made her way on foot, against the flow of retreating soldiers and civilians, reaching Krichev, 120 kilometres to the south-west, four days later. 'She was almost black with dust and grime, when she arrived,' recalls Leonid, 'and totally exhausted from the journey.'

The people of Krichev hurried to pack up their belongings and head east. The 2,000 Jews, almost half the town's population, were among the first to leave, worried by the rumours they had heard of the Nazis' brutality; they were soon followed by the Communists, who had just as much to fear from the invading troops. As the relatives of a senior Soviet official, the Makhnach family needed to get out as fast as possible. Maria delayed the family's departure from the town for as long as possible in the hope that her husband would contact them. On 16 July, the day before the Germans took Krichev, she had still not heard from Vladimir, so she wrote him a letter in Moscow, packed some belongings on a horse and cart and set off with Leonid and her parents, moving slowly east on the smallest country roads to avoid the German planes, which dropped their bombs on the main highways. She had no idea that Vladimir was speeding west towards them in his chauffeured limousine. 'Travelling on the highway from Smolensk, he could not have been more than a few kilometres away when we passed each other,' concludes Leonid.

Vladimir got to Krichev just in time to see the Germans entering the town. From the meadows on the opposite bank of the Sozh River he watched the town's wooden houses go up in flames, he heard the screams, and then the shots. Thinking that his family was about to be massacred, Vladimir tried to cross the river and reach the town by foot to rescue them, but he was stopped by the retreating Soviet troops. Believing that his family had probably been killed, he returned to Moscow. The next day the letter from his wife arrived: she was heading towards Briansk, 200 kilometres east of Krichev, and would travel on to Stalingrad, where she had relatives. Maria thought it would be safer than going back to Moscow, which, it was rumoured, was about to fall to the Germans.

Going back to Moscow proved to be Vladimir's undoing. Shortly after his return he was arrested and sentenced to ten years in a labour camp for 'defeatist talk and panic-mongering'. In a conversation with a work colleague at the Mosgaz Trust he had talked about the chaos he had witnessed at the front. Many people were arrested for such talk in the first months of the war, when the Soviet authorities desperately tried to suppress all news about the military catastrophe. The NKVD in Moscow built the arrest of Makhnach into a 'Trotskyist conspiracy' among the city's leading energy officials and made dozens of arrests. It was not until the autumn that Vladimir was able to get word to his wife about his whereabouts. On the long train journey to Siberia, he threw a letter from the window of his carriage addressed to her in Stalingrad. A peasant picked it up and posted it:

My dear ones! I am alive and well. Circumstances prevented me from writing to you earlier. Do not worry about me. Look after yourselves. Maria, my beloved, it will be hard for you. But do not give up hope. I am going to Siberia. I am innocent. Wait for me, I will return.[1]

The German assault was so powerful and swift that it took the Soviet forces completely by surprise. Stalin had ignored intelligence reports of German preparations for an invasion. He even dismissed last-minute bulletins confirming a massive German build-up on the frontier as a British ploy to lure the Soviet Union into war (he had the bearers of this information shot as 'British spies'). The Soviet defences were in total disarray. After the signing of the Nazi–Soviet Pact the old defensive lines had been abandoned; the new fortifications, hastily constructed in the occupied Baltic states, had hardly any heavy guns, radio equipment or minefields. They were easily overrun by the nineteen Panzer divisions and fifteen motorized infantry divisions that spearheaded the German invasion force. Soviet units were rushed towards the front to plug the gaps, only to be smashed by German tanks and planes, which had control of the sky. By 28 June, six days into the invasion, German forces had advanced in a huge pincer movement through Belorussia to capture Minsk, 300 kilometres into Soviet territory, while further north they had cut through Lithuania and Latvia to threaten Leningrad.

Konstantin Simonov saw much of the chaos on the Belorussian Front. When the war began he was called up to the front as a correspondent for an army newspaper and sent to join the political department of the

Third Army near Grodno on the border with Poland. Travelling by train, he arrived in Borisov early in the morning of 26 June, but could not travel any further because the line to Minsk was under heavy bombardment. Simonov disembarked and found a driver to take him on to Minsk by car, but they soon came up against the Soviet forces falling back in disarray. German planes flew overhead, firing on the troops with machine-guns and dropping bombs on to the road. The soldiers fled into the woods. An officer was standing in the middle of the road, shouting at the men that he would shoot them if they did not turn around. But they simply ignored him. The woods were swarming with soldiers and civilians trying to find cover from the German planes, which swooped above the trees, firing on the crowds below. Simonov was nearly killed when a captured Soviet plane mowed down several people around him: it flew so low above the trees that he could see the faces of its German crew. When it was dark he stumbled back on to the road and found a commissar, 'a young unshaven man with a *pilotka* [fore-and-aft cap], a winter coat and for some reason a spade in his hands'. Simonov introduced himself as a journalist and asked for directions to the Front Headquarters. 'What headquarters?' asked the officer. 'Can't you see what's happening here?'[2]

Simonov retreated with the army to Smolensk. The roads were full of soldiers and civilians – women, children, old people, many of them Jews – heading east on every type of cart, or walking on the road with heavy bundles of household possessions on their backs. In the first days of July he passed through Shklov and Orsha – 'quiet rural towns' inhabited by numerous Jewish families, including his wife's relatives, the Laskins. Stopping for water at a house in Shklov, Simonov was asked by the frightened Jews if he thought they should flee. He advised them to stay, assuring them that the Germans would be routed by the Red Army before reaching Shklov. A few days later, the Germans captured Shklov. They killed nearly all the Jews, some 6,000 men, women and children, whom they shot and buried in a pit outside the town. On 16 July, the Germans took Orsha, and set about building a Jewish ghetto. Most of Orsha's Jews were transported to the Nazi death camps in 1943, although some, like Samuil Laskin's brother Iakov, a doctor in Orsha, ran away to join the Red Army.[3]

Looking back on the catastrophe of 1941, Simonov would come to realize that its origins were rooted in the policies of the Stalinist regime.

By the middle of the 1950s, when he began to write his great war novel *The Living and the Dead* (1959), Simonov had come to recognize that Stalin was to blame for the disaster, not just because he had failed to understand the situation and prepare for war in 1941, but more fundamentally because his reign of terror had created so much fear and mistrust that the country was virtually incapable of coordinated action in its self-defence. Simonov did not see this at the time – his advice to the Jews of Shklov was clear evidence of his belief in the propaganda version of reality – but from 1942 he began to grapple with these troubling ideas in his war diaries (on which he later drew for *The Living and the Dead*). It became clear to him that the fundamental problem of the Soviet armed forces in 1941 was the climate created by the military purges of 1937–8. He saw that the Terror had undermined the officers' authority and made them fearful of taking responsibility for military decisions and initiatives in case they were punished by superiors, or denounced by the commissars and other political officers (*politruki*) who watched their every move. They waited passively for decisions from above, which always came too late to make a positive difference to the military situation on the ground.[4]

None of these ideas was printable, of course, in the war years (or, for that matter, at any other time before the 'Thaw' of 1956). What Simonov had written in his diaries could never have been published in *Krasnaia zvezda*, the main Red Army newspaper, for which he worked as a correspondent from July 1941. Censorship was tightened on the outbreak of the war. Through the Soviet Information Bureau (Sovinform-biuro), created on the third day of the war to control all printed and radio reports, the government attempted to conceal the military catastrophe from the public and manipulate the news to boost morale. Journalists like Simonov were expected to give their reports a positive and optimistic gloss, even when they were writing about disasters at the front, and what they wrote was in any case nearly always cut or changed by the censors.

Simonov was in a particularly difficult position. Arriving in Moscow on 19 July, three days after the German capture of Smolensk, he was the first correspondent to return from the Belorussian Front. People in the capital had no idea about the extent of the military debacle. News of the fall of Smolensk had been suppressed to avoid causing panic (it was not until 13 August, following the failure of Soviet forces to regain a foothold in the town, that the information was finally released). Muscovites bombarded Simonov with questions about the military situation. But he could not answer truthfully without running the risk of being denounced, like Makhnach, for 'defeatist talk and panic-mongering'. So he resolved to hold his tongue and keep to himself his depression, which, he noted in his diary, 'even people close to me mistook as a sign of exhaustion'. Writing in the press, Simonov struggled to find something positive to say about the events he had seen. 'It seemed impossible to write about what had actually happened,' he recalls. 'Not just because it would not have been printed, but also because there was something inside me' that would not accept so dark an outcome. He needed to find some sign of hope in the catastrophe. The incident he focused on had taken place amidst the chaos of the retreat to Smolensk. Simonov had seen two men, a captain and a brigadier, walking west, against the human tide, towards the front. The last remaining men of their platoon, which had been wiped out by a German bomb, the two men were driven, it seemed to Simonov, by some innate sense of patriotic duty, in which, as time went on, he came to see the seeds of a future Soviet victory.[5]

In the absence of any reliable information from the Soviet media, rumours spread and people started to panic. It was said that the government had fled; that there was treason in the army staff; that the Soviet leadership was preparing to abandon Moscow and Leningrad. It was even rumoured that the German bombing of the capital, which began in mid-July, had been led by the famous Soviet aviator Sigizmund Levanevsky, who had disappeared on a flight across the North Pole to the USA in 1937. The journalist N. K. Verzhbitsky recorded in his diary a conversation with 'a lively old man' in a Moscow street: 'Why hasn't anybody spoken to us on the radio?' the old man said. 'They should say something – anything, good or bad. But we are completely in a fog, and must all think for ourselves.' Stalin's absence from the public scene added to this feeling of uncertainty. Apparently, he had suffered some sort of breakdown in the first days of the war: he locked himself away in his dacha and took no interest in anything. It was not until 1 July that Stalin returned to the Kremlin and not until two days later that he made his first war speech to the nation. Pausing frequently, as if distressed, to take a drink, Stalin addressed the Soviet people as 'my brothers and sisters, and my friends'. He called on them to unite for 'the life-or-death struggle', which he described as a 'war of the entire Soviet nation'. It was the first time that Stalin had defined the Soviet people in such fraternal and inclusive terms: there was no longer mention of the class struggle or ideology. Simonov recalls the impression the speech made on himself and the soldiers at the front: 'Nobody had spoken to us like that for a long time. All those years we had suffered from the lack of friendship. And in that speech, as I recall, it was the words "My friends" that moved us to tears.'[6]

Despite the galvanizing effect of Stalin's speech, the outbreak of the war witnessed an explosion of open talk and criticism of the Soviet regime, prompted perhaps by the uncertainty or the release from fear. 'One hears conversations that only a short time ago would have led to a tribunal,' Verzhbitsky noted in his diary on 18 October, when the Germans were a few miles from the capital. Much of this disgruntlement came from peasants and workers, who criticized the lack of preparation for the war, the stringent labour discipline, the reduction of food rations, the coercive conscriptions and the flight of the Party bosses to the rear, which had left ordinary people to face the invasion on their own. In Leningrad, where half the city's Party members took flight in the first six months of the war, the anti-Soviet mood of the workers was so strong that some even welcomed the prospect of a German victory. The many strikes and workers' demonstrations in the first months of the war signalled a return to something like the revolutionary atmosphere of 1917. At one demonstration in the Ivanovo region, in October 1941, when the Party bosses tried to calm the crowds, the strike leaders shouted to the workers: 'Don't listen to them! They know nothing! They've been deceiving us for twenty-three years!' At factory meetings workers showed that they were not afraid to blame the Communists for the outbreak of the war and the defeats at the front. According to the NKVD's surveillance groups, there were many workers and peasants who welcomed the invasion on the grounds that it would sweep away the Soviet regime. It was a commonplace that only Jews and Communists had anything to fear from the Germans.[7]

The government responded to this vocal opposition by declaring war on 'panic-mongerers'. Thousands were arrested and many people shot for loose ('defeatist') talk about the situation at the front. Roza Vetukhnovskaia was arrested on the third day of the war and charged with treason against the motherland. When she got to her prison cell she found that she was one of many women who had been arrested for something they had said: 'This one said that the German army is stronger'; 'That one said that our crops are poor'; 'Yet another said that we work like slaves in the kolkhoz'. Most of these women were ordinary workers and peasants. Irina Shcherbov-Nefedovich was arrested in Leningrad on 30 July, one week after she had been denounced for 'panic-mongering and spreading rumours' by a Party worker at the Institute of Vaccines where she worked. It turned out that all she had done was to tell a friend about the bombing of Smolensk, which she had heard about in a radio broadcast by Sovinformbiuro. Sentenced to seven years in a labour camp near Khabarovsk, she died there in 1946. Irina's husband and daughter were never told what had happened to her. They assumed that she had died in the bombing of Leningrad. It was not until 1994 that they learned the truth about her death.[8]

On 20 July, after the fall of Smolensk, Stalin assumed control of the military command (Stavka) by appointing himself Commissar of Defence. He sent Marshal Timoshenko, the former defence chief, to take command of the Western Front and launch a counter-offensive for the recapture of Smolensk. For a while the German advance towards Moscow was slowed down, not least because part of the German army was diverted to the south to seize the rich agricultural land, the mines and industries of Ukraine. Convinced that economics was the key to victory, Hitler thought control of these resources would help make the Third Reich invincible. During August, Hitler focused on the conquest of Ukraine, allowing the Red Army to push the Germans back on the Smolensk–Moscow front. On 6 September, Soviet forces briefly regained control of the outskirts of Smolensk, before falling back for lack of basic military equipment. Further north, on 25 September, the Germans reached the shores of Lake Ladoga, effectively surrounding Leningrad. Wanting to preserve his northern troops for the battle of Moscow, Hitler decided to lay siege to Leningrad and starve its population out of existence rather than to try to conquer it. In strictly military terms the fate of Leningrad had little real significance for the outcome of the war, which would be decided on the Moscow and the southern fronts. But as the birthplace of the Russian Empire and the Revolution, and as a citadel of European values and culture in Russia, Leningrad had a huge symbolic importance. This goes a long way towards explaining why it was not abandoned by the Soviet command; and indeed why most of its population chose to stay in the besieged city in the autumn of 1941, when Leningrad was cut off from virtually all its food and fuel supplies (perhaps a million people, or one-third of the pre-war population, died from disease or starvation, before the siege was lifted in January 1944). Meanwhile, to the south, the German advance continued slowly, because the bulk of the Soviet forces had been stationed here to protect the rich industrial and food resources of the Ukraine. A huge pincer movement by the Germans managed to encircle Kiev and its eastern hinterlands. After several weeks of desperate fighting by the Soviet troops, in which nearly half a million soldiers were killed or taken prisoner, the Germans took the city on 19 September, though much street fighting continued after that. By the start of October, with Kiev captured and Leningrad besieged, Hitler concentrated his forces on the conquest of the Soviet capital. He vowed that Moscow would be totally destroyed, its ruins flooded by an artificial lake.[9]

As the Germans swept across the country, millions of families were broken up, as relatives were caught behind the front. Many children were at summer camps when the invasion began and could not be returned to their families before the German troops arrived. Decades later parents were still trying to trace them through public organizations and advertisements. Thousands of children ended up in orphanages or roamed across the country, joining children's gangs or even units of the Red Army (according to one estimate there were as many as 25,000 children who marched with the army at some point in the war).[10]

Iurii Streletsky was twelve years old and living in an orphanage in Leningrad in 1941. His father had been arrested in 1937, and his mother exiled to Vyshnyi Volochek, half-way between Leningrad and Moscow. When the war broke out the orphanage was evacuated to Arzamas near Gorkii. During the journey, Iurii jumped off the train and ran away. He had been unhappy at the orphanage. He joined a children's gang, which lived off petty thefts from railway travellers, but he soon became disgusted by their criminality and turned himself in to the police. The police handed him over to the NKVD, which sent Iurii to a military aerodrome in Arzamas, where he worked as an apprentice engineer. The engineers stationed there adopted Iurii as their mascot. They gave him alcohol and cigarettes and set him up with girls, who were attached to their unit. When twenty of the engineers were transferred to Tbilisi in the spring of 1942, they took the boy with them. Iurii had pleaded with the soldiers to let him go along. He knew that he had been born in the Georgian capital, though his family had left when he was very young, and remembered going there as a child to visit his godparents. He also knew that his older sister had gone to live with them after the arrest of their parents. During the journey to Tbilisi the soldiers concealed Iurii. He had no papers for the trip and would have been arrested, had he been discovered. 'They were very kind to me,' Iurii recalls:

They were risking a great deal by taking me along, but none of them complained, and they all gave me food from their own rations. They were fond of me and felt sorry because I had no family. When we approached Stalingrad our train was stopped by a patrol. The two NKVD guards asked to see my papers. They wanted to arrest me when I said that I had none. But the soldiers insisted that I was one of them, and refused to give me up to the two guards, who agreed to let me go for a hundred grams [of vodka].

In Tbilisi Iurii parted company with the soldiers and wandered round the city, hoping he would recognize the place where his godparents lived. Eventually he went to the city offices and obtained a copy of his birth certificate, which proved to be the start of a paper trail leading to them. From then on, Iurii lived with his godparents, who were both engineers, and his sister. Iurii became an engineer as well.[11]

The evacuation of the population from the western regions of the Soviet Union also broke up families. Eight million children were evacuated to the rear. The main priority was to rescue the industrial stock from cities under threat from the Germans. Three thousand factories were dismantled and transported east – to the Volga and the Urals and beyond – in more than a million railway trucks between June and December 1941. Factory workers and their families travelled east with them. Entire institutions were relocated with their staffs: government and public offices, universities and research institutes, libraries, museums, theatre companies and orchestras.[12]

For many families evacuation was a mixed blessing. Natalia Gabaeva was eleven years old when she was evacuated from Leningrad to Omsk, to a special children's home belonging to the Union of Artists. Her mother, a painter, remained in Leningrad, so she could be close to her husband Sergei, a former exile who lived in Peterhof, near the city, and worked in the Agricultural Institute. In 1941, he moved to live with his sick and elderly father, a retired museum worker, in the basement of

Leningrad's Hermitage. Every day he visited his ailing mother, who was divorced from his father, in a distant suburb of the former capital. Natalia was a 'spoiled young girl', as she herself recalls. From Omsk she wrote 'frightful letters' to her mother, begging her to come and join her. 'In one letter I even threatened to walk to Leningrad, if my mother did not come.' In September 1941, she got her wish. Natalia's mother arrived in Omsk. She had left Leningrad just before the Germans put up the blockade. Sergei suffered in her absence. He fell ill in the first weeks of the siege. He wrote to friends of his desperate need to see Natalia. But when he had the chance to leave Leningrad on one of the last flights from the city, in October 1941, he turned it down. As the sole support of his parents, he could not bring himself to leave them. Sergei understood that he would not survive the siege: people all around him were dying. On 1 January 1942, he wrote to his mother that his only wish was to see Natalia once more before he died. Five days later he was killed when the Hermitage received a direct hit from a German bomb. Throughout her life Natalia was haunted by a sense of guilt about her father's death: she felt she was to blame for his abandonment by her mother, who might have helped him to survive if she had stayed with him in Leningrad. 'I've been tormented by the same question since my childhood,' Natalia recalls: 'if my parents were threatened by some terrible danger, and I had it in my power to save only one of them, which one would I choose? I tried to banish the question from my mind, I couldn't answer it, but it kept coming back.'[13]

Natalia Gabaeva with her parents, 1934

Marianna Fursei was four years old in 1941. She came from an intelligentsia home in Arkhangelsk. Her father Nikolai was an artist and a musician. Her mother, Vera German, was a teacher from a family of famous pedagogues in Leningrad. They met in the Solovetsky prison camp, where both of them were prisoners, in 1929, and were exiled together to Arkhangelsk, where their son Georgii was born in 1933, and Marianna in 1937. In January 1941, Nikolai was arrested for 'anti-Soviet agitation' and sentenced to ten years in a labour camp near Arkhangelsk. Vera died of typhus in 1942. Marianna and her brother remained in the care of their grandmother, Anastasia Fursei, who had lived with the family in Arkhangelsk. During the first year of the war, food supplies to Arkhangelsk were drastically reduced: the town became a near-famine zone. The children became ill. By the spring of 1942, Marianna was so weak with hunger that she could no longer walk; it seemed only a matter of time before she would die. Anastasia could not cope. The doctor she consulted, a well-known TB specialist called Zina Gliner, advised her to give the girl away for adoption to a family that could afford to feed her and perhaps save her life. At first Anastasia refused, in the hope that Nikolai would soon return from the labour camp. But when she found out that he had been shot (in September 1942), she reluctantly took the doctor's advice, gave away her grand-daughter and went with Georgii to stay with friends in Irkutsk in Siberia. 'Forgive me. I beg you not to curse me,' she wrote to the German family in Leningrad. 'I gave away Marinka [Marianna]. It was the only way to save her life.' There was little else that Anastasia could do: Marianna was too sick to make the journey to Irkutsk; there were no other relatives in Arkhangelsk to care for her; and while the German family had kept in touch with Anastasia, the siege of Leningrad had ended any hope of delivering the girl to them.

Marianna was adopted by Iosif and Nelly Goldenshtein, who came from a large Jewish family in Mariupol, in south-east Ukraine. Iosif was a senior-ranking Communist in the Soviet air force who had been sent to Arkhangelsk in 1942. When, at the end of September 1942, the German army attacked Mariupol, Iosif flew back to try to save his family. Instead he witnessed a dreadful massacre. As he approached his family's house, he heard screams from the courtyard. He could only watch from a distance as Hitler's troops lined up nineteen of his relatives, including three of his own children, and shot them through the head. Traumatized by this experience, the Goldenshteins were desperate for a child to love, even – or perhaps especially – one as sick as Marianna, whom they could care for and nurse back to health.

Anastasia with Marianna and Georgii Fursei, Arkhangelsk, 1939

Marianna's maternal grandmother, Vera German, wrote to Anastasia in Irkutsk, asking for the name and address of the family that had adopted her granddaughter. But here there was a critical mistake: instead of writing Goldenshtein, Anastasia wrote the name Goldshtein in her reply. By the time the siege of Leningrad had been lifted, and Vera's family was able to begin their search for Marianna, the Goldenshteins had moved to Tbilisi, and all trace of them in Arkhangelsk had vanished. In 1946, Georgii returned to Leningrad, where he was determined to study at the university: he was just thirteen years of age, too young to remember the Goldenshteins' real name; and he never spoke with the Germans about his lost sister. Georgii had left behind his grandmother in Irkutsk, promising to come back for her later, but he never did. She died there in a home for invalids in 1957.[14]

The Goldenshteins were kind, well-meaning people, who loved Marianna as their own daughter. Knowing that her parents had been arrested as 'enemies of the people', and that her father had been shot, they tried to protect Marianna (and perhaps themselves) by keeping this information from her. They told Marianna nothing about her parents, although they encouraged her to become a musician like her father (in fact, she became a teacher, like her mother). The Goldenshteins belonged to the Communist military establishment in Tbilisi. Marianna grew up in this privileged environment and adopted many of its values and customs. She always thought of the Goldenshteins as her parents, and called them 'Mama' and 'Papa'. But some time around the age of eleven she began to realize that she had once belonged to a different family. The traumatic memories of her early childhood, so deeply buried in her consciousness, began to surface. The catalyst, it seems, was an incident at a Pioneer camp when Marianna was excluded by the other children from an expedition into the forest because, as they said, she was a 'foundling'. Slowly, Marianna began to piece together the fragments of her former life in Arkhangelsk. She never spoke about these recollections to the Goldenshteins. But her growing sense that she was not 'family' focused her unhappiness, and perhaps her teenage resentments, both against the Goldenshteins, who were very strict with her, and against her real parents, who, she concluded, had abandoned her. Marianna explains:

Every night Papa would inspect my school work. I could not go to bed until it was perfect . . . And Mama was too ill to protect me. She had TB. At the age of thirteen or fourteen, I was expected to do all the household chores . . . When my mother and father were angry with me, I would think: if only I was living nearer Arkhangelsk, I would run away and find my grandmother [Marianna did not know that she had died]. My parents might be cross with me, but my grandmother would surely not be so angry. Then I would remember that I had no real mother or father. And that made me totally shut down. I was only rarely able to cry.[15]

On 1 October 1941, Stalin ordered the evacuation of the government from Moscow to Kuibyshev on the Volga. Panic spread in Moscow as the bombing of the city became more intense. There were reports that German troops had broken through the Soviet defences at Viazma, a few days' march from the capital, on 16 October. At railway stations there were ugly scenes as crowds struggled to board trains for the east. Verzhbitsky reported that people were paying 20,000 roubles to go by car from Moscow to Kazan. The panic was partly based on memories of famine from the Civil War. And indeed the food situation quickly became desperate. Huge queues formed at all the shops, and there was widespread looting, which mass arrests did little to control. Verzhbitsky summed up the public mood in his diary on 17 October:

Who is the author of all this mess, this general flight, this thievery, this confusion in our minds? People talk quite openly in a manner that three days ago would have got them arrested. Queues, endless queues, nervous people on the edge. The hysteria has spread from the leadership to the masses. They've begun to remember and count up all the insults, oppressions, injustices, the bullying and bureaucratic machinations of officialdom, the contempt and arrogance of Party members, the draconian orders, deprivations, deceptions and the boastful self-congratulations of the newspapers. It is terrible to hear. People now speak from the heart. Can a city really hold out when it is in such a mood?[16]

On the same day, Stalin made a radio broadcast pledging to stand by the city to the end: it was a decisive turning-point. People rallied to the defence of the capital, motivated more by local patriotism for Moscow than by any allegiance to the Soviet regime. Muscovites recall that the inhabitants of the city all congregated in the centre – the outskirts were almost completely empty – as if from a collective impulse of self-defence or an unconscious need to unite against the enemy. A quarter of a million civilians dug ditches, carted food and medicines to the front and took injured soldiers into their homes. Tens of thousands volunteered for the citizens' defence to fight alongside the regular soldiers, scratched together from the shattered armies that had fallen back from the Belo-russian Front and reinforcements from Siberia who were thrown into battle directly on their arrival in Moscow. Under General Zhukov, military discipline was gradually restored. The new spirit of determination was symbolized by Stalin's decision to hold the Revolution Day (7 November) parade on Red Square as usual: the troops marched past the Lenin Mausoleum, and were then sent straight off to the front. According to K. R. Sinilov, the Commandant of Moscow, the parade had a critical effect on the public mood. Before the parade the letters he received had been mostly defeatist: many people wanted to abandon Moscow rather than expose its population to danger. But afterwards people wrote with messages of defiance.[17]

These few weeks of desperate fighting determined the outcome of the war. By mid-November the German forces were bogged down in winter mud and snow. They were unprepared to survive a Russian winter and exhausted after marching for five months without a break. For the first time since the invasion had begun, they were taking heavy casualties. In December, the Soviets launched a counter-offensive and by April they had pushed the Germans back towards Smolensk. The defence of the capital was a huge boost for Soviet morale. People started to believe in victory. The country was still in a terrible position. By the end of 1941, it had lost 3 million troops, more than half the number that had begun the war; much of Soviet industry had been destroyed; while 90 million citizens, nearly half the pre-war Soviet population, lived in territories occupied by the Germans. But Moscow's survival was crucial: having failed to capture the Soviet capital, Hitler's forces stood no further realistic chance of defeating the Soviet Union.

2

Simonov went to war with a photograph of Valentina Serova in his breast pocket. He kept her image near his heart. In the last six months of 1941, when Valentina was evacuated to Sverdlovsk, he overwhelmed her with love poems. The poet fell in love with the woman he imagined in his poetry:

> I want to say you are my wife,
> Not so I can tell them you're my own,
> Not because our true relationship
> Has long been guessed and generally known.
>
> I do not boast of your beauty
> Nor of the fame and fortune you have found.
> Enough for me the gentle, secret woman
> Who came into my house without a sound.[18]

Simonov did not write to his real wife. Zhenia Laskina had been evacuated with their son Aleksei, her parents, Samuil and Berta, and her two sisters, Fania and Sonia, to Cheliabinsk in the Urals in September 1941. The three sisters worked in the Cheliabinsk Tractor Factory, the biggest of the plants to be reassigned to the manufacture of tanks in a city that was nicknamed Tankograd. Sonia and Zhenia worked in the procurements offices, while Fania was a norm-setter (responsible for fixing the targets of production and the rates of pay). The Laskins all lived together in one room of a two-room flat which they shared with another family. 'It was cramped, but warm and friendly,' remembers Fania: 'we were all very close.' Simonov's parents had also been evacuated to the Urals, to Molotov. Unlike Simonov, they stayed in touch with Zhenia, whom both of them adored. Towards the end of December,

Simonov was given a few days' leave for the New Year. He did not come to Cheliabinsk or Molotov, but went instead to visit Valentina in the nearby city of Sverdlovsk. She refused to receive him – she was about to return to Moscow – so he flew to the Crimea, where a major offensive had just been launched to retake the Kerch peninsula from the Germans.[19]

Valentina continued to resist Simonov's approaches. Her affections lay elsewhere. She had, it seems, a brief affair with Stalin's son, Vasily, and then fell in love with the military hero General Rokossovsky, whom she had met in the spring of 1942 whilst performing at a Moscow hospital, where he was recovering from battle wounds. A veteran of the Civil War, Rokossovsky was arrested in 1937, but released from the Butyrki jail in 1940, when he and his wife and daughter settled in Kiev. On the outbreak of the war, Rokossovsky was recalled by Stalin to Moscow and given the command of the Fourth Army near Smolensk. He took part in the crucial battles for Moscow in the autumn of 1941. When Kiev was occupied by the Germans, he lost contact with his wife. Rokossovsky believed – or wanted to believe – that he was free for Serova. He did not expect to see his wife again. But two months after he met Serova, Rokossovsky's wife appeared with their daughter in Moscow. They had been evacuated from Kiev just before the Germans occupied the Ukrainian capital. In Moscow she soon heard of the romance between her husband and the film actress, who was still pursued by Simonov. The love-triangle had become the gossip of the Soviet elite, which dubbed it the 'USSR' (Union of Serova, Simonov and Rokossovsky). Determined to break up the affair, Rokossovsky's wife complained to Stalin, who disapproved of his leading generals being distracted by personal affairs. In July 1942, Stalin ordered Rokossovsky to take up the command of the Briansk Front, south of Moscow, and focus his attentions on the war. Throughout that summer Valentina tried to revive the romance. Hopelessly in love with the handsome general, she flew out to the front to visit him. But after Stalin's intervention, Rokossovsky refused to receive her. As it became clear that her passion for the general would not be reciprocated, Valentina softened towards Simonov, who had continued to send her gifts and poetry. She slept with him but said she was not in love with him. Sometimes she exploited him in cruel and humiliating ways. Once she even made him deliver one of her love letters to Rokossovsky at the front.[20]

By this time the 'romance' of Simonov and Valentina had become the subject of a cycle of lyric poems known by everyone. Their love affair became an established fact in the nation's literary imagination even before it existed in reality.

The most famous of these poems was 'Wait For Me', written in the summer of 1941, when Simonov was a long way from conquering Valentina's heart:

> Wait for me, and I'll come back,
> But wait with all your might,
> Wait when dreariness descends
> With the yellow rains,
> Wait when snowdrifts sweep the ground,
> Wait during the heat,
> Wait when others are given up
> And together with the past forgotten.
> Wait when from distant places
> Letters do not arrive,
> Wait when all who've waited together
> Are already tired of it.
>
> Wait for me, and I'll come back,
> Don't give your approval
> To those who say you should forget,
> Insisting they are right.
> Even though my son and mother
> Believe I'm already gone,
> Though my friends get tired of waiting,
> Settle by the fire and drink
> A bitter cup,
> So my soul should rest in peace . . .
> Wait. Do not make haste to join them
> In their toast to me.
>
> Wait for me, and I'll come back,
> Just to spite all deaths.
> Let the ones who did not wait
> Say: 'It was his luck.'
> It's hard for them to understand,

For those who did not wait,
That in the very heat of fire,
By waiting here for me,
It was you who saved me.
Only you and I will know
How I survived –
It's just that you know how to wait
As no other person.[21]

Simonov had written these love poems for Valentina and himself. He did not think that they were suitable for publication, because they lacked the mandatory 'civic content' of Socialist Realist poetry. 'I thought these verses were my private business,' Simonov said in 1942. But living in the dug-outs at the front, he had recited them to the soldiers, who wrote them down and learned them by heart. The men found an echo of their own emotions in these poems and encouraged Simonov to publish them in *Krasnaia zvezda*. In December 1941, when Simonov returned on leave to Moscow, several of his poems were broadcast on the radio and then published in *Pravda*. 'Wait For Me' had the greatest response. The poem was reprinted hundreds of times in the press. It was copied out and circulated in millions of private versions by soldiers and civilians. It became a hit song. In 1942, Simonov wrote the screenplay for a film (*Wait For Me*) in which Valentina played the leading role. A stage version was produced by theatres in cities across the land. Soldiers copied out the poem in their albums and notebooks. They kept it in their pockets as a talisman. They engraved the poem's main refrain on tanks and lorries and tattooed it on their arms. Lost for words to express their own emotions, they simply copied out the verse in letters to their sweethearts, who responded with the same pledge. 'My darling Volodenka,' wrote one woman to her lover at the front. 'I have not heard from you for a long time. But I'll wait for you, and you'll come back.' Soldiers wrote their own love poems in imitation of 'Wait For Me', often adding some individual details from their own experience.[22]

The main reason for the poem's huge success was its ability to voice the private thoughts and emotions of millions of soldiers and civilians, who linked their hopes of survival to the idea of reunion with somebody they loved. One group of soldiers wrote to Simonov in May 1942:

Whenever your poems appear in the newspapers, there is huge excitement in our regiment. We cut the poems out and copy them and pass these copies round by hand, because there are not enough copies of the newspapers, and we all want to read the poems and discuss them. We all know 'Wait For Me' by heart. It says exactly what we feel. For all of us have wives, fiancées or girlfriends back home, and we all hope that they will wait for us, until we return with victory.[23]

Everybody was involved in his own private version of the universal romance encapsulated by the poem – a tale of 'You' and 'I' against the background of the war. But romantic yearning was only half of it. The poem also voiced the soldiers' deep anxiety about the fidelity of wives and girlfriends left behind. Many soldiers' songs expressed that worry. One of the most popular had its origins in a song sung by women after the departure of their menfolk, but it had a resonance among the troops, who sang it as they went into battle:

> I wanted to say so much to you,
> But did not say a word.
> Quietly but firmly you whispered in my ear:
> 'Don't love anybody except me!'
>   . . .
> Do not worry when you go to war,
> I will be true to you,
> You will return from victory, my soldier,
> And I will hold you firmly in my arms!

Variations on 'Wait For Me' also stressed fidelity. One group of soldiers from the Urals sang:

> I shall wait for you, my darling,
> I shall wait steadfastly.
> I shall wait for the Urals winter,
> For the flowers in the spring . . .

Another version added motifs, like the nightingale, from traditional Russian folk songs:

> I shall wait, you will return, I know.
> Let the yellow rains fall,
> I shall wait for you, my sweet nightingale,
> And believe with all my strength in our happiness . . .[24]

Soldiers passed harsh judgement on wives who were unfaithful to their husbands at the front. As the war went on, the suspicion of infidelity placed a growing strain on many families, not least because the majority of women (who had to live in the real conditions of the war) could not hope to match the ideal image of Soviet womanhood (the waiting girlfriend, the loyal and faithful wife) portrayed in propaganda films, plays and poems such as 'Wait For Me'.[25]

Simonov himself became involved in a case of soldiers' outrage against an unfaithful wife. In September 1943, he was attached to the Third Army on the Briansk Front. A few days after one of the commanders had been killed in action, a letter for him arrived from his wife in Vichuga, northeast of Moscow, in which she told her husband that she was leaving him for another man. Having opened the letter, the soldiers felt that they should answer it. They asked Simonov to write on their behalf, and told him what they wanted to say. But Simonov was called away to a different sector of the front before he had time to pen the text. Two months later, when he was in Kharkov to report for *Krasnaia zvezda* on the Nazi murders of the Jews there, he suddenly recalled his unfulfilled promise to the soldiers. Simonov still had the woman's name and address, but instead of writing directly to her, he wrote the poem 'An Open Letter to the Woman of Vichuga' to give public voice to the sentiments of the soldiers. As he explained to the Party Secretary of Vichuga, in the poem he 'cited many of the exact phrases and expressions the troops had used themselves' when telling him what he should write to the unfaithful wife.[26]

> I am obliged to inform you
> That the addressee did not receive
> The letter which you posted
> Without a hint of shame.
>
> Your husband did not get the letter,
> He was not wounded by your vulgar words,
> He did not wince, or lose his mind,
> He did not regret the past.
>
> . . .
>
> So your former husband has been killed.
> All is well. Live with your new one.
> The dead cannot hurt you
> In a letter with superfluous words.

> Live, without fear or guilt,
> He cannot write, he won't reply
> He won't return to your town from the war
> And meet you holding another's hand.[27]

According to the poet Margarita Aliger, the key to the appeal of 'Wait For Me' and the other poems in the collection *With You and Without You* (1941–5) was the way they managed to express universal feelings in such an intensely personal voice. Soviet readers had rarely encountered such emotional and erotic poetry as they found in Simonov's wartime verse. Before the war, the public and the private had been counterposed as cultural and political opposites. During the 1920s and 1930s there was no room for intimate or private themes in the public-oriented poetry of the Soviet Union. Couched in terms of 'We' (or 'He' in poems that portrayed Stalin as the voice of every Soviet citizen), poetry was dominated by the grand collective themes of the Revolution (even Mandelshtam declared that lyric verse was inappropriate for Soviet art, because the historical epoch no longer had 'any interest in the human fate of the individual'). But wartime Soviet culture saw the gradual merging of the private and public. Poetry became more intimate. It took on personal themes. It talked about emotions and relationships, which gave it a new status and authority. In the words of the poet Semyon Kirsanov:

> War does not lend itself to odes
> And much in it is not suitable for books,
> But I believe that the people needs
> The spirit of this open diary.
>
> ('Duty', 1942)

'Wait For Me' was the first major sign of this aesthetic shift. It conjured up a private world of intimate relationships independent of the state. Because it was written from the feelings of one person, it became necessary to millions. With the noise of battle everywhere, with shouting officers and barking commissars, people needed poetry to speak to their muted emotions; they yearned for words to express the sorrow and anger, hatred, fear and hope that agitated them. 'Your poems live in our feelings,' a group of soldiers wrote to Simonov in 1945. 'They teach us how to act with other people, especially with women, and for that reason they are loved by all of us. You alone have managed to express our deepest thoughts and hopes.'[28]

For all the private impact of this poetry, its propaganda uses were clear for all to see. Poems such as 'Wait For Me' were powerful weapons in the Soviet campaign to maintain morale. The emotions they expressed helped to foster a kind of primary-level patriotism, centred on the family, comradeship and love, which, in turn, provided a foundation for the broader Soviet concept of national solidarity. Although Stalin was rumoured to have said that only two copies of 'Wait For Me' should have been printed ('one for him and one for her'), the regime was in fact very quick to exploit the poem's popularity. According to Aleksandr Shcherbakov, the head of the Main Political Department of the Red Army, the Kremlin even considered moving Simonov away from the danger of the front because of his value as a poet. The Party leadership had become alarmed by a stanza in one of his poems that hinted at martyrdom (it was a romantic gesture to Valentina) and Shcherbakov was ordered to advise him to be careful. After the success of 'Wait For Me', Simonov quickly rose to the top of the Soviet cultural establishment. He won the Stalin Prize in 1942 and again in 1943. He was rewarded with a luxury flat in a new building on the Leningrad Highway in Moscow (until then, when he had been in Moscow, he had lived in the editorial offices of *Krasnaia zvezda*). For the first time in his life he had a maid. Well paid for his journalism and his poetry, he became rich, all the more so since there was nowhere to spend his earnings at the front and most of his personal expenses were picked up by the authorities. He only had to draw on his royalties when he wanted to send money to his parents, or to Zhenia for his son.[29]

As Simonov's fame and fortune increased, he became more attractive to Valentina. She had always been drawn towards powerful and influential men, who could protect her from the consequences of her spoilt biography. Thanks to Simonov, Valentina was getting leading roles in films and plays. By the spring of 1943, the glamorous, romantic couple were regularly featured in the Soviet press, sometimes appearing together at the front. The image of the separated lovers of 'Wait For Me' reunited in reality was too good for the regime to resist as a morale boost for the soldiers. But in fact the two were not married until October 1943, and all the evidence suggests that it was only shortly before then that

Valentina agreed to marry Simonov. At the time of their wedding, Simonov was still legally married to Zhenia Laskina (there is no record that he ever divorced her), although he had left her three years previously. The wedding itself was hastily arranged. There were only a few guests, among them Stalin's daughter Svetlana and his son Vasily, who brought a personal blessing from Stalin. After the ceremony, Simonov left immediately for the Briansk Front. Apart from two brief spells, when Valentina came to visit Simonov, once in 1943 on the Briansk Front, and another, when she toured the front near Leningrad with him, the newly married couple did not see each other until the end of the war. Even when the war was over, Valentina and Simonov led quite separate lives: they had their own apartments, each with a maid, on the same floor of the building on the Leningrad Highway. Valentina began to drink a lot. She was often drunk in the middle of the day. According to the memoirs of her friend, the actress Tatiana Okunevskaia, Valentina was unhappy in the marriage, and drinking was her way of getting through the day (for Simonov, by contrast, it was a way to get her into bed). One may question the reliability of Okunevskaia's memoirs, which are deeply coloured by her intense hatred of her former husband, Boris Gorbatov, a close friend of Simonov, against whom she also bore a grudge.* It may well be that Valentina had at some point been in love

---

*According to her memoirs, published in 1998, Okunevskaia had married Gorbatov in 1937 in the hope that, as a well-known writer and *Pravda* journalist, he might protect her from arrest (her father, who had been arrested as a tsarist officer in 1925, was rearrested with her grandmother and sent to a labour camp in 1937, while she herself was dropped from the film she had been shooting and could not find any other acting work). For the next ten years the couple lived the luxurious lifestyle of the Soviet elite. They were always to be seen at receptions in the Kremlin, where Tatiana's beauty attracted the attentions of NKVD chief Lavrenty Beria. In 1947, she was raped repeatedly by Beria. The event became common knowledge in the Soviet leadership. In her memoirs Okunevskaia claims that Gorbatov did nothing to protect her. He had just been promoted to the Central Committee and did not want to rock the boat. Tatiana became wild and outspoken. She drank heavily and acted indiscretely at Kremlin receptions. Afraid of her arrest, Gorbatov pleaded with his wife to try to save herself by joining the Party. But she refused. To save himself, according to Okunevskaia, Gorbatov gave evidence about his wife's activities to the authorities. Tatiana was arrested and sentenced to ten years in the Kolyma camps for espionage (she had often been abroad and was well known for her affairs with foreign men, including Josip Tito, the Yugoslav Prime Minister). Okunevskaia's arrest was a cause of frequent arguments in the Simonov household. In her memoirs Okunevskaia is deeply hostile towards Simonov, depicting him, like Gorbatov, as a loathsome Party careerist. Recalling her first meeting with Simonov, at Peredelkino in 1937, when she claims he tried to force himself on her, she describes the writer as 'the most unsympathetic [of all Gorbatov's friends], coarse and blunt,

Serova and Simonov on tour,
Leningrad Front, 1944

with Simonov – possibly when she looked up to him as a figure of importance in the Soviet cultural world – and that her drinking had a different origin. But there is no doubt that their marriage was a stormy one, a long way from the propaganda image of domestic bliss produced by the Soviet authorities to give the public something happy to believe. There were constant arguments, interrupted by passionate exchanges, not least in Simonov's love letters and poems to Valentina from the front; but there were no children, until Maria, born in 1950, by which time Valentina had betrayed Simonov in numerous affairs.[30]

Not everybody was so fond of 'Wait For Me'. Some people thought that it was sentimental, that the intimate emotions of which it spoke were inappropriate for public consumption.[31] Simonov's own mother, Aleksandra, was one such person, though her reservations had as much to do with her personal dislike of Valentina and her disapproval of her son's behaviour towards his family as with her natural aristocratic reserve about the display of emotion. She took particular exception to the lines 'Even though my son and mother / Believe I'm already gone',

---

lacking graciousness, dirty and unkempt', a description radically at odds with the cultured and respectable figure described by others at the time (T. Okunevskaia, *Tat'ianin den'* (Moscow, 1998), pp. 65–6).

which she thought showed a lack of respect for her and for every mother in the Soviet Union. After attending a poetry reading in Moscow where Simonov recited 'Wait For Me' to Valentina, seated at the front of a packed hall, Aleksandra wrote to her son from Molotov in December 1944:

Kirunia! We talked today on the telephone, which prompted me to finish my letter . . . because it contains all the thoughts and worries I've had in recent times. You've arranged your life in such a way that I can't talk openly with you. I cannot say what is in my heart, what I feel and think, in snatches of conversation while we're being driven around by your chauffeur, and yet I feel I must keep trying.

And so, my dear, I have to speak the bitter truth and tell you that I am troubled by your private life. I felt this at the reading, and I felt it painfully for a long time afterwards . . . I understood a lot that evening . . .

As I see it, K. Simonov has done something great, he has summoned youth to love, he has spoken about love in a clear voice, which is something new in our literature and poetry, where heroes loved and lived their lives in a strictly regimented way . . . To do so, he drew on his own intimate feelings, and as the rumours circulated, people became curious. The audience in the hall that night was not made up of thinking people who had come to listen and reflect. They were a mob, which had no qualms about standing up and jostling for a better view of 'that woman' – a woman they measured and envied but did not like very much, a woman you undressed in front of them. I don't think she could have enjoyed the experience . . . These theatrical performances show your character in a bad light; they do not make amends for your mistakes. It is painful to watch you surround yourself with this grubby crowd of hangers-on, as you have done in recent years; you've found neither the strength within yourself nor the understanding of life in general to see them for what they are . . . You and she, she and you, that is all we've heard in the past few years . . . and it seems to me that in this vulgar show there is only egoism and caprice, but no real love for anyone.[32]

Only a mother could have written such a letter. No one else could have given Simonov such a stern and bitter reprimand. Aleksandra had strict ideas about 'decency' and 'correct behaviour' and, being something of a pedagogue, did not hesitate to tell people how they should behave. She disapproved of her son's marriage to Valentina, a 'selfish, capricious and moody woman, whose behaviour I simply cannot stand', as she wrote in a letter to her husband, Aleksandr, in May 1944. She did not like the way her son had 'crawled' into the Soviet elite, and, judging from the tone of her letters congratulating him, did not put much store by his receipt of the Stalin Prize and various other honours. She accused him of being selfish, of neglecting her, of failing to appreciate the sacrifices she had made to bring him up. Although Aleksandra had a tendency to dramatize events and, like every mother, wanted more attention from her son, there was a moral basis to her reprimands. In one revealing letter, in which Aleksandra reproached her son for not writing to her for two months ('and then suddenly a two-line note typed out by your secretary arrives . . . Cela brusque!' [sic]), she berated him for thinking only of his own ease and happiness with Valentina, whilst she and Aleksandr lived in poverty, 'as do all of us in Cheliabinsk':

The comfort you enjoy, which you have earned, is the sort of comfort that you once knew only from history books and from the stories of my previous life, which I told you when you were growing up – a time when your well-being was my only joy. I was born in another world. The first twenty-five years of my life [1890–1915] were spent in conditions of luxury, I did not even have to undress myself. Then suddenly, that life was destroyed. But I began to live again – through my hopes for you. I washed and cooked and went to the shops and worked all day, and it was all for your sake. I say frankly: I think I have earned the right to live half as well as the son I raised. I have earned the right to live in a comfortable room, with somewhere I can wash.[33]

But the main reason for her disapproval lay elsewhere. Aleksandra was concerned for Zhenia and her grandson, Aleksei, a sickly little boy, who suffered periodically from TB. Neglected by Simonov, Aleksei was growing up in the shadow of a famous father whom he rarely saw. 'Wake up, Kirunia, what is wrong with you?' Aleksandra wrote to Simonov in 1944:

What has happened to the decency that marked you so clearly as a child? You have kept it in your conduct at the front but lost it in your private life, in your behaviour towards the people who should be the closest to your heart! . . . In the nursery where Alyosha [Aleksei] spends his days there is a boy whose father, who is just a sailor, picks him up every evening. And he's just an ordinary boy. Alyosha's spiritual qualities are fast developing . . . You could learn to be a better person, a richer person spiritually, by staying close to him . . . The other day he came back from the nursery and declared that he had the best granny in the world, the best mummy, and then he thought, and said: 'and the best daddy in the world'. Kirunia, your son still believes in you, in his dear childish heart the belief in a papa still exists, he wants to have a papa, a real papa, and there is still time for you to become one. Believe in yourself, my son, as Alyosha believes in you. Return to yourself, to your true and decent self, believe in yourself, in your work, which for you was always the most valuable aspect of your life, and then believe in us, the people close to you, who love you and believe in you. Concentrate your will – you were always proud of it and now you need it more than ever if you are to become your true self again.[34]

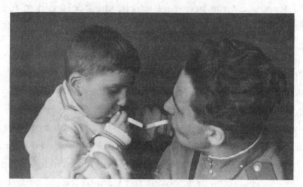

Aleksei and Simonov, 1944

If Simonov's relations with his mother deteriorated during the war, his relations with his stepfather, Aleksandr, became closer. 'It appears that Papa and I have exchanged places in your affections,' Aleksandra wrote to Simonov in 1944, 'and that you have become more affectionate to him than you are to me. I understand the reason why – you need him now at a time of war – and I value it.'[35] Aleksandr was a military man. He had brought up his stepson to be conscientious and obedient, disciplined and orderly – military values which Simonov had placed at the centre of his own identification with the Stalinist regime during the 1930s. But the young Simonov, acutely aware of having the wrong class background, had always felt uncertain of his position. It was only in the war, when rank was defined less by social class than by the performance of one's duties to the state, that he found his place in the system.

Army service itself was thrilling to him. Promoted to lieutenant-colonel in 1942, Simonov wore his new authority with graceful ease and style. The writer Iraklii Andronnikov remembers him as 'a real Russian

Simonov in 1941

officer with fine bearing, calm and self-assured in his uniform, with shiny leather boots and a pistol in his belt. He had white teeth and a sunburned face. He wore his cap tilted slightly to one side.' The war years were the happiest in his life: they defined it. 'I have quickly grown accustomed to the military uniform and way of life,' Simonov wrote in 1942, 'so much so that I cannot even imagine how I will get on when the war is over and I have no military reports to write, no trips to make to the front, and I have to manage without the thousands of friends I've made in dozens of armies.' Margarita Aliger recalls that he spent the war in a sort of fury of activity. 'He wrote from all the crucial fronts, rushed back to Moscow, "wrote himself out", and rushed off again to the places where the fighting was most dangerous. He would never stay in Moscow for more than a day or so, and often only for a few hours, enough to go drinking with some friends.' Through the war Simonov gained in self-possession and proved his courage to himself. Sexually, too, he grew in confidence. He had many lovers, including Marina Chechneva, the ace bomber pilot and Hero of the Soviet Union. According to one of his later lovers, Simonov had a special attraction to women dressed in military uniforms. He liked to have sex on a Nazi flag, which he had recovered from the front.[36]

The war shaped Simonov's entire outlook on the world. His values were measured on a military scale. 'The army is a sort of school,' he later said. 'Serving in the army teaches one for life to carry out one's duties to society. Not to have this strict sense of duty is not to be a complete human being.' Simonov was meticulous and diligent in performing his duties, rigidly adhering to routines and rules, rational to the point of seeming cold and uncaring, and sometimes rather domineering in his dealings with people. In many ways his model of behaviour was a figure he had introduced to Russian prose: the officer-*intelligent* who understands the logic of the orders handed down by the authorities and carries them out conscientiously. In later years, he tended to judge people by the way they had behaved during the war:

> Not to blacken the name of someone
> But to know them in the dark
> The winter of forty-one
> Gave us a true mark
>
> And if you will, it is useful from here on,
> Not letting it slip from our hands,
> With that mark, straight and iron,
> To check now how someone stands.[37]

Simonov applied this harsh measure to Lugovskoi, his charismatic teacher at the Literary Institute who had inspired a whole generation of Soviet poets. Lugovskoi was badly shaken by an incident in 1941 when he was serving at the front and fell under heavy bombardment. Retreating through a town that had been attacked by the Germans, he had stumbled on a bombed-out house where he found the blown-up bodies of several women and children. Lugovskoi suffered a nervous breakdown. He was evacuated to Tashkent. Many friends came to Lugovskoi's assistance, including Elena Bulgakova, the widow of the writer Mikhail Bulgakov, who tried, unsuccessfully, to lift the ban on the publication of Lugovskoi's poetry (which had been condemned as 'politically harmful' in 1937). Sonia and Zhenia Laskina also reached out to Lugovskoi. They wrote to him with deep affection and friendship. 'You must come to Moscow,' Zhenia wrote in 1943, shortly after the Laskins had returned to the capital from Cheliabinsk. 'You are needed here, and people always come when they are needed. We are not just people, but your friends, you cannot refuse friends.' Sonia even promised to marry Lugovskoi ('I shall surround you with the comforts of a family') if he returned and lived with them in the Laskin apartment in Sivtsev Vrazhek, where eight people were already cramped in the three tiny rooms. But Simonov had no such sympathy. He considered Lugovskoi's remove to Tashkent a sign of cowardice and ceased to count him as a close friend.[38]

The war was the making of Simonov as a 'Stalinist': that was when he placed his faith in Stalin at the centre of his life, when he assumed his place in the regime's hierarchy of political and military command, internalized the values of the system and accepted the directions of the Party leadership. Simonov had joined the Party as a candidate member on the outbreak of the war, becoming a full member in 1942. As he later explained, he had joined the Party because he wanted to have a say in the direction of the war effort – he thought that was his duty as an officer – and he did not think the war could be won without the Party's leadership. The Party 'alone was a mass force, capable of making the necessary decisions and sacrifices in the conditions of war', and he wanted to be part of that force. Simonov identified with the Party, and in particular with its leader, even to the point of growing a moustache, brushing back his hair in the 'Stalin style', and posing with a pipe.

Simonov in 1943

According to Dolmatovsky, Simonov did not smoke the pipe but adopted it as a 'way of life'.[39]

Simonov's major service to the Party was through his writing. He was an outstanding military journalist, at least the equal of Vasily Grossman and Ilia Ehrenburg, although Grossman, who is better known to Western readers because of his later novels, such as *Life and Fate* (published in the West in the 1980s), was the better novelist and morally perhaps the more courageous man. This was not a matter of physical bravery. Simonov never shied away from the fiercest point of the fighting. He reported from all the major fronts in 1942: from the Kerch peninsula, where the Soviet attempt to retake the Crimea from the German forces ended in catastrophe during the spring; from the Briansk Front, where the Red Army lost Voronezh in July as the Germans drove south-east towards the grain supplies of Ukraine and the Don and the rich oil-fields of the Caucasus; from Stalingrad, where the Germans launched their first attack, fighting street by street for the Soviet stronghold, in August; and from the northern Caucasus, where the Germans pushed the Soviet forces south to Krasnodar and Ordzhonikidze by December. The only front from which Simonov did not report was Leningrad, where the city continued under siege for a second year, though he did write from the ports of Murmansk and Arkhangelsk, where Lend-Lease supplies from the Western Allies began to arrive on British ships in the summer of 1942.

As a military man, who had himself experienced the bloody fighting at Khalkin Gol, Simonov understood the war from the soldiers' point of view as well as from the viewpoint of the officer who was obliged to carry out his orders from above. His war reporting was distinguished by its direct observation and humanity. But he also fully accepted the propaganda role the regime assigned him as a journalist. All his war reports were written with the aim of strengthening morale and discipline, fostering love for Stalin and hatred of the enemy. He wrote that patriotic Soviet troops were fighting for the glory of Stalin. 'United by their iron discipline and Bolshevik organization,' he reported from Odessa, 'our Soviet forces are dealing to the enemy a heavy blow. They are fighting without fear, without tiring in the struggle, as we have been taught by the great Stalin . . . For our Odessa! For the Motherland! For Stalin!' In Simonov's reports Stalin's leadership was a constant inspiration to the Soviet troops. For example, he wrote about an officer he had encountered on the front near Stalingrad who 'gained all his strength from the idea that our great leader directs everything in our enormous cause from his office in Moscow and thus invests in him, an ordinary colonel, part of his genius and spirit'. He had expressed the same idea in his poem commemorating the anniversary of the Revolution on 7 November 1941:

> Comrade Stalin, do you hear us?
> You must hear us, we know that.
> Neither son nor mother in this frightful hour,
> It is you we remember first.

Simonov's belief in Stalin was genuine. In later years he never tried to deny it. In his memoirs, he acknowledged that the huge significance which he had attributed to Stalin in this poem 'had not been an exaggeration' of his true opinion.[40]

Some of his war correspondence served the regime's campaign to get the troops to fight. In August 1941, after the collapse of the Soviet front, Stalin had issued his merciless Order Number 270, condemning all those who surrendered or were captured as 'traitors to the motherland'. Several senior commanders were arrested and shot, including the commander of the Western Army Group, General Dmitry Pavlov, who had made a desperate effort to hold the front together in the first weeks of the war. The wives of captured officers were also subject to arrest (even the wife of Stalin's son, Iakov, who was captured by the Germans in July, was arrested and sent to a labour camp). Simonov accepted – and argued in his reports of 1941 – that the collapse of the Soviet front had been caused by the 'criminal behaviour of certain generals, at best cowards and at worst German agents', who 'were shot deservedly'. He also peddled the idea that the bravest soldiers were the ones least likely to be killed – a propaganda myth that encouraged many troops to fight in situations where they were almost bound to die.[41]

Alongside this service to the Stalinist regime, Simonov pursued yet another objective in his war writings, especially in the unpublished notes and observations which he later used for his great war novel *The Living and the Dead*. A Soviet patriot and firm believer in the Soviet Union's victory, he attempted to discern the signs of that victory in the actions, ideas and emotions of the people. He had spotted the first sign amidst the chaos of the Soviet retreat in June 1941, when he had seen the two junior officers walking west towards the front at Minsk to locate their military command.[42] Simonov could not forget this scene – it symbolized for him the patriotic spirit of the ordinary people – and he would return to it in his later writings as he struggled to develop a populist conception of the Soviet victory. But at the time he had only a vague sense of the forces that moved the people to fight.

3

Simonov arrived in Stalingrad in September 1942, at the height of the battle for the streets. The last Soviet defenders were confined to the factory districts of the north, the area around the railway station and the small hill in the centre, while all around them the city had collapsed under the bombardment of the German tanks, artillery and planes. Simonov was astonished by the extraordinary determination of the Soviet soldiers to fight for every street, and every ruined building, against the superior German forces. Even as the Germans pushed them back towards the river bank, the Soviet soldiers would not give up the city and evacuate to the eastern shore of the Volga, where the main Soviet army was massed. It was this determination – a spirit that cannot be explained by military discipline or ideology – that tipped the scales in this decisive battle of the war.

In his diary on 16 September, A. S. Chuianov, the head of the Stalingrad Defence Committee, recorded a conversation he had overheard between a group of newly arrived troops and a wounded soldier who had been evacuated from the burning city:

'What is going on in the city?' [the men asked the wounded soldier].

'There's no making head or tail of it. Look,' he pointed with his good arm towards the Volga – 'the whole town is on fire.'

'But why is it burning for so long?' the troops asked in astonishment.

'Everything is on fire: the houses, the factories, the land, all the metal is melting . . .'

'And the people?'

'The people? They are standing! Standing, and fighting! . . .'

The courageous determination of the Soviet forces was indeed decisive in the war and cannot be dismissed as a propaganda myth. Yet its origin has never been satisfactorily explained. Why did so many Soviet soldiers fight with such fierce disregard for their own lives in the battles for Moscow, Kiev, Stalingrad and a dozen other Soviet cities?

Terror and coercion provide part of the explanation. The practices of the pre-war terror system were reimposed to keep the soldiers fighting in the war. At the height of the Soviet collapse, on 28 July 1942, as the Germans threatened Stalingrad, Stalin issued the notorious Order Number 227 ('Not One Step Backwards!'), calling on the troops to defend every metre of Soviet territory 'to the last drop of blood' and threatening the severest punishments for 'panickers' and 'cowards' who shirked their duty.* Special 'blocking units' (*zagradotriady*) were set up to bolster the existing NKVD units: their orders were to sweep behind the Soviet front and shoot any soldiers who lagged behind or tried to run from the fighting. During the course of the war approximately 158,000 soldiers were sentenced to be shot (many more were shot without any formal sentencing or record of their deaths); 436,000 were imprisoned; while 422,000 were made to 'atone with their blood' for the crimes they had 'committed before the motherland' by serving in the special penal battalions (*shtrafroty*) used for the most dangerous tasks, such as clearing minefields or storming German fortifications. The impact of Order Number 227, like the terror system in the army as a whole, should not be exaggerated, however. The Order was enforced at desperate moments, like the battle for Stalingrad, when an estimated 13,500 Soviet troops were shot in the space of a few weeks. But otherwise the Order was frequently ignored by the commanders and their political officers, who learned from experience that military unity and effectiveness were not served by such wholesale drastic punishments. Indeed, despite the introduction of the Order, desertion from the army continued to increase, prompting even Stalin to acknowledge that terror was becoming ineffective as a way to make the soldiers fight, and that other means of persuasion should be developed.[43]

Appeals to the patriotism of the Soviet people were more successful. The vast majority of Soviet soldiers were peasant sons: their loyalty was not to Stalin or the Party, which had brought ruin to the countryside, but to their homes and families, to their own vision of the 'motherland'. As Stalin put it to Averell Harriman in September 1941, the Russian people were fighting 'for their homeland, not for us'. To appeal to them, Soviet propaganda increasingly jettisoned Soviet symbols in favour of

---

*The Order was not made known to the Soviet public until 1988, when it was published as part of the policy of glasnost, or openness, although it had been distributed to all units of the Soviet armed forces in 1942.

older images of Mother Russia that carried greater weight among the troops. Thus Stalin's picture became less conspicuous in 1941–2, the period of military catastrophe (although he reappeared as the national figurehead and inspiration of the Soviet victories in 1943–5); the 'Internationale' was replaced by a new national anthem; new Soviet medals were produced featuring military heroes from Russian history; and the Church was granted a new lease on life, as the state lifted many of its pre-war political controls on religious activities in exchange for Church leaders' moral support in the war. The result of this communion between Church and state was a curious blend of religious faith and Soviet belief. The journalist Ralph Parker saw a Siberian soldier at a Moscow railway station preparing to leave for the front. He was listening to a broadcast on the loudspeaker, and when he recognized Stalin's voice, he crossed himself and cried out 'Stalin!'[44]

Soviet propaganda also played on the emotions of hatred and revenge. By the winter of 1941, the German invasion had brought so much suffering to Soviet families that all it took to get the people fighting was to fan their rage against the enemy. According to Lev Pushkarev, a young soldier and ethnographer who made a detailed study of the culture and beliefs of the Red Army rank and file, it was hatred of the Germans, more than anything else, that made the soldiers fight. The force of this emotion was so powerful and unpredictable – containing as it did much pent-up fury over the suffering people had endured long before the war – that it needed to be carefully manipulated by propagandists to focus it against the foreign enemy. Poets played a vital part. Simonov was one of several Soviet writers, along with Ilia Ehrenburg and Aleksei Surkov, who lent their literary talents to the hate campaign. 'Kill Him!' was the best known poem in this call to arms. Written by Simonov in July 1942 – at a desperate moment of the war when the Germans threatened to break through to the Volga and the Caucasus – it was essentially a reiteration of the fight-to-the-death spirit of Order Number 227. Officers would read the poem to their men before they went into battle to instil in them the spirit of defiance and determination to fight to the end:

> If you cherish your mother,
> Who fed you at her breast
> From which the milk has long since gone,
> And on which your cheek may only rest;

If you cannot bear the thought,
That the Fascist standing near her,
May beat her wrinkled cheeks,
Winding her braids in his hand;

. . .

If you have not forgotten your father,
Who rocked you in his arms,
Who was a good soldier
And fell in the Carpathian snows,*

Who died for the Volga and the Don,
For the future of your native land;
If you cannot bear the thought
That he will turn in his grave,

That his soldier's portrait on the cross
Should be smashed on to the ground
And stamped on by a German
Before your mother's eyes . . .

. . .

Then kill a German – make sure to kill one!
Kill him as soon as you can!
Every time you see him,
Make sure that you kill him every time!

Simonov's play *The Russian People* strove for a similar effect. Published in the pages of *Pravda* at the end of July 1942, it was performed in theatres across the Soviet Union. The play was very weak, but extremely timely, and its message – that all Russians were united against the enemy – caught the mood of defiance (it won the Stalin Prize in 1943). Aleksandr Werth, who was in Moscow to report for the *Sunday Times*, witnessed a performance at the Moscow Art Theatre:

There was complete silence for at least ten seconds after the curtain had fallen at the end of the third act; for the last words had been: 'See how Russian people are going to their death.' Many women in the audience were weeping.[45]

Coercion, patriotism, hatred of the enemy all played a part, but perhaps the most important element in the soldiers' determination to

*The Russian army fought in the Carpathian mountains in the First World War.

fight was the cult of sacrifice. The Soviet people went to war with the psychology of the 1930s. Having lived in a state of constant revolutionary struggle, where they were always being called upon to sacrifice themselves for the greater cause, they were ready for war. As Simonov remarked, the people were prepared for the privations of the war – the sharp decline in living standards, the breaking up of families, the disruption of ordinary life – because they had already been through much the same in the name of the Five Year Plans.[46]

This readiness for personal sacrifice was the Soviet Union's greatest weapon. In the first year of the war, especially, it was essential to the Soviet Union's survival, as it struggled to recover from the catastrophic summer of 1941. The actions of ordinary soldiers and civilians, who sacrificed themselves in huge numbers, made up for the failures of the military command and the paralysis of nearly all authority. The ethos of sacrifice was particularly intense in the 'generation of 1941' (people born in the 1910s and early 1920s), which had been raised on the legendary tales of Soviet heroes who consecrated themselves to the interests of the state: record-breaking pilots and Stakhanovites, Arctic explorers, soldiers of the Civil War, Communists who went to fight in Spain. It was in emulation of their feats that so many youthful volunteers rushed into war. The call to arms in 1941 connected them to the heroic tradition of the Russian Civil War and the Five Year Plan of 1928–32 – the two great romantic episodes in Soviet history when great things were supposedly achieved by collective enterprise and sacrifice. In the words of the poet David Samoilov (who was twenty-one when he joined the army in 1941): 'The Civil War – that was our fathers. The Five Year Plan – that was our older brothers. But the Patriotic War of '41 – that is us.' Many soldiers derived the strength to fight from a sense of being part of this continuum: 'I am following in the footsteps of our father, who died fighting in the Civil War in 1919,' wrote Leonid Kurin, a junior lieutenant, to his sister in 1943.

He fought for my life. Now I am fighting for the lives of your children . . . Sonia, I have thought a lot about dying – is it frightening or not? It is not frightening when you know that you will die for a better future, for the happiness of our children. But you have to kill a dozen Germans before you die.[47]

The generation of 1941 fought with selfless dedication and heroic bravery, even recklessness, from the first day of the war. It bore the greatest human cost. Only 3 per cent of the male cohort of soldiers born in 1923 survived until 1945.* Older men fought more cautiously – and were the ones who tended to survive. Viacheslav Kondratiev, born in 1920 and injured several times during the war, recalls that the older soldiers tried to help the younger ones:

They fought more skilfully, more soberly, they did not charge ahead, but held us young ones back, because they understood the value of life more than we did. I had one such protector, a forty-year-old man, who often told me that I had to respect my own life, even in a war.[48]

Rita Kogan was just eighteen when she joined the army in 1941. She was one of the million Soviet women who served in the Red Army and its partisan units – a number representing about 8 per cent of all Soviet combatants (though many more women were active in supporting roles, such as transport, supplies and medical assistance).[49] Rita was born in 1923 to a Jewish family in Rechitsa, a small industrial town in Belorussia. It was, she says, a 'modern family of the Soviet type'. Her father was a factory manager, her mother an accountant, and Rita and her sister were brought up in the 'Soviet spirit of those times', without Jewish customs or beliefs or the influence of grandparents. Rita's worldview was shaped by her school, the Pioneers and the Komsomol. 'I saw the Pioneers and the Komsomol as a type of children's army that fought against injustice wherever it appeared,' she recalls. 'If at school I saw a boy who was bullying a girl or a smaller boy, I would deal with him so harshly that he would run to the teachers to complain.' The ethos that inspired her was enshrined in the widely read children's book by Arkadii Gaidar, *Timur and His Team* (1940), which tells the story of a juvenile militia in a dacha settlement near Moscow that guards the homes of Red Army officers who are away at the front. Timur's story encouraged the military aspirations of many adolescents. And the training they had received in the Pioneers and the Komsomol (the organized marching and drilling, the strict discipline and subordination to authority, the paramilitary games) served explicitly as preparation for the Red Army. Being a girl was no bar: propaganda put forward positive images of

---

*In the Golovin family three of Nikolai's four sons were killed in the fighting of 1941: Ivan (then aged thirty-four), Nikolai (twenty-eight) and Anatoly (twenty-one).

Soviet women bearing arms and generally promoted the militarization of women as a mark of sexual equality.

Rita was finishing her last year at school when the war broke out. Evacuated with her family to Stalingrad, she found work as an accountant in a school, but desperate to do something more directly for the war effort, she pleaded with the local Komsomol to enrol her in their military school. The Komsomol refused (at eighteen she was too young, they said) but sent her to work in a munitions plant, where she assembled parts for aeroplanes. In the summer of 1942, the Soviet press publicized the heroic feats of young Red Army women volunteers who were fighting as snipers and anti-aircraft gunners during the defence of Stalingrad; barely out of school, few of them had fired guns before. Rita was determined to follow their example and once again appealed to the Komsomol. Again she was refused and told to continue working in the factory. 'I was furious,' she recalls. 'I had volunteered to fight, I said that I was ready to sacrifice my life, and they treated me like a little girl. I went straight home and cried.' Rita formed her own group of young Komsomol women; together they ran away from the factory and applied to a military school that was training telegraph and radio operators in preparation for the launching of Operation Uranus, the Soviet counter-offensive against the German forces around Stalingrad, in November 1942. Rita joined the class for Morse-code signallers. She was sent with a group of girls to the headquarters of the South-west Front, between Stalingrad and Voronezh. During late December, she took part in Operation Little Saturn, when the combined forces of the South-west and Voronezh Fronts broke through to the rear of the German armies on the Don. 'The senior communications officer to whom we reported at the front headquarters was an elderly gentleman, who had served in the tsarist army in the First World War,' recalls Rita. 'He had no idea how to deal with us girls, and spoke to us in a kindly manner, instead of giving us firm orders. But he was a first-rate specialist and protected us from the other officers, who looked for sex from us.' In January 1943, Rita was stationed in an observation point on the front near Kharkov when it was overrun by German troops: struggling to escape with her radio equipment, she had her first taste of battle, killing two attackers in hand-to-hand fighting before managing to get away, severely wounded. After she recovered she went on to serve as a radio operator on several fronts; she fought as a gunner in Marshal Konev's First Ukrainian Front against the Germans near Lvov in July 1944, before eventually reaching Budapest with the Fifty-seventh Army in January 1945.

Reflecting on her determination to fight against the Germans, Rita could be speaking for the whole 'generation of 1941'.

I was just eighteen, I had only recently left school, and I saw the world in terms of the ideals of my Soviet heroes, the selfless pioneers who did great things for the motherland, whose feats I had read about in books. It was all so romantic! I had no idea what war was really like, but I wanted to take part in it, because that was what a hero did . . . I did not think of it as 'patriotism' – I saw it as my duty – that I could and should do everything in my power to defeat the enemy. Of course, I could have simply worked in the munitions factory and sat out the war there, but I always wanted to be at the centre of events: it was the way I had been brought up by the Pioneers and the Komsomol. I was an activist . . . I did not think of death and was not afraid of it, because, like my Soviet heroes, I was fighting for the motherland.[50]

This was the spirit that Simonov attempted to explain in *Days and Nights* (1944), a story based on his diary observations of the battle for Stalingrad. For Simonov it was not fear or heroism that made the soldiers fight, but something more instinctive, connected to the defence of their own homes and communities, a feeling that grew in strength, releasing the people's energy and initiative, as the enemy approached:

The defence of Stalingrad was essentially a chain of barricades. Together they were linked as a large battlefield, but separately each one depended on the loyalties of a small group who knew that it was essential to stand firm, because if the Germans broke through in one place, the whole defence would be threatened.[51]

As Stalingrad showed, soldiers fought best when they knew what they were fighting for and linked their fate to it. Leningrad and Moscow proved the same. Local patriotism was a powerful motivation. People were more prepared to fight and sacrifice themselves when they identified the Soviet cause with the defence of a particular community, a real network of human ties, than with some abstract notion of a 'Soviet motherland'. The Soviet propaganda that invoked the defence of '*rodina*' (a term that combines the local and the national meaning of 'homeland') tapped into this sentiment.

Contrary to the Soviet myth of wartime national unity, Soviet society was more fractured during the war than at any previous time since the Civil War. Ethnic divisions had been exacerbated by the Soviet state, which scapegoated certain national minorities, such as the Crimean Tatars, the Chechens and the Volga Germans, and exiled them to regions where they were not welcomed by the local populace. Anti-Semitism, which had been largely dormant in Soviet society before the war, now became widespread. It flourished especially in areas occupied by Hitler's troops, where a large section of the Soviet population was directly influenced by the Nazis' racist propaganda, but similar ideas were imported to places as remote as Kazakhstan, Central Asia and Siberia by Soviet soldiers and evacuees from the western regions near the front. Many people blamed the Jews for the excesses of the Stalinist regime, usually on the reasoning of Nazi propaganda that the Bolsheviks were Jews. According to David Ortenberg, the editor of *Krasnaia zvezda*, soldiers often said that the Jews were 'shirking their military responsibilities by running away to the rear and occupying jobs in comfortable Soviet offices'.[52] More generally, this gulf between the front-line servicemen and the 'rats' who remained in the rear became the focus of a widening divide between the common people and the Soviet elite, as the unfair distribution of the military burden became associated in the popular political consciousness with a more general inequality.

But if there was no genuine national unity, people did unite for the defence of their communities. By the autumn of 1941, 4 million people had volunteered for the citizens' defence (*narodnoe opolchenie*), which dug trenches, guarded buildings, bridges and roads, and, when their city was attacked, carted food and medicine to the soldiers at the front, brought back the injured and joined in the fighting. In Moscow the citizens' defence had 168,000 volunteers from over thirty nationalities, and another half a million people prepared for defence work; in Leningrad, there were 135,000 men and women organized in units of the citizens' defence, and another 107,000 workers on a military footing, by September 1941.[53] Fired up with civic patriotism, but without proper training in warfare, they fought courageously but died in shocking numbers in the first battles.

Comradeship was also crucial to military cohesion and effectiveness. Soldiers tend to give their best in battle if they feel some sort of loyalty to a small group of trusted comrades, or 'buddies', according to military theorists.[54] In 1941–2, the rates of loss in the Red Army were so high that small groups seldom lasted long: the average period of front-line service for infantrymen was no more than a few weeks, before they were removed by death or injury. But in 1942–3, military units began to stabilize, and the comradeship that men found within them became a decisive factor in motivating them to fight. The closeness of these friend-ships naturally developed from the dangers the men faced. The mutual trust and support of the small collective group was the key to their survival. 'Life at the front brings people closer very fast,' wrote one soldier to the fiancée of a comrade, who had been killed in the fighting.

At the front it is enough to spend a day or two together with another man, and you will find out about all his qualities and feelings, which on Civvy Street you would not learn in a year. There is no stronger friendship than the friendship of the front, and nothing can break it, not even death.

Veterans recall the intimacy of these wartime friendships with idealism and nostalgia. They claim that people then had 'bigger hearts' and 'acted from the soul', and that they themselves were somehow 'better human beings', as if the comradeship of the small collective unit was a cleaner sphere of ethical relationships and principles than the Communist system, with all its compromises and contingencies. They often talk as if they found in the collectivism of these groups of fellow soldiers a type of 'family' that was missing from their lives before the war (and would be missing afterwards).[55]

By January 1943, Uranus and Little Saturn had forced the Germans back to the Donets River, 360 kilometres west of Stalingrad, where the spearhead of the German army, a quarter of a million men, was cut off by the Soviet troops. Battling as much against the cold and hunger as against the Soviet enemy, the trapped Germans kept up an intense resistance – they were terrified of capture by the Soviet troops – losing more than half their number before finally surrendering on 2 February. The victory was greeted by the Soviets as a major turning-point. It was a huge boost to morale. 'Up till then,' wrote Ehrenburg, 'one believed in victory as an act of faith, but now there was no shadow of doubt: victory was assured.' From Stalingrad, the Soviet army pushed on towards Kursk, where it concentrated 40 per cent of its soldiers and three-quarters of its armoured forces to defeat the bulk of the German forces in July. Kursk definitively ended German hopes of a victory on Soviet soil. The Red Army drove the demoralized Germans back towards

Kiev, reaching the outskirts of the Ukrainian capital by September and finally recapturing it on 6 November, just in time for a massive celebration in Moscow for the anniversary of the Revolution the next day.[56]

The bravery and resilience of the rank and file was a decisive factor in the Soviet military success. Another was the transformation in the structure of authority within the Red Army after the first disastrous twelve months of the war. Stalin at last recognized that the intervention of the Party in the military command (not least his own as the Supreme Commander) made it less efficient and that commanding officers were best left on their own. Zhukov's appointment as Deputy Supreme Commander in August 1942 – enabling Stalin to step back from the active control of the armed forces – signalled a new relationship between the Party and the military command. The stategic planning and running of the war effort were gradually transferred from the politicians of the Military Council to the General Staff, which now took the lead and merely kept the Party leadership informed. The power of the commissars and other political officers, a legacy of the military purges of the 1930s, was drastically reduced in military decisions and eliminated altogether in many of the smaller army units, where the commanding officers were left in sole authority. Released from the Party's tight control, the military command developed a new confidence; autonomy encouraged initiative and produced a stable corps of military professionals, whose expertise was crucial to the victories of 1943–5. To reinforce this professional ethos, in January 1943, the Party leadership restored the epaulettes that had been worn by tsarist officers, a hated symbol of the old regime that was destroyed in 1917; in July the title 'officer' was brought back to replace the egalitarian 'comrade'. Gold braid was imported from Britain, whose officials were incensed at shipping what to them were fripperies, although in fact the braid was far more significant than that.[57] Medals also played a vital role as a reward for the military professional. Eleven million medals were awarded to Soviet servicemen between 1941 and 1945 – eight times more than awarded by the United States. It took only a few days for the Soviet soldier to receive his reward after an operation, whereas US soldiers usually waited for six months. Soldiers who had distinguished themselves in battle were also encouraged to join the Party by a lowering of the requirements for entry from the ranks.

Changes in the industrial economy also contributed to the Soviet military revival. In 1941–2, the Red Army had been poorly equipped compared to its adversary and therefore suffered enormous losses. But during 1942–3, dramatic improvements in the production of tanks, planes, cars, radars, radios, artillery, guns and ammunition enabled the formation of new tank and mechanized divisions, which fought more effectively and at far less human cost. The rapid reorganization of Soviet industry was where the planned economy (the foundation of the Stalinist system) really came into its own. Without state compulsion, none of the necessary changes could have been achieved in such a short period of time. Thousands of factories and their workers were evacuated to the east; virtually all industrial production was geared towards the needs of the military; railways were built or redirected to connect the new industrial bases of the east with the military fronts; and factories were placed under martial law to tighten labour discipline and productivity. Under the new work regime there were severe punishments for negligence, absenteeism and unauthorized leave, or simply being late for work (failure to arrive within twenty minutes was counted as 'desertion from the labour front'). There were a staggering 7.5 million court convictions for these crimes during the war years.[58] In most factories seventy-hour weeks became the norm, with many workers taking all their meals and sometimes even sleeping in their factories, for fear of being late in the morning. Comprehensive rationing was introduced to reduce costs and keep people at their place of work (where they received their rations). Finally, a vast new army of Gulag labourers was mobilized through mass arrests to supply the country with much needed fuel and raw materials.

One of the least-known aspects of the Soviet war effort is the role of the so-called 'labour army' (*trudovaia armiia*), which numbered well over a million conscripts. It was used for various tasks that could not be performed by free labour. There is no mention of the 'labour army' in official documents, which talk euphemistically of the 'labour service' (*trudovaia povinnost'*) and 'labour reserves' (*trudovye rezervy*), both terms that conceal the element of compulsion, but in fact the conscripts in these categories were unpaid labourers, subject to the same conditions as the prisoners of the Gulag. They worked in convoys under guard and were used for the same labour tasks (timber felling, construction, factory and agricultural work). Unlike the Gulag prisoners, many of the conscripts of the labour army had never been arrested or sentenced by a court. Most of them were simply rounded up by the NKVD and military units from deported nationalities, especially the Soviet Germans, who were exiled from the Volga region to Siberia and Kazakhstan on the outbreak of the war, although the labour army also contained large numbers of Crimean Tatars, Chechens, Kalmyks, Finns, Romanians, Hungarians and Koreans.

Rudolf Gotman was born in 1922 to a Lutheran German family from the Crimea. The Gotmans were categorized as 'kulaks' and exiled to the wilderness near Arkhangelsk in 1931. When the war broke out Rudolf was picked up by the NKVD as a 'German national' (in fact his ancestors had lived in Russia since 1831) and sent to work in the coal mines of the Donbass. There he was conscripted by a labour brigade made up of a hundred young men from 'German' families and sent to work in a food-processing factory in Solikamsk, in the northern Urals. In the autumn of 1942, the men were sent to a nearby logging camp to fell timber. They lived in barracks, slept on wooden benches, and were given starvation-level rations. Made to work in freezing temperatures, more than half the brigade members died in the first winter. The NKVD guards, who supervised the brigade, showed no mercy for the 'German' boys and called them 'Fascist scum'. Rudolf survived by virtue of the fact that he was injured and taken to hospital: otherwise he would have died from exhaustion. He remained in the labour army for the next fourteen years. He worked in factories, Soviet farms and construction sites and was even sent to the Caucasus to build dachas for Stalin, Molotov and Beria. He did not receive any pay until 1948, and was not allowed to leave the labour army until 1956, as part of the general amnesty for Gulag prisoners.[59]

It was not just 'non-Russians' who were rounded up by the labour army. Former 'kulaks' were also vulnerable to conscription. Ivan Bragin from the Suksun region in the Urals was mobilized by the labour army in the autumn of 1943, ten years after he had been exiled as a 'kulak' to a 'special settlement' attached to the pulp-and-paper mill at Krasnok-amsk near Perm. Almost blind from the chemicals used at the mill and semi-paralysed with rheumatic pains, Ivan was sent to work at a logging camp near Kotlas. Conscription was a punishment for complaining after he had not received his full ration at the mill. Unable to cope with the heavy labour at the logging camp (he could barely see the trees he was meant to cut), Ivan soon fell ill in the freezing temperatures. 'My legs have swollen up,' he wrote to his family in Krasnokamsk. 'They are so big that I cannot even put my trousers on.' The food in the camp was very bad and not sufficient to maintain his strength. The work was terribly hard. One day in the autumn of 1943 Ivan collapsed from exhaustion. He was taken to a hospital, where he slowly recovered. In January 1944, Ivan wrote to tell his family that his feet were 'showing signs of life at last'. He was hopeful that he would soon be released from the hospital and that as an invalid he would be allowed to return to his family. It was a treacherous winter journey from Kotlas to Suksun, 1,000 kilometres away, and Ivan was afraid to leave before the spring, in case he became 'dizzy from the frosty air and fell down on the ice', but he was determined to walk back once he had regained his strength. 'All I need is a pair of large felt boots and I shall come home.' Ivan was released from the labour camp in February 1944, long before he was fit to begin his long journey. He never made it home. A few hundred metres from the hospital he slipped and fell on the icy road and froze to death.[60]

Ivan Bragin and his family, 1937

Gulag labour also played an important part in the wartime economy, producing perhaps 15 per cent of all Soviet ammunition, a large proportion of the army's uniforms and much of its food. The population of the camps declined during 1941–3, as half a million prisoners were released to 'redeem their guilt' by fighting at the front, but from the end of 1943 it increased sharply, as the Soviet army swept across the territories abandoned by the Germans and the NKVD units, which followed in its wake, arrested hundreds of thousands of people suspected of collaborating with the enemy or of supporting nationalist insurgencies opposed to the Soviet regime. The exploitation of this Gulag labour force became more intense during the war. In mines and logging camps, prisoners were driven to the brink of death to increase fuel supplies, while rations were reduced to the bare minimum required to keep them alive. In 1942, the rate of mortality in the Gulag labour camps was a staggering 25 per cent – that is, one in every four Gulag workers died that year.[61]

Alongside the logging camps and mines, a new type of Gulag economy developed in the war, one in which prison labour was attached to factories and construction sites in large-scale industrial zones (Gulag cities) under the control of the NKVD. The Norilsk complex in the Arctic Circle is a good example of this new type of industrial development. The Norilsk region's huge reserves of nickel, platinum and copper were discovered by geologists in the 1920s, but the first large survey was not carried out until 1930, when the precious ores became essential to the programme of industrialization. Norilsk contained about a quarter of the world's known deposits of nickel (used in the production of high-grade steel) and over one-third of its reserves of platinum. The natural conditions of the region were highly favourable for mining and processing these ores because of the large deposits of coal, which served as a power supply for smelting and transportation to the Kara Sea. But the region was virtually uninhabitable. Winter temperatures dropped to minus 45 degrees. There were almost constant snow blizzards. It was dark for several months a year. And then in the summer the ground turned into marshland, and human beings were eaten by the mosquitoes. No labourers would go to Norilsk of their own accord.

In 1935, the development of the region was handed over to the Gulag administration of the NKVD, which had a growing reputation for managing large-scale building projects in remote regions where the civilian ministries were reluctant to operate (the Ministry of Heavy Industry, which was responsible for metallurgy, had refused to take on the Norilsk project). The Norilsk camp and mining complex were dug from the permafrost by 1,200 Gulag prisoners using only pickaxes and wheelbarrows. By 1939, the number of prisoners had risen to 10,000, though many more had died in the meantime. The Gulag administration in Moscow became impatient with the slow progress. In 1939, the first director of Norilsk, Vladimir Matveyev, was arrested and sent to a labour camp for fifteen years. He was replaced by Avraam Zaveniagin, the dynamic former head of the mining complex at Magnitogorsk. The appointment was a sign of the importance which the regime attached to the project at Norilsk. The military demand for high-grade steel made the nickel of Norilsk vitally important in the war. Norilsk's work regime intensified. From 1941 to 1944, Group A prisoners (who worked in production or construction) had less than three days off each month (many former prisoners do not recall any days off work at all); all the prisoners worked eleven-hour shifts; and fewer days were lost through bad weather (during snow-storms they would walk to work by holding on to ropes). Zaveniagin introduced a system of incentives and rewards – better living quarters, clothes and food rations, even small monetary rewards – for 'Stakhanov-ite' prisoners who exceeded their norms (about one in five in 1943). He also increased the number of free workers and 'volunteers' (there were about 10,000 by the end of the war) by offering them managerial and specialist positions. But the biggest growth took place in the number of prison labourers, which reached 100,000 by 1944.[62]

Prisoners were brought to Norilsk from all corners of the Soviet Union, especially from Ukraine, the northern Caucasus and the Baltic region, where the mass arrests of 'nationalists' and 'collaborators with the enemy' were largely motivated by the need to supply the Gulag with labour. The long journey to Norilsk began by train to Krasnoiarsk, the capital of the Siberian administrative region in which Norilsk was located, 2,000 kilometres to the south of the labour camp. From Krasno-iarsk the prisoners were brought by steamboat on the Yenisei River to Dudinka, the port for the Norilsk complex, and then transported to the camp by rail. The Arctic wilderness around Norilsk was so remote that there was no need to build a fence for the labour camp. No prisoner in his right mind would think of trying to escape, and no one ever did (although there were tales about escapes across the Arctic Sea to Alaska, 5,000 kilometres away).[63]

Vasilina Dmitruk was fifteen when she was sent to Norilsk. Born into a large peasant family in the Ternopol region of western Ukraine, she was one of several dozen women accused of supporting the Ukrainian nationalist partisans and rounded up by the NKVD units attached to the Red Army after the recapture of her village in 1943 (the young men were all conscripted by the Red Army). Taken to the local town, the girls were beaten by their Russian NKVD interrogators until they

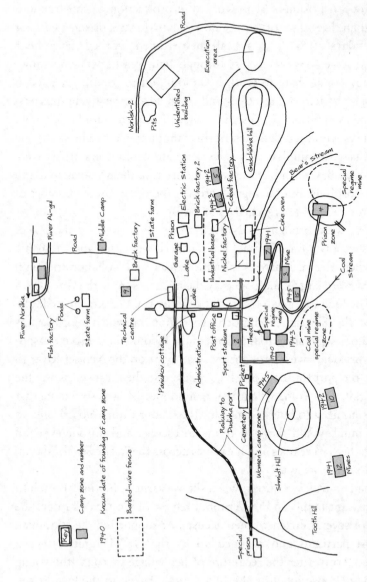

Norilsk Labour Camp and Mining Complex (Gorlag)
Based on a map drawn by Leonid Konovalov, a prisoner of Norilsk, in 1949.
Konovalov's map is unreliable in the numbering of the camp zones, and the
'execution area' may not have been as large as the prisoners imagined it.
(source: MM, f. 1, op. 1, d. 242)

confessed to 'treason against the motherland' (a charge which many of them could not understand because they did not speak Russian). They were then tried (again in Russian) by a military tribunal, which sentenced them to ten years in Norilsk. They were put to work on the construction of the Norilsk aerodrome. Despite the freezing temperatures, their only shelter was a large tent, which they shared with several hundred other young Ukrainian women, who had been brought to Norilsk in a similar fashion.[64]

Anna Darvina was sixteen and studying at a school in the town of Uiar, 120 kilometres east of Krasnoiarsk, when she was rounded up as a 'voluntary labourer' and sent to Norilsk. She was one of about a thousand so-called 'Komsomol volunteers' who were brought to Norilsk by force from the Krasnoiarsk region in September 1943. 'A large crowd met us at the station in Norilsk. There was a choir and an orchestra,' Anna remembers.

It was cold when we stepped out of the train. We had left in our sandals, but there was already snow on the ground. The people were very poor. They were dressed in rags. But they gave us blankets and felt boots. They thought that we were volunteers. They had been told that we were the orphans of soldiers who had been killed in the war. But in fact all of us had been captured and sent by the military, without any choice on our part. There was a war, and the military needed all of us, however weak, as labourers.[65]

Semyon Golovko was eighteen when he came to Norilsk in 1943. He was born in the Stavropol region of the northern Caucasus, the second of eleven children in a Cossack family which was categorized as 'kulak' and lost all its property during collectivization. Semyon's father and older brother were both killed in the Red Army near Smolensk in June 1941. As the oldest surviving male, Semyon was left in charge of his family. He gave up school and went to work as a tractor driver on a collective farm to support his mother and the other nine children. In September 1942, as the Germans overran the northern Caucasus, Semyon joined the Red partisans, but he was captured by the Germans, who forced him to join their auxiliary police (*Schutzmannschaft*) by threatening to shoot his family. Four months later, the area was recaptured by the Red Army. Semyon was arrested as a 'collaborator with the enemy' and sent to Norilsk. He worked in various mines and factories and soon became a brigade leader and even a Stakhanovite. He won several medals for his contribution to the war effort as a Gulag labourer.[66]

Olga Lobacheva, a leading mineralogist, was sent to Norilsk in 1944. Following the arrest of her husband in 1938, she was sentenced to eight years for 'counter-revolutionary agitation' and ultimately ended up in a labour camp in Siberia. While in the camp, she gave birth to a son who was sent to an orphanage. In the autumn of 1943, Olga was drafted as a specialist by the NKVD and assigned to the Norilsk mines. For six weeks she was imprisoned in Marinsk, 350 kilometres west of Krasnoiarsk, where a whole convoy of geologists and other mining specialists was gradually assembled from the labour camps of Siberia. Transferred to Krasnoiarsk for the long journey north, Olga was declared unfit to travel by a medical commission (she had pneumonia) and was sent to the Taishet labour camp, 400 kilometres to the east. Taishet was known by prisoners as the 'camp of death' because it was full of invalids and old people who were left to die. Shortly after her arrival in Taishet, Olga was drafted once again by the NKVD. Despite her pneumonia, she was reassigned for immediate transfer to Norilsk. She travelled in a convoy of engineers, electricians, metallurgists and builders, flying from Krasnoiarsk in a special NKVD plane to speed up the arrival of these specialists. Olga worked as a geological researcher in the technical sector, where she was reunited with many of her friends from university.[67]

Among those friends was Elizaveta Drabkina, the young girl who had recognized her long-lost father Sergei Gusev, the Bolshevik revolutionary, in the canteen of the Smolny Institute in October 1917. Elizaveta had been arrested as a 'Trotskyist' in December 1936 and sentenced to five years in the Iaroslavl jail. In 1939, her sentence was extended to fifteen years, and she was sent to serve them in the Norilsk labour camp. For the first three years she worked in the coal mines, but then she was transferred to the technical sector, where she was employed as a translator of imported books and manuals. Elizaveta worked like a real Stakhanovite, from genuinely patriotic commitment. She felt that she was contributing to the Soviet economy through her work in the labour camp. Between 1941 and 1945 she appealed to join the army at the front on four separate occasions. Her appeals were denied, but Elizaveta was nonetheless rewarded for her industry with a room in the zone for specialists. She lived there with her husband, Aleksandr Daniets, the son of a repressed Bolshevik, who had been arrested in 1938. They had previously been friends in Leningrad. Their former neighbours from Norilsk recall them as a quiet couple with a dog. Drabkina was deaf, the result of an accident in the mines, and this made it hard for them to socialize. They had a small circle of friends with whom they formed a Marxist study group – the works of Marx and Lenin were available in the camp's library – but they were suspicious of outsiders. In 1945, a member of their circle was arrested and later executed for 'counter-revolutionary agitation'. Suspecting that their circle had been infiltrated by a prisoner working for the NKVD, they closed down their study group and went underground, meeting their friends secretly on the road to the graveyard when they walked their dog. Elizaveta and her husband were both fluent in several languages. When they were at home, they spoke in French to protect themselves against unwanted listeners in the next room.[68]

4

Some time at the end of the 1940s Akhmatova was walking with Nad-ezhda Mandelshtam in Leningrad when she suddenly remarked: 'To think that the best years of our life were during the war when so many people were being killed, when we were starving and my son was doing forced labour.' For anyone who suffered from the terror of the 1930s, as Akhmatova had done, the war must have come as a release. As Pasternak would write in the epilogue of *Doctor Zhivago* (1957), 'When the war broke out, its real horrors, its menace of real death, were a blessing compared with the inhuman power of the lie, a relief because it broke the spell of the dead letter.' The relief was palpable. People were allowed to act in ways that would have been unthinkable before the war. By necessity, they were thrown back on their own initiative – they spoke to one another and helped each other without thinking of the political dangers to themselves; and from this spontaneous activity a new sense of nationhood emerged. The war years, for this reason, would come to be recalled with nostalgia. They were remembered as 'a period of vitality', in the words of Pasternak, as an 'untrammelled, joyous restoration of the sense of community with everyone'.[69]

For the writer Viacheslav Kondratiev, that feeling of belonging was the defining feature of the time:

We are proud of those years, and this nostalgia for the front stirs all of us, not because they were the years of our youth, which is always recalled with fondness, but because then we felt ourselves to be citizens in the truest sense of the word. It was a feeling which we did not have before or afterwards.[70]

The renewed sense of personal and collective responsibility was evident, especially in the period from 1941 to 1943, when the infrastructure of the Stalinist regime had virtually collapsed as a result of the German invasion, and people had to rely on their own resources and make their own decisions about how to act. The historian Mikhail Gefter, then an army doctor, describes these years as a period of 'spontaneous de-Stalinization':

Before our eyes – a person subject to the whim of fate, unexpectedly, in the face of death, finds the freedom to take command of himself . . . As an eye-witness and a historian I can attest: in '41 and '42 there were a multitude of situations and decisions that constituted a process of spontaneous de-Stalinization . . . We remained Russian, Soviet, but in those years the universal human spirit also entered into us.

For Ada Levidova, who spent the war years working in a medical institute, this spontaneous de-Stalinization was reflected in a shift of power from the Party officials, who formally controlled the hospital, to the doctors and nurses: 'There were far too many instances when a crucial life-and-death decision needed to be made by the people on the job, without authorization from the authorities, when we had to act, or improvise, without regard for the official rules.'[71]

People had a sense of being needed by the war effort. They felt that they could make a difference. From this feeling of involvement they derived a sense of civic freedom and individual responsibility. Hedrick Smith records a conversation in the house of a Jewish scientist in the early 1970s. The scientist had said that the war was 'the best time of our lives' and explained to his shocked friends:

Because at that time we all felt closer to our government than at any other time in our lives. It was not their country then, but our country. It was not they who wanted this or that to be done, but we who wanted to do it. It was not their war, but our war. It was our country we were defending, our war effort.

According to Kondratiev, a veteran of the front, even the most humble soldier, who was constantly abused and made to feel insignificant by his commanding officers, became his own general when he went into the attack on the battlefield:

There nobody can command you. There you're in control of everything. And in defence too you have to have your wits about you ... otherwise the Germans will break through ... You feel as if you hold the fate of Russia in your hands, and that everything might turn out differently, but for you. In peacetime in our society, nothing depended on the individual. But in the war it was different: everybody felt their personal involvement in the victory.[72]

For the 'generation of 1941', which had grown up in the shadow of the cult of Stalin and the Party, this new freedom was a shock to the system. 'The military catastrophe of 1941–2 forced us for the first time to question Stalin,' recalls the literary historian Lazar Lazarev, who went to war directly from high school in 1941:

Before the war we had not questioned anything, we believed all the propaganda about Stalin, and believed in the Party as the embodiment of justice. But what we saw in the first years of the war forced us to reflect on what we had been told. It made us question our beliefs.[73]

The atmosphere presaged the change of values in 1956, the opening year of the Khrushchev 'thaw', when Julia Neiman wrote the poem '1941':

Those Moscow days ... The avalanche of war ...
Uncounted losses! Setbacks and defeats!
Yet, comrades of that year, tell the whole truth:
Bright as a torch it flamed, that shining year!
Like crumbling plaster, subterfuge flaked off,
And causes were laid bare, effects revealed;
And through the blackout and the camouflage
We saw our comrades' faces – undisguised.
The dubious yardsticks that we measured by –
Forms, questionnaires, long service, rank and age –
Were cast aside and now we measured true:
Our yardsticks in that year were valour, faith.
And we who lived and saw these things still hold

> Fresh in the memory, and sacred still,
> The watches, rooftops, and barrage balloons,
> The explosive chaos that was Moscow then,
> The buildings in their camouflage attire,
> The symphony of air raids and all-clears –
> For then at last seemed real
> Our pride as citizens, pure-shining pride.[74]

As citizens claimed new freedoms, the ideological influence of the Party and the cult of Stalin inevitably weakened. Although it nearly doubled in its size during the war years, the Party lost much of its pre-war revolutionary spirit, as the most committed Bolsheviks were killed in the fighting of 1941–2. By 1945, over half the Party's 6 million members were serving in the armed forces, and two-thirds of them had joined it in the war. This rank and file differed significantly from the Stalinist Party of the 1930s: it was more pragmatic, not so ideological (or even trained in Marxist-Leninist ideology), less inclined to view the world in terms of class and impatient with bureaucracy.[75] The new mood was summarized by *Pravda* when it argued, in June 1944, in sharp contrast to the Party's pre-war principles, that the 'personal qualities of every Party member should be judged by his practical contribution to the war effort' rather than by his class origins or ideological correctness. According to Lazarev, who joined the Party from the ranks, Bolshevik ideology played almost no role in the war, and the pre-war slogans that advanced the cult of Stalin and the Party lost much of their power and significance:

There is a legend that the soldiers went into attacks shouting, 'For Stalin!' But in fact we never mentioned Stalin, and when we went into battle it was 'For the Motherland!' that we shouted. The rest of our war cries were obscenities.

The war gave rise to a whole new repertoire of anti-Stalin rhymes and songs, like this one from 1942:

> Dear Joseph Stalin!
> Now you've lost Tallin!
> The food we get is bad!
> You'll lose Leningrad![76]

For many people the war was a time of liberation from fear of the regime. It was a time, perhaps the only time in their entire lives, when they were forced to act without regard for the political consequences of their actions. The 'real horrors' of the war focused all their attention, while the potential terrors that awaited them at the hands of the NKVD somehow seemed less threatening, or easier to cope with in the general struggle. During the conversation recorded by Hedrick Smith, the Jewish scientist recalled an incident from the war years:

I was in Kazan in my room sleeping . . . and in the middle of the night someone from the Cheka came and woke me up, and I was not afraid. Think of it! He knocked on my door in the middle of the night and woke me up and I was not afraid. If some Chekist had done that in the thirties, I would have been terrified. If it had happened after the war, just before Stalin died, it would have been just as frightening . . . But then, during the war, I was absolutely unafraid. It was a unique time in our history.[77]

To an important extent, the new sense of freedom was a product of the regime's relaxation of political and even religious controls after 1941. Children born to 'enemies of the people' especially benefited. If they were willing or qualified to work in areas that met an urgent wartime need, their spoilt biographies were much less of an obstacle than they had been before the war. Though not official policy, it was common practice for pragmatic officials to turn a blind eye to the social background of applicants for jobs and student courses that needed to be filled.

Yevgeniia Shtern was born in 1927 to a family of Bolshevik officials in Moscow. Her father was arrested and shot two years later as a 'German spy'. Her mother was sentenced to five years in the labour camps of Kolyma. Yevgeniia was sent to live with her grandmother in the Altai region of Siberia. In 1943, she returned to Moscow and lived with her aunt. The teachers at her school, where she was allowed to study as an external student, recognized her capabilities and protected her. One day in the summer of 1944, Yevgeniia was passing by the university when she saw a notice inviting high-school students to apply to the Physics Faculty of Moscow University. She had never liked physics, she was not good at it, but she recognized the opportunity to enter Moscow University, the most prestigious university in the Soviet Union. Encouraged by her aunt, she decided to try. 'I was just sixteen,' recalls Yevgeniia.

In the questionnaire [which she was obliged to fill out as part of the application process] I did not mention that my parents had been arrested. I wrote that my father had been killed ... I think that they would have taken me in any case, because there were not enough people wanting to study physics, and at that time, in 1944, there was an urgent need for physicists.[78]

The war years offered similar opportunities to Antonina Golovina, the 'kulak' daughter who learned to conceal her social origins. Antonina's ambition had been to study at the Institute of Medicine in Leningrad. She applied in 1941, but while her high-school grades were certainly good enough for her to be accepted at the institute, she was refused admission probably, as she believes, on the grounds of her suspicious social origins. The outbreak of the war ended her dreams of Leningrad, which came under siege. Antonina worked as an assistant teacher in the village school at Pestovo and then in 1943 applied to Sverdlovsk University. An old school friend, who was a student there, had suggested that she might get in because Sverdlovsk needed doctors and the university had relaxed the rules of admission to the Faculty of Medicine. Despite her 'kulak' origins, Antonina was admitted to the university. She soon emerged as one of the best students in the faculty. She had the full support of her professors, who kept the secret of her social origins. 'For the first time in my life I was allowed to progress on my own merits,' she reflects. After the siege of Leningrad was lifted, in January 1944, Antonina applied to the Leningrad Institute of Pediatrics to continue with her studies. She did not have a passport to live in Leningrad, and her 'kulak' origins would normally have disqualified her, despite the warm letters of support from her teachers at Sverdlovsk. But Leningrad desperately needed pediatricians to care for the tens of thousands of sick and disturbed children orphaned by the siege. In the words of the official who recommended Antonina's admission to the institute, it would have been 'a sin to reject such a student at this time'. Without a passport to live in Leningrad, Antonina could not be officially registered as a student at the institute, so she became one of fourteen 'illegals' (all from 'alien class backgrounds') studying *ex officio*, all housed together in a basement room. As an *ex officio* student Antonina could not get a stipend. She could not take out library books, or eat in the student cafeteria. She worked illegally as a waitress in the evenings to support herself. In 1945, the fourteen students were at last put on a legal footing, provided with passports and registered at the institute. The director of the institute, a pragmatic Communist, had appealed on their behalf to the Leningrad Party Committee, insisting that the students were urgently required for the city's needs. For Antonina this official recognition was a major boost to her confidence. It partially released her from the fear that she had felt so acutely before the war, enabling her to think more critically about the nature of the Soviet regime and its consequences for her family.[79]

The regime's concessions in the religious sphere also had wide-ranging effects. The relaxation of controls on the Church led to a dramatic revival of religious life from 1943 to 1948 (when most of the concessions were reversed). Hundreds of churches reopened, attendances increased, and there was a revival of religious weddings, baptisms and funerals.

Ivan Bragin's family had strong connections to the Church. He counted several priests among his relatives, and his wife, Larisa, was the daughter of a priest. Those connections were rigorously concealed in the 1930s, when the family was dispossessed as 'kulaks' and sent into exile in Krasnokamsk: Ivan and Larisa did not go to church; they did not wear crosses; they hid their icons in a chest and hung a portrait of Stalin above the doorway where the icons were traditionally displayed. They encouraged their children to join the Pioneers and participate in anti-religious activities in order to avert suspicion. But after 1944 the family began to return to religious ways. The children were all baptized in a nearby village church, which had been reopened in 1944 after the villagers collected money for a tank. Larisa brought out her most precious icon from the chest and fixed it in a corner of the room, where it was half-hidden only by a curtain. She crossed herself before the icon when she entered or left the room. 'Gradually,' recalls her daughter Vera,

we began to celebrate religious holidays, and Mama told us about them. She would prepare a special dish, although that was difficult during the war. She always said: 'We have food on the table, so it is Shrovetide. And if there is none, then it is Lent.' We celebrated Christmas, Epiphany, the Annunciation, Easter, Trinity.[80]

Perhaps the most striking aspect of the war years was a new freedom of expression. People spoke openly about the loss of relatives, they related feelings and opinions in a way that would previously have been unthinkable and they engaged in political debates. The war's uncertainties, including the uncertain survival of Soviet power, had removed the fear of talking about politics and even criticizing the regime.

Vera Pirozhkova recalls returning to her home town of Pskov in 1942: 'Everyone was talking openly about politics and without any fear.' She records an argument between two sisters: one aged twenty-two, the wife of a Red Army officer at the front, the other, seventeen, who was an 'ardent anti-Communist'. When the elder sister denied any knowledge of the labour camps, the younger one was scornful: 'You didn't know?' she said. 'The whole country knew about the camps, and you didn't? You didn't want to know, you hid behind the back of your officer and pretended to yourself that everything was fine.' On another occasion, the younger woman criticized her older sister for claiming not to know about the problem of unemployment, even though a number of their relatives had not been able to find jobs before the war. 'How could you not know? Unless after your marriage you completely forgot about your family and did not care how poor we were.' Before the war, comments Vera, when the older sister's husband had been living with the rest of the family, no one would have dared to speak so freely, if only from the fear that he might report them.[81]

Food queues were a particularly fertile breeding ground for political discussion and complaint. Anger and frustration united people there and gave them courage to speak out (which is also why the queues were frequented by informers and police). 'Anti-Soviet views are openly expressed when supplies run out,' reported one group of informers from various lines outside Moscow shops in April 1942. An old man in a queue for kerosene was heard to say: 'The Party-parasites are everywhere. The bastards! They have everything, while we workers have nothing but our necks from which to hang.' To which a woman added: 'And that's why we are in a mess.' In another Moscow queue the following conversation was reported by informers:

DRONIN [a soldier]: It would be better if we were living now as we lived before 1929. As soon as they introduced the kolkhoz policy everything went wrong. I ask myself – what are we fighting for? What is there to defend?

SIZOV [a soldier]: It is only now that I have understood that we are slaves. There were people like [the Bolshevik leader] Rykov who tried to do something good for us, but they got rid of him. Will there ever be another person who thinks of us?

KARELIN [a carpenter]: They told us that the Germans were all ragged and louse-ridden, but when they arrived in our village near Mozhaisk, we saw how they were eating meat and drinking coffee every day . . .

SIZOV: We are all hungry, but the Communists say that everything is fine.[82]

Tongues were loosened to a remarkable degree. Roza Novoseltseva recalls an encounter with a Moscow shoemaker in 1942. She had just returned to the capital, five years after the arrest of her parents. She had never really questioned the Soviet regime about their arrests. Although she believed in her parents' innocence, she was prepared to accept that 'enemies of the people' actually existed, 'alien elements that needed to be cleared away', as she herself described them in 1938. But her visit to the shoemaker changed her view. While he fixed her shoes, he cursed the Soviet government, blaming it for all the country's woes and telling her the story of his own unjust arrest during the 1930s. He clearly did not think about the dangers of talking in this way to a complete stranger like Roza. The frankness with which he spoke – something she had never before encountered – made her 'stop and think about these things' for the first time in her life.[83]

The army's ranks were also an important arena for criticism and debate. The small groups of trusted comrades formed by the soldiers at the front produced a safe environment for talk. 'We cursed the leadership,' recalls one veteran. 'Why were there no planes? Why were there not enough artillery rounds? What was the reason for all the chaos?' Another veteran recalls that soldiers had no fear of repression for speaking their minds: 'They thought little about it . . . Soldiers living with the risk of death were not afraid of anything.' In the spring of 1945, Lazar Lazarev returned from the front to spend some time in a Kuibyshev hospital:

Like all soldiers, I had a loose tongue in 1945. I said exactly what I thought. And I spoke about the things in the army that I thought were a scandal. The doctor in the hospital warned me to 'watch my tongue', and I was surprised, because I thought, like the rest of the soldiers, that I had a right to speak, having fought for the Soviet state . . . I often heard the soldiers from villages complain about the collective farms, and how it was necessary to sweep them all away when the war was won. Freedom of speech was at such a level that it was thought entirely normal to air views like these.[84]

From this kind of talk the outline of a new political community began to emerge. The increased trust and interaction between people gave rise to a renewed civic spirit and sense of nationhood. At the heart of this transformation was a fundamental change of values. Before the war the climate of general mistrust was such that no community was capable of forming on its own, without direction by the Party; all civic duties were performed as orders from the state. But in the war civic duties addressed something real, the defence of the country, which brought people together, independent of state control, and created a new set of public attitudes.

Many people remarked on the change. The writer Prishvin felt, as he noted in his diary in 1941, that 'people have got kinder since the war began: everybody is united by their fear for the motherland'. He also felt that class divisions had been erased by the national spirit that had arisen in the war. 'Only now do I begin to understand that "the people" is not something visible, but something deep within us,' he wrote in 1942. 'The "people" means much more than peasants and workers, even more than writers like Pushkin, Dostoevsky or Tolstoy, it is something within all of us.' Others experienced this wartime national unity as a new feeling of solidarity in their work place. Ada Levidova noted a new 'closeness' among the staff of her medical institute in Leningrad, which cut across the old professional hierarchies:

The institute became our home. The boundaries between the professors and the ordinary workers disappeared. There was the feeling of a common cause, of a shared responsibility for the institute, for the patients, for our colleagues, which made us very close. This spirit of democracy (for that is what it was), the feeling that we were one family, was sensed by all who survived the siege of Leningrad. It remained with us after the war.

The commander of an infantry platoon reported that the war had made him think again about human values and relationships:

At the front people soon discovered what the most important qualities in others were. The war was a test, not just of their strength but of their humanity as well. Baseness and cowardice and selfishness were immediately revealed. Instinctively, if not intellectually, human truths were understood in a very short time – truths which can take many years to learn, if they are learned at all, in times of peace.

Little wonder that the war appeared to many as a sort of spiritual purification, a violent purging of the 'inhuman power of the lie' that had stifled all political discussion in the years before. 'The war forced us to rethink our values and priorities,' remarks Lazarev, 'it enabled us, the ordinary soldiers, to see a different kind of truth, even to imagine a new political reality.'[85]

This rethinking became more widespread as the war neared its end and much of the vast Soviet army entered into Europe, where the soldiers were exposed to different ways of life. By the start of 1944, the Soviets had amassed an army of 6 million men, more than twice the size of the German army on the Eastern Front. In June 1944, just as the Allies launched the invasion of northern France, the Red Army burst through the bulk of the German forces on the Belorussian Front, retaking Minsk by 3 July and pushing on through Lithuania to reach the Prussian border by the end of August. Meanwhile the Soviet troops on the Ukrainian Front swept through eastern Poland towards Warsaw. In the southern sector, where the German forces soon collapsed, the Red Army swept across Romania and Bulgaria to reach Yugoslavia by September 1944. The Soviet advance was relentless. By the end of January 1945, the troops of the Ukrainian Front had penetrated deep into Silesia, while Zhukov's Belorussian Front had reached the Oder River and had Berlin in its sights.

Hardly any of the Soviet soldiers had ever been to Europe. Most of them were peasant sons who had come into the army with the small-world views and customs of the Soviet countryside and an image of the wider world shaped by propaganda. They were not prepared for what they discovered. 'The contrast between the standard of living in Europe and our own in the Soviet Union was an emotional and psychological shock, and it changed the views of millions of troops,' observed Simonov. Soldiers saw that ordinary people lived in better houses; they saw that the shops were better stocked, despite the war and looting by the Red Army; and that the private farms they passed on their way to Germany, even in their ruined state, were far superior to the Soviet collective farms. No amount of propaganda could persuade them to discount the evidence of their own eyes.

The encounter with the West shaped the soldiers' expectations of the future in their own country. Peasant soldiers were convinced that with the end of the war the collective farms would be swept away. There were many rumours of this sort in the army, most of them involving promises by Zhukov to the troops. Retold in a million letters from the soldiers to their families, these expectations spread throughout the countryside, resulting in a series of peasant strikes on the collective farms. Other soldiers talked about the need to open the churches, about the need for more democracy, even about the dismantling of the Party system root and branch. The film director Aleksandr Dovzhenko remembered a discussion with a military driver, a 'Siberian lad', in January 1944. 'Our life is bad,' the driver had said. 'And all of us, you know, just wait for changes and improvements in our lives. We all wait. All of us. It's just that we don't all say it.' 'I was astonished by what I heard,' Dovzhenko noted in his diary afterwards. 'The people have a tremendous need for some other kind of life. I hear it everywhere. The only place where I don't hear it is among our leaders.'[86]

Officers were in the forefront of this army movement for reform. They openly expressed their criticisms of the Soviet system and their hopes for change. One lieutenant wrote to the Soviet president Mikhail Kalinin in 1945 with a 'series of considerations to put to the next meeting of the Presidium of the Supreme Soviet'. Having been to Maidanek, the Nazi death camp in Poland, and having seen the consequences of a dictatorship in Germany, the officer demanded an end to arbitrary arrests and imprisonment in the Soviet Union, which, he said, had its own Maidaneks; the abolition of the collective farms, which he knew were a disaster from what he had been told by his own troops; and a list of other, more minor grievances, which his soldiers had asked him to convey to the president.[87]

Party leaders were understandably anxious about the return of all these men with their reformist ideas. For those who cared to look back at history, there was an obvious parallel with the war against Napoleon in 1812–15, when the returning officers brought back to tsarist Russia the liberal thought of Western Europe which then inspired the Decembrist uprising of 1825. Political activists attending a conference at the Second Belorussian Front in February 1945 called for efforts to counteract the pernicious influence of the West:

After the war of 1812 our soldiers, having seen French life, compared it with the backward life of tsarist Russia. At that time the French influence was progressive ... The Decembrists came to see the need to struggle against the tsarist dictatorship. But today it is different. Maybe the estates of East Prussia are better off than some collective farms. That impression might lead a backward person to conclude in favour of the landed estates against the socialist economy. But that is regressive. So there must be a merciless struggle against this frame of mind.[88]

There was particular concern about the influence of these Western ideas on Party members, more than half of whom were serving in the military by 1945. Their demobilization, the leadership assumed, was bound to infect civilian organizations with dangerous liberal notions of political reform.

In fact such ideas were already spreading among civilians, especially within the political and educated classes. The alliance with Britain and the USA had opened Soviet society to Western influence long before the end of the war. After years of isolation, Soviet cities were flooded with Hollywood films, Western books and goods imported by the Lend-Lease agreement with America. Millions of people got a taste of what life in the West was really like – not the ideal of Hollywood perhaps, but a long way from the gloomy images retailed by Soviet propaganda during the 1930s. Restaurants and commercial shops reappeared on Moscow's streets, suggesting perhaps that something like the NEP might be restored. All this fuelled the expectation that life in the Soviet Union would become easier and more open to the West once the war was over. As the writer and propagandist Vsevolod Vishnevsky put it in a speech to the Society for External Cultural Relations in the summer of 1944:

When the war is over, life will become very pleasant ... There will be much coming and going, and a lot of contacts with the West. Everybody will be allowed to read whatever he likes. There will be exchanges of students, and foreign travel for Soviet citizens will be made easy.

Ideas of political reform were openly discussed by the intelligentsia without fear of censorship (and perhaps with the approval of the Party leadership, which was willing to offer such inducements to keep the people fighting until the end of the war). 'A large circle of the intelligentsia was for liberalization,' recalls Simonov. 'There was a general atmosphere of ideological optimism.' For most people in these circles liberalization meant a 'dialogue' with the government about reform. Few people were prepared to challenge the Communist dictatorship openly, but many wanted greater involvement in political decision-making so that they could open up the system from within. In the words of the poet David Samoilov:

Civic duty to our minds consisted of serving political missions in whose usefulness we believed ... It was our sense that if we took on a civic mission, we were entitled to honesty from the government ... We needed an explanation of its ideas and to be convinced of the wisdom of its decisions. We certainly did not want to be the witless executors of whatever the government was pleased to do.

Even economic reform was an acceptable topic for discussion. Ivan Likhachyov, the director of the Stalin Factory in Moscow, the biggest car producer in the Soviet Union, advanced the idea of introducing an internal market into the industrial economy with more finanicial freedom at the local level to stimulate the workers through higher rates of pay – a programme that would change the fundamental nature of the planned economy. Some economists, too, were openly critical of the planning system and suggested a return to the market to stimulate production after the war.[89]

In this atmosphere of public openness, people felt emboldened to question the principles and values of the Soviet regime in their private lives as well.

Elga Torchinskaia, a teenage Stalinist before the war, recalls a particular episode that made her reconsider her political beliefs. As an activist in the Komsomol, Elga had been sent with a group of students from the university to dig ditches outside Leningrad during the defence of the city in 1941. The students slept in the trenches. One of them was less than satisfied with the conditions and complained to the leader of the brigade, who responded by punishing him, bullying him and finally denouncing him at a meeting of the Komsomol. The student was arrested and sent to jail. For Elga this act of persecution was a moment of awakening. When her father had been arrested, in 1937, she had assumed that he must have done something wrong. She had believed the regime's propaganda about 'enemies of the people'. But now she saw that people were arrested for no reason. She joined a group of students to protest against their friend's arrest, but to no effect. From this point Elga began to view the Komsomol and Party in a different light, not as democratic institutions, but as enclaves of an elite that abused its power. She thought about resigning from the Komsomol and ceased to attend its meetings. Her new perceptions carried over to her actions in the communal apartment where she lived throughout the siege of Leningrad:

It was a pleasant apartment. There were rarely arguments. But there was a woman who lived in the room at the back: she was always arguing with her husband, a drunkard, who beat her. Then she joined the Party. Suddenly she became very self-important. She took over our room. She had bread, she had furniture, she had everything. And I actually dared tell her that I did not agree with the Party. I remember it very well. I could have been arrested.[90]

For Marksena Karpitskaia, working in the Public Library in Leningrad and living on her own in a communal apartment after the arrest of her parents, the moment of awakening came when she herself was summoned to the NKVD headquarters and pressured to join in the denunciation of a retired tsarist officer who hung around in the library and helped the staff with petty tasks in order to stay warm. When she refused, the NKVD interrogator turned to her and said that it was no wonder because she herself was the daughter of an 'enemy of the people and therefore you protect such enemies'. The insult caused something to snap in Marksena, and from some inner sense of justice, some need to defend both the harmless officer and her parents, she launched herself into a brave if foolish act of defiance:

I exploded with rage. I said that nobody had yet proved that my parents were enemies of the people, and that what he was saying was itself a crime. For me that was suddenly clear. But imagine my saying it! Only the foolishness of youth could have possessed me to be so brave! He jumped up and came towards me, as if to hit me. No doubt he was used to beating people. I stood up and grabbed my stool, as if to protect myself. He would have hit me had it not been for the stool. He came to his senses, sat down at his desk and asked for my papers.

A few days later, Marksena received an NKVD order to leave Leningrad. But she refused to go. 'Leningrad was my home, it was everything to me, and the idea of leaving it was inconceivable,' recalls Marksena. 'I thought, why should I go? The only thing I have is this little corner [in the communal apartment]. Let them arrest me, I will not leave.' The next day Marksena was helped by one of the senior librarians, Liubov Rubina, a courageous Party member, who defended many Leningraders from the NKVD terror in the war and post-war years. Rubina had known Marksena's stepfather – a former secretary of the district Party cell – and considered him a decent man. She herself had lost a brother and a sister in the purges of the 1930s (she would lose more relatives in the anti-Jewish Terror of 1948–53). An outspoken Communist, 'she did not mince her words in criticizing Stalin and the other leaders of the Party,' Marksena recalls: 'they were all "reptiles" in her view'. Rubina made up a bed for Marksena in her office and told the library staff to conceal her whereabouts from the police. Hiding the girl was a courageous act that could have landed Rubina in jail, but such was her moral authority among the librarians that no one said a word, and Marksena lived there for the better part of a year. 'She took care of me as if I was her child,' recalls Marksena. Their conversations in Rubina's office were a political education for Marksena, reconnecting her to the values of her parents, who had never had the freedom to speak so openly:

Rubina was an extraordinary person, brave and strong, a Communist idealist, with a deep commitment to justice for everyone. She allowed herself to speak openly to me. We talked about everything – not just about Stalin. There was one conversation in which she told me that collectivization had been a terrible mistake that had ruined the country; and others where she said that the White Sea Canal and other building projects had all been built by prisoners . . . She talked about the arrests [of 1937–8] and said that my parents had been innocent. She explained many things that I had not understood. She talked all night. She knew that I would not betray her, that I would not say a word to anyone, and when she talked to me she opened up her heart.[91]

5

Simonov was in Berlin for the final battle of the war. 'Tanks, more tanks, armoured cars, Katiushas, lorries in their thousands, artillery of every size,' he wrote in his diary on 3 May:

It seems to me that it is not divisions and army corps but the whole of Russia that is entering Berlin from every side . . . In front of the huge and tasteless monument to Wilhelm I a group of soldiers and officers are being photographed. Five, ten, a hundred of them at a time, some with guns and some without, some exhausted, some laughing.[92]

Five days later Simonov was in Karlshorst to report on the signing of the German surrender. He then returned to Moscow for the victory celebrations and parades.

The centre of Moscow was filled with soldiers and civilians for the festivities on 9 May. Samuil Laskin's nephew Mark was struck by the crowds outside the US Embassy on Manezh Square who had 'gathered with home-made placards in support of the Allies and cheered wildly when the American diplomats and soldiers waved to them, many of them holding whiskey bottles, from the windows and the balconies'. It seemed to him the closest thing that he had seen since 1917 to a 'street demonstration for democracy'. Later, Mark returned to the Laskin apartment at Sivtsev Vrazhek for a family celebration. All the Laskins – Samuil and Berta, Fania, Sonia, Zhenia and her son Aleksei – had returned to Moscow from Cheliabinsk in 1943. 'We drank a toast to the victory,' Mark recalls, 'we drank to Stalin (a toast to him was mandatory), and there was joy in all our hearts.' That evening there were even more people in the centre of Moscow to salute a giant portrait of Stalin, the 'father of the nation', which was raised above the Kremlin and illuminated by projectors for crowds to see from miles around.[93]

Six weeks later, on 24 June, there was a formal victory parade on Red Square. Riding on a white Arab stallion, Marshal Zhukov led the column of troops and tanks out on to the square in pouring rain, while military bands played Glinka's patriotic hymn 'Slavsya!' ('Glory to You!'). Two hundred soldiers carrying Nazi flags marched to the Lenin Mausoleum, where they turned to face Stalin and flung their flags to the ground. At a grand banquet for his senior commanders, Stalin made a famous toast to the 'tens of millions' of 'simple, ordinary, modest people . . . who are the little screws (*vintiki*) in the great mechanism of the state, but without whom all of us, marshals and commanders of the fronts and armies, would not be worth a damn'.[94]

The victory was greeted by the Soviet people with universal joy. This was a moment – perhaps the only moment during Stalin's rule – of genuine national unity. Even prisoners in the Gulag's labour camps received the end of the war with patriotic pride: they felt that they had made their contribution to the victory and no doubt hoped that it would mean an amnesty for them. 'Never in my life have I kissed so many people out of simple joy and happiness,' wrote one ALZhIR prisoner to her son on the evening of 9 May:

I even kissed the men. This was the first day in our seven-and-half-year separation when I forgot all my sorrows and suffering. In the settlement [the outer zone of the prison camp] they are playing the accordion, the young ones are dancing. It is as if we were not here, but there, with you.[95]

Gradually the soldiers returned home. Many men and women experienced enormous problems of adjustment to civilian life. Two million came back from the war as invalids. Criminally neglected by the Soviet authorities, from which they received a tiny allowance, they found it hard to get jobs; many ended up as beggars on the street. An even greater number returned from the war with psychological wounds, battle stress or trauma or schizophrenia, but since few of these illnesses were recognized by the Soviet medical profession and veterans themselves were far too stoical to report them, the true scale of the problem remains unknown.[96]

For others the return to 'normal life' was full of disappointments. The loss of homes and families, the difficulty of communicating their experiences in the war to friends and relatives, the absence of the comradeship and sense of mutual understanding they shared with other soldiers at the front – all led to widespread depression in the post-war years. 'Most of my old comrades from the army drank themselves to death or killed themselves when the war ended – one killed himself only recently,' Kondratiev wrote in the 1990s.

We felt unwanted, handicapped ... We were insulted when Stalin compared us to nothing more than the 'little screws' in a machine. That is not how we felt at the front. We thought then that we held the destiny of Russia in our hands, and we acted accordingly, in the belief that we were citizens.

Reflecting on these years, Kondratiev wrote:

We had beaten the Fascists and liberated Europe, but we did not return feeling like victors, or rather, we felt that way for a very short time, while we still had hopes for change. When those hopes did not come true, the disappointment and the apathy, which we had at first explained to ourselves as physical exhaustion from the war, seized hold of us completely. Did we really understand that, by saving Russia, our Motherland, we had also saved the Stalinist regime? Perhaps not. But even if we had understood it, we would have fought in the same way, preferring our own home-grown totalitarianism to the Hitlerite version, because it is easier to bear violence from one's own people than from foreigners.[97]

Families were harder to reconstitute than the soldiers had imagined in their letters home: sweethearts did not wait for them; women did not match up to the soldiers' dreams; and marriages collapsed from the strains of separation and return. In his play *So It Will Be*, written in the summer of 1944, Simonov tells the story of an officer who returns to Moscow from the front. His wife and child have long gone missing in German-occupied territory, and the officer is sure that they are lost, so he starts a new life, marrying the daughter of a professor. The play's main idea, that people would need to move on when the war ended, could not have been further from the message of 'Wait For Me'.

The ending of the war coincided with the first mass release of prisoners from the Gulag. The eight-year sentence received by millions of 'politicals' in 1937–8 came to an end in 1945–6 (other prisoners, whose sentences expired before 1945, had to wait until the ending of the war for their release). Families began to piece themselves together again. Women took the lead in this recovery, sometimes travelling across the country in search of husbands and children. There were tight restrictions on where former prisoners could live. Most of them were banned from residing in the major towns. So families who wanted to be together often had to move to remote corners of the Soviet Union. Sometimes the only place they could find to settle was in the Gulag zone.

Nina Bulat was released from a labour camp in Magadan in 1945. She travelled 16,000 kilometres to retrieve her daughter Inessa from an orphanage in Iaroslavl (where she had ended up following the death of her grandmother) and bring her back to live with her in the camp in Magadan. She had little choice in this matter: she had been released with 'minus 100', a legal restriction limiting the movement of many former prisoners and prohibiting them from settling in a hundred listed towns.[98]

Maria Ilina's odyssey was even more arduous. Formerly the director of a large textile factory in Kiev, she was arrested as the wife of an 'enemy of the people' in 1937 (her husband was a high-ranking Party official) and sentenced to eight years in the Potma labour camps in Mordovia. She was released in 1945 and set about finding her children. At the time of her arrest, Maria's two-year-old daughter, Marina, and her two older sons, Vladimir and Feliks, were taken to a distribution centre. Their grandmother, already burdened with several grandchildren after the arrest of her other daughter in 1936, had refused to take in the children. Vladimir, who turned sixteen shortly after his arrival in the distribution centre, was arrested there as an 'enemy of the people' and sentenced to five years in a labour camp in Magadan. Feliks was sent to an orphanage in Kiev; Marina to a different orphanage in the nearby town of Bucha and then, in 1939, to another one in Cherkassy, 200 kilometres to the south of the Ukrainian capital. From the Potma camps, Maria had written to officials throughout the Soviet Union to learn where her children had been sent. She found no trace of Vladimir, who died an unrecorded death in Magadan some time before 1942. It took Maria eighteen years to discover anything about Feliks, who had been evacuated with his orphanage to the Terekty region of western Kazakhstan after the outbreak of the war. She finally learned that in 1943, when he was only twelve, Feliks ran away from the orphanage and wandered through the country on his own for several months, ending up in the remote town of Cheremkhovo in the Irkutsk region of Siberia, 2,500 kilometres to the east, where he got a job in a factory.

She had better luck with Marina. It so happened that one of the doctors in the orphanage at Cherkassy, Antonina Mazina, had a sister who was in the same labour camp as Maria. Through her, Maria received regular reports on her daughter's health from the workers of the orphanage. Marina had fallen ill with scarlet fever shortly after her arrival at the Bucha orphanage. She was close to death. But when she arrived at Cherkassy, Antonina nursed her back to health. She took Marina home to live with her own daughter (also called Marina) until she was well enough to return to the orphanage. Antonina brought her food, halva and sweets and told her they were sent by her mother. It was not often true – small amounts of money came irregularly from Potma (and there were some food parcels from Marina's grandmother until the outbreak of the war) – but the doctor understood that the young girl needed hope, she needed to believe in a loving mother, if she was to survive. 'I had no recollection of my mother,' recalls Marina.

I had no real idea what a mother was. But the older children in the orphanage would often speak about their mothers and say how kind they were – they would talk about how happy they had been before the war, about how they were never hungry, because there was always bread and butter, and nice sweet things to eat – so in my mind these sweets, the chocolate and the halva, became symbols of the kind and ideal mother I imagined for myself . . . These were not just sweets that I had been given by anyone – they were 'Mama's sweets'.[99]

Antonina Mazina with her daughter Marina and
Marina Ilina (left), Chimkent, 1944

In 1941, the orphanage was evacuated from Cherkassy to Chimkent
in southern Kazakhstan. But through the workers at the orphanage,
who went on writing to Maria, the family connection was maintained.
Marina was still too young to write to her mother by herself (she did
not receive any schooling until the age of ten) but the caretakers wrote
on her behalf, adding their own standard phrases to present the orphanage in a positive light:

> Chimkent, 1 January 1944
>
> Greeting res[pected] Maria Markovna!
>
> I am writing to you from your daughter Marinochka: 'Mama I remember you.
> Will you be home soon? I miss you very much. I am living well, they feed us well. I
> can sing and dance and soon I will go to school. Mama, send me your photograph.
> Goodbye, I kiss you, your daughter Marinochka.'
>
> I asked her what else she wanted to say, and she said this was enough. Her
> health is fine. She is a happy child, loved by all the other children in our collective
> ... We are writing regularly to her grandmother in Kiev. Photographs cost 22
> roubles in a private booth ... Send the money if you want one ...
>
> Care[taker] Aleksandra Zakharovna Gerasimchuk.[100]

The orphanage returned from evacuation in 1945, but it was relocated
in the ruined buildings of an estate near Lvov, on the Ukrainian border
with Poland, instead of Cherkassy. Antonina disappeared. Marina

waited for her mother. 'I had never seen her picture, I did not know what she looked like, but I felt that I was waiting for my mother, as one might wait for God, a saviour,' she recalls. Mothers came for other children at the orphanage. 'I was madly jealous of them all, and dreamed that my turn would come next.' Marina did not realize that these other children were different from her – their parents were not 'enemies of the people' but had simply been separated from their children in the war – but she overheard the 'whispered conversations' of the caretakers at the orphanage and registered the phrase 'an enemy of the people', which she 'sensed meant something bad that could not be talked about'. Throughout 1945, Marina wrote to her mother on a regular basis. She was by now in the second class at the school in the orphanage and could write in her own hand. Typically the teachers told the children what to write, again including some standard phrases to let their parents know that they were happy at the orphanage. But Marina's letters managed to communicate a different mood. On 17 August she wrote to her mother:

Hello Mama, how are you? Mama, write to me, just one letter, so I know you have got mine. I have written to you seven letters but maybe you have not got one of them. Mama, I am well, I am not sick. It is already winter here and very cold but even so we go to school. Mama, come for me or send for me soon, I am sick of being here . . . The other girls do not hit me but there are sometimes fights. Mama, I suppose that you will come and get me in the spring.

Marina did not know what it would mean to be with her mother, but she was unhappy in the orphanage. She presumed that, like the other children, she had been separated from her mother because of the war and that with the war's end her mother would come for her; then she would enjoy the happy life which the other children had told her all about from their memories of living with their families before the war.[101]

Marina's mother was released from the labour camps at the end of 1945. Forbidden to return to Kiev, she stayed with friends in various towns, while she went in search of her children. Through the husband of her niece, a Party activist and historian, she made contact with the poet Pavlo Tychina, a member of the Stalinist elite in the Ukrainian capital (although in private he was critical of the regime), who found out her daughter's whereabouts. Marina remembers the arrival of her mother in a chauffeur-driven car used by members of the government.

A crowd of children had gathered at the entrance to see who had come for the lucky girl:

'Someone's come for you,' everyone was telling me . . . I came out. There was a strange woman there. I did not know what to do. I was afraid of being punished if I ran up to her and embraced her. I knew that the caretakers did not like it when the children flung their arms around someone who had come for them, because it showed the orphanage in a bad light. We had to give the impression that everything was fine, that we were reluctant to leave . . . But also I was very shy. Mama later said that there was no joy at our meeting, that I looked afraid. I was afraid of everything . . . I remember thinking that I might not be taken. No one had told me that the woman was my mother. And I didn't know it was her, because I had never seen her, not even in a photograph. She was no longer young. She was wearing an old shawl on her head which looked as if it had been loaned to her to help her look respectable. She was not dressed like a lady, she had no furs, no hat, no pretty things. She looked poor and unhappy, like an old woman. She did not look like a mother, not as I had pictured her. What was a mother in my mind? Someone beautiful and smartly dressed, young and striking, full of life . . . But this woman had grey hair.[102]

Marina's mother took her to Lvov, where they stayed in a hotel. They ate soft rolls with cocoa for breakfast, Marina's first experience of such luxuries, which she would remember all her life. After a few days, they went to Cherkassy, where they lived together in a small room in a hostel. Marina went to school. It was very difficult for the two of them to overcome their estrangement. 'For the first weeks I did not talk at all with my mother,' recalls Marina.

I was a wild child from the orphanage and did not want to speak. And she didn't try to force me, she was afraid of me herself . . . Maybe she saw something wild in me and was trying to figure out how to handle it . . . My mother later said that I was not just very shy but also timid and frightened. I would not go to her when she called and would never call for her. For a long time I would say 'vy' [the formal 'you'] to her, and would not call her 'Mama'. Something stopped me saying that, a wall inside me. I had to force myself to call her 'Mama' – it took a long time.

Although they lived together for the next twelve years, they never formed a close relationship. They were both too damaged to open up to each other. Marina's mother died in 1964. She never talked to her daughter about what she had experienced in the labour camps. 'She was too afraid to tell, and I was too afraid to ask,' recalls Marina. Whatever she found out about her mother's life in the labour camps she learned from Maria's Gulag friends. She did not even know about her lost brothers, until 1955, when Feliks reappeared and Maria learned that Vladimir had died. Falling into deep depression, Maria withdrew into herself and never spoke about the past. 'We lived together in almost total silence,' remembers Marina.

It was terrible. To this day, I do not understand. Why was she so frightened to speak? I think she did not want to burden me. She wanted me to be happy, not to make me bitter about life in the Soviet Union. She knew that everything that had been done to our family had been an injustice, but she did not want me to think that.[103]

7

Ordinary Stalinists

(1945–53)

I

The Bushuevs returned to Perm from the ALZhIR labour camp in December 1945. Zinaida and her three children – Nelly, Angelina and their younger brother Slava – moved into a communal apartment on Soviet Street. They shared a room, 11 metres square, with Zinaida's mother and her brother Tolia and his wife, who had two young children of their own. Zinaida slept with her three children in a single bed; Tolia and his wife in another bed with their baby daughter; and the grandmother slept with Tolia's other child. 'It was a nightmare, how we lived,' recalls Angelina, who was then aged ten. 'I don't know how we managed to survive.' When the Bushuevs came back from the labour camp all their possessions fitted into a single bag. 'We had nothing,' recalls Nelly, who was twelve, 'only our bedding and the clothes we were wearing. My mother used to say: "I wonder if we'll ever see the day when we each have a bed?"' The housing block they lived in was totally run down. No repairs had been carried out since the beginning of the war. There was no water or electricity, the roof had fallen in, the sewage system had broken down, and vermin were everywhere.

Perm was a long way from the fighting, but although it was never bombed, it was, like many cities in the rear, in a terrible condition. The mass influx of evacuees from the war zone had placed enormous pressure on the city's housing, food and fuel supplies. The main streets had been turned into allotments for growing vegetables. There were no cars in the city, just a few trucks around the factories. Many of the city's wooden pavements, its benches, fences and most of its trees had disappeared, all chopped up for firewood.[1]

No other country suffered more from the Second World War than the

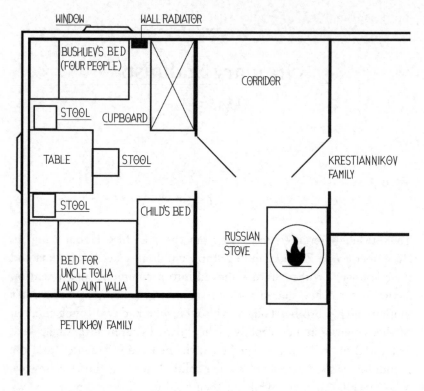

The Bushuev 'corner' room in the communal apartment at
77 Soviet Street, Perm, 1946–8

Soviet Union.* According to the most reliable estimates, 26 million
Soviet citizens lost their lives (two-thirds of them civilians); 18 million
soldiers were wounded (though far less were recognized as such by the
Soviet authorities);† and 4 million disappeared between 1941 and 1945.
The demographic consequences of the war were catastrophic. Three-
quarters of the people killed were men between the ages of eighteen and
forty-five. By the end of the war, there were twice as many women as
men in this age range, and in areas of heavy fighting, such as Stalingrad,

*Proportionately it is arguable that Poland suffered more, but in absolute numbers the Soviet
loss of human life and property was much greater.
†The Soviet authorities took the view that a wounded veteran who had the capacity to work
was not a war invalid. It encouraged wounded veterans to find employment – to toughen up
and thus recuperate – and paid only a small invalidity pension to about 3 million veterans
(B. Fieseler, 'The War Disabled in the Soviet Union 1945–64', paper presented at the School
of Slavonic and East European Studies, London, September 2006).

Voronezh, Kursk and Krasnodar, the ratio was three to one. The imbalance was especially acute in rural areas, because so many peasant soldiers chose not to return to their villages, but settled in the towns, where the demand for factory labour promised jobs. There were villages where no soldiers came back from the war. Soviet agriculture never really recovered from this demographic loss. The kolkhoz became a place for women, children and old men.[2]

The material devastation was unparalleled: 70,000 villages, 1,700 towns, 32,000 factories and 40,000 miles of railway track were destroyed. In areas occupied by the Germans half the housing stock was damaged or destroyed. In Moscow, which was not the worst affected, 90 per cent of the city's buildings had no heating, and 48 per cent no running water or sewage systems, in 1945. In all, 20 million people were left homeless by the war. The Soviet authorities were very slow to respond to the urban housing crisis, which was exacerbated by the massive in-migration of people from the countryside as rural living standards steadily declined. As late as the 1950s, there were still millions of people living in the ruins of buildings, in basements, sheds or dug-outs in the ground.

Simonov, who became a Soviet deputy for the Smolensk region in 1947, received hundreds of appeals for help with housing from his constituents. One typical letter came from an officer and Party member who was demobilized in 1946. He was living in Kaluga with his family of six, including three young children and his elderly mother, in a small unheated basement room, where the roof leaked and water ran down the walls. They had been there since 1941, when their house in Smolensk had been bombed. For two years, the officer petitioned for new accommodation, but there was no reply from the Soviet authorities. With Simonov's assistance the family was finally scheduled for rehousing in Smolensk, but because of bureaucratic delays the move was not completed until 1951.[3]

The Soviet economy emerged from the war in a catastrophic state. Two poor harvests, in 1945 and 1946, brought the country to the brink of famine with at least 100 million people suffering malnutrition. Between 1946 and 1948, an actual famine developed, and in the worst-affected areas, such as the Ukraine, some 2 million people died of starvation.[4] The production of consumer goods had come to a virtual standstill in the war, when industry was geared towards the army's needs. Despite the propaganda promises of a return to the good life, the military demands of the Cold War meant that for another decade the main priorities of Soviet industry would remain the production of steel and iron, energy and armaments. Basic household items were in short supply, especially in provincial towns like Perm, where everybody wore patched-up clothes and worn-out shoes.

Zinaida Bushueva found a job in the offices of a state insurance agency, but her ration was not adequate to feed the family, so she got a job for Nelly as an office messenger, which meant that they received a second ration card. Even so, the Bushuevs only had enough money for bread, soup and potatoes. They could not afford soap, which disappeared entirely from the state shops and could be purchased only in the countryside, where it was made and sold illegally by the peasants. They had only a single pair of shoes for the three children, so they took turns going to school. Zinaida's salary was not enough to buy clothes for the children, so she made them clothes from rags she bought on the market. The children were embarrassed to go out. Angelina recalls an occasion when they were invited by an aunt to the theatre. It was a few years later, in 1950, when material conditions had improved somewhat and all the children had some clothes and shoes, but they still had feelings of embarrassment:

We could not go to the theatre, we were too ashamed. All I had to wear was a three-rouble pair of lace-up canvas sandals, which I wore throughout the year, and the cotton dress which my mother had made for me in 1946. We did not have the money to buy me a coat until 1957. It was a black woollen coat, very poorly made, which we purchased second-hand.[5]

In September 1945, a commission of the Central Committee was appointed to look into a series of large-scale strikes and demonstrations in the defence plants of the Urals and Siberia – just one of many workers' protest movements at that time. The commission concluded that the main reason for the strikes was the chronic shortage of housing and consumer goods which affronted the workers' dignity. Reporting on the strike by the 12,000 workers of Factory No. 174 in Omsk, the commission reported:

The workers and their families are in desperate need of clothes, shoes and linen. In 1945, the average worker received 0.38 items of clothing and 0.7 pairs of shoes. Because of the shortage of shoes and clothing, 450 children did not go to school in 1944, and this year there are about 1,300 children in this situation. Many workers have become so ragged that they cannot show themselves in public places. The workers' families have no cutlery or kitchen utensils, spoons, cups, bowls; they do not have enough beds, stools, washbasins and other essential items. There are long delays in the distribution of rations, which are mostly surrogates. The workers receive barely any soap, salt or kerosene.[6]

Emboldened by their wartime experience, people were no longer frightened to express their discontent. In 1945–6, alone, the NKVD of the Russian Republic received well over half a million letters from Soviet citizens, who wanted to complain about the situation in the country as a whole. One factory worker even gave his own name and address in his angry letter:

So this is what we have come to! This is what you call the state's concern for the material needs of the working people in the Fourth Stalinist Five Year Plan! Now we understand why there are no meetings to discuss these concerns – they might turn into revolts and uprisings. The workers will all say: 'What did we fight for?'[7]

At the end of the war people had been convinced that life in the Soviet Union would improve. According to the writer Ilia Ehrenburg:

Everybody expected that once victory had been won, people would know real happiness. We realized, of course, that the country had been devastated, impoverished, that we would have to work hard, and we did not have fantasies about mountains of gold. But we believed that victory would bring justice, that human dignity would triumph.

The expectation of reform, the greater sense of independence, and the vision of a better life fostered by the encounter with Europe and with Western books and films all came together to create the stirrings of a new political community. People had been altered by the war; they lost some of their old fear and felt freer to talk. In veterans' clubs and student meeting-places, in cafés and beer halls, people allowed themselves the kind of liberty they had first experienced in the war. Everybody spoke about the need to improve the standard of living. Even in the highest circles change was acknowledged as a political necessity. 'Absolutely everyone says openly how they are discontented with life,' one senior general told another in a private telephone conversation, which was

taped by the NKVD in 1946. 'It's what everyone is saying everywhere.'
The Politburo member Anastas Mikoian believed, as he recalls in his
memoirs, that with the ending of the war the country would return to
something like the NEP of the 1920s.[8]

Anti-Stalinist opinions were seldom expressed openly, but they were
a tacit element in the unofficial discourse uniting certain social, ethnic
and occupational groups, prisoners and exiles, and sometimes even
whole cities with reason to be hostile to the regime. In Leningrad the
wartime experience of the siege fostered in the city's population a strong
anti-Moscow feeling, which was widely understood by Leningraders
as a sign of their own civic independence and even opposition to the
Kremlin. This dissent was subtly articulated in the folklore of the siege,
in public monuments to its victims, in the city's jargon, jokes and
anecdotes.

Marianna Gordon was seventeen when she returned to Leningrad
in 1945 from evacuation in Cheliabinsk. Her father had remained in
Leningrad throughout the siege. He was a translator for Soviet trade
delegations, an active theosophist, who had been imprisoned several
times during the 1920s and 1930s. On her return, Marianna noticed
that her father had become more open in voicing his dislike of the
Stalinist regime. She recalls an incident in 1945 when her father made a
comment which, even in the privacy of their home, he would never have
allowed himself to make before the war:

The radio was on, my father was lying on the bed reading, and I was washing
the floor. The singer [Iurii] Levitan came on the radio and sang the song that was
then everywhere, 'Glory to Comrade Stalin! Our Great Leader!' Papa said:
'Marianna, strangle that *kleine Sachs*!'* He was just asking me to switch off the
radio, but I was completely taken aback. Until then I had more or less accepted
the idea that comrade Stalin was the author of our victory, and although I had
my doubts, I had always suppressed them. Papa's words made me think more
sceptically.[9]

Scepticism and dissent were particularly developed in the post-war
student community, where open expressions of opposition were more
common. The generation of students that had grown up during the war
proved to be more independent in their thinking than the children who

---

*'Little [Hans] Sachs' (from Wagner's opera *The Mastersingers of Nuremburg*).

had come of age before 1941. Many of these young people had been exposed to the world of adults in the war, a time when criticisms of the regime were often heard. Their experience bred a special kind of independence and distance from Soviet propaganda and the conformist culture of the Komsomol, although most of them continued to believe in the Communist ideal. Valentina Aleksandrova, the daughter of a Bolshevik official arrested in 1938, describes this clash of values among her fellow students at the Polytechnic Institute in Leningrad, where she enrolled in 1947:

We were definitely patriotic in the spirit of those times: our Motherland was great, we had won the war; we thought of ourselves as the Young Guard and even formed a club by that name.* But we also reacted against what we saw as the corruption of society – the girl who studies badly but gets good grades because she's the daughter of a model worker or an engineer, and so on. There were many things like that which we disliked: the compulsory lectures on the history of the Party; the teacher who made us write the number of our Komsomol membership on the cover of our exercise books; the lack of sincerity we sensed in the propaganda efforts to make us respond a certain way. To us, the Komsomol seemed a place for careerists, and we stayed away from it, forming our own circle at the institute, where we would meet to drink and discuss political ideas. If anyone had overheard our conversations, we would have been arrested, but our dangerous talk just united us more firmly. In our circle to be in opposition to the cult of Stalin was a mark of belonging. After a few drinks somebody might become very daring and sarcastically propose a toast: 'To comrade Stalin!' And we would all laugh.[10]

There were many such informal student groups. Most were small discussion circles where independent thinking was encouraged, along with the reading of a wider range of books than officially approved. But there were also more-political groups, usually watched by the NKVD, which espoused some form of Communist regeneration in reaction to what they saw as the domination of the Komsomol by 'careerist elements'. Although these groups were small, rarely numbering more than a handful of students, the views they expressed were shared by

---

*A reference to *The Young Guard* by Aleksandr Fadeyev, a semi-factual novel about an underground youth organization in occupied Ukraine during the Second World War, which won the Stalin Prize in 1946.

many young people. In Cheliabinsk, for example, the NKVD uncovered a student circle which published its own almanac with mystical poetry and political articles calling for the restoration of the Leninist revolutionary spirit in the Komsomol. A report by a local Party commission in September 1946 found that many of these attitudes were broadly shared by the students of Cheliabinsk, who were just as alienated by the Komsomol, because it failed to address their interests in foreign literature, sexual matters and philosophy.[11]

In 1945, Elena Shuvalova returned with her mother from evacuation to Leningrad and began her studies at the university. During the 1930s, the family had been exiled to Voronezh, as punishment for her father's correspondence with his mother in Germany. Elena's parents were divorced in 1939. The stigma of growing up in exile had left its mark on Elena, who became 'withdrawn' and 'inwardly resistant' to the Soviet system, in her own words. This internal resistance was reinforced by her mother, an artist who specialized in portraits of Stalin, whom she sardonically referred to as 'the father of the nation' when they were alone at home. Brought up by her mother 'to believe in God and always speak the truth', Elena felt increasingly estranged from the social milieu of the university, where she had to hide the truth about her past. Openness and plain speaking became synonymous for her with the assertion of her personality. She started up a discussion circle with her two most trusted friends, Natasha and Elena, who also had spoilt biographies. 'The idea was to be entirely open with each other,' she recalls. 'We held our first session (*zasedanie*) in Elena's room in the communal apartment. We discussed how to attract new members. We needed "our" sort of people – non-conformist types.' The circle never developed, because Elena explained what she was doing to her grandfather, a former tsarist official, who took fright and made her stop. He revealed a family secret to discourage her from her activities: Elena's parents had been punished in the 1930s, not just for their German connections but also for their involvement in a clandestine religious organization.[12]

Liudmila Eliashova enrolled as a student at Leningrad University in 1940, two years after the arrest and execution of her father, a veteran Bolshevik and well-known Leningrad neurologist. Evacuated with the university to Saratov in 1941, she returned with it to Leningrad in 1944 and graduated in 1946. By this time she had already formed dissenting views on the Stalinist regime. A major influence on her thinking was the rector of the university, the brilliant political economist Aleksandr Voznesensky, who rescued many children of the 'enemies of the people' by getting them admitted to the university. Morally courageous and humane, charismatic and handsome, Voznesensky was 'my ideal Soviet man', recalls Liudmila. 'I even wrote to him to tell him so. To some extent he took the place of my father, who had been my ideal man.' Voznesensky's lectures introduced Liudmila to Marx, whose early works, in particular, became her gospel and the basis of her moral opposition to the Stalinist regime. 'Marx was a great humanist,' reflects Liudmila.

After I had listened to Voznesensky's lectures and read Marx's works, I began to understand that true socialism, the Communist idea, was not at all what we had under Stalin. Our task was to return to the true socialist society, in which people like my father would never have been arrested.

Instead of a picture of Stalin, Liudmila kept a portrait of Marx among her things. Every day she would cross herself before it and say, as if in prayer: 'Karl Marx, teach me how to live!' Together with some friends from the university, she formed a Marxist study group, which met once a week in the Public Library. As in the underground revolutionary circles of the nineteenth century, friendships in the study group were made and broken on the basis of political principles. Liudmila remembers a typical incident:

One day in the Public Library, a few of us were standing on the staircase, talking. Somebody said: 'Why has there been such a long delay in the convocation of the Nineteenth Party Congress? Surely it is an infringement of the Party rules!' Since the Eighteenth Party Congress [in 1939] well over five years had gone by [the Nineteenth Congress was not convened until 1952] and this seemed to us to be against the principles of Party democracy [which had called for a Congress every year between 1917 and 1925 and would guarantee one every five years between 1956 and 1986]. Then this girl said: 'Stalin must know best!' I looked at her and thought: 'That's it!' For me she ceased to exist as a human being.*

The group began to read beyond the literature they were offered in classes. Not unlike the later dissidents, they were trying to discern a

---

*That person (who is still alive) went on to become the head of the Department of Party History at Leningrad University.

'moral code', as Liudmila puts it, 'by which we might live more honestly, without dissimulation, in a society whose basic principles negated any moral code'.

From Marx we learned about Dante, whose motto he quotes: 'Follow your own path and let the others talk.' We often discussed this and came to the conclusion that, though it is impossible to ignore the opinions of others completely, one should generally try to follow one's own path, without compromising one's principles or conforming to the crowd.[13]

Stalin was quick to rule out any idea of political reform. In his first major speech of the post-war era, on 9 February 1946, he made it clear that there would be no relaxation of the Soviet system. Speaking against the backdrop of mounting Cold War tensions, Stalin called for renewed discipline and sacrifices on the part of the Soviet people to recover from the damage of the war and prepare for the next global conflict, which the capitalist system was bound to bring about ('as long as capitalism exists there will be wars and the Soviet Union must be prepared'). Stalin ordered his subordinates to deliver 'a strong blow' against any talk of democracy, even before such talk had become widespread. Censorship was tightened, particularly in regard to memoirs of the war, in which the collective experience tended to prompt ideas of reform.[14] The NKVD was strengthened and reorganized as two separate bureaucracies in March 1946: the MVD was henceforth to control domestic security and the Gulag system; while the MGB (the forerunner of the KGB) was placed in charge of counter-intelligence and foreign intelligence, although since the regime's enemies were *ipso facto* 'foreign spies', the MGB's mandate spilled over into the surveillance of the domestic scene as well. The post-war years saw no return to the level of the terror of the 1930s, but every year several tens of thousands of people – many of them Jews and other nationalities accused of siding with the West in the Cold War – were arrested and convicted by the courts for 'counter-revolutionary' activities.[15]

Immediately after the end of the war, Stalin launched a new purge of the army and the Party leadership, where rival power-centres, formed by groups perceived as 'liberal' reformers, had emerged as a challenge to his personal authority. Stalin's first priority was to cut down the top army leaders, who enjoyed enormous popularity as a result of the victory of 1945 and, in the case of Marshal Zhukov, had become the focus of the people's hopes for reform.* The MGB began to monitor the telephone conversations of senior military commanders. A file was kept on Zhukov, whose grandeur had reached intolerable proportions. As the military administrator of the Soviet zone of occupation in Germany, Zhukov had given a press conference in Berlin, at which he claimed the lion's share of the credit for the Soviet victory. Denounced by Stalin for his boastfulness, Zhukov was recalled to Moscow, summoned before the Military Council and condemned by Politburo members as a Bonapartist threat to the Soviet state (all but one of the generals at the meeting spoke up in defence of the marshal). On Stalin's orders, Zhukov was demoted to commander of the Odessa Military District; he was later sent to an obscure posting in the Urals (it could have been much worse, for there were rumours that Zhukov had been plotting a military coup against Stalin). Zhukov's name vanished from the Soviet press. He was written out of Soviet accounts of the Great Patriotic War, which portrayed Stalin as the sole architect of victory. Other popular military heroes shared a similar fate: Marshal Antonov, the former Chief of Staff, was exiled to the command of the Transcaucasian Military District; the names of Rokossovsky, Konev, Voronov, Vatutin and many others were erased from the public record of the war; and several senior commanders were executed or imprisoned on trumped-up treason charges between 1946 and 1948.[16]

Stalin also turned against the Party leadership of Leningrad, a city with a strong sense of independence from Moscow and a vibrant literary culture rooted in the European values of the nineteenth century, which made it a stronghold of the intelligentsia's reform hopes. Leningrad's Party leaders were neither liberals nor democrats: they were technocrats who believed in the rationalization of the Soviet system. During the war, a number of them had risen to senior positions in Moscow, largely due to the powerful patronage of Andrei Zhdanov, the former Party boss of Leningrad. In the post-war years, Zhdanov was in charge of the Party apparatus and oversaw ideological matters as well as foreign policy. By the time he died of a heart attack in 1948, the Politburo contained a

---

*There is a legend about the victory parade in Moscow on 24 June 1945, when Zhukov led the columns of troops across Red Square riding on a white Arab stallion. It was said that Stalin had intended to lead the parade but that at the rehearsal he had been thrown by the stallion. The legend is untrue, but it suggests the popular desire for Stalin to be toppled by Zhukov.

disproportionate number of Leningraders, including two, Nikolai Voznesensky and Aleksei Kuznetsov, who were widely seen as potential
successors to Stalin. Like his brother Aleksandr, Rector of Leningrad
University, Nikolai Voznesensky was a political economist. He was
young, dynamic and good-looking. As the Director of Gosplan, Voznesensky had been the mastermind behind the planning of the Soviet war
economy. After 1945, he looked for ways to rationalize the reconstruction of Soviet industry, embracing many ideas from the NEP,* which
had done so much to revitalize the country after the destruction of the
Civil War. Kuznetsov was the Central Committee secretary in charge of
security affairs, but he was better known as a military hero from the
siege of Leningrad, which was the main reason for his popularity in
Leningrad, as well as a source of constant irritation to Stalin.

In 1949, Stalin sent Grigorii Malenkov, the head of the Party Secretariat and a bitter enemy of Voznesensky and Kuznetsov, to inspect the
work of the Leningrad Party organization. The pretext of Malenkov's
visit was to investigate allegations of fixed elections by the district Party
committees, but his real purpose was to break the city's power-base.
The first target was the Museum of the Defence of Leningrad, whose
exposition presented the history of the siege as a collective act of heroism
by the city's people largely independent of the Party's leadership. The
Museum was closed down and its leaders arrested. The Museum's
invaluable depository of personal documents and recollections was
destroyed, as if to erase all memory of the city's independence and
bravery. Then, in August 1949, Kuznetsov and Voznesensky were
arrested, along with several other independent-minded Leningrad
officials, including the rector of the university, in what became known
as the 'Leningrad Affair'. Accused of various trumped-up charges, from
spying for Britain to debauchery, Voznesensky and the others were
found guilty in a secret trial and shot on the same day in October 1950.

The post-war political clampdown was matched by a return to the
austerity of the planned economy. As Stalin warned in his 9 February
1946 speech, there could be no relaxation in a situation of international

---

*Voznesensky did not advocate a restoration of the mixed economy but he did favour lifting
state controls on prices so that they would better reflect supply and demand. He also
advocated an expansion of the cooperative sector, and more investment in consumer industries, such as textiles, both measures which had been important to the early success of
the NEP.

tension. A new Five Year Plan was introduced that year. Huge building projects were drawn up for the restoration of the country's infrastructure. The fantastic targets set for industrial production could only be fulfilled by a workforce of Stakhanovites. Soviet propaganda cajoled the population to brace itself for one more period of sacrifice, sweetening its message with the usual promise that hard work would be rewarded with cheap consumer goods. However, for most of the population, there was little reason for faith in such promises. Rising prices on the few available basic household goods were deflating real wages. To deal with the problem of inflation the regime introduced a currency reform in 1947, exchanging old for new money at a rate of ten to one, which drastically reduced the spending power of the rural population, in particular. It wiped out peasant savings from the market sale of garden vegetables and handicrafts during the war, when there had been a relaxation of restrictions against petty trade.[17]

Forced labour played an increasingly important part in the post-war Soviet economy, according to a policy dictated by Stalin and his 'kitchen cabinet' of advisers. With the ending of the war the pool of unpaid labour available for exploitation by the state grew enormously. Apart from Gulag prisoners and labour army conscripts, there were 2 million German POWs, and about another million from other Axis nationalities, who were mostly used for timber-felling, mining and construction, although those with skills were employed occasionally in Soviet industry. In some factories German POWs were so integral to production that detention camps were built on the factory grounds and officials tried to block the prisoners' repatriation to Germany. The Gulag population also grew, despite the release of many prisoners in the amnesty of 1945; the camps took in well over a million new prisoners between 1945 and 1950, largely as a result of the mass arrest of 'nationalists' (Ukrainians, Poles, Belorussians, Latvians, Lithuanians and Estonians) in territories captured or reoccupied by the Red Army but never really reconciled to Soviet power. The Gulag system expanded into a vast industrial empire, with 67 camp complexes, 10,000 individual camps and 1,700 colonies, employing a captive labour force of 2.4 million people by 1949 (compared with 1.7 million before the war). Overall, it is estimated that conscript labourers represented between 16 and 18 per cent of the Soviet industrial workforce between 1945 and 1948. They were especially important in the mining of precious metals in cold and remote regions where free labour was very expensive, if not impossible, to employ (hence their contribution to the Soviet economy was even more significant than the figures would suggest). Slave labour also made up the workforce in the big construction projects of the late 1940s which came to symbolize, officially at least, the post-war confidence and achievements of the Soviet system: the Volga–Don Canal; the Kuibyshev hydro-electric station; the Baikal-Amur and Arctic railways; the extensions to the Moscow Metro; and the Moscow University ensemble on the Lenin Hills, one of seven wedding-cake like structures ('Stalin's cathedrals') in the ostentatious 'Soviet Empire' style which shot up around the capital in these years.[18]

The post-war years saw a gradual merging between the Gulag and civilian economies. Every year about half a million Gulag labourers were contracted out to the civilian sector, mostly in construction, or wherever the civilian ministries complained of labour shortages; about the same number of free labourers, mostly specialists, were paid to work in Gulag industries. The Gulag system was increasingly compelled to resort to material incentives to motivate even its forced labourers. The population of the camps had become more unruly and difficult to control. With the amnesty of about a million prisoners in 1945, mainly criminals, who had their sentences either reduced or annulled, the camps were left with a high proportion of 'politicals' – not the intellectual types who filled the camps in the 1930s but strong young men who had fought as soldiers in the war, foreign POWs, Ukrainian and Baltic 'nationalists' – who were hostile to the Soviet regime and not afraid of violence. Without a system of rewards, these prisoners simply refused to meet the set targets. The cost of guarding the prisoners was also becoming astronomical. By 1953, the MVD was employing a quarter of a million guards within its camps, spending twice as much on the upkeep of the Gulag than it received in revenue from its output. Several senior MVD officials were seriously questioning the effectiveness of using forced labour at all. There were even mooted plans, supported by Beria and Malenkov, to dismantle sections of the Gulag and convert the prisoners into partially civilian workers, but since Stalin was a firm supporter of the Gulag system, none of these ideas was seriously proposed.[19]

The Norilsk complex is a good example of the post-war convergence between the Gulag and civilian economies. Its population tripled, from 100,000 to nearly 300,000 prisoners between 1945 and 1952. Most of the new arrivals were Soviet POWs who had passed through the 'filtration camps' (where 'collaborators with the enemy' were weeded out by interrogation) on their return from Europe and the former zones of Nazi occupation; or soldiers and civilians who were rounded up as 'nationalists' from the Baltic region and Ukraine. But there was also a steady increase in the number of free labourers, who represented about one-third of the total workforce by 1949, if one includes prisoners who remained (or were made to remain) on paid contracts in the Norilsk complex after their release. Finally, there was a large contingent of Komsomol enthusiasts who came to Norilsk as volunteers; and relatives of prisoners who came to be united with their families.[20]

Lev Netto was born in 1925 to an Estonian family of Communists that had come to Moscow in 1917. His father was a member of the Latvian Rifle Brigade that played a vital role in Lenin's seizure of power; his mother, who became an official in the Ministry of Foreign Affairs, named Lev after Trotsky, who was her hero. In 1943, Lev was mobilized by the Red Army and assigned to a special NKVD unit of partisans which was sent to fight behind the German lines in Estonia. Captured by the enemy in 1944, Lev was imprisoned in Dvinsk in Latvia and then sent to a POW camp near Frankfurt-am-Main in Germany. In April 1945, the POWs were forced by the Germans to march west. Lev and a few of the other prisoners ran away from the convoy and were liberated by US troops. Lev spent two months in a camp run by the Americans. Despite their attempts to persuade him not to return to his native land, he went back to the Soviet Union in May 1945. He was twenty years old and wanted to study at a university. When Lev reached the Soviet border, he was sent to a filtration camp and then put back into the Red Army. For the next three years Lev served as an ordinary soldier in the newly occupied territories of western Ukraine. In April 1948, he was arrested in Rovno, charged with spying for the USA and, after weeks of torture by his NKVD interrogators, accused of having betrayed his partisan brigade to the Germans during the war. Threatened with the arrest of his parents, Lev signed a full confession to his crimes, and was sentenced to twenty-five years of hard labour followed by five years of exile in Norilsk.[21]

Maria Drozdova was sent to Norilsk after being arrested in Berlin by the Red Army in April 1945. Four years earlier, when she was seventeen, Maria had been captured by the Germans in Krasnoe Selo, near

469

Leningrad, the town she lived in with her parents. She was taken by the German army to Estonia, where she worked as a nurse in a field hospital, and then to Berlin, where she was employed as a servant in the house of a senior Nazi official. Maria resisted several attempts by the Germans to recruit her as a spy – she was beaten by them many times – but her wounds were not enough to persuade the Soviet military tribunal which sentenced her to ten years in Norilsk for 'treason against the Motherland'.[22]

The precious metals of Norilsk played an important role in Stalin's thinking about the post-war reconstruction of the Soviet economy. To stimulate the Norilsk labour force the camp administration made increasing use of work credits and monetary rewards. By 1952, money wages had become the norm for the majority of Norilsk prisoners, who each earned on average 225 roubles a month, about one-third the normal rate of pay for civilian workers, although in Norilsk food and housing were 'free of charge'. Many of the voluntary workers received special ('northern') rates of pay which were far higher than they could have earned outside the Gulag system.[23] A strange hybrid system was evolving in Norilsk: a prison system where the prisoners were paid. But no amount of pay could make up for the loss of dignity and the inhumane conditions in which they were forced to live and work. It was only a matter of time before they rebelled.

2

The post-war years witnessed the consolidation of a new type of educated Soviet 'middle class'. From 1945 to 1950, the number of students in universities and higher schools doubled, giving rise to a young professional class of technicians and managers who would become the leading functionaries and beneficiaries of the Soviet system over the next few decades. This new elite was different from the Soviet cadres of the 1930s: its members were better educated, less ideological in outlook and more stable. Their professional qualifications not only assured them senior positions in the Soviet system, but virtually guaranteed them immunity from demotion on account of class or ideological impurity. Professional capacity began to take the place of proletarian values in the ruling principles of the Soviet elite.

The creation of this professional class was a conscious policy of the Stalinist regime, which recognized the need for a larger and more reliable stratum of engineers, administrators and managers, both to compete with the capitalist economies and to stabilize the Soviet system by providing it with a more solid social base. The regime needed the support of a loyal middle class, if it was not to be overwhelmed by broader social pressures for political reform after 1945; and the most direct means of winning that loyalty was to cater to people's bourgeois aspirations. This new Soviet bourgeoisie was rewarded with secure and well-paid jobs, private apartments and the domestic pleasures of a comfortable home. There were few consumer goods to meet their aspirations in the immediate post-war years, but, as in the 1930s, there were plenty of promises of 'the good life'. Soviet propaganda, films and fiction conjured up an image of the personal and material happiness that lay ahead for those who studied hard and worked diligently. In post-war films and fiction, personal enrichment was promoted as a just reward for industry and loyalty; the pursuit of private happiness, domesticity and material goods was represented as a newly positive ('Soviet') value.[24]

The expansion of the higher education system was the key to the creation of this middle class. By the early 1950s, there were 1.7 million students in Soviet universities, and well over 2 million students in the higher technical schools and colleges.[25] The student population was basically a mix of children from intelligentsia families, a larger share of children from the existing Soviet elite and a sizeable proportion of young men from humble backgrounds who had risen through the ranks of the army in the war and were now given favoured access to higher education. Promoted to the managerial and technical elite, they owed their success, not to their class origins or political zealotry, as did the *vydvizhentsy* of the 1930s, but rather to their training in Soviet schools and universities. Their identification with the system was closely linked to their professional identity. As engineers and technicians, managers and planners, whose careers were defined by the aim of ensuring that the Soviet system worked effectively, they readily accepted the rationality of the planned economy and society, even if politically, or because of their family's repression, they had reasons to oppose the Stalinist regime.

To succeed on this career path people had to conform, at least outwardly, to the demands of the regime. As an engineer explained in 1950,

To advance on the job, one needs to be energetic and persistent, one must be able to keep one's mouth shut and to wear a mask ... If one can manage to shout, 'Long Live Stalin!' ... and sing the popular song, 'I know of no other country in which a man breathes so freely', then one will succeed.

According to a group of émigrés interviewed at this time, the most common type of Soviet functionary was no longer the Communist believer and enthusiast of the 1930s, but the careerist who might not believe in the Party or its goals but carried out its orders nonetheless.[26] Through these ordinary Stalinists, the millions of technocrats and petty functionaries who did its bidding, the regime was routinized, its practices bureaucratized, and the revolutionary impulses that had led to the Terror gradually transformed into the stable culture of a loyal professional elite.

Dissimulation had always been a necessary survival skill in Soviet Russia, but in the post-war years, when the requirements of class and political commitment became secondary to the outward display of conformity, the art of wearing masks was perfected. Czesław Miłosz, who had lived under the post-war Communist system in Poland, thought that people had become so practised at acting in public that it began to seem natural:

After long acquaintance with his role, a man grows into it so closely that he can no longer differentiate his true self from the self he simulates, so that even the most intimate of individuals speak to each other in Party slogans. To identify one's self with the role one is obliged to play brings relief and permits a relaxation of one's vigilance. Proper reflexes at the proper moment become truly automatic ... Acting on a comparable scale has not occurred often in the history of the human race.[27]

Few people lost themselves entirely in their public role. A split identity was probably more representative of the Soviet mentality. Like an actor with an eye to his performance, most citizens remained acutely conscious of the difference between their private and their public selves and they had many ways to keep the two identities apart, from strategies to suppress potentially dangerous thoughts and impulses to methods for resolving the moral dilemmas that nagged at their consciences.

The young professional class of the late 1940s and early 1950s faced new dilemmas compared to those their parents faced in the 1930s. In many cases burdened with a spoilt biography they had inherited from their parents, they were forced to find a way through the system, in which few of them (in contrast to their parents) actually believed – a complex strategic game involving dissimulation (and self-deception), conformism and moral compromise. The first moral choice that many people faced on their career path was whether to declare the arrest of their relatives in the questionnaire (*anketa*) they were required to fill out on entering a job or university. To reveal a spoilt biography was to run the risk of rejection; but to conceal it could potentially entail even more serious consequences, if the truth was discovered by the authorities.

Irina Aleksandrova concealed the arrest of her father when she enrolled as a student in the Economics Department at the Polytechnic Institute in Leningrad in 1946. However, in her second year, she revealed the truth in another questionnaire which the students were required to fill out before going on a study trip. Irina thought that 'times had changed, they had become more free', and that 'there was no longer any shame in coming from a family of enemies of the people', although, looking back on these events, she thinks that she was influenced by the liberal hopes of friends whose families had never been repressed. When it received her second questionnaire, the Komsomol at the institute organized a 'purge meeting' of all the students in Irina's year at which she was made to answer hostile questions about why she had 'concealed her social origins'. The leaders of the Komsomol accused Irina of behaving 'shamefully', in an 'anti-Soviet manner', just as her father, an 'enemy of the people', had behaved. The meeting passed a resolution to recommend the expulsion of Irina from the institute. Irina was rescued by one of the lecturers, the vice-director of the department, who had himself been arrested during the industrial purges of the early 1930s and had recently returned from fighting at the front. 'Back then, the moral tone of the institute was still dominated by the soldiers who had returned from the front,' recalls Irina. 'They would not tolerate the restoration of the culture of the purge, and they kept a firm grip on the faculties and dormitories to ensure that student activists did not bully others like myself.' The lecturer made sure that Irina was not expelled – he even got her reinstated to the study trip – and she graduated from the institute with honours. But in 1949 the lecturer was himself dismissed in a general purge of the institute connected with the Leningrad Affair.[28]

Many people thought it was 'the honest thing to do' to declare the arrest of their parents in the questionnaire. Brought up in the Soviet way, in the belief that private life should be open to public scrutiny, they felt that the most important thing was to live in truth. Others thought that denying their parents' arrest was tantamount to betraying them for egotistical reasons; conversely to accept the inheritance of their parents' spoilt biography was in some way to keep faith with them. Inna Gaister enrolled as a student at Moscow University in 1944. She always wrote the truth about the arrest of her parents because she was afraid that if she wrote some half-truth, or a lie, she would be getting dangerously close to renouncing them.

I was very frightened of that . . . I was afraid that if I lied about my parents, I would be somehow letting go of them . . . By stating openly that I was the daughter of an enemy of the people, I felt that I protected myself from being put under pressure to renounce my father, which seemed to me a very bad thing to do, even though I knew that he was dead.[29]

Inna Gaister (centre) with two friends at Moscow University, 1947

Some people chose to hide their spoilt biography in order not to jeopardize their career. There were many ways to justify this action in their mind: that their parents were not really 'enemies of the people' and that they were therefore not concealing any crime; that their parents would have wanted them to get on in society; or that such concealment was the only way to become honest Soviet citizens. Thus Leonid Makhnach, in his application to the Moscow Film School in 1949, wrote that his father Vladimir (who had been arrested and sentenced to ten years in a Siberian labour camp in 1941) had simply 'vanished without trace' during the war.[30] And Vladimir Vlasov swapped his real name (Zikkel) for the surname of his aunt, Olga Vlasova, who had brought him up in her home in Leningrad after the arrest of his parents. Vladimir found a job in a secret military installation in 1948. He recalls:

I always wrote the same thing on every questionnaire. My older sister helped me make a crib sheet I could consult so that I was sure to give the same answer every time. I always put down the same false place and date of birth, and always wrote that I had lost my parents at an early age. 'I have no information about my father,' I would add. As for my mother, I always gave the [false] name Nina Ippolitovna. I invented the story that she had won three medals in the war, and that she had never been married. I allowed her a lover called Boris Stepanovich, who had come to Russia from Paris, though I was too little to remember much about him, except that he was some sort of artist and did many sketches of my mother. I kept up this fiction until 1980, when I finally killed off my mother. By then, she had reached the age of eighty-six.[31]

Only in the Soviet Union, the most bureaucratic and yet absurdly inefficient country in the world, was it possible to keep such lies going for so long.

For those who wanted to leave their past behind, there was bound to be a change in their relation to parents who had been repressed. As Inna Gaister feared, it was always a temptation to let go of such parents. Angelina Bushueva became an active member of the Komsomol in Perm. She had already joined the Pioneers in the ALZhIR labour camp, from which she had returned with her mother and her sister in 1946. More than anything, she wanted recognition as 'an equal Soviet citizen', to enjoy the same rights as other citizens and overcome the stigma of her parentage. At the Pedagogical Institute in Perm, where she enrolled as a student in 1951, Angelina soon became the secretary of the Komsomol. She loved Stalin. She refused to believe that he had been responsible for the arrest of her father, in 1937, or for the destruction of her family, following the arrest of her mother in 1938. Because her mother took a different view – a view that was still dangerous to hold in the early 1950s – the family never talked about the past. Angelina tried not to think about her father. Only by denying him could she move on and

Nelly and Angelina Bushueva, 1953

pursue a career in a factory in Perm. She certainly never talked about him to her husband, a Communist official in the factory:

In my family we used to say: 'The more you know – the quicker you grow old!' Or: 'The less you know – the easier to live!' I never talked to anyone about my father – not until I retired from the factory and collected my pension in 1991.[32]

Leonid Saltykov was born in 1927 to the family of a priest, who was arrested in 1937. As the eldest of five children, Leonid felt responsible for his mother, a postal worker who did not earn enough to support the family. Although he was a bright boy, he finished only four classes before he was expelled from school, because of his spoilt biography. After several casual jobs, he managed to enrol in a factory school by hiding the arrest of his father. He wanted to become an engineer, to prove himself as a 'first-class Soviet citizen', as he recalls, by doing well in a profession highly valued by the regime. In 1944, Leonid got a job as an electrical engineer in a munitions factory in Cheliabinsk. In the evenings he studied at a technical college. On all the forms he wrote that his father had died in 1942: it suggested that he had been killed during the war. 'Nobody would check up on a date like that,' reasoned Leonid.

I stuck to this version of events for many years – right up until 1958, when I became the head of the special sector in the 'secret group' of operations in the munitions factory. Then I felt that I should put the record straight . . . I was afraid that in this 'secret group' they would check my story and that, when they found out that I had been lying, they would accuse me of being a spy.

Leonid in 1944

Leonid only found out what had happened to his father in 1963 (he had been shot in 1938). Until then, he continued to deny all knowledge about his fate. 'My only interest was to climb the career ladder,' he admits, 'and to do that I had to keep the secret of my past ... The truth about my father's arrest would have blackened my reputation and ruined my career.' In 1965, Leonid joined the Party. He became the secretary of the Party Committee in the factory where he worked, effectively the leader of 1,500 Communists. He was an ardent Stalinist, grieved when Stalin died and kept his picture on his desk until his retirement in 1993. Leonid did not believe that Stalin was responsible for the arrest of his father (a view he still holds today). On the contrary, he was grateful to Stalin for the opportunity to rise from a humble background, the son of a village priest, and become a senior factory boss.[33]

Breaking from the past for career purposes damaged many family relationships. In 1946, Iurii Streletsky graduated with top marks from high school in Tbilisi. He wanted to return to Leningrad, where he had grown up, to study engineering at the Polytechnic Institute, but he was rejected when he admitted on his application that his parents had been arrested as 'enemies of the people'. Iurii managed to find part-time work in various factories in Leningrad, which enabled him to sit in as an external student on the evening classes at the institute, although he could not take the final examinations or receive certification. In 1948, he was employed unofficially as a technical designer at the main Party press in

Leningrad, just when the press was introducing new technology from Germany. Iurii played a vital role in setting up the new machinery, but as an unofficial employee, he received no reward or recognition for his achievement. In fact, as soon as the new printing works was up and running, he was dismissed because of the arrest of his father, which he had recorded in a questionnaire. For the next three years Iurii held a series of casual jobs. In 1951, his mother returned from exile in Kazakhstan to Leningrad. Deeply damaged by her husband's death and by years of exile, she could not find a job and lived very poorly on her own. Iurii did not visit her, or even try to help her financially. His own bitter experiences had made him selfish, as he confesses in an interview.

I became an egotist, and my feelings towards others, even towards my own mother, hardened. I put her out of my mind and forgot about her, because I saw her as a burden which I could do without. It is shameful to admit, but it is true.

In 1953, Iurii applied for a job as a senior technician at the Pulkovo Observatory. This time he did not declare his spoilt biography – he wrote down that his parents were both dead – and as a result he got the job.[34]

Some young people were so desperate to make a career for themselves that they became informers for the NKVD. The security organs recruited many of its informers from children of 'enemies of the people'. They knew that they were vulnerable and that many of them had a strong desire to prove themselves as worthy Soviet citizens.

Tatiana Elagina was born in Leningrad in 1926 to a family of merchants that had been very wealthy before 1917. The Elagins were exiled to Kazakhstan in 1935 following the murder of Kirov. In 1945, Tatiana applied to study mathematics at Moscow University. Although she had top grades, she was rejected on the basis of her 'alien social origins'. So she enrolled instead at the Moscow Electromechanical Institute for Transport Engineers, where the demand for able students meant that less attention was paid to her family background. Studying in Moscow was the fulfilment of Tatiana's dreams. But shortly after she began her studies, the institute announced a general purge to remove 'social undesirables'. Tatiana fled to Leningrad, where she joined the Institute of Electrical Engineering: the authorities there were glad to have a student with such high grades apply and turned a blind eye to her spoilt biography. But in her final year, when the students were involved in 'secret' work at power stations, the weeding-out of unreliables was intensified. She was picked to write reports on her classmates:

They said there was nothing shameful about this, and somehow I managed to convince myself that they were right. They told me that if I heard the students saying something negative about the institute, or complaining about anything, even if it was in a private conversation among themselves, I was to report it immediately, making sure that the people I reported did not know.

Tatiana did her best to report as little as she could: she passed on rumours she had heard without mentioning specific names. But there was growing pressure on her to provide more-concrete information, not least because, if she refused, she might be sent to work, as others from the year before had been, in the remote regions of the Arctic North by the Ministry of Electric Power, which had first call on the graduates of the institute. Before she took her last exams, Tatiana submitted a report that led to the arrest of three students. She got a prestigious job in Moscow in the Trust of Hydro-electricity.[35]

Valentina Kropotina made her whole career by informing. She was born in 1930 into a Belorussian peasant family that was repressed as 'kulaks' during the collectivization of agriculture. The family house and farm were destroyed. Valentina's father was sent into exile, leaving her mother to survive with their two young daughters in a shack she built from the rubble of their house. Banned from school as a 'kulak' daughter, Valentina spent her childhood working with her mother in various low-paid jobs, before moving to Irkutsk and then to Abakan, in the Altai region of Siberia. In Abakan she and her mother were reunited with Valentina's father. Sick and broken from his years in the labour camps, he found a job as the caretaker in a school, where Valentina's mother worked as a cleaner. Valentina only started attending classes when she was thirteen. Until then she could not read, as she recalls:

I was basically a street-child, dressed in rags, barefoot . . . All my childhood memories are dominated by the feeling of hunger . . . I was afraid of hunger, and even more, of poverty. And I was corrupted by this fear.

At school Valentina suffered acutely from the stigma of her 'kulak' origins. She became increasingly ashamed of her parents' poverty, of their Belorussian background and their ignorance (they were illiterate and could not speak Russian). Determined to liberate herself by studying hard, Valentina joined the Pioneers and then the Komsomol. Only that path 'offered hope of an escape from the poverty and hunger in which I had grown up', she explains. Valentina grew up to believe that Stalin was 'the greatest human being in the whole of history'. She totally accepted the Party's propaganda about 'spies' and 'enemies'. She even wanted to become a lawyer so that she could help the government to hunt them down. 'Like Stalin,' she recalls, 'I was not at all sorry for people who were sent to the Gulag.'

In 1948, when she was eighteen, Valentina ran away from home. She enrolled at a college for accountants and then took a job as a trainee accountant at a naval base on the island of Sakhalin, where she received the higher rates of pay and food rations reserved for special military personnel. Valentina married a naval officer. She became a trusted member of the naval base, where she worked in the staff building, with special access to the files of all the personnel. In this capacity she was recruited by the MVD to inform on the wives of other naval officers. Her task was to strike up friendships with these women and report to her controller on their private lives and opinions:

In some cases I would approach the women and ask them to make something I could buy: many women spent their spare time sewing and knitting. In others I would befriend the women and get myself invited to their place for tea. Or I would visit them at work. My controller gave me money for these 'commissions' (I still have lots of items, mainly coats and pullovers, which my 'clients' made for me). He also gave me money to buy a cake for tea, or some other offering so that I could make that first contact and win the women's trust. The main thing was to make a connection. It was really easy. There was just one rule: you had to be alone with somebody before striking up a conversation about something important. Only then would they speak freely.

Valentina worked as an informer for several years. She wrote dozens of reports on people who were subsequently arrested. She was well paid – well enough to send large sums of money to her aged parents and to buy a house in Abakan, where she retired with her husband in 1959 (at the age of thirty-nine). During interviews she still insists that she was forced to work against her will. She sees herself as a victim of repression too:

It was impossible to refuse, they knew everything about my parents and their kulak origins . . . I knew that they had imprisoned my father and I was afraid

Valentina Kropotina and her
husband, Viktor, 1952

that they would imprison me ... Besides, my husband might have suffered, if
I had refused to cooperate.

On the other hand, Valentina insists that the people she denounced were
truly enemies of the people, 'proven spies'. She feels no remorse for what
she did. Indeed, she is proud of the honours she received for what she
calls her work in 'counter-espionage'.[36]

3

Simonov's career rose to new heights after 1945. The writer returned
from the war with a chestful of medals for his reports from the battle-
fields. Now a trusted Party member in Stalin's inner circle of favoured
intellectuals, Simonov was put in charge of a small delegation of influential journalists sent by the Kremlin to the USA in May 1946, when the
world stood on the brink of the Cold War. Briefed in the Kremlin by
Molotov, the Foreign Minister, Simonov was charged by Stalin with
persuading the Americans that the Soviet Union did not want a war.
The trip gave Simonov his first real taste of governmental privilege. He
was shocked by the huge advance that he received for the trip; perhaps
he was even unnerved by the disparity between his situation and what

he knew of the conditions of ordinary Soviet people, but, if so, the feeling was momentary. Simonov revelled in the pleasures of the West. In the USA Simonov was greeted as an international celebrity. His novel *Days and Nights* was a national bestseller. Everybody knew his poem 'Wait For Me'. His plays were running in theatres in New York, Boston, Washington and San Francisco. Simonov himself was photographed in the company of luminaries such as Gary Cooper, Lion Feuchtwanger and Charlie Chaplin, who became his regular correspondent.[37]

The American tour was one of several foreign trips made by Simonov in the immediate post-war years. On each occasion he was entrusted by the Soviet government with an important task. In London, which he visited in 1947, Simonov reported on the possibility of recruiting leading writers (including J. B. Priestley and George Bernard Shaw) to the Soviet cause.[38] In Paris, where he stopped on his way to America, Simonov attempted to persuade the émigré Russian writer Ivan Bunin to return to the Soviet Union. The only Russian to have won the Nobel Prize for Literature, Bunin had been living abroad since 1920, when he fled the Revolution in disgust. He was now in his mid-seventies, but Stalin hoped that patriotic sentiment and nostalgia might yet convince him to return to his native land. Many émigrés were seduced by the favourable image of the Soviet Union in 1945 and some indeed decided to go back. Simonov met Bunin in Paris in a series of fashionable restaurants. He paid the bills with money given him by the Soviet government. Emphasizing his own noble ancestry, Simonov waxed lyrical about life in the Soviet Union. And when Bunin invited him to dinner in his home, Simonov suggested a 'collective meal', for which Valentina Serova was flown in from Moscow with a huge hamper of Russian delicacies (herrings, pork fat, black bread and various types of vodka) designed to heighten the old man's nostalgia. Valentina even sang him Russian songs. But Bunin did not change his anti-Soviet attitudes. He refused to return to the Soviet Union, even for a visit.[39]

In 1946, the Writers' Union was reorganized on the lines of the Politburo, with a General Secretary, Aleksandr Fadeyev, and three deputies, including Simonov. The writer Kornei Chukovsky noted in his diary on 16 November 1946: 'The leaders of the Writers' Union are very stony-faced. Frozen still. The worst is Tikhonov. He can listen for hours without an expression on his face . . . Fadeyev and Simonov are also very stony-faced. It must be from the habit of chairmanship.' Two weeks after his election to the leadership of the Writers' Union, Simonov was made the editor of *Novyi mir* ('New World'), the oldest and most prestigious literary journal in the Soviet Union. In March 1950, he left *Novyi mir* to assume the editorship of the country's main literary newspaper, *Literaturnaia gazeta*, with personal instructions from Stalin to use its editorials to articulate an alternative perspective on the cultural politics of the Cold War, one that would appear sufficiently different from the Kremlin's position to satisfy the literary intelligentsia's desire for independence without really departing from its hardline policies towards the West. It was a sign of Stalin's trust in Simonov that he gave him such a delicate and awkward task.[40]

Simonov in 1946

Elevation to the Soviet elite led to a dramatic transformation of Simonov's appearance. He abandoned the 'military look' of the war years and began to dress in elegantly tailored English suits, or more casually in turtleneck sweaters from America, a camel coat and the short-peaked cap fashionable in the post-war years. Tall and strikingly handsome, Simonov cut the figure of a European gentleman. He reclaimed many of the manners of the aristocracy into which he had been born. He was a bon viveur and generous host; he was loyal and kind to servants, especially to secretaries and chauffeurs; he opened doors for women, helped them with their coats and greeted them with a chivalrous kiss on the hand.[41]

Simonov's lifestyle, too, underwent dramatic transformation. He had several homes. There was a spacious dacha in the prestigious literary resort of Peredelkino, just outside Moscow, which he bought in 1946 from the writer Gladkov for a quarter of a million roubles, a large fortune in those days; a house in Gulripshi, a village near Sukhumi, overlooking the Black Sea, which he bought in 1949; and a large apartment on Gorky Street, in Moscow, where he lived with Valentina after 1948. The couple kept two maids, a housekeeper, a secretary and a private chauffeur for the limousine they had imported from America. The apartment was filled with elegant and expensive antiques. There were precious paintings on the walls, including one by Kuzma Petrov-Vodkin, which must have come from a private collection that had been confiscated by the state. The apartment was the scene of fashionable parties for the elite of Moscow's literary and theatre world. Simonov was a keen cook and sometimes he would make elaborate meals for these parties; but more often he would call on the head chef of the nearby famous Aragvi Georgian restaurant who would bring his team of chefs to prepare a banquet in the apartment.[42]

Among his staff at *Novyi mir* Simonov was known for his 'seigneurial' manner. Lydia Chukovskaia, who was in the poetry division, was struck by the youthful appearance of the new editor, who was then just thirty-one. Yet at the same time she remarked on his enormous confidence, which gave him the authority of a much older man. At work Simonov was serious and measured in his deliberations, drawing on his briar pipe, in the Stalin style, as he handed down instructions to subordinates (there were always half a dozen different pipes on Simonov's desk). According to Chukovskaia, Simonov was arrogant and domineering in his dealings with the staff at *Novyi mir*. In her diary she compared the editorial offices to a nineteenth-century manor with 'minions and lackeys' running everywhere at the lord's beck and call. She was especially offended by Simonov's high-handed treatment of two poets, whom she had persuaded to submit work to *Novyi mir* in 1946. One was Nikolai Zabolotsky, who had just returned from eight years in a labour camp. Simonov agreed to publish one of his poems but then forced him to change some lines for political reasons. The other was Boris Pasternak, a huge figure in the Soviet literary world who was then, at the age of fifty-six, old enough to be Simonov's father. Pasternak had asked for an advance on a poem which Simonov had accepted for publication in *Novyi mir*. But Simonov refused because he saw the request as a veiled threat to withdraw the poem if the advance was not paid. He told Chukovskaia that it was unethical for Pasternak to 'threaten me, after everything that I have done for him. If I were in his position, I would not behave that way.' To teach Pasternak a lesson Simonov decided not to publish the accepted poem after all. For Chukovskaia, herself the daughter of a writer (Kornei Chukovsky), brought up on the values of the old intelligentsia, Simonov's behaviour was appalling, because it signalled his acceptance of the primacy of state power over the autonomy of art. 'He [Simonov] wants to be a patron and demands gratitude,' she wrote in her diary.

But people don't want charity. They want the respect which they deserve. Zabolotsky should be published, not because he spent eight years in the camps, but because his poem is good. Simonov is obliged to support Pasternak, not to do him favours, but *obliged* to support him, because he is in charge of poetry and, in this domain, Pasternak should be his most important responsibility . . . Simonov does not understand that it is his duty to Russian culture, and to the people, to give money to Pasternak. He thinks of it as a personal favour, for which Pasternak should be grateful.[43]

Like all power-holders in the post-war Stalinist system, Simonov was able to exercise enormous patronage. As head of *Novyi mir* and deputy of the Writer's Union, he could make or ruin the career of almost any writer in the Soviet Union. He could help people in many other ways – to get housing or a job, even to protect them from arrest – if only he was brave enough to use his influence with the authorities. That was how the system worked. Simonov was inundated with personal requests from colleagues, friends, friends of friends, casual acquaintances, soldiers he had met during the war. He could not help them all, of course, but how he chose the people he would help was revealing.

He was very protective and kind towards his private secretary, Nina Gordon, for example, a small attractive woman in her mid-thirties, who had come to *Novyi mir* in 1946. Nina had previously worked for the writer Mikhail Koltsov, whose articles on the Spanish Civil War had been an inspiration to the young Simonov. Her husband, Iosif Gordon, a film editor from a noble family, had been arrested in 1937 and sentenced to five years in a labour camp near Magadan. In 1942, Iosif was released so that he could fight at the front. Nina informed Simonov about her disgraced husband when he wanted to promote her to become his personal secretary. At that point Iosif was living in exile in Riazan, where he was working as an engineer. Nina offered to decline the promotion. But Simonov would not hear of it. He even said that he would write to the MVD to help Iosif – an offer she rejected because she did not want to exploit his kindness. As it was, her employment in the offices of *Novyi mir* could have had unpleasant consequences for Simonov, as shown by an incident in 1948, when Iosif, who had been given permission to visit Moscow for a few days, turned up unexpectedly at the editorial offices. A journalist from the newspaper *Izvestiia* happened to be there and paid close attention to Iosif, who clearly had the look of an exile. The next day, Nina was called in for questioning by the journal's Special Department, which served as the eyes and ears of the MVD (every Soviet institution had its own Special Department). Her interrogators wanted to know why Nina had concealed that she was married to a political exile, and threatened to report her for lack of vigilance. When Simonov heard about the incident he was furious. He saw it as an infringement of his editorial authority. Nina received a reprimand by the Special Department, which also issued a statement that 'suspicious persons' were not to be admitted to the offices, but there was no further action against her.[44]

If Simonov was often kind towards people in his personal sphere and brave in helping them with the authorities, he was far less courageous when it came to people in the public sphere. Many writers turned to him for help during the repressions of the post-war years. Simonov was cautious in his response. He was helpful to some, less so to others, depending on his personal feelings, but he was always careful not to risk his own position or to raise suspicions about himself. For example, in September 1946, Simonov wrote a letter of recommendation for his old classmate from the Literary Institute, the poet Portugalov, who had applied to join the Writers' Union. He did not mention Portugalov's arrest (in 1937) or the years that he had suffered in the labour camps of Kolyma, referring instead to the 'seven years that Portugalov spent in the army' as the reason why he had not published anything, so as not to give the impression that he was pleading for a former 'enemy of the people'. Portugalov was turned down by the Writers' Union in 1946, but he reapplied in 1961, at the height of the Khrushchev thaw. On that occasion, Simonov was more forthcoming in his letter of recommendation, pointing to the 'injustice of his arrest' as the only reason why his first book of poetry, which appeared in 1960, had not come out twenty years before.[45] Simonov also wrote to support the publication of the poet Iaroslav Smeliakov, a committed Communist and close friend of the Laskins, who had been arrested in 1934, served five years in a labour camp and fought bravely in the war, after which he served another term in the Gulag, working in a coal mine near Moscow.[46] But other writers who appealed to him were not as fortunate. Simonov refused to help his old teacher at the Literary Institute, the poet Lugovskoi, who had suffered a nervous breakdown during the first battles of 1941 and spent the war years in evacuation in Tashkent. After his return to Moscow, Lugovskoi wrote to Simonov with a request for help in finding a new apartment. Lugovskoi was living with his wife in a communal apartment, but his fragile mental state required privacy. 'I am no longer young,' he wrote to his old pupil,

I am a sick person. I cannot bear to live in a communal apartment, with a family of six in the next room . . . My nerves are constantly on edge and if I end up in a lunatic asylum it will not be surprising . . . It is hard to ask for help . . . but you are a humane person, and that encourages me to turn to you. Forgive me! I love you and am proud of you.[47]

Simonov did not reply. As he saw it, Lugovskoi did not deserve help. For one thing, he already had an apartment, and worse, he had lacked courage in the war – an unforgivable crime in Simonov's eyes.

Simonov's firm commitment to the Soviet ideal of military sacrifice goes some way to explain his entanglement in Stalin's post-war campaigns of repression, starting with his involvement in the 'Zhdanovshchina', the official clampdown against 'anti-Soviet' tendencies in the arts and sciences, which was led by Andrei Zhdanov, Stalin's chief of ideology.

The Zhdanovshchina had its origins in the military victory of 1945, which gave rise to a xenophobic nationalism in the Soviet leadership. Pride in the Soviet victory went hand in hand with the promotion of the USSR's cultural and political superiority (by which the regime really meant the superiority of the Russians, who were described by Stalin as the most important group in the Soviet Union). Soviet-Russian nationalism replaced the internationalism of the pre-war years as the ruling ideology of the regime. Absurd claims were made for the achievements of Soviet science under the direction of Marxist-Leninist ideology. National pride led to the promotion of frauds and cranks like the pseudo-geneticist Trofim Lysenko, who claimed to have developed a new strain of wheat that would grow in the Arctic frost. The aeroplane, the steam engine, the radio, the incandescent bulb – there was scarely an invention or discovery that the Soviets did not claim for themselves. With the onset of the Cold War, Stalin called for iron discipline to purge all anti-patriotic – meaning pro-Western – elements in cultural affairs. He argued that historically, since the start of the eighteenth century when Peter the Great had founded St Petersburg, the intelligentsia in Russia had prostrated itself before Western – science and culture: it needed to be cured of this 'sickness' if the Soviet Union was to defend itself against the West.

On Stalin's orders, Zhdanov launched a violent campaign against Western influences in Soviet culture.* For Stalin the starting-point of this campaign was Leningrad, a European city he had never liked, whose independence from Moscow had been greatly strengthened by the war. The clampdown began on 14 August 1946, when the Central Committee published a decree censoring the journals *Zvezda* and *Leningrad* for publishing the work of two great Leningrad writers, Mikhail Zoshchenko and Anna Akhmatova. In singling out these writers for attack the Kremlin aimed to demonstrate to the Leningrad intelligentsia its subordination to the Soviet regime. Akhmatova had acquired immense moral influence during the war. Although her poetry had been rarely published in the Soviet Union since 1925, she remained for millions of Russians a living symbol of the spirit of endurance and human dignity that enabled Leningrad to survive the siege. In 1945, the Oxford philosopher Isaiah Berlin, who had then just arrived as First Secretary of the British Embassy in Moscow, was told that in the war Akhmatova

received an amazingly large number of letters from the front, quoting from both published and unpublished poems, for the most part circulated privately in manuscript copies; there were requests for autographs, for confirmation of the

---

*It has often been suggested that Zhdanov was a political moderate, a liberal reformer, who lost out to hardliners, such as Malenkov, in Stalin's ruling clique, as relations with the West deteriorated in 1945–6. According to this view, the hardline cultural policies were in fact imposed by Zhdanov's rivals in the Party leadership. But the archives show that Zhdanov had no independent political ideas, and that policy positions within the ruling clique were developed in response to various signals from Stalin, who used Zhdanov to impose on all the Soviet arts and sciences a rigid ideological conformity to the Party's anti-Western stance.

authenticity of texts, for expressions of the author's attitude to this or that problem.

Zoshchenko believed that the Central Committee decree had been passed after Stalin heard about a poetry reading by Akhmatova before a packed house at the Polytechnic Museum in Moscow. After Akhmatova finished reading, the audience erupted in applause. 'Who organized this standing ovation?' Stalin asked.[48]

Zoshchenko was just as much a thorn in the dictator's side. He was the last of the Soviet satirists – Maiakovsky, Zamiatin and Bulgakov had all perished – a literary tradition Stalin could not tolerate. The immediate cause of the attack on him was a children's story, 'Adventures of a Monkey', published in *Zvezda* in 1946, in which a monkey escapes from a zoo and is trained as a human being. But in fact Stalin had been irritated by Zoshchenko's stories for years. He recognized himself in the figure of the sentry in 'Lenin and the Guard' (1939), in which Zoshchenko portrayed a rude and impatient 'southern type' with a moustache, whom Lenin treats like a little boy.[49]

As a leading member of the Writers' Union, Simonov had little choice but to go along with this campaign. In his first issue as editor of *Novyi mir* he published the decree of the Central Committee alongside a transcript of a speech by Zhdanov which described Akhmatova as 'one of the standard bearers of a hollow, empty, aristocratic salon poetry which is absolutely foreign to Soviet literature' and (in a phrase that had been used by Soviet critics in the past) as a 'half-nun, half-harlot or rather harlot-nun whose sin is mixed with prayer'.[50]

Perhaps Simonov felt some discomfort as the persecutor of the Leningrad intelligentsia, with which his own mother's family identified, but whatever feelings he may have had on this score, he refused to let them hold him back from what he understood as his higher duty to the state. Reflecting on these events in the last year of his life, Simonov confessed that he had gone along with the Zhdanovshchina because he believed that 'something really needed to be done' to counteract the 'atmosphere of ideological relaxation' that had taken hold of the intelligentsia. Unchecked, it would lead to 'dangerous expectations of liberal reform' precisely at a time when the Soviet Union needed to prepare for the intensified ideological struggle of the Cold War. This is what he argued at the time. As he put it in a letter to the Central Committee:

On the ideological front a global struggle of unprecedented violence is being waged. And yet, despite the circumstances there are people spouting theories about a 'breathing space' – the idea that we should all sit around in a coffee house and talk about reform. These are mostly people, by the way, who have no need for breathing space, because they laboured very little in the war; in fact, most of them did nothing . . . If they want, we can give them their breathing space by stopping them from working in the field of Soviet art, but meanwhile the rest of us will go on working and fighting.[51]

This contempt for intellectuals who shied away from 'struggle' – a long-standing view of Simonov's – explains his hostility to Zoshchenko, in particular. With Akhmatova his attitude was different. He did not like, or even really know, her poetry, but he took exception to the violent language used by Zhdanov against her, because it seemed to him that 'nobody should speak in such a way about a person who had suffered with the people as Akhmatova had done during the war'.* By contrast, Zoshchenko had spent the war years in evacuation in Tashkent, and according to the Soviet press, which accused the satirist of cowardice, he had fled from Leningrad to avoid fighting at the front. Simonov believed the charge of cowardice. He did not know the truth, or did not bother to discover it: that Zoshchenko, who was in his mid-forties and in poor health, had been ordered by the authorities to leave Leningrad at the beginning of the war. He judged Zoshchenko by the same harsh measure he applied to every man who did not fight, and extended it to the intellectuals who failed to recognize the need to join the ideological struggle of the Cold War. The theatre critic Aleksandr Borshchagovsky, who knew Simonov as well as anyone, points out that this rush to condemn people like Zoshchenko was entirely based on prejudice. Simonov, he writes, had a tendency to

mistrust anyone – especially an intellectual – who had spent the war years working in the rear, and had not shared in the bloody sacrifices of the soldiers at the front. This generalized suspiciousness – which was formed without the slightest effort

---

*For the same reason Simonov defended the writer Vasily Grossman, whose play *If We Are to Believe the Pythagoreans* was savagely attacked in *Pravda* in September 1946. Simonov wrote to the paper's editor, defending Grossman on the grounds that a writer who had spent 'the whole war fighting at the front' did not deserve to be criticized in the abusive language used by the critic, even if he had made 'serious ideological errors' (RGALI, f. 1814, op. 9, d. 1384, l. 2).

to look deeper into the biography of each individual – did not take into account the fact that millions of people in the rear worked themselves into the ground so that millions of their comrades at the front could be armed for victory.[52]

Simonov joined in the attacks on Zoshchenko but not directly in the slander against Akhmatova. When *Pravda* asked him to write an article condemning the two, Simonov replied that he would speak only against Zoshchenko, and the resulting article was almost wholly focused on the prose writer. However, Simonov reversed his campaign a few months later when he learned the truth about Zoshchenko's evacuation and heard from the writer Iurii German that Zoshchenko was a courageous man, who had fought with honour in the First World War. Realizing his mistake, Simonov made some efforts to correct the situation: he recommended to Zhdanov the publication of Zoshchenko's *Partisan Tales*, written in 1943, which Simonov personally edited, even though he did not think that they were very good. Zhdanov refused to read the tales, but at a meeting with Stalin, in May 1947, Simonov again brought up the issue of their publication on the grounds that Zoshchenko was in a desperate state and needed help. It was a bold and courageous step to go above Zhdanov and ask for Stalin's help directly for a writer so disliked by the Soviet leader. Stalin told Simonov that he could print the tales on his own editorial authority, but that after they were published, he would read them and form his own opinion about Simonov's decision to print them. As Simonov recalls, there was more than a 'hint of a threat in Stalin's humour', but he went ahead with the publication of the tales, which appeared in *Novyi mir* in September 1947.[53]

And yet, despite this effort at setting things right, Simonov then refused to show compassion for Zoshchenko. In 1954, a group of English students came to Leningrad and requested a meeting with Akhmatova and Zoshchenko. The meeting was attended by several Party members from the Writers' Union in Leningrad. The foolish students, who made their anti-Soviet feelings clear, asked Akhmatova and Zoshchenko for their opinion of the Central Committee decree of August 1946. Akhmatova replied that the decree had been correct. She was no doubt frightened of the consequences of saying otherwise. But Zoshchenko was less careful. He replied that the decree had been unjust, and he violently rejected the accusations of cowardice against himself. The Party leadership of the Writers' Union immediately accused Zoshchenko of 'anti-patriotic behaviour', and sent a delegation headed by Simonov to

Leningrad to 'work him over'. In a heart-rending speech of self-defence that bordered on hysteria, Zoshchenko declared that his writing life was finished, that he had been destroyed, and he pleaded with his accusers to let him die in peace. Simonov rejected Zoshchenko's pleas and went after him in the manner of a prosecutor at a purge meeting. 'Comrade Zoshchenko is appealing to our feelings of compassion, but he has learned nothing, and he ought to be ashamed,' Simonov declared, referring once again to his war record and his 'anti-patriotic' conduct after 1945.[54]

The attacks against Akhmatova and Zoshchenko were soon followed by a series of repressive measures against 'anti-Soviet elements' in all the arts and sciences. The State Museum of Modern Western Art was closed down. A campaign against 'formalism' and other 'decadent Western influences' in Soviet music led to the official blacklisting of several composers (including Shostakovich, Khachaturian and Prokofiev) charged with writing music that was 'alien to the Soviet people and its artistic taste'. In January 1947, the Politburo issued a decree against a *History of European Philosophy* (1946) by G. F. Aleksandrov, the head of Agitprop (the Central Committee's Department of Agitation and Propaganda), accusing the book of having undervalued the Russian contribution to the Western philosophical tradition. Aleksandrov was soon removed from his post. Later that year, in July 1947, the Central Committee published an ominous letter censuring the scientists Nina Kliueva and her husband Grigorii Roskin for 'obeisances and servility before foreign and reactionary bourgeois Western culture unworthy of our people'. The scientists had been accused of giving information about their cancer research to the Americans during a tour of the USA in 1946. On their return they were dragged before an 'honour court', a newly founded institution to examine acts of an anti-patriotic nature in the Soviet establishment, where they were made to answer hostile questions before 800 spectators.[55]

As the Cold War intensified, fear of foreigners took hold of society. The American journalist Harrison Salisbury recalls returning to Moscow as a foreign correspondent in 1949. None of the Russians he had known from his previous stay in 1944 would acknowledge him. He wrote to his old acquaintances Ehrenburg and Simonov, but not even they replied to him. In 1944, it seemed to Salisbury, the country had been poor, but, compared with the 1930s, there was a new mood of freedom and a buoyant atmosphere that arose from the people's hopes for victory. By contrast, in 1949 the country had reverted to a state of fear, and there was a

complete severance of any kind of ordinary human relations between Russians and foreigners which, in turn, simply reflected the impressive xenophobia of the Soviet government and the degree to which they had made it plain to all Russians that the most certain, if not the quickest, way to obtain a one-way ticket to Siberia or places even more distant lay in having anything to do with a foreigner.

The briefest of contacts with foreigners could lead to arrest for espionage. The Soviet jails were filled with people who had been on trips abroad. In February 1947, a law was passed to outlaw marriages between Soviet citizens and foreigners. Police kept watch over hotels, restaurants and foreign embassies, on the lookout for Soviet girls who met with foreign men.[56]

After the foundation of Israel, in May 1948, and its alignment with the USA in the Cold War, the 2 million Soviet Jews, who had always remained loyal to the Soviet system, were portrayed by the Stalinist regime as a potential fifth column. Despite his personal dislike of Jews, Stalin had been an early supporter of a Jewish state in Palestine, which he had hoped to turn into a Soviet satellite in the Middle East. But as the leadership of the emerging state proved hostile to approaches from the Soviet Union, Stalin became increasingly afraid of pro-Israeli feeling among the Soviet Jews. His fears intensified as a result of Golda Meir's arrival in Moscow in the autumn of 1948 as the first Israeli ambassador to the USSR. Everywhere she went she was cheered by crowds of Soviet Jews. On her visit to a Moscow synagogue on Yom Kippur (13 October), thousands of people lined the streets, many of them shouting '*Am Yisroel chai*' ('The People of Israel live!') – a traditional affirmation of national renewal to Jews throughout the world but to Stalin a dangerous sign of 'bourgeois Jewish nationalism' that subverted the authority of the Soviet state.[57]

The enthusiastic reception of Meir prompted Stalin to step up the anti-Jewish campaign that had in fact been underway for many months. In January 1948, Solomon Mikhoels, the director of the Jewish Theatre in Moscow and the leader of the Jewish Anti-Fascist Committee (JAFC), was killed in a car accident arranged by the MVD. The JAFC had been established in 1942 to attract Western Jewish aid for the Soviet war effort, but for many of the Soviet Jews who had joined it, among them leading writers, artists, musicians, actors, historians and scientists, its broader aim was to encourage Jewish culture in the USSR. The immediate post-war years were relatively favourable for this goal. In 1946, Mikhoels was awarded the Stalin Prize. Jewish plays were often broadcast on the radio. The JAFC developed a major project to commemorate the Nazi destruction of the Soviet Jews: a collection of documents edited by Vasily Grossman and Ilia Ehrenburg known as *The Black Book*. Stalin had hoped to use the JAFC to curry favour with the nascent Jewish state in the Middle East. But as it became clear that the new state would more likely be allied to the USA, he changed his attitude. The MGB was instructed to build up a case against the JAFC as an 'anti-Soviet nationalist organization'. The publication of *The Black Book* was postponed indefinitely. After the murder of Mikhoels, the Jewish Theatre was closed down. In December 1948, over a hundred JAFC members were arrested, tortured to confess to their 'anti-Soviet activities' and executed or sent to labour camps.[58]

In the Soviet literary world the assault against the Jews took the form of a campaign against 'cosmopolitans'. The term was first coined by the nineteenth-century literary critic Vissarion Belinsky to refer to writers ('rootless cosmopolitans') who lacked or rejected national character. It reappeared in the war years, when Russian nationalism and anti-Jewish feelings were both on the rise. For example, in November 1943, Fadeyev attacked the Jewish writer Ehrenburg for coming from 'that circle of the intelligentsia that understands internationalism in a vulgar cosmopolitan sense and fails to overcome the servile admiration of everything foreign'.[59] After 1945, the term appeared with increasing regularity in the Soviet literary press.

The campaign against the 'cosmopolitans' began when Fadeyev forwarded a letter he had received from an obscure journalist (Natalia Begicheva) to Stalin on 10 December 1948. Originally written as a denunciation to the MVD, the letter claimed that there was a group of 'enemies' at work within the literary establishment, and cited as the leaders of this 'anti-patriotic group' seven critics and writers, all but one of them Jewish. Under pressure from Stalin, Fadeyev made a speech in the Writers' Union on 22 December. He attacked a group of theatre critics, naming four of the six Jews denounced by Begicheva (Altman, Borshchagovsky, Gurvich and Iuzovsky), who, Fadeyev claimed, were 'trying to discredit our Soviet theatre'. It was a relatively moderate speech: Fadeyev was apparently reluctant to play the role of Stalin's henchman. Once a decent man, Fadeyev had been reduced to a trembling alcoholic by the moral compromises he had been forced to make. Stalin

Fadeyev at the Writers' Union, 22 December 1948.
Far left: Simonov. Next to him: Ehrenburg.
The banner under the portrait reads: 'Glory to the Great Stalin!'

kept up the pressure, enlisting *Pravda* to attack Fadeyev for not being vigilant enough against the 'cosmopolitans', and putting rumours out that he was about to be replaced as the leader of the Writers' Union. Unable to resist any longer, Fadeyev gave his endorsement to an anonymous article in *Pravda* on 29 January 1949 ('About One Anti-Patriotic Group') which, in language strongly reminiscent of the rhetoric of the Great Terror, denounced several theatre critics as 'rootless cosmopolitans' and accused them of fomenting a 'bourgeois' literary conspiracy to sabotage the healthy principles of 'national pride' in Soviet literature.[60] All the critics named were Jews. The article was almost certainly written by the Party hack and *Pravda* journalist David Zaslavsky. A former Menshevik and active Zionist until he joined the Bolsheviks in 1921, Zaslavsky had written several hatchet jobs for Stalin to expiate his sins and expedite his rise into the Soviet elite.*

*Zaslavsky was probably the author of the infamous *Pravda* article of 1936 ('Muddle Instead of Music') denouncing Shostakovich's opera *Lady Macbeth of Mtsensk*. In 1929, Zaslavsky had denounced his own brother as a 'Trotskyist' to demonstrate his loyalty to the Party. On Fadeyev's initiative, and with the agreement of Stalin, Zaslavsky and Ehrenburg were both

The *Pravda* article was soon followed by a series of attacks on 'rootless cosmopolitans' in the rest of the Soviet press. Stalinists competed with each other to denounce the 'anti-patriotic groups' which they claimed were undermining Soviet poetry, music, art and cinema.[61] For the Jews named by these vicious articles, the consequences were harsh. Many lost their jobs, or were expelled from the Party or their union, effectively depriving them of their livelihood. Some were arrested. A few saved themselves by confessing their 'mistakes' or by distancing themselves from the 'rootless cosmopolitans'. Of the theatre critics denounced by Fadeyev, only one man was arrested, Iogann Altman, the victim of an ugly article, filled with hatred and thinly veiled anti-Semitism, in the journal *Soviet Art*. 'In the name of the Soviet people, we pronounce that the Altmans of this world pollute Soviet culture like living corpses,' it declared. 'We must get rid of their rotten stench to purify the air.' Altman was denounced in the Writers' Union by Anatoly Sofronov, a fanatical supporter of the anti-Semitic campaign and a major power in the Union during the long absences of the alcoholic Fadeyev. Expelled from both the Writers' Union and the Party, Altman was arrested on the night of Stalin's death in March 1953. Altman and Fadeyev had been good friends for many years. It was Fadeyev who had insisted that he should work with Mikhoels in the Jewish Theatre. 'He needs an adviser, a commissar: think of it as a Party command!', Fadeyev had said. When Altman was asked by his interrogators how he came to work with Mikhoels, he said nothing about Fadeyev. He knew that he might save himself by naming the leader of the Writers' Union, but he did not want to implicate Fadeyev in what was being styled as a 'Zionist conspiracy'. Undoubtedly, Altman hoped that Fadeyev would respond in kind, would intervene to rescue him. But Fadeyev did nothing. Fadeyev was absent from the meeting at the Writers' Union when Altman was expelled, and nobody could find him in Moscow (Simonov believed that he had disappeared on a drinking binge to escape his responsibilities). Altman never recovered from Fadeyev's betrayal. Released from jail in May 1953, he died two years later, a broken man.[62]

Simonov too was dragged into the 'anti-cosmopolitan' campaign. At first he tried to hold a moderate line. If he did not openly protest against

---

removed from the list of members of the JAFC shortly before the arrest of its other members in December 1948 (RGALI, f. 2846, op. 1, dd. 75, 101, 187, 310, 311).

the campaign, he also didn't align himself with Sofronov and the other hardliners. Simonov was not an anti-Semite. As the editor of *Novyi mir*, he had published several writers of Jewish origin. His first two wives were Jewish; the second, Zhenia Laskina, was a cousin of the writer Boris Laskin, who had been named as an 'enemy of Soviet literature' in Begicheva's original denunciation to the MVD. Simonov's moderate position irritated the hardliners in the Party and the Writers' Union. Simonov had many enemies: critics who were jealous of his status as 'Stalin's favourite' which had done so much to promote him, as a young man, to the top of the Soviet establishment; and members of the Central Committee who thought that Stalin's protection had made Simonov insubordinate to the rest of the Party leadership. To drive a wedge between the writer and Stalin, these hardliners accused Simonov of trying to protect the 'cosmopolitans'. The most vicious of these accusations came from Viktor Vdovichenko, the editor of *Soviet Art*. Vdovichenko sent Malenkov a long denunciation, listing more than eighty Jewish names in what he claimed to be a Zionist organization within the Writers' Union. Much of the denunciation was directed against Simonov. Vdovichenko accused him of protecting Zionists. He pointed to the editorial staff of *Novyi mir*, which he said included many Jews ('people without kith or kin'), and singled out for criticism Aleksandr Borshchagovsky, who had been brought by Simonov to Moscow from the Ukraine, where the theatre critic had been in disgrace for criticizing a play by Khrushchev's favourite writer, Aleksandr Korneichuk. Simonov was fond of Borshchagovsky, 'a quiet and modest man', whose literary opinions were indispensable at *Novyi mir*, according to Natalia Bianki, a member of the editorial staff. 'Simonov decided almost nothing without him. "Let's see what Borshchagovsky has to say", was his frequent comment.' Vdovichenko claimed that Borshchagovsky had not produced 'a single work that made him worthy of being on the staff of *Novyi mir*', and that his influence at the journal was purely a function of Simonov's Jewish sympathies. He pointed out that Simonov had been married to a Jew and that he had many Jewish friends.[63]

Like Fadeyev, Simonov ultimately gave in to the pressure of the hardliners. He was afraid of losing his position in the Stalinist elite and thought he had to prove his loyalty by joining in the campaign against the Jews. In a letter to the editor of *Pravda*, he countered the hardliners' accusations of Judaeophilia by distancing himself from Borshchagovsky and the other Jewish critics he had employed at *Novyi mir*.[64] The Kremlin urged Simonov to expand on the themes of the anonymous *Pravda* article ('About One Anti-Patriotic Group') in a keynote speech in the Writers' Union. Fadeyev had been reduced to a drunken wreck, and Sofronov was keen to do the job, but Malenkov believed that Simonov would give more authority to the 'anti-cosmopolitan' campaign precisely because of his well-known moderate stance. Simonov was further pressed by Fadeyev, who warned that Sofronov would give the speech if Simonov refused. A hardline anti-Semite with political ambitions in the Writers' Union, where he hoped to replace Simonov as the Kremlin's favourite to succeed Fadeyev, Sofronov was certain to add another dozen names to the existing list of Jewish writers and critics destined for expulsion from the Writers' Union. Fearful that power would fall into Sofronov's hands, Simonov agreed to give the speech. He delivered it at the Plenum of the Writers' Union on 4 February 1949. Simonov's first wife, the Jewish writer Natalia Sokolova (née Tipot), described in her diary the dreadful atmosphere as he delivered his denunciation of the 'anti-patriotic group':

The speech lasted an hour and a half, then there was a break, and then another session for an hour and a half. People listened, looking tense and guarded, no one spoke except for a rare whispered, 'Has he named someone new?' . . . 'Did you hear?' . . . 'Yet another cosmopolitan?' . . . 'A new cosmopolitan?' Some people made a list of all the names, as I did.[65]

In later years, Simonov continued to maintain that he had made the speech to keep the extremist Sofronov from taking control of the 'anti-cosmopolitan' campaign. Although remorseful about his role, Simonov insisted that it had been his aim to moderate the campaign against Jewish writers by taking up the leadership of it himself. This is supported by the memoirs of his friend, the theatre critic Borshchagovsky, who was with Simonov in his Gorky Street apartment when Malenkov phoned to say that Stalin wanted him to make the speech. Putting down the receiver, Simonov 'looked at me sadly and gazed out of the window', recalls Borshchagovsky. 'It took him less than ten minutes to reach his decision.' Then he said:

'I am going to make the speech, Shura [Aleksandr]. It is better if I do it, and not someone else.' Having yielded on that point, he looked for some argument to justify his 'active engagement', for an honest point of view he could hold to in this dishonest campaign. 'All this thuggishness (*khamstvo*) and rudeness we must end. We must learn to argue on a different level, to civilize our language. We have had, and we still have, the problem of the formalists, constructivist apologists, people who want to enslave us to the culture of the West, and we must talk about them.'[66]

It is also true that in his speech Simonov attempted to set the 'anti-cosmopolitan' campaign in a broader political and intellectual context rather than offering up some crude Zionist cabal. In a series of articles for the Soviet press, in which he built on the ideas of his speech of 4 February, Simonov accused the 'cosmopolitans' of 'putting [Jean-Paul] Sartre in the place of Maksim Gorky and the pornography of [Henry] Miller in the place of Tolstoy'.[67] The Cold War undoubtedly influenced his thinking on the need to defend the Soviet Union's 'national culture' against the 'rootless cosmopolitans' who would sell it into 'slavery to American imperialism . . . and the international power of the dollar'. But otherwise there is little evidence that Simonov's participation was crafted as a civilizing influence on the campaign against the Jews. His language was inflammatory. He called the 'anti-patriotic group' a conspiracy of 'criminals' and 'enemies' of Soviet culture who were not to be mistaken for mere 'aesthetes', because they had a 'militantly bourgeois and reactionary programme', namely working for the West in the Cold War. He blamed the Jews for bringing many of their problems on themselves. They had, he said, refused to assimilate into Soviet society and had embraced 'Jewish nationalism' after 1945. He sacked all the Jews from the editorial staff at *Novyi mir*. He even wrote to Stalin on behalf of the Writers' Union, calling for the exclusion from the Union of a long list of inactive writers, all of whom were Jews.[68]

His friend Borshchagovsky was included on that list. From the start of the 'anti-cosmopolitan' campaign, Simonov had been gradually distancing himself from the theatre critic, who had been singled out as one of the main leaders of the 'anti-patriotic group'. He knew that in the end he would be forced to denounce his friend, whose career he himself had promoted. After the phone call from Malenkov, when he agreed to give the speech against the 'anti-patriotic group', Simonov attempted to justify himself to Borshchagovsky by explaining: 'If I do it, it will put me in a stronger position. I will be able to help people, which at the

Aleksandr Borshchagovsky, 1947

moment is the most important thing.' He warned him not to come to the plenum, saying to the theatre critic as he left: 'If you come, I shall feel obliged to denounce you in even stronger terms.' Borshchagovsky did not read the speeches or the articles in which he was named by Simonov as a 'saboteur of the theatre', as a 'bourgeois enemy' of Soviet literature and 'literary scum'.* He had trusted Simonov – he had viewed him as a friend – and stoically claimed to understand that he was forced to 'perform a ritual ideological dance'.

Borshchagovsky was expelled from the Writers' Union and the Party. He lost his job at *Novyi mir* and was sacked from the Red Army Theatre, where he was the head of literature. Borshchagovsky and his family – his mother, his wife and their young daughter – were kicked out of their Moscow flat. For a while, they were put up by their friends, who let them sleep on floors or stay at their dachas (they even stayed at Simonov's dacha at Peredelkino). Borshchagovsky took repression in his stride: a survivor of the 1930s, he had learned to carry on as best he could. To make ends meet, he sold his possessions (mostly books) and borrowed money from friends, including Simonov, who gave him money, as Borshchagovsky understood, 'to ease his own conscience', and refused to let him pay it back.[69]

Filled with guilt towards his friend, Simonov went on seeing him as

*The phrase 'literary scum' (*literaturnye podonki*) had been used to characterize Zoshchenko in the Central Committee's decree of 14 August 1946.

often as he could between 1949 and 1953, when the ban on Borsh-chagovsky was finally lifted, but he never spoke to him about the speech. It seemed to Borshchagovsky that when they met, Simonov would 'look at me in an anxious way, as if he thought he needed to explain'. In July 1950, Simonov supported the publication of *The Russian Flag*, Borshchagovsky's patriotic novel set in the Crimean War. 'The book is accomplished, serious and necessary,' Simonov concluded in his report to the censors. 'I am convinced that its deeply patriotic content will touch readers' hearts ... Borshchagovsky has committed serious mistakes of an anti-patriotic character, that is evident, but he has suffered and he has acknowledged his mistakes.' The book was finally passed for publication in 1953.[70]

Interviewed fifty years later, in 2003, Borshchagovsky was still stoical about the injury Simonov had done him. 'One grows accustomed to the pain', was all he would say. But according to his wife, in the last years of his life, he was increasingly haunted by the events of 1949.* In his memoirs he concluded that Simonov had not found the civic courage to defend his friends and fellow writers from the hardline anti-Semites in the Writers' Union. He didn't feel Simonov was moved by fear or that he lacked a conscience. Rather, he believed that Simonov was driven by personal ambition, and especially by a kind of political servility: he was simply too devoted to Stalin, too infatuated with the aura of his power, to adopt a more courageous stand.[71]

The 'little terror' of the post-war years was very different from the Great Terror of 1937–8. It took place, not against the backdrop of apocalypse, when frightened people agreed to betrayals and denunci-ations in the desperate struggle to save their lives and families, but against the background of a relatively mundane and stable existence, when fear no longer deprived people of their moral sensibility. The repressions of the post-war years were carried out by career bureaucrats and functionaries like Simonov. These people did not have to participate in the system of repression. Simonov was probably not in danger of expulsion from the Writers' Union, let alone arrest. Had he refused to add his voice to the denunciation of the Jews, he might at most have suffered demotion from the leadership of the Writers' Union and dis-missal as the editor of *Novyi mir*, although of course he may have feared

---

*Aleksandr Borshchagovsky died in May 2006 at the age of ninety-four.

much worse. But the point is, people like Simonov had a choice. They could have followed a career path that skirted the pitfalls of political responsibility, as millions of others did, albeit at the cost of losing out on privileges and material rewards. For those unable to take a public stand, there were quieter ways to avoid involvement in political decisions that compromised their moral principles. As Borshchagovsky wrote of the people who betrayed him in 1949, could easily have chosen not to speak, they could have not shown up at the Plenum of the Writers' Union, or pretended to be ill: they were not subject to Party discipline. For Borshchagovsky, the persecutions of that period, and the behaviour of those who facilitated them, were rooted in an all-pervasive compliance with the Stalinist regime – the defining characteristic of ordinary Stalinists. As he wrote:

The phenomenon of 1949, and not only of that year, is not explained by fear – or if so, a fear that had long before dissolved into other elements within the human soul ... [more to the point is] the servility of officious hangers-on, who had so little courage and morality that they were unable even to stand up to the semi-official directives of the lowest bureaucrats.[72]

There were certainly people in a similar position of responsibility to Simonov who refused to get involved in the 'anti-cosmopolitan' campaign. The President of the Academy of Sciences, Sergei Vavilov, for example, quietly resisted intense pressure to denounce an 'anti-patriotic group' in the Academy and sabotaged his own bureaucracy to prevent the dismissal of Jewish scientists (his brother Nikolai, the geneticist, had been arrested in 1940 and starved to death in prison in 1943).[73] In the Writers' Union there were people such as Boris Gorbatov, the Party Secretary of the Writers' Union Presidium and a close friend of Simonov, who refused to go along with the campaign against the Jews. A Jew himself, Gorbatov had more cause to fear than Simonov: his wife had been arrested in 1948 and sentenced to ten years for 'foreign espionage', while he himself was not above political suspicion (in 1937, Gorbatov had been accused of propagating 'Trotskyist' opinions in his first novel, *Our Town*, a proletarian epic about the Five Year Plan in the Donbass; although he had narrowly avoided expulsion from the Party, his brother had been arrested as a 'Trotskyist' and shot in 1938). Yet despite the intense pressure of the Stalinist hardliners in the Writers' Union, who denounced him as a 'Jewish sympathizer' of the 'anti-patriotic group',

Gorbatov refused to join the persecution of his fellow Jews. For this he was forced to give up all his posts in the Party and the Writers' Union. Borshchagovsky recalls meeting him in 1949 at Simonov's dacha in Peredelkino. Having fallen out of favour with Stalin, Gorbatov was 'a broken man who had been driven into a corner', but he had managed to retain his moral dignity and principles.[74]

Simonov was an altogether more complex, perhaps even tragic, character. He clearly had a conscience: he was troubled and even repulsed by some aspects of the 'anti-cosmopolitan' campaign. But he lost himself in the Stalinist system. The military ethos and public-service values he inherited from the aristocracy were so closely harnessed to the moral categories and imperatives of the Soviet system that he was left with few other means to judge or regulate his own behaviour. Simonov had a hypertrophied sense of public duty and responsibility that defined his outlook on the world. 'Without the discipline of public duty,' Simonov once said, 'a person cannot be a complete human being.' He was an activist by temperament; he could never have pretended to be ill to avoid being forced to make a difficult moral choice. In Simonov's opinion, the avoidance of public responsibility was tantamount to cowardice. He had no time for people who were prone to indecisiveness, weakness or procrastination – all of which he considered human failings. He admired people who were rational and logical. These were the moral qualities he assigned to his fictional heroes – men like himself, only more courageous, who were able to draw the right conclusions from objective evidence and act decisively.[75]

It was the elevation of duty to a supreme virtue that determined Simonov's political obedience: he confused public virtue with submission to the Party line. He was in awe of Stalin. His post-war notebooks are filled with synopses of Stalin's works, quotations from his speeches and lists of the leader's phrases and ideas which he set out to learn in order to become more politically literate.[76] Simonov was infatuated with Stalin's power. He felt his presence, felt Stalin watching over him, in virtually everything he did. Stalin was his patron and protector, his teacher and his guide, his critic and confessor, and at times perhaps, in his imagination, his jailer, torturer and executioner.

The slightest criticism from the Soviet leader was enough to reduce Simonov to a state of total misery. In 1948, Simonov's novella *Dym otechestva* ('Smoke of the Fatherland') was savagely attacked by

Simonov (seated third from right) at the Congress of
Soviet Writers in the Belorussian Republic, Minsk, 1949

Agitprop's main journal (*Kul'tura i zhizn'*) with the personal backing of
Stalin, who, concluded Simonov, 'disliked the story intensely'. Frightened and depressed, Simonov could not understand what was wrong
with the book, which was one of his own favourites. 'When I wrote it,'
he later told a friend, 'I thought I was fulfilling my duty to the Party . . .
and to Stalin, who was then, two years after the end of the war, the
supreme authority for me.' The central figure in the novella is a Communist veteran of the war who returns from abroad to the Soviet Union in
1947. Believing that his duty to the nation has been done, he tries to
rebuild his private life in the difficult conditions of the post-war years.
The novella accurately portrayed a certain mood that was common at
that time, and it was a patriotic work, full of favourable comparisons
between the Soviet Union and the USA. But it did contain some straight
talk, about the famine of 1946–7 in particular, which was not done at
the time (it was not until the Khrushchev thaw that social problems were
addressed at all by Soviet literature), and it was this that had attracted
censure from the Party leadership. Simonov was shaken by the attack
on his work. It coincided with the attack on Fadeyev's novel *The Young
Guard* (1947), which had also been initiated by Stalin, and also in the
Agitprop journal, giving rise to the suspicion that the tyrant was

preparing a purge of the leaders of the Writers' Union. Desperate to understand why Stalin had disliked his work, and eager to correct it so that it would meet with his approval, Simonov went to Zhdanov for advice, but Stalin's chief of ideology had no light to shed on the matter – Zhdanov himself liked the novella – so Simonov resolved 'not to publish *Smoke of the Fatherland* again'.[77]

Shortly afterwards, Simonov was called by one of Zhdanov's secretaries, who asked him when he would be delivering his play about Kliueva and Roskin, the disgraced scientists, whom Stalin had accused of subservience towards the West. Stalin had originally proposed the idea of a novel on this subject at a meeting in the Kremlin with Fadeyev and Simonov in May 1947. There was a need, he said, for more patriotic works of fiction to expose the intelligentsia's submission to the West. Simonov agreed but suggested that the theme was better suited to a play. At that time Simonov was still writing *Smoke of the Fatherland*, so he put off working on the play, a serious political commission that he felt as a burden, although he did go to Zhdanov's offices to look at the materials on Kliueva and Roskin. Coming as it did so quickly after the attack on him by Agitprop, the call from Zhdanov's secretary was a clear message to Simonov that Stalin would forgive him for the mistakes he had made in his novella, if he delivered the play Stalin had been waiting for. Desperate to redeem himself, in the early months of 1948 Simonov produced the first draft of *Alien Shadow*, a crude propaganda play about a Soviet microbiologist whose infatuation with the West leads him to betray his motherland. In a shameful act of political toadying, Simonov sent the draft to Zhdanov for his approval, and on his advice to Molotov and Stalin for their approval as well. Stalin telephoned Simonov and gave him precise instructions on how to rewrite the play. He advised Simonov to place greater emphasis on the egotism of the scientist-protagonist (Stalin: 'he sees his research as his own personal property') and to highlight the government's benevolence by ending the play with the Minister of Health implementing Stalin's orders to forgive the errant scientist and let him carry on with his research. 'That is how I see the play,' Stalin said. 'You need to correct it. How you do it is your own business. Once you have corrected it, the play will be passed.' Simonov reworked the ending of the play, making the changes suggested by Stalin, and sent him the second draft for his approval. 'I wrote the play in agony, under duress, forcing myself to believe in the necessity of what I was doing,' recalled Simonov. 'I could have chosen not to write it, if only I had found the strength of character to resist this self-violation. Today, thirty years later, I am ashamed that I lacked the courage to do that.'[78]

The episode ended in tragicomedy. The play was published in the journal *Znamia* and nominated for the Stalin Prize, along with several other plays, whose merits were considered by the Secretariat of the Writers' Union, before being passed up to the committee of the Stalin Prize. At the meeting of the Secretariat, where Simonov was present, several of his colleagues criticized the ending of the play (the one suggested by Stalin) on the grounds that it was 'too weak, too liberal, almost a political capitulation, to forgive the scientist rather than to punish him'. Simonov said nothing about his telephone conversation with Stalin. 'I sat there in silence listening to my colleagues censuring Stalin's liberalism.' The play won the Stalin Prize.[79]

Simonov was accustomed to self-criticism and self-censorship. He wrote many letters to the Soviet leadership confessing to mistakes. He drafted several stories which he then put in the drawer because he knew the censors would never pass them for publication. In 1973, Simonov was asked by the German writer Christa Wolf whether he had ever felt pressure to write what he knew to be politically acceptable. Simonov admitted to a life-long struggle between the writer and the censor in himself and even acknowledged feelings of disgust when his cowardice gained the upper hand.[80]

Occasionally, the writer in Simonov did rebel against the censor, and the poet spoke up for his political conscience. In October 1946, at the height of the Zhdanovshchina, for example, Simonov wrote an angry letter to Aleksei Surkov, the editor of the journal *Ogonyok*, to which he had previously sent a number of poems for publication. Simonov expressed his bitter disagreement, 'in substance and in principle', with the petty cuts and changes Surkov had made to his work, including the removal of the names of foreigners (on 'patriotic' grounds) and the names of Soviet figures who had been politically disgraced. Simonov took particular exception to the cutting of a poem dedicated to his old friend David Ortenberg, who had been dismissed as the editor of the Red Army newspaper *Krasnaia zvezda* in 1943 after he had refused an order from the Kremlin to sack several fellow Jews from his editorial staff. Ortenberg had bravely written to the Party leadership to voice his discontent with the 'unchecked anti-Semitism' which he had detected in some sections of the military and in many areas of the Soviet rear. 'I want to include this poem,' Simonov insisted, 'I like it as a whole. It is dedicated to a person I love, and I want it to remain as I wrote it.'[81]

Perhaps Simonov attached more significance to his poem about Ortenberg as he became entangled in the literary persecution of the Soviet Jews. His conscience often troubled him, even when he was involved in the repressive measures of the Stalinist regime, and the conflict nearly broke him as a writer and a man. The physical and mental stress of his political responsibilities showed up in his changing appearance: in 1948, Simonov, aged thirty-three, seemed a young man in the prime of life; just five years later, he looked grey and middle-aged. His hands suffered from a nervous skin condition, and only heavy drinking calmed his nerves.[82]

Simonov in 1948 (left) and in 1953 (right)

In his memoirs, composed in the last year of his life, Simonov recalls an incident that particularly troubled his conscience and brought him face to face with the realization that Stalin's tyranny rested on the cowardly complicity of functionaries like himself. The incident occurred in 1952 at a meeting in the Kremlin to judge the Stalin Prize. It was more or less agreed to give the prize to Stepan Zlobin's novel *Stepan Razin*, but Malenkov objected that Zlobin had behaved badly in the war because he had let himself be captured by the Germans. In fact, as everybody knew, Zlobin had behaved with extraordinary courage; he had even led a group of resistance fighters in the concentration camp where he was held. After Malenkov had made his statement there was a deathly hush. Stalin stood up and paced around the room, passing by the seated Politburo members and the leaders of the Writers' Union and asking out loud, as if to himself, but also for them to consider, 'Shall we forgive him or not?' There was silence. Stalin continued to pace around the room and asked again, 'Shall we forgive him or not?' Again there was silence: no one dared to speak. Stalin went on with his pacing and asked for a third time, 'Shall we forgive him or not?' Finally he answered his own question: 'Let's forgive him.' Everyone had understood that the fate of an innocent man had been hanging in the balance: either he would win the Stalin Prize or he would be sent to the Gulag. Though all the writers at the meeting were at least acquainted with Zlobin, no one spoke in his defence, not even when invited to do so by Stalin. As Simonov explains: 'In our eyes it was not just a question of whether to forgive or not forgive a guilty man, but whether to speak out against a denunciation' made by a figure as senior as Malenkov, a denunciation that had evidently been accepted as truth by Stalin, for whom the question was whether to forgive a guilty man. Looking back on this event, Simonov came to the conclusion that Stalin had always been aware of the accusations against Zlobin, and that he had himself deliberately nominated his book for the Stalin Prize so that he could stage this 'little game'. Knowing that there would be nobody with the courage to defend Zlobin, Stalin's aim had been to show that he, and only he, decided the fate of men.[83]

4

The 'anti-cosmopolitan' campaign opened the floodgates to anti-Semitism in the Soviet Union. Anti-Semitism had a long history in the Russian Empire. After 1917, it continued to exist, especially among the urban lower classes, whose hatred of the Jews in trade was a major factor in the popular resentment of the NEP which Stalin had exploited during his rise to power. The widespread indifference of the lower classes towards the purges of the 1930s was also partly shaped by the perception that the Party leaders, the main victims of the Terror, were all 'Jews' in any case. But generally before the war the Soviet government made serious attempts to stamp out anti-Semitism as a relic of the tsarist past, and Soviet Jews were relatively untroubled by discrimination or hostility. All this changed with the German occupation of the Soviet Union. Nazi propaganda released the latent force of anti-Semitism in Ukraine and Belarus, where a significant proportion of the non-Jewish population silently supported the destruction of the Jews and took part as auxiliaries in rounding up the Jews for execution or deportation to the camps. Even in the remote eastern regions of the Soviet rear there was an explosion of anti-Semitism, as soldiers and civilians evacuated from the western regions of the Soviet Union stirred up hatred of the Jews.[84]

With the post-war adoption of Russian nationalism as the ruling ideology of the Stalinist regime, the Jews were recast as 'alien outsiders' and potential 'spies' and 'enemies', allies of Israel and the USA. Borshch-agovsky recalls the atmosphere of 'Kill the Yids!' which developed under cover of the 'anti-cosmopolitan' campaign:

'Rootless', 'cosmopolitan', 'anti-patriot' were useful words for the Black Hundreds* – masks behind which the old term 'Yid' could hide. To take away the mask and speak that sweet primeval word was full of risks: the Black Hundred was a coward, and anti-Semitism is strictly punished by the Criminal Code.[85]

The language of officials who broadened the campaign against the Jews was similarly masked. Between 1948 and 1953, tens of thousands of Soviet Jews were arrested, dismissed from their jobs, expelled from their universities or forcibly evicted from their homes, yet they were never told (and it was never mentioned in the paperwork) that the reason for these actions had to do with their ethnic origins. Officially, at least, such discrimination was illegal in the Soviet Union.

Before the war most of the Jews of Russia's major cities were only partly conscious of themselves as Jews. They came from families that had left behind the traditional Jewish life of the shtetl and embraced the urban culture of the Soviet Union. They had exchanged their Judaism and their Jewish ethnicity for a new identity based upon the principles of Soviet internationalism. They thought of themselves as 'Soviet citizens', and immersed themselves in Soviet society, rising to positions that had been closed to Jews before 1917, even if they retained Jewish

---

*Anti-Semitic Russian nationalists of the tsarist era.

customs, habits and beliefs in the privacy of their own homes. The anti-Jewish campaigns of the post-war years compelled these Jews to see themselves as Jews again.

The Gaister family was typical of those Jews who had left the Pale of Settlement and found a new home in the Soviet Union. Before his arrest in 1937, Aron Gaister was a leading member of the Soviet government, the Deputy Commissar of Agriculture; his wife, Rakhil Kaplan, was a senior economist in the Commissariat of Heavy Industry. Their daughters Inna and Natalia were brought up as Soviet citizens, immersed in the universal culture and ideas of Russian literature and barely conscious of the Jewish elements that remained in their Moscow home – from the food they ate to the family rituals on Soviet holidays and the tales of the pogroms which their grandmother told. In 1944, Inna enrolled as a student in the Physics Faculty of Moscow University. She worked in the evenings at the laboratory of one of her professors to support herself and help her mother, who, after her release from the ALZhIR labour camp in 1945, had settled in Kolchugino, 100 kilometres north-east of Moscow. In 1948, Inna's younger sister was refused entry to Moscow University. When Inna went to find out why, she was told by the secretary of the Party committee that she should look at her sister's questionnaire: Natalia had entered 'Jewish' under nationality.* This was the first time Inna was made conscious of her Jewishness, she says. A Russian boy with lower grades was admitted to the university instead of Natalia. He went on to become a professor.

In April 1949, Inna was arrested during her defence of her diploma at the university. Convicted as 'the daughter of an enemy of the people', she was sentenced to five years of exile in Kazakhstan, where she found a job as a schoolteacher in Borovoe, a bleak and remote steppeland town. Two months later, Natalia was arrested too: she had failed to record the arrest of her parents in the questionnaire she had filled out to join the Komsomol at the Moscow Pedagogical Institute, where she was accepted as a student in 1948. The fact that she had kept a photograph of her father, instead of renouncing him, was taken by her interrogators as an admission of her guilt as a 'socially dangerous element'. Natalia was also sentenced to five years of exile in Kazakhstan. She

---

*Natalia was not asserting her own Jewishness: nationality, or ethnic origin, was a required category in all official documents.

ended up in Borovoe with Inna and her mother, who joined them there.[86]

Vera Bronshtein was born in 1893 to a Jewish family in western Ukraine. She joined the Bolsheviks as a schoolgirl in Odessa in 1907 and became an active member of the revolutionary underground, taking part in the Bolshevik seizure of power in Moscow in October 1917. She married a Russian factory worker, had a daughter, Svetlana, born in 1926, and then left her husband (who turned out to be an anti-Semite) when he threatened to denounce her as a 'Trotskyist' in 1928. Vera worked in the administration of the State Archives. She studied history at the Institute of Red Professors and went on to become a history professor, handing down the certainties of Stalin's *Short Course* to the soldiers of the Frunze Military Academy in Moscow, where she taught from 1938. Untouched by the Great Terror, Vera and her daughter enjoyed the comforts of the Soviet elite until 1948, when Vera was arrested on the basis of a denunciation by her ex-husband. Convicted of 'counter-revolutionary activity', she was sentenced to five years in the Potma labour camps. At that time Svetlana was a student and an activist in the Komsomol at Moscow University. Threatened with expulsion from the university, she was put under growing pressure to denounce other students and professors as 'Jewish nationalists', but she refused, unable to believe the propaganda about 'Zionist conspiracies'. Naively, she even wrote to Stalin to complain about discrimination against Jewish students at the university, an action which led to her own arrest in 1952 and a sentence of ten years in the Viatka labour camp.[87]

Olga Loputina-Epshtein was born in 1913 to a Jewish family that left the Pale of Settlement for Poltava after 1917. She moved to Leningrad in the early 1930s when she married Boris Epshtein, another Jew from the Pale, and became an accountant in the Lenin Factory. Their son Mark was born in 1937. During the war, Olga and her son were evacuated to Cheliabinsk. Boris was killed on the Belorussian Front in 1944. Olga remarried and returned with her new husband and Mark to Leningrad in 1945. The city had a chronic housing shortage and, even with the help of Olga's brother, who worked in the MVD, they could only find a tiny room in a communal apartment. Among their neighbours, who were mostly workers, anti-Semitic attitudes were strongly held, and they frequently surfaced during arguments. 'The apartment was a tinderbox of ethnic hatred waiting to explode,' recalls Mark.

The neighbours, who were often drunk, would swear at us, curse and threaten us, tell us we should go to Palestine, whenever they had some complaint, and then my mother would say to my stepfather, who was a pure Russian: 'Kolia, why don't you deal with your fellow tribalists?' The atmosphere was poisonous. Sometimes the threats became so serious that my mother would run to the Party headquarters [in the Smolny building opposite the apartment], but nothing ever came of her complaints.

At school Mark was bullied by the other children, who refused to sit next to 'the dirty Yid'. They painted 'Yid' on the door of the building where he lived. Olga complained many times to the school authorities. She even wrote to the Party leadership, but without effect. Nor was there any point in taking her complaint to the MVD, because her brother had been arrested, along with many other Jewish officers of the MVD, in connection with the Leningrad Affair. Olga became ill with anxiety and suffered several heart attacks between 1949 and 1953 which left her practically an invalid. After the death of her second husband, in 1955, she became wholly dependent on her son. They continued living in the same apartment, with the same anti-Semitic neighbours, until Olga died in 1987. At the age of sixty-five, Mark got married and moved out.[88]

The anti-Jewish campaigns also took their toll on the Laskin family. In 1943, the Laskins had returned to Moscow from Cheliabinsk, where they had been evacuated in the war. Samuil and Berta lived in the apartment of their eldest daughter, Fania, in the Arbat, where Zhenia's son Aleksei and her sister Sonia also lived (Zhenia lived at the family apartment on Zubov Square). Samuil returned to the world of trade, supplying salted fish to Gastronom, the state's network of food stores. Fania continued working in the administration of the tractor industry, while Sonia went to work at the Stalin Factory, the huge car plant in Moscow, where she soon rose to become the head of metal and technical supply. It was an important job because in the post-war years the Stalin Factory was introducing new technology and higher grades of steel for the mass production of lighter cars and lorries. Sonia was devoted to her work. Her husband, Ernst Zaidler, a Hungarian Communist working for the Comintern, had been arrested and shot in December 1937, and they did not have children. Zhenia worked as a radio editor and coped as best she could with Aleksei, who was often ill. She did not want to call on Simonov for help, so her parents took care of the child. Simonov's parents also helped. In 1947, they took Aleksei on an extended seaside holiday to help him recover from TB.[89]

Simonov himself had little time for Aleksei. He saw him only once or twice a year. His mother Aleksandra needed to remind him to write to Aleksei on his birthday. In 1952, on Aleksei's thirteenth birthday, a telegram from Simonov had failed to reach his son, so he later wrote to him:

Dear Alyosha!

I have been feeling unwell, and was not in Moscow, and only today did I realize that, by some misunderstanding, they did not dispatch the telegram which I wrote to you on your birthday ... I believe in your future and I hope that with the passing years you will grow up to become a little friend. Another year has brought you closer to that ... Twice a week I pass by the new building of Moscow University, and I always think that you will study there some day, and then you'll start on your working life – going where the state sends you. Think of that with joy, and work joyously towards the happy calling that waits for you and millions of children just like you ... .[90]

Aleksei was not offended by the formality of this letter: all his relations with his father were like that, and since there were so few communications he treasured each one of them. His father's letters were usually typed, meaning they had been dictated to a secretary. Pedagogical in tone, they were more like the letters of a Party functionary than those of a father to a son. This one was written in the summer of 1948, when Aleksei was eight years old:

Dear Alyosha,

I received your letter and drawing. As far as the drawing is concerned, it is not bad in my opinion, especially the cockerel. But there is no cause for pride. Remember, your father at your age could draw better than you can, so you must work even harder to catch up. I hope that your promise to get top marks will be true not just on paper but in reality as well. I would be very glad of that.[91]

Aleksei recalls his father often telling him that 'ties of blood' had no special significance for him: it was one of his 'democratic principles' to treat his family on the same terms as colleagues and subordinates. Aleksei paid the cost of his father's principles. He could not understand why his famous father, who was so popular with everybody else, had so little time for him. On the few occasions when his father came to take him out, Aleksei felt awkward, there were long silences, but his father never noticed his unease. In the spring of 1947, Simonov sent his son a suit (brown jacket, brown shorts and a cap) which he had brought back from a trip to the USA. Aleksei did not like the shorts – the boys in the yard would laugh at him and even beat him when he wore them – so he put them in a drawer. Several weeks later a government car turned up at the house on Zubov Square to take Aleksei to visit his father. He had not seen him for a year. Berta, Aleksei's grandmother, made him wear the brown suit to show his father that he liked the gift. In front of all the other boys, who had gathered in the yard to inspect the limousine, Aleksei walked out and got into the car. He was driven to the Grand Hotel, where Simonov had taken a private dining room to entertain his friends. The seven-year-old boy was presented to the company and called on by his father to give them a 'report' on how he had fared during the past year at school. Having been informed of his son's success at school, Simonov had planned a surprise for him: a cook in a white suit and a big white hat came in carrying a 'surprise omelette' (made of ice cream) on a silver dish. Aleksei was left to eat the 'omelette' on his own while his father went on talking with his friends. To Aleksei, his father seemed 'all-powerful and almost magical'. At one point Simonov turned towards his son and asked him if he liked his suit. Aleksei gave him a polite response. Shortly afterwards Aleksei was driven home – 'to wait', as he recalls, 'for the next meeting with my father, maybe in a month, maybe six, depending on how busy he was with his work for the government'.[92]

Apart from his mother Aleksandra, Sonia was the only person who

Samuil and Berta, Sonia, Aleksei and Zhenia, *circa* 1948

dared to criticize Simonov for neglecting Aleksei. In October 1947, Sonia wrote to Simonov. Aleksei had been ill and needed food and medicines which the Laskins could not get:

It is distasteful to have to remind you for a second time (only the second?) of your obligations to your son. You allow yourself to ignore him to a degree that I find astonishing. Believe me, neither I nor Zhenia would approach you if it was not necessary for your child, but it is wrong to make Alyosha suffer because we feel uncomfortable about asking you for a favour – a feeling which is wholly the result of your behaviour. If things were different, I would write you off, I would stop your son from loving a father who cannot even spare two hours for him. I have told you this before.[93]

In May 1950, Sonia was arrested and held in solitary confinement in the Lefortovo prison in Moscow, where she was interrogated in connection with the Stalin Factory Affair, in which the Jewish workers of the car plant were accused of spying for the USA. The origins of the affair went back to 1948, when some of the factory's workers had begun organizing group trips to the Jewish Theatre in Moscow. The Stalin Factory had a large contingent of Jewish workers, mostly engineers and administrators, who were supportive of the JAFC and the foundation of Israel. Their cultural activities were encouraged by the deputy director of the factory, Aleksandr Eidinov, who also gave a tour of the car plant to the American ambassador. This was enough for the MGB to fabricate an 'anti-Soviet group of bourgeois Jewish nationalists at the Stalin Factory', which, it claimed, was passing industrial secrets to the USA. The initiative for the investigation came from Nikita Khrushchev, the Moscow Party boss from December 1949, although he was probably following instructions from Stalin, who by this time was seeing 'Jewish spies' and 'plotters' everywhere. Convicted by a military tribunal, Eidinov was one of fourteen 'leaders' who were later shot. More than a hundred other Jewish workers from the factory, and several hundred more from factories across the Soviet Union, were sent to various labour camps.[94]

Sonia was sentenced to twenty-five years of hard labour in the camps of Vorkuta in the Far North. Fania and Zhenia concealed the length of her sentence from Samuil and Berta, telling them that she had been given just five years, because they feared the truth would kill them. Sonia was sent to the brick factory in Vorkuta, where she worked with her usual energy and initiative. Even in the Gulag she was entirely dedicated to the cause of Soviet industry. Sonia was rewarded with a privileged position as a librarian in the labour camp, but in her letters home she frequently expressed her frustration that she could have served the country better as a senior industrialist than by filing books.

Sonia's arrest took a heavy toll on Samuil's health. Throughout her absence he seemed to be weighed down by an immense sadness, according to Fania. Samuil was seventy-one when Sonia was arrested. He had always been a sprightly man, full of life and energy, but after her arrest he became old and frail. He could no longer work at the same pace he had worked before. Still, traditions continued. Every Sunday for the next five years the family and friends would meet as usual for the famous 'Laskin suppers', when Berta would prepare delicious Jewish dishes and Samuil would hold his kitchen parliament. Simonov was never there, but his parents often were. 'They were different people, from a different class,' recalls Fania, 'but they got on well with our parents, and they loved Zhenia and Aleksei.' The opening toast would always be the same: 'To the return!' If a letter from Sonia had arrived during the previous week, it would be read out and the assembled guests would discuss her news. There would always be some tears. Everyone would give their greetings to Sonia for the reply which Zhenia would write.

By the early 1950s, conditions in many of the camps had begun to improve, as the administrators of the Gulag looked for ways to get the prisoners to make greater efforts, and weekly letters were not unusual for star workers like Sonia. Censors still read the correspondence, but the rules were more relaxed, and it was possible for prisoners and relatives to write with a new openness. There were even occasions when Sonia was allowed to call her family on the telephone – occasions when emotions ran too high for proper talk. 'My dear girl,' Zhenia wrote to Sonia after one such call,

You cannot understand what a joy it was for all of us, but especially for Mama and Papa. It makes it easier for them to wait. Papa was trembling and could not say a word for the first minute. I cannot tell you how happy they are to have heard your voice . . . Aleksei – he has grown up so much that you would not recognize him – he was very nervous when he spoke to you, that's why his voice sounded strange. He said something stupid about shaving and then got depressed because of it.

In 1952, Zhenia went to stay with Sonia in Vorkuta. It was part of the relaxation of the Gulag system to allow relatives to visit prisoners. Zhenia was one of the first visitors to Vorkuta. On the night before her departure she asked Simonov to come to the house at Zubov Square. Aleksei overheard his parents' conversation. Zhenia was afraid that she might be arrested in the labour camp (it was a common fear of relatives) and she wanted Simonov to give a solemn promise that, should anything happen to her, he would let their son remain with Samuil and Berta until she returned. Zhenia was generally a diplomat in life. She had an extraordinary capacity for getting on with people of all kinds, without judging them, but on this matter she was adamant – it was a question of principle: Aleksei was not to live with Simonov.

Zhenia (left) and Sonia at Vorkuta, 1952

Zhenia never asked Simonov for anything for herself. In 1951, she had been sacked from her radio job, as part of a general purge of Jews in radio. For a long time she could not find work. She applied to dozens of literary magazines and newspapers and sent along articles she hoped they might publish, but she did not turn to Simonov. For Sonia, though, she would do it. Much of Zhenia's energy at the time was taken up with the appeal for Sonia's release. She wrote to all the relevant authorities: to the Military Tribunal that had sentenced Sonia; to the Military Procurator responsible for the review of its cases; she even wrote to the editor of *Pravda* in the hope that justice would be done. Finally, Zhenia appealed to Simonov. Over a period of six months, she met him several times, hoping to get information and advice. Simonov was unwilling to become involved, as Zhenia wrote to Sonia:

You cannot imagine how Kostia [Simonov] has changed. Nothing remains of the person we once knew. In the past few years I have seen him very little, and never for more than a few minutes, so I'm struck all the more – as you would be too – by his new personality . . . It is not just a question of his getting older (he is still comparatively young), nor of his becoming wiser with experience or as a result of his exalted position and prosperity. No, it is something else entirely . . . Kostia promised to get us the information we need. I thought it was worth waiting for because the information was likely to be reliable, but he still hasn't done it. No doubt he is too busy . . . He could have done more but – God go with him – let him live his quiet and comfortable life. I have simply stopped respecting him.

In Simonov's defence there was probably not a lot that he could have done, even had he chosen to intervene on Sonia's behalf. Certainly that was the view taken by the rest of the Laskin family, who continued to treat him with affection and esteem. On the rare occasions when they saw him, they never raised the question of Sonia's release. 'We knew that he was close to Stalin and that he could have had a word with him,' Fania explains, 'but none of us ever brought that up – we just couldn't allow ourselves to do it.'[95]

In any case, by this time Simonov had become so entangled in the Stalinist campaigns against the Jews that he would have put himself in a difficult position if he had tried to act for the Laskins. When Simonov took charge of the literary newspaper *Literaturnaia gazeta*, in 1950, he had been instructed by the Kremlin to bring it into line with its own position in the 'anti-cosmopolitan' campaign. The previous editor had been too soft, and Stalin was depending on Simonov to turn the influential newspaper into the vanguard of the Party's 'struggle against alien bourgeois elements' in Soviet culture. On taking over as its editor, Simonov dismissed eleven members of the paper's staff (all of them Jews) for 'poor work and political mistakes'. Under his control the newspaper regularly published articles and editorials whose anti-Semitism was only thinly disguised by the 'ideological struggle' with 'comopolitanism' and 'servility towards the West'. Having been a 'moderate' in the early stages of the anti-cosmopolitan campaign, Simonov, it seems, was becoming one of its hardliners. He maintained this position right until the end of the Stalinist regime. On 24 March 1953, more than two weeks after

Stalin's death, Simonov wrote on behalf of the Secretariat of the Writers' Union to the Central Committee with a list of names of Jewish writers who needed to be purged (as 'dead-weight') from the Writers' Union. Even later, he wrote to insist on the purge of his old friend and war comrade Aleksandr Krivitsky, the editor of the international section of *Literaturnaia gazeta*, because of 'certain biographical facts', as he put it in his denunciation to the Central Committee, not least Krivitsky's lack of vigilance against Jewish nationalists.[96]

Vigilance was exactly what Simonov was trying to display. Under growing pressure from a series of attacks by anti-Semites who, it seemed, had the support of the Kremlin, Simonov reacted as he always had: he frantically tried to demonstrate his loyalty. The campaign against Simonov began in 1951 with a public argument about the use of pseudonyms by Jewish writers. At a meeting to discuss the Stalin Prize, Stalin asked why the writer Orest Maltsev did not use his Jewish name (Rovinsky) and proposed that anyone using a Russian pseudonym should henceforth be required to include his Jewish name in brackets on all official forms.* This had been official custom during tsarist times, when Jews and revolutionaries were seen as practically synonymous, but after 1917 the practice had been dropped because it was considered anti-Semitic. The use of pseudonyms was widely discussed in the Soviet press, starting in 1949, with hardliners urging the return to the system of identifying Jewish names. In February 1951, an article appeared in *Komsomolskaia pravda* by Mikhail Bubennov ('Are Literary Pseudonyms Still Necessary?'). It was a nasty article, openly anti-Semitic in character, in which Bubennov taunted Jewish writers for adopting pseudonyms and accused them, 'chameleon-like', of 'hiding from society'. As the editor of *Literaturnaia gazeta*, Simonov responded to the article, claiming that the use of pseudonyms was a private matter and citing laws from the 1920s that gave writers the right to adopt them. He signed off the article as 'Konstantin (Kirill) Simonov'. It was a courageous argument. *Komsomolskaia pravda* then came out with a defence of Bubennov by no less a person than Mikhail Sholokhov, the celebrated author of *Quiet Flows the Don*. Simonov was doubtful that Sholokhov had really written it. He wanted to call him and ask him, man to man, what sort of pressure

---

*Maltsev (Rovinsky) was in fact a Russian but he shared the name of a well-known Jewish editor called Rovinsky at *Izvestiia* (Stalin had probably confused the two). He changed his name from Rovinsky to Maltsev after an anti-Semitic reaction against one of his earlier novels.

had been placed on him, but then thought better of it. Instead he wrote a second article in *Literaturnaia gazeta*, accusing Sholokhov and the Bubennov campaign of 'cheap sensationalism' and claiming that he would not write another word about the controversy.[97]

Thousands of other people did. The controversy produced an avalanche of letter-writing to the press. Some people wrote in support of Simonov – many of them Jews, others choosing to remain anonymous. But most correspondents agreed with Bubennov, either because in their view there was no need for any pseudonyms in the Soviet Union, where 'everyone is equal regardless of their race', or because they thought the Jews had something to conceal. Many of the letters were violently anti-Semitic and accused Simonov of 'acting as defender of the Jews'.[98]

By this stage a whispering campaign had started against Simonov. It was rumoured that he was a Jew. Towards the end of 1952, Simonov was approached by Aleksei Surkov, a leading member of the Writers' Union and an opponent of the anti-Semitic campaign. Surkov told him that during the past year he had been involved in a number of discussions with senior bureaucrats from the Central Committee about a series of denunciations claiming that Simonov was a 'secret Jew'. Some people said that his real name was Simanovich, that he was the son of a Jewish craftsman on the estate of 'Countess Obolenskaia', who had adopted him; others that he was the son a baptized Jew from St Petersburg. They all pointed to his 'Jewish looks' and to the fact that he used a pseudonym (Konstantin instead of Kirill). Simonov's initial reaction was to dismiss all these rumours as ridiculous: his mother was a princess, not a countess, and she had no estate. But the Simanovich story found its way into a threatening denunciation by a veteran member of the Party, Vladimir Orlov, who accused Simonov of promoting Jews to the editorial staff of *Literaturnaia gazeta* in order to transform the newspaper into a 'Zionist organization'. The threat loomed larger in January 1953, when Surkov visited Simonov again and told him he had been approached by the writer Vladimir Kruzhkov, who claimed to have evidence of a literary group in Moscow with connections to Jewish nationalists throughout Eastern Europe and the Soviet Union: according to Kruzhkov, the leader of this group was Simonov. Surkov was taking a huge personal risk by telling Simonov, because he had been sworn by Kruzhkov not to say a word. 'There are some bastards digging around under you,' Surkov warned. 'They're digging your grave.'[99]

The anti-Jewish campaign reached its climax around this time. The final episode was the absurd Doctors' Plot. The plot had its origins in 1948, when Lydia Timashuk, a doctor in the Kremlin Hospital who also worked for the MGB, wrote to Stalin two days before Zhdanov's death, claiming that his doctors had failed to recognize the gravity of his condition. The letter was ignored and filed away, but three years later it was used by Stalin to accuse the Kremlin doctors of belonging to a 'Zionist conspiracy' to murder Zhdanov and the rest of the Soviet leadership. None of the doctors who had treated Zhdanov was Jewish, so Stalin had to find a way to link his death with Zionists. The fabrication of the plot hinged on the confession beaten out of Dr Iakov Etinger, a leading diagnostician, who had been arrested in November 1950 for uttering anti-Soviet thoughts to relatives and friends. Etinger confessed that he was a Jewish nationalist and that he had the protection of Viktor Abakumov, the head of the MGB. After the arrest of Abakumov, in July 1951, hundreds of doctors and MGB officials were arrested and tortured into making confessions, as Stalin concocted a huge international conspiracy that linked Soviet Jews in the medical profession, the Leningrad Party organization, the MGB and the Red Army to Israel and the USA. The country seemed to be returning to the atmosphere of 1937 with the Jews in the role of the 'enemies of the people'. In December 1952, Stalin told a meeting of the Central Committee that 'every Jew is a potential spy for the United States', thus making the entire Jewish people the target of his terror. Thousands of Jews were arrested, expelled from jobs and homes, and deported as 'rootless parasites' from the major cities to remote regions of the Soviet Union. Stalin ordered the construction of a vast network of new labour camps in the Far East, where all the Jews would be sent. Throughout the Soviet Union people cursed the Jews. Patients refused to visit Jewish doctors, who were hounded out of practice and, in many cases, forced to work as labourers. Rumours spread of doctors killing babies in their wards. Pregnant mothers stayed away from hospitals. People wrote to the press calling on the Soviet authorities to 'clear out' the 'parasites', to 'exile them from the big cities, where there are so many of these swine'.[100]

And then at the height of this hysteria, Stalin died.

5

Stalin had suffered a stroke and lay unconscious for five days before he died on 5 March 1953. He might have been saved if doctors had been called on the first day, but amidst the panic of the Doctors' Plot none of Stalin's inner circle dared take the initiative. Stalin's own doctor was tortured for saying he should rest. If Stalin awoke from his coma to find doctors by his bed, he might consider the act of calling them a sign of disloyalty.[101] It is a fitting irony that Stalin's death was hastened by his politics.

On the evening Stalin died, Simonov was in the Kremlin for a general meeting of the Soviet leadership: 300 members of the Supreme Soviet and the Central Committee. Everybody was aware of the grave situation, and most of the delegates had turned up early in the Sverdlov Hall. 'We all knew each other,' recalls Simonov, 'we recognized each other and had met many times through our work.'

We sat there, shoulder to shoulder, we looked at each other, but no one said a word. Nobody asked anything of anybody else. It seems to me that no one even felt the need to talk. Until the start [of the session] there was such a silence in the hall that, if I had not sat there for forty minutes myself, I would not believe that it was possible for three hundred people to sit so close to each other without making a sound.

At last the Presidium members arrived* and announced that Stalin was dying. Simonov had the strong impression that, with the exception of Molotov, the other members of this inner circle were relieved by the news: it was visible on their faces and audible in their voices.[102]

From the Kremlin Simonov went to the *Pravda* offices, where he was with the editor when the call came informing him of Stalin's death. Although he had been expecting it, the news was a shock. 'Something shuddered inside me,' Simonov recalls. 'Some part of my life had ended. Something new and unknown had begun.' At that moment he felt a sudden need to record his thoughts in poetry: he did not know if he

---

*In the autumn of 1952, Stalin had replaced the Politburo with a larger Presidium of twenty-five members in preparation for a new purge of the Party leadership.

could write, but he was certain he couldn't do anything else. He went home and began:

I wrote the first two lines and suddenly, unexpectedly, I burst into tears. I could deny it now, because I don't like tears, neither mine nor anybody else's, but only those tears properly conveyed the shock I had experienced. I did not cry out of sorrow, nor out of pity for the deceased: these were not sentimental tears, they were the tears that result from shock. A revolution had happened, and its impact was so enormous that it had to be expressed in something physical, in this case in the convulsive weeping that seized hold of me for several minutes.

Speaking later with his fellow writers, Simonov discovered that they had felt the same. Many followed his example, penning heartfelt eulogies on Stalin's death. The sense of shock and grief, it seems, affected people who had experienced Stalin's reign in widely different ways. On the night after Stalin died, Simonov wrote:

> There are no words to communicate
> All the unbearable pain and sorrow,
> There are no words to narrate
> How we mourn for you, comrade Stalin!

Tvardovsky, the 'kulak' son who had renounced his family in the 1930s, wrote:

> In this hour of great sorrow
> I cannot find the words,
> To express fully
> All our people's loss . . .

Even Olga Berggolts, who spent two years in prison during the Great Terror, wrote a mournful poem to her torturer:

> The heart bleeds . . .
> Our own, our dear one!
> Holding your head in its arms,
> The nation weeps for You.[103]

Stalin's death was announced to the public on 6 March. Until the funeral, three days later, his body lay in state in the Hall of Columns near Red Square. Huge crowds came to pay their respects. The centre

of the capital was mobbed by mourners, who had travelled to Moscow
from all corners of the Soviet Union; hundreds of people were killed in

Stalin's body lies in state

the crush. Simonov was among those chosen to stand guard over Stalin's
body. He had a unique opportunity to observe the reactions of ordinary
people as they filed past. He noted in his diary on 16 March:

I do not know how to give an accurate description of the scene – or even how to put
it into words. Not everybody cried, not everybody sobbed, but somehow everybody
showed some deep emotion. I could sense a kind of spiritual convulsion inside
every person filing past at the very moment they first saw Stalin in his coffin.[104]

This 'spiritual convulsion' was felt across the Soviet Union. Mark
Laskin, who had no reason to love Stalin, broke down in tears when he
heard the news. Surprised by his own emotional reaction, he thought
it might have to do with the overwhelming role Stalin had played in
his life:

I had spent my entire adult life in Stalin's shadow – I was sixteen when Lenin
died in 1924 – and all my thoughts had been shaped by the presence of Stalin. I
waited on his words. All my questions were addressed to him, and he gave all
the answers, laconically, precisely, without room for doubt.[105]

For people of Laskin's age, or younger, Stalin was their moral reference-
point. Their grief was a natural reaction to the disorientation they were

bound to feel upon his death, almost regardless of their experience in Stalin's reign.

Some victims of the Terror even felt genuine sorrow on Stalin's death. When Zinaida Bushueva heard the news, she burst into tears, although her husband had been arrested in 1937, and she had spent the best years of her life in the ALZhIR labour camp. Her daughter Angelina recalls her mother coming home that day:

They were all crying, my mother and my sister and my grandmother. My grandmother said that it would have been better if she had died instead of him. She was four years older than Stalin. She loved him. She often wrote to him. She believed that it was Stalin who had allowed her to write to her daughter [in the labour camp] so that she could reunite the family . . . 'It would be better if I had died and he had lived,' my grandmother kept saying. I didn't contradict her – I loved Stalin too. But today [in 2003] I would say to her: 'Granny, what on earth are you saying?' She herself had suffered so much. Her daughter had been arrested. Her grandchildren had been sent to orphanages. Her son-in-law had been shot. Even her own husband had been persecuted for being a priest . . . Yet she was prepared to lay down her life to save Stalin.[106]

But for some of the older generation, whose views had been formed in an earlier age, the death of Stalin was just as likely to be a cause for rejoicing.

Svetlana Sbitneva was born in 1937 in Barnaul in the Altai region of Siberia. Her father was arrested before she was born and was shot in 1938. Her mother came from Omsk, where her family had been active in the Social Democratic movement before 1917. Sixteen of her mother's relatives were arrested in the Great Terror: all but one, Svetlana's grandmother, were either shot by the Bolsheviks or perished in the camps. Svetlana was told very little about her family. She grew up to become a model Soviet schoolgirl and, like all schoolgirls, loved Stalin. On the day his death was announced, she came home from school with black ribbons in her hair: there had been a mourning ceremony at her school – the children had decorated Stalin's portrait with palm leaves and white lilies – and this had left her deeply moved. 'We were all crying,' she recalls. 'We thought that it was the end of the world.' As soon as she got home, Svetlana climbed up to the roof, where she liked to go to be alone. There she found her grandmother:

She was sitting there, crying quietly and crossing herself in a way I had never seen before. She saw that I had been crying and she said: 'Don't worry, dear, I am crying from happiness. Because he killed my family: my sons, my brothers, my husband, my father – Stalin killed them all – leaving only me and your mother.' That was the first time I heard any of this. And then the two of us sat down and cried together, from joy and grief.[107]

For the vast majority of the Soviet people, whatever Stalin's death meant, it was not a release from fear. In fact, it was likely to increase their fear: they did not know what would happen next. Nadezhda Mandelshtam recalls a conversation with her dressmaker, one of the few people with whom she shared her feelings, shortly after Stalin's death:

'What are you howling for?' I asked her. 'What did he mean to you?' She explained that people had somehow learned to live with him, but who knew what would come now? Things might get even worse . . . She had a point.[108]

Boris Drozdov was living with his parents in Magadan after the release of his father, one of Berzin's close associates, from a labour camp in 1951. 'Everyone was frightened when Stalin died,' recalls Boris. 'My father was afraid. People feared that Beria would come to power, and they were scared of him. The Gulag system was associated with Beria and the MVD, not with Stalin, who many people thought had not even known the truth about the camps.'[109]

Vera Bragin's mother worshipped Stalin, even though she had been exiled as a 'kulak' and her husband sent to the labour army, where he died in 1944. 'When Stalin died, my mother did not throw out his portrait,' recalls Vera. 'She kept it on the wall, next to the picture of my father.' At a village meeting,

Everyone was crying . . . People associated Stalin with our victory in the war, with the lowering of prices and the end of rationing. They thought that life was slowly getting better and they were afraid that now it would get worse.

Many rural people felt a similar anxiety. 'Things had been so hard for us during the war, but then in the last years [before Stalin's death] life had got a little better,' recalls the 'kulak' daughter Klavdiia Rublyova, who also spent the war years in the labour army, and then worked in a kolkhoz near Krasnoiarsk. 'When Stalin died we did not know what would happen, and people were afraid.'[110]

Mourning ceremony at the Gorky Tank Factory in Kiev, 6 March 1953

Fears that Stalin's death would lead to a new wave of mass arrests agitated many families, especially those who had lost a relative in the Terror. As Elga Torchinskaia remembers:

The general reaction in our family was, 'What will happen next?' We were afraid of the government, we did not know what to expect from it, and we were scared that it might retaliate for Stalin's death by making more arrests.[111]

The fear only abated when the Doctors' Plot was exposed as a government fabrication. The decision to reveal the truth about the Doctors' Plot appears to have come from Beria – a critic of the anti-Semitic campaigns and potential victim of the MGB purge that followed from the Plot – who took control of the 'collective leadership' that assumed power on 5 March. Despite his background in the security police, which made him widely feared by the population, Beria was something of a political reformer. He wanted to dismantle the Gulag system ('on the grounds of economic ineffectiveness'), to end the use of torture by the Soviet police, to reverse the Sovietization of the western Ukraine, the Baltic lands and East Germany and to rid the country of the cult of Stalin – a programme which he thought would help build popular support for his own dictatorship. On 4 April, Beria called off the investigation into the Doctors' Plot. *Pravda* announced that the people responsible for the 'incorrect conduct of the investigation' had been arrested and 'brought to criminal responsibility'. Public opinion was divided.

Judging from a sample of workers' letters to *Pravda*, many people continued to believe that there were 'elusive enemies' behind the scenes of power and that the rehabilitation of the doctors was itself a sign of 'Jewish influence' in the highest spheres of government ('Without comrade Stalin our government has bowed before the Jews,' etc.). But others were incensed by what turned out to be malicious slander against Jewish physicians and demanded an explanation for the unjust arrests.[112]

For the Torchinsky family the conclusion of the Doctors' Plot was a huge relief. They took it as emphatic proof that all the 'plots' by 'enemies' were fabrications by the state and that they need not fear a new wave of arrests. Released from fear, Elga grew in confidence and began to speak out against people who had bullied her. Elga worked as an assistant at the Ethnographic Museum in Leningrad. One of her senior colleagues, an ardent Stalinist and a 'frightful anti-Semite' called Maria Nesterova, had given loud support to the 'anti-cosmopolitan' campaign, writing dozens of denunciations of Jewish workers at the museum, some of whom were dismissed from their jobs. During the mass hysteria of the Doctors' Plot, Nesterova became even more vociferous in her denunciations of the Jews, telling everybody, for example, that babies delivered by Jewish doctors were born blue because their blood had been sucked out by the Jews. Elga knew that it was pointless to argue with Nesterova, who obviously hated her. She was afraid to lose her job, so she had remained silent and withdrew into herself. But after the exposure of the Doctors' Plot, Elga chose to confront her:

I told her that she did not know what she was talking about, and that everything she said had been picked up from people in food queues . . . Maria began to threaten me: 'Do you know what I can do to you? You shut up!' And then from somewhere, I don't know where, I found the courage to reply: 'Please, don't threaten me, I'm not afraid of you.'[113]

Those who felt joy at Stalin's death were mostly too cautious to show it in public. Any sign of pleasure had to be concealed. Zinaida Belikova, a factory worker in Krasnodar, recalls that many of the town's intelligentsia, doctors, teachers, even Party officials, found it hard to hide their excitement when Stalin died. 'The mourning ceremonies in Krasnodar were more like a holiday. They put on a mournful face, but there was a sparkle in their eyes, the hint of a smile beneath their greeting, that made it clear that they were pleased.'[114]

When the Gaisters heard the news of Stalin's death, they were still living in exile in Kazakhstan, expecting to be rearrested any day in connection with the Doctors' Plot. On 6 March, Inna's mother Rakhil came home from the shop with a kilogram of sugar. There was never any sugar in the shop, but for some reason, that day the shop had it. No one else in the settlement had dared to buy the sugar. It might be seen as evidence of celebration. But Rakhil saw no harm in taking advantage of her good fortune in finding some. When she showed the sugar to her daughters, they were terrified. 'We threw ourselves at poor Mama, and became hysterical,' recalls Inna. 'How could she have bought sugar on a day like this? What would they think of us? Poor Mama! Fear had deprived us of reason.'[115]

The one place where the death of Stalin was welcomed with undisguised rejoicing was in the Gulag's camps and colonies. There were, of course, exceptions, camps where the vigilance of the authorities or the presence of informers prevented prisoners from showing their happiness, but generally the news of Stalin's end was greeted with spontaneous outbursts of joy. On 6 March, in the Inta camp Iurii Dunsky and Valerii Frid met with their friend, the poet Smeliakov, to organize a midnight party. They could not get hold of any alcohol (everybody wanted some that day) so they bought a bag of sweets and 'ate them all in one sitting . . . as if we were children at a tea-party'. In the Viatka labour camp Vera Bronshtein and her fellow prisoners set down their tools and began to sing and dance when they heard the news: 'We are going home! We are going home!' Among the prisoners it was commonly assumed that they would be released on Stalin's death. Hopes and expectations were extremely high. When Olga Adamova-Sliuzberg heard the news, she was living in exile in Karaganda in Kazakhstan. Covering her face so that her workmates could not see her joy, she began to tremble with nervous excitement: 'It's now or never. Everything has to change. Now or never.'[116]

In several labour camps expectations ran so high that, when the prisoners were not released on Stalin's death, there were mass protests and uprisings. During the spring and early summer of 1953, major strikes and protests erupted in the labour camps of Norilsk and Vorkuta, followed by smaller demonstrations in many other camps in 1953–4.[117] These 'slave rebellions' were an important turning-point, not just because they helped to bring about the abolition of the Gulag system, which was already being questioned by the Soviet leadership, but because they were the first real protest on a major scale against the tyranny of the Stalinist regime.

The Norilsk uprising was the biggest in the history of the Gulag. It involved nearly 20,000 prisoners in six camp zones of the Gorlag prison, the mining and industrial complex of Norilsk, where the work regime was particularly harsh. Most of the Gorlag prisoners were former Red Army soldiers, foreign POWs and Ukrainian and Baltic nationalists, many of them serving sentences of twenty-five years for their part in resistance movements against Soviet forces in 1943–5. They were hostile to the Stalinist regime, ready for a fight and did not have a lot to lose. During the autumn of 1952, a large contingent of prisoners had been transferred to Gorlag after taking part in an armed uprising in the Karaganda camps. The influx of these rebels had a radical effect on the political mood within the Norilsk camp. *Ad hoc* 'strike committees' sprang up in all the Gorlag zones. In the fourth zone, where Lev Netto was a prisoner, there was even a secret reading and discussion club called the 'Democratic Party' (also known as the 'True Leninists'). Here prisoners studied Lenin's ideas on the revolutionary underground as a model for how to organize themselves along military lines.

Stalin's death raised their hopes of a release. But when Beria declared an amnesty on 27 March, it applied to prisoners whose sentences were shorter than five years (mainly criminals). Conditions at Gorlag became even worse. The working day was lengthened, prisoners were forced to work in severe frost, and rations were reduced to a minimum. The guards began to treat the prisoners with calculated cruelty. They provoked the remaining criminals to start fights with the 'politicals' and then suppressed the 'politicals' with brutal violence. More than twenty 'politicals' were murdered by the guards between March and May. As in other camps where there were rebellions, the guards' provocations were almost certainly aimed at keeping the Gulag system going. Beria had made it clear that he wanted to dismantle the Gulag system, releasing all but the most dangerous criminals, so unless it could be shown that the release of 'politicals' was a danger to society, tens of thousands of Gulag guards and administrators would find themselves without a job.

The prisoners in the Gorlag strike committees and conspiratorial groups were divided about what to do. Some were in favour of an uprising, but others thought that it was doomed to fail. They decided to arm themselves defensively. 'We made knives from bits of steel,' recalls Netto, who organized their secret manufacture in a workshop. There was no plan for an uprising, but in this atmosphere of heightened tension it was only a question of time before some further provocation led to a rebellion.[118]

For Lev Netto these events were the culmination of a long process of political awakening that began in 1944, when Lev was dropped behind the German lines to organize the partisans in Estonia. Born into an Estonian family in Moscow, Lev had always thought of himself as a Soviet Russian with an Estonian background and he saw his mission in patriotic terms, but what he witnessed in his parents' native land (the Red Army was guilty of pillage, rape and village-burning) made him think again about the Soviet forces as the 'liberators' of Estonia. The native population called the Soviet forces 'Stalinist bandits', and he couldn't help but agree.

Captured by the Germans, Lev was imprisoned in a camp with thousands of other Soviet POWs. This too was a moment of awakening, for he had always believed, in line with Soviet propaganda, that there were no Soviet POWs, only deserters. But here, as he recalls, were

thousands of ordinary men, just like me, canon fodder for the Soviet regime . . . I began to feel a kind of revulsion against Stalin and the Soviet system, which had so deceived me and treated us [the soldiers] as less than human.

Later, in the spring of 1945, when he was in a camp run by the US forces, Lev was able to contrast the Soviet system with the attitude of the Americans:

Whenever the Americans came back from some operation they would hand in their guns. The next day they would get a different gun. But [in the Soviet army] each man was responsible for his own gun and, if he lost it, he would be dragged before a tribunal, to be imprisoned or even shot. The Americans placed a higher value on the individual. With us the individual counted for nothing.

On his return to the Soviet Union, Lev was sent to a filtration camp and readmitted to the Red Army. In 1948, he was arrested as a 'foreign spy' and sent to Norilsk. There he fell in with Fyodor Smirnov, the leader of the Democratic Party, who encouraged him to see the Stalinist regime as a deviation from Marxist principles. The Democratic Party was held together by informal ties of trust and comradeship.* Because informers were a constant danger, nothing was written down, and everyone who joined had to have the personal recommendation of an existing member, who remained responsible for him. In this environment prisoners like Lev could develop and express their own political identity.[119]

The uprising began on 25 May. Some guards had shot at a convoy of prisoners on their way to work. A protest strike quickly spread through all of Gorlag, including the female section, although its stronghold was in the fourth and fifth zones, where the prisoners – west Ukrainians, Poles and Balts – were militant and organized. They were armed with axes, knives and picks, but their main weapon was a hunger strike to put pressure on the camp authorities. 'Our slogan was "Freedom or Death",' recalls Netto. 'We wanted to be freed, and we were determined to fight for freedom even unto death. We thought it would be better to die fighting than to keep working and living in this inhuman way.' It was time for Stalin's slaves to prove themselves as citizens. The insurgents locked themselves into their barracks and raised black flags as a symbol of their protest against the arbitrary killing of their comrades. Each zone had its own strike leaders, but a general strike committee was quickly organized to present demands to the authorities. Netto served as a messenger and coordinator between the various zones, a dangerous task because he ran the risk of being shot every time he moved from one zone to another.[120]

The strikers' demands were all about respect and dignity. Despite their apocalyptic slogans, what the strikers actually asked for was relatively moderate and by no means anti-Soviet.[121] They wanted the guards to call them by their names, not by the numbers on their prison clothes, which they asked to be removed. They wanted windows without bars in the barracks. They wanted an end to beatings by the guards, and for

*One of Lev's most important friendships within the party was with Andrei Starostin, one of the four famous Starostin brothers, all footballing stars with Spartak Moscow. Lev had known Starostin since the 1930s, when his younger brother Igor had played for the youth team of Moscow Dinamo (Igor Netto went on to become a stylish midfielder with Spartak Moscow, and from 1952, when Lev was in the Gulag, the captain of the Soviet national side). Lev was deeply influenced by Starostin's ideas, which he recorded in a notebook. One idea, which Lev now sees as the 'guiding principle' of his whole life, was borrowed from Tolstoy: 'Do what is necessary, and what you think you should, and whatever will be, will be.'

the guards who had killed prisoners to be punished. They wanted a normal ten-hour working day instead of the fifteen-hour shifts which most prisoners were forced to work. They wanted to be able to write freely to their relatives instead of only twice a year. The strike committee refused to negotiate with the Norilsk authorities and demanded talks with the government in Moscow, aware that the local bosses could not make concessions without clearance from Moscow in any case. A few days later, on 5 June, Beria sent one of his senior officials to talk to the leaders of the strike. It was an extraordinary precedent: never before had the Kremlin responded to prisoners' demands with anything but brutal force. Beria's emissary promised to convey the strikers' demands to the government. But he pleaded with them to resume their work, which he said was highly valued and important for the country as a whole. It was a clever ploy, because more than anything the strikers wanted recognition for their labour. In Netto's words:

We had made great sacrifices to provide the country with nickel, we were proud of our work, and when we heard these words of gratitude – and from no less a personage than Beria's representative – it was like spiritual nourishment. It lifted our spirits and made us ready to go on. We were prepared to make further sacrifices, if only they would treat us as human beings, if only they would talk to us as human beings.[122]

Among the rebels divisions arose between those who wanted to continue with the strike and those who preferred to return to work in the hope of wresting concessions from Moscow through cooperation. In truth, the fighters had no real prospect of holding on, let alone of winning: they were isolated in the prison zone, surrounded by soldiers and had minimal support from the rest of the Norilsk population. So when the chief prosecutor of Norilsk addressed the strikers over the loudspeaker system, calling on them to disperse and promising that they would not be punished, most of the prisoners obeyed. They were sorted into groups by the camp guards. The ringleaders were led away, the rest allowed to return to their barracks. A few thousand strikers resisted. In the sixth zone, on 7 July, 1,000 women formed a human circle, four rows deep, around a black flag and began to scream and whistle when the soldiers tried to drag them away; they kept up their din for five hours and were only broken up by water canon. In the fifth zone, 1,400 prisoners refused to leave and fought pitched battles with the soldiers, who opened fire, killing twenty prisoners. According to reports, the most stubborn resistance was in the third zone, where several hundred strikers locked themselves in the barracks and held out against the troops until 10 July. The unexpected leader of these rebels was Semyon Golovko, the young Cossack from the northern Caucasus, who suddenly discovered the courage in himself to lead this desperate fight. 'I did not realize that I had it in me,' he recalls. 'At the beginning, when the soldiers were banging on the doors and threatening to shoot, I was very scared. I kept saying the Lord's Prayer. But once I had taken charge, I no longer felt this fear.' An estimated 500 prisoners were killed and 270 injured before the camp was taken by the troops.[123]

The strikes were suppressed. But the labour camps were never really pacified. The prisoners' demand for human dignity was ultimately irrepressible. Smaller strikes and demonstrations continued during 1953–4, until at last the regime recognized that it could not go on with the Gulag system and began to release the prisoners.

8
Return
(1953–6)

I

After long delays, Sonia Laskina finally returned from Vorkuta in November 1955. The entire Laskin family waited at the Iaroslavl Station to meet her train. Apart from her sister Zhenia, who had been to visit her in the labour camp, none of them had seen her for the past five years. At last Sonia's train arrived, and she emerged from the crowd of passengers alighting from her carriage, looking very tired, pale and thin. Sonia walked towards her family. Standing before Samuil and Berta, she dropped her bags, fell on to her knees on the platform and begged her parents to forgive her for all the misfortune that she had brought them.

Like so many of the people who returned from Stalin's labour camps, Sonia was burdened with a sense of guilt for the grief her arrest had caused. In Vorkuta, she had starved herself of food so that she could send some money home and had become dangerously thin. After her return, she lived for her family. At the age of forty-four, without a husband or children of her own, she dedicated herself to the welfare of her parents and to the children of her two sisters. 'There was nothing she would not do for us,' recalls her nephew Aleksei. 'She was ready to drop everything if she felt that she was needed, to search the shops for medicine or run some errand. Her devotion to the family had an almost religious character, it had an element of self-negation and self-sacrifice, although she herself was not a religious person in the least.'[1]

Following the Russian tradition of freeing prisoners on the death of a tsar, a million prisoners were released from the labour camps by the amnesty of 27 March 1953, a figure representing about 40 per cent of the total population in the Gulag. In addition to convicts serving sentences of less than five years, the amnesty applied to prisoners convicted of economic crimes, women with young children, juveniles and prisoners who had reached retirement age. Political prisoners were excluded from the amnesty. Their cases needed to be reviewed by the Soviet Procuracy, a process that could take several years, especially in cases such as Sonia's, where senior Party leaders (in her case Khrushchev) had been implicated in the creation of 'anti-Soviet plots'. By the end of April 1955, the Soviet Procuracy had reviewed 237,412 appeals from political prisoners (less than a quarter of the appeals it had received since March 1953) but only 4 per cent had resulted in the release of the prisoners concerned.[2]

There was no rhyme or reason to these decisions. For example, the Stalin Factory Affair, in which Sonia was involved, had its origins in the 'Zionist conspiracy', supposedly organized by Solomon Mikhoels, the former head of the Jewish Theatre in Moscow. Mikhoels himself was posthumously rehabilitated on 3 April 1953, and after that he was praised frequently as a loyal patriot in the Soviet press. Yet in November of that year Sonia was informed by the General Procurator that there were no grounds to justify a review of her case. A prisoner in the Inta labour camp who had also been arrested in connection with the Stalin Factory Affair was outraged when he got a similar response. It came in a letter with the single sentence, 'No grounds for a review of the case', which he was meant to sign and return to the Procurator to acknowledge its receipt. 'There is no logic in it,' he compained to his fellow prisoners. If Mikhoels was innocent, why wasn't he? One of the other prisoners replied: 'Sign the letter now – and they will send the logic later on.'[3]

The Soviet leadership was divided over how far to go with the release of prisoners. Immediately after Stalin's death, Beria had argued for a general amnesty for all prisoners who 'did not represent a serious danger to society', including 1.7 million political exiles. Beria was the dominant figure in the collective leadership of Politburo members that took control on Stalin's death. With his power base in the MVD and MGB, he ran the government in partnership with Malenkov (Chairman of the Council of Ministers) and Voroshilov (Chairman of the Presidium of the Supreme Soviet), although Khrushchev (the Secretary of the Party's Central Committee) was bitterly opposed to Beria and campaigned against him from the start with the support of Nikolai Bulganin (the new Defence Minister). Senior Party and military leaders were certainly suspicious of Beria's programme, which involved the immediate dismantling of the Gulag system and the relaxation of Soviet policies in the newly annexed territories of western Ukraine, the Baltic region and East Germany. In the spring of 1953, Beria imposed a series of reforms on the East German leadership. The Communist hardliners in Berlin dragged their heels over implementing the measures, resulting in a week of mass demonstrations on the streets of East Berlin that were put down by Soviet tanks. Back in Moscow, Beria was blamed for the uprising by Khrushchev, Bulganin, Molotov and even Malenkov. On 26 June, he was arrested in a Kremlin coup, organized by Khrushchev with senior army personnel in the Soviet capital. Held in an underground bunker at the Staff Headquarters of the Moscow Military District, he was tried in secret and then shot in December 1953 (it is even possible that he was shot before his trial). There was no legal basis for the coup: the charges against Beria were extremely vague (there was nothing he had done without the agreement of the collective leadership); and the verdict against him was announced to the Party long before his trial was held. But none of the leaders opposed the coup, or even questioned its legality. Trained in the traditions of Stalinist obedience to the Party line, they were a docile group of functionaries, quick to bend their principles when they sensed a shift of power at the top. Khrushchev emerged from the coup with new confidence. Simonov recalls the Party Plenum of 24 December when the execution of Beria was announced. He was struck by the 'passionate satisfaction' with which Khrushchev recounted the 'capture' of Beria: 'You could tell from his account that it was Khrushchev himself who had played the main role . . . that he had instigated the action, and had turned out to be more discerning, more talented, more energetic, and more decisive than the other leaders,' who had no choice but to submit.[4]

Although Malenkov was formally the head of the Soviet government, Khrushchev was the growing force inside the collective leadership. The coup had nothing to do with policies: it was a naked struggle for power. Khrushchev had supported Beria's programme and he now took it for his own. From the end of 1953, Khrushchev introduced a series of reforms to reinforce the principles of 'socialist legality', a term used throughout the Soviet period but never taken very seriously. He ordered a review by the Soviet Procurators of all cases involving 'counter-revolutionary crimes' since 1921. Khrushchev took a particular interest in the Leningrad Affair, in which his rival Malenkov had served as Stalin's main henchman. In April 1954, several MGB officials closely linked to Malenkov at the time of the Leningrad Affair were arrested. Malenkov was clearly under threat. For the moment, Khrushchev held back the evidence he had gathered against Malenkov – he still needed his support in the collective leadership – but in the early months of 1955, as Khrushchev launched his bid for the control of the Party, he saw to it that Malenkov was charged with 'moral responsibility' for the Leningrad Affair and demoted from Chairman of the Council of Ministers to Minister of Electrification.

Khrushchev used the exposure of Stalin's crimes to strengthen his position and undermine his rivals in the leadership (what he did to Malenkov in 1955 he would do to Kaganovich, Molotov and Voroshilov at the Party Congress in 1961). It was a dangerous game to play, because Khrushchev had himself been deeply implicated in the mass repressions of the 1930s, first as the Moscow Party boss in 1935–8, and then as Party chief of Ukraine, when he oversaw the arrest of at least a quarter of a million people. But Khrushchev was able to limit the Procurators' activities if they went against his own interests. The Stalin Factory Affair was one such example. Because Khrushchev was involved, there were long delays in the review of prisoners' appeals that might throw up incriminating evidence against him. In June 1954, Sonia Laskina was promised a response to her appeal by August; in August she was told that it would be done by September; in September this became October, then November; and then in February 1955, she heard that it would be completed by the end of March. The case was finally considered in September 1955.[5]

Like the other Party leaders, Khrushchev was afraid of what might happen if all of Stalin's victims were suddenly released. 'We were scared,' he wrote in his memoirs. 'We were afraid that the thaw might unleash a flood, which we wouldn't be able to control and which would drown us all.' According to Mikoian, a Politburo member for over thirty years, it would have been politically impossible for all the 'enemies of the people' to be declared innocent at once, because that would make it clear that 'the country was not being run by a legal government, but by a group of gangsters'. The Party leadership had no real interest in speeding up the release of political prisoners. Nor did the officials of the Procuracy, who were reluctant to admit mistakes in the prosecution of politicals, let alone to confess their part in the fabrication of evidence against them during Stalin's terror. In 1954, serving the interests of both

The Laskin family at their Ilinskoe dacha near Moscow, 1956.
From left: Zhenia, Berta, Sonia, Samuil, Fania

institutions, the staff of the Soviet Procuracy was cut by two-thirds, thereby prolonging the procedural delays.[6]

The Laskin family was one of the lucky ones. They were able to return to the old rhythms of domestic life, and in many ways they became even closer after Sonia came back from the labour camps. Sonia herself was invited to take up her old job at the Stalin Factory. After months of writing applications to the Procuracy and battling with officials in Soviet offices, she received a certificate of rehabilitation, clearing her of all the charges against her, restoring her civil rights and entitling her to a small sum in compensation for the five years she had wasted in the labour camp. Sonia was given a small room in a communal apartment on the outskirts of Moscow, which was used by various relatives, as were all the places where the Laskins lived. The famous Laskin suppers at Zubov Square carried on as usual on Sunday evenings. The apartment was always full of family and friends, including some, like the poet Lugovskoi, Simonov's old teacher at the Literary Institute, who became part of the extended clan. Aleksei, who was already sixteen when Sonia returned, recalls the atmosphere of the Laskin home:

It was a place of extraordinary warmth and hospitality governed by the outlook of my grandfather [Samuil Laskin]. He ran it by this rule: anyone who came into our home was welcomed as a member of the family. Once I tried to test this rule:

for several Sundays in a row I brought home to dinner various girls I had picked up on the streets. No one said a word, not even my mother, who was morally very strict, because those were Samuil's rules.[7]

The return of relatives from the labour camps drew many families closer. Years of separation brought home the joys of domestic life even to those Bolsheviks who had once lived entirely for politics. Before her arrest in 1937, Ruth Bonner had taken little interest in the upbringing of her two children. She was totally committed to her work in the Party. The letters she wrote to her teenage daughter Elena from ALZhIR were cold and loveless, with instructions for her to study hard, 'help your grandmother', and 'be a model Komsomol'. Her main concern was to petition Mikoian (an old friend) to save her husband, who had been arrested in the purge of the Comintern in 1937, insisting in her letters that he 'had always been faithful to the Party'. Released in 1946, Ruth was not allowed to return to Leningrad, so she settled in Luga, 135 kilometres to the south, where, with the help of Elena's friends, young poets, she got a job as a housemother at the Writers' Union Pioneer camp. Meanwhile, Elena had returned to Leningrad from the army, having spent the war years serving as a military nurse, and was studying pediatrics at the Medical Institute. She shared a room with several girlfriends (including Ida Slavina) and, during the winter, when the Pioneer camp was closed, Ruth would come to visit her. At first their relations were tense. 'I could tell that she didn't share our post-war jollity and didn't approve of our way of life,' recalls Elena in her memoirs.

Now I understand that each of us had her own experiences. She had the death of her husband, prison, and camp. I had my own losses and, as it seemed then, a completely different life. Neither of us knew how to be open with the other, and I didn't want that. I was annoyed by the way Mama still treated me like the fourteen-year-old she had left, and her questions drove me crazy: 'Where are you going?' 'When will you be back?'

Reflecting on these years in interview, Elena admits: 'I often wished my mother would just go to hell. I couldn't kick her out, but I could drop out of the institute and run away somewhere, anywhere to earn a living, as long as I was free from her.' After the birth of Elena's daughter Tania in 1950, there was a dramatic change in Ruth's priorities. 'We found a common focus – the upbringing of her granddaughter – and that brought us closer,' recalls Elena. From that moment, Ruth ceased to have any real interest in politics. Although she rejoined the Party after her return to Leningrad and her rehabilitation in 1954, she never played an active role and, according to Elena, remained a member 'mainly because she was afraid for us, above all for her grandchildren'.* 'Only the grandchildren [Tania and her brother Aleksei] mattered,' Elena recalls. 'It was amazing how much warmth and inner radiance she had preserved for them.' Ruth was rediscovering the values of her own mother, Elena's beloved grandmother Batania, who had taken charge of her grandchildren while her children dedicated themselves to their Party work. Reflecting on this transformation in her mother's character, Elena Bonner remembers the morning of Ruth's funeral in December 1987:

I was getting tablecloths from the cupboard, setting the tables for the wake. The first to fall on me was a heavy cloth with coloured embroidery . . . Under it was the pink one! Now, after innumerable washings, it merely gave off a pink tint, and Mama's beautiful and fine mending stood out in bright pink. Could I have ever imagined that my mother, a Party worker, antibourgeois and maximalist, who never allowed herself to use a tender word to Egorka or me, would be mending tablecloths, sewing dresses for me, dressing up Tania, that she could turn into a 'crazy' grandmother and great-grandmother, for whom her grandchildren and great-grandchildren would be the 'chief light in the window', the justification for all the losses of her entire life? I couldn't even imagine that she would come to love potted flowers on the windowsill and tend them, making them grow and live. Or that she would turn in her Party card with a certain pride and challenge. This was not a demonstration for the sake of the Party or a settling of accounts . . . It was simply that with that difficult, almost impossible step she fully gave herself to us, her warm, living love, which was higher and greater than abstract ideas and principles. She said almost before her death that in life you must simply live in a good and kind way.[8]

Families had a miraculous capacity for survival despite the enormous pressures arrayed against them during Stalin's reign. The family emerged

---

*She left the Party as soon as Tania and her brother Aleksei emigrated to the USA – at the height of the Kremlin's campaign against Elena Bonner and her second husband Andrei Sakharov – in 1978. Elena Bonner had joined the Party in 1956. She stopped paying her Party dues after the Soviet invasion of Czechoslovakia in 1968, but out of fear for the welfare of her grandchildren, Ruth Bonner secretly went on paying them for her until 1972 (interview with Elena Bonner, Boston, November 2006).

from the years of terror as the one stable institution in a society where virtually all the traditional mainstays of human existence – the neighbourhood community, the village and the church – had been weakened or destroyed. For many people the family represented the only relationships they could trust, the only place they felt a sense of belonging, and they went to extraordinary lengths to reunite with relatives.

Few people made quite as many sacrifices as Valentin Muravsky. He was born in 1928 to the family of a radio engineer in Leningrad. In 1937, after the arrest and execution of his father as an 'enemy of the people', Valentin was exiled with his sister Dina and his mother to Uzbekistan, from which they returned to Leningrad in 1940. During the war, when they were evacuated to Cherkessk, near Stavropol, the three of them were captured by the Germans and sent to work in various factories in Austria and Germany. In 1945, Dina was working at a factory near Nuremberg that was liberated by US troops. She married an American officer and emigrated to the USA. But Valentin returned to Leningrad, where he was reunited with his mother. The war had made him think more critically about the Soviet system and about the reasons for the arrest of his father. His experience in Germany had led him to conclude that one could live more freely in the West, a view he expressed in letters to his sister in America. In 1947, Valentin was arrested and interrogated by the MGB, which tried to persuade him to convince his sister to return to the Soviet Union. When Valentin refused, he was charged with 'anti-Soviet propaganda' and sentenced to three years in a labour camp near Krasnoiarsk. His mother was arrested in 1948, also on the basis of her correspondence with Dina, and sentenced to ten years in the ALZhIR labour camp. Valentin was released in 1950. He went to live with an aunt in Anapa, on the Black Sea coast near Krasnodar, and found a job in a cement factory. But he was soon conscripted by the Soviet navy and sent to Sevastopol, where he was forced to serve for the next four years. He married a nineteen-year-old girl from Sevastopol, and they had a daughter, who was born in 1953.

In 1954, Valentin was released from the navy. He decided to go and live near his mother in Kazakhstan rather than to return to his native Leningrad, and took with him his wife and their daughter. Valentin gave up good job prospects in Leningrad. He had excelled in the navy and left it with an excellent report. But his conscience told him that he should help his mother, who, at the age of sixty-one, was physically weak and mentally damaged by the years of living in the labour camp. Looking back on his decision, Valentin explains it in terms of the principles he was taught in his childhood:

My mother always told me to be moral and honest, to live a life of truth, as preached by the great Russian writers of the nineteenth century, Herzen in particular, whose works she read to us when we were young ... When I got married I told my wife that I would not hide the fact that my mother had been in a labour camp and that I would live in such a way to help her as best I could ... I could not have acted otherwise. It was my moral duty to help her.

Valentin's decision to follow his mother into exile was partly influenced by the example of the Decembrist wives, the noblewomen who had followed their husbands into political exile in Siberia after the failure of their uprising in December 1825. As he himself admits, there was perhaps in his decision a conscious element of political dissent, a deliberate withdrawal from the Soviet system and the career path that awaited him in Leningrad, which was born from his own injury and sense of injustice.[9]

Valentin Muravsky with his daughter
Nina, Karaganda, Kazakhstan, 1954

In Kazakhstan Valentin worked as the driver of a combine harvester on a large collective farm in the middle of the steppe. The Soviet government was just then investing in new technology as part of the Virgin

Lands Campaign, an optimistic and ultimately disastrous project to open up vast new tracts of arid steppeland in Kazakhstan and Siberia for wheat cultivation. Valentin's kolkhoz was among the first to launch the campaign in 1954, when no less than 19 million hectares of grazing land went under the plough. Valentin lived with his wife and daughter in a primitive barracks in a remote steppeland settlement. Once a week he walked the 100 kilometres to Akmolinsk to visit his mother in the ALZhIR labour camp and bring her clothes and food. The burden of caring for his sick and aged mother, and the hardships of the steppe, placed an unbearable strain on Valentin's relations with his wife, who was not prepared for such a sacrifice. In 1956, she left Valentin and went back to her family in the Crimea, leaving Valentin with their three-year-old daughter and his mother to care for. In the same year, Valentin's mother was released from the camp. Valentin returned with her to Leningrad, where they lived together in a small room in a communal apartment. He got a job as a labourer in the construction of the Leningrad Metro. In 1957, his mother died: eight years of life in the labour camp had broken her entirely. Two years later, Valentin was rejoined by his wife; they had two more children; but then, in 1964, she left them once again. Valentin brought up their three children on his own.[10]

Marianna Fursei was reunited with her family in the most extraordinary way. Four years old and dangerously ill, in 1942 she had been given away for adoption to the Goldenshteins by her grandmother, who had then gone with Marianna's brother Georgii to Irkutsk. After the war, Georgii returned to his mother's family in Leningrad. They had no way of finding Marianna, because they had lost all contact with the Goldenshteins and did not even know their proper name. Marianna grew up with the Goldenshteins in Tbilisi. She thought of them as her parents and had no memory of her real family. But things began to change in her teenage years.

Marianna first began to suspect that the Goldenshteins were not her real parents in 1949, when other children at a Pioneer camp teased her as a foundling. The incident brought back traumatic memories of her early childhood in Arkhangelsk. She had a vague memory of her grandmother and could recall that she had a brother. As she grew older and began to rebel against the strict discipline of the Goldenshtein household, she attached even more importance to these distant memories, building them into an almost mythical picture of her long-lost family. Recalling that she had been in a hospital in Arkhangelsk, Marianna set out to trace her brother:

I was sixteen years old – it was 1954. I wrote a letter to Arkhangelsk. To the Medical Institute. On the envelope I wrote: First Year, First Group, to the First Female Student in Alphabetical Order. I told this girl that I had lived in Arkhangelsk as a child, on Pavlin Vinogradov Street, that I had a brother, and that there was a female doctor who might know something about him. Could she find her? And, would you believe it, this girl tracked down the doctor! The doctor told the girl how my grandmother and Georgii had been destitute and hungry. She also found out through acquaintances that my brother was studying physics somewhere in Leningrad. When the girl wrote back to me with all this information, I was in a frenzy of excitement. I sent letters to all the institutes in Leningrad, asking them to find a student called Georgii who had come from Arkhangelsk. It turned out that he was studying in the Polytechnic Institute. He wrote to me and sent a photograph.[11]

Georgii spent three months with Marianna in Tbilisi during the summer of 1954. He remembers their reunion as a joyous occasion, although he sensed some jealousy on his sister's part, as he recalls, 'that I had lived with grandma while she had been given away to strangers'. The Goldenshteins were decent people who loved Marianna as their own daughter. They never told her anything about her real parents, partly because they were trying to protect her from the facts of their arrest, but mainly, it seems, because they were afraid that she would leave them if she found out. Their 'materialistic values', according to Georgii, were very different from those of the Fursei family, who were artists and musicians, and from those of the German family, on their mother's side, who were part of the cultural elite in Leningrad. In the autumn of 1954, Marianna spent a week with the Germans in Leningrad. They showed her photographs of all her relatives, including pictures of herself in Arkhangelsk, but did not tell her that her parents had been arrested, or that they had died in labour camps, only that they had been killed during the war. Looking back on that visit, Marianna thinks that there must have been some agreement between the Germans and the Goldenshteins to keep the truth from her, and perhaps there was.* Her

*This is not confirmed by Marianna's cousin Katia Bronshtein (née German), who was eighteen at the time.

Marianna with Iosif and Nelly Goldenshtein, Tbilisi, 1960

brother Georgii, who also knew about the fate of their parents, concealed it from her as well. 'The truth was an inconvenience for him,' concludes Marianna, seeking to explain the silence of her brother, who was then a physics student at Leningrad University (he went on to become a professor). 'The only thing that was important for him was to study and get ahead.'[12]

Marianna enrolled at the Institute of Light Industry in Tbilisi and then worked as a schoolteacher in the Georgian capital. She did not discover the true story about her parents until 1986, when she received an invitation to view an exhibition of her father's paintings in Ark-hangelsk, where she was told everything by his old friends and colleagues. Having grown up in a strictly Communist household, and having always thought that her father had been killed as a soldier in the war, it was a shock for Marianna to discover, at the age of nearly fifty, that he had been shot as an 'enemy of the people'. It opened her eyes to a history of repression in the Soviet Union which she had previously ignored in the naive belief that it had not affected her own family. 'I felt sorry for these people (my blood parents),' she recalls:

I sympathized with them and wondered how it could have been that such good and law-abiding people could have been repressed so unjustly ... I could not understand. I mean if they were suspected of some crime, why was there no investigation? Why didn't the courts function properly? I began to question the

Soviet system, which I had been brought up [by the Goldenshteins] to accept uncritically ... Gradually, I came to realize that I shared the values of my real parents, even though I had been apart from them since the age of three.[13]

Along with the return of prisoners, the years after Stalin's death witnessed the release of tens of thousands of children from orphanages and other children's homes, where many of them had grown up without any knowledge of their relatives.

Nikolai Kovach had no idea of family life when he was released from his orphanage, at the age of sixteen, in 1953. He had no memory of his parents, who had both been shot in labour camps when he was only one, nor any recollection of his older sister, who had been sent to a different orphanage. His earliest experience of living with a family occurred after he was sent by the Komsomol to help with the first harvest of the Virgin Lands Campaign in Kazakhstan (more than 300,000 people were recruited by the Komsomol as volunteers for the harvest of 1954). One of the leaders of the tractor brigade, an older worker, took a paternal interest in Nikolai. He brought him back to live with his wife and their three children, who all accepted him as an equal member of their home. 'It was just an ordinary Russian household. The three children were all younger,' recalls Nikolai, 'and they fell in love with me. I played games with them and loved them too.' Nikolai lived with them for eighteen months, until 1957, when he was mobilized by the army. 'I had never known what a family was,' he says:

But I observed how this family functioned, how all the relations worked, and the experience was good for me. Later on I read books by psychologists which explained that children grow up like their families. When I was a child I did not have a family, and I was an adult before I knew any kind of family life. I was lucky to meet such wonderful people. I married [in 1962] and brought up a family of my own. I could not have achieved that without that experience in Krasnoiarsk ... It taught me the importance of respect and love – they were always helping each other, thinking of each other and of me – and I had never seen that before, certainly not in the orphanage.[14]

Elizaveta Perepechenko knew nothing about her father when he came to collect her from an orphanage in 1946. She was just a baby when he was arrested in 1935, and he had not been heard from in the ten years he had spent in a labour camp and exile in Kazakhstan. Elizaveta's mother had died in a labour camp, and she had no other family. So she had little choice but to join her father in Alma-Ata, where he worked as a geologist. They lived in the basement of a large communal house, which was shared by several other families. Although she was only a teenager, Elizaveta took on all the household duties for her father, a taciturn and difficult character who had been deeply damaged by his experience in the camp. It was particularly hard for Elizaveta to get on with him and to relate to him as a father, because she had never been close to any men (all the workers at her orphanage had been women). Like many parents who had returned from the labour camps, Elizaveta's father was strict and controlling. He would not let her go out in the evenings without knowing exactly where she was and with whom. There were frequent conflicts, as they each tried to impose their will on the other. Elizaveta remembers 'one occasion when we sat at a table facing each other for more than an hour, because I refused to eat a piece of bread. We were both equally stubborn.' Her father never spoke to her about his past, and she never spoke to him about the orphanage. So they lived together in a state of mutual estrangement. In 1953, Elizaveta moved to Leningrad and applied for a job in the MVD: she had no idea that her father had once been arrested as an 'enemy of the people'. When he found out about his daughter's application, he came immediately to Leningrad to tell her prospective employers about his spoilt biography. He was afraid she might be punished if it was discovered that she had not declared it in the questionnaire. On his request the MVD agreed not to tell Elizaveta about her father's history. She did not find out about his arrest until 1959.[15]

During the years of separation from their parents, children naturally constructed an image of their mothers and their fathers in their minds. It was often very different from the reality they encountered on their reunion.

Galina Shtein was eight years old when her father, Aleksandr Sagatsky, was arrested in 1936.* Galina grew up without knowing anything about what had happened to her father, an economics professor from Leningrad. Her mother, who was sacked from the library where she worked after the arrest of Aleksandr, cut all ties with him and reverted

---

*Galina took her mother's name.

to her maiden name. During the war, when Galina was evacuated with her mother to Siberia, she began to feel a desperate need for a father. She recalls:

Everyone was talking about their 'papa at the front', about how their papa was a hero, or how he had died. I began to feel inadequate. I did not have a father. I did not even know who or where or what he was. I did not know what he looked like, because Mama had destroyed all the photographs of him.

Galina wrote to the Bureau of Addresses in Leningrad in the hope of tracking down her father's younger brother, but she was told that he had died in the siege of Leningrad. She gave up hope of finding her father, until 1947, when chance put her on his tracks. Galina was studying biology at Leningrad University. One day, while standing in a library queue, she heard a student say the name Sagatskaia. The student was referring to a lecturer in Marxism-Leninism. Galina waited for the lecturer outside one of the lecture halls:

A middle-aged woman with an attractive face came out of the hall. I was very nervous, apologized profusely for disturbing her and then asked: 'You aren't by any chance a relative of Aleksandr Pavlovich Sagatsky?' She was silent for a moment. Then she said: 'Are you Galina?' It turned out that she was my father's first wife.[16]

Galina's father was in Norilsk. He had been sentenced to ten years in the labour camp and then, after his release in 1948, to another five years of exile in the Gulag settlement. Galina wrote to him, giving her address at the central post office in Leningrad. 'I did not want to worry my mother,' she explains.

I went to the post office every day to see if my father had replied. I started going there in the autumn [of 1947] and was still going there in the winter. There was never a reply. Finally, in April 1948, I decided that I would make just one more journey to the post office, and if there was nothing, then I would give up. It was fortunate that I made that final trip. At the counter they gave me four fat envelopes. They were made by hand out of some sort of crude paper. Inside each of them, on light-blue writing paper, was a long letter.

The first letter was full of feeling:

4 April 1948. Norilsk
Letter No. 1
(I am sending three letters all at once on 6.IV)

My darling daughter Galia!
Your letter filled my heart with joy . . . One of the greatest tragedies of my life is to have been separated for so many years from the child I love. You write: 'My letter, no doubt, will be a surprise, but I hope, nonetheless, that it is a pleasant one.' And I reply: 1. A surprise – yes; 2. Pleasant – more than that – it is a joy. Even in the way you phrase your thoughts, that 'nonetheless', I recognize myself! In your place I would have written just the same. It makes me smile to notice traces of myself in you . . . Believe me, Galia, you have found your father, who lost you for so many years but never stopped loving you.[17]

Through their letters, Galina started an intense relationship with her father. She imagined him to be the sort of romantic hero she had read about in books: 'I admired courageous men, bold scientists, fearless explorers, or people like my father who had survived against the odds. I had never come across such people in my life.' In the early correspondence her father matched her ideal image. His letters were passionate and emotionally engaging, full of details about how he lived, what he read and how his views had changed in recent years. Galina fell in love with this literary persona. 'In my mind I had a fantasy of the father I had yearned for all those years,' she recalls.

He seemed the sort of man with whom I could be open, to whom I could say absolutely anything, and he would always listen, give me advice, and so on. A new life began for me, and I was entirely absorbed by it. Despite my reserved character, and my general reticence, it seemed that I, like him, was an emotional person after all. Now of course I understand that it was easier for me to be emotional in these letters than it was in real life.[18]

In 1956, Aleksandr visited Galina in Leningrad. But the meeting was a disappointment: they could not re-create the connection they had forged in their letters. Recently released from exile in Norilsk, Aleksandr had been rehabilitated by the Party; he was preoccupied with the resurrection of his political career. According to Galina, he was too busy with his work in the Party to engage with her. 'I had the impression that he was no longer interested in me,' she recalls.

I even think he disapproved of me. I remember he once said to me, 'You have become such a slut.' Why did he think that? Because I didn't show an interest in the poetry of Mao Tse-tung. Because I hadn't read some political article that he wanted me to read. I wasn't interested in politics. But he lived for it.

Aleksandr and Galina, Leningrad, 1956

In 1956, Aleksandr moved to Ulianovsk, Lenin's birthplace on the Volga. He taught political economy at the university and wrote on the subject for various journals. 'My father hated Stalin,' Galina recalls, 'but he remained a convinced Leninist. Despite everything he had suffered, he continued to believe that there was no other way. He had been unjustly treated, but Soviet history was correct.' This unshakeable belief in the Communist ideal, so necessary for his own survival, became an obstacle to Aleksandr's communication with Galina, who was more sceptical but saw no point in political debate. 'What was the point of arguing with a believer? He was totally rigid in his opinions. Politics, which was at the centre of his life, became a subject we could not talk about.' Galina went to see her father in Ulianovsk in 1958. It was her only visit there. They barely said a word to each other, except to ask some polite questions about each other's work. Out of duty, Galina went on writing letters to her father until the early 1960s. But, as she admits,

I did not really have anything to say. I no longer felt like opening my heart to him, as I had in the early years. And the letters he wrote to me were really nothing more than political reports. They were all about the Party conferences he had attended, or about the books that he had read. There was nothing personal in them. I had lost the father of my dreams.[19]

2

Bulat Okudzhava tells the story of how he met his mother when she returned from the labour camps in his 'autobiographical tale' *The Girl of My Dreams* (1988). The future poet and songwriter was just twelve years old when his mother was arrested and sentenced to ten years in the Karaganda labour camps in 1937, following the arrest of her husband, a Communist official of Georgian origin. Bulat was brought up by his grandmother in Moscow and then went to live with his father's family in Tbilisi. In 1941, at the age of seventeen, just before his graduation from high school, he volunteered for the army. After his demobilization in 1945, he became a student at Tbilisi University. His mother spent a total of eighteen years in the Gulag, returning from the camps in 1955.

In *The Girl of My Dreams* Okudzhava revisits the night of her return. The narrator is a student, 'an innocent young man', who lives with a flatmate in a one-room apartment. He is happy because he is in love. The one source of sadness in his life is the absence of his mother. He keeps a photograph of her when she was young, 'with big brown almond eyes', and recalls her gentle smile and tender voice. One day a telegram arrives: 'Meet the 501. Mama.' On his way to the station he imagines their reunion as a happy and simple occasion:

I meet her. We eat at home. The two of us. She tells me about her life, and I tell her about mine. We don't analyse, or try to understand the motives of those who were to blame. What took place is over, and now we are together again . . . And then I take her to the cinema and let her relax a bit.

But things turn out differently. The arrival of the special train, the 501, with prisoners, is delayed several times, and when he comes at midnight to meet it, he learns that it arrived an hour earlier. He finds his mother walking to his house. They embrace and walk home together in silence. At his apartment she sits at the kitchen table and smokes constantly. When he looks into her eyes, he does not see the 'big, brown almond eyes' but something else:

Her eyes were cold and remote. She looked at me, but she did not see me. Her face was frozen, turned to stone, her lips slightly open, her sunburned hands resting weakly on her knees. She did not say a word.

She cannot hold a conversation. She does not understand what her son says. When he asks her if she wants something to eat, she says, 'What?' And when he asks again, she says, 'Me?' She does not ask her son about his life. She mutters only isolated words, the names of places near her camp. She is frightened of her son's flatmate and asks him if he comes from the camps as well, suspecting that he might be an informer. She is afraid to leave the house. When her son drags her to the cinema, she leaves after a few minutes, before the film begins.[20]

People returned from the labour camps physically and mentally broken. A few years in the Gulag was enough to make a person prematurely old. Some prisoners had aged so much that they were barely recognized by relatives when they came home. Ivan Uglitskikh was thirty-three when he was released from Kolyma and returned to Cherdyn. In an interview he recalls his homecoming:

I came back in November 1953. I had not seen my family for thirteen years. My younger brother was living in our old house. He was not in, he had gone to get some hay, and his wife did not know who I was. We sat down for some tea, and when she said that I looked like her husband, I told her that I was his brother, but that she was not to tell him when he arrived. I wanted to surprise him. My brother arrived with the hay, put it in the barn and came to join us ... He saw that there were guests – the samovar was on the table, and there was a bottle of vodka ... His wife said to him: 'Do you know who this is?' And he said: 'No, who is it? An old man passing through?' And then he said to me: 'Where are you going, old man?' He did not know who I was at all. We sat there drinking tea ... [*Ivan breaks down and ends the interview*].[21]

People came back from the camps with physical deformities and chronic illnesses. Fruza Martinelli, the wife of the director of the Dallag Gulag complex until his arrest in 1937, returned to Moscow from the labour camps of Kazakhstan as an invalid. She had been tortured and beaten heavily in the labour camps, and her body was covered with the marks. Her daughter Elena never knew about these beatings, until her mother's death in 1960, when the doctors questioned her about scars and bruises. 'They said they had never seen a body so damaged,' Elena recalls. 'Even the heart had been beaten out of place.'

'Was your mother in a labour camp?' they asked. They could not imagine how my mother could have survived in such a state. It was only then that I understood why my mother was so coarse and cruel when she returned from the camp. She was always swearing, hitting us and breaking things in one of her temper fits. I used to ask her if she had been beaten in the camp, but she refused to say. 'There are things one cannot talk about,' she used to say. And I never asked her again.

Fruza Martinelli, 1956

Elena found it increasingly difficult to live with her mother, who became fanatically religious and showed signs of mental derangement after her return from the labour camp. Fruza was violent towards Elena's son, who was born handicapped in 1953. She would break his toys and steal his sweets, which she hid with other food in her bedding. Unable to cope with her behaviour, Elena moved to Leningrad in 1958.[22]

Gertrud Ielson-Grodzianskaia had pictured her mother in the ALZhIR labour camp as 'good and beautiful and living in a distant land'. It was an image she had formed from the letters that her mother had sent her, and from the little presents she had made for her, like the embroidered towel with pictures of animals. When Gertrud was fourteen, her mother was released from the labour camp and allowed to settle outside an exclusion zone of 100 kilometres from Moscow. She chose to live near Vladimir, where she found a job as an agronomist on a collective farm. She passed through Moscow, where Gertrud lived with her uncle's family, on her way from ALZhIR to Vladimir. Gertrud went to meet her at the station:

Suddenly a woman stepped off the train. She was dressed in a sheepskin and had a plywood case and a rucksack. Her head was shaved. She smelled frightfully. She had been travelling for a week. We brought her home, and I was asked to help her wash . . . I heated the water on the kitchen stove and helped her to undress. The smell was overpowering. It was a real shock. She had lice all over her body and cockroaches in her clothes. I was repulsed. I did not see this woman as my mother but as someone else.[23]

Esfir Slavina was released from the ALZhIR labour camp in 1943. Forbidden to return to Leningrad, or to any of the other major cities in the Soviet Union, she was rescued by her daughter Ida, who was already working as a teacher in Novosibirsk and arranged for them to live in an empty office at the school. Ida recalls her mother's appearance:

She was very thin and brown, burned by the sun of Kazakhstan and showing all the signs of having suffered from malaria. She did not look at all like her old self. She was not the mother I had known. She was sick and hardly able to move, and relied on me for everything.

In 1944, Esfir moved to Moscow, where her son, a research scientist, had received permission for her to live with him. Ida married a school-teacher in Novosibirsk. In 1945, she returned to Leningrad, where she lived in a communal apartment with five other families. Esfir lived illegally with them so that she could help with Ida's new-born son, who was often ill. In 1949, Esfir was rearrested for breaking passport regulations (she was not registered to live in Leningrad) and exiled to the town of Malaia Vishera, 110 kilometres to the south-east, where she lived in terrible conditions, unable to cope on her own, without work and constantly harassed by the local residents, who took against her as a 'political', which in their eyes made her a 'fascist'. Six months after her arrival in Malaia Vishera, Esfir was arrested yet again, this time as an 'anti-social element', and exiled to Shadrinsk, in western Siberia, where she lived in the cheapest rented room on the outskirts of the town. Without a job, she lived on the money Ida sent each month. In 1951, Esfir was finally allowed to return to Leningrad. 'She was completely broken,' recalls Ida, who took care of her:

She was silent nearly all the time. She was afraid to speak and spoke only in whispers. You had to coax every word from her: as soon as she said anything she would immediately regret it. She never told me anything about the camp. I tried to get it out of her, my brother tried as well, but it was no use. She was afraid to go out of the house. If she was in the street and saw a policeman she would run to hide in the entrance of a building and not come out until she was sure that the policeman had disappeared. This was totally out of keeping with her character; she had always been strong and confident. But she came home from the camp a different person. Her confidence was gone, so was her health; she had two strokes in the first three years after her return. And she had lost all her liveliness and sociability. She never wanted to see anyone. She spent her last years bed-ridden.[24]

Left: Esfir and Ida in 1938. Right: Esfir in 1961.

The ALZhIR camp had a different effect on Zinaida Bushueva. It made her cold and strict, according to her daughter Angelina, who was ten years old when her mother was released. Zinaida did not like to talk about the past. She was emotionally withdrawn. 'It was very hard to live with her,' recalls Angelina.

She was silent all the time. She never talked to us about what she was thinking or feeling. And I blamed her for that. I wanted her to talk. But perhaps she wanted to protect us from everything she had suffered . . . She was always very distant from us. She would never show affection, she would never stroke our hair or hold us close. Her idea of being a mother was to make sure that we were fed, that we went to school and that we remained physically healthy – but that was all. She gave us nothing spiritually or emotionally. The truth is, after the camp, she had nothing left to give.

Angelina attributes her mother's emotional austerity to the labour camp, where Zinaida had requested heavy manual work so as not to have time to think about the children she had lost. Closing herself off had become a mechanism of survival, and it continued as a means of coping with the problems of return. This same instinct for survival manifested itself in her obsessive eating: she would carry bits of bread around with her, hoard supplies of food and get up in the night to eat something because she was afraid of feeling hunger.[25]

Liuba Babitskaia came back to Moscow from the ALZhIR labour camp in 1947. Forbidden to settle in the capital, she came back illegally in search of work and family and friends. Despite his earlier efforts to persuade her to return to him, her first husband, the filmmaker Anatoly Golovnia, had begun an affair with a young production assistant (and probably an agent of the NKVD) called Tatiana Lobova, who exercised a malign influence on him and alienated all his relatives, most of all his daughter Oksana, who saw their romance as a betrayal. Physically exhausted, her film-star looks all gone, Liuba was shunned by most of

Liuba after her return, Moscow, 1947

her old friends in Moscow. 'As soon as people recognized her as the former wife of Golovnia, the widow of the executed Babitsky, they crossed the street to avoid her,' recalls Oksana. The one person who came to Liuba's aid was the actress Liubov Orlova, an old friend who may have felt some guilt because her husband, the film director Grigorii Aleksandrov, who had close ties to the NKVD, had been behind the denunciations at the Mezhrabpomfilm studios that led to the arrest of

Babitsky. Orlova took Liuba in and suggested that she contact Mikhail Gurevich, the Deputy Minister of Geology, who, she said, might help her get permission to remain in Moscow and find a job. 'All his life he has been in love with you,' Orlova explained, calling Gurevich and passing the receiver to Liuba. Gurevich asked Liuba where she was, and then said: 'Wait for me, I am coming now. We will get married.' Thanks to their marriage Liuba got rights of residence and a job in Moscow; Gurevich was dismissed from his post.

When Liuba was arrested in 1938, her daughter Oksana was eleven years old; by the time she returned, just nine years later, the girl had become a wife and mother. 'Relations between us were very difficult,' recalls Oksana. 'Something had broken in our relationship – there was so much pain, love, jealousy, all mixed up with estrangement, a yearning for closeness, to understand each other, and at the same time an inability to find the words to communicate.' Liuba wanted to control Oksana's life. In 1948, when her daughter started an affair with an American diplomat, she became frightened and threatened to report her to the MVD for contacts with a foreigner unless she broke it off. Oksana's husband, Albert Rikhter, a naval officer from a German-Jewish family in Odessa, had already been arrested and sentenced to ten years in Magadan for 'espionage', so the report would probably have led to her arrest. In the end, Liuba used her connections with Gurevich to send Oksana to Siberia as an assistant on a geological expedition, which brought the affair to an end.

Liuba returned from the camps with a different personality: the warmth and affection that she had once shown as a mother had all gone, and in its place was a new harshness and insensitivity. She never gave affection to her grandchildren. If they fell and hurt themselves, she would tell them to get up and stop crying, because there was 'much worse' that could happen to hurt them, 'things that would really make [them] cry'. Liuba brought home the customs of the camps. She was selfish, even greedy, when it came to food; short-tempered, sometimes cruel and violent; emotionally closed to everyone. 'She kept a suitcase packed with winter clothes and dried food beneath her bed in case they came for her again,' recalls her granddaughter. 'She was terrified of the telephone and doorbell when they rang at night, and took fright when she saw policemen in the street.' These camp traces remained in her character. 'A person who is released from the camps is afraid of freedom,' Liuba wrote in her last notebook, just before she died in 1983. 'Deeply wounded once, you are forever easily hurt again.'[26]

Many people came back from the camps with nervous habits and obsessions. Elena Cherkesova would count the steps she took at home. It was a habit she had picked up in the Temnikovsky camps as a way of maximizing her efficiency and avoiding all unnecessary exertions. Elena had never worked before she was sent to the camps, and she was exhausted by the regime there, which pushed her to the brink of starvation. During the war years, in particular, when the work quotas for Gulag prisoners were raised, Elena had often failed to meet her quota, which meant that she received less bread. To save her energy she taught herself to keep her steps to a minimum. A similar obsession was brought back from the labour camps by Aleksandra Fillipova. She was paranoid about people stealing her food. Living with her daughter in a communal apartment, she would conceal bits of food in hiding-places in their room and then forget having eaten them. When she looked for the food and found that it was gone, she would accuse her daughter, or the other neighbours, of having taken it. Relations with her daughter became so bad that Aleksandra forced her to move out of the apartment.[27]

Mikhail Nikolaev had grown up in a children's home. He did not know who his parents were. He spent his teenage years in the Red Army, and then fifteen years in various labour camps. In every institution where he had lived there had been a struggle over food – a constant battle to get the glass or plate that was most full – so that he had learned to grab whatever he could without thinking about anybody else. The thirty-six-year-old who was released from the labour camps had no idea how to behave in a normal family home, never having been in one. A large handsome man with a thick beard, he was known in the literary circles of Moscow as a 'wild man from Mars', recalls Viktoriia Shweitser, who fell in love with him and married him. When she introduced him to her family, she was shocked by his table manners. She could not understand how he could help himself to all the food from the table without offering it to others first. For a long time, she said nothing, but one day she finally lost her patience and told him off for grabbing the last orange instead of leaving it for the children, as was the custom in their household. 'Mikhail replied: "I didn't know, nobody ever taught me that, why didn't you explain it to me?",' recalls Viktoriia. 'He was not greedy, but as he said about himself, he was tight-fisted', perhaps even selfish, because of the way he had grown up. As she recalls in interview, it was at this point that she realized that she had fallen in love with a man whom she did not really know. 'I had to learn to fall in love with him again, only this time with the real Misha, the boy from the orphanage, so that I could understand him properly and help him live a normal life.'[28]

It was often very hard for people who returned from the labour camps to re-establish relationships with relatives. After years of living in the Gulag, what sort of 'normal family life' could they hope to lead? There was no counselling or psychoanalysis for these people, no help for their physical and behavioural disorders, not even any recognition of the traumas they experienced. At the same time, those who returned often had little understanding of the tension under which their families had lived or the horrors they had suffered in the intervening years. People on all sides – those who had returned from the camps and those who had remained at home – felt rejected and estranged.

For various reasons, survivors of the camps found it difficult to talk about what they had been through 'on the other side', and closed themselves off from their families. Some people were afraid to talk for fear of punishment (on their release, prisoners were told not to discuss what had happened to them in public, and many feared, in consequence, to talk about their past in private too). Others did not tell their relatives because they were reluctant to burden them, or because they were afraid that they would not and could not understand what they had suffered. Parents were afraid to tell their children, in particular, because they did not want to say anything that might alienate them from the Soviet system or get them into trouble with the authorities.

Even within families where talk became the norm, parents remained cautious about what they said to their children. On her return from Kolyma, Olga Adamova-Sliuzberg discovered that her son had grown up in her absence to become an active member of the Komsomol, fanatically devoted to Stalin. One day over dinner, she asked whether it was true that Stalin had been ill:

Nobody knew, but my son answered in a meaningful tone: 'I don't know whether he's ill or not, but if he were ill and I had to give my life's blood and die for him, I'd gladly do it.' I understood that this was intended as a lesson and as a warning to me, and I bit my tongue.[29]

Adamova-Sliuzberg's experience in the labour camps had made her sceptical of the regime, but she knew that she could not say that, even though she wanted her son to understand what she had been through. She recalls:

I was afraid to tell him what I had discovered 'on the other side'. I could probably have persuaded him that there was a great deal wrong in our country, that his idol, Stalin, was far from perfect, but my son was only seventeen. Had I explained everything to him, and had he agreed with me, he would have been unable to applaud Stalin's name, to write letters to Stalin, to proclaim in class that our country was just. And if he could not have done that, he would have died. Perhaps he would have found a way to live a double life. But I could not make him go through that. I was afraid to be frank with him. But somehow, gradually, I did win him over. He would look at me carefully. After several months he said to me: 'Mama, I like you.'[30]

The opposite dynamic was more prevalent. Parents who remained committed to the Bolshevik ideals of the 1930s often came home from the labour camps to discover that their children had developed altogether different ideas and attitudes in the relatively liberal climate of the Khrushchev thaw, when censorship was gradually relaxed and the Stalin era was re-evaluated in the Soviet media. Young people turned away from politics and took up the pursuit of personal happiness, stimulated by the economic boom of the Khrushchev years, when private housing blocks were constructed, more consumer goods became available, and new technologies, fashions, art and music were imported from the West. Yet this inevitably gave rise to the fear, voiced by Communists whenever the regime relaxed control on the private sphere, that individualistic tendencies would lead to the demise of social activism, collectivism and other Soviet values in the young. There were thus renewed calls for Soviet youth to join the Komsomol as well as to become 'enthusiasts' of collective projects like the Virgin Lands Campaign.[31]

When she returned from the Potma labour camps, Maria Ilina encountered this form of the generation gap with her daughter Marina. Before her arrest, in 1937, Maria had been the director of a large textile factory in Kiev; her husband was the Party boss, until his own arrest and execution that same year. On her release, in 1945, Maria found Marina, then aged ten, in a Ukrainian orphanage. She had not seen her daughter since she was two. Mother and daughter lived together for the next twelve years, first in Cherkassy, and then Moscow, until 1958, when Maria moved back to Kiev. Until Maria's death in 1964, they would visit one another on every holiday. Yet their relationship was difficult. Maria wanted to direct the way her daughter lived. She wanted her to be a model Communist, to be the sort of youth that she had been until her own arrest. Rehabilitated in 1956, Maria rejoined the Party and became an active propagandist of the Party cause. According to her daughter, 'she needed to believe in the Communist ideals that had sustained her and my father when they had been young: otherwise the sacrifices she had made would have been too much to bear'.

Maria gave herself entirely to the political education of her daughter. She organized a programme of reading, a mixture of Soviet and Russian classics, designed to inculcate the correct Communist ideas and attitudes. Tolstoy's *Anna Karenina* was considered bad, for example, because Anna was selfish, and 'the main thing for a woman was not love but comradeship and duty to society'.

She wanted me to be strong and resolute, brave and courageous, an active member of the Pioneers and the Komsomol . . . She wanted me to be the master of myself, to overcome the negative in me, to improve myself constantly, like the heroes of Soviet literature. For Mama that was the most important thing – to become the master of oneself . . . I was always being told that I had to do things I did not want to do.

Maria intervened in all sorts of ways. Her daughter wanted to study literature and become a schoolteacher, but she made her go to the prestigious Moscow Power Engineering Institute. Marina joined the Komsomol and became the chairman of the Komsomol committee at the institute. Having qualified as an engineer, she worked at a research institute in Moscow. Maria wanted her to join the Party and pleaded with her to accept the invitation to do so from the Party secretary of her factory, which she had worked hard to arrange. But Marina now had different ideas. Like many of her friends, she was inspired by the liberal climate of the Khrushchev thaw. Self-assured and independent in her thinking, she became increasingly sceptical about politics. She thought that joining the Party would demand too much from her – far more than she was prepared to give to activities in the public sphere. These ideas were reinforced by her new husband, Igor, whom she had married during her third year at the institute. Igor was critical of the Soviet system, and argued frequently with Maria, but Marina was not interested in their political debates. She rejected the Party, and politics, not because she had reflected deeply on the reasons for her family's tragedy, but, on the contrary, because she wanted to forget about the past and begin a 'happy life'. Her main interests were music and the cinema, dancing, and socializing with her friends. She was encouraged to pursue these interests by Igor, who was paid well as an engineer, and dreamed of keeping her at home. Marina's attention to her personal appearance met with constant disapproval from her mother, whose Communist convictions and Spartan attitudes left no room for such 'petty-bourgeois' diversions. Maria was always neat and tidy. She had a good figure. But after her return from the labour camps, she never made the most of her appearance or even cared that much about the way she looked. Poorly paid, she could not afford to spend a lot on clothes or cosmetics. But according to her daughter, there was another reason for her lack of interest in such things: the experience of the camps had left her in a deep state of depression which became even worse after 1955, when she found out about the death of her son Vladimir in the Gulag. 'After everything she had been through,' Marina says,

she gave up on herself and let herself go. She never looked at herself in the mirror . . . or wore perfume or make-up . . . Only once she bought a coat that fitted her well, and from the back she looked very good. She was tall and slim with slender legs and fine ankles. Men would overtake us in the street and look back at her – but they could not understand. She looked completely different from the front . . . Her hair was grey and thin, and her face marked with cuts.

Short of money, Maria sold the coat and wore instead a quilted jacket, like those worn by prisoners in the Gulag.[32]

Vladimir Makhnach, the former boss of the Mosgaz Trust, which controlled Moscow's gas supply, returned to the Soviet capital in June 1955 after fourteen years in the Taishet labour camp. His son Leonid, now a young man of twenty-two, had long resented the stigma of his 'spoilt biography'. Born into the privileged conditions of the Soviet elite, he had lived with his mother in a desperate state of poverty following the arrest of his father. His mother had no income of her own. They occupied a room in a communal apartment which was raided several times by the police in search of incriminating evidence against the 'relatives of enemies of the people'. Anxious to get on, Leonid lied about the arrest of his father when he applied to join the Moscow Film School (VGIK). By the time his father came back, Leonid was moving in the bohemian circles of the film world, which flourished in the liberal climate of the thaw. He had also developed connections with the MGB. His fiancée Tamara was the stepdaughter of Naftaly Frenkel, the man responsible for the conception of the Gulag system in 1929, who lived as a recluse in the Soviet capital. Frenkel took a keen interest in Leonid.

Vladimir's return was bound to ruffle Leonid's feathers. The young man was suddenly confronted by a father who insisted on asserting his authority over wife and child. Vladimir 'was a difficult character', according to his son.

He was moody and taciturn. He would not speak about the camps. Emotionally he was closed to us. He brought into the house the habits and the fears he had acquired in the camps and expected us to adapt to them. He would not sleep in the same bed as my mother, who was then forty-six. I remember how she said to him in tears one day: 'I have stopped being a woman for you!'

Vladimir in 1956

Despite his years in labour camps, Vladimir remained a staunch Leninist; he continued to believe that Stalin's policies of the early 1930s – the forced collectivization of agriculture and the industrialization programme of the Five Year Plans – were essentially correct. He himself had played a leading role in the execution of these policies. In his opinion, it was only in the later 1930s that Stalin ceased to be a Communist. For

Vladimir the process of return was a question of putting the clock back. He rejoined the Party, which retroactively recognized his membership to 1921. He re-entered his old sphere of work and was appointed Deputy Director of Moscow's Fuel and Energy Administration in 1956. He even received a chauffered car and a dacha near the one the Makhnaches used to have in Serebrianyi Bor. But Vladimir had little sense of the social changes that had taken place since his arrest. He came from the generation of peasants who had risen to the Soviet elite during Stalin's industrial revolution of the early 1930s. His politics were radical, but his social attitudes were conservative (he had made Maria give up work when Leonid was born because he thought that 'a senior party leader should have a wife who stays at home'). Now Vladimir fully expected to become the patriarchal head of the household once again. He did not like it when Leonid stayed out late at night, not least because the camps had left him with severe insomnia. There were constant arguments between the two. One night, Leonid returned from a party at midnight. There was an argument which became a fight. Vladimir punched his son in the face. Leonid stormed out of the apartment and went straight to Frenkel's house, where he remained until his marriage to Tamara in 1958. As Leonid recalls, after the break with Vladimir, Frenkel became the main paternal figure in his life. An opponent of the Khrushchev thaw, Frenkel retained strong connections with the MGB, which promoted Leonid as a film director and commissioned his first film, a propagandist story about Soviet spies in the Cold War.[33]

A widespread feeling among survivors of the camps was a sense of the incommunicability of their experience, of an unbridgeable gap between themselves and those who had not been in the camps. In 1962, Maria Drozdova returned to her family in Krasnoe Selo after twenty years of imprisonment and exile in Norilsk. 'What could I tell them?' she writes:

That I was alive and had returned. But what could I say about my life out there? How I travelled in a convoy to Norilsk? How could they understand what the word 'convoy' really meant? However much detail I described, it would still be incomprehensible to them. Nobody can understand what we went through. Only those who know what it was like can understand and sympathize.[34]

Like many former prisoners, Maria felt much closer to her Norilsk friends than to her own family, and she continued to see them regularly after her release. 'The friendships formed in the labour camps were friendships for life,' writes one ex-prisoner. According to many Gulag survivors, people who had been in the camps together tended to be more supportive of each other than relatives and friends at home. In a society where former prisoners were frequently the victims of prejudice and malice, they forged special bonds of trust and mutual reliance. While prisoners did not talk to their families about the camps, they did talk with their friends from the Gulag. They would correspond, meet on holidays, visit one another and arrange reunions. Sonia Laskin had a large network of old friends from the Vorkuta camp. She was always putting someone up in her apartment in Moscow. Some of them were practically members of the Laskin extended family and attended all the Laskin anniversaries. 'The spirit of comradeship was extraordinary,' recalls Valerii Frid of his old friends from the Inta labour camp. 'Without any affectation, without long conversations, we would simply help each other out.' According to Frid, the great writer of the Gulag, Varlam Shalamov, was wrong when he wrote that there was nothing positive a prisoner could take from his experience in the camps. His own life-long friendship and collaboration with the film-maker Iurii Dunsky was strengthened by the years they spent together in Inta. 'I was grateful to the camps for teaching me the meaning of friendship,' recalls Frid, 'and for giving me so many friends.'[35]

Some prisoners returned home with new husbands, or new wives, whom they had met 'on the other side'. For women, in particular, these 'Gulag marriages' had sometimes been motivated by the struggle to survive. But they were also based on the understanding and trust that frequently developed between prisoners.

After her release from the Norilsk labour camp in 1946, Olga Loba-cheva, the specialist in mineralogy, stayed on in Norilsk as a voluntary worker. She married a geologist called Vladimir, a student volunteer from Saratov University, who was twenty years younger than herself. In 1956, they returned together to Semipalatinsk, where, before her own arrest, Olga had been living in exile, following the arrest of her first husband Mikhail. Olga did not know what had happened to Mikhail. Without any news of him, she had presumed that he was dead, and on that understanding she agreed to marry Vladimir. In fact Mikhail had been sentenced to ten years of labour in the Karaganda camps. There he had married a fellow prisoner, a young and beautiful Hungarian Jew called Sofia Oklander, who gave him a daughter in 1948. 'They too had been brought together by their need for love and friendship in the camps,' reflects the son of Olga and Mikhail. 'It was not their fault, but both my parents fell in love with younger people and ended up betraying each other.' In 1956, Mikhail moved with his new wife and their daughter to Alma-Ata. He got in touch with Olga and went to visit her in Semipalatinsk. He even tried to persuade her to return to him. But Olga refused to forgive her former husband for marrying Sofia without trying to locate her first.[36]

Liudmila Konstantinova also married someone she had met in the labour camps. Mikhail Yefimov, a strong and handsome peasant man from Novgorod, had been sent to Kolyma on some petty charge of 'hooliganism' in 1934 and was part of a team of labourers that built the town of Magadan. By 1937, Yefimov had served his three-year sentence, but he did not have the money to return to Novgorod, so he stayed in Magadan as a volunteer. Liudmila met him in 1938, when she had been working as a prisoner in a cotton factory where Yefimov was building ventilation pipes. Liudmila had been in Kolyma since 1937; she did not know what had happened to her husband after his arrest in 1936. Shortly after she met Yefimov, Liudmila became very ill with a kidney infection. Yefimov nursed her back to health, buying special medicines and food for her. In 1944, she learned that her daughters Natalia and Elena had been rescued from an orphanage by their grandmother, who had brought them up in exile in the remote steppeland town of Ak-Bulak. A year later, when Natalia and Elena returned to Leningrad with their grandmother, Yefimov began to send them parcels and money. Liudmila was released from the labour camp in the autumn of 1945, but she remained in Magadan to be with Yefimov, who was refused permission to move to Leningrad. In 1947, she married Yefimov. Ten years had passed since the arrest of Liudmila's husband, and she had not heard from him. She could not get any information from the Soviet authorities, so she presumed that he was dead.* 'You cannot keep someone waiting for ever,' she wrote to her mother in 1945, after she was granted a divorce from her first husband. 'People need to live in the real world.'

Liudmila was not in love with Yefimov. In her letters to her mother she describes him as 'a good comrade from the first painful days in

---

*In 1989 she discovered that he had been shot in 1937.

Kolyma'. He was strong and kind and supportive, they had a lasting friendship based on their experience of the Gulag, and she relied on him for emotional sustenance after her release. In 1948, Liudmila moved with Yefimov to Novocherkassk, near Rostov-on-Don, where she would live until her death in 1992. Once a year she visited her daughters and mother in Leningrad. Sometimes Yefimov would come with her. He remained a distant figure to his stepdaughters, who addressed him with the polite 'you' (*vy*) normally used for speaking to strangers. 'Only shortly before Mama died did I start to use [the informal] *"ty"*,' recalls Natalia. Elena and Natalia remained with their beloved grandmother until she died in 1968; they were never reunited with their mother as a family.[37]

From left to right: Elena Konstantinova, her mother Liudmila,
her grandmother Elena Lebedeva, and her sister Natalia, Leningrad, 1950

Ilia and Aleksandra Faivisovich were hairdressers in Osa, a small town in the Urals, south of Perm. They were both arrested in 1939, following reports by clients that they had complained about shortages. Ilia was sentenced to ten years in a labour camp near Gorkii; Aleksandra to five years in a camp near Arkhangelsk. Their daughter Iraida was brought up by her grandmother, until Aleksandra returned in 1945. Four years later, Ilia was released. Aleksandra had waited patiently for his return. Finally, the day came. The house was full of Aleksandra's relatives; Aleksandra had prepared a special meal for Ilia's homecoming. But Ilia did not appear. Instead his sister Lida came from Perm and told them that he had arrived at her house with a young woman, his new wife. Aleksandra and her daughter went to visit him, a scene Iraida remembers:

The door opened and there was Father – we had not seen him for ten years. He gave me a hug and kissed me . . . Nina [his new wife] was standing in the room. Mama started crying. Lida tried to calm her down: 'What do you expect if you don't see each other for ten years?' she said. Mama went on crying. Father held me close to him, as if to say that there was nothing I could do. He had been drinking heavily and he was drunk, I think. Mama began to curse him. 'You have ruined my life! You have destroyed our family!' she kept shouting . . . 'Why couldn't you have written to me telling me not to wait?'

Aleksandra suffered a nervous breakdown and spent four months in a psychiatric hospital. Ilia and Nina settled in a small town near Sverdlovsk where they lived in an old bath-house. They had met in the labour camp, where Nina, a young Jewish doctor from Leningrad, was working in the hospital. Nina had saved Ilia's life. He had been brought to the

Nina and Ilia outside their house, near Sverdlovsk, 1954

hospital with severe frostbite after he had collapsed from exhaustion, felling timber without food, and had not been found for several days. Nina gradually nursed him back to health. She fell in love with him. Ilia returned from the labour camps an invalid. He relied on Nina to help him walk. Once a year he would visit Aleksandra and Iraida in Osa. Sometimes he wrote to them, but the family was never close again. After Nina's death, in 1978, Iraida tried to persuade her father to return to Aleksandra, but he married someone else instead. Aleksandra did not remarry. She never got over Ilia's betrayal. According to her daughter, she was still in love with him. She kept his photograph by her bedside and had it with her when she died.[38]

Zinaida Levina was one of the founders of the Pioneer Organization in the Ukraine, where she was born into a Jewish family in 1904. She was arrested in 1937 and sentenced to eight years in the Kolyma labour camps. Her husband, Daniil, an engineer, was arrested too, as a 'relative of an enemy of the people', and exiled for three years to Turkmenistan (after his release he served in the army, was wounded at the front and evacuated to Siberia). Their daughter Larisa, who was four years old on the arrest of her parents, was brought up by her grandmother in the communal apartment the family shared in Kiev. In 1945, Daniil returned from Siberia with a new wife, Regina, and their daughter. They moved into two small rooms where Daniil's three sisters also lived. Larisa went to live with them. She got on well with her half-sister but was hated by Regina and her aunts. According to Larisa, Daniil had chosen to renounce and divorce Zinaida because he was afraid he might be rearrested on his return from exile if he was still married to an 'enemy of the people'. But Zinaida's mother, who viewed her son-in-law as a womanizer, thought that he had simply taken advantage of his wife's arrest to marry Regina, who was young and beautiful, and refused to visit them. Cut off in this way from her grandmother, Larisa's situation in her father's home became more difficult.

After her release in 1946, Zinaida was ordered by the state to live in Zvenigorodka, a small town near Kiev. One day, she turned up at her mother's apartment with a little boy called Valerii and introduced him as her son. In the Kolyma camps Zinaida had learned about the massacre of Kiev's Jewish population at Babi Yar in September 1941. Fearing that her family had been destroyed, she resolved to have another child before it was too late (she was then thirty-seven) and gave birth to Valerii in 1942. She refused to say who the father was (and took her secret to her grave) but everyone assumed that it was a prison guard. In 1949, Zinaida was rearrested as an 'anti-social element' (it was the height of the campaign against the Jews) and sentenced to three years in the Potma labour camps (she was later exiled to Dzhambul in Kazakhstan). Valerii was taken in by his grandmother; but a few months later the old woman died. Larisa begged her father to rescue Valerii. She felt responsible for her half-brother, a difficult boy with severe behavioural problems: 'Something made me love him. I had this feeling of responsibility. It came from the heart. I had no family, and wanted to protect him as my own.' Valerii, however, was given to an orphanage by Daniil's sisters, who took the view that the son of a prison guard should be looked after by the state. Valerii disappeared until 1953, when he wrote to Larisa from another orphanage, in Uzhgorod, in western Ukraine. Larisa went to collect him and took him to their mother in Dzhambul, where they all lived for the next two years. 'At that time,' recalls Larisa,

I hardly knew my mother. I had never really lived with her, and that time, from 1953 to 1954, was the first I had spent with her . . . She drowned me with her love . . . I was overwhelmed by it. I was not used to it . . . But I soon discovered the joy of family love.

In 1955, Zinaida fell in love with another Jewish exile in Dzhambul, a man who had lost his family at Babi Yar. He helped her with Valerii and loved him as if he were his own. They were married in 1956. Released from exile, they returned to Kiev, where they began a new life as a family.[39]

For some prisoners, family life itself was no longer possible. They were too afraid – of disappointment, of being a burden, of being unable to connect.

Natalia Iznar was born in 1893 to a family of lawyers in St Petersburg. In the 1920s she worked as a graphic artist and stage designer for the Moscow Art Theatre and Stanislavsky's Opera Studio. In 1932, she divorced her first husband and married Grigorii Abezgauz, a minor official in the Commissariat of Education and the Arts. In 1937, Abezgauz was arrested and shot. Natalia was arrested and sentenced to eight years in the ALZhIR labour camp. After her release, in 1946, she remained in Dolinka, where she worked as a decorative artist for the MVD's Political Department, which was responsible for propaganda art and theatre in the labour camps. Natalia had relatives in Moscow and in Leningrad. She had a daughter from her first marriage. But she chose to remain in the Gulag settlement rather than return to her family. Years of separation in the labour camp had broken something inside her and it could no longer be repaired. Natalia wrote to her sister-in-law in Moscow to explain:

Chistye Prudy 15, Apt. 27
Elena Moiseyevna Abezgauz

My dear, it is fortunate that Liudmila Aleksandrovna [a friend from ALZhIR] can deliver this by hand. At last I can explain in a way that you may understand. Six weeks have past since I gained my freedom, and yet this is my first letter. How can I explain? It is painful to have to recognize that after the long years of separation there is now an unbridgeable division between us. In the short period of my so-called freedom I have come to realize that I can't feel close to you again. When I think of coming back to you, I am overcome by the terrifying thought that I will not be needed, that I will be out of place, and that I will be no help to you. I have lost the confidence of a mother. I am a different person after all these years – I have become more sober. I want to work. I am trying to educate myself to live without the feeling that I need a family, to eradicate that feeling to such a degree that it might never have existed in me in the first place. There is nothing that I need except my work . . . Liudmila Aleksandrovna will tell you everything about the way I live, my character, appearance, and so on. She is the dearest person to me in the world, closer to me than any family could be, because she has been with me and experienced the same things in the camp. It is such a joy when you meet a person who is absolutely good . . . I feel that I have lost you all internally. I no longer feel the need for a family – that feeling has died inside of me . . . It's not a bad thing. It's just how it is . . .[40]

3

When Sonia Laskina was released from the Vorkuta labour camp, she was given two things: a certificate of release signed by two administrators of her labour camp and a second-class train ticket to Moscow. Sonia had a family, a job and an apartment to return to in Moscow. Other prisoners were far less fortunate. They had nowhere to go: either their families had broken up or moved away, or their homes had disappeared or been taken over by others, or they were forbidden to return to the cities where they had once lived. Banned from the major centres, many ex-prisoners were forced to live a marginal existence in temporary

Sonia's certificate of release. It gives the dates of her
imprisonment, cites the decision of the Military Collegium
of the Supreme Court to close the case against her 'for
failure to prove the charges', and allows her to return to
Moscow as her place of residence

housing, wherever they were able to get registered as residents by the
Soviet authorities, which were often reluctant to give such rights to
former 'criminals'. The struggle to overcome the legal obstacles and
institutionalized discrimination that prevented them from returning to
their towns and homes was long and complicated.

In 1953, at the age of seventy-eight, Liudmila Tideman (née Obolenskaia) returned to Leningrad from Orenburg, where she had been living
in exile since 1935. The eldest of Simonov's three Obolensky aunts,
Liudmila was the only one to have survived the hardships of exile (Dolly
and Sonia had both died in Orenburg). After much petitioning, she
received permission from the city Soviet to move back to her old room
in the communal apartment where she had lived with her son and
daughter before her arrest. When she returned to the apartment, however, the house committee refused to register her as a resident, on the
grounds that three people in her family had previously been living there,

so she could not live there on her own. For several weeks Liudmila stood in queues at the police station, the local housing department, the city Soviet and various other offices in an effort to establish her right to occupy the room alone. 'The most disgusting aspect of it all was that everywhere they thought I was a swindler,' she wrote to Simonov. 'They said I had listed extra names [on the housing order from the Soviet] to receive more living space.' The authorities would not let her live there on her own, nor would they change the names on the housing order, claiming, as she put it, that 'they do not make mistakes', so the case dragged on. Months later, Liudmila was finally allowed to return to her home.[41]

Simonov's personal secretary, Nina Gordon, had an equally difficult time. Her husband, Iosif, had been rearrested and sent as a punishment to Krasnoiarsk, where Nina joined him in 1951. On the couple's return to Moscow in 1954, they stayed with Simonov until they could find a place to live. Although Nina and Iosif were Muscovites, it proved impossible to get them registered as residents, even with the help of Simonov, who wrote to the city Soviet and even to the head of the Moscow militia on behalf of this 'honest working couple who have suffered such misfortune during recent years'. Eventually, they were permitted to stay in Moscow for a year, and they moved into a room in a communal apartment obtained for them by Simonov. Iosif got a job at the Gorky Film Studios, while Nina went back to work for Simonov. But their rights of residence were soon annulled, for no apparent reason, and the couple were informed that they would have to leave the capital within a month. As Simonov protested in a letter to the head of the Moscow MVD,

The conclusion is simple: a person who for no crime whatsoever has spent many years in prison and exile, and who at last has returned to the work from which he was unjustly torn away, is being forced to leave that work again and go away. His wife, who already gave up her own job once to be with her husband, must now give up her job and again leave her native city, if she wants to be with him. It is not only unjust, it is inhumane.

Thanks to Simonov's petitioning, the couple were allowed to stay on a temporary basis in Moscow. They lived in eight different rooms and apartments over the course of the next four years, until at last they were registered as permanent residents. In 1958, Simonov got them put on a waiting list for an individual flat in an apartment block, which was then being built for the workers of the Gorky Film Studios. But the building was delayed, forcing Iosif and Nina to find yet more temporary accommodations. It was not until 1966, shortly before Iosif's death, that the couple finally got a small flat of their own.[42]

Finding work was just as onerous as finding a place to live. Soviet officials were generally mistrustful of former prisoners, and many employers continued to regard them with suspicion as potential troublemakers and 'enemies of the people'. The return of political prisoners followed the release of common criminals from the labour camps as a result of the amnesty of March 1953. The mass of the Soviet population did not distinguish between 'politicals' and criminals. They associated all the releases from the Gulag with the rise of crime and 'hooliganism' after 1953 (just as they connected them with the reappearance of 'internal threats and enemies' after the Hungarian Uprising of 1956, when the Soviet press was full of propaganda on that score). Even after their rehabilitation, many former prisoners were refused work. The very fact of their rehabilitation was frequently a cause of prejudice and suspicion among employers, who did not want to run the risk of taking on a person who had been labelled as a political 'criminal' only a few years before. One ex-prisoner recalls being told by a factory boss in Kharkov that 'even though I had been rehabilitated, in his eyes I was still a person with a shameful past'. Until Khrushchev's explicit condemnation of Stalin's crimes, at the Twentieth Party Congress in 1956, the public attitude towards the returning Gulag prisoners wavered between mistrust and hostility. People were afraid to have any connection with the former 'enemies' who came back from the camps. The sight of these returning prisoners stirred up awkward memories, perhaps even feelings of guilt and shame, in many citizens, who had had a relatively comfortable existence while their compatriots had languished in the labour camps. Most people preferred to put the returning ex-prisoners out of sight and out of mind, just as during Stalin's reign they had avoided any mention of the missing millions. Lev Kopelev recalls that, after his return from the labour camps, he felt uncomfortable with successful people who had managed to avoid the purges of the Stalin years and that he preferred the company of people who had been 'unlucky in some way'. With them at least he could be sure that he was not in the presence of someone who had made his or her career by collaborating with the system of repression.[43]

The problem of finding work and housing was so acute that some ex-prisoners ended up returning to the labour camps. After 1953, many of the camps remained in operation as special economic zones employing nominally free labour, mainly released prisoners. They received a wage but were not free to leave the remote settlements because of legal restrictions on their movements. There were also those who chose to remain in the camps and settlements because they felt unready to return to society. In some labour camps the old barracks were inhabited by ex-prisoners well into the 1960s. There were even cases of former prisoners committing minor crimes in order to be arrested and sent back to the camps, where at least they could be sure of a bread ration.[44]

After his return from the Kolyma camps in 1953, Ivan Uglitskikh was unable to find a job or a place to live in his home town of Cherdyn; the police had refused to grant him the necessary passport for rights of residence. He travelled round the country in search of work, living from the money he had saved as an electrician in Kolyma. First he went to Moscow. It was his great ambition to see Red Square. But he was so badly dressed in his patched-up wadded camp jacket that he was immediately stopped by the police and deported. He was, in any case, prohibited from going to Moscow. Next he went to Novozybkov, a small town in the Briansk region, south-east of the capital, where his former wife was living with her new husband and their two children, but he could not find work there. Then he went to the Donbass, hoping for a job in the mines, but there was nowhere for him to live, and without registration as a resident no one would hire him. He encountered the same problem in Zhdanov and Taganrog. After months of desperate searching, Ivan ended up on a state farm near the Azov Sea where all the workers lived in dug-outs in the ground, but even here he could not find a job: one look at his release certificate from Kolyma was enough for the farm officials to reject him. Ivan finally got work just as he decided to return to Kolyma. On the way there he stopped in Krasnokamsk to visit his brother's family, who were living in the barracks of a former labour camp. Ivan approached an official at the brick factory attached to the camp, asking for a job. Although he was turned down initially, a bribe of a watch persuaded the official to change his mind. Ivan remained at the brick factory until his retirement in 1981.[45]

Between 1953 and 1957, an estimated 612,000 former prisoners were rehabilitated, many of them posthumously, by the Soviet authorities. In the rhetoric of the Soviet leadership the process of rehabilitation was about restoring truth – about reviving faith in the principles of justice established in 1917 – and seen from the outside it had something of this idealistic quality. But from the perspective of the ordinary people trying to regain their civil rights the practical reality was very different. For them it meant a long and humiliating series of visits to offices, where they were made to stand in queues, fill out forms and battle with officials who were often hostile to their cause. It was not unusual for a former prisoner to write a dozen letters before his appeals were granted by the Soviet authorities, although the process of judicial review and rehabilitation was speeded up after 1956. Sometimes appellants were summoned to appear before a commission in the offices of the MVD or the Justice Ministry, places that inspired fear among former prisoners, who would often turn up in their winter coats, accompanied by weeping relatives, convinced that they were about to be sent back to the labour camps. Not surprisingly, such fears and obstacles deterred many people from applying for rehabilitation altogether (which was probably the intention of the authorities). The required judicial reviews and bureaucratic procedures were carried out extremely grudgingly. Soviet officials had an obvious motive to drag their feet: many had been promoted on the basis of cases they had fabricated against 'enemies of the people', and they were afraid of being prosecuted if these injustices were revealed. Some of their attempts to salvage something from these cases were petty and ridiculous. One war veteran, for example, had been sentenced in 1947 to ten years in a labour camp for 'anti-Soviet propaganda' (he had told some 'anti-Soviet' jokes). In 1954, he had his sentence reduced to five years on appeal and he was immediately released. The investigating procurator in his judicial review had decided that the jokes were not anti-Soviet after all. But he had justified the original prosecution (and thus refused to overturn the case and rehabilitate the prisoner) on the grounds that one of them was capable of being understood as anti-Soviet.[46]

Finally, when rehabilitation was granted, it came with no apology for the citizen's unjust arrest, let alone for the years wasted in a labour camp. In the eyes of most officials, the rehabilitation of a former criminal did not expunge all his guilt. As one ex-prisoner was reminded by a KGB major in 1960: 'Rehabilitation does not mean that you were innocent, only that your crimes were not all that serious. But there's always a bit left over!'[47]

For many people the need for rehabilitation was so strong that no obstacle could deter them. It was particularly important to former Party members and to those who had dedicated themselves to the public values of the Revolution of 1917. The recognition of their civic worthiness was fundamental to their personal dignity. For the same reason, many of these people wanted reinstatement in the Party. Only when they were given back their Party cards did they feel fully revalidated as Soviet citizens. The widow of an 'enemy of the people' who spent twelve years in the ALZhIR labour camp recalls her pride when she got her husband's pension and notice of his posthumous reinstatement in the ranks of the Party. As the widow of a Party member, she got many special benefits which were not given to other repressed families (and this gave her a distorted view of the position of the rehabilitated generally), but these advantages were important to her first and foremost as a symbol of her reintegration in society:

Politically and as a citizen I felt that I had finally become a whole person again. More than that, I was in a sense a 'hero of the day'. Those in the Party who were rehabilitated rose in social status. We were placed at the head of the queue for living quarters, holidays, financial help and so on.[48]

For others rehabilitation was important because it restored meaning to their lives and political beliefs. Despite the injustices they had suffered, many people still held firm to their commitment to the Soviet ideal. This belief gave meaning to their lives, and perhaps to their sacrifice. Many even took pride in the idea that their labour in the camps had made a contribution to the Soviet cause, as Aleksandr Degtiarev, a scholar at the Lenin Agricultural Institute, explained to the journalist Anatoly Zhukov in the 1970s:

I dug by hand so many precious metals in the labour camp that I could have ended up a multi-millionaire. That was my contribution to the Communist system. And the most important factor that ensured my survival in those harsh conditions was my unflinching, inextinguishable belief in our Leninist Party and its humanist principles. It was the Party that gave me the strength to withstand these trials. The Party kept alive our spirits and our consciousness, it helped us fight. Reinstatement in the ranks of the Communist Party was the greatest happiness of my entire life.[49]

There was another category of people who sought rehabilitation because they thought it would lift the shame that had been attached to their name. Maria Drozdova, who was released from the Norilsk camps, did not feel she was really free until she had been rehabilitated: 'It was only then that I could look people in the eye with a sense of honour and with pride. Nobody could curse me any more.'[50]

Rehabilitation was a huge relief for the Turkin family, which had been stigmatized as the relatives of an 'enemy of the people' since 1936, when Aleksandr Turkin, the veteran Bolshevik and journalist from Perm, was arrested as a 'Trotskyist'. For twenty years, Aleksandr's wife and their two daughters believed that Aleksandr was guilty of some crime against the state: it was the only way they could explain the hostility of former friends and neighbours. Aleksandr's mother-in-law had cut his face out of the family portrait in the living room ('If we have an enemy among us, we must clear him out') and since then the family had avoided all mention of him. So when Aleksandr's wife was told that her husband had been innocent, and she then received his rehabilitation on appeal, it was a liberation for the family. At last they could talk, without a sense of shame, about the husband and the father they had lost.* 'Once people learned that my father had been rehabilitated, they began to soften in their attitude towards us,' recalls Aleksandr's daughter Vera. 'It was important for us morally, because we had doubted him as well, and it turned out that we had been wrong.'[51]

Not everyone saw rehabilitation as an adequate response. Some took the view that they had always known that they were innocent, that they did not need the vindication of a system that had proved itself unjust. This viewpoint was often to be found among older Party members, the followers of Lenin, who regarded Stalin as a 'counter-revolutionary'. Others, such as Lev Netto, one of the leaders of the Norilsk uprising, who was released from the labour camp in 1956, refused to apply for rehabilitation, 'on principle'. Speaking for his comrades in the uprising, Netto explains, 'we all felt that we did not need forgiving by the state, which was guilty of a crime against us. It was a matter of our self-respect and dignity.'[52]

For many Party members and their families, rehabilitation was not

---

*With the certificate of rehabilitation the Turkins received information that Aleksandr had died in a labour camp a few weeks after his arrest in 1936. He was fifty-two.

enough to restore justice without reinstatement in the Party (which also meant they received extra compensation from the state). But the process of reinstatement was extremely slow, particularly in the provinces, where many Party organizations continued to be ruled by the old bosses, who had risen to the top by fabricating cases against 'enemies of the people' and risked losing everything if they now acknowledged their mistakes. Aleksandr Turkin was one of thirty Bolsheviks in Perm unjustly arrested as 'Trotskyists' in 1936. At the time of his rehabilitation, in 1956, the local press had raised the issue of their reinstatement in the Party, but despite the efforts of their families, the question was then buried by the Party organization, until it resurfaced in the glasnost period of the 1980s. But even then, the city's leaders dragged their heels: not one of the thirty Bolsheviks was reinstated in the Party before its abolition in 1991.[53]

Unless they were reinstated in the Party, the compensation given to ex-prisoners on their rehabilitation was so derisory that many refused to take it. When Zinaida Bushueva was rehabilitated in 1957, she was given two months' wages, calculated at the values of 1938, the year of her arrest, in compensation for the eight years she had spent in the ALZhIR labour camp, and another two months' wages for her husband, who was shot in 1938 and rehabilitated posthumously 'for failure to prove the charges' against him. She used the money to buy a coat for her two daughters, a suit for her son and a table with six stools for the one-room flat they were given by the Soviet in Perm.[54]

Olga Adamova-Sliuzberg applied for rehabilitation for herself and her husband in 1954. She waited for two years before receiving the usual certificate, in which it was stated that her case had been reviewed and the charges dropped for lack of evidence. 'I had paid for this mistake with twenty years and forty-one days of my life,' she writes. In compensation, she was entitled to two months' pay for herself and her dead husband, and a further 11 roubles and 50 kopecks to compensate for the 115 roubles which had been in the possession of her husband at the time of his death. In the waiting room outside an office in the Supreme Soviet building in Moscow, where she was presented with this gift, there were twenty other women, all receiving similar certificates. Among them was an old Ukrainian, who became hysterical when she was told what her son's life was worth:

The old Ukrainian woman began to shout: 'I don't need your money for my son's blood. Keep it yourselves, murderers!' She tore up the certificate and threw it on the floor.

The soldier who had been handing out the certificates approached her: 'Calm down, citizen,' he began.

But the old woman started shouting again: 'Murderers!' She spat in his face and began to choke in a fit of rage. A doctor ran in with two assistants and took her away. Everyone was silent and subdued. Here and there were the sounds of stifled sobs. I too found it hard to contain myself . . . I returned to my apartment, from which no policeman could evict me now. There was nobody at home, and I was free to weep. To weep for my husband, who perished in the cellars of the Lubianka when he was thirty-seven years old and at the height of his powers and talent; for my children, who grew up as orphans, stigmatized as the children of enemies of the people; for my parents, who died of grief; for the twenty years of torture; and for friends who never lived to be rehabilitated but lie beneath the frozen earth of Kolyma.[55]

Millions of people never came back from the camps. For their relatives, who were seldom told where they were or what had happened to them, the years after 1953 were a long and agonizing wait for their return, or for information about their fates. In many cases it was not until the 1980s, when 'openness' or glasnost became the watchword of the Soviet government, or even after the collapse of the Soviet regime in 1991, that this wait came to an end.

Zinaida Bushueva never found out that her husband had been shot in 1938. Until her death, in 1992, she did not know whether he was dead, in which case she would have mourned for him, or whether he was still alive but had chosen not to return to his family, in which case she would have probably concluded that he had been guilty after all.[56]

Afanasia Botova continued to believe that her husband might still be alive until she died in 1981. Her husband had been arrested in 1937 at his work in the engineering workshops attached to the railway station at Perm. He was sent to Bamlag, the Gulag complex organized for the construction of the Baikal–Amur railway line, and from there to a camp near Magadan, where, as his daughter Nina was informed in 1989, he died from exhaustion in November 1940. None of this was known to Afanasia, who received a note from him in January 1941: 'So far still alive. The temperature is minus 50 degrees.' For forty years this tiny scrap of faded paper was enough for Afanasia to hold on to the hope that her husband would return.[57]

Elena Cherkesova clung to the belief that her husband was alive until she died in 1982. Her husband, Vsevolod, a geologist at the Mining Institute in Leningrad, was arrested in 1937 and sentenced to be shot in February 1938. Before his execution Vsevolod was allowed to phone his wife. He told her that they would never see each other again, but he did not say that he was about to be executed, telling her instead, as no doubt instructed by his executioners, that he had been sentenced 'without rights to correspond'. Like millions of other relatives with loved ones in the labour camps, Elena did not understand that 'without rights to correspond' was Gulag code for the death sentence. After 1953, she presumed that his sentence must have ended, so she tried to track him down. She made inquiries at the MVD headquarters in Leningrad and wrote to the Soviet Procuracy in Moscow, but none of the officials would tell her anything. Shortly after her trip to the MVD headquarters, Elena was visited by a strange woman, who told her that she had been a prisoner in the same labour camp as Vsevolod and that she had seen him there a few years before. The woman encouraged Elena to believe that her husband was still alive.[58]

It was a common ploy of the MVD to deceive the relatives of executed prisoners in this way. Soviet officials took great care to cover up the facts of their killings. Their main concern was to hide the huge death toll of 1937–8 by claiming that the people executed in those years had died later, usually during the war years. They fabricated death certificates and informed relatives that prisoners had died from heart attacks or other illnesses when in fact they had been killed many years before.

Ida Slavina successfully appealed for the rehabilitation of her father in 1955. With the certificate of rehabilitation she received a death certificate from the registry in Leningrad which stated that her father had died of a heart attack in April 1939. Ida was puzzled because in 1945 she had been told by the Soviet authorities that her father was alive. She went to the headquarters of the MVD in Leningrad, where she was advised to trust the evidence of the death certificate. Ten years later, in 1965, when she applied for information from the KGB in Moscow, she received the same advice. Ida continued to believe this version until 1991, when she gained access to her father's file in the KGB archives and discovered that he had been shot, only three months after his arrest, on 28 February

1938. In his file she also found an order from a KGB official in 1955, which stated that 'for reasons of state security' Ida should be misinformed that her father died of a heart attack in 1939.[59]

Irina Dudareva never gave up hope that she would find her husband after his arrest in the southern town of Azov, where he was the leader of the Party committee, on 30 August 1937. Ten years later, she had not heard anything from him, but he was due to be released, so she began to write to the MVD and to all the labour camps whose names and addresses she had collected from the relatives of other prisoners arrested in the Rostov region where she lived. Shortly afterwards she received a visit from a man, one of her husband's former Party colleagues from Azov, who claimed that he had seen him in a labour camp, where, he said, he was alive and well. Irina went on writing to the authorities, who informed her that her husband was alive but still serving his sentence in a labour camp 'without rights to correspond'. After 1953, she wrote with increasing frequency, assuming that her husband must surely now have been released, since she had never heard of anybody serving more than fifteen years in the labour camps; she thought she would have been told if his sentence had been extended for some reason. Finally, in 1957, Irina received a certificate stating that her husband had died from an illness in 1944. This is all Irina knew until her death in 1974. But in 1995, her daughter Galina was given access to her father's file in the KGB archives, in which it was stated that he had been executed on the night of his arrest.[60]

4

'Now those who were arrested will return, and two Russias will look each other in the eye: the one that sent these people to the camps and the one that came back.'[61] With these words the poet Akhmatova anticipated the drama which unfolded as prisoners returned from the camps to confront the colleagues, neighbours, friends who had informed on them.

In 1954, Maria Budkevich came back to the communal apartment in Leningrad where she had lived with her brother and their parents until their arrest in 1937. Their two rooms had been taken over by the next-door neighbours, a married couple with three children. The wife had been on very friendly terms with the Budkeviches until the mass arrests of 1937, when she denounced them as 'counter-revolutionaries' and 'foreign spies' (Maria's father was of Polish origin). She had even claimed that Maria's mother was a prostitute who brought clients to the house. In 1954, the same woman, now grown old and thin with long white hair, was living in the rooms, her children having grown up and left the apartment, and her husband sent to a labour camp in 1941. Maria needed the woman to sign a document testifying to the fact that her family used to live there. She had recently received the rehabilitation of her parents, who had both been shot in 1937, and needed the document to apply for compensation for the living space and personal property which had been confiscated from the Budkeviches at the time of their arrest. The woman's face went white when she heard Maria say her name. 'I didn't think you would come back,' she said. Maria explained the purpose of her visit and reassured the woman that she had no intention of making any claim to her living space. The woman invited Maria to sit down while she read and signed the document. Maria looked around the room. She recognized her mother's collection of ceramic pots, the leather sofa which her father had brought back from Minsk, cushions, lamps and chairs, familiar to her from her childhood. When she had signed the document, the woman asked Maria to sit down with her on the sofa. 'There is something I must tell you,' she whispered. The woman told Maria that, shortly after his arrest, her husband had written her a letter from the labour camp, which she had destroyed out of fear. He had written to tell her that during his interrogation they had knocked out all his teeth, that he did not think he would return from the labour camp, and that she should not wait for him but should marry someone else. Her husband never returned from the labour camps. She was telling Maria this, she explained, because she wanted her to understand that she had suffered too and that she was sorry about what had happened to her parents.[62]

Iurii Shtakelberg was arrested in 1948 on charges of belonging to a group of 'Jewish nationalist students' at Leningrad University. It was claimed that the group was organized and financed by a German baron as a 'spy-ring' against the Soviet Union. Iurii was accused of trying to set up a secret printing press to spread anti-Soviet propaganda in the university. The charges had no foundation. They were based entirely on a made-up story and denunciation signed by four of his fellow students

at the university, who, it seems, were motivated largely by their xenophobia and had picked on Shtakelberg because of his foreign name (it
is also possible that they knew about the arrest of Iurii's father for
'disseminating German propaganda' in December 1941). In March
1949, Iurii was sentenced by a court in Leningrad to twenty-five years
of hard labour. He was sent to the Bamlag camp (where his father had
perished in 1942) and put to work building bridges for the railway. In
1956, he was seriously injured from a fall and released as an invalid. At
first he lived in Luga and then finally he returned to Leningrad, taking
a job in the Public Library. When Iurii was invited by the KGB to
look at the records of his trial, he saw the names of his fellow students
who had reported him. He paid a visit to each one in turn. 'They all
understood that I knew what they had done,' recalls Iurii.

One woman told me that it made no difference that I had returned, that it
changed nothing, because I had been a bastard then, and I was a bastard now
. . . She said that I should have been shot. One of the men – the one who had
always been a provocateur, and a stupid one at that – took me to his home and
in the entrance showed me a large bundle of paper. It was the sort of consignment
that was sometimes sold in the big shops. He said: 'If you want some, help
yourself. Perhaps now's the time to start your printing press.' I laughed it off,
but it sent a shiver down my spine. I thought of telling him that the paper was of
no use for a printing press because it was cut too small, but I said nothing.[63]

Ibragim Izmail-Zade was a senior professor of medicine and a depart-
mental head at the Institute of Medicine in Baku at the time of his arrest,
in 1938, on charges of belonging to an 'anti-Soviet group of Azerbaijani
nationalists'. After his release from the Kolyma camps, he returned to
Baku, where he took up a junior position in the same institute. Instead
of the cutting-edge research he had done in the 1930s, he was now
employed in routine clinical work. During the trial of M. D. Bagirov,
the former Party boss of Azerbaijan, in 1955, Ibragim appeared as a
witness for the prosecution, in which capacity he was allowed to look
at his own file from 1938, when Bagirov had led the terror campaign in
Baku. Ibragim discovered that he had been denounced by his favourite
student, who had since gone on to become the head of his department
at the institute. While Ibragim was in Kolyma, the former student had
often visited his wife and daughter, who treated him as a member of the
family. The old student was noticeably cooler in his behaviour after

Ibragim's return, rarely coming to the house, and never in the evening, when he would have been obliged to eat or drink with him. After his discovery of the denunciation, Ibragim and his family were forced to see the former student several times, and while they never spoke to him about his actions, it was clear that the Izmail-Zades now knew of the betrayal. One day the political director of the institute appeared at the Izmail-Zade house. He wanted Ibragim to sign a document stating that his family had no grievance against the former student, and that they would remain on friendly terms. Ibragim refused to sign. He had to be restrained from throwing the official out on the street. According to his daughter, Ibragim was crushed by the betrayal. He felt humiliated at being forced to work beneath someone who, he felt, was hardly qualified. Being asked to sign the document had been the final straw.[64]

In 1953, Kolia Kuzmin, the former leader of the Komsomol in Obukhovo, who had denounced the Golovins as 'kulaks' during the collectivization campaign of 1930, came to live in Pestovo, the small town near Vologda, where the Golovins had settled after their return from exile in Siberia. Before his denunciation of the Golovins, Kolia had often been a guest in their house. He had even been employed in the leather workshop of Nikolai Golovin, who had taken pity on the teenage boy, because he came from the poorest family in the village. Nikolai and his wife Yevdokiia were religious believers. When Kolia came to visit them shortly after Stalin's death and asked for their forgiveness, not just for his denunciation but for his part in the murder of Nikolai's brother, they not only forgave him but invited him to come and live with them in Pestovo. Their daughter Antonina, who was then working as a doctor in Kolpino, near Leningrad, took exception to her parents' generosity and tried to persuade them to change their minds. 'He killed Ivan [Nikolai's brother] and destroyed our family. How can one forgive a man for that?' she reasoned. But Yevdokiia believed that 'a truly Christian person should forgive his enemies'. Kolia settled in a house next door to the Golovins. He was ashamed of his actions in the past and tried to make amends by running errands for the Golovins. On Saturdays he would go with Nikolai to the public baths; on Sundays he would go with both of them to church. In 1955, Yevdokiia died, followed three years later by Nikolai, and in 1970 by Kolia Kuzmin. They are all buried in the same churchyard in Pestovo.[65]

Many former prisoners were surprisingly forgiving towards the people who had informed on them. This inclination to forgive was seldom rooted in religious attitudes, as it was with the Golovins, but it was often based on the understanding, which was shared by everyone who had experienced the prisons and the camps of the Gulag system, that virtually any citizen, no matter how good they might be in normal circumstances, could be turned into an informer by pressure from the NKVD. The journalist Irina Sherbakova recalls a meeting of the Moscow Memorial Society (established to represent the victims of repression) during the late 1980s:

one woman, who had been arrested in about 1939, said to me in a completely calm voice: 'Over there is the man who informed on me.' And she greeted him quite normally. Catching my perplexed expression, she explained: 'Of course we were just eighteen then, his parents were Old Bolsheviks who were repressed, and they [the NKVD] tried to recruit me too. And of course he himself was repressed later on.' I felt that what she said was motivated, not by a lack of concern for the past or a desire to forget it, but by the realization of the shameful things the system had done to people.[66]

That realization was certainly more likely to develop in the 1980s, when painful memories had perhaps softened over time, and the victims of repression, informed by history, had arrived at a more objective understanding of the Soviet system. But the tendency to refrain from the condemnation of individuals was already noted in the 1950s, when Soviet émigrés, apparently, were not hostile to ordinary Party functionaries, because they understood that they were really powerless and perhaps themselves victims of the same system.[67]

Not surprisingly, the return of Stalin's prisoners provoked great fear in the people who had helped to send them to the camps. 'All the murderers, provocateurs and informers had one feature in common,' recalls Nadezhda Mandelshtam: they never thought that their victims might return one day:

They thought that everybody sent to the next world or to the camps had been eliminated once and for all. It never entered their heads that these ghosts might rise up and call their grave-diggers to account. During the period of rehabilitations, therefore, they were utterly panic-stricken. They thought that time had gone into reverse and that those they had dubbed 'camp dust' had suddenly once more taken on flesh and reassumed their names. They were seized by terror.

One 'wretched woman informer' was constantly summoned to the Prosecutor's office to retract testimony she had given against the living and the dead. After every session, recalls Mandelshtam, she would run to the families of those she had denounced and plead, 'as God was her witness', that she had 'never said anything bad' about them, and that 'her only reason for going to the Prosecutor's office now was to say good things about all the dead people so they would be cleared as soon as possible'. Mandelshtam concluded that

the woman had never had anything remotely resembling a conscience, but this was more than she could stand, and she had a stroke that left her paralysed. She must at some moment have got so scared that she really believed these rehabilitations were serious and that all the slanderers and other minions might be brought to trial.[68]

Mandelshtam also tells the story of a senior MVD official in Tashkent who was pensioned off after Stalin's death but 'occasionally summoned to interviews with former victims who had by some miracle survived and returned from the camps'. The man could not stand it and hanged himself. Mandelshtam was able to read a draft of the suicide letter he addressed to the Central Committee. The official wrote that he had always worked hard for the Party, and that it had never crossed his mind

that he might have been serving not the people, but 'some kind of Bonapartism'. He tried to put the blame on others: on the people he had interrogated for signing all kinds of bogus confessions, thereby misleading the officials in charge of their cases; on the officials sent from Moscow with instructions concerning 'simplified interrogration procedures' and demands that the quotas be fulfilled; and, last but not least, on the informers who volunteered the denunciations which forced the secret police to act against so many people.

The death of the MVD official was hushed up. He had named too many functionaries and informers before his suicide. But his daughter was determined to get even 'with those who had caused her father's death'. As Mandelshtam noted:

Her anger was directed against the ones who had stirred up this nightmarish business. 'They should have shown some consideration for the people in official positions at the time! They didn't start all this, they were just carrying out orders.'[69]

Another one of Stalin's henchmen to commit suicide was Aleksandr Fadeyev, the alcoholic leader of the Writers' Union, who was removed from that post in 1954. Fadeyev had been suffering from depression for a long time, but Stalin's death completely unhinged him. 'My illness is not in my liver,' he wrote to a fellow Union member, 'it is in my mind.' Fadeyev confessed to Simonov that he was 'bankrupt' as a writer. He gave up working on his last novel, a Socialist Realist tale about the Party's struggle against industrial sabotage, which made use of materials from the 1930s trials, after he had realized, as he explained to several friends, that its moral import was completely wrong: there had been no industrial sabotage. Fadeyev was overcome by feelings of remorse for his part in the repression of writers during his leadership of the Writers' Union. 'I was such a scoundrel,' he wrote to Chukovsky. He was particularly remorseful about his old friend Iogann Altman, who died in 1955, two years after his release from jail. Fadeyev had denounced Altman during the 'anti-cosmopolitan' campaign and had done nothing to save his friend when he was arrested and imprisoned in 1949. After Altman's death, Fadeyev went on a drinking binge. He confessed to a friend that he had sanctioned the arrest of many writers he had known were innocent.[70]

After 1953, Fadeyev attempted to redeem himself by petitioning the authorities for the release and rehabilitation of writers who had been sent to the labour camps. He wrote to Malenkov and Khrushchev, calling on the Party to loosen its ideological control of the cultural sphere, but he was ignored and then removed from his leadership position. By 1956, Fadeyev had become an isolated figure, widely denounced as an unreconstructed Stalinist by the literary intelligentsia, which knew nothing of his later efforts on behalf of repressed writers. Just before he shot himself, on 13 May 1956, Fadeyev wrote a letter to the Central Committee which remained hidden in the Party archives until 1990:

I see no possibility of living any longer, because the cause of [Soviet] art, to which I gave my life, has been destroyed by the arrogant and ignorant leadership of the Party ... Our best writers have been exterminated or died before their time because of the criminal connivance of those in power ... As a writer, my own life has lost all sense, and it is with joy, with a sense of liberation from this vile existence, where the soul is crushed by malice, lies and slander, that I depart this life.[71]

Fadeyev was broken by the conflict between being a good Communist and being a good human being. He was by nature a kind person, as many of his victims recognized, but his conscience, his identity and in the end his will to live were gradually destroyed by the compromises and accommodations he had made in his many years of service to the Stalinist regime.[72]

Despite Fadeyev's pessimism about the state of literature, Soviet writers played a leading role in the beginning of the thaw. As the regime ceased to exercise a direct veto over writers, literature became the focus for a new emphasis on the individual and private life, and on the rejection of the meddling interference of the Stalinist bureaucracy. Soviet writers moved away from the public themes and heroes of Socialist Realism and strove to portray real people in their domestic and social context. The most daring work of fiction in those years, Ehrenburg's *The Thaw* (1954), was deliberately provocative, as if it were a test to see how far it was possible to go in the new climate. The novel tells the story of a despotic factory boss, a 'little Stalin', who becomes increasingly corrupt and inhumane, stealing money assigned for workers' housing to invest in the factory, as he struggles to fulfil the production quotas of the Five Year Plan. The boss's wife cannot bear to stay with such a heartless man, and the spring thaw, which promises a new and better life, gives her the courage to leave him. In the political climate of 1954, when the thaw had only just begun, it was too early for Soviet readers to discuss the novel's anti-Stalinism, which was not obvious in any case. Instead they concentrated on the novel's other theme, the independence of the artist, which was contained in its sub-plot about a painter. The artist churns out works to order by the state and lives comfortably as a consequence, but he recognizes his own mediocrity compared with other painters whose art has not been compromised by service to the system.

The publication of *The Thaw* split the Soviet literary world. Liberal journals such as *Novyi mir*, where the novel was first published, hoped it would mark the start of a new era, when writers could at last be honest and sincere, when they would return to their true role of shaping private sensibilities rather than reflecting the interests of the regime. In a discussion of his work at a Moscow library in 1954, Ehrenburg maintained that the purpose of art was to express the 'culture of emotions' and help the 'individual understand his fellow human beings'.[73] Alarmed by all this liberal talk, conservatives in the Soviet establishment began to organize a series of attacks on the liberal writers of the thaw. In August 1954, they secured the dismissal of Tvardovsky, the 'kulak' son and poet, from the post of editor of *Novyi mir*. The task of criticizing Ehrenburg fell to Simonov, who replaced Tvardovsky as the editor of *Novyi mir*. Simonov was chosen because he was regarded as a moderate conservative, and therefore more authoritative than Stalinist hardliners such as Sofronov. In two long articles in *Literaturnaia gazeta* Simonov attacked *The Thaw*, arguing that its portrayal of Soviet Russia was too dark and that the conclusion of its sub-plot was simplistic: it was possible, Simonov argued, to be a good artist and to serve the state.[74]

Simonov remained in the Stalinist camp until 1956, when he began to embrace the spirit of reform. Like many people who had lived in Stalin's shadow, Simonov was confused and disoriented by the leader's death. At first, it was far from clear which way Kremlin politics would go: a return to the Terror was quite plausible. In this climate of uncertainty it was not unreasonable for people in positions such as Simonov's to play it safe by sticking to the political ground they had occupied before Stalin died. 'In those years,' recalls Simonov, 'my attitude to Stalin kept changing. I wavered between various emotions and points of view.' For much of 1953, his main feeling was a 'profound sense of grief at the loss of a great man', which led Simonov to write a startling eulogy in *Literaturnaia gazeta* ('The Sacred Duty of the Writer') in which he argued that it was 'the highest task of Soviet literature to portray the greatness and the genius of the immortal Stalin for all nations and all future generations'. The article enraged Khrushchev, who insisted on Simonov's removal from the newspaper's staff. Simonov remained loyal to his Stalinist origins throughout 1954, placing a portrait of Stalin on his desk. It was a picture he particularly liked: Stalin gazing on that monument to Gulag labour, the Volga–Don Canal. During Stalin's lifetime, Simonov had never hung a portrait of the ruler in his office or his house. He did so now because he was repulsed by the 'turncoats' and 'careerists' who had proclaimed their love for the Soviet leader when he was alive but renounced him as soon as he was dead. 'It was not Stalinism that inspired me [to display the photograph],' recalls Simonov, 'but something closer to the noble or intelligentsia idea of honour.' This same refusal to renounce his past led Simonov, in 1955, to include in a collection of his verse a truly awful 'Ode to Stalin' that he had written in 1943 but not published, in which he praised the Soviet leader as the greatest human being in the whole of history.[75]

Simonov with his son Aleksei, 1954

Simonov followed his critique of Ehrenburg with a series of attacks on other writers in the vanguard of the liberal thaw. In a major *Pravda* article, in July 1954, Simonov decried the literary rejection of the traditions of Socialist Realism and the growing trend towards satire, singling out for criticism the Ukrainian dramatist Aleksandr Korneichuk for abandoning the theatre's responsibility, as Simonov defined it, 'to teach the Soviet people how to love and cherish the Soviet system'.[76]

As the editor of *Novyi mir*, Simonov was also critical of Vladimir Dudintsev's explosive novel *Not by Bread Alone*, submitted to the journal for publication in serial form. The novel tells the story of an inventor, a physics teacher dedicated to the betterment of life in the Soviet Union, whose creativity is stifled and destroyed by the petty corruption and inefficiency of Soviet officialdom. Simonov forced Dudintsev to tone down his attack on the bureaucracy, fearing that the novel might raise doubts about the system as a whole, before he published it in *Novyi mir* in 1956. Despite the changes demanded by Simonov, the book was still hailed by the reformers as a battering ram against the establishment. The first public discussion of the novel drew so many people to the Writers' Union, with students climbing water-pipes to listen to the debate from the windows on the second floor, that mounted police had to be called in to disperse the crowds.[77]

Simonov was also responsible for *Novyi mir*'s crucial decision not to publish Pasternak's *Doctor Zhivago*. In September 1956, he wrote to Pasternak on behalf of the journal's editorial board, outlining their political objections to his novel, an epic human drama set against the backdrop of the Revolution and the Civil War. The letter was used and prominently cited by the Soviet leadership in 1958 during its campaign to force Pasternak to turn down the award of the Nobel Prize.* Simonov had a very low opinion of the novel, 'a vile and spiteful work of philistinism and in places simply anti-Soviet', as he described it in a letter to his son. Simonov took the view that in posing the central question of his novel – whether the Russian intelligentsia had made the right decision to accept the October Revolution of 1917 – Pasternak had set things up so that it could only be answered in the negative: that by deciding to go along with the Bolsheviks, the intelligentsia had betrayed their duty to the Russian people, to Russian culture and humanity. In Simonov's opinion, not only did this bias make the novel anti-Soviet; it was also an insult to a whole generation of professionals, to people like his mother and his stepfather, who had remained in Soviet Russia and worked for the Bolsheviks, not out of political choice, but because they were Russian patriots first and foremost.[78]

As the thaw developed and Khrushchev's reformers gained the upper hand in the Soviet leadership, Simonov became an increasingly isolated figure in the Moscow literary world. The liberal spirit of reform was not tolerant of Stalinist believers who refused to change their views. As Simonov put it in 1956:

> The editor can ask to cut away
> The name of Stalin from my verse,
> But he cannot help me
> With the Stalin who is left within my soul.

It was only very gradually, after Khrushchev's speech denouncing Stalin at the Twentieth Party Congress in 1956, that Simonov began to purge that inner Stalin from himself.[79]

---

*Smuggled out of the Soviet Union and first published in Italy in 1957, *Doctor Zhivago* became an international bestseller, and Pasternak was nominated for the Nobel Prize for Literature in 1958, but under pressure from the Writers' Union, and a storm of nationalist abuse against him in the Soviet press, he was forced to refuse the prize.

Khrushchev's speech was a crucial watershed, more important than the death of Stalin, in the slow demise of the terror system that had ruled the Soviet people since 1917. With Khrushchev's speech, it became clear that the Soviet government was finally distancing itself from Stalin's reign of terror, and the people's fear and uncertainty about the future gradually began to lift.

The Twentieth Party Congress, the first since Stalin's death, convened in the Great Kremlin Palace on 14 February 1956. The 1,355 voting delegates assembled in the expectation that the leadership would at last explain its post-Stalin line and clarify the status of the dead leader. The decision to expose and denounce Stalin's crimes was made by the collective leadership – though there were bitter arguments about how far they should go – following the report by a special commission on the repression of Party members between 1935 and 1940 presented to the Central Committee on 9 February. The leadership was surprised by the commission's findings – both by the huge scale of the mass arrests and executions and by the fabrication of the evidence on which this wave of terror had been based – and on the eve of the Party Congress it resolved to tell the truth to a closed and secret session of its delegates. The text of the speech was prepared collectively and Khrushchev, who had been the main driving force behind disclosure, took responsibility for its delivery on 25 February.

Khrushchev's motives were complex. It was certainly courageous to argue for disclosure when other Party leaders, such as Kaganovich, Molotov and Voroshilov, were clearly uncomfortable with the idea of exposing the crimes of a regime in which they had played such important roles. During the discussions on 9 February, Khrushchev called for bold action:

What sort of leader destroys everyone? We have to be courageous and tell the truth . . . We all worked with Stalin, but that does not implicate us. As the facts emerge, we have to speak of them, otherwise we are justifying his actions . . . We can speak with a clear voice. We are not ashamed. We have nothing to fear, and no reason to be satisfied by small-minded arguments.

Disclosure also suited Khrushchev's bid for power. He used the exposure of Stalin's crimes to undermine or threaten his main rivals for the leadership, and to build a base of support in those sectors of society that embraced the thaw and political reform. But above all, perhaps, like the rest of the Party leaders, Khrushchev feared that, if they did not speak of Stalin's crimes, the public would speak in their place, and that in the climate of the thaw critics of the Party would hold the entire leadership responsible. 'Either you tell them at the upcoming congress, or you will find yourself under investigation,' Khrushchev was warned by an old Party comrade, recently returned from the labour camps, whose testimony featured in his speech. By giving the impression that the Party leaders had discovered the truth about the Terror only recently, as a result of the commission which reported on 9 February, Khrushchev was able to shift the blame on to Stalin and clear the other leaders from suspicion, on the grounds that they 'did not know'. To the same end Khrushchev offered a rather exculpatory explanation of the injustices committed by the Party since 1935: Stalin was held personally responsible for all of them, but other Party leaders were portrayed as victims of his 'monstrous' crimes (even the followers of Trotsky and Bukharin had not deserved to die). There was no question of blaming the Soviet system – only of struggling to 'overcome the cult of personality'. The whole purpose of the speech was to restore Leninism to power.[80]

Khrushchev ended his speech with a plea for secrecy:

This subject must not go beyond the borders of the Party, let alone reach the press. That is why we are talking about this at a closed session . . . We must not provide ammunition for our enemies, we must not bare our injuries to them. I assume congress delegates will understand this and act accordingly.

After he had finished speaking there was a 'deathly silence' in the conference hall. Aleksandr Iakovlev, later to become a leading figure in Gorbachev's policies of glasnost, was one of the congress delegates. He recalls the scene:

I sat in the balcony. I remember well the sense of profound disturbance, if not desperation, which took hold of me after Khrushchev spoke. The silence in the hall was profound. There was no sound of squeaking chairs, no coughing, no whispering. No one looked at anyone – whether from the unexpectedness of what had just occurred or from nervousness and fear . . . We left the conference hall with our heads bowed.

Among the delegates who spilled out into the entranceway was Simonov, who stood there for a long time in a state of shock and confusion, smoking and talking with Igor Chernoutsan, the Central Committee's cultural adviser. 'We already knew a lot,' recalls Chernoutsan, 'but we were stunned by the way the truth caved in on us. But was it the whole truth?'[81]

9
Memory
(1956–2006)

I

Khrushchev's 'secret speech' did not remain secret very long. A transcript was printed in a brochure and sent to Party organizations across the Soviet Union with instructions for it to be read to Communists in all workplaces. In the weeks following the Twentieth Party Congress, the speech was heard by 7 million members of the Party and 18 million members of the Komsomol in Soviet factories and offices, universities and schools. The speech was also sent to the Communist governments of Eastern Europe. Walter Ulbricht, the East German leader, tried to conceal it from the population of the GDR, but the Polish leaders published it, and a copy reached the *New York Times*, which ran it on its front page on 4 June. From the West, the text of Khrushchev's speech filtered back to the GDR and the rest of the people of the Soviet Union.[1]

The speech threw the Party into confusion. In local Party offices throughout the land there were animated discussions about what to make of the revelations, with some Party members blaming leaders who had failed to speak out earlier and others criticizing Khrushchev for raising these questions at an awkward time. By June 1956, the Central Committee was so concerned by these voices of dissent in the rank and file that it sent out a secret circular to local Party leaders calling on them to clamp down on criticism by purging and even imprisoning members who overstepped the accepted boundaries.[2]

Outside the Party, some fearless people took Khrushchev's speech as a signal to discuss and question everything. The intelligentsia was the first to speak. 'The congress put an end to our lonely questioning of the Soviet system,' recalls Liudmila Alekseyeva, a graduate of Moscow University who later joined the dissidents and emigrated to the USA.

Young men and women began to lose their fear of sharing views, information, beliefs, questions. Every night we gathered in cramped apartments to recite poetry, read 'unofficial' prose and swap stories that, taken together, yielded a realistic picture of what was going on in our country.[3]

Khrushchev's speech took away the fear that had silenced many prisoners after their return from the Gulag – and now they began to speak as well. 'The Twentieth Congress was the beginning of a thaw inside of us,' recalls Larisa Levina, whose mother, Zinaida, returned to Leningrad from exile in 1956.

My mother hardly said a word about her life in the labour camps [Kolyma from 1937 to 1946 and the Potma camps from 1949 to 1953] ... But after the Twentieth Congress she started talking. And the more we talked, the more our ideas changed – we became more sceptical. Our relationships changed as well – freed from my mother's fears, we became closer as a family.[4]

Children of Stalin's prisoners, burdened with the disadvantages of a 'spoilt biography', suddenly felt encouraged to voice their sense of injustice. Angelina Yevseyeva was working at a munitions factory in Leningrad when the text of Khrushchev's speech was read out to the Party workers at the plant. Someone told her of the reading, which she managed to attend by slipping in unnoticed to the Party offices. At the end of the reading, Angelina became hysterical and sobbed uncontrollably. She recalls:

No one understood what was wrong with me. I had a perfect *curriculum vitae* (*anketa*) and had even been elected as a deputy to the city Soviet. No one knew that my father had been arrested as an enemy of the people in 1937. I had never said a word to anyone. And I was always afraid that they would discover my secret. But when I listened to the speech, I felt released from this fear. That is why I cried. I could not help myself. After that, I started telling people the truth about my past.[5]

For Lydia Babushkina, whose father had been shot in 1938, Khrushchev's speech gave official sanction to the feelings of injustice she had harboured since her childhood, when her father disappeared. Before 1956, she was too frightened to talk about her feelings even to her mother and her grandmother, who were themselves afraid to talk about the arrest of Lydia's father, mainly because they both worked in a munitions factory where they feared they would be sacked if their spoilt biography were discovered. Their silence had sometimes made her doubt her father's innocence. But after Khrushchev's speech, Lydia no longer had such doubts. At last she summoned up the courage, not just to question her mother about the arrest of her father, but also to express her feelings to her fellow workers at the clothing factory where she worked near Smolensk. One night in the dormitory attached to the factory, Lydia told the other girls that Stalin had been 'the real enemy of the people' because he had ordered the arrest of innocent citizens like her father. The other girls became frightened: 'Quiet, quiet, they can arrest you for talk like that!' But Lydia was not put off: 'Let them. I'll tell them, loud and clear, that I'm saying exactly what Khrushchev said. Let them listen, and they'll realize that it's the truth.'[6]

But such talk was still exceptional. Even after 1956, the vast majority of ordinary people were still too cowed and frightened by the memory of the Stalinist regime to speak as openly or critically as Lydia did. The accepted understanding of the Khrushchev thaw – as a time of nation-wide debate and political questioning – was largely shaped by the memoirs of the talkative intelligentsia, which are hardly representative. Open talk was possibly the norm among city intellectuals, who used the thaw to grapple with the history of the Terror, but for the mass of the Soviet population, who remained confused and ignorant about the forces that had shaped their lives, stoicism and silence were more common ways of dealing with the past.

In 1957, Aleksandra Faivisovich, the hairdresser from Osa, spoke for the first time to her daughter Iraida about her arrest and the years which she had spent in the labour camp near Arkhangelsk, where she was then still living. Aleksandra's rehabilitation, which she had just received, had given her the confidence to tell Iraida something about her past. Iraida recalls their conversation:

She told me that she had a new passport [given to her on her rehabilitation], that the record of her arrest had been 'wiped clean', that she was innocent, and that therefore she could talk. But all she could bring herself to say was that my father had been put in prison 'for his loose tongue' [he had been overheard complaining about shortages in the shops] . . . and that she had been arrested because he was her husband. She said that many people had died in the camps – 'they dropped like flies' – that they got sick and no one cared for them. 'They treated us like dogs.' That was all she said.

For the next quarter of a century, until her death in 1980, Aleksandra did not say another word to Iraida about her arrest or the labour camp. All she would say, when her daughter questioned her, was: 'I have a new passport. I am clean.'[7]

Zinaida Bushueva never spoke about the camps. She did not tell her children about the circumstances of her own arrest, or of the arrest of her husband, who was shot in 1938. Even in the last years of her life, in the late 1980s, she would put up her defences whenever she was questioned about the past. 'In our family,' recalls Angelina,

no one talked about the reasons for my mother's arrest, or why we had no father. It was a closed subject. After the Twentieth Party Congress, I tried to find out more, but Mama would just say: 'The less you know, the easier to live,' or 'The more you know, the quicker you grow old.' She had many of these expressions to close the conversation down.

Zinaida Bushueva (centre) with her daughter
Angelina and her son Slava, 1958

According to her daughter, Zinaida took no interest in politics. 'She could not allow herself.' The fear she had brought back from the camps led her to adopt a position of 'uncritical acceptance' of everything she was told by the Soviet regime. She saw the contradictions between propaganda and reality, she had direct experience of the injustices of the regime, but, like millions of other ordinary Soviet citizens, she 'never stopped to reflect critically' on the reality she had observed. Acceptance of Soviet reality was a coping mechanism that helped her to survive.[8]

Nadezhda Maksimov grew up completely unaware of her family's history. Her father, a peasant from the Novgorod region, had worked as a carpenter in Leningrad. Arrested twice in the 1920s, he was re-arrested in 1932, when Nadezhda was only three, and sent into exile with his family to Arkhangelsk, where Nadezhda spent her childhood oblivious to their reason for living in the Arctic Circle. Her father was arrested and imprisoned briefly yet again in 1938 (Nadezhda believed he was away on a work trip) before the family settled in Penza. In 1946, Nadezhda enrolled as a student at the Medical Institute in Leningrad and went on to become a physician. It was only shortly before her mother's death in 1992 that Nadezhda found out about her father's multiple arrests and the eight years he had spent in various prisons, labour camps and 'special settlements'. She saw her father's name in the newspaper, along with the names of her grandfather and her uncle, in a list of former political prisoners, posthumously rehabilitated after the collapse of the Soviet regime. Nadezhda showed the list to her mother, who at first said: 'It was all so long ago. Why drag all that up again?' But after Nadezhda insisted, her mother told her everything. Her parents had wanted to protect her by not putting her in a position where she would feel obliged to declare her spoilt biography. 'Throughout my life, whenever I was asked to complete a questionnaire,' explains Nadezhda,

I was able to write 'No' in the section where they asked if I had any relatives who had been repressed, and because I did not know about my father, I was able to say that with a clear conscience, without any of the anxiety which I would have felt if I had been forced to lie. I'm sure that's why I always got away with it.

Her parents had maintained their silence even after 1956; they still thought it was too dangerous to tell her about their past, in case she told her friends, or the political circumstances changed. As a consequence, until the age of sixty-three, Nadezhda, as she herself admits, had little concern for the victims of the Stalinist regime – an indifference that was no doubt shared by other Soviet citizens whose lives were unaffected directly by the terror. Reflecting on her life in the 1930s and 1940s, Nadezhda recalls:

I had heard about the repressions, but they made no impression on me whatsoever. In 1946, for example, there were mass arrests in the neighbouring village in Penza, but somehow they passed me by, I did not understand or even try to understand what was going on ... Today I find it hard to explain this – that these events took place in parallel with my own life, but didn't affect me in the least. Somehow I managed to avoid it all.[9]

The grave of Nadezhda's father,
Ignatii Maksimov, Penza, 1994

Tamara Trubina did not find out for over fifty years what had happened to her father. All her mother, Kapitolina, told her was that he had disappeared in the Far East, where he had gone as a voluntary worker on various construction sites. Kapitolina had met Konstantin, an engineer, in 1935, when she, a young doctor, was sent by the Komsomol to work in the Gulag administration in Sychan, a small town near Vladivostok, where he was working as a penal labourer on a building site attached to the Gulag. In 1938, Konstantin was rearrested. Kapitolina had no idea where her husband was. She knew only that he had been sent to a labour camp somewhere in the Dalstroi Gulag network in north-east Siberia. After leaving the young Tamara with her mother in Perm, Kapitolina returned to work as a doctor in the labour camps of Kolyma. Because her marriage to Konstantin had not been registered and she had kept her maiden name, she was able to conceal her spoilt biography for several years. Eventually the commandant of the Gulag section where she worked found out about Konstantin, but the need for doctors in the camps was so acute that he kept Kapitolina's secret and protected her. For thirty years, Kapitolina continued to work as a doctor for the NKVD, and then the MVD, rising to become a major in the Medical Division of the KGB, before her retirement in 1965. Until 1956,

Tamara and Kapitolina, 1948

she never gave up hope that in the course of her travels around the labour camps of Kolyma she might discover Konstantin, or find out something about him. By helping other prisoners like him, she felt, at least, as she herself expressed it, that she was maintaining a link indirectly with her lost husband. Then, in 1956, she was told the truth: Konstantin had been executed in November 1938.

For nearly twenty years, Kapitolina had lived in constant fear that her colleagues would find out that her husband was an 'enemy of the people'. She was afraid to speak of Konstantin even with her family. So the revelation that he had been shot – which she took as evidence that he may well have been guilty of a serious crime – made her even more withdrawn and silent about him. She said nothing to her daughter, who asked about her father with increasing frequency. 'Mama never spoke about my father,' recalls Tamara.

She kept all his letters [from the 1930s] and some telegrams, but she never showed them to me. She always steered the conversation on to other subjects. She would say, 'I don't know what he did.' The most she would say was, 'Perhaps his tongue got him into trouble.'

After her mother's death, in 1992, Tamara was advised by her uncle, a senior official in the KGB, to write to his police colleagues in Vladivostok and ask for information about Konstantin. The reply she received informed her that her father had been shot in 1938 on charges of belonging to a 'Trotskyist organization', but it made no mention of his imprisonment in any labour camp. So she continued to believe that Konstantin was a voluntary worker in the Far East, as her mother had told her, and that he had fallen out of favour with the Soviet authorities only during 1938. It was only in 2004, when Tamara was interviewed in Perm in connection with this book, that she learned the whole story. Shown the documents which proved that her father was a long-term prisoner in the Gulag, she at first refused to believe them and insisted that there must be a mistake. Mentally she was not prepared to see herself as a 'victim of repression' in the Soviet system where she had enjoyed a successful career as a teacher and perceived herself as a member of the Soviet establishment. Perhaps, Tamara acknowledged, she owed her success to her mother's silences: had she known the truth about her father, she might well have hesitated to make a career for herself.[10]

The suppression of traumatic memories has been widely noted as a psychic self-defence for victims of repression in all totalitarian regimes, but in the Soviet Union there were special reasons for Stalin's victims to forget about the past. For one thing, nobody was sure whether Khrushchev's thaw would last. It was possible that it would soon be followed by a return to repression; and, as it turned out, the thaw was brief and limited. Throughout the Khrushchev period, the regime made it clear that it was not prepared to tolerate any discussion of the Stalinist repressions that might lead to criticism of the Soviet system as a whole. Even at the height of the Khrushchev thaw in the early 1960s – a time when Stalin's body was removed from Lenin's Mausoleum, when Stalinist hardliners such as Kaganovich, Molotov and Malenkov were expelled from the Party, and when the perception of the Stalinist regime was changed for good by the publication of Solzhenitsyn's searing Gulag tale *One Day in the Life of Ivan Denisovich* (1962) – there was no official recognition of the millions who had died or been repressed, no public monument, no government apology, no proper reparation for the victims, whose rehabilitation was granted only grudgingly.

In 1964, Khrushchev was replaced by Leonid Brezhnev, and the relatively liberal climate of the thaw came to an abrupt end. Censorship was tightened. Stalin's reputation as a 'great war leader' was resurrected for the twentieth anniversary of the Soviet victory, when a bust of the dictator appeared by his grave near the Kremlin Wall. Brezhnev clamped down on the 'dissidents', who were first organized by the protest movement against the show trial of the samizdat writers Iulii Daniel and Andrei Siniavsky in February 1966. The persecution of the dissidents was a powerful deterrent against the discussion of Stalin's crimes. Millions of people whose memory of the Stalinist regime might have made them think or speak more critically about the Soviet system pulled back, afraid of giving the impression that they sympathized with the dissidents, whose references to Stalin's crimes were a form of opposition to the Brezhnevite regime. People again suppressed their memories – they refused to talk about the past – and conformed outwardly to the loyal and silent Soviet majority.

Among Stalin's former prisoners the threat of rearrest was real enough to reinforce this silence for several decades after 1956. The KGB may have been defanged by the ending of the Terror, but it still had access to a huge range of draconian punishments, and its powers of surveillance, which reached everywhere, instilled fear in anyone who dared to think or speak or act in ways that could be seen as anti-Soviet.

Inna Gaister was working as an engineer in the Tsvetmetavtomatika Laboratories in Moscow in 1977 when she was called to the telephone to speak to an operative from the KGB who asked her to come in to the Lubianka. 'Naturally, I began to get the shakes,' recalls Inna. 'I could not think at all.' Her mind raced back to her arrest in April 1949, when she had been summoned in a similar manner in the midst of her thesis defence at Moscow University; to the arrest of her sister in June 1949; and to the arrest of both her parents forty years before, in 1937, when Inna had been twelve. Inna responded that she was in the middle of an experiment and so couldn't come in straight away. The KGB official told her that he would ring again in half an hour. Inna frantically began to call her friends, both to warn them that they might be summoned too and to let them know where she was going, in case she did not return. When the KGB rang back, Inna once again refused to go to the Lubianka, so the operative began to question her about her acquaintance with Lev Kopelev, the former Gulag prisoner, dissident and writer, who was soon to be expelled from the Soviet Union. Kopelev was an acquaintance of Inna, as he was of hundreds of other Muscovites, and had given readings at her house. Somehow the KGB had found this out, perhaps by tapping her telephone, or more probably from an informant who had been at one of the readings. Inna was terrified. For the next few days, she lived in expectation of her imminent arrest. She threw out all the dissident literature she had been storing in her apartment, in case it was searched by the KGB, and cancelled any further readings in her home. Inna was not arrested. The incident had no further repercussions. But the call had stirred up painful memories and had left her with feelings of anxiety and fear that disturbed her for many years. 'All my life I have struggled with this fear,' reflects Inna, 'I am always afraid.' It is hard to say what frightens her. 'It's nothing concrete,' she explains. 'It's more like a feeling of inferiority, of some vague defectiveness.'[11]

This anxiety was widely shared by Stalin's former prisoners. Zinaida Bushueva lived in constant worry and even expectation of her rearrest throughout the 1960s and 1970s. It was not until 1981, when she received a clean passport, without the mark to signify that she had been imprisoned in a labour camp, that her fear began to diminish, although even then, according to her daughter, she 'was frightened all her life that the Terror might return, right until the day she died'. Maria Vitkevich, who spent ten years in the Norilsk labour camp after her arrest in 1945, remains frightened to this day. 'I cannot rid myself of fear,' she explains.

I have felt it all my adult life, I feel it now [in 2004], and I will feel it on the day I die. Even now, I am afraid that there are people following me. I was rehabilitated fifty years ago. I have nothing to be ashamed of. The constitution says that they can't interfere in my private life. But I am still afraid. I know that they have enough information about me to send me away again.

Svetlana Bronshtein, who was sentenced to ten years in a labour camp in 1952, still has nightmares of the Viatka labour camps, where she served three years of her sentence before her release in 1955. If she could find the energy to do the paperwork and stand in the queues at the

American Embassy, she would try to emigrate to the USA, where she believes her fear would disappear.[12]

Cowed and silenced, the majority of Stalin's victims stoically suppressed traumatic memories and emotions. 'A human being survives by his ability to forget,' wrote Varlam Shalamov in *Kolyma Tales*. People who had suffered terribly did not talk about their lives. They very rarely cried. 'To this day I cannot weep,' reflects Inna Gaister. 'In Stalin's time people did not cry. Within me there has always been some sort of internal prohibition against crying which comes from that time.'[13]

This stoicism has been widely noticed by historians. In her book on death and memory in Soviet Russia, the British historian Catherine Merridale notes that the Russians became so used to suppressing their emotions and remaining silent about their suffering – not so much in the sense of unconscious avoidance ('denial') but as a conscious strategy or coping mechanism – that one might wonder whether 'notions of psychological trauma are genuinely irrelevant to Russian minds, as foreign as the imported machinery that seizes up and fails in a Siberian winter'.[14]

Psychiatry suggests that talking has a therapeutic influence on the victims of trauma, whereas the repression of emotions perpetuates the trauma, the anger and the fear.[15] The longer the silence continues the more these victims are likely to feel trapped and overwhelmed by their unspoken memories. Stoicism may help people to survive but it can also make them passive and accepting of their fate. It was Stalin's lasting achievement to create a whole society in which stoicism and passivity were social norms.

Nobody is more stoical or accepting of his fate than Nikolai Lileyev. Born in 1921, Nikolai was conscripted by the Red Army at the age of eighteen, captured by the Germans in 1941 and taken as a POW to work on a farm in Estonia, and then in various mines and factories in Germany. In 1945, Nikolai returned to the Soviet Union, where he was arrested and sentenced to ten years in the Komi labour camps. On his release in 1955, Nikolai was not allowed to return to his native Leningrad, so he lived in Luga until 1964. In 2002, he wrote his memoirs, 'The Unlucky Do Not Live', which begins with this prologue, written, he insists, without the slightest hint of irony or black humour:

I have always been extremely fortunate, particularly in the difficult periods of my life. I am lucky that my father was not arrested; that the teachers at my school were good; that I did not fight in the Finnish War; that I was never hit by a bullet; that the hardest year of my captivity I spent in Estonia; that I did not die working in the mines in Germany; that I was not shot for desertion when I was arrested by the Soviet authorities; that I was not tortured when I was interrogated; that I did not die on the convoy to the labour camp, though I weighed only 48 kilograms and was 1.8 metres tall; that I was in a Soviet labour camp when the horrors of the Gulag were already in decline. I am not bitter from my experience and have learned to accept life as it really is.[16]

2

In 1956, Simonov divorced the actress Valentina Serova and married his fourth wife, Larisa Zhadova, who was then pregnant with his child. Larisa was an art historian, the daughter of a senior general, the Second-in-Command of all Soviet Ground Forces. Her father had been furious when she married her first husband, the poet Semyon Gudzenko, who died in 1953; when she announced that she would marry Simonov, he threatened to expel her and her three-year-old daughter from the family house ('Isn't one poet enough?'). Larisa was a serious and rather stern woman, cold by comparison with Valentina. She took charge of Simonov's private life and became his close companion, but she did not inspire him to write romantic poetry.[17] Perhaps he wanted order and quiet in his life.

The break-up with Valentina had been as turbulent as the rest of Simonov's relationship with her. Things began to fall apart after the birth of their daughter Masha (Maria) in 1950. Valentina, who had always been a heavy drinker, became a chronic alcoholic as her beauty faded and her career in the theatre steadily declined. There was a series of scandalous affairs at the Maly Theatre, for which she was reprimanded several times and then dismissed by the authorities in 1952. Valentina's behaviour was a huge embarrassment for Simonov, who at the time was under growing pressure from the Stalinist hardliners in the campaign against the Jews. Simonov had constant fights with Valentina, whose drinking bouts and violent fits grew worse as she sensed that he was preparing to leave her. In 1954, he moved out of their apartment on Gorky Street. He was already seeing Larisa, as Valentina was aware. In a last effort to rescue their relationship, he got Valentina the leading role in a play at the Moscow Soviet Theatre, and promised that he would return to her if she 'pulled herself together'. But Valentina, as he must have known, was incapable of doing that. She was sick and needed help.

Simonov and Valentina Serova, 1955

In the spring of 1956, Simonov finally decided to divorce Valentina: Larisa had told him that she was pregnant, and he could not risk another scandal, if he refused to marry her. Valentina did not want a divorce. Like many of the couple's friends, she took the view that her husband was abandoning her just when she most needed his support. Perhaps this was unfair. There was little understanding of alcoholism in the Soviet Union, where heavy drinking was commonly regarded as a part of the Russian national character, and without medical support there was not much Simonov could do for her. Valentina fell into despair and drank so heavily that she ended up in hospital. Just then the divorce was legalized. Valentina had a nervous breakdown. She was confined to a psychiatric hospital five times over the course of the next four years. Masha lived with Valentina's mother for most of this period. The girl was profoundly disturbed by the strains of living with her alcoholic mother and by the disappearance of her father.[18]

In 1960, Dr Zinaida Sinkevich, the main consulting psychiatrist in the hospital where Valentina was confined, wrote to Simonov, accusing him of having caused Valentina's breakdown:

Valentina Vasilevna gave herself to you entirely ... There was no aspect of her life that was not in your hands – her self-esteem as a woman, her career as an actress in the theatre and the cinema, her success and fame, her family and friends, her children, her material well-being ... And then you left, and your departure destroyed everything! She lost all confidence, her ties to the theatre and the cinema, her friends and family, her self-esteem ... Wine was all she had left, the one thing on which she could rely, but without you it became an escape from reality.

Looking back on these events in 1969, Simonov confessed in a letter to Katia (Larisa's sixteen-year-old daughter from her first marriage who had lived with Simonov since 1956) that by the time of his divorce from Valentina he had felt 'not a shred of respect, let alone of friendship' for his alcoholic wife, and that his 'one regret', for which he blamed himself, was that he had not left her 'many years before'.[19]

Simonov had always had this cold and rational capacity to cut people out of his life if he disapproved of them or calculated that they were of little use to him. In the 1930s and 1940s, when political loyalties were considered higher than personal ones, Simonov had broken off many relationships, and for that reason he was left without close friends when his manoeuvring came back to haunt him after 1956. Perhaps it goes to show that in the end it is impossible to be a Stalinist in public life and not let the morals of the system infect personal relationships.

After the divorce, Simonov made a conscious effort to cut out of his life everything to do with Valentina, although he continued to help her financially until her death in 1975. He bought a new apartment and dacha. He excluded their daughter Masha from the rest of his family, not inviting her to birthday celebrations, family anniversaries, book or film parties. In his 1969 letter to Katia, who had demanded to know why she had not been allowed to meet Masha, Simonov explained why it was for the best for them to be kept apart.*

Today there is a nineteen-year-old girl [Masha] who has been brought up by her mother with very different views and rules to my own – and therefore, although she carries my name, she is spiritually alien to me. I don't consider her part of my life, even though for many years I devoted much time and energy to ensuring

---

*Interviewed in Moscow in 2004, Masha Simonova did not know about the existence of this letter, nor about the sentiments which it expressed.

that she have a more or less normal existence, an almost impossible task since she was living with her mother, who for more than twenty years had drunk, then cured herself, then drunk and cured herself again.

I have never wanted you to know or meet this girl or to have any relations with her, because it would have made her and you unhappy. And I don't think there's a reason why you should know her now. Neither of you needs that. In life there are difficult decisions to be made, times when a man must take responsibility and do what he believes to be right, without asking others to carry the burden.[20]

It was only in the 1970s that Simonov softened in his attitude towards Masha, who then appeared at family events.

For Simonov the marriage to Larisa and the birth of their daughter Aleksandra meant the start of a new life. 'As for your sister, she is eight weeks old today,' Simonov wrote to his son Aleksei in March 1957.

She is losing her dark colouring and slowly turning red – so there is hope: that she will be a strong person, with healthy views on life, that she will walk and eat and talk as a person should – in a word, that she will become someone with good principles.

Domestic happiness coincided with the Khrushchev thaw. For Simonov the changes of 1956 represented a spiritual release, even though at first he had his reservations about the rejection of Stalin. After 1956, recalls Aleksei,

my father became happier and more relaxed. He was not so overburdened and pressured by his work. His hands, which had suffered from a nervous condition for as long as I remembered as a child, became normal once again. He became more attentive and warmer towards people close to him. It was as if the thaw in politics had thawed out his heart, and he began to live again.[21]

In August 1957, the Laskin family celebrated the golden wedding anniversary of Samuil and Berta with a banquet in a Moscow restaurant. The festivities were organized by Samuil's nephew, the writer Boris Laskin, who was well known as a humourist and satirist. The printed invitations and decorations in the restaurant were a lampoon of Soviet propaganda, with slogans such as '50 Years of Happiness – An Easy Burden!' and 'Your Family Union is a School of Communism!' Simonov joined in the celebrations and even contributed to the costs, despite his usual disapproval of jokes ridiculing Soviet power. Simonov had good relations with the Laskin family after 1956. He remained friends with Zhenia, helped her with money, often took her advice on literary affairs and advanced her career as an editor at the pro-thaw journal *Moskva* by sending her the manuscripts of poetry and prose that came his way.* There was perhaps an element of guilt in Simonov's attentiveness towards his former wife. As he embraced the spirit of the thaw, he must have been troubled by the moral contrast between Zhenia – a fearless champion of samizdat who helped to publish censored writers – and his own role in the Soviet literary establishment. At Zhenia's fiftieth birthday celebrations in 1964, an evening with family and friends at Zhenia's new apartment near the Airport Metro station in northern Moscow, some of these writers recited poems they had composed for her. The mood was warm and humorous, full of tenderness and love for Zhenia. Simonov made an awkward speech that went on far too long. He was visibly uncomfortable talking about Zhenia in a room full of writers who admired her for her moral courage and generosity, her willingness to help other people regardless of the dangers to herself. Simonov was rescued by his seven-year-old daughter Aleksandra, who walked into the room and ran towards him. He grabbed hold of her and asked her to 'congratulate her auntie Zhenia – quickly!' Aleksandra took hold of the microphone: 'Dear auntie Zhenia, happy fiftieth birthday, and tell Alyosha [Aleksei] to shave his beard!'[22]

For Aleksei the thaw marked the start of a new relationship with Simonov. In 1956, the sixteen-year-old boy wrote a letter to his father in which he spoke about their previous estrangement when he had lived with Valentina, and about his hope that they might become closer in the years ahead:

I believe in you, not just as a father but as a good, intelligent and honourable man, as an old friend. This belief is a source of strength for me, and, if it helps you, even just a bit, then I am happy. Remember that your son, although very young and not very strong, will always support you . . . We have rarely talked about your private life – only once I think . . . I never felt at home in your house – it wasn't anything obvious but when you were 'away' there were conversations that were difficult for me. I avoided going to your house when you were not

*Zhenia worked at *Moskva* from 1957 to 1969, when she was sacked for 'grave ideological errors' (she had published Yevgeny Yevtushenko's poetry).

there. My relations with Masha were also difficult – I could not accept her as a sister ... None of that is important any more. Now I feel that things will be different. It is good that you are calmer, happier. I am sure that I will be friends with your new wife – my feelings for her are already very warm. We will become closer, Father, and I will not be just a guest in your house.[23]

In the summer of 1956, at the age of sixteen, Aleksei finished school and, encouraged by his father, joined a scientific expedition to the remote region of Iakutsk in eastern Siberia. For Aleksei the expedition was all about proving himself as a man, in the image of his father, who had left school and gone to work at a similar age. 'Tell Father that I will not let him down,' Aleksei wrote to his mother Zhenia in his first letter home. In his letters to his father Aleksei compared the expedition to Simonov's own 'university of life' in the factories of the First Five Year Plan. His father responded with a tenderness and informality that Aleksei had never seen from him before. In one letter, which Aleksei would treasure all his life, Simonov wrote:

It is customary in these letters for a father to give advice to his son. Generally I don't like to do this – but one piece of advice I will give you before you go off for the winter. You no doubt have heard, or can imagine from what I have written on the subject, that I was not guilty of cowardice during the war. Here is what I want to say to you: I did what I had to do, according to my understanding of human dignity and my own pride as a man, but remember, if you now have the satisfaction of having a living and healthy father, not just a tombstone or a memory, it is because I never took stupid risks. I was very attentive, restrained and careful in all situations where there was a real danger, although I never ran away from it. It should be clear why I am writing this to you ...

And now, my friend, I must run to the Writers' Union and tell the young writers how they should and should not write – and you meanwhile feel free to put in any missing punctuation marks and correct my grammatical mistakes. Yes?

I kiss you, my sweet one, and squeeze your paw. Father. 31 August 1956.[24]

In September, Simonov joined Aleksei in Iakutsk for three days. He enjoyed the primitive conditions and comradeship of the expedition, which reminded him of life during the war ('He is very pleased that he can still go hiking with a rucksack on his back,' Zhenia explained to Aleksei). For the first time in his life, he sat with his son, drank with him by the camp fire and talked openly about his life, about politics and about his hopes for the future. Isolated in literary society, Simonov now found a soul-mate and a loyal supporter in his son. 'He is very pleased with you in all respects,' Zhenia wrote to Aleksei after seeing Simonov on his return. 'He is pleased with the way you have turned out, physically and spiritually, and with the way that you are seen by your contemporaries.' As for Aleksei, he had never known his father so happy and excited: 'He was full of the Twentieth Congress, of his new family, his daughter, his new house, and his new novel, *The Living and the Dead*. It seemed to him that he could turn over a new leaf and live his life in a different way.' During those three days in Iakutsk Aleksei fell in love with Simonov. The ideal father he had pictured all these years had finally materialized, and Aleksei flourished; his new connection with his father gave him a sense of independence and maturity. In his letters from Iakutsk, Aleksei explained to Simonov his ideas on literature and life, and asked for his advice, man to man. 'I have great hopes for our forthcoming meeting,' he wrote to him in February 1957. 'There is so much I must tell you, so much to ask you, which I cannot put in a letter.'[25]

Aleksei's closeness with his father was short-lived. The intimacy they had achieved in Iakutsk could not be repeated in Moscow, where Simonov had no time for his son. Politics divided them. Aleksei was swept along by the democratic spirit of the thaw, towards which his father remained sceptical, if not totally opposed. Aleksei was too young, politically too immature, to mount an articulate opposition to his father's politics. He had no real thoughts, for example, on the Kremlin's bloody suppression of the Hungarian uprising in 1956, when his father had supported sending in the tanks to crush the anti-Soviet demonstrators in Budapest. Yet there was in Aleksei an element of latent protest and dissent, which was perhaps connected to the history of the Laskin family. In 1956, Aleksei applied for his first passport. In the section where every Soviet citizen was required to register his ethnic origin, he was determined to write down Jewish, even though he had the right to register as Russian, the nationality of his father's family, which would make his life much easier. It took the concerted efforts of all the Laskins – and the insistence of Samuil and Berta in particular – to talk him out of it. For Aleksei, identifying with his Jewish origins was a conscious act of political dissent from the values of the Soviet regime. His views on other matters displayed the same attitude. Aleksei was repulsed by the falsity and hypocrisy of the Komsomol. He was deeply impressed by Dudintsev's *Not by Bread Alone*, a blistering attack on Soviet official-dom, and wrote to its author to tell him that it was a work of genius that was badly needed for the country's political reform. He signed the letter with his grandfather's name ('Aleksei Ivanishev') rather than his father's, so as to avoid the connection being made with Simonov, who had criticized the novel for giving rise to anti-Soviet sentiments, and had forced Dudintsev to tone down its assault on the bureaucracy before printing it in *Novyi mir*. Simonov was far more cautious than his son towards the reformist spirit of the thaw. 'If one steps back for a minute and looks at the country and the spirit of the people,' he wrote to Aleksei in February 1957, 'one can say without exaggeration that we have travelled an enormous distance since 1953. But when some writer considers it his duty to stir up unnecessary rebellion, then I have no sympathy for him.'[26]

Simonov's own de-Stalinization progressed very slowly. The revelations of the Twentieth Party Congress had both excited and shaken him, and it took a while for him to come to terms with them. For Simonov the crucial moral test of the Stalinist regime remained its conduct in the war. It was while working on his great war novel, *The Living and the Dead* (1959), that Simonov began to grapple with the central moral question raised by the war: the regime's appalling waste of human life. The novel deals with many of the issues that had been excluded from the public discourse on the war: the devastating effect of the Terror on the military command; the chaos and confusion that overwhelmed the country in the first weeks of the war; the climate of mistrust and the incompetence of the officers which cost so many innocent young lives. Drawing on his diaries and memories of the war, Simonov retells the story of the fighting through a series of vivid scenes where officers and men struggle to make sense of events and carry out their duty in the face of all these obstacles. He shows how people were changed by their experience in the war, becoming more determined and united against the enemy, and implies that this human spirit was the fundamental cause of the Soviet victory. Simonov had always seen the leadership of Stalin as a crucial factor in the war. But in *The Living and the Dead* he began to reassess Stalin's role and moved towards the populist conception – which he would develop in his final years – that it was the Soviet people who had won the war and that they had done so in spite of Stalin's leadership. As Simonov suggests, the chaos and mistrust that Stalin's reign of terror had fostered in the army led directly to the military catastrophe of 1941; only the patriotic spirit and initiative of ordinary people like the heroes in his book had reversed the crisis and turned disaster into victory. Simonov had touched on some of these ideas in his diaries of 1941–5, which he filled with observations of the war. He had discussed them with his friends, including the writer Lazar Lazarev, before 1953. But as Simonov himself confessed at a literary evening in the Frunze Military Academy in 1960, he had 'lacked sufficient civic courage' to publish these ideas while Stalin was still alive.[27]

Throughout his life Simonov retained an emotional attachment to Stalin's memory. His own personal history and identity were too closely bound up with the regime to reject the legacy of Stalin root and branch. For this reason, Simonov could never quite bring himself to embrace wholeheartedly the Khrushchev thaw, which seemed to him a betrayal of Stalin as a man and a leader, and as a betrayal of his own past. He could not deny Stalin any more than he could deny himself. Even at the height of the Khrushchev thaw, Simonov held firm to many of the dogmas of the Stalinist dictatorship. He took a hardline position on the Hungarian crisis of 1956. 'Several thousand people were killed in the events in Hungary,' Simonov wrote to Aleksei from Calcutta in 1957, 'but the British spilled more blood during the partition of India, and not in the interests of the people [the motive of the Soviet actions in Budapest, according to Simonov] but simply to stir up religious hatred and rebellions.'[28]

After 1956, Simonov was seen by liberal reformers as an unreconstructed Stalinist, and by the old Stalinists as a dangerous liberal, but in fact throughout the Khrushchev years he was a moderate conservative. He recognized Stalin's mistakes and saw the need for limited political reform, but he continued to defend the Soviet system that Stalin had created in the 1930s and 1940s as the only solid basis for the progress of humanity. 'We have made mistakes on the road to Communism,' he wrote to Aleksei, 'but the acknowledgement of our mistakes should not lead us to waver for a moment in our conviction that our Communist principles are correct.'[29]

When Brezhnev came to power, in 1964, Simonov's moderate conservatism found official favour, as Khrushchev's policies of de-

Stalinization were gradually reversed and the Kremlin opposed any real political reform in the Soviet Union or the other countries of the Warsaw Pact. From the mid-1960s, Simonov emerged as an elder statesman in the Soviet literary establishment. His books were widely published and made standard reading in Soviet schools and universities; he frequently appeared in the Soviet media; he travelled round the world as the official face of Soviet literature; and even by the standards of the Soviet elite, he enjoyed a privileged lifestyle.

Aleksei and Konstantin Simonov, 1967

On the twenty-fifth anniversary of the Soviet victory in 1945, 9 May 1970, Simonov gave an interview to the newspaper *Socialist Industry* in which he clarified his position on Soviet history since the end of the war:

I have spent a lot of time studying the history of the Great Patriotic War and I know a lot more now than I did when the war had just ended. Of course, a lot has changed in my understanding. But my main feeling, which you get when you travel round the country and see the building going on today, when you see what has been done and what is being done, is that our cause in those times was just. However hard it was, however many lives were lost, our people did what needed to be done during the war. If they had failed in that difficult endeavour, our country would not be what it is today, there would be no other socialist countries, no world struggle for freedom and independence from colonial rule. All of that was made possible only by our victory.[30]

For people of Simonov's generation the war was the defining event of their lives. Born around the time of the Revolution of 1917, this generation reached maturity in the 1930s, when basic values were reshaped by the Stalinist regime, and moved towards retirement in the Brezhnev period. From the vantage point of the 1960s and 1970s, these people recalled the war years nostalgically as the high-point of their youth. It was a time of comradeship, of shared responsibilities and suffering, when 'people became better human beings' because they had to help and trust one another; a time when their lives had greater purpose and meaning because, it seemed to them, their individual contribution to the war campaign had made a difference to the destiny of the nation. These veterans recalled the war as a period of great collective achievement, when people like themselves made enormous sacrifices for victory. They looked back at 1945 as an almost sacred time-space in Soviet history and memory. In the words of the war veteran and writer Kondratiev:

For our generation the war was the most important event in our lives, the most important. That is what we think today. So we are not prepared to belittle in any way the great achievement of our people in those terrifying, difficult and unforgettable years. The memory of all our fallen soldiers is too sacred, our patriotic feelings are too pure and deep for that.[31]

The commemoration of the Great Patriotic War served as a reminder of the success of the Soviet system. In the eyes of its loyal citizens, including Simonov, the victory of 1945 justified the Soviet regime and everything it had accomplished after 1917. But the popular memory of the war – in which it was recalled as a people's war – also represented a potential challenge to the Soviet dictatorship. The war had been a period of 'spontaneous de-Stalinization', when, more than at any other time, the Soviet people had been forced to take reponsibility for their own actions and organize themselves for the war effort, often in the absence of effective leadership or control by the Party. As the post-war regime feared, the collective memory of this freedom and initiative could become dangerous if it gave rise to ideas of political reform.

For many years the memory of the war was downplayed in the public culture of the Soviet regime. Until 1965, Victory Day was not even an official Soviet holiday, and it was left to veterans' groups to organize their own celebrations and parades. Publications on the war were tightly censored, and war novels politically controlled.* Wartime newspapers were withdrawn from public libraries. After 1956, there was a partial relaxation of these controls on the memory of the war. Memoirs by war veterans appeared in print. Writers who had fought in the war as young men published stories and novels drawing on their own experience to portray the reality of the soldiers' war – the 'truth of the trenches' (*okopnaia pravda*) as it was often termed – which functioned as a moral counter-balance to the propaganda version of the war.† But these publications were pushing at the boundaries of what was permitted by the Khrushchev thaw: the Party was prepared to blame Stalin for the military setbacks but not to challenge the official narrative of the war as a triumph of Communist discipline and leadership. In 1962, Grossman was told by Mikhail Suslov, the Politburo chief of ideology, that his war novel *Life and Fate*, which had been seized by the KGB after its submission to the journal *Znamia*, could not be published for at least 200 years (it was first published in Russia in 1988).

The memory of the war was even more tightly controlled by the Brezhnevite regime, which used the commemoration of the Soviet victory to create a powerful display of public loyalty and political legitimacy for itself. In 1965, Victory Day became an official Soviet holiday, celebrated with enormous pomp by the entire Party leadership and featuring a military parade on Red Square. A new Museum of the Armed Forces was opened for the anniversary; its vast display of memorabilia elevated the remembrance of the war to the level of a cult. Two years later, the Tomb of the Unknown Soldier was erected near the Kremlin Wall, quickly becoming a sacred site for the Soviet state and a place of ritual homage for Soviet brides and grooms. In Volgograd (previously Stalingrad) a monumental site of mourning was completed in 1967. At its centre stood a vast sword-bearing Mother Russia, the tallest statue in the world at 52 metres high. It was at this time that the endlessly repeated statistic of '20 million dead' entered Soviet propaganda as a messianic

---

*The one really notable exception is Viktor Nekrasov's *In the Trenches of Stalingrad* (1946), a vivid re-creation of the ordinary soldiers' war which avoids the usual clichés about the wise leadership of the Party. Perhaps surprisingly, it won the Stalin Prize in 1946.
†Four works of fiction in this category: Simonov's *The Living and the Dead*; Nekrasov's *The Second Night* (1960); Okudzhava's *Good Luck, Schoolboy* (1961); and Vasil Bykau's *The Dead Feel No Pain* (1965).

Mother Russia, part of the Mamaev Kurgan
War Memorial complex in Volgograd

symbol of the Soviet Union's unique sacrifice for the liberation of the world.

Simonov was too much of a soldier, he had seen too much of the war's realities, to have any part in the manipulation of its public memory. He had thought for many years about the meaning of the war and about the reasons for the Soviet victory. His thinking on the war became a sort of moral contemplation about Stalin and the Soviet system as a whole: whether it was justified to spend so many lives to win the war; and whether it was force that had spurred the people on to victory or something deeper inside them, the spiritual force of patriotism or stoical endurance, unconnected to any politics. During the last decade of his life, Simonov collected soldiers' memoirs and testimonies. By his death, in 1979, he had amassed a large archive of memoirs, letters and several thousand hours of taped interviews.* Many of these testimonies were recorded in *A Soldier Went* (1975), a 'film-poem in seven chapters', each one reflecting on a different aspect of the soldiers' experience, with interviews and readings from the works of Simonov. In a way that was extraordinary for its time, the film brought to life the horrors of the war and the suffering of the soldiers, who were portrayed as ordinary human beings behaving with courage and resilience in the most difficult circum-

*In the last year of his life Simonov attempted to establish a special collection of soldiers' memoirs at the Ministry of Defence archives in Podolsk, just outside Moscow, but high-ranking army leaders were opposed to the idea ('O popytke K. Simonova sozdat' arkhiv voennykh memuarov', *Otechestvennye arkhivy*, 1993, no. 1, pp. 63–73).

stances. One of the film's longest chapters dwells on the soldiers' injuries, featuring an infantryman who was wounded seven times yet still marched on to Berlin. The film was a homage to the Red Army rank and file – to the courage and endurance of millions of unknown and neglected heroes who brought about the Soviet victory – by a man whose writings on the war had usually taken the perspective of the officer. According to Marina Babak, the film's director (and Simonov's lover at that time), there was a strong personal motive in this act of homage, because 'Simonov felt that he had never shown sufficient courage' in his life. 'Simonov insisted that he should not be seen in the film at all,' recalls Babak. 'He said that he was unworthy to appear alongside a soldier.'[32]

The film ran into trouble with the military establishment, which took exception to its gritty realism and populist conception of the war (the censors insisted on the addition of a sequence paying homage to Brezhnev as a war leader). The Brezhnev leadership regarded all attempts to commemorate the suffering of the people in the war as a challenge to the government. From the mid 1960s, many of Simonov's writings on the war were either banned from publication or published in a censored form. His war diaries from 1941, prepared for publication as a book (*A Hundred Days of War*) in 1967, were turned down by the Soviet censors, despite Simonov's personal appeal to the Party leadership (the book was finally published in 1999). The same fate befell his essays on Zhukov and his war diaries of 1941–5 (*Various Days of War*), which were published with major cuts in 1977.[33] His documentary film *If Your House Is Dear to You* appeared in 1966 only after a long battle with the censors, who cut it heavily, while the film version of his novel *Soldiers Are Not Born* (1964), the second volume of *The Living and the Dead*, was so badly butchered by the Soviet censors that Simonov withdrew the title of the novel and even his own name from the final version of the film, which was screened as *Retribution* in 1967.

These battles with censorship strengthened Simonov's determination to search for the truth about the war and about the Stalinist regime. His notebooks from this time are filled with reminiscences about his encounters with Stalin, with self-interrogations about what he knew and did not know (or did not want to know) about Stalin's crimes when he had been part of the dictator's court. The more he learned of Stalin's lies and murders, the more he tried to distance himself from his past.

'There was a time when, although I had some doubts, I loved Stalin,' Simonov wrote in 1966. 'But today, knowing all the things that I know about him, I do not and cannot love him any more. If I had known then what I know now, I would not have loved him then.'[34]

During the last years of his life Simonov became increasingly remorseful about his role in the Stalinist regime. As if to redeem his sins, he tried hard to promote the work of writers and artists who had been censored or repressed in Stalin's time. Encouraged by his wife, Simonov became a private collector and champion of the Soviet avant-garde in art (he organized a major retrospective of the long-forgotten artist Vladimir Tatlin). He played a leading role in the campaign for the publication of works by Osip Mandelshtam, Kornei Chukovsky, Vsevolod Ivanov and for the Russian translation of Jaroslav Hašek's *The Good Soldier Schweik*. He gave money to writers who had suffered in the past – including Borshchagovsky, Vera Panova and Nadezhda Mandelshtam – and petitioned on behalf of many others for housing, jobs and readmission to the Writers' Union.[35]

In 1966, Simonov set in motion a process that culminated in the publication of Mikhail Bulgakov's subversive masterpiece *The Master and Margarita*, a fantastic social satire in which the devil comes to Moscow and brings out the worst in everybody through his anarchic pranks. Impossible to publish while Stalin was alive, the manuscript had been hidden in a drawer since the writer's death in 1940. In 1956, Simonov had been made the chairman of the commission in charge of Bulgakov's literary estate by the writer's widow Elena Bulgakova, who was an old acquaintance of Simonov's mother. Simonov gave the manuscript of *The Master and Margarita* to Zhenia Laskina, who was then working at *Moskva*, a journal much in need of exciting prose to boost its falling subscription sales (upon which its standing and subsidies depended) after the ending of the literary thaw, when it had become a rather dull and quiet magazine. Simonov was doubtful that Zhenia would succeed in getting the book past the censors, who were tightening up on literature. He had even advised Elena Bulgakova to accept some cuts to get the book published. Having read the manuscript at his dacha over a weekend, Yevgeny Popovkin, *Moskva*'s editor, confessed to Zhenia that he was afraid to publish it, even though he knew that it would make his name. Popovkin advised Zhenia to take the manuscript to one of *Moskva*'s editors, a retired censor who had good connections at Glavlit, the committee in charge of literary censorship, and who, as an editor, had never had a manuscript rejected by the censors. With the help of this retired censor, Bulgakov's manuscript was passed with relatively minor cuts and published in instalments in *Moskva* from November 1966. The November issue (150,000 copies) sold out overnight. There was a huge demand to subscribe to the journal for the next two years, the period it took to serialize Bulgakov's extraordinary novel, which appeared to Soviet readers as a miracle in the oppressive atmosphere of the early Brezhnev years. Delighted by their success, Zhenia and Simonov commemorated the historical event by compiling a scapbook of all the passages that had been cut by the censor. They made three copies of the book: one for Simonov, one for Zhenia and one for Elena Bulgakova.[36]

Simonov's support for these initiatives was a public statement about his politics. By setting out to rescue suppressed works of art and literature, he was aligning himself with the liberal wing of the Soviet establishment. These efforts, which he undertook on his own initiative (he had no official position in any Soviet institution or journal), earned him the respect of many artists and writers, who made him the chairman of literary commissions and organizations like the Central House of Literature in the 1960s and 1970s. Simonov had not become a liberal in the sense of the dissidents, who were pro-Western and anti-Soviet, but like many Communist reformers in the Brezhnev era, he was open to the idea of a fundamental change in the politics and culture of the Soviet system. Simonov did not openly criticize the Brezhnev government. But privately he was opposed to many of its policies – not least to the invasion of Czechoslovakia in August 1968 in order to suppress the 'Prague Spring' of Alexander Dubček's reformist government. The crisis of 1968 was a major turning-point in Simonov's political development. It radicalized him. He began to question whether it was possible or even desirable for the one-party system to survive in the stagnant form which it had developed under Brehznev's leadership. According to his son, if Simonov had lived a few more years, he would have welcomed Gorbachev's reforms:

As a senior Party member there was only so far he could go, of course. He would have had to break his Party mould completely to come out in support of Solzhenitsyn, for example, and he could not do that. I do not know what he really thought, and what he forced himself to think in order to keep himself in check, but I know that he went on evolving politically to the end. That, for me, was his strongest quality – he never lost the capacity to change.[37]

The development of Simonov's political ideas in his final years was intimately linked to his re-examination of his past. Simonov became increasingly remorseful about his own conduct during Stalin's reign. As he admitted his errors to himself, he grew more critical of the political system that had led him to make them. His feelings of contrition were sometimes so intense that they bordered on self-loathing, according to Lazar Lazarev, who was as close as anyone to Simonov at that time. Lazarev recalls that Simonov would castigate himself, both as a writer and as a man, at public occasions. Simonov was known for his self-deprecating irony. His friends and admirers took it to be part of his personal charm. But there were times when they must have realized that his self-criticisms came from darker impulses. At his fiftieth-birthday celebration at the Central House of Literature in 1965, an evening of speeches in praise of Simonov attended by more than 700 guests, he seemed to grow impatient with the kind things said of him. At the end of the evening, shaking visibly with emotion, he approached the microphone to deliver these extraordinary words:

On these sorts of occasions – when someone reaches fifty years of age – of course people mainly like to recall the good things about them. I simply want to say to the people here, to my comrades who have gathered here, that I am ashamed of many of the things I have done in my life, that not everything I have done is good – I know that – and that I did not always behave according to the highest moral principles – neither the highest civic principles, nor the highest human principles. There are things in my life that I remember with dissatisfaction, occasions when I acted without sufficient willpower, without sufficient courage. I know that. And I am not saying this for the purposes, so to speak, of some sort of repentance, that is a person's private business, but simply because, by remembering, one wants to avoid repeating the same mistakes. And I shall try not to repeat them ... From now on, at whatever cost, I will not repeat the moral compromises I made.[38]

These feelings of remorse intensified over time. He regretted the way that he had written about Stalin and the White Sea Canal during the 1930s. He felt remorse for his participation in the wartime propaganda of the Stalinist regime, for having gone along with Stalin's lies about the 'criminal behaviour' and 'treason' of those Soviet generals who ordered the retreat of 1941. He felt remorse for his shameful actions in the Writers' Union between 1946 and 1953 – years he found it 'painful to recall', as he wrote in an essay on Fadeyev: 'There are many things that are hard to remember without dissembling one's feelings, and many more that are even harder to explain.' In the last years of his life Simonov engaged in a long struggle to understand his actions in the Writers' Union. He interrogated his own memory and wrote several drafts of a personal account about his role in the 'anti-cosmopolitan' campaign, which remained locked away in his archive. Yet he never tried to defend or justify his actions in those years. Lazarev recalls an evening at Simonov's house to celebrate his fifty-fifth birthday in 1970. Proposing a toast to the assembled guests, the writer Aleksandr Krivitsky passed around a photograph of Simonov in 1946 and said that they should drink to the words of a well-known song, 'As he was then, so he is now'. Lazarev took exception to the implication – that Simonov remained a Stalinist – and, proposing the next toast, he said they should drink to the courage of their host, who was 'not afraid to change and break with the past'. A heated argument began about whether Simonov had changed and whether that was a good thing or not. The next day Lazarev called Simonov to apologize. But Simonov saw nothing wrong. 'On the contrary,' recalls Lazarev, 'he said that the discussion had been highly educational, because it had helped him make up his mind about himself: of course it was better when a person changed, if he changed for the better.'[39]

Many of Simonov's activities in the 1970s were driven by his need to make up for his past actions. Haunted by memories of the Stalinist attacks on Jewish writers, he led a brave campaign in defence of Lilia Brik, the muse of much of Maiakovsky's later poetry. Brik was the subject of a violent and openly anti-Semitic attack by literary critics working for Suslov, who demanded that she should be expunged from accounts of Maiakovsky's life to purge the memory of the great Soviet poet of all Jewish elements. Filled with regret for his attacks on Ehrenburg in 1954, Simonov organized the publication of the writer's war journalism. The collection included an article by Simonov, written in 1944, in which he had described Ehrenburg as the best of all the war-time journalists. The book was published in 1979, not long before Simonov's death. Simonov was in hospital when he received a copy from the publishers. He called Lazarev, who had edited the book, and told him that he was extremely happy and relieved that he had 'made his peace' with Ehrenburg.[40]

Many people in the reformist circles of the literary intelligentsia were sceptical of Simonov's late repentant liberalism. To them it seemed unlikely that a veteran Stalinist could reconstruct himself so radically. There was always the suspicion of hypocrisy when Simonov came out for some liberal cause. 'Simonov the man of many faces,' Solzhenitsyn wrote, 'Simonov simultaneously the noble literary martyr and the esteemed conservative with access to all official quarters.'[41]

There were indeed times when Simonov behaved with anything but liberal inclinations. He took part, for example, in the Kremlin's persecution of *Metropol*, a literary almanac compiled and edited by Viktor Erofeev, Yevgeny Popov and Vasily Aksyonov, which was published (with 'Moscow, 1979' as the given place and date) by Ardis in the USA. *Metropol* was not a dissident publication but, as Erofeev later described it, 'an attempt to struggle with stagnation in conditions of stagnation'. Furious at this attempt to undermine their control of the printed word, the ailing leaders of the Brezhnevite regime took revenge on the editors of *Metropol*. Erofeev and Popov were expelled from the Writers' Union, while several other writers in the almanac resigned in protest from the Union or emigrated from the Soviet Union. Simonov was drawn into the campaign against *Metropol* by Suslov, who put pressure on him to denounce the publication as 'anti-Soviet'. Simonov had a vested interest. His daughter Aleksandra, then aged twenty-two, was in love with the brother of Viktor Erofeev, a young art historian called Andrei, to whom she had become recently engaged. Aleksandra and Andrei had been mixing with a group of bohemian friends, all of them children of the Soviet elite (Andrei's father was a high-ranking diplomat), who dressed like hippies and listened to rock music, then a form of dissidence. Once the literary scandal broke, Simonov resolved to end their love affair, determined to distance himself and his family from the Erofeevs, whose association with the dissidents, or circles close to them, was potentially dangerous to him. Perhaps, as Andrei thinks, he wanted Aleksandra to marry someone from a family that conformed more closely to the Soviet establishment. Perhaps he was afraid that the Metropol Affair might become more problematic (it had raised a storm of protest in the West) and that Aleksandra might suffer from the consequences of her close involvement with the Erofeevs. Fear was never absent from Simonov's relations with the Soviet regime – even in these final years when he enjoyed the status of a major figure in the Soviet establishment and, it would seem, should have had no fears. In Suslov's office Simonov compiled a literary report on *Metropol* in which he denounced not just Viktor but Andrei Erofeev as 'anti-Soviet dissidents'. When Aleksandra was told this by Andrei, she refused to believe him, accused him of slandering her father and broke off their engagement. But later she found out that he had told the truth.[42]

Simonov in 1979

Simonov's death from chronic bronchitis was slow and painful. The Kremlin doctors were afraid to take responsibility for his treatment (a common problem in the Soviet Union in the decades following the Doctors' Plot) and failed to give him the right drugs. During his last months, when he was in and out of hospital, Simonov continued to reflect on his past, to ask himself why he had not done more to help the people who had turned to him during the Stalinist terror. In some of his final notes, drafted for a play (*The Four 'I's*) which was meant to take the form of a conversation between his present self and three 'other selves' at various moments in the past, he put himself on trial:

'So, how did you act, when someone whom you knew appeared before you and needed you to help?'

'It depended. Sometimes they would call, sometimes they would write, and sometimes they would ask me directly.'

'What would they ask?'

'It depended. Sometimes they would ask me to intervene to help someone, they would say how good that person was. Sometimes they would write to me to say that they could not believe that somebody they knew could be guilty, that they could not believe that he had done what he was accused of – they knew him too well to believe that.'

'Did people actually write that?'

'Yes, sometimes. But more often they wrote that they knew it wasn't their business, that they could not judge, that perhaps it was right, but . . . And then they would try to write down all the good things they knew about that person to try and help him.'

'And you tried to help?'

'Well, there were times when I did not reply to the letters. Twice. Once because I had never liked the person and I thought I was correct not to help a person I did not like and about whom I did not know anything. The other time I knew the person well, I had even been at the front with him and had liked him very much, but when they imprisoned him during the war, I believed that he was guilty, that he might be involved in some conspiracy, although no one spoke about such things – it was impossible to talk. He wrote to me. I didn't reply, I didn't help. I didn't know what to say to him, and so I delayed. Then, when he was released, I was ashamed. All the more so, because it turned out that one of our comrades, a man I considered even weaker and more of a coward than myself, had replied to him, and had helped as many people as he could – he had sent them parcels and money.'[43]

It was during one of these last spells in hospital that Simonov dictated his memoirs, *Through the Eyes of a Person of My Generation*, which remained unfinished at his death.[44] Simonov constructed his memoirs as another conversation with his former selves, recognizing that it was impossible to know what he had really thought at any moment in the past, but searching for the truth about his life through this dialogue with his own memory. Struggling to explain his long preoccupation with Stalin, his collaboration with the regime and the nature of the Stalinism that had taken possession of him, he interrogated himself without flinching – and judged himself harshly.

Simonov died on 28 August 1979. His ashes were scattered on a former battlefield near Mogilyov, the resting place of several thousand men who had fallen in the battles of June 1941. The press around the world announced the death of a great Soviet writer, 'Stalin's favourite'. During the 1980s, Simonov's works continued to be read as classics in Soviet schools and universities. They were translated into many languages. But after the collapse of the Soviet regime, his literary reputation fell and his sales declined dramatically. To younger Russian readers, who wanted something new, his prose seemed dated and too 'Soviet'.

3

After 1956, millions of people who had collaborated in some way in Stalin's crimes, some directly as NKVD men or prison guards, others indirectly as bureaucrats, went on living 'normal' lives. Most of them were able to avoid any sense of guilt by contriving, consciously or not, to forget their actions in the past, by rationalizing and defending their behaviour through ideology or some other justifying myth, or by pleading innocence on the basis that they 'did not know' or were 'only carrying out orders'.[45] Few had the courage to confront their guilt with the honesty displayed by Simonov.

By most estimates, there were something in the region of a million former camp guards living in the Soviet Union after 1956. Few of those who talked about their past showed much sign of contrition or remorse. Lev Razgon recalls meeting a Siberian Tatar named Niiazov in a Moscow hospital in the 1970s. Niiazov turned out to be a former guard at the Bikin transit camp near Khabarovsk, where he had overseen the execution of thousands of prisoners. His story was simple. The son of a janitor, Niiazov had been the bully at his school and had become a petty thief and gangster by the time he was a teenager. Picked up by the police, he was first employed as a prison guard in Omsk and then transferred to the Gulag as a guard. The Bikin transit camp between Khabarovsk and Vladivostok was one of many 'special installations' (spetsob'ekty) in the Gulag system where prisoners were held for a few days before being shot. Niiazov was involved in a large proportion of the estimated 15,000 to 18,000 shootings carried out in the Bikin camp during its brief existence from 1937 to 1940. He was given vodka before and after the shootings. He felt no regret, according to Razgon, nor any guilt when he was told many years later that his victims had been innocent.

Niiazov told Razgon that he slept well. During the war, Niiazov was mobilized by the Red Army. He fought in Germany, where he took part in the looting of a bank. After 1945, Niiazov was put in charge of security at a military warehouse; he grew rich from thefts and scams. Sacked from his job by a new Party boss, he had a heart attack and was brought to the hospital where he met Razgon.[46]

Ivan Korchagin was a guard at the ALZhIR Camp for Wives of Traitors to the Motherland. The son of a poor peasant, he had only four years of rural schooling and could not read or write when he joined the army at the age of sixteen in 1941. After the war he was part of a military unit mobilized for various tasks in the Gulag. Korchagin was employed as a camp guard at ALZhIR from 1946 to 1954. Interviewed in 1988, he was aware that the mass arrests which filled the labour camps had been unjust, but he felt no contrition for his actions. He rationalized and justified his participation in the system of repression through his own brand of half-baked ideology, moral lessons drawn from life and class hatred for his prisoners:

What is Soviet power, I ask you? It is an organ of coercion! Understand? Say, for example, we are sitting here and talking, and two policemen knock at the door: 'Come with us!' they say. And that's that! That's Soviet power! They can take you away and put you in prison – for nothing. And whether you're an enemy or not, you won't persuade anybody of your innocence. That's how it is. I get orders to guard prisoners. Should I believe these orders or should I believe you? Maybe I feel sorry for you, maybe I don't, but what can I do? When you kill a pig you don't feel sorry for it when it squeals. And even if I did feel sorry for somebody, how could I help them? When we were retreating from the front in the war, we had to abandon wounded soldiers, knowing they would die. We felt sorry, but what could we do? In the camp I guarded mothers with sick children. They cried and cried. But what could I do? They were being punished for their husbands. But that was not my business. I had my work to do. They say that a son does not answer for his father, but a mother answers for her husband. And if that husband is an enemy of the people, then what sort of son could the mother be raising? There were lots of children in the camp. But what could I do? It was bad for them. But maybe they were better off without mothers like that. Those enemies were really parasites. They had trips abroad. They were always showing off, with their music and their dachas and their finery. And the poor people were hungry, they had no fat, they lived worse than animals. So who's the enemy of

Ivan Korchagin, Karaganda, 1988

the people? Why should I cry for anyone? Besides, my job did no one any harm. I did a service for the government.[47]

During the period of glasnost in the late 1980s, when the role of the Gulag administrators began to be debated in the public media, many former guards wrote letters to ex-prisoners asking them to confirm for the historical record that they had been kind and decent to them in the camp. One such guard was Mikhail Iusipenko. Iusipenko was born in 1905 to the family of a landless labourer in Akmolinsk. He had only three years of rural schooling before the outbreak of the First World War and the departure of his father for the army forced him to go out to work. His father never returned from the war. During the 1920s, Iusipenko worked as a farm hand to support his mother and his younger brothers and sisters. He lost his wife and their two children in the famine of 1931. From 1934, Iusipenko was a Party worker in Karaganda, the administrative centre of the Gulag camps in Kazakhstan. He was soon recruited by the NKVD, which appointed him the Deputy Commandant of the ALZhIR labour camp near Akmolinsk. During his five years at the camp, from 1939 to 1944, Iusipenko allegedly raped a large number of the female prisoners, but there was no criminal investigation of his activities, only lots of rumours, which, it seems, began to trouble Iusipenko in the years of the Khrushchev thaw. Between 1961 and 1988, Iusipenko wrote to several hundred former prisoners, including many children of the women who had died since their release from ALZhIR, asking them to write a testimonial about his good conduct. He received testimonials from twenty-two of these women, who wrote to say that

Mikhail Iusipenko, Karaganda, 1988

they remembered him as a kind and decent man, certainly compared to many of the other guards at the ALZhIR labour camp (several of these testimonials were written by women who were said to be among his rape victims). In 1988, after an article about the ALZhIR camp in the newspaper *Leninskaia smena* implied that he was guilty of sexually assaulting prisoners, Iusipenko forwarded these testimonials to the editors of various national and local newspapers, as well as to the Party offices of Kazakhstan, with a long commentary intended to 'put the historical record straight'. Iusipenko claimed that he had 'always known' that the prisoners were innocent and that 'from the start' he had 'shown them profound sympathy', had 'never talked to them in a commanding tone', and had done 'everything possible to ease their burden', allowing them to write and receive more letters and parcels than officially allowed, and filing reports to get them released early, at 'great risk' to his position and even to his life. 'I could easily have been accused of sympathizing with the enemies of the people,' Iusipenko wrote, 'and then it would have been the end for me. But I was convinced, as I am now, that I was doing the right thing.' By getting the newspapers to publish the testimonials with his commentary, Iusipenko aimed not just to demonstrate that he had a clear conscience. He intended to show that he had even been opposed to the 'Stalinist repressions' (a phrase coined in the era of glasnost) and, indeed, that he had been a victim of them too.[48]

Many former Gulag officials invented similar myths about their past. Pavel Drozdov, Chief Accountant of the Planning Section and Inspector of the Dalstroi Gulag complex, was arrested in 1938 and later sentenced to fifteen years in the labour camps of Magadan. After his release in 1951, he remained in Magadan as a voluntary worker, and was soon joined by his wife and son. According to the story Pavel told his son, the former Gulag chief had been nothing but a humble specialist with no real authority in the Dalstroi Trust, which managed the camps. The tale had an element of truth in so far as, after the arrest of his patron Eduard Berzin, the head of the Dalstroi Trust, in 1937, Pavel had been demoted to the rank of simple accountant – his own arrest following shortly thereafter. Towards the end of the Khrushchev era, Pavel began to carry out research for his memoirs of the Dalstroi Trust. His aim was to honour Berzin's memory by presenting him as a visionary economic reformer and as a humane and enlightened man. But some of Pavel's correspondence with former Dalstroi prisoners disturbed him deeply. He had not realized, or had somehow banished from his mind, the full extent of the human suffering over which he had presided in the Planning Section of the Dalstroi Trust. Pavel had a series of heart attacks. On medical advice, he gave up writing his memoirs. The truth about his past was too upsetting to confront. Pavel died in 1967. His son continues to believe that his father was a blameless bureaucrat, a mere accountant in the Dalstroi Gulag complex at a time when Berzin ran it 'in a relatively humane and progressive way', who fell victim to the Stalinist regime.[49]

The intermingling of myth and memory sustains every family, but it played a special role in the Soviet Union, where millions of lives were torn apart. Psychoanalysis suggests that trauma victims can benefit from placing their experiences in the context of a broader narrative, which gives them meaning and purpose. Unlike the victims of the Nazi war against the Jews, for whom there could be no redeeming narrative, the victims of Stalinist repression had two main collective narratives in which to place their own life-stories and find some sort of meaning for their ordeals: the survival narrative, as told in the memoir literature of former Gulag prisoners, in which their suffering was transcended by the human spirit of the survivor; and the Soviet narrative, in which that suffering was redeemed by the Communist ideal, the winning of the Great Patriotic War, or the achievements of the Soviet Union.

The Gulag memoirs published in the decades after Khrushchev's thaw have had a powerful impact on the way that ordinary people remember their own family history in the Stalin period. Their influence has rested partly on the way that trauma victims deal with their own memories.

As psychoanalysts have shown, people with traumatic memories tend to block out parts of their own past. Their memory becomes fragmentary, organized by a series of disjointed episodes (such as the arrest of a parent or the moment of eviction from their home) rather than by a linear chronology. When they try to reconstruct the story of their life, particularly when their powers of recall are weakened by old age, such people tend to make up for the gaps in their own memory by drawing on what they have read, or what they have heard from others with experiences similar to theirs.[50] In the opening pages of his memoirs, written in the 1970s, Alexander Dolgun, a US consul clerk arrested for 'espionage' in 1948 and imprisoned in a labour camp in Kazakhstan, explained these lapses in his memory:

Most of my story is what I actually remember, but some is what must have been. There are episodes and faces and words and sensations burned so deeply into my memory that no amount of time will wear them away. There are other times when I was so exhausted because they never let me sleep or so starved or beaten or burning with fever or drugged with cold that everything was blurred, and now I can only put together what must have happened by setting out to build a connection across these periods.

Although he claimed to have an 'extremely good memory', Dolgun had 'absolutely no recall' of a two-week period between leaving Moscow on a convict train and starting work in a stone quarry in the camp in Kazakhstan.[51]

To fill these gaps people borrowed from each other's memories. Many of the scenes described by amateur memorists of the Stalin period bear a striking resemblance to scenes in well-known books about the Terror such as Yevgeniia Ginzburg's *Into the Whirlwind* (1967) or Solzhenitsyn's *Gulag Archipelago* (1973). Though both of these books, originally published in the West, did not officially come out in Russia until the late 1980s, they circulated widely through samizdat long before, helping to give rise to a boom in amateur memoir-writing from that time.* It is

---

*Thousands of such memoirs may be found in the archives of the Memorial Society, which was established in towns across the Soviet Union during the late 1980s to commemorate the victims of repression and record their memories. There are also rich collections of unpublished memoirs from this period in the Archive of the Moscow Historical-Literary Society ('Vozvrashchenie'), established in 1989; and in the Andrei Sakharov Public Centre and Museum, opened in Moscow in 1996.

not clear if the scenes that figure in these memoirs represent a direct memory, as opposed to what the writer surmises took place or imagines 'must have happened', because others wrote about such episodes. Irina Sherbakova, who interviewed many Gulag survivors in the 1980s, suggests how this borrowing of memories occurred:

Over many decades, life in the Gulag gave birth to endless rumours, legends, and myths, the most common being about famous people – long believed to have been executed in Moscow – who were said to have been seen by someone in some far distant camp somewhere. There were constantly recurring themes and details in such stories. For example, at least four women described to me exactly the same scene: how, many years later, when they were able to look in a mirror again and see themselves, the first image they saw was the face of their own mother. As early as the 1970s, I recognized incidents recounted to me orally that exactly matched scenes described in Solzhenitsyn's *Gulag Archipelago* or in other printed recollections. By now [in 1992] story-telling about the camps has become so general that recording oral memory has become much more difficult. The vast amount of information pouring out of people often seems to happen through an immolation of their own memories to the point where it begins to seem as if everything they know happened to them personally.[52]

Many Gulag survivors insist that they witnessed scenes described in books by Ginzburg, Solzhenitsyn or Shalamov, that they recognize the guards or NKVD interrogators mentioned in these works, or even that they knew the writers in the camps, when documentation clearly shows that this could not be so.[53]

There are a number of reasons why Gulag survivors borrowed published recollections in this way. In the 1970s and 1980s, when books like *The Gulag Archipelago* circulated in samizdat, many victims of Stalinist repression identified so strongly with their ideological position, which they took to be the key to understanding the truth about the camps, that they suspended their own independent memories and allowed these books to speak for them. The victims of repression frequently lacked a clear conceptual grasp of their own experience, having no structural framework or understanding of the political context in which to make sense of their memories. This gap reinforced their inclination to substitute these writers' coherent and clear memories for their own confused and fragmentary recollections. As one historian has observed from the experience of interviewing survivors of the Great Terror:

Should you ask the seemingly straightforward question 'How many people did you know who were arrested in 1937?', the response would probably be one of wide-eyed amazement, 'Haven't you read Solzhenitsyn? Don't you know that everyone was arrested?' If you continue with: 'But were any members of your family arrested?', there may well be a pause ... 'Well, no, not in my family, but everybody else was.' Then you ask: 'How many people were arrested in the communal apartment you lived in?' There's a very long pause, followed by, 'Well, hmm, I don't really remember, but yes, yes there was one, Ivanov, who lived in the room down at the end, yes, now I remember.'[54]

This example shows why oral testimonies, on the whole, are more reliable than literary memoirs, which have usually been seen as a more authentic record of the past. Like all memory, the testimony given in an interview is unreliable, but, unlike a book, it can be cross-examined and tested against other evidence to disentangle true memories from received or imagined ones.

The published Gulag memoirs influenced not only the recollection of scenes and people, but the very understanding of the experience. All the memoirs of the Stalin Terror are reconstructed narratives by survivors.[55] The story they tell is usually one of purgatory and redemption – a journey through the 'hell' of the Gulag and back again to 'normal life' – in which the narrator transcends death and suffering. This uplifting moral helps to account for the compelling influence of these literary memoirs on the way that other Gulag survivors recalled their own stories. Ginzburg's memoirs, in particular, became a model of the survivor narrative and her literary structure was copied by countless amateur memoirists with life-stories not unlike her own. The unifying theme of Ginzburg's memoirs is regeneration through love – a theme which gives her writing powerful effect as a work of literature. Ginzburg explains her survival in the camps as a matter of her faith in human beings; the flashes of humanity she evokes in others, and which help her to survive, are a response to her faith in people. In the first part of her memoirs, *Into the Whirlwind*, Ginzburg highlights her work in a nursery at Kolyma where caring for the children reminds her of her son and gives her the strength to go on. In the second part, *Within the Whirlwind* (1981), Ginzburg is transferred from the nursery to a hospital, where she falls in love with a fellow prisoner serving as a doctor in the camp. Despite the anguish of repeated separations, they both survive and somehow keep in touch until Stalin's death; freed but still in exile from the major Russian cities, they get married and adopt a child.[56] This narrative trajectory is endlessly repeated in the memoir literature. The uniformity of such 'family chronicles' and 'documentary tales', which are virtually identical in their basic structure, in their form and moral tone, is remarkable and cannot be explained by literary fashion on its own. Perhaps these memoirists, who all lived such extraordinary lives, felt some need to link their destiny to that of others like themselves by recalling their life-story according to a literary prototype.

The Soviet narrative offered a different type of consolation, assuring the victims that their sacrifices had been in the service of collective goals and achievements. The idea of a common Soviet purpose was not just a propaganda myth. It helped people to come to terms with their suffering by giving them a sense that their lives were validated by the part they had played in the struggle for the Soviet ideal.

The collective memory of the Great Patriotic War was very potent in this respect. It enabled veterans to think of their pain and losses as having a larger purpose and meaning, represented by the victory of 1945, from which they took pride. The historian Catherine Merridale, who conducted interviews with veterans in Kursk for her book on the Soviet army in the war, found that they did not speak about their experiences with bitterness or self-pity, but accepted all their losses stoically, and that 'rather than trying to relive the grimmest scenes of war, they tended to adopt the language of the vanished Soviet state, talking about honour and pride, of justified revenge, of motherland, Stalin, and the absolute necessity of faith'. As Merridale explains, this identification with the Soviet war myth was a coping mechanism for these veterans, enabling them to live with their painful memories:

Back then, during the war, it would have been easy enough to break down, to feel the depth of every horror, but it would also have been fatal. The path to survival lay in stoical acceptance, a focus on the job at hand. The men's vocabulary was businesslike and optimistic, for anything else might have induced despair. Sixty years later, it would have been easy again to play for sympathy or simply to command attention by telling bloodcurdling tales. But that, for these people, would have amounted to a betrayal of the values that have been their collective pride, their way of life.[57]

People who returned from the labour camps similarly found consolation in the Stalinist idea that, as Gulag labourers, they too had made a contribution to the Soviet economy. Many of these people later looked back with enormous pride at the factories, dams and cities they had built. This pride stemmed in part from their continued belief in the Soviet system and its ideology, despite the injustices they had been dealt, and in part, perhaps, from their need to find a larger meaning for their suffering. In *Within the Whirlwind* Ginzburg recalls her impression on her return to Magadan, a city which was built by her fellow prisoners in the Kolyma camps:

How strange is the heart of man! My whole soul cursed those who had thought up the idea of building a town in this permafrost, thawing out the ground with the blood and tears of innocent people. Yet at the same time I was aware of a sort of ridiculous pride . . . How it had grown, and how handsome it had become during my seven years of absence, our Magadan! Quite unrecognizable. I admired each street lamp, each section of asphalt, and even the poster announcing that the House of Culture was presenting the operetta *The Dollar Princess*. We treasure each fragment of our life, even the bitterest.[58]

Norilsk, July 2004

In Norilsk this pride continues to be strongly felt among the older segments of the city's population (approximately 130,000 people), which consists largely of former Gulag prisoners and their descendants, with a small minority of former labour camp administrators and voluntary workers, whose families remained in this Arctic settlement after the Gulag was dismantled. Many people stayed on because they had nowhere else to go. After 1953, when the administration of the industrial complex was transferred from the Gulag to the Ministry of Heavy Industry, the people of Norilsk were fully integrated into all the usual institutions of Soviet rule (schools, Pioneer and Komsomol organizations, Party cells and so on), which helped to create a Soviet consciousness – and to some extent a local Soviet patriotism based on their pride in Norilsk – that overlaid the memory of the Gulag. To this day, the town is celebrated in song and story. People still sing:

> Here is a town which is called Norilsk,
> We dig for nickel and copper.
> Here the people have a strong spirit,
> In Russia everybody knows about Norilsk.

Books and films commemorate the men and women who braved the elements to build Norilsk, often glossing over the fact that most of them were prisoners (in this haunted city, where survival is forgetting, the memory of the Gulag is kept just beneath the surface of public consciousness). Pride in the town is connected with the romantic and pioneering spirit of Arctic exploration, which continues to find expression in the popular idea that a special strength of spirit is required to survive the harsh conditions of Norilsk:

> People here are made of special stuff.
> The weak at once will run away.
> There is no place for them in this harsh land,
> Where the winds blow,
> And snowstorms rage,
> And there is no summer.[59]

There is also a popular belief that the people in the town have a special warmth and sense of comradeship born from the shared experience of the Gulag and the common struggle to survive in these conditions. But above all this civic pride is rooted in the labour of the people of Norilsk, like Vasily Romashkin, a town hero, who in 2004, was still living there with his children and grandchildren.

Vasily Romashkin, 2004

Vasily was born in 1914 to a peasant family in the Moscow region, arrested as a 'kulak' in 1937, and imprisoned in Norilsk from 1939, where he remained in the mining complex – first as a prisoner and then as a 'voluntary worker' – until his retirement in 1981. Vasily has been decorated many times for his labour in Norilsk. Even as a prisoner, he was known as a real Stakhanovite. He is particularly proud of his contribution to the Soviet war effort, as he explains in an interview:

These medals are all for winners [of Socialist Competitions] – Winner of Metallurgy, Winner of the Ninth Five Year Plan [1971–5] . . . I forget what that one is . . . And these ones are 'Veteran of the [Norilsk] Complex' and 'Veteran of the USSR' – for valiant and dedicated labour. And this one is a jubilee medal for veterans of the Great Patriotic War, when the complex was militarized . . . I am proud of the part I played in the war – I carried out my patriotic duty as a citizen.[60]

Vasily speaks for the older generation which celebrates the labour camp's contribution to the Soviet economy, especially in the war, when the precious metals which they dug in freezing temperatures were essential for the Soviet victory. This sense of achievement is partly what they mean when they declare their love for the 'beauty' of Norilsk, as they often do, a city which they built with their own hands (no one seems to notice that its atmosphere is permanently poisoned with toxic yellow fumes in which no trees can grow). 'It is a beautiful city,' declares Olga Iaskina, who was imprisoned in the Norilsk labour camp in the early 1950s and never left the town. 'It is our little Leningrad.'[61] Many of the buildings in the centre are indeed built in the neo-classical style of St Petersburg (another city constructed by slaves). Norilsk represents a startling paradox: a large industrial city built and populated by Gulag prisoners, whose civic pride is rooted in their own slave labour for the Stalinist regime.

A similar paradox underlies the popular nostalgia for Stalin, which more than half a century after the dictator's death continues to be felt by millions of people, including many of his victims. According to a survey carried out by the All-Russia Centre for the Study of Public Opinion in January 2005, 42 per cent of the Russian people wanted the return of a 'leader like Stalin' (60 per cent of the respondents over sixty years of age were in favour of a 'new Stalin').[62] This nostalgia is only loosely linked with politics and ideology. For older people, who recall the Stalin years, it has more to do with the emotions invested in the remembrance of the past – the legendary period of their youth when the shops were full of goods, when there was social order and security, when their lives were organized and given meaning by the simple goals of the Five Year Plans, and everything was clear, in black and white, because Stalin did the thinking for them and told them what to do. For these people, nostalgia for 'the good old days' of Stalin reflects the uncertainty of their lives as pensioners, particularly since the collapse of the Soviet regime in 1991: the rising prices that put many goods beyond their means; the destruction of their savings by inflation; and the rampant criminality that frightened old people in their homes.

The people who succumbed to this nostalgia included not just those who had held a certain status – the vast army of Soviet officials and petty functionaries, camp guards, policemen, chauffeurs, railways clerks, factory and kolkhoz bosses, house elders and janitors, who looked back to the days when they had been connected, as 'little Stalins' in their own sphere of power, to the Great Leader in one continuous chain of command. But ordinary citizens were nostalgic as well, people who had no special place in the Stalinist regime, but whose lives had become entangled in its destiny. Mikhail Baitalsky recalls meeting one old

Stalinist in the 1970s, a comrade from the Komsomol in the 1920s, who had risen to become a middle-level engineer in one of Stalin's factories. The engineer remained a fanatical supporter of Stalin. He did not try to defend the dictator (he knew the facts), although there were many Stalinist assumptions, like the guilt of Tukhachevsky and other 'enemies of the people', which he still believed and refused to question. Baitalsky came to the conclusion that his old friend was clinging not to any Stalinist ideology, but rather to his 'pride in the qualities which he himself had had in those young and ardent years'. He did not want to renounce the beliefs which he had held in the 1920s and 1930s, beliefs that had become a part of his own personality, and refused to admit that precisely those qualities had fostered 'his internal readiness to accept everything, positively everything, up to and including the execution of his closest comrades'.[63]

Leonid Saltykov, 1985

This nostalgia was also not unknown to Stalin's victims and their descendants. Leonid Saltykov was the son a priest who was shot in 1938. Leonid concealed the arrest of his father when he became a factory worker and then an engineer. In 1965, he joined the Party, ending up as the secretary of the Party Committee in the factory where he worked. Leonid was a fanatical supporter of Stalin all his life. He mourned Stalin's death and kept a picture of him on his desk until his retirement from the factory in 1993. During interviews Leonid denied that Stalin was responsible for the mass arrests of the 1930s, including the arrest of his father:

Yes, my father suffered, and so did many others too, but Stalin was still better than any of the leaders that we have today. He was an honest man, even if the people around him were not ... Don't forget, thanks to him we won the war, and that is a great achievement. If today someone tried to fight a war like that, there would be no guarantee that Russia would win it, no guarantee. Stalin built our factories and our railways. He brought down the price of bread. He spurred us all to work because we knew that if we studied hard and went to an institute we were guaranteed a good job, and could even choose a factory. Everything depended on how hard you worked.[64]

Vera Minusova was seventeen years old when her father, a railway engineer in Perm, was arrested and shot in 1937, and since then, as she herself admits, she has lived in almost constant fear, despite the fact that she was married in 1947 to a senior Party official in Perm. During interviews in 2004, she was still afraid to talk about many subjects connected to the Terror, and at several points she insisted that the tape-recorders be turned off. In these interviews Vera looked back with nostalgia to the years of Stalin's reign as a time when 'the basic necessities of life were affordable to all' and there was 'more discipline and order than we have today'. Vera worked for over fifty years as a bookkeeper in the offices of the Soviet railway. She complained that people 'do not

Vera Minusova at the Memorial Complex for Victims of Repression near Yekaterinburg, May 2003. The candle she has lit is by the name of her father (which is incorrectly spelt)

want to work today' and claimed that it was better during Stalin's time, when 'everyone was made to work'.

Discipline is fundamental. You have to keep the people under control, and use the whip if necessary. Today they should go back to the methods Stalin used. You can't have people coming late for work, or leaving when they want. If they want the job they should be made to work according to the rules.[65]

Iraida Faivisovich was four years old when both her parents, the hairdressers from Osa, were arrested and sent to the Gulag in 1939. During interviews in 2003, she too argued that life was better under Stalin. 'People did not kill each other in the streets! It was safe then to go out at night.' According to Iraida, political leaders were honest during Stalin's day: 'Of course, there were sometimes shortages of food or clothes, but on the whole they delivered on their promises.' Like many older people who grew up in a communal apartment, Iraida misses the collectivism of those years, which she remembers as a happier existence compared to her lonely life as a pensioner:

Life under Stalin was spiritually richer – we lived more peacefully and happily. Because we were all equally poor, we didn't place much emphasis on material values but had a lot of fun – everything was open, everything was shared, between friends and families. People helped each other. We lived in each other's rooms and celebrated holidays with everyone together on the street. Today every family lives only for itself.

People then had greater hope and meaning in their lives, Iraida says:

We believed that the future would be good. We were convinced that life would get better, if we worked well and honestly . . . We didn't imagine that we were creating heaven on earth but we did think that we were building a society where there would be enough for everyone, where there would be peace and no more wars . . . That belief was genuine, and it helped us to live, because it meant that we concentrated on our education and our work for the future instead of on our material problems. We took more pride in our work then than we do today. It is hard to live without beliefs. What do we believe in today? We have no ideals.[66]

4

Nostalgia notwithstanding, the ruinous legacies of the Stalinist regime continued to be felt by the descendants of Stalin's victims many decades after the dictator's death. It was not only a question of lost relationships, damaged lives and families, but of traumas passed from one generation to the next.[67]*

From her parents, both executed in 1937, Elizaveta Delibash inherited a life-long fear of the Soviet authorities, which she passed down to her children. Brought up by her grandparents in Tbilisi and then by her aunt, an ardent Stalinist, in Leningrad, Elizaveta had overcome that fear in her teenage years by joining the Komsomol and becoming a student activist. She studied hard and got high grades at school, enabling her to enrol as a language student at Leningrad University in 1947. But her fear never went away. 'I always felt inferior and unsure of myself because of what had happened to my parents,' she recalls. 'All my life I had this inner fear, a sense of loss and vulnerability, a feeling that I was not fully worthy as a human being, and that at any moment I could be insulted or humiliated by people in authority.' Fearing her arrest in Leningrad, Elizaveta abandoned her ambitions of graduate research and fled to Krasnodar, a quiet town in the Kuban, where she worked as a school-teacher until 1954, when she returned to Leningrad with her husband, a physics student called Iosif Liberman, and got a job as a librarian.

Iosif came from a Jewish family in Leningrad that quietly dissented from the Soviet regime. The contrast with the orthodox opinions of her aunt was a revelation for Elizaveta, who, encouraged by the revelations

---

*This psychological inheritance can be handed down in various ways: in parents' anxieties and phobias, in their over-protection of children, in the expectations with which they burden them, and even in the games they play with them. The Hungarian psychoanalyst Terez Virag, who specialized in the treatment of Holocaust survivors and their children, cites the case of a mother, for example, who lived through the siege of Leningrad as a child. The mother's two-year-old daughter would not eat Father Christmas biscuits, and would cry in protest when she was given them. As a child herself, the mother had been traumatized by stories she was told of people killing children to eat them during the siege of Leningrad. According to Virag, the mother had passed on this trauma in the form of a bath-time game she played with her daughter in which she would take the infant's foot in her mouth and say, 'Now I will eat you' (T. Virag, *Children of Social Trauma: Hungarian Psychoanalytic Case Studies* (London, 2000), p. 43).

of the Twentieth Party Congress, began to think more critically about the events surrounding her parents' disappearance. In 1958, she finally discovered that they had both been shot. It was a shock because she had hoped that her mother might still be alive and had always looked to the Great Bear in the night sky, as her mother had advised her in her final letter from the Solovetsky labour camp, as a symbol of that hope. The discovery intensified Elizaveta's sense of alienation from the Soviet system. She and Iosif fell in with the opposition student group started up by Mikhail Molostvov, arrested and exiled from Leningrad in 1958. They were part of Iosif Brodsky's circle, the Leningrad poet who was put on trial for 'parasitism' in 1964 and sentenced to five years of exile in the North (a sentence commuted in 1965 after protests from around the world). In the later 1960s they had close connections to the refuseniks, Soviet Jews denied an exit visa to leave the Soviet Union, whose protests became an important part of the human rights movement.

All this time, Elizaveta lived in fear. She was afraid for Iosif, who was not awarded his doctoral degree (qualifying him for an academic salary) for many years after the completion of his dissertation – a relatively small punishment for his involvement in opposition circles but one that retained the threat of worse to come. Elizaveta became increasingly withdrawn. She was afraid for her children, Aleksandr (born in 1955) and Anna (1960). Elizaveta lived a 'secret life', terrified that her dissident convictions would lead to her arrest and deprive her children of a mother, as she herself had been when she was a child. 'The loss of my mother was the strongest feeling in my life,' she recalls. 'It made me frightened for my own children.'

As a mother, Elizaveta was excessively protective, according to Anna.* She did not tell her daughter about her family's history. 'It was a taboo subject throughout my childhood,' Anna remembers. When she was fourteen, Anna found out from her brother that their grandparents had been shot in the Terror. But when she asked her mother about it, she was told that they had been killed during the war. Elizaveta kept the truth about her parents from her daughter until the glasnost period. As a child Anna was completely unaware that her parents were involved in opposition circles: 'They protected me and kept me at a distance from

---

*Aleksandr died in a climbing accident in 1991.

their activities.' She did not realize until the 1980s that many of her parents' friends were dissidents, that Brodsky visited their apartment, or that the manuscripts her parents read were illegal samizdat.

The one thing on which her mother always insisted was that she should study hard. 'She drummed it into us that we had to try much harder than the other children at our school,' recalls Anna, 'because with our Jewish names we would be marked down.' Anna felt this pressure as a burden, as if she was expected to make up for her mother's interrupted studies after university: 'God forbid, if I had ever failed to come in the top group at school. I was forced to be clever – I was not allowed to be anything else.' Anna was forbidden to mix with children from proletarian backgrounds because her mother feared that they might pose a danger if her family's history was revealed. 'Looking back,' reflects Anna, 'I realize now that my mother wanted me to become friends with children from educated families that, like ours, had been repressed.' Anna was brought up to be modest, not to put herself above the crowd, to be conformist, politically loyal, to join the Pioneers and the Komsomol, although instinctively she sensed that this obedience to the authorities was 'purely for appearances'.

Anna recognizes in herself a deep-seated fear, a lack of confidence and social inhibition, which she thinks are the inheritance of her mother's upbringing:

It is hard to say what the fear is, because I have felt it since I was a child. I am afraid of any sort of contact with bureaucracy . . . It is a fear of being humiliated . . . This was something I was taught when I was young, to retreat from any situation where my conduct could be criticized by the authorities . . . From my teenage years I was open among friends, but withdrawn socially . . . I was afraid to be with strangers and always tried not to stand out.

Anna's fear was menacing, but vague and ill-defined, because as a child she was never really told about her family's repression. It hit her with full force only when she first became aware of the consequences of her spoilt biography. Anna recalls the moment well: she had said to one of her teachers that she would like to go to university, and he had questioned if she could, not because of her abilities, but because, as he explained, 'they don't give the highest marks to people with [Jewish] names like yours'. Anna became 'hysterical'. This was the humiliation she had feared.

To make it possible to go to university, where she studied tourism, Anna took her mother's Georgian nationality rather than her father's Jewish one when she registered for her Soviet passport. She joined the Komsomol, and then, when she became disillusioned by its ideology, stayed in, afraid that leaving it might get her into trouble with the university authorities. She took no interest in politics, never got involved with the dissidents, and though she claims she always knew that the Soviet system was unjust, she censored her own thoughts and interests, and never let herself behave in any way to raise suspicions about her loyalty.[68]

This 'genetic fear', as Anna herself calls it, affected the children of Stalin's victims in many different ways, from the friends they made at school to their choices of career. Vladimir Korsakov, for example, was born into an old intelligentsia family in Leningrad which suffered in the purges of the 1930s and 1940s. Deeply traumatized by his childhood memories of the siege of Leningrad, he turned down the chance of a career as a dancer in the Kirov Ballet in the late 1950s and went to work instead in the Baltic Factory, a huge shipbuilding and engineering plant, because even then, as he recalls, he was afraid of being stigmatized as the son of an 'enemy of the people', and he wanted to protect himself by 'merging with the proletarian mass'.[69]

Aleksei Iurasovsky grew up in the communal apartment of the Khaneyevsky family in Moscow in the 1950s and early 1960s. His mother was the daughter of the military doctor Aleksei Khaneyevsky, who had been given noble status in the First World War, and his father the descendant of a noble Russian-Georgian clan. Aleksei's paternal grandfather and several great-uncles had fought in the White Army in the Civil War. Because his parents and grandmother were extremely wary of their proletarian neighbours, Aleksei learned to hold his tongue and mistrust everyone. 'I was taught to fear the regime,' he recalls.

My grandmother added a lot of irrationality to the issue, because her warnings were rather fantastic, though convincing to a child. For example, she told me the story of a boy who put one foot on the front steps of the Finnish Embassy and was immediately arrested – never to be seen again. This story really frightened me. She had a lot of fairy-tales like that.

Fear made Aleksei exceedingly cautious. As a student at Moscow University, he lived an isolated existence; his only trusted contact with the outside world was through a short-wave radio he had built as a school-boy to listen to the BBC. Having shunned the Komsomol and all involve-ment in student politics, which he found repugnant, Aleksei concluded that his most sensible strategy was to avoid friends, who might become suspicious about his political loyalties. He maintained that strategy throughout his twenties and thirties, as he trained to become an archae-ologist and Arabist. Looking back on his career, Aleksei reflects that his choices were determined by a 'desire to escape' from the political pres-sures of the Soviet system, which he perceived as a 'minefield' of rules and dangers that were always changing unpredictably. The fear he had felt as a child gradually dissolved – to be replaced, in his own words, by 'gloominess and scepticism' about Russia and the Soviet regime. His caution also played a role in his choice of a wife; Anna was his third cousin, and her immediate relatives had been repressed by the Stalinist regime. 'It helped of course that we had come from the same back-ground,' Aleksei recalls. 'It drew us closer together and gave our relation-ship a special understanding and solidarity.'[70]

The inheritance of fear had a direct impact on many marriages. It was not uncommon for a woman whose own parents had been arrested, for example, to marry someone like a Party official, who she believed would protect her. Vera Minusova, whose father was arrested and then shot in 1937, married the local Party boss, a man nearly twice her age, even though she found him physically repugnant, because she felt, as her mother had advised her, that he would provide for her materially and enable her to bring up her children without fear for their future. 'I cried when I got married,' she recalls, 'but Mother kept on saying, "Marry him! Marry him!" I did not love him, he was repulsive, but I had a daughter, she grew up, and I loved her.' Marksena Karpitskaia, the teenage girl from Leningrad who lived on her own after the arrest and execution of both her parents in 1937, later married a senior military scientist and Party official in Leningrad. She told her husband everything about her family history, because she wanted to be sure that he knew what their marriage would involve. However, she insisted that they did not register their marriage, because, in her words: 'Even after the rehabilitation of my parents, I wanted him to have the opportunity to walk away from me, if at any time he felt that it was too much for him to be married to the daughter of former enemies of the people.'[71]

Many people with a spoilt biography told their future spouses about it only when they were about to marry. Like Marksena, they wanted them to know about their past before they joined their lives together, but to tell their spouses beforehand might have frightened them away. It took Lydia Babushkina nearly three years of courting before, on the eve of her wedding in 1965, she summoned up the courage to tell her fiancé ('a convinced Stalinist from a military family of convinced Stalinists') about the arrest and execution of her father as an 'enemy of the people'. Boris Kashin also waited until just before his wedding to tell his fiancée that his father had been shot as a 'counter-revolutionary' in 1938. 'It was taking a huge risk,' recalls Boris, 'but I trusted her, and did not want to ruin her life by marrying her under false pretences. She reacted calmly and told me that her own grandfather had been repressed as a kulak, so she knew about such things.'[72]

It is striking how many marriages were formed by couples who both came from repressed families. Something seemed to draw these people together. Larisa and Vitalii Garmash fell in love when they were first-year students at the Moscow Institute of Economics and Statistics in 1955. Larisa was the daughter of Zinaida Levina, who had spent eight years in the Kolyma camps (from which she returned in 1946 with a boy fathered, it would seem, by a prison guard) and then three years in the Potma camps, followed by exile in Kazakhstan. Larisa had lived with her mother in exile before going to Moscow. Vitalii had been arrested as a student in 1949 and had only just been rehabilitated when he met Larisa on the first day at the institute. As she recalls, their mutual attraction was linked to the sense, which they both had, that for the first time in their lives they could talk about their past to someone they could trust and who would understand. As Larisa remembers:

He sat next to me in the lecture hall. I knew nothing about him, absolutely nothing, but we began to talk ... Of course he talked with his Moscow friends, who knew about his arrest, and his closest friend had himself recently returned from the labour camps, but perhaps he did not feel the same emotional openness with them as with me, because, suddenly, his whole past came pouring out ... Our relations developed very quickly after that. The fact that we had shared the same problems, that our family histories were not simple, that played an enormous role.[73]

When Nikolai Meshalkin met his fiancée, Elfrida Gotman, in 1956, he did not tell her that his family had been driven out of Penza as 'kulaks' in 1933 and that they were still living in penal exile in the Komi region.* He knew nothing about Elfrida's family – Soviet Germans from the Crimea who had also been deported to the Komi region in the war – but he sensed that they too had suffered from the Stalinist regime (the Komi region was full of Soviet Germans in exile), and this drew him to her. Nikolai bombarded her with love letters. For several years Elfrida was reluctant to open her heart to a Russian. 'I thought that I would settle down with a nice German boy,' recalls Elfrida. But Nikolai persisted, and Elfrida, who was nearly thirty and worried that she might not find a mate, at last agreed to marry him. Slowly, Nikolai and Elfrida began to tell each other about their families, and their common history and sympathy drew them tightly together. After nearly fifty years of marriage, Nikolai believes that this mutual understanding was the most important element in their relationship:

I call this understanding solidarity. I have always had this feeling, this feeling of solidarity with this woman, because she also suffered, she was also repressed . . . I think that she's had the same feeling about me. I think what we had together was not love but solidarity, which was more important for us both. Love goes away, but solidarity has nowhere else to go.[74]

Nikolai and Elfrida Meshalkin with their daughters,
Marina and Irina, Perm, 2003

*It was only in the 1990s, when he did his own researches in the Penza archives, that Nikolai discovered a family secret his parents had kept from him: that they had owned a village tavern and a bakery – enough property by Soviet standards to make them members of the bourgeoisie.

Nikolai and Elfrida did not tell their daughters about their spoilt biographies until 1992, after they had read about a new decree offering compensation to victims of repression. Before that they had been afraid to tell them the whole history, in case it burdened them or alienated them from the Soviet system. They always steered the conversations about the past to more positive episodes, such as the role which both their fathers played during the Great Patriotic War.[75]

The Meshalkins were not unusual in this respect. Even in the last years of the Soviet regime, in the liberal climate of glasnost, the vast majority of ordinary Soviet families did not talk about their histories, or pass down stories of repression to their children. The influence of glasnost was confined largely to the major cities, and in the provinces, in towns like Perm where the Meshalkins lived, Stalin's ghost was still alive. In the words of the poet Boris Slutsky, writing just before his death in 1986:

> The provinces, the periphery, the rear,
> Where it was too frozen for the thaw,
> Where to this day Stalin is alive.
> No he died! But his body is still warm.[76]

Fifteen years after the collapse of the regime, there are still people in the provinces who are too afraid to talk about their past, even to their own children.[77]

Antonina Golovina lived virtually her entire life with the secret of her spoilt biography. She only told her daughter about her 'kulak' background in the 1990s, more than sixty years after she was exiled to Siberia as a young girl. Antonina concealed the truth about her family's history from her two husbands, each of whom she lived with for over twenty years. When she met her first husband, Georgii Znamensky, in 1947, in her final year as a medical student at the Leningrad Institute of Pediatrics, Antonina was already living with the assumed name of an old boyfriend to hide her past. Without a legal right of residence in Leningrad, she was frightened of the possibility of her rearrest and exile as an 'anti-social element' – a fate that befell many former 'kulaks' (including her own father) in the post-war years, when the regime was committed to a comprehensive purge of the cities – if it was discovered that she had concealed her 'kulak' origins when she was admitted to the institute. Antonina recalls her situation:

All my documents were false. I was terrified of being stopped by a policeman on the street. My passport was full of stamps and signatures that had been forged, some of them by my sister in Sverdlovsk . . . My right of residence [in Leningrad] had expired more than six months earlier.

Antonina was living in a communal apartment where the house elder was an ardent Stalinist, widely suspected as an informer, who made her suspicions of Antonina clear. On one occasion, when a neighbour showed off a new pair of shoes, Antonina had let her guard down by saying that her father would have made them better because he had been a shoemaker (a trade associated with the 'kulaks' in the countryside). Frightened that she would be exposed, it was a huge relief for Antonina when Georgii Znamensky asked her to marry him. Marriage to Znamensky, an engineer and native citizen of Leningrad, would give her a new name and a new set of documents to let her stay in Leningrad.

For the next forty years Antonina kept the secret of her 'kulak' origins from Georgii. They rarely spoke to one another about their previous lives. When she talked about her family she was always careful to refer to them as poor peasants. She concealed the truth from all her friends and colleagues at the Institute of Physiology (she only came to realize much later that all her friends had come from repressed families). In 1961, she even became a member of the Party (which she would remain until 1991), not because she believed in its ideology (there were many occasions when she quietly subverted Party rules to help a friend) but because she thought that joining would divert suspicion from herself. She wanted to promote her medical career and gain some protection for her daughter, who was then fourteen and fast approaching the time when she would need to apply to university. 'I was very worried about my daughter's future,' recalls Antonina.

I did not want her ever to find out about my past. I wanted her to feel that she had a normal mother, just like the mother of every other girl at her [elite] school, where all the parents, or at least the fathers, were members of the Party.

Antonina continued to conceal her spoilt biography from Georgii, even after he had divorced her in 1968, and she had married an Estonian called Boris Ioganson. In 1987, Antonina received a visit from an elderly aunt of Georgii who let slip that he was the son of a rear-admiral in the Imperial Navy, a man dedicated to the tsar, who had fought for the

White Army in the Civil War. All this time, just like Antonina, she now realized, Georgii had concealed his origins. Having spent his early years in labour camps and 'special settlements', Georgii had decided to become an engineer in a conscious effort to forge a proletarian identity for himself. When he had applied for his first factory job he had made up the biographical details he entered on his questionnaire; throughout his life he kept a crib sheet with this invented biography close at hand in order to make sure that there were no discrepancies when he filled out another form. By some strange intuition, Georgii and Antonina had found in each other a mirror image of themselves.

Boris Ioganson had also come from a repressed family – his father and grandfather were both arrested in 1937 – although Antonina did not discover that or tell him of her own spoilt biography until the early 1990s, after the collapse of the Soviet system, when, emboldened by the public revelations and debates about the repressions of the Stalinist regime, they at last began to talk about their past. It was also at this time that Antonina and Georgii opened up their secret histories, which they had concealed from one another for over forty years. However, they agreed to keep this information from their daughter, Olga, who was then established in her own career as a schoolteacher. They thought that ignorance would protect her if the Stalinists returned. Gradually Antonina overcame her life-long fear and summoned up the courage to tell her daughter about her 'kulak' origins. Two things happened to bring about this change.

The first took place in 1995, when, at the age of seventy-two, Antonina returned to Obukhovo, the village where her family had lived until they were exiled to Siberia in 1931. The last time she had visited Obukhovo had been in 1956, with her brother and her father, a few weeks before her father's death. The ground where their house had stood was empty. Weeds had grown around the millstone where they used to sit and talk with the other villagers. As they had stood looking at the space, Antonina heard a voice behind her: 'The kulaks have returned! The kulaks have returned! They got rid of them and now they have come back wearing nice new clothes.' As Antonina turned towards the voice, the speaker disappeared. The memory of that last visit had always troubled Antonina. 'I wanted to return to my birthplace and feel that it was somewhere I could still call home,' she recalls. 'I wanted the people to acknowledge me, to talk with me and accept me as one of them.'

Antonina Golovina, 2004

Antonina returned to Obukhovo on 2 August 1995, the sixty-fifth anniversary of the arrest of her father in 1930. There was not much left of the old village. Only nine of the houses were still inhabited. Sixty years of collectivization had sapped Obukhovo of youth and energy, just as it had done to thousands of other villages like it. In 1930, Obukhovo had been a poor but vibrant farming community with a population of 317 people, nearly half of them children. It had its own village church and school, its own cooperative store, and many of the households, like the Golovins', had their own leather workshops which manufactured shoes and other goods. By 1960, the population of Obukhovo had declined to sixty-eight, most of them old couples or single pensioners, and by the time of Antonina's visit, in 1995, there were only thirteen people left in the village, all but two of them in their sixties or their seventies. The old religious holiday on 2 August had long been forgotten by the villagers, but the Russian peasant tradition of hospitality had not died out, and on her arrival an evening meal in Antonina's honour was soon arranged by the village women in the house of Ivan Golovin, the last remaining household of her family in the village. Once the initial tension had passed, the villagers recalled Antonina's father as a good farmer, whose industry was missed in the collective farm. 'The Golovins were honest, clean and sober people,' recalled one old woman. 'It was wrong to arrest them. Tonya [Antonina], you are one of us, a real peasant woman, we need more like you.'[78]

The other turning-point in Antonina's reconciliation with her past came when she made a pilgrimage to the Altai region of Siberia to see Shaltyr, the 'special settlement' where she had lived with her family in exile between 1931 and 1934. The settlement had been abandoned many years before, but the ruins of the barracks were still standing behind a high barbed-wire fence and could be seen from the road. Nearby, Antonina came across a local woman of about the same age as herself. She asked her whether it was possible to get inside the settlement, and they began to talk. The woman told her that she had lived there when she was a child. 'I am a kulak daughter,' the woman said. 'I was sent here in 1930, but my real home is in Barnaul.' Antonina recalls her reaction to these simple words.

I was shaken. I had never heard anybody say that they were the daughter of a kulak, like myself. It had never occurred to me that it was possible to say these words without feeling shame, let alone to say them with the pride this woman evidently felt. All my life I had tried to hide my kulak origins. When the woman spoke, I looked around to see if anybody else had heard. Later, I began to think. Why had I looked around to see if there was anybody listening? What was there to fear? Suddenly, I felt ashamed of my own fear. And then I said aloud: 'I am a kulak daughter.' It was the first time I had ever said those words aloud, although in my head I had whispered them a thousand times. There was nobody around to hear me. I was on my own on a deserted road. But even so I was proud that at last I had spoken. I went down to the river bank and washed myself in the river. And then I said a prayer for my parents.[79]

Afterword and Acknowledgements

The Whisperers has a long history. The idea of the book goes back to middle of the 1980s, when I was a graduate researcher in Moscow. As a student of the Russian Revolution and the Civil War, I was eager to meet anyone who could still recall that period. I had become friends with Zhenia Golovnia, the granddaughter of the film-maker Anatoly Golovnia. Her mother, Oksana, told me many stories about the family's history in the 1920s and 1930s, and put me into contact with some friends, who had been born in the 'peaceful times', as she liked to call the years before the First World War. Over the next months, I visited the homes of about a dozen of Oksana's friends, mainly elderly ladies, who were too young to recall anything about the Civil War and, it seemed, too nervous to speak in depth about the history that had really shaped their lives: the years of Stalin's rule.

That first attempt at an oral history taught me to appreciate the importance of family memory as a counterweight to the official narrative of Soviet history. After 1991, I thought again about the possibility of researching for a book on the subject of *The Whisperers*. The sudden outpouring of personal memoirs about the Stalinist repressions encouraged the idea. But my instinct was that older people, on the whole, would keep their thoughts and feelings to themselves until they were sure that the Communists would not return, and that might take many years. In some ways I was wrong: the early 1990s are now widely seen as the heyday of oral history in the former Soviet Union, certainly compared with the Putin years, when the restoration of authoritarian government encouraged many Russians to return to their reticent habits. But in other ways my instinct had been right: for what people wanted to record in that first rush of commemoration were the facts of their repression, the details of arrest, imprisonment and rehabilitation, rather than the damage to their inner lives, the painful memories of personal betrayal and lost relationships that had shaped their history.

By 2002, when I finished working on *Natasha's Dance*, I felt at last the time had come to approach this uncharted territory. The last generation to reach adulthood before 1953 was disappearing fast, so there was a sense of urgency that this was our last real chance to understand the Stalin period through the internal life of ordinary families and individuals. The average age of the people giving interviews and archives to the research project for *The Whisperers* was eighty. To the best of my knowledge, at least twenty-seven of them died (about 6 per cent of the total sample) before the completion of the book.

My first inquiries were directed to the Russian state and public archives, where I hoped to locate private papers about family life and then conduct interviews with the people who donated them. This involved a very long and ultimately rather fruitless trawl through collections of letters, notebooks, diaries and memoirs, often written in a barely decipherable scrawl, yielding bits of information from which it was difficult to draw any conclusions (almost nothing from these archives went into *The Whisperers*). At this stage of my research I was helped by several employees: Katia Bunina and Julia Sharapova, who worked with me in the Moscow archives; Nikolai Mikhailov, who collected materials from the archives in St Petersburg; and Nikolai Kuzmin, who worked in the archives in Orel and elsewhere. I would also like to thank my two old teachers and comrades for their support in these early stages of research: Viktor Danilov (1925–2004), the historian of the Soviet peasantry, who took a keen interest in my research and helped to open doors in RGAE; and Teodor Shanin, who gave my project the backing of the Moscow School of Social and Economic Science.

Simultaneously with my searching through the archives, I would visit people in their homes, listening to their stories from the Stalin period and asking whether they had private papers they could give. The project spread by word of mouth – still the most efficient means of working in Russia – as contacts I developed told their friends about my work. I was overwhelmed by the interest from people asking to be interviewed, offering a family memoir, letters, notebooks or some other precious manuscript they wanted me to publish (or perhaps hoped to sell). It is impractical to thank everyone who helped me at this stage (they are named in the List of Interviews) but I owe a special debt to Sasha

Kozyrev, who kindly agreed to interview a number of his friends and acquaintances in St Petersburg; Ida Slavina, who gave me several interviews, many documents and photographs from her archives and sent me articles and information about her family; Yevgeniia Vittenburg, Ada Levidova, Bella Levitina. Olga Ramenskaia and Galina Petrova, who all gave interviews and family archives to the project; Leonid Makhnach, who put his recollections into lucid prose and handed over precious documents; Vakhtang Mikheladze, who gave several interviews and put me into contact with his family in Tbilisi; and Zhenia Golovnia, who not only transcribed and scanned her family archives, but also made available the many interviews and documents she had collected from former prisoners and administrators of the ALZhIR labour camp for her film *Izmennitsy* (1990). Zhenia advised me on the complex history, the rumours, intrigues and personalities of the Soviet film world and introduced me to many families with interesting stories and archives from the Stalin period.

It was through Zhenia that I met Aleksei Simonov, to whom I owe the greatest debt of all. I had already known of Aleksei as a film director, journalist and activist for human rights and press freedom (in 1999 he became the President of the Foundation for the Defence of Glasnost in Moscow), but I did not know his family's extraordinary history, for the story of the Laskins, on his mother's side, had been almost totally excluded from the biographies of his famous father which I read in preparation for my first meeting with him in his Moscow flat, just around the corner from Konstantin Simonov Street. Aleksei had kept the Laskin family archive in a drawer following the death of his mother, Zhenia Laskina, in 1992. From these materials he had written his own touching memoir of his parents (*Chastnaia kollektsiia*) in 1999, but from the start he welcomed my interest and put his trust in me to become what he called 'the family's historian'. Aleksei allowed me to copy the Laskin archive. He gave up many hours from his busy working schedule to brief me on the details of his family's history and correct my mistakes. Aleksei is a marvellous raconteur. In our many interviews and conversations around the kitchen table in his flat, often lasting late into the night, he conjured up so vividly the special atmosphere of the Laskin household – a warmth and informality that Aleksei and his wife Galina have managed to preserve in their home – that I began to feel that I was not just a historian but practically a member of the extended family. I had the same sensation whenever I visited Aleksei's aunt, Fania Samuilovna, or Dusia, as she is called, the last surviving Laskin sister, who lives with her son on the eleventh floor of a modern tower block near Ilich Square. Fania was moved to the apartment in 1990, after she and her sister Sonia were evicted from their home in Sivtsev Vrazhek, where the family had lived for nearly sixty years. Sonia died in 1991. Fania's memory is faltering. She was ninety-seven when she gave me her final interview. But sometimes, when I asked her about something we had discussed many times before, she would suddenly recall a long-forgotten detail about the Laskin family which otherwise would never have been known. For this reason, but mainly for her charm, I learned to cherish every moment spent in Dusia's company.

I am deeply grateful to Aleksei for giving me complete and unrestricted access to his father's huge archive in RGALI. Most of the papers I received from the previously closed sections of Simonov's personal archive (in *opis* 9 and 10) had not been seen by any scholars previously. Indeed it soon became apparent that some of their most sensitive materials were unknown to the family itself. Unfortunately, as a result of my discoveries, which stirred up painful memories for some members of the family, in October 2005 Katia Simonova (Gudzenko), the head of the Commission in charge of Simonov's literary estate, took the decision to close his archive to researchers until 2025.

Apart from the revelations of Simonov's archives, I learned a lot about the writer's life and character from interviews with colleagues, friends and relatives. I am particularly grateful to Maria Simonova, Lazar Lazarev, Nina Arkhipova, Aleksei and Sofia Karaganov, Andrei Erofeev and Marina Babak; and to many others who helped fill out my understanding of the world in which Simonov moved, including Iunna Morits, Viktor Erofeev, Viktoriia Shweitser, Galina Kravchenko and Aleksei Schmarinov.

By the spring of 2003, I had ongoing projects with a dozen families, but I desperately needed a research team to expand my work and put it on a more systematic footing. So it was a crucial breakthrough to receive two major grants, one from the Arts and Humanities Research Council and the other from the Leverhulme Trust, in 2003. Without the generous support of these British institutions, it would have been impossible to write *The Whisperers* or complete the broader research project connected to the book, and I am extremely grateful to them both.

Supported by these grants, I employed the Memorial Society in St Petersburg, Moscow and Perm to interview survivors of the Stalin years and collect their family archives for transcription and scanning. The choice of these three branches of Memorial was not difficult. They had an excellent record in oral history, although in many ways the work they did for me, with its emphasis on the inner world of the individual and family relationships, was different from the projects they had done before which focused on the history of the Gulag. They all had large and active memberships, from which our participants were largely drawn, although the three went well beyond their natural constituency (victims of repression) to involve a much broader range of families, including many that had done very well by the Stalinist regime. In St Petersburg and Moscow the main advantage was the relatively high proportion of educated families that had retained written documents. In Perm it was the fact that the city had remained outside the occupied zone during 1941–5, so that the memory of the Stalin period was not confused with the trauma of the war, as well as the large number of former exiles and Gulag prisoners in the population of this area, which was once full of labour camps and 'special settlements'.

The team in St Petersburg was led by Irina Flige, whose clever insights and advice, as well as her criticisms, were invaluable to the project. I have enjoyed and learned a lot from working with Irina and will always remain in her debt. The rest of the team in St Petersburg was made up by Tatiana Kosinova, a sympathetic listener who, like Irina, somehow managed to get far more from her interviews than anybody could have expected; and Tatiana Morgacheva, who took interviews and organized the archives with great skill. Irina Flige and Tatiana Kosinova also led the expedition to Norilsk, and Irina travelled on her own to Moscow, Saratov, Petrozavodsk, Krasnoiarsk and Stavropol to conduct interviews and collect materials.

Alyona Kozlova led the Moscow team with calm authority, always giving thoughtful and intelligent advice. Irina Ostrovskaia, Olga Binkina, Natalia Malykhina and Alyona Kozlova conducted the interviews with great sensitivity, while Galia Buvina organized the archives with exemplary efficiency. I am deeply grateful to them all.

In Perm the team was organized by the able and enthusiastic Aleksandr Kalykh, assisted by Elena Skriakova, with interviews conducted by Robert Latypov, Andrei Grebenshchikov, Svetlana Grebenshchikova and Mikhail Cherepanov. I would like to thank them all, particularly Robert and Andrei, who did most of the interviewing, always producing interesting results, and wrote helpful commentaries.

A few words are in order on the methodology of the project. I made the selection of the families to be included in the project from a database assembled by the research teams through telephone interviews with more than a thousand people in total. My main concern was to ensure that the final sample was drawn from a representative social base (it would have been very easy to skew it towards the intelligentsia, especially in Moscow and St Petersburg) whilst sticking to the principle that every family should have some sort of archive to corroborate the testimony given during interviews. In Perm this was difficult. It is a region heavily populated by former 'kulaks', uprooted from their homes, and other victims of the Stalinist regime. The vast majority of the people interviewed by telephone had no personal documents at all (many did not even have a photograph of their parents). But those who did have family archives were well worth hunting out.

During the first interview, people were allowed to reconstruct their life-story with minimal intervention (a standard practice of oral history), although I prepared a questionnaire for the interviewers and asked them to develop certain themes that had emerged already from the database. These interviews were very long, usually lasting several hours and often stretching over several days. Having analysed the edited transcripts, I would then decide the main direction and set questions for the secondary interviews, which explored in depth specific themes. There were usually two or three interviews for every family. About once a month, I would meet the research teams to discuss the interviews and select the materials from the families' archives for transcription and scanning. The selection of the archives was relatively straightforward: we took as much as possible – personal documents, diaries, memoirs, notebooks, runs of letters in their entirety – as long as these were written before 1960 or shed light on the Stalin period. In the interviews, by contrast, we encountered many challenges, most of which will be familiar to prac-titioners of oral history in the former Soviet Union. Techniques had to be developed to get people to think more reflectively about their lives; to disentangle direct memories from received impressions and opinions; to see the past and recall what they had thought without hindsight; and to overcome their fear of talking to strangers. The gradual building up of trust was essential. It would often taken a dozen visits before precious documents were handed over to our teams for copying (portable scanners and digital cameras made it possible to do this quickly in the home).

I am deeply grateful to all the families who contributed to the project with Memorial. It is impractical to thank them individually (they are all named in the List of Interviews) but special thanks must go to Antonina Znamenskaia, Inna Shikheyeva, Marksena Nikiforova, Elizaveta Delibash, Angelina Bushueva, Valentina Tikhanova, Nina Feofilaktova, Maria Vitkevich, Marianna Barkovskaia, Georgii Fursei, Maria Kuznetsova, Yevgeniia Vasileva, Nikolai Kovach, Valentin Muravsky, Rada Poloz, Anzhelika Sirman, Zoia Timofeyeva, Nikolai Lileyev, Vladimir Piatnitsky, Lev Netto, Julia Volkova, Larisa and Vitalii Garmash, Maia Rodak, Galina Adasinskaia, Roza Novoseltseva, Veronika Nevskaia, Svetlana Khlystova, Vera Minusova, Nikolai Meshalkin, Elfrida Meshalkina, Leonid Saltykov, Dmitry Streletsky, Irina Mikueva, Rezeda Taisina, Liubov Tetiueva, Vera Vasiltseva, Natalia Stepantseva, Ivan Uglitskikh, Sofia Ozemblovskaia, Valentina Kropotina, Tamara Trubina and Vera Turkina, who all gave many hours of their time and precious documents to the project. I would also like to thank Elena Bonner, who was interviewed as part of the Memorial project by Irina Flige in Boston, for giving me permission to cite extracts from Antonina W. Bouis's translation of her book *Mothers and Daughters* (London: Hutchinson, 1992).

These people are the heroes of *Whisperers*. In a real sense this is their book: I have only given voice to them. For us these are stories, for them it is their lives.

At every stage of working on this book, I have been acutely conscious of my duty as a historian to tell these people's stories in a way that they can recognize as a truthful reflection of their experience. There is no anonymous testimony in this book: with one or two exceptions, all the people who have given interviews or documents have agreed to have their names revealed. For this reason, sections of the later drafts were translated into Russian and given to the families concerned, so that they could make the necessary corrections and suggest alterations to the text. This was a long and complex process – not least because the way a person sees his own biography is often very different from the view of him that can be formed from a reading of his memoirs, letters, diaries and recorded words – but it was important that the subjects of this book should have a chance to correct it. There was no case where I was forced to change my overall interpretation, but many where my views were enriched and improved by the family's input. A problem arose with just one family, the Shikheyevs (Gaisters): some members of the family took exception to the testimony of Inna's older daughter, which was cut from the proofs on their request. Inna saw and corrected all the remaining Gaister passages but later closed her archive in Memorial. I would like to thank Zhanna Bogdanovich and Natalia Leshchenko for translating sections of the book into Russian; Irina Flige, Alyona Kozlova and Irina Ostrovskaia for checking the final drafts; Leo Viprinski for his generous and thoughtful assistance with the Slavin sections; and Aleksei Simonov, not just for correcting the English text on the Laskins and the Simonovs, but for showing me the need to think again about the enigma of 'K.M.'

Most of the materials generated by the research project of *The Whisperers* are available on line (http://www.orlandofiges.com). Here you will find the main family archives together with the transcripts and sound extracts of the interviews. Some of the materials have been translated into English. Without the website, many of these archives would have been lost when their owners passed away, for the younger generation in Russia has little interest in the Soviet past and not much storage space to keep such things. I would like to thank Emma Beer, Aibek Baratov and Ding Zhang for their help in the design and construction of the website. With the support of Jerry Kuehl, Emma also took the lead in trying to get interest going in a video project, the aim of which was to create a film archive of interviews with the heroes of *The Whisperers* delivered via streaming from the website.

Working on this project has involved a lot of travelling, months spent away from my family, Stephanie, Lydia and Alice, who have put up with a lot but will now see, I hope, that it was worthwhile. Through their love and support they have reminded me of the meaning of a family.

I must thank my friend Robert (Lord) Skidelsky for his generous hospitality in Moscow, and Aleksei Iurasovsky for being such a good landlord. I would also like to thank Elena (Helen) Volkonskaia for inviting me to stay in her lovely home in Tuscany, where much of the second draft was written in the summer of 2006.

As a writer, I am blessed with wonderful support. My agent Deborah Rogers has been as kind and passionate as ever in her efforts on my behalf, and Melanie Jackson, in the United States, has also helped in many ways. Simon Winder at Penguin and Sara Bershtel at Metropolitan are a dream editorial team for any writer. In their different ways – Simon inspiring with enthusiastic comments and encouragement, Sara editing the typescript line by line with extraordinary passion and attention to detail – they have each had an immense influence on the writing of this book. I owe a huge debt to them both. I would also like to thank David Watson for his copy-editing, Merle Read for checking the transliteration of the Russian names, Alan Gilliland for drawing the floorplans and Donald Winchester for extra editorial support. I am also grateful to Andrei Bobrov at the ITAR-TASS Photo Agency for helping to track down some elusive photographs.

I would like to thank the scholars who have helped me with points of detail and directed me to sources that I did not know: Valerii Golofast, Katerina Gerasimova, Stephen Wheatcroft, Catriona Kelly, Boris Kolonitsky, Jonathan Haslam, Daniel Beer and Daniel Pick. I also owe a debt to Rob Perks, who shared his wisdom on the challenges of oral history. Jennifer Davis gave me good advice on the legal aspects of the contracts with Memorial, for which many thanks. Raj Chandarvarkar gave loyal support and help in countless ways. I only wish he was alive to discuss the book with me.

Finally, I would like to thank my old friend and colleague, Hiroaki Kuromiya, one of the finest and most careful historians of the Stalin period, who read the manuscript with strict instructions to challenge anything that could be construed as a flaw. Any errors that remain are mine.

London
April 2007

Permissions

With the following exceptions (listed by the pages on which they appear), all the photographs are reproduced with the permission of their owners from private family archives and the archives of Memorial (MM, MP, MSP): GARF: 21; GMPIR: 330; RGAE: 23, 225, 226; RGALI: 2, 61, 135, 140, 199, 403, 407, 409, 495, 507, 617; TASS: 229, 232, 375, 500; TsGAKFD: 152, 486, 504, 524, 527, 609, 627.

Notes

Introduction

1. MSP, f. 3, op. 14, d. 2, l. 31; d. 3, ll. 18–19.
2. I have based my estimate on the figures in M. Ellman, 'Soviet Repression Statistics: Some Comments', *Europe-Asia Studies*, vol. 54, no. 7 (November 2002), pp. 1151–72. Ellman gives a figure of 18.75 million Gulag sentences between 1934 and 1953, but many Gulag prisoners served more than one sentence in this period. He also gives the following figures for these years: at least 1 million executions; 2 million people in the labour army and other units of forced labour subordinated to the Gulag; 5 million people among the deported nationalities. According to the most reliable estimates, about 10 million people were repressed as 'kulaks' after 1928. That gives a total of 36.5 million people; allowing for the duplication of Gulag sentences, an overall figure of 25 million people is reasonable and probably an underestimate.
3. Interview with Elena Dombrovskaia, Moscow, January 2003.
4. MP, f. 4, op. 25, d. 2, ll. 9–10.
5. M. Gefter, 'V predchuvstvii proshlogo', *Vek XX i mir*, 1990, no. 9, p. 29.
6. See e.g. V. Kaverin, *Epilog: Memuary* (Moscow, 1989); K. Simonov, *Glazami cheloveka moego pokoleniia* (Moscow, 1990).
7. The literature is enormous, but see e.g. A. Barmine, *One Who Survived* (New York, 1945); V. Kravchenko, *I Chose Freedom: The Personal and Political Life of a Soviet Official* (London, 1947); A. Gorbatov, *Years off My Life* (London, 1964); N. Kaminskaya, *Final Judgment: My Life as a Soviet Defence Attorney* (New York, 1982); N. Mandelstam, *Hope Against Hope* (London, 1989); same author, *Hope Abandoned* (London, 1990); E. Ginzburg, *Journey into the Whirlwind* (New York, 1967); same author, *Within the Whirlwind* (New York, 1981); L. Bogoraz, 'Iz vospominanii', *Minuvshee*, vol. 2 (Paris, 1986); L. Kopelev, *No Jail for Thought* (London, 1979); same author, *The Education of a True Believer* (London, 1980); T. Aksakova-Sivers, *Semeinaia khronika*, 2 vols. (Paris, 1988); Mikhail Baitalsky, *Notebooks for the Grandchildren: Recollections of a Trotskyist Who Survived the Stalin Terror* (New Jersey, 1995).
8. A. Krylova, 'The Tenacious Liberal Subject in Soviet Studies', *Kritika: Explorations in Russian and Eurasian History*, vol. 1, no. 1 (Winter 2000), pp. 119–46.
9. Again the literature is voluminous, but among the more interesting are: O. Adamova-Sliuzberg, *Put'* (Moscow, 1993); A. Raikin, *Vospominaniia* (St Petersburg, 1993); I. Diakonov, *Kniga vospominanii* (St Petersburg, 1995); Iu. Liuba, *Vospominaniia* (St Petersburg, 1998); I. Shikheeva-Gaister, *Semeinaia khronika vremen kul'ta lichnosti (1925–53 gg.)* (Moscow, 1998); I. Dudareva, *Proshloe vsegda s nami: vospominaniia* (St Petersburg, 1998); E. Evangulova, *Krestnyi put'* (St Petersburg, 2000); K. Atarova, *Vcherashnyi den': vokrug sem'i Atarovykh-Dal'tsevykh: vospominaniia* (Moscow, 2001);

L. El'iashova, *My ukhodim, my ostaemsia. Kniga 1: Dedy, ottsy* (St Petersburg, 2001); N. Iudkovskii, *Rekviem dvum semeistvam: vospominaniia* (Moscow, 2002); E. Vlasova, *Domashnyi al'bom: vospominaniia* (Moscow, 2002); P. Kodzaev, *Vospominaniia reabilitirovannogo spetspereselentsa* (Vladikavkaz, 2002); E. Liusin, *Pis'mo-vospominaniia o prozhitykh godakh* (Kaluga, 2002); A. Bovin, *XX vek kak zhizn': vospominaniia* (Moscow, 2003). See also: I. Paperno, 'Personal Accounts of the Soviet Experience', *Kritika: Explorations in Russian and Eurasian History*, vol. 3, no. 4 (Autumn 2002), pp. 577–610.

10. See e.g. S. Fitzpatrick, *Stalin's Peasants: Resistance and Survival in the Russian Village After Collectivization* (New York, 1994); S. Davies, *Popular Opinion in Stalin's Russia: Terror, Propaganda and Dissent, 1934–1941* (Cambridge, 1997); S. Kotkin, *Magnetic Mountain: Stalinism as a Civilization* (Berkeley, 1997).

11. See e.g., N. Kosterina, *Dnevnik* (Moscow, 1964); O. Berggol'ts, 'Bezumstvo predannosti: iz dnevnikov Ol'gi Berggol'ts', *Vremia i my*, 1980, no. 57, pp. 270–85; A. Mar'ian, *Gody moi, kak soldaty: dnevnik sel'skogo aktivista, 1925–1953 gg.* (Kishinev, 1987); M. Prishvin, *Dnevniki* (Moscow, 1990); E. Bulgakova, *Dnevnik Eleny Bulgakovoi* (Moscow, 1990); N. Vishniakova, *Dnevnik Niny Vishniakovoi* (Sverdlovsk, 1990).

12. See e.g. V. Vernadskii, 'Dnevnik 1938 goda', *Druzhba narodov*, 1992, no. 2, pp. 219–39; no. 3, pp. 241–69; same author, 'Dnevnik 1939 goda', *Druzhba narodov*, 1993, nos. 11/12, pp. 3–41; A. Solov'ev, *Tetradi krasnogo professora (1912–1941 gg.)*, *Neizvestnaia Rossiia. XX vek*, vol. 4 (Moscow, 1993), pp. 140–228; '"Ischez chelovek i net ego, kuda devalsia – nikto ne znaet": iz konfiskovannogo dnevnika', *Istochnik*, 1993, no. 4, pp. 46–62; *Golgofa. Po materialam arkhivno-sledstvennogo dela no. 603 na Sokolovu-Piatnitskuiu Iu. I.*, ed. V. I. Piatnitskii (St Petersburg, 1993); A. Afinogenov, 'Dnevnik 1937 goda', *Sovremennaia dramaturgiia*, 1993, no. 1, pp. 219–33; no. 2, pp. 223–41; no. 3, pp. 217–39; K. Chukovskii, *Dnevnik 1930–1969* (Moscow, 1994); M. Prishvin, '"Zhizn' stala veselei . . .": iz dnevnika 1936 goda', *Oktiabr'*, 1993, no. 10, pp. 3–21; same author, 'Dnevnik 1937 goda', *Oktiabr'*, 1994, no. 11, pp. 144–71; 1995, no. 9, pp. 155–71; M. Prishvin and V. Prishvin, *My s toboi: dnevnik liubvi* (Moscow, 1996); A. Kopenin, 'Zapiski nesumashedshego: iz dnevnika sel'skogo uchitelia', *Rodina*, 1996, no. 2, pp. 17–29; *Dnevnye zapiski ust'-kulomskogo krest'ianina I. S. Rassukhaeva (1902–1953)* (Moscow, 1997); M. Krotova, *Bavykinskii dnevnik: vospominaniia shkol'nogo pedagoga* (Moscow, 1998); A. Tsember, *Dnevnik* (Moscow, 1997); V. Sitnikov, *Perezhitoe: dnevnik saratovskogo obyvatelia 1918–1931 gg.* (Moscow, 1999); E. Filipovich, *Ot sovetskoi pionerki do cheloveka-pensionerki: moi dnevniki* (Podol'sk, 2000); A. Man'kov, *Dnevniki tridtsatykh godov* (St Petersburg, 2001); Iu. Nagibin, *Dnevnik* (Moscow, 2001); N. Lugovskaya, *I Want to Live: The Diary of a Soviet Schoolgirl 1932–1937* (Moscow, 2003); M. Shirshova, *Zabytyi dnevnik poliarnogo biologa* (Moscow, 2003). Extracts from ten diaries were published in translation in V. Garros, N. Korenevskaya and T. Lahusen (eds.), *Intimacy and Terror: Soviet Diaries of the 1930s* (New York, 1995).

13. The historian Jochen Hellbeck has pioneered the study of Soviet diaries in the 1930s, particularly the diary of Stepan Podlubny, which is reproduced in J. Hellbeck (ed.), *Tagebuch aus Moskau, 1931–1939* (Munich, 1996). See also Hellbeck's discussion of four Soviet diaries from the 1930s in *Revolution on My Mind: Writing a Diary Under Stalin* (Cambridge, Mass., 2006). Hellbeck's controversial view is that Soviet citizens in the 1930s thought in Soviet categories because they had no conceptual alternative, and that in their diaries they tried to mould themselves into the New Soviet Person by purging from themselves all non-Soviet elements of their personality (which they experienced as a 'crisis of the self'). See further: J. Hellbeck, 'Self-Realization in the Stalinist System: Two Soviet Diaries of the 1930s', in M. Hildermeier (ed.), *Stalinismus vor dem Zweiten Weltkrieg: neue Wege der Forschung* (Munich, 1998), pp. 275–90. Hellbeck's view has been heavily criticized, particularly by A. Etkind, 'Soviet Subjectivity: Torture for the Sake of Salvation?', *Kritika: Explorations in Russian and Eurasian History*, vol. 6, no. 1 (Winter 2005), pp. 171–86; and S. Boym in 'Analiz praktiki sub'ektivizatsii v rannestalinskom obshchestve', *Ab Imperio*, 2002, no. 3, pp. 209–418.

14. See e.g. J. Hellbeck, 'Fashioning the Stalinist Soul: The Diary of Stepan Podlubnyi (1931–1939)', *Jahrbücher für Geschichte Osteuropas*, 44 (1996), pp. 344–73; I. Halfin and J. Hellbeck, 'Rethinking the Stalinist Subject: Stephen Kotkin's "Magnetic Mountain" and the State of Soviet Historical Studies', *Jahrbücher für Geschichte Osteuropas*, 44 (1996), pp. 456–63; I. Halfin, *Terror in My Soul: Communist Autobiographies on Trial* (Cambridge, Mass., 2003); C. Kaier and E. Naiman (eds.), *Everyday Life in Early Soviet Russia: Taking the Revolution Inside* (Bloomington, 2006).

15. This is the main argument of Hellbeck (see the references to his work above).

16. MP, f. 4, op. 18, d. 2, ll. 49–50.

17. See in particular the two books by Catherine Merridale, *Night of Stone: Death and Memory in Russia* (London, 2000) and *Ivan's War: The Red Army 1939–1945* (London, 2005), both partly based on interviews.

18. See e.g. *Golos krest'ian: Sel'skaia Rossiia XX veka v krest'ianskikh memuarakh* (Moscow, 1996); *Sud'ba liudei: Rossiia xx vek. Biografii semei kak ob'ekt sotsiologicheskogo issledovaniia* (Moscow, 1996); D. Bertaux, P. Thompson and A. Rotkirch (eds.), *On Living through Soviet Russia* (London, 2004); V. Skultans, *The Testimony of Lives: Narrative and Memory in Post-Soviet Latvia* (London, 1998); A. Shternshis, *Soviet and Kosher: Jewish Popular Culture in the Soviet Union, 1923–1939* (Bloomington, 2006). Many books have been drawn from interviews, among them notably: N. Adler, *Beyond the Soviet System: The Gulag Survivor* (New Brunswick, 2002); A. Applebaum, *Gulag: A History of the Soviet Camps* (London, 2003).

19. The first major oral history was the Harvard Project on the Soviet Social System (329 interviews with Soviet refugees in Europe and the USA carried out in 1950–51). Most of the interviewees had left the Soviet Union between 1943 and 1946, and their views, which were coloured by the experience of living in the West, were consciously anti-Soviet in a way that was not representative of the Soviet population as a whole. Nonetheless, the project resulted in the publication of several sociological books, which influenced the Western view of Soviet daily life during the Cold War: R. Bauer, A. Inkeles and C. Klukhohn, *How the Soviet System Works: Cultural, Psychological and Cultural Themes* (Cambridge, Mass., 1957); J. Berliner, *Factory and Manager in the USSR* (Cambridge, Mass., 1958); M. Field, *Doctor and Patient in Soviet Russia* (Cambridge, Mass., 1958); and A. Inkeles and R. Bauer, *The Soviet Citizen: Daily Life in a Totalitarian Society* (Cambridge, Mass., 1959), which was specifically dedicated to studying 'how Soviet society impinges on the individual and how he fits into the functioning pattern of Soviet life' (p. 3). Smaller oral history projects adopting a sociological approach were carried out in the early 1990s by Daniel Bertaux and Paul Thompson (published in *Sud'ba liudei* and *On Living Through Soviet Russia*) and by the Moscow School of Social and Economic Science (published in *Golos krest'ian*). The oral history of the Gulag has been pioneered by the Memorial Society (http://www.memo.ru), although of course the first great oral history of the subject was Aleksandr Solzhenitsyn's *Gulag Archipelago*, 3 vols. (London, 1974–8), which relied heavily on interviews with survivors of the labour camps.

1: Children of 1917 (1917–28)

1. RGALI, f. 3084, op. 1, d. 1389, l. 17; f. 2804, op. 1, d. 45.

2. E. Drabkina, *Chernye sukhari* (Moscow, 1975), pp. 82–3.

3. S. Sebag Montefiore, *Stalin: The Court of the Red Tsar* (London, 2003), p. 61.

4. RGALI, f. 2804, op. 1, d. 22, l. 4; f. 3084, op. 1, d. 1389, l. 3; Drabkina, *Chernye sukhari*, pp. 23–9; N. Burenin, *Pamiatnye gody: vospominaniia* (Leningrad, 1961), pp. 150–51.

5. *Partiinaia etika: dokumenty i materialy diskussii dvadtsatykh godov* (Moscow, 1989), p. 16; M. Gorky, *Untimely Thoughts: Essays on Revolution, Culture and the Bolsheviks, 1917–18* (London, 1970), p. 7.

6. Cited in E. Naiman, *Sex in Public: The Incarnation of Early Soviet Ideology* (Princeton, 1997), pp. 91–2.

7. RGALI, f. 2804, op. 1, dd. 22, 40, 1389; V. Erashov, *Kak molniia v nochi* (Moscow, 1988), p. 344.

8. O. Figes, *A People's Tragedy: The Russian Revolution, 1891-1924* (London, 1996), pp. 752-68.

9. I. Stalin, *Sochineniia*, 13 vols. (Moscow, 1946-55), vol. 6, p. 248.

10. K. Geiger, *The Family in Soviet Russia* (Cambridge, Mass., 1968), p. 61.

11. L. Kirschenbaum, *Small Comrades: Revolutionizing Childhood in Soviet Russia, 1917-1932* (New York, 2001), p. 48.

12. O. Maitich, 'Utopia in Daily Life', in J. Bowlt and O. Maitich (eds.), *Laboratory of Dreams: The Russian Avant-garde and Cultural Experiment* (Stanford, 1996), pp. 65-6; V. Buchli, *An Archaeology of Socialism* (Oxford, 1999), pp. 65-8.

13. W. Goldman, *Women, the State and Revolution: Soviet Family Policy and Social Life, 1917-1936* (Cambridge, 1993), p. 107; N. Lebina, *Povsednevnaia zhizn' sovetskogo goroda: normy i anomalii, 1920-1930 gody* (St Petersburg, 1999), p. 272.

14. I. Halfin, 'Intimacy in an Ideological Key: The Communist Case of the 1920s and 1930s', in same author (ed.), *Language and Revolution: Making Modern Political Identities* (London, 2002), pp. 187-8.

15. L. Trotsky, *Problems of Everyday Life: Creating the Foundations of a New Society in Revolutionary Russia* (London, 1973), p. 72; A. Inkeles and R. Bauer, *The Soviet Citizen: Daily Life in a Totalitarian Society* (Cambridge, Mass., 1959), p. 205.

16. Trotsky, *Problems of Everyday Life*, p. 48.

17. MSP, f. 3, op. 16, d. 2, ll. 2, 7, 46-62.

18. See O. Figes, *Natasha's Dance: A Cultural History of Russia* (London, 2002), pp. 119-30.

19. MSP, f. 3, op. 18, d. 2, ll. 24, 26.

20. MSP, f. 3, op. 12, d. 2, l. 15.

21. E. Bonner, *Mothers and Daughters* (London, 1992), pp. 40, 46, 61-2, 101.

22. Buchli, *An Archaeology of Socialism*, p. 131.

23. V. Maiakovskii, *Polnoe sobranie sochinenii*, 13 vols. (Moscow, 1955-61), vol. 2, pp. 74-5.

24. V. Dunham, *In Stalin's Time: Middle-Class Values in Soviet Fiction* (Durham, 1990), p. 64 (translation slightly altered for clarity).

25. W. Rosenberg (ed.), *Bolshevik Visions: First Phase of the Cultural Revolution in Soviet Russia*, 2 vols. (Ann Arbor, 1990), vol. 1, p. 37 (translation slightly altered for clarity).

26. MM, f. 1, op. 1, dd. 167, 169; f. 12, op. 27, d. 2, ll. 47-54.

27. MSP, f. 3, op. 47, d. 2, ll. 32-3, 59-64; d. 3, ll. 1-6; L. El'iashova, *My ukhodim, my ostaemsia. Kniga 1: Dedy, ottsy* (St Petersburg, 2001), pp. 191-4.

28. OR RNB, f. 1156, d. 597, ll. 3, 14; IISH, Vojtinskij, No. 11 (Box 3, file 5/b); VOFA, A. Levidova, 'Vospominaniia', ms., p. 11; interview with Ada Levidova, St Petersburg, May 2004.

29. OR RNB, f. 1156, d. 576, ll. 4, 12-19; d. 577, l. 1; d. 597, l. 51; VOFA, A. Levidova, 'Vospominaniia', ms., p. 12.

30. V. Zenzinov, *Deserted: The Story of the Children Abandoned in Soviet Russia* (London, 1931), p. 27.

31. A. Lunacharskii, *O narodnom obrazovanii* (Moscow, 1948), p. 445.

32. E. M. Balashov, *Shkola v rossiiskom obshchestve 1917-1927 gg. Stanovlenie 'novogo cheloveka'* (St Petersburg, 2003), p. 33; J. Ceton, *School en kind in Sowjet-Rusland* (Amsterdam, 1921), p. 3. On work and play in kindergartens see L. Kirschenbaum, *Small Comrades: Revolutionizing Childhood in Soviet Russia, 1917-32* (New York, 2001), pp. 120-23.

33. MP, f. 4, op. 18, d. 2, ll. 1-2; RGAE, f. 9455, op. 2, d. 154; L. Holmes, 'Part of History: The Oral Record and Moscow's Model School No. 25, 1931-1937', *Slavic Review*, 56 (Summer 1997), pp. 281-3; S. Fitzpatrick, *Education and Social Mobility in the Soviet Union 1921-1934* (Cambridge, 1979), p. 27; SFA, I. Slavina, 'Tonen'kii nerv istorii', ms., p. 16.

34. RGAE, f. 9455, op. 2, d. 30, ll. 241–56; d. 51, ll. 113–14; d. 154, ll. 47–8.
35. RGAE, f. 9455, op. 2, d. 154, l. 397; d. 155, ll. 5, 8, 9, 15; d. 156, ll. 11–12, 171; d.157, ll. 98–103.
36. R. Berg, *Sukhovei: vospominaniia genetika* (Moscow, 2003), p. 29.
37. A. Mar'ian, *Gody moi, kak soldaty: dnevnik sel'skogo aktivista, 1925–1953 gg.* (Kishinev, 1987), p. 17; E. Liusin, *Pis'mo – vospominaniia o prozhitykh godakh* (Kaluga, 2002), pp. 18–19. See further C. Kelly, 'Byt, Identity and Everyday Life', in S. Franklin and E. Widdis (eds.), *National Identity in Russian Culture: An Introduction* (Cambridge, 2004), pp. 157–67.
38. Balashov, *Shkola v rossiiskom obshchestve*, p. 137.
39. MSP, f. 3, op. 37, d. 2, ll. 8–9; op. 14, d. 3, ll. 24–6; MP, f. 4, op. 24, d. 2, ll. 41–2; op. 3, d. 2, l. 24; V. Frid, *58½: zapiski lagernogo pridurka* (Moscow, 1996), p. 89.
40. MSP, f. 3, op. 8, d. 2, ll. 1, 7; MP, f. 4, op. 9, d. 2, ll. 11–12.
41. C. Kelly, 'Shaping the "Future Race": Regulating the Daily Life of Children in Early Soviet Russia', in C. Kaier and E. Naiman (eds.), *Everyday Life in Early Soviet Russia: Taking the Revolution Inside* (Bloomington, 2006), p. 262; Rosenberg, *Bolshevik Visions*, vol. 2, p. 86; MP, f. 4, op. 24, d. 2, l. 43.
42. Interview with Vasily Romashkin, Norilsk, July 2004.
43. Interview with Ida Slavina, Cologne, June 2003.
44. MSP, f. 3, op. 17, d. 2, l. 8.
45. P. Kenez, *The Birth of the Propaganda State: Soviet Methods of Mass Mobilization, 1917–1929* (Cambridge, 1985), pp. 168–9.
46. N. Vishniakova, *Dnevnik Niny Vishniakovy* (Sverdlovsk, 1990), pp. 28–9.
47. E. Dolmatovskii, *Bylo: zapiski poeta* (Moscow, 1982), pp. 22–3.
48. V. Pirozhkova, *Poteriannoe pokolenie* (St Petersburg, 1998), pp. 46–7.
49. Interview with Vasily Romashkin, Norilsk, July 2004; D. Hoffman, *Stalinist Values: The Cultural Norms of Stalinist Modernity* (Cornell, 2003), pp. 121–2.
50. M. Baitalsky, *Notebooks for the Grandchildren: Recollections of a Trotskyist Who Survived the Stalin Terror* (New Jersey, 1995), pp. 56, 68, 71 (translation slightly altered for clarity).
51. Lebina, *Povsednevnaia zhizn'*, p. 274.
52. Baitalsky, *Notebooks for the Grandchildren*, pp. 94–6, 161–2.
53. Stalin, *Sochineniia*, vol. 6, p. 46; *Partiinaia etika*, p. 287.
54. M. Rubinshtein, *Sotsial'no-pravovye predstavleniia i samoupravleniia u detei* (Moscow, 1925), pp. 69–70.
55. *Partiinaia etika*, p. 329.
56. O. Khakhordin, *The Collective and the Individual in Russia: A Study of Practices* (Berkeley, 1999), pp. 35–74, 212–28. In a similar manner 'proletarian consciousness' required proof of consciousness (ideological commitment to the Party's cause); it was not enough to be born into the proletariat, for there were many people of working-class origin who had developed a 'petty-bourgeois' mentality.
57. L. Schapiro, *The Communist Party of the Soviet Union* (London, 1970), p. 385.
58. See further I. Halfin, 'From Darkness to Light: Student Communist Autobiography During NEP', *Jahrbücher für Geschichte Osteuropas*, 45 (1997), pp. 210–36; same author, *Terror in My Soul: Communist Autobiographies on Trial* (Cambridge, Mass., 2003).
59. Khakhordin, *The Collective and the Individual in Russia*, pp. 123–5.
60. V. Kozlov, 'Denunciation and Its Functions in Soviet Governance: A Study of Denunciations and Their Bureaucratic Handling from Soviet Police Archives, 1944–1953', *Journal of Modern History*, 68 (December 1996), p. 867; C. Hooper, 'Terror from Within: Participation and Coercion in Soviet Power, 1924–64' (Ph.D. dissertation, Princeton University, 2003), p. 13.
61. *XIV s'ezd VKP(b): stenograficheskii otchet* (Moscow, 1926), p. 600.
62. Ibid., p. 615.
63. Bonner, *Mothers and Daughters*, p. 148.

64. *Partiinaia etika*, p. 329.
65. Interview with Elena Dombrovskaia, Moscow, January 2003.
66. MSP, f. 3, op. 48, d. 2, ll. 1, 23, 32–4.
67. MSP, f. 3, op. 42, d. 2, ll. 5–6.
68. MP, f. 4, op. 9, d. 1, ll. 4–8; d. 2, l. 13.
69. MP, f. 4, op. 12, d. 2, l. 7.
70. Bonner, *Mothers and Daughters*, p. 17.
71. V. Semenova, 'Babushki: semeinye i sotsial'nye funktsii praroditel'skogo pokoleniia', in *Sud'ba liudei: Rossiia xx vek. Biografii semei kak ob'ekt sotsiologicheskogo issledovaniia* (Moscow, 1996), pp. 326–54.
72. Bonner, *Mothers and Daughters*, pp. 14, 15, 16, 27, 40, 78, 145; interview with Elena Bonner, Boston, November 2006.
73. GFA, O. Golovnia, 'Predislovie k pis'mam', ms., p. 20; interview with Yevgeniia Golovnia, Moscow, November 2004.
74. Interview with Vladimir Fomin, St Petersburg, September 2003.
75. Interview with Yevgeniia Yevangulova, St Petersburg, March 2004; E. P. Evangulova, *Krestnyi put'* (St Petersburg, 2000), pp. 7–9, 36; RGAE, f. 5208, op. 1, d. 28.
76. Interview with Boris Gavrilov, St Petersburg, June 2003.
77. 'Obydennyi NEP (Sochineniia i pis'ma shkol'nikov 20-x godov)', in *Neizvestnaia Rossia xx vek*, vol. 3 (Moscow, 1993), pp. 285–7; HP, 59 A, vol. 5, p. 25; Inkeles and Bauer, *The Soviet Citizen*, p. 216. See similarly, S. Tchouikina, 'The "Old" and "New" Intelligentsia and the Soviet State', in T. Vihavainen (ed.), *The Soviet Union – A Popular State?* (St Petersburg, 2003), pp. 99–100.
78. Inkeles and Bauer, *The Soviet Citizen*, p. 223; MSP, f. 3, op. 52, d. 2, l. 19.
79. E. Olitskaia, *Moi vospominaniia*, 2 vols. (Frankfurt, 1971), vol. 2, p. 56; MP, f. 4, op. 8, d. 2, l. 6. See also, MM, f. 12, op. 31, d. 2, ll. 1–2; MSP, f. 3, op. 53, d. 2, ll. 11–12; f. 3, op. 8, d. 2, ll. 1–7.
80. *Partiinaia etika*, p. 437; Liusin, *Pis'mo*, p. 11; MP, f. 4, op. 32, d. 4, l. 7.
81. Bonner, *Mothers and Daughters*, pp. 41, 138–9, 200–202.
82. MSP, f. 3, op. 16, d. 2, ll. 3–4, 7.
83. MSP, f. 3, op. 37, d. 2, ll. 13–15; I. Shikheeva-Gaister, *Semeinaia khronika vremen kul'ta lichnosti: 1925–1953* (Moscow, 1998), pp. 5–6.
84. V. Danilov, *Sovetskaia dokolkhoznaia derevnia: naselenie, zemlepol'zovanie, khoziaistvo* (Moscow, 1977), p. 31.
85. MSP, f. 3, op. 14, d. 3, ll. 34–5.
86. On the peasant revolution see O. Figes, *Peasant Russia, Civil War: The Volga Countryside in Revolution, 1917–1921* (Oxford, 1989).
87. MSP, f. 3, op. 14, d. 3, ll. 8, 104; G. Dobronozhenko, *Kollektivizatsiia na Severe, 1929–1932* (Syktyvkar, 1994), pp. 27–8.
88. MSP, f. 3, op. 14, d. 3, ll. 7–8.
89. MSP, f. 3, op. 14, d. 2, ll. 18, 69.
90. MSP, f. 3, op. 2, d. 2, ll. 20, 43–5.
91. VFA, E. Vittenburg, 'Pamiati P. V. Vittenburga', ms., p. 4; interviews with Yevgeniia Vittenburg, St Petersburg, August 2003, September 2004; E. Vittenburg, *Vremia poliarnykh stran* (St Petersburg, 2002), pp. 44–74.
92. RGALI, f. 1814, op. 9, d. 351, l. 3; interview with Aleksei Simonov, Moscow, November 2003.
93. RGALI, f. 1814, op. 9, d. 2613, ll. 7, 13; K. Simonov, *Segodnia i davno* (Moscow, 1978), p. 65. Family legend has it that Aleksandra blamed Mikhail for the miscarriage of a baby daughter and decided to leave him (interview with Aleksei Simonov, Moscow, June 2003).
94. RGALI, f. 1814, op. 10, d. 360; op. 9, d. 2613, ll. 3, 13.
95. RGALI, f. 1814, op. 9, d. 2698, l. 1.
96. RGALI, f. 1814, op. 10, d. 360, l. 31.

97. RGALI, f. 1814, op. 9, d. 353, l. 38; d. 337, l. 7.

98. RGALI, f. 1814, op. 10, d. 339, l. 11; op. 9, d. 1534, l. 31.

99. RGALI, f. 1814, op. 6, d. 70, l. 103; d. 170, l. 17; op. 9, d. 2613, l. 13; dd. 23, 24.

100. RGALI, f. 1814, op. 9, d. 1533, l. 18; d. 24, l. 16; d. 25, ll. 6, 17, 26; d. 1010, ll. 9–10; Simonov, *Segodnia i davno*, p. 66.

101. K. Simonov, *Glazami cheloveka moego pokoleniia* (Moscow, 1990), pp. 25–6.

102. RGALI, f. 1814, op. 9, d. 25, l. 12; d. 1010, ll. 16–19; op. 10, d. 339, l. 11.

103. SLFA, M. Laskin, 'Vospominaniia', ms., p. 2.

104. SLFA, 'Lichnyi listok po uchety kadrov' (Samuil Laskin); interviews with Fania Laskina, Moscow, November 2003, March 2005.

105. A. Ball, *Russia's Last Capitalists: The NEPmen 1921–1929* (Berkeley, 1987), p. 39.

106. Interviews with Fania Laskina, Moscow, June, November 2003, February, July 2004; interviews with Aleksei Simonov, Moscow, November 2003; SLFA, M. Laskin, 'Vospominaniia', ms., pp. 20, 21, 29.

107. Y. Slezkine, *The Jewish Century* (Berkeley, 2005), p. 217; *Vsesoiuznaia perepis' naseleniia. 1937 g. Kratkie itogi* (Moscow, 1991), p. 90.

108. A. Shternshis, *Soviet and Kosher: Jewish Popular Culture in the Soviet Union, 1923–1939* (Bloomington, 2006), pp. 35–43; J. Veidlinger, *The Moscow State Yiddish Theatre: Jewish Culture on the Soviet Stage* (Bloomington, 2000).

109. Interviews with Fania Laskina, Moscow, June, November 2003; interview with Aleksei Simonov, Moscow, November 2003; SLFA, M. Laskin, 'Vospominaniia', p. 19.

110. Interview with Rebekka (Rita) Kogan, St Petersburg, May 2003.

111. I. Slavin, *Protsess v Novikakh* (Vitebsk, 1920).

112. SFA, I. Slavina, 'Tonen'kii nerv istorii', ms., p. 11; interview with Ida Slavina, Cologne, October 2003.

113. Interview with Fania Laskina, Moscow, March 2005.

114. A. Barmine, *One Who Survived: The Life Story of a Russian Under the Soviets* (New York, 1945), pp. 124–5; H. Kuromiya, *Stalin's Industrial Revolution: Politics and Workers, 1928–1932* (Cambridge, 1988), p. 110; RGAE, f. 9455, op. 2, d. 157, l. 183.

115. V. Danilov, 'Vvedenie: sovetskaia derevnia v gody "Bol'shogo terrora"', in *Tragediia sovetskoi derevni: kollektivizatsiia i raskulachivanie. Dokumenty i materialy v 5 tomakh 1927–1939*, 5 vols. (Moscow, 1999–2004), vol. 5: *1937–1939*, Part 1, 1937, p. 9; A. Meyer, 'The War Scare of 1927', *Soviet Union/Union Soviétique*, vol. 5, no. 1 (1978), pp. 1–25; S. Fitzpatrick, 'The Foreign Threat During the First Five Year Plan', *Soviet Union/Union Soviétique*, vol. 5, no. 1 (1978), pp. 26–35; Stalin, *Sochineniia*, vol. 11, pp. 170–72.

116. R. Davies, *The Industrialization of Soviet Russia 3: The Soviet Economy in Turmoil, 1929–1930* (London, 1989), p. 76; Ball, *Russia's Last Capitalists*, pp. 76–7.

117. SLFA, 'Lichnyi listok po uchety kadrov' (Samuil Laskin); interviews with Fania Laskina, Moscow, November 2003, March 2005.

118. N. Mandelstam, *Hope Abandoned* (London, 1989), p. 551.

2: The Great Break (1928–32)

1. MSP, f. 3, op. 14, d. 2, l. 38; d. 3, l. 10.

2. AFSBVO, Arkhivno-sledstvennoe delo N. A. Golovina.

3. MSP, f. 3, op. 14, d. 2, ll. 102–4.

4. MSP, f. 3, op. 14, d. 2, l. 93.

5. AFSBVO, Arkhivno-sledstvennoe delo N. A. Golovina; MSP, f. 3, op. 14, d. 2, l. 69; d. 3, ll. 7–8.

6. GAVO, f. 407, op. 1, d. 98, l. 7.

7. AFSBVO, Arkhivno-sledstvennoe delo N. A. Golovina; MSP, f. 3, op. 14, d. 3, l. 9.

8. AFSBVO, Arkhivno-sledstvennoe delo N. A. Golovina.

9. MSP, f. 3, op. 14, d. 3, l. 11.

10. *Tragediia sovetskoi derevni: kollektivizatsiia i raskulachivanie. Dokumenty i materialy,*

5 vols. (Moscow, 1999–2004), vol. 1, pp. 36, 148–50, 228–30, 742; *Izvestiia TsK KPSS*, 1991, no. 5, pp. 196–202.

11. Cited in M. Lewin, *Russian Peasants and Soviet Power: A Study of Collectivization* (London, 1968), p. 257.

12. R. Davies, *The Soviet Economy in Turmoil, 1929–30* (London, 1989), pp. 198–9; *Pravda*, 1 September, 10 November, 1929.

13. *Pravda*, 7 November 1929; I. Stalin, *Sochineniia*, 13 vols. (Moscow, 1946–55), vol. 12, p. 174.

14. R. Davies, *The Socialist Offensive: The Collectivization of Soviet Agriculture, 1929–1930* (London, 1980), p. 111; *Tragediia sovetskoi derevni*, vol. 1, pp. 702–10, 716–27; M. Hindus, *Red Bread: Collectivization in a Russian Village* (Bloomington, 1988), p. 246.

15. Davies, *The Socialist Offensive*, p. 218; V. Kravchenko, *I Chose Freedom* (New York, 1946), p. 91.

16. M. Vareikis, 'O partiinom rukovodstve kolkhozam', *Na agrarnom fronte*, 1929, no. 8, p. 65; *Izvestiia*, 19 April 1930; GARK, f. 3, op. 1, d. 2309, l. 6.

17. Davies, *The Socialist Offensive*, p. 198.

18. M. Fainsod, *Smolensk Under Soviet Rule* (Cambridge, Mass., 1958), p. 250.

19. R. Conquest, *The Harvest of Sorrow: Soviet Collectivization and the Terror-Famine* (London, 1986), pp. 120–21; S. Fitzpatrick, *Stalin's Peasants: Resistance and Survival in the Russian Village After Collectivization* (New York, 1994), pp. 54–5.

20. GAVO, f. 22, op. 1, d. 37, l. 41; GARK, f. 136, op. 1, d. 121, l. 153; MSP, f. 3, op. 14, d. 3, l. 75; *Tragediia sovetskoi derevni*, vol. 3, pp. 66–8.

21. MP, f. 4, op. 18, d. 2, l. 44.

22. Conquest, *Harvest of Sorrow*, p. 137; *Tragediia sovetskoi derevni*, vol. 3, p. 15; Lewin, *Russian Peasants and Soviet Power*, p. 508.

23. MP, f. 4, op. 18, d. 5, l. 15.

24. MP, f. 4, op. 7, d. 2, l. 39.

25. MP, f. 4, op. 5, d. 2, l. 30.

26. VFA, 'Vospominaniia', ms., p. 8; *Komsomol'skaia pravda*, 8 September 1989, p. 2.

27. LFA, 'Roditeli', p. 24.

28. A. Zverev, *Zapiski ministra* (Moscow, 1973), p. 54.

29. L. Kopelev, *The Education of a True Believer* (London, 1981), p. 235.

30. *Tragediia sovetskoi derevni*, vol. 1, pp. 8–9; R. Davies and S. Wheatcroft, *The Years of Hunger: Soviet Agriculture, 1931–1933* (London, 2004), p. 451.

31. Davies, *The Socialist Offensive*, pp. 442–3; *Tragediia sovetskoi derevni*, vol. 3, pp. 8–9; Davies and Wheatcroft, *The Years of Hunger*, pp. 31, 37; *Politbiuro i krest'ianstvo: vysylka, spetsposelenie 1930–1940*, 2 vols. (Moscow, 2006), vol. 2, p. 43.

32. AFSBVO, Arkhivno-sledstvennoe delo N. A. Golovina; MSP, f. 3, op. 14, d. 2, ll. 82–101, 122–3; d. 3, ll. 11, 56–8.

33. Hindus, *Red Bread*, p. 142.

34. E. Foteeva, 'Coping with Revolution: The Experience of Well-to-do Russian Families', in D. Bertaux, P. Thompson and A. Rotkirch (eds.), *On Living through Soviet Russia* (London, 2004), p. 75.

35. Interviews with Olga Ramenskaia (née Zapregaeva) and Galina Petrova, Strugi Krasnye (Pskov oblast), August 2003.

36. RGAE, f. 7486, op. 37, d. 101, ll. 61–2; M. Tauger, 'The 1932 Harvest and the Soviet Famine of 1932–33', *Slavic Review*, vol. 50, no. 1 (Spring 1991); Davies and Wheatcroft, *The Years of Hunger*, pp. 181–224, 411, 415; Conquest, *Harvest of Sorrow*, pp. 3, 196, 272–3, 441. The charge of genocide is also made by J. Mace, 'The Man-Made Famine of 1933 in the Soviet Ukraine: What Happened and Why?', in I. Charny (ed.), *Toward the Understanding and Prevention of Genocide: Proceedings of the International Conference on the Holocaust and Genocide* (Boulder, 1984), p. 67; and 'Famine and Nationalism in Soviet Ukraine', *Problems of Communism*, vol. 33, no. 3 (May–June 1984), p. 39.

37. For the link between the famine and the introduction of the passport system, in December 1932, see RGASPI, f. 81, op. 3, d. 93, ll. 24–5; f. 558, op. 11, d. 45, l. 109.

38. Fitzpatrick, *Stalin's Peasants*, p. 80; Conquest, *Harvest of Sorrow*, p. 237.

39. G. Kessler, 'The Passport System and State Control over Population Flows in the Soviet Union, 1932–1940', *Cahiers du Monde Russe*, vol. 42, nos. 2–4 (2001), pp. 477–504; D. Shearer, 'Social Disorder, Mass Repression and the NKVD during the 1930s', *Cahiers du Monde Russe*, vol. 42, nos. 2–4 (2001), pp. 505, 519–20. See also D. Shearer, 'Elements Near and Alien: Passportization, Policing, and Identity in the Stalinist State, 1932–1952', *Journal of Modern History*, vol. 76 (December 2004), pp. 835–81.

40. *Tragediia sovetskoi derevni*, vol. 3, p. 63; A. Applebaum, *Gulag: A History of the Soviet Camps* (London, 2003), p. 333; GARF, f. 5207, op. 3, d. 49, l. 190; f. 8131, op. 37, d. 137, l. 4.

41. L. Viola, 'Tear the Evil From the Root: The Children of Spetspereselentsy of the North', in N. Baschmakoff and P. Fryer (eds.), *Modernization of the Russian Provinces*, special issue of *Studia Slavica Finlandensia*, 17 (April 2000), pp. 4, 44, 48–9 (translation of quotation slightly changed for clarity), 51; *Politbiuro i krest'ianstvo*, p. 47. For more on the 'special settlements' see L. Viola, *The Unknown Gulag: The Lost World of Stalin's Special Settlements* (Oxford, 2007); N. Werth, *Cannibal Island: Death in a Siberian Gulag* (Princeton, 2007).

42. MSP, f. 3, op. 14, d. 2, ll. 25–6; d. 3, ll. 12–18, 125.

43. MP, f. 4, op. 18, d. 2; d. 5, ll. 16–17.

44. MP, f. 4, op. 5, d. 2, ll. 37, 38.

45. *Politbiuro i krest'ianstvo*, pp. 467–553; Viola, *The Unknown Gulag*, p. 232.

46. MP, f. 4, op. 9, d. 5, ll. 2–7.

47. AMILO, M. A. Solomonik, 'Zapiski raskulachennoi', ts., pp. 7–34.

48. *Pravda*, 7 November 1929.

49. AFA, A. M. Alekseyev, 'Vospominaniia', p. 18.

50. See e.g. GARF, f. 9414, op. 1, d. 368, l. 115. See also the revealing hindsight comments by Aleksei Loginov, the director of the Gulag mining complex in Norilsk from 1954 to 1957, in A. Macqueen, 'Survivors', *Granta*, 64 (Winter 1998), p. 45.

51. For a classic political interpretation of the Gulag system see R. Conquest, *The Great Terror: A Reassessment* (London, 1992), and same author, *Kolyma: The Arctic Death Camps* (New York, 1978). The economic dimension has been emphasized by M. Jakobson, *Origins of the Gulag: The Soviet Prison Camp System, 1917–1934* (Lexington, 1993); G. Ivanova, *Gulag v sisteme totalitarnogo gosudarstva* (Moscow, 1997); and by several scholars in P. Gregory and V. Lazarev (eds.), *The Economics of Forced Labor: The Soviet Gulag* (Stanford, 2003). For a scholarly account of the Gulag's early years that combines both these views see O. Khlevniuk, *The History of the Gulag: From Collectivization to the Great Terror* (New Haven, 2004).

52. *Sistema ispravitel'no-trudovykh lagerei v SSSR, 1923–1960. Spravochnik* (Moscow, 1998), p. 395; Applebaum, *Gulag*, pp. 31–40.

53. GARF, f. 5446, op. 11a, d. 555, l. 32; RGASPI, f. 17, op. 3, d. 746, l. 11; *Sistema ispravitel'no-trudovykh lagerei v SSSR*, p. 38.

54. GARF, f. 9414, op. 1, d. 2920, l. 178; Applebaum, *Gulag*, pp. 62–5; C. Joyce, 'The Gulag in Karelia, 1929–41', in Gregory and Lazarev (eds.), *The Economics of Forced Labor*, p. 166; N. Baron, 'Conflict and Complicity: The Expansion of the Karelian Gulag, 1923–33', *Cahiers du Monde Russe*, vol. 42, nos. 2–4 (2001), p. 643; A. Solzhenitsyn, *The Gulag Archipelago 1918–1956: An Experiment in Literary Investigation*, 3 vols. (London, 1974–8), vol. 2, p. 99.

55. MSP, f. 3, op. 19, d. 2, ll. 1–4.

56. GARF, f. 5515, op. 33, d. 11, ll. 39–40; GASO, f. 148, op. 5, d. 26, l. 75.

57. GARF, f. 9414, op. 1, d. 3048, ll. 25–36; V. Shalamov, *Vishera: antiroman* (Moscow, 1989), p. 23.

58. D. Nordlander, 'Magadan and the Economic History of the Dalstroi in the 1930s', in Gregory and Lazarev (eds.), *The Economics of Forced Labor*, p. 110.

59. V. Shalamov, *Kolyma Tales* (London, 1994), pp. 368–9. Shalamov arrived at Kolyma in 1937, so much of what he writes about the Berzin period is based on camp legend.

60. MP, f. 4, op. 10, d. 1, ll. 1–4, 14–17.
61. A. Barmine, *One Who Survived: The Life Story of a Russian Under the Soviets* (New York, 1945), p. 196.
62. C. Ward, *Stalin's Russia* (London, 1999), p. 56; A. Smith, *I Was a Soviet Worker* (London, 1937), p. 43.
63. Interviews with Lydia Pukhova, St Petersburg, May, October 2004.
64. MSP, f. 3, op. 14, d. 2, ll. 23–4, 26, 29; d. 3, ll. 20, 63–70.
65. Y. Druzhnikov, *Informer 001: The Myth of Pavlik Morozov* (London, 1997), pp. 45–6, 155–6; C. Kelly, *Comrade Pavlik: The Rise and Fall of a Soviet Boy Hero* (London, 2005), p. 66.
66. Druzhnikov, *Informer*, pp. 19–20, 30–31, 42, 114, 152; Kelly, *Comrade*, pp. 13, 94. Kelly (who has seen the secret police file) doubts that there was a trial of Morozov. In her view, Pavlik's denunciation was fabricated by the police and the press (pp. 251–8).
67. Kelly, *Comrade*, pp. 26–72.
68. Druzhnikov, *Informer*, pp. 9–11; Kelly, *Comrade*, p. 14.
69. Kelly, *Comrade*, p. 156 (translation slightly altered for clarity).
70. See ibid., pp. 22, 26–9, 169–71.
71. M. Nikolaev, *Detdom* (New York, 1985), p. 89.
72. V. Danilov, *Sovetskaia dokolkhoznaia derevnia: naselenie, zemlepol'zovanie, khoziaistvo* (Moscow, 1977), p. 25; P. Kenez, *The Birth of the Propaganda State: Soviet Methods of Mass Mobilization, 1917–1929* (Cambridge, 1985), p. 186; *Ocherki byta derevenskoi molodezhi* (Moscow, 1924), pp. 10–12.
73. Interviews with Nina Gribelnaia, St Petersburg, March, June, October 2004; AFSBTO, Arkhivno-sledstvennoe delo F. Z. Medvedeva.
74. Conquest, *Harvest of Sorrow*, p. 295; Fitzpatrick, *Stalin's Peasants*, p. 256.
75. *Vskhody kommuny*, 19 December 1932; K. Geiger, *The Family in Soviet Russia* (Cambridge, Mass., 1968), p. 308 (translation slightly altered for clarity).
76. A. Mar'ian, *Gody moi, kak soldaty: dnevnik sel'skogo aktivista, 1925–53* (Kishinev, 1987), pp. 55, 71, 78–9.
77. Cited in Geiger, *The Family in Soviet Russia*, p. 140.
78. A. Shternshis, *Soviet and Kosher: Jewish Popular Culture, 1923–1939* (Bloomington, 2006), p. 61. My thanks to Anna Shternshis for making available a transcript of the interview with Sofia G.
79. V. Baevskii, 'Syn kulaka i vrag naroda: A. T. Tvardovskii v Smolenske v 1937 g.', in *Stalinizm v rossiiskoi provintsii: smolenskie arkhivnye dokumenty v pochtenii zarubezhnykh i rossiiskikh istorikov* (Smolensk, 1999), p. 256.
80. *Istoriia sovetskoi politicheskoi tsenzury* (Moscow, 1997), p. 109; Baevskii, 'Syn kulaka', pp. 255–8.
81. I. Tvardovskii, 'Stranitsy perezhitogo', *Iunost'*, 1988, no. 3, pp. 14, 18.
82. Ibid., p. 23.
83. Ibid., p. 26.
84. Ibid., p. 27.
85. E. Iaroslavskii (ed.), *Kak provodit' chistku partii* (Moscow, 1929), p. 10.
86. See S. Fitzpatrick, 'The Problem of Class Identity in NEP Society', in S. Fitzpatrick, A. Rabinowitch and R. Stites (eds.), *Russia in the Era of NEP: Explorations in Soviet Society and Culture* (Bloomington, 1991), pp. 21–33.
87. G. Alexopoulos, 'Portrait of a Con Artist as a Soviet Man', *Slavic Review*, vol. 57, no. 4 (Winter 1998), pp. 774–90. See further, S. Fitzpatrick, 'Making a Self for the Times: Impersonation and Imposture in 20th Century Russia', *Kritika: Explorations in Russian and Eurasian History*, vol. 2, no. 3 (Summer 2001), pp. 469–87; and same author, *Tear off the Masks! Identity and Imposture in Twentieth-Century Russia* (Princeton, 2005).
88. E. Bonner, *Mothers and Daughters* (London, 1992), p. 317.
89. S. Fitzpatrick, *Everyday Stalinism: Ordinary Life in Extraordinary Times: Soviet Russia in the 1930s* (Oxford, 1999), pp. 118–38.

90. Geiger, *The Family in Soviet Russia*, pp. 141–2. See further Fitzpatrick, *Everyday Stalinism*, p. 133.

91. B. Engel and A. Posadskaya-Vanderbeck, *A Revolution of their Own: Voices of Women in Soviet History* (Boulder, 1997), pp. 29–32 (translation slightly altered for clarity).

92. Geiger, *The Family in Soviet Russia*, p. 143; N. Novak-Decker (ed.), *Soviet Youth: Twelve Komsomol Histories* (Munich, 1959), p. 99.

93. RGALI, f. 1814, op. 10, d. 339, l. 6.

94. RGALI, f. 1814, op. 10, d. 339, l. 3.

95. K. Simonov, *Glazami cheloveka moego pokoleniia* (Moscow, 1990), pp. 29–30.

96. RGALI, f. 1814, op. 10, d. 339, l. 5.

97. Simonov, *Glazami cheloveka*, p. 32.

98. Ibid., p. 33.

99. Ibid., pp. 35–6.

100. W. Leonhard, *Child of the Revolution* (London, 1957), p. 143.

101. J. Hellbeck, 'Fashioning the Stalinist Soul: The Diary of Stepan Podlubnyi (1931–1939)', *Jahrbücher für Geschichte Osteuropas*, 44 (1996), pp. 350, 353–5 (translation slightly altered for clarity).

102. MSP, f. 3, op. 14, d. 3, l. 22.

103. MSP, f. 3, op. 14, d. 2, l. 31; d. 3, ll. 18–19.

104. MSP, f. 3, op. 14, d. 2, l. 38.

105. MSP, f. 3, op. 14, d. 2, l. 84.

106. MSP, f. 3, op. 14, d. 2, ll. 119–20.

3: The Pursuit of Happiness (1932–6)

1. SLFA, letter from Fania and Sonia Laskina to Gavril Popov, 18 May 1990; M. Laskin, 'Vospominaniia', ms., p. 31; interviews with Fania Laskina and Aleksei Simonov, Moscow, July 2004, March 2005.

2. T. Colton, *Moscow: Governing the Socialist Metropolis* (Cambridge, Mass., 1995), pp. 214, 270ff.

3. RGALI, f. 2772, op. 1, d. 93, l. 2; Colton, *Moscow*, pp. 280, 327.

4. RGALI, f. 2772, op. 1, d. 6, l. 24; d. 87, l. 5.

5. RGALI,, f. 2772, op. 1, d. 94, l. 55; D. Neutatz, *Die Moskauer Metro: Von den ersten Planen bis zur Grossbaustelle des Stalinismus (1897–1935)*, *Beitrage zur Geschichte Osteuropas* 33 (Vienna, 2001), pp. 173, 181–2; Colton, *Moscow*, p. 257; *Pravda*, 20 May 1935, p. 3.

6. RGALI, f. 2772, op. 1, d. 97, ll. 17–18.

7. RGALI, f. 2772, op. 1, d. 87, l. 87; d. 90, ll. 20–21; interview with Fania Laskina, Moscow, November 2003.

8. E. Zaleski, *Planning for Economic Growth in the Soviet Union, 1918–1932* (Chapel Hill, 1971), p. 120; N. Lampert, *The Technical Intelligentsia and the Soviet State: A Study of Soviet Managers and Technicians 1928–1935* (London, 1979), p. 71; S. Fitzpatrick, *Education and Social Mobility in the Soviet Union 1921–1934* (Cambridge, 1979), pp. 199–200; R. Davies, *The Soviet Economy in Turmoil, 1929–30* (London, 1989), pp. 134–5.

9. A good sampling of these letters can be found in *Obshchestvo i vlast' 1930-e gody: povestvovanie v dokumentakh* (Moscow, 1998) and *Stalinism as a Way of Life: A Narrative in Documents*, edited by L. Siegelbaum and A. Sokolov (New Haven, 2000).

10. See L. Viola, *Peasant Rebels Under Stalin: Collectivization and the Culture of Peasant Resistance* (Oxford, 1996); same author, 'Popular Resistance in the Stalinist 1930s: Soliloquy of a Devil's Advocate', *Kritika: Explorations in Russian and Eurasian History*, vol. 1, no. 1 (Winter 2000), pp. 45–69; J. Rossman, 'The Teikovo Cotton Workers' Strike of April 1932: Class, Gender and Identity Politics in Stalin's Russia', *Russian Review*, vol. 56, no. 1 (January 1997), pp. 44–69.

11. Interviews with Lev Molotkov, St Petersburg, May 2003; Zinaida Belikova, St Petersburg, October 2003; MUFA, A. Golovanov, 'Tetradki', ms., p. 16.

12. TsKhDMO, f. 1, op. 23, d. 1265, l. 43.

13. J. Arch Getty and O. Naumov, *The Road to Terror: Stalin and the Self-Destruction of the Bolsheviks, 1932–1939* (New Haven, 1999), pp. 52–4.

14. Ibid., p. 126.

15. S. Fitzpatrick, *The Cultural Front: Power and Culture in Revolutionary Russia* (Ithaca, 1992), pp. 160–61; same author, *Education and Social Mobility*, pp. 178, 246.

16. A. Man'kov, *Dnevniki tridtsatykh godov* (St Petersburg, 2001), pp. 82–3.

17. *Stalinism as a Way of Life*, pp. 124–5 (translation slightly altered for clarity).

18. L. Trotsky, *The Revolution Betrayed* (New York, 1972), pp. 136, 138.

19. J. Gronow, *Caviar with Champagne: Common Luxury and the Ideals of the Good Life in Stalin's Russia* (Oxford, 2003), p. 36; Fitzpatrick, *The Cultural Front*, p. 224.

20. RGASPI, f. 17, op. 120, d. 138, ll. 78–9.

21. D. Hoffman, *Stalinist Values: The Cultural Norms of Stalinist Modernity* (Ithaca, 2003), pp. 126, 131; N. Timasheff, *The Great Retreat: The Growth and Decline of Communism in Russia* (New York, 1946), pp. 317–18. On the ideological role of *kul'turnost'* ('cultured life') in the 1930s: V. Volkov, 'The Concept of *Kul'turnost'*: Notes on the Stalinist Civilizing Process', in S. Fitzpatrick (ed.), *Stalinism: New Directions* (London, 2000), pp. 210–30.

22. L. Trotsky, *Problems of Everyday Life: Creating the Foundations of a New Society in Revolutionary Russia* (London, 1973), p. 98.

23. K. Gerasimova, 'Public Privacy in the Soviet Communal Apartment', in D. Crowley and S. Reid (eds.), *Socialist Spaces: Sites of Everyday Life in the Eastern Bloc* (Oxford, 2002), p. 210; V. Buchli, *An Archaeology of Socialism* (Oxford, 1999), p. 78.

24. S. Fitzpatrick, *Everyday Stalinism: Ordinary Life in Extraordinary Times: Soviet Russia in the 1930s* (Oxford, 1999), pp. 150–55; K. Clark, *The Soviet Novel: History as Ritual* (Chicago, 1981), p. 115; J. Brooks, 'Revolutionary Lives: Public Identities in *Pravda* during the 1920s', in S. White (ed.), *New Directions in Soviet History* (Cambridge, 1992), p. 34; Timasheff, *The Great Retreat*, pp. 199–200, 202; C. Kelly, *Comrade Pavlik: The Rise and Fall of a Soviet Boy Hero* (London, 2005), p. 158.

25. Interview with Marina Ivanova, St Petersburg, March 2004.

26. I. Shikheeva-Gaister, *Semeinaia khronika vremen kul'ta lichnosti: 1925–1953* (Moscow, 1998), pp. 15–17.

27. J. Barber, 'The Worker's Day: Time Distribution in Soviet Working-Class Families, 1923–36', paper presented to the Centre for Russian and East European Studies, University of Birmingham, 1978.

28. Trotsky, *The Revolution Betrayed*, p. 156.

29. MFA, L. Makhnach, 'Oskolki bylogo s vysoty nastoiashchego', ms., pp. 2–5; interviews with Leonid Makhnach, Moscow, March, July 2004.

30. MFA, L. Makhnach, 'Otets', ms., pp. 2–4.

31. MFA, Vladimir to Maria Makhnach, 29 November 1935.

32. GFA, O. Golovnia, 'Predisloviia k pis'mam . . .' ms., pp. 3–4, 6, 12, 14, 47.

33. GFA, O. Golovnia, 'Mezhdu kratovym i otdykhom', ms., p. 1; 'Predisloviia k pis'mam . . .', ms., p. 31; A. Golovnia, 'Dnevnik'; interviews with Yevgeniia Golovnia, Moscow, March, July, October 2004.

34. GFA, 'Predisloviia k pis'mam . . .', ms., pp. 40–43, 58–61.

35. Ibid., p. 51.

36. E. Osokina, *Za fasadom 'stalinskogo izobiliia'. Raspredelenie i rynok v snabzhenii naseleniia v gody industrializatsii, 1927–41* (Moscow, 1998), pp. 128, 134; Man'kov, *Dnevniki tridtsatykh godov*, p. 272. See also Gronow, *Caviar with Champagne*, pp. 126–7.

37. A. Ledeneva, *Russia's Economy of Favours: Blat, Networking and Informal Exchange* (Cambridge, 1998); Fitzpatrick, *Everyday Stalinism*, p. 63.

38. Fitzpatrick, *Everyday Stalinism*, p. 46.

39. S. Kotkin, *Magnetic Mountain: Stalinism as a Civilization* (Berkeley, 1997), pp. 161, 171, 175–6, 477.

40. N. Mandelstam, *Hope Against Hope* (London, 1989), p. 135.

41. See e.g. MSP, f. 3, op. 36, d. 2, ll. 3–9.

42. MSP, f. 3, op. 44, d. 2, l. 57.

43. The following section is based on interviews with thirty-seven residents of communal apartments during the 1930s. See the List of Interviews.

44. K. Gerasimova, 'Public Privacy in the Soviet Communal Apartment', p. 208; V. Semenova, 'Ravenstvo v nishchete: simvolicheskoe znachenie "kommunalok" ', in *Sud'ba liudei: Rossiia xx vek. Biografii semei kak ob'ekt sotsiologicheskogo issledovaniia* (Moscow, 1996), p. 374.

45. K. Gerasimova, 'Public Spaces in the Communal Apartment', in G. Rittersporn, M. Rolfe and J. Behrends (eds.), *Public Spheres in Soviet-Type Societies* (Sonderdruck, 2003), p. 167; I. Utekhin, *Ocherki kommunal'nogo byta* (Moscow, 2001), pp. 148–9.

46. Interviews with Aleksei Iurasovsky, Moscow, March, June 2005.

47. P. Messana, *Kommunalka. Une histoire de l'Union soviétique à travers l'appartement communautaire* (Paris, 1995), pp. 16–17. See also R. Berg, *Sukhovei. Vospominaniia genetika* (Moscow, 2003), p. 140.

48. SSEES, Pahl-Thompson Collection, E. V. Mamlin, pp. 1–7.

49. Interview with Minora Novikova, Moscow, May 2005.

50. Interview with Nina Paramonova, St Petersburg, June 2005.

51. Interview with Ninel Reifshneider, Moscow, April 2005.

52. MSP, f. 1, op. 16, d. 2, ll. 65–6; op. 23, d. 2, l. 93; Berg, *Sukhovei*, p. 141; interview with Elena Baigulova, St Petersburg, May 2005; SSEES, Pahl-Thompson Collection, E. V. Mamlin, p. 4.

53. Gerasimova, 'Public Spaces', pp. 185–6.

54. Interview with Nina Paramonova, St Petersburg, June 2005.

55. V. Semystiaha, 'The Role and Place of Secret Collaborators in the Informational Activity of the GPU–NKVD in the 1920s and 1930s (on the Basis of Materials of the Donbass Region)', *Cahiers du Monde Russe*, vol. 42, nos. 2–4 (2001), pp. 231–44. See also P. Holquist, ' "Information is the Alpha and Omega of Our Work": Bolshevik Surveillance in its Pan-European Context', *Journal of Modern History*, 69 (September 1997), pp. 415–50.

56. Interview with Nina Paramonova, St Petersburg, June 2005; M. Baitalsky, *Notebooks for the Grandchildren: Recollections of a Trotskyist Who Survived the Stalin Terror* (New Jersey, 1995), p. 144.

57. Interview with Natalia Grigoreva, St Petersburg, May 2005.

58. Interview with anonymous, Moscow, March 2003.

59. Interview with Yevgeniia Moiseyenko, St Petersburg, September 2005.

60. Interview with Minora Novikova, Moscow, May 2005; SSEES, Pahl-Thompson Collection, G. E. Mamlina, p. 6.

61. Interview with Nina Paramonova, St Petersburg, June 2005; interview with Yevgeniia Moiseyenko, St Petersburg, September 2005; MSP, f. 3, op. 16, d. 2, ll. 71–2.

62. Gerasimova, 'Public Privacy', p. 224.

63. Interviews with Inna Shikheyeva (Gaister), Moscow, May 2005; Elizaveta Chechik, Moscow, April 2005; Minora Novikova, Moscow, May 2005; Maia Rodak, Moscow, October 2004; Tatiana Vasileva, St Petersburg, May 2005; Elena Baigulova, St Petersburg, May 2005.

64. Interviews with Elizaveta Chechik, Moscow, April 2005; Inna Shikheyeva (Gaister), Moscow, May 2005; Minora Novikova, Moscow, May 2005; SSEES, Pahl-Thompson Collection, E. V. Gavrilova, pp. 6–7; G. E. Mamlina, p. 12; MSP, f. 3, op. 16, d. 2, ll. 64–5.

65. SSEES, Pahl-Thompson Collection, A. A. Dobriakova, pp. 5–8.

66. Interview with Aleksei Iurasovsky, Moscow, March 2005. See also E. A. Skriabina, *Stranitsy zhizni* (Moscow, 1994), p. 84.

67. Interviews with Inna Shikheyeva (Gaister), Moscow, May 2005; Elizaveta Chechik, Moscow, April 2005; Minora Novikova, Moscow, May 2005; Maia Rodak, Moscow, October 2004; Tatiana Vasileva, St Petersburg, May 2005; SSEES, Pahl-Thompson Collection, E. V. Gavrilova, p. 7; E. V. Mamlin, p. 12.

68. Utekhin, *Ocherki*, pp. 94–5, 151, 153, 166; interview with Galina Markelova, St Petersburg, June 2004. See also MM, f. 12, op. 7, d. 2, ll. 12–15; TsGASP, f. 7384, op. 42, d. 343, ll. 421–4.

69. N. Lebina, *Povsednevnaia zhizn' sovetskogo goroda: normy i anomalii, 1920–1930 gody* (St Petersburg, 1999), p. 195; interview with Elizaveta Chechik, Moscow, April 2005.

70. Interviews with Minora Novikova, Moscow, May 2005; Inna Shikheyeva (Gaister), Moscow, May 2005.

71. K. Mannheim, *Ideology and Utopia: An Introduction to the Sociology of Knowledge* (London, 1991), pp. 184, 219. See also A. Kelly, 'In the Promised Land', *New York Review of Books*, vol. 48, no. 19 (29 November 2001), from which I have drawn for this paragraph.

72. N. Patolichev, *Ispytaniia na zrelost'* (Moscow, 1977), p. 170.

73. V. Petrov, *Byt derevni v sochineniiakh shkol'nikov* (Moscow, 1927); T. Egorov, *Kem khotiat byt' nashi deti? Sbornik detskikh pisem dlia ottsov* (Moscow and Leningrad, 1929); G. Petelin, *Dadim slovo shkol'niku* (Moscow, 1931).

74. MSP, f. 3, op. 47, d. 2, l. 7.

75. R. Orlova, *Vospominaniia o neproshedshem vremeni* (Ann Arbor, 1983), p. 30.

76. *Izvestiia*, 14 July 1935, p. 2; A. Tertz, *On Socialist Realism* (New York, 1960), p. 78; *Soviet Writers' Congress, 1934: The Debate of Socialist Realism and Modernism* (London, 1977), p. 157; S. Fitzpatrick, *The Cultural Front: Power and Culture in Revolutionary Russia* (Ithaca, 1992), p. 217; W. Leonhard, *Child of the Revolution* (London, 1957), p. 22.

77. N. Kaminskaya, *Final Judgment: My Life as a Soviet Defence Attorney* (New York, 1982), pp. 18–21.

78. *The Correspondence of Boris Pasternak and Olga Freidenberg, 1910–1954* (New York, 1982), p. 154; N. Mandelstam, *Hope Against Hope: A Memoir* (London, 1989), p. 115.

79. L. Kopelev, *No Jail for Thought* (London, 1975), pp. 11–13.

80. Leonhard, *Child of the Revolution*, p. 81.

81. D. Shearer, 'Social Disorder, Mass Repression and the NKVD During the 1930s', *Cahiers du Monde Russe*, vol. 42, nos. 2–4 (2001), pp. 505–34; P. Hagenloh, ' "Socially Harmful Elements" and the Great Terror', in S. Fitzpatrick (ed.), *Stalinism: New Directions* (London, 2000), pp. 286–308.

82. RGALI, f. 1604, op. 1, d. 21, l. 32; A. Avdeenko, 'Otluchenie', *Znamiia*, no. 3 (1989), p. 11.

83. C. Ruder, *Making History for Stalin: The Story of the Belomor Canal* (Gainesville, Fl., 1998), p. 50; G. Smith, *D. S. Mirsky: A Russian-English Life, 1890–1939* (Oxford, 2000), p. 209; Avdeenko, 'Otluchenie', p. 18; *Belomorsko-baltiiskii kanal imeni Stalina: istoriia stroitel'stva 1931–1934 gg.* (Moscow, 1934).

84. A. Starkov, *Mikhail Zoshchenko: sud'ba khudozhnika* (Moscow, 1990), p. 139.

85. S. and B. Webb, *Soviet Communism: A New Civilization?*, 2 vols. (London, 1935), vol. 2, p. 591; Ivan Chukhin, *Kanalo-armeitsy: istoriia stroitel'stva Belomorkanala v dokumentakh, tsifrakh, faktakh, fotografiiakh, svidetel'stvakh ychastnikov i ochevidtsev* (Petrozavodsk, 1990), p. 37.

86. Ruder, *Making History for Stalin*, pp. 56–9.

87. Avdeenko, 'Otluchenie', p. 8; RGALI, f. 1814, op. 1, d. 944, ll. 6, 14.

88. RGALI, f. 1814, op. 10, d. 339; d. 360, ll. 33, 35–6. On Simonov and Pudovkin: K. Simonov, 'O Vsevolode Illarionoviche Pudovkine', in *Pudovkin v vospominaniiakh sovremennikov* (Moscow, 1989), pp. 274–81.

89. K. Simonov, *Glazami cheloveka moego pokoleniia* (Moscow, 1990), pp. 39–41.

90. RGALI, f. 1814, op. 10, d. 360, l. 34; Simonov, *Glazami*, pp. 39, 41, 45.

91. RGALI, f. 1814, op. 1, d. 1, ll. 13–14, 60; d. 848, l. 5; op. 10, d. 360, ll. 34–5.

92. RGALI, f. 1814, op. 10, d. 339, l. 4.

93. RGALI, f. 1814, op. 10, d. 360, l. 36.

94. RGALI, f. 632, op. 1, d. 1; d. 16, ll. 5, 12.

95. N. Tipot (Sokolova), 'Dnevnik', private archive.

96. RGALI, f. 632, op. 1, d. 15, ll. 23–7; d. 16, ll. 7–8; f. 1814, op. 9, d. 2606, l. 6; op. 10, d. 339, l. 11; interview with Lazar Lazarev, Moscow, November 2003.

97. L. Lazarev, *Konstantin Simonov. Ocherk zhizni i tvorchestva* (Moscow, 1985), pp. 18, 35; A. Karaganov, *Konstantin Simonov vblizi i na rasstoianii* (Moscow, 1987), pp. 9, 10; RGALI, f. 1814, op. 1, d. 71.

98. Simonov, *Glazami*, pp. 42–5; RGALI, f. 1814, op. 9, d. 25, l. 13; d. 1010, ll. 16–19, 25.

99. Simonov, *Glazami*, pp. 46–7.

100. Ibid., pp. 48–9.

101. Ibid., p. 47.

102. TsGAIPD, f. 1278, op. 1, d. 439869, l. 4.

103. SFA, I. Slavina, 'Tonen'kii nerv istorii', ms., pp. 16–17, 30; interview with Ida Slavina, Cologne, September 2003.

104. I. Slavin, *Vreditel'stvo na fronte sovetskogo ugolovnogo prava* (Moscow, 1931), p. 76; SFA, I. Slavina, 'Put' na plakhu', ms., p. 29.

105. I. Slavin, 'K voprosu o prinuditel'nykh rabotakh bez soderzhaniia pod strazhei', *Ezhenedel'nik sovetskoi iustitsii*, 1922, no. 36; 'Proizvodstvennye tovarishcheskie sudi i revoliutsiia', *Sovetskoe gosudarstvo i pravo*, 1931, no. 7; 'Nekotorye voprosy praktiki proizvodstvenno-tovarishcheskikh sudov', *Sovetskoe gosudarstvo i pravo*, 1932, nos. 5–6.

106. SPbF ARAN, f. 229, op. 1, d. 100, ll. 44–5.

107. TsGAIPD, f. 1816, op. 2, d. 5095, l. 66.

108. SPbF ARAN, f. 229, op. 1, d. 93, ll. 4, 6; d. 100, l. 67; d. 120, ll. 7–12; d. 122, ll. 6–10; SFA, 'Put' na plakhu', pp. 79–81; interviews with Ida Slavina, Cologne, June, October, 2003; TsGAIPD, f. 563, op. 1, d. 1467, l. 117.

109. S. Wheatcroft, 'The Scale and Nature of German and Soviet Repression and Mass Killings, 1930–45', *Europe-Asia Studies*, vol. 48, no. 8 (1996), pp. 1338–40.

110. Interview with Yevgeniia Vittenburg, St Petersburg, August 2003; E. Vittenburg, *Vremia poliarnykh stran* (St Petersburg, 2002), pp. 106–12.

111. I. Flige, 'Osoblag Vaigach', *Vestnik Memoriala*, no. 6 (St Petersburg, 2001), pp. 12–19.

112. VFA, letter from Zinaida to Veronika and Valentina Vittenburg, 26 August 1933.

113. Interview with Yevgeniia Vittenburg, St Petersburg, August 2003.

114. Interview with Yevgeniia Vittenburg, St Petersburg, September 2004.

115. VFA, 'Sotsdogovor ambulatornogo vracha sanotdela vaigachskoi ekspeditsii NKVD Vittenburg Z.I. ot 2 marta 1933'; letter from Zinaida to Veronika and Valentina Vittenburg, undated [1935]; interview with Yevgeniia Vittenburg, St Petersburg, September 2004.

116. Interviews with Yevgeniia Vittenburg, St Petersburg, August 2003, September 2004; VFA, letter from Zinaida to Yevgeniia Vittenburg, 3 November 1935; 'Dnevnik v pis'makh P. V. Vittenburga docheri Evgenii', p. 54; Vittenburg, *Vremia poliarnykh stran*, p. 134.

117. VFA, letter from Pavel to Yevgeniia Vittenburg, 13 September 1936; 'Dnevnik v pis'makh P. V. Vittenburga docheri Evgenii', ms., p. 7.

118. MM, f. 1, op. 4, Trudovaia kniga; f. 12, op. 9, d. 2.

119. MM, f. 12, op. 2, d. 2, l. 13; d. 3, l. 43.

120. S. Rosefield, 'Stalinism in Post-Communist Perspective: New Evidence on Killings, Forced Labour and Economic Growth in the 1930s', *Europe-Asia Studies*, vol. 48, no. 6 (1996), p. 969.

121. MSP, f. 3, op. 1, d. 2, ll. 1–14; d. 5, ll. 1–5, 12–15; *Pravda*, 3 November 1929, p. 5; P. Broué, *Trotsky* (Paris, 1988), p. 638.

122. MSP, f. 3, op. 1, d. 5, ll. 10, 19.

123. MSP, f. 3, op. 1, d. 4 (citations from the letters can be found by their date).
124. MSP, f. 3, op. 1, d. 2, ll. 21, 59.
125. MSP, f. 3, op. 1, d. 2, l. 58.
126. MSP, f. 3, op. 1, d. 2, l. 50.
127. MSP, f. 3, op. 1, d. 2, l. 52.
128. MSP, f. 3, op. 1, d. 5, ll. 7, 8, 21, 25–6.
129. *Stalin's Letters to Molotov*, edited by L. Lih, O. Naumov and O. Khlevniuk, translated by C. Fitzpatrick (New Haven, 1995), p. 200.
130. RGAE, f. 769, op. 1, d. 23–35.
131. RGAE, f. 769, op. 1, d. 25, l. 10.
132. RGAE, f. 769, op. 1, d. 31, l. 9.
133. RGAE, f. 769, op. 1, d. 13.
134. RGAE, f. 769, op. 1, d. 29, l. 44.

4: The Great Fear (1937–8)

1. *Pravda*, 31 January 1932; *Golgofa. Po materialam arkhivno-sledstvennogo dela no. 603 na Sokolovu-Piatnitskuiu Iu. I.*, ed. V. I. Piatnitskii (St Petersburg, 1993), p. 42.
2. Ibid., pp. 8–9.
3. V. Piatnitskii, *Zagovor protiv Stalina* (Moscow, 1998), p. 198.
4. *Golgofa*, p. 9.
5. J. Haslam, 'Political Opposition to Stalin and the Origins of the Terror, 1932–1936', *Historical Journal*, vol. 29, no. 2 (June 1986), p. 412. See also same author, 'The Soviet Union, the Comintern and the Demise of the Popular Front, 1936–39', in H. Graham and O. Preston (eds.), *The Popular Front in Europe* (London, 1987), pp. 152–60; K. McDermott, 'Stalinist Terror in the Comintern: New Perspectives', *Journal of Contemporary History*, vol. 30, no. 1 (January 1995), pp. 111–30.
6. *The Diary of Georgi Dimitrov, 1933–1949* (New Haven, 2003), p. 110; McDermott, 'Stalinist Terror', p. 118.
7. B. Starkov, 'The Trial That Was Not Held', *Europe-Asia Studies*, vol. 46, no. 8 (1994), p. 1303.
8. *Golgofa*, pp. 20, 21, 24; interviews with Vladimir Piatnitsky, St Petersburg, September 2005.
9. *Golgofa*, pp. 62–3.
10. Ibid., pp. 25, 39–40.
11. Ibid., pp. 26, 34; interviews with Vladimir Piatnitsky, St Petersburg, September 2005.
12. M. Ellman, 'Soviet Repression Statistics: Some Comments', *Europe-Asia Studies*, vol. 54, no. 7 (November 2002); H. Kuromiya, 'Accounting for the Great Terror', *Jahbücher für Geschichte Osteuropas*, 53 (2005), p. 88; A. Applebaum, *Gulag: A History of the Soviet Camps* (London, 2003), pp. 516, 519. The figures for 1929–32 are from V. Popov, 'Gosudarstvennyi terror v sovetskoi Rossii. 1923–1953 gg.', *Otechestvennyi arkhiv*, 1992, no. 2, p. 28.
13. J. Getty, *Origins of the Great Purges: The Soviet Communist Party Reconsidered, 1933–1938* (Cambridge, 1985).
14. P. Solomon, *Soviet Criminal Justice Under Stalin* (Cambridge, Mass., 1996), chap. 5; O. Khlevniuk, 'The Politburo, Penal Policy and "Legal Reforms" in the 1930s', in P. Solomon (ed.), *Reforming Justice in Russia, 1864–1996: Power, Culture, and the Limits of Legal Order* (Armonk, 1997), pp. 190–206.
15. J. Getty, ' "Excesses Are Not Permitted": Mass Terror and Stalinist Governance in the Late 1930s', *Russian Review*, 61 (2002), no. 1, pp. 113–38.
16. S. Fitzpatrick, 'Varieties of Terror', in same author (ed.), *Stalinism: New Directions* (London, 2000), p. 258. For a similar view: B. McLoughlin and K. McDermott, 'Rethinking Stalinist Terror', in same authors (eds.), *Stalin's Terror: High Politics and Mass Repression in the Soviet Union* (New York, 2003), pp. 1–18.

17. O. Khlevniuk, 'The Reasons for the "Great Terror": The Foreign Political Aspect', *Annali della Fondazione Giangiacomo Feltrinelli*, vol. 34 (1998), pp. 163ff.; same author, 'The Objectives of the Great Terror, 1937–38', in J. Cooper, M. Perrie and E. Rees (eds.), *Soviet History, 1917–1953: Essays in Honour of R. W. Davies* (London, 1995), pp. 158–76. See also H. Kuromiya, 'Accounting for the Great Terror', upon which I have drawn for the following paragraphs.

18. Kuromiya, 'Accounting for the Great Terror', p. 94; S. Payne, *The Spanish Civil War, the Soviet Union, and Communism* (New Haven, 2004), p. 309.

19. S. Allilueva, *Twenty Letters to a Friend* (London, 1967), pp. 88–9; J. Getty and O. Naumov, *The Road to Terror: Stalin and the Self-Destruction of the Bolsheviks, 1932–1939* (New Haven, 1999), pp. 157, 256–7.

20. V. Kravchenko, *I Chose Freedom* (London, 1947), p. 213.

21. V. Rogovin, *Partiia rasstreliannykh* (Moscow, 1997), pp. 487–9; *Reabilitatsia. Kak eto bylo*, 3 vols. (Moscow, 2000–2004), vol. 1, p. 30; O. Suvenirov, *Tragediia RKKA, 1938–1938* (Moscow, 1998), p. 315.

22. *Istochnik*, 1994, no. 3, p. 80; N. Khrushchev, *Khrushchev Remembers* (London, 1971), p. 283; M. Jansen and N. Petrov, *Stalin's Loyal Executioner: People's Commissar Nikolai Ezhov, 1895–1940* (Stanford, 2002), pp. 89, 201.

23. F. Chuev, *Sto sorok besed s Molotovym* (Moscow, 1991), pp. 390, 413; Piatnitskii, *Zagovor protiv Stalina*, p. 65; Kuromiya, 'Accounting for the Great Terror', p. 96.

24. *Tragediia sovetskoi derevni: kollektivizatsiia i raskulachivanie. Dokumenty i materialy*, 5 vols. (Moscow, 1999–2004), vol. 5: *1937–1939*, Part 1, 1937, pp. 32, 33, 46, 54, 387; Kuromiya, 'Accounting for the Great Terror', pp. 92–3.

25. N. Petrov and A. Roginskii, ' "Pol'skaia operatsiia" NKVD 1937–1938 gg.', in L. Eremina (ed.) *Repressii protiv poliakov i pol'skikh grazhdan* (Moscow, 1996), pp. 40–43. On the 'national operations' as a form of 'ethnic cleansing' see T. Martin, *The Affirmative Action Empire: Nations and Nationalism in the Soviet Union, 1923–1939* (Ithaca, 2001), pp. 328–43.

26. V. Garros, N. Korenevskaya and T. Lahusen (eds.), *Intimacy and Terror* (New York, 1995), p. 357.

27. Interview with Vladimir Piatnitsky, St Petersburg, September 2005.

28. R. Thurston, *Life and Terror in Stalin's Russia* (New Haven, 1996), pp. 72–7.

29. V. Frid, *58½: zapiski lagernogo pridurka* (Moscow, 1996), p. 91.

30. Interview with Viacheslav Kolobkov, St Petersburg, May 2004.

31. E. Ginzburg, *Journey into the Whirlwind* (New York, 1967), pp. 21–2.

32. E. Bonner, *Mothers and Daughters* (London, 1992), p. 263.

33. MP, f. 4, op. 4, d. 2, ll. 2, 25; op. 5, d. 5, ll. 3–4; L. Il'ina, *Moi otets protiv NKVD* (St Petersburg, 1998), pp. 16–21.

34. MSP, f. 3, op. 12, d. 2, ll. 35–40, 116–17.

35. SFA, I. Slavina, 'Tonen'kii nerv istorii', ms., pp. 9–13.

36. R. Conquest, *The Great Terror: A Reassessment* (London, 1992), pp. 75, 87, 89, 127.

37. V. Bronshtein, 'Stalin and Trotsky's Relatives in Russia', in T. Brotherstone and P. Dukes (eds.), *The Trotsky Reappraisal* (Edinburgh, 1992), pp. 8–15.

38. Getty and Naumov, *The Road to Terror*, pp. 486–7; Chuev, *Sto sorok besed*, p. 415.

39. *Golgofa*, p. 29.

40. See also MSP, f. 3, op. 34, d. 2; MP, f. 4, op. 16, dd. 2, 3.

41. *Golgofa*, pp. 31, 34, 35–6, 43, 45; interview with Vladimir Piatnitsky, St Petersburg, August 2005.

42. *Golgofa*, p. 37.

43. M. Prishvin, 'Dnevnik 1937 goda', *Oktiabr'*, 1995, no. 9, p. 168.

44. Conquest, *The Great Terror*, p. 256; M. Prishvin and V. Prishvin, *My s toboi. Dnevnik liubvi* (Moscow, 1996), p. 13.

45. MP, f. 4, op. 25, d. 2, ll. 9–10.

46. MSP, f. 3, op. 8, d. 2, l. 9.

47. MP, f. 4, op. 6, d. 2, ll. 18, 37.
48. E. Gerstein, *Moscow Memoirs* (London, 2004), p. 79.
49. MM, f. 12, op. 14, d. 2, ll. 15–16.
50. MM, f. 12, op. 7, d. 2, l. 23.
51. Gerstein, *Moscow Memoirs*, p. 214.
52. MP, f. 4, op. 8. d. 2, l. 22.
53. MM, f. 12, op. 28, d. 2, ll. 12, 35–6.
54. GFA, O. Golovnia, 'Dom na Vasil'evskoi', ms., pp. 2–3.
55. Prishvin, 'Dnevnik 1937 goda', *Oktiabr'*, 1995, no. 9, p. 158.
56. A. Man'kov, *Dnevniki tridtsatykh godov* (St Petersburg, 2001), p. 144.
57. Prishvin, 'Dnevnik 1937 goda', *Oktiabr'*, 1995, no. 9, p. 165.
58. For a different view of the role of diary-writing see the works of Jochen Hellbeck cited in the Introduction.
59. ' "Zhizn' stala veselei . . ." Iz dnevnika 1936 goda', *Oktiabr'*, 1993, no. 10, p. 4; M. Prishvin, 'Dnevnik 1937 goda', *Oktiabr'*, 1994, no. 11, p. 144; same author, *Sobranie sochinenii*, 8 vols. (Moscow, 1986), vol. 8, p. 473.
60. J. Hellbeck, *Revolution on My Mind: Writing a Diary Under Stalin* (Cambridge, Mass., 2006), pp. 304–5, 306, 308–9, 311–22; RGALI, f. 2172, op. 3, d. 5, l. 249.
61. E. Evangulova, *Krestnyi put'* (St Petersburg, 2000), pp. 68, 81, 83.
62. Man'kov, *Dnevniki*, p. 59.
63. Prishvin and Prishvin, *My s toboi*, pp. 22–3, 35, 37.
64. MM, f. 12, op. 25, d. 2, l. 136; Kravchenko, *I Chose Freedom*, p. 448; Thurston, *Life and Terror in Stalin's Russia*, p. 71. A lower figure of 10,000 informers for Moscow in 1930 is given by an OGPU official cited in G. Agabekov, *GPU: zapiski chekista* (Moscow, 1931). See also V. Semystiaha, 'The Role and Place of Secret Collaborators in the Informational Activity of the GPU-NKVD in the 1920s and 1930s (on the Basis of Materials of the Donbass Region)', *Cahiers du Monde Russe*, vol. 42, nos. 2–4 (2001), pp. 231–44.
65. On these low-level networks of informers see C. Hooper, 'Terror from Within: Participation and Coercion in Soviet Power, 1924–64' (Ph.D. dissertation, Princeton University, 2003), pp. 154–64.
66. K. Simonov, *Glazami cheloveka moego pokoleniia* (Moscow, 1990), p. 50.
67. W. Leonhard, *Child of the Revolution* (London, 1957), pp. 100–102.
68. Frid, *58½*, pp. 160–61.
69. MP, f. 4, op. 9, d. 2, ll. 25–7; d. 5, ll. 8–9.
70. O. Adamova-Sliuzberg, *Put'* (Moscow, 2002), p. 172.
71. TsAODM, f. 369, op. 1, d. 161, ll. 1–2.
72. Interviewed in *The Hand of Stalin* (Part 2), October Films, 1990.
73. Adamova-Sliuzberg, *Put'*, pp. 19–20.
74. Cited in Thurston, *Life and Terror in Stalin's Russia*, p. 154.
75. MSP, f. 3, op. 16, d. 2, ll. 3–4, 63–5.
76. Interview with Lev Molotkov, St Petersburg, May 2003.
77. N. Adler, *Beyond the Soviet System: The Gulag Survivor* (New Brunswick, 2002), p. 216; I. Shikheeva-Gaister, *Semeinaia khronika vremen kul'ta lichnosti: 1925–1953* (Moscow, 1998), p. 32.
78. Conquest, *The Great Terror*, p. 222; V. Kozlov, 'Denunciation and Its Functions in Soviet Governance: A Study of Denunciations and Their Bureaucratic Handling from Soviet Police Archives, 1944–1953', *Journal of Modern History*, vol. 68, no. 4 (December 1996), p. 875. On apartments see V. Buchli, *An Archaeology of Socialism* (Oxford, 1999), pp. 113–17.
79. MSP, f. 3, op. 36, d. 2, ll. 3, 13–14; d. 3, ll. 4–6.
80. Simonov, *Glazami*, pp. 55, 62.
81. RGALI, f. 1814, op. 9, d. 5, ll. 65–7; interview with Lazar Lazarev, Moscow, November 2003.

82. RGALI, f. 632, op. 1, d. 12, ll. 28–9; d. 13, l. 10; interview with Semyon Vorovsky, Moscow, June 2005.

83. RGALI, f. 631, op. 15, d. 242, ll. 6–8; f. 618, op. 3, d. 27, ll. 5–14.

84. RGALI, f. 653, op. 1, d. 1087, l. 4.

85. RGALI, f. 631, op. 15, d. 226, l. 72.

86. RGALI, f. 1814, op. 1, d. 437, ll. 1–7.

87. RGALI, f. 632, op. 1, d. 15, l. 23.

88. RGALI, f. 632, op. 1, d. 12, l. 13.

89. E. Dolmatovskii, *Bylo: zapiski poeta* (Moscow, 1982); interview with Lazar Lazarev, Moscow, November 2003.

90. RGALI, f. 1812, op. 1, d. 96, l. 7.

91. RGALI, f. 631, op. 15, d. 265, l. 34.

92. A. Granovsky, *All Pity Choked: The Memoirs of a Soviet Secret Agent* (London, 1952), p. 101.

93. Ginzburg, *Journey into the Whirlwind*, pp. 90–92.

94. A. Gorbatov, *Years off My Life* (London, 1964), pp. 103–4.

95. Conquest, *The Great Terror*, pp. 203–4. It may be that part of Iakir's motives may have been to save his family (who were all later shot or sent to camps).

96. F. Beck and W. Godin, *Russian Purge and the Extraction of Confession* (London, 1951), p. 86.

97. S. Vilenskii (ed.), *Till My Tale is Told* (London, 1999), pp. 124–6.

98. Interviewed in *The Hand of Stalin* (Part 2), October Films, 1990.

99. Kravchenko, *I Chose Freedom*, p. 206. See further: S. Davies, *Popular Opinion in Stalin's Russia: Terror, Propaganda and Dissent, 1934–1941* (Cambridge, 1997), pp. 131–5; Thurston, *Life and Terror in Stalin's Russia*, pp. 143–6.

100. Interview with Ida Slavina, Cologne, June 2003.

101. MM, f. 12, op. 21, d. 2, ll. 28–9; op. 32, d. 2, l. 17.

102. MP, f. 4, op. 18, d. 2, ll. 32–5, 49–50.

103. VFA, letter from Pavel to Yevgeniia Vittenburg, [February] 1937.

104. TsMAMLS, f. 68, op. 1, d. 76, l. 77; d. 124, l. 19; d. 141, l. 88.

105. N. Kaminskaya, *Final Judgment: My Life as a Soviet Defence Attorney* (New York, 1982), p. 19.

106. MM, f. 12, op. 23, d. 2, ll. 37–8.

107. Simonov, *Glazami*, pp. 54–5.

108. Adamova-Sliuzberg, *Put'*, p. 11.

109. *Deti GULAGa 1918–1956, Rossiia XX vek. Dokumenty* (Moscow, 2002), pp. 272–3.

110. O. Khlevniuk, 'The Objectives of the Great Terror, 1937–1938', in D. Hoffman (ed.), *Stalinism* (London, 2003), p. 98; Jansen and Petrov, *Stalin's Loyal Executioner*, pp. 187–8, 192.

111. SLFA, Mark Laskin, 'Vospominaniia', ms., p. 41.

112. Simonov, *Glazami*, p. 59.

113. V. Shentalinsky, *The KGB's Literary Archive* (London, 1993), pp. 186–7.

114. RGALI, f. 1712, op. 1, d. 21, l. 4, op. 4, d. 8, l. 37.

115. RGALI, f. 1712, op. 3, d. 13, l. 1.

116. GARF, f. 5446, op. 82, d. 66, ll. 287–8. See also L. Siegelbaum and A. Sokolov (eds.), *Stalinism as a Way of Life: A Narrative in Documents* (Yale, 2000), pp. 237–41.

117. Adamova-Sliuzberg, *Put'*, pp. 77–8.

118. P. Solomon, *Soviet Criminal Justice under Stalin* (Cambridge, 1996), p. 234.

119. M. Shreider, *NKVD iznutri: zapiski chekista* (Moscow, 1995), p. 42.

120. Ibid., p. 91.

121. Ibid., pp. 104–5.

122. Ibid., p. 120.

123. Bonner, *Mothers and Daughters*, p. 304.

124. A. Solzhenitsyn, *The Gulag Archipelago 1918–1956: An Experiment in Literary Investigation*, 3 vols. (London, 1974–8), vol. 2, p. 637.
125. Adamova-Sliuzberg, *Put'*, pp. 11–12.
126. MSP, f. 3, op. 37, d. 2, l. 93.
127. MSP, f. 3, op. 12, d. 2, ll. 42–3.
128. MP, f. 4, op. 6, d. 2, ll. 6–10, 39–41, 45–9; d. 3, ll. 1–6.
129. *Golgofa*, pp. 30, 32, 35; interview with Vladimir Piatnitsky, St Petersburg, August 2005.
130. MSP, f. 3, op. 18, d. 1, l. 1; d. 2, ll. 2–3, 7–10.
131. MP, f. 4, op. 25, d. 2, ll. 7–8, 13–16, 18, 19, 21–2, 26–30.
132. See e.g. MSP, f. 3, op. 4, d. 2; MP, f. 4, op. 4, d. 2; V. Shapovalov (ed.), *Remembering the Darkness: Women in Soviet Prisons* (Lanham, 2001), pp. 228–9; N. Ulanovskaia and M. Ulanovskaia, *Istoriia odnoi sem'i* (New York, 1982), p. 135.
133. MM, f. 12, op. 2, d. 2, ll. 16–20.
134. O. Liubchenko, 'Arbat 30, kvartira 58', *Istochnik*, 1993, nos. 5–6, pp. 26–9.
135. SFA, I. Slavina, 'Tonen'kii nerv istorii', ms., p. 31; interview with Ida Slavina, Cologne, June 2003.
136. Bonner, *Mothers and Daughters*, pp. 254–5 (where Bonner mistakenly names the school director as Klavdia Vasileevna); interview with Elena Bonner, Boston, November 2006.
137. Interview with Ida Slavina, Cologne, September 2004.
138. MSP, f. 3, op. 46, d. 2, ll. 17–18, 42–3.
139. MP, f. 4, op. 18, d. 2, l. 53.
140. MSP, f. 3, op. 37, d. 2, ll. 23–5, 37.
141. MM, f. 1, op. 1, d. 169 (Sofia to Vladimir Antonov-Ovseyenko, 16 October 1937).
142. GARF, f. 7523, op. 123, d. 202, ll. 16–19.
143. GARF, f. 5446, op. 26, d. 105, ll. 35–6.
144. Adamova-Sliuzberg, *Put'*, pp. 60–63.
145. MP, f. 4, op. 6, d. 2, ll. 37–8.
146. MSP, f. 3, op. 4, d. 2, l. 24.
147. *The Diary of Nina Kosterina* (London, 1972), pp. 35, 44, 53, 85, 163, 165.
148. M. Baitalsky, *Notebooks for the Grandchildren: Recollections of a Trotskyist Who Survived the Stalin Terror* (New Jersey, 1995), pp. 334–5.
149. MSP, f. 3, op. 10, d. 1, l. 1; d. 3, ll. 7, 10–11.
150. *Golgofa*, pp. 41, 46, 53–4; interview with Vladimir Piatnitsky, St Petersburg, September 2005.
151. *Golgofa*, pp. 33, 42.
152. Ibid., pp. 41–2.
153. Interview with Vladimir Piatnitsky, St Petersburg, September 2005. She was receiving psychiatric help from May 1938 (see *Golgofa*, p. 88).
154. *Golgofa*, pp. 42–3, 58.
155. Ibid., pp. 57, 100.
156. Ibid., pp. 52, 61; interview with Vladimir Piatnitsky, St Petersburg, September 2005.
157. L. Razgon, *True Stories* (London, 1997), p. 131.
158. Starkov, 'The Trial', p. 1307.
159. *Lubianka. Stalin i glavnoe upravlenie gosbezopasnosti NKVD, 1937–1938* (Moscow, 2004), p. 544.
160. *Golgofa*, p. 80.
161. Ibid., pp. 83–4.
162. Ibid., p. 99.
163. Interview with Vladimir Piatnitsky, St Petersburg, September 2005.
164. *Golgofa*, pp. 114–16.

5: Remnants of Terror (1938–41)

1. MP, f. 4, op. 2, d. 2, ll. 7–10.
2. MP, f. 4, op. 2, d. 2, l. 5. See similarly MM, f. 4, op. 11, d. 2, ll. 40–41.
3. MP, f. 4, op. 2, d. 2, l. 10.
4. MSP, f. 3, op. 41, d. 2, l. 10.
5. MSP, f. 3, op. 41, d. 2, ll. 6, 11, 31–2, 54, 59, 62–3, 65.
6. MSP, f. 3, op. 6, d. 2, ll. 6, 10, 25–6.
7. For the first-born children assuming adult roles in single-parent families see MP, f. 4, op. 24, d. 2, ll. 39–40; op. 13, d. 2, ll. 42–4.
8. MSP, f. 3, op. 37, d. 2, ll. 11–12, 40; I. Shikheeva-Gaister, *Semeinaia khronika vremen kul'ta lichnosti: 1925–1953* (Moscow, 1998), pp. 36–8, 41–7, 50, 53–4, 187.
9. MP, f. 4, op. 22, d. 2, ll. 3–4, 24–6, 34–5.
10. See S. Davies, *Popular Opinion in Stalin's Russia: Terror, Propaganda and Dissent, 1934–1941* (Cambridge, 1997), pp. 131–2.
11. MM, f. 1, op. 3, d. 905 (25 January 1939).
12. See in particular MM, f. 1, op. 1, d. 5401; op. 3, d. 5923; f. 12, op. 25, d. 2; op. 31, d. 2.
13. MM, f. 1, op. 3, d. 905 (25 August 1940); f. 12, op. 3, d. 2, l. 31.
14. L. Siegelbaum and A. Sokolov (eds.), *Stalinism as a Way of Life: A Narrative in Documents* (Yale, 2000), p. 401.
15. GMPIR, f. 2, nos. 51291–1345; VS 11026; f. 6, VS 1937, VS 1937 VS 1938.
16. MM, f. 12, op. 22, d. 1, l. 1; d. 2, ll. 5–6, 14.
17. MSP, f. 3, op. 40, d. 2, ll. 10, 22; d. 5 (20 May 1940).
18. MSP, f. 3, op. 40, d. 2, ll. 7, 18, 24, 34–5.
19. MSP, f. 3, op. 16, d. 2, ll. 71–2.
20. MSP, f. 3, op. 16, d. 1; d. 2, ll. 25–7.
21. GARF, f. 5207, op. 3, d. 49, l. 190; d.56, l. 18.
22. A. Applebaum, *Gulag: A History of the Soviet Camps* (London, 2003), p. 300.
23. MSP, f. 3, op. 29, d. 2, ll. 1, 3, 14, 20–21.
24. MM, f. 12, op. 27, d. 2, ll. 4, 72.
25. MSP, f. 3, op. 13, d. 2, ll. 4–6, 21–4.
26. MSP, f. 3, op. 24, d. 2, ll. 10, 41; d. 4, l. 25.
27. MSP, f. 3, op. 24, d. 2, ll. 37–8.
28. MSP, f. 3, op. 24, d. 2, ll. 20, 39–40.
29. M. Nikolaev, *Detdom* (New York, 1985), pp. 48–9, 89.
30. Ibid., pp. 42, 65, 101.
31. Ibid., pp. 77–9, 126; interview with Viktoriia Shweitser (Mikhail Nikolaev's widow), Moscow, July 2004.
32. MSP, f. 3, op. 24, d. 2, l. 16; d. 4, l. 21.
33. MSP, f. 3, op. 12, d. 2, l. 68.
34. MSP, f. 3, op. 12, d. 2, ll. 127–30.
35. E. P. Evangulova, *Krestnyi put'* (St Petersburg, 2000), pp. 59, 69, 75, 77, 81.
36. SFA, I. Slavina, 'Na vesakh nadezhdy i otchaianiia', ms., p. 1.
37. MSP, f. 3, op. 42, d. 2, l. 23; d. 3, ll. 1–2.
38. MP, f. 4, op. 12, d. 2, ll. 10, 14, 32, 63–4.
39. MSP, f. 3, op. 11, d. 2, ll. 39, 61, 62, 63–4, 72.
40. Lynne Viola, 'Tear the Evil From the Root: The Children of Spetspereselentsy of the North', in Natalia Baschmakoff and Paul Fryer (eds.), *Modernization of the Russian Provinces*, special issue of *Studia Slavica Finlandensia*, 17 (April 2000), pp. 60–61.
41. MP, f. 4, op. 18, d. 2, ll. 11, 16, 50, 52, 65, 76; d. 5, ll. 22–3.
42. MP, f. 4, op. 2, d. 2, l. 14.
43. Interviews with Oksana Kozmina (Moscow, 1988), Klavdiia Goncharova (Moscow, 1986), Inna Ilina (Moscow, 1988), Lydia Violina (Moscow, 1988), Klavdiia Babaeva

(Moscow, 1988); GFA, interviews with Sergei Barinov (Akmolinsk, 1988); *Leninskaia smena*, 2 June 1988, p. 2; M. Shreider, *NKVD iznutri: zapiski chekista* (Moscow, 1995), p. 117. See further A. Kukushkina, *Akmolinskii lager' zhen 'izmennikov rodiny'. Istoriia i sud'by* (Karaganda, 2002).

44. MP, f. 4, op. 2, d. 2, ll. 4, 45, 51.

45. A. Applebaum, *Gulag*, p. 234; I. Shikheeva-Gaister, *Semeinaia khronika vremen kul'ta lichnosti: 1925–1953* (Moscow, 1998), pp. 47–8.

46. SFA, I. Slavina, 'Na vesakh nadezhdy i otchaianiia', ms., pp. 6–7.

47. Interview with Oksana Kozmina, Moscow, 1988.

48. The most detailed discussion of the trusties is in A. Solzhenitsyn, *The Gulag Archipelago 1918–1956: An Experiment in Literary Investigation*, 3 vols. (London, 1974–8), vol. 2, pp. 251–91.

49. MM, f. 12, op. 29, d. 2, ll. 1, 18.

50. H. Volovich, 'My Past', in S. Vilenskii (ed.), *Till My Tale is Told: Women's Memoirs of the GULAG* (Bloomington, 1999), pp. 260–64.

51. Applebaum, *Gulag*, p. 293.

52. Interviews with Oksana Kozmina (Moscow, 1988), Klavdiia Goncharova (Moscow, 1986), Inna Ilina (Moscow, 1988), Lydia Violina (Moscow, 1988), Klavdiia Babaeva (Moscow, 1988), Mikhail Iusipenko (Akmolinsk, 1988).

53. On this see Solzhenitsyn, *Gulag*, vol. 2, pp. 229–34; Applebaum, *Gulag*, pp. 285–91.

54. MIFA, Tina Mikheladze, 'Vospominaniia', ms., pp. 1–8; interview with Vakhtang Mikheladze, Moscow, April 2003.

55. MSP, f. 3, op. 41, d. 2, ll. 10–12, 40–41, 83–91.

56. GFA, Oksana Golovnia, 'Vospominaniia', ms., pp. 5–7.

57. GFA, letter from Anatoly to Liuba Golovnia, 22 June 1940; letters from Polina Eisner to Liuba Golovnia, 11 December 1940, 22 March 1941.

58. GFA, Oksana Golovnia, 'Predislovie k pis'mam', ms., p. 42; Polina Eisner (Ivanova), 'Avtobiografiia' (February 1942); interview with Oksana Kozmina, Moscow, 1988; letters from Anatoly to Liuba Golovnia, 23 July 1939; 1 March, 27 March, 3 April 1940.

59. Interview with Aleksei Simonov, Moscow, November 2003.

60. RGALI, f. 632, op. 1, d. 14, ll. 26–7.

61. RGALI, f. 631, op. 2, d. 453, l. 21; f. 2897, op. 1, d. 114; A. Simonov, *Chastnaia kollektsiia* (Nizhny Novgorod, 1999), pp. 35–6, 49; interviews with Aleksei Simonov, Moscow, November 2003; SLFA, Yevgeniia Laskina to Aleksandra Ivanisheva, 8 September 1939; Konstantin Simonov to Yevgeniia Laskina, August 1939.

62. RGALI, f. 1814, op. 1, d. 93, l. 20.

63. J. Colvin, *Nomonhan* (London, 1999), pp. 169–75.

64. RGALI, f. 1814, op. 1, d. 480, l. 106; op. 6, d. 170, l. 46; op. 10, d. 339, l. 11; K. Simonov, *100 sutok voiny* (Moscow, 1999), p. 295.

65. G. Roberts, 'The Soviet Decision for a Pact with Nazi Germany', *Soviet Studies*, vol. 44, no. 1 (1992), pp. 57–78; R. Overy, *The Dictators: Hitler's Germany and Stalin's Russia* (London, 2004), p. 486.

66. C. Merridale, *Ivan's War: The Red Army 1939–45* (London, 2005), p. 44.

67. RGALI, f. 1814, op. 6, d. 170, ll. 44–6; K. Simonov, *Glazami cheloveka moego pokoleniia* (Moscow, 1990), p. 67; Simonov, *100 sutok voiny*, pp. 292–3.

68. Simonov, *100 sutok voiny*, pp. 297–8.

69. *Konstantin Simonov v vospominaniiakh sovremennikov* (Moscow, 1984), pp. 18–20.

70. N. Pushnova, *Valentina Serova* (Moscow, 2003), pp. 10, 298–9; interview with Maria Simonova, Moscow, March 2004.

71. Pushnova, *Valentina Serova*, pp. 48–9.

72. Ibid., p. 96.

73. Interview with Fania Laskina, Moscow, July 2004.

74. Pushnova, *Valentina Serova*, p. 115; M. Simonova, 'Ia pomniu', *Ogonek*, 1993, no. 6, pp. 22–3; interview with Fania Laskina, Moscow, November 2003.

6: 'Wait For Me' (1941–5)

1. MFA, L. Makhnach, 'Oskolki bylogo s vysoty nastoiashchego', ms., pp. 1–14; Vladimir to Maria Makhnach, November 1941; TsAODM, f. 3, op. 52, d. 27, l. 21.

2. RGALI, f. 1814, op. 10, d. 339, l. 6; K. Simonov, *100 sutok voiny* (Moscow, 1999), pp. 6–17.

3. Simonov, *100 sutok voiny*, pp. 51–2; SLFA, M. Laskin, 'Vospominaniia', ms., p. 55.

4. RGALI, f. 1814, op. 4, d. 5, ll. 7, 58. For more on the development of Simonov's ideas about the Terror during the wars years: A. Karaganov, *Konstantin Simonov vblizi i na rasstoianii* (Moscow, 1987), pp. 88–9. On the legacy of the Terror in the Soviet armed forces: E. Seniavskaia, 'Dukhovnyi oblik frontovogo pokoleniia: istoriko-psikhologicheskii ocherk', *Vestnik MGU: Istoriia*, 1992, no. 4, pp. 39–51; M. von Hagen, 'Soviet Soldiers and Officers on the Eve of the German Invasion: Toward a Description of Social Psychology and Political Attitudes', in R. Thurston and B. Bonwetsch (eds.), *The People's War: Responses to World War II in the Soviet Union* (Urbana, 2000), pp. 193ff.

5. Simonov, *100 sutok voiny*, pp, 17–21, 53, 121, 409–11.

6. *Moskva voennaia 1941–1945: memuary i arkhivnye dokumenty* (Moscow, 1995), p. 475; C. Merridale, *Ivan's War: The Red Army 1939–1945* (London, 2005), p. 84; Simonov, *100 sutok voiny*, p. 50.

7. *Moskva voennaia*, p. 478; R. Bidlack, 'The Political Mood in Leningrad During the First Year of the Soviet–German War', *Russian Review*, vol. 59, no. 1 (January 2000), pp. 101–11; G. Bordiugov, 'The Popular Mood in the Unoccupied Soviet Union: Continuity and Change during the War', in *The People's War*, pp. 59–60; M. Gorinov, 'Muscovites' Moods, 22 June 1941 to May 1942', in *The People's War*, pp. 119–20.

8. V. Shapovalov (ed.), *Remembering the Darkness: Women in Soviet Prisons* (Lanham, Maryland, 2001), pp. 150–51; MSP, f. 3, op. 35, d. 1, l. 1; d. 2, l. 34.

9. R. Overy, *Russia's War* (London, 1997), p. 94.

10. E. Maksimova, *Deti voennoi pory* (Moscow, 1988), pp. 235–308; Merridale, *Ivan's War*, p. 216.

11. Interviews with Iurii Streletsky, St Petersburg, May 2003, February 2004.

12. J. Dunstan, *Soviet Schooling in the Second World War* (Basingstoke, 1997), p. 82; J. Barber and M. Harrison, *The Soviet Home Front, 1941–1945: A Social and Economic History of the USSR in World War II* (London, 1991), p. 128.

13. MSP, f. 3, op. 3, d. 2, ll. 14–15, 34–42; d. 3, l. 28.

14. MSP, f. 3, op. 45, d. 2, ll. 9, 53, 88, 165.

15. MSP, f. 3, op. 45, d. 2, ll. 11, 46.

16. *Moskva voennaia*, pp. 478, 481.

17. Ibid., pp. 149, 152.

18. K. Simonov, *Sobranie sochinenii*, 12 vols. (Moscow, 1979–87), vol. 1, p. 171. I have borrowed from the translation by Mike Munford (www.simonov.co.uk).

19. Interview with Fania Laskina, Moscow, February 2003; interview with Aleksei Simonov, Moscow, September 2003; SLFA, Sonia Laskina's papers; RGALI, f. 1814, op. 10, d. 339, l. 41.

20. N. Pushnova, *Valentina Serova: krug otchuzhdeniia* (Moscow, 2003), pp. 150–52, 161–5; interview with Aleksei Simonov, Moscow, November 2003; RGALI, f. 1814, op. 9, d. 2788, l. 1.

21. A. Todd and M. Hayward (eds.), *Twentieth-Century Russian Poetry* (London, 1993), pp. 623–4 (translated by L. Yakovleva).

22. L. Lazarev, *Konstantin Simonov. Ocherk zhizni i tvorchestva* (Moscow, 1985), pp. 66–7, 71, 78–9; L. Pushkarev, *Po dorogam voiny: vospominaniia fol'klorista-frontovika* (Moscow, 1995), pp. 56–7; B. Pankin, *Chetyre Ia Konstantina Simonova* (Moscow 1999), p. 80; *Poslednie pis'ma s fronta. Sbornik*, 5 vols. (Moscow, 1992), vol. 3 (1943), p. 257.

23. RGALI. f. 1814, op. 1, d. 765, l. 9.

24. Pushkarev, *Po dorogam voiny*, pp. 31, 57–8.
25. On this see Merridale, *Ivan's War*, pp. 93, 208, 272–4.
26. RGALI, f. 1814, op. 8, d. 93, ll. 61–2.
27. Simonov, *Sobranie sochinenii*, vol. 1, pp. 129–32.
28. Lazarev, *Konstantin Simonov*, pp. 38–9, 70–72; same author, *Pamiat' trudnoi godiny*. *Velikaia otechestvennaia voina v russkoi literature* (Moscow, 2000, pp. 47–9; *Autobiographical Statements in Twentieth-Century Russian Literature* (Princeton, 1990), p. 13; R. Stites, 'Soviet Russian Wartime Culture: Freedom and Control, Spontaneity and Consciousness', in *The People's War*, p. 175; V. Dunham, *In Stalin's Time: Middle-Class Values in Soviet Fiction* (Durham, 1990), pp. 70–71; RGALI, f. 1814, op. 1, d. 772, l. 362.
29. L. Lazarev, *Shestoi etazh. Kniga vospominaniia* (Moscow, 1999), pp. 202–3.
30. RGALI, f. 1814, op. 9, d. 1532, l. 4; d. 775, l. 1; interviews with Fania Laskina, Moscow, June and September 2003; Pushnova, *Valentina Serova*, pp. 181–2, 290; T. Okunevskaia, *Tat'ianin den'* (Moscow, 1998), pp. 119–20.
31. See e.g. RGALI, f. 1814, op. 1, d. 765, ll. 15, 66, 68, 77.
32. RGALI, f. 1814, op. 9, d. 1530, l. 2; d. 1533, ll. 29–30.
33. RGALI, f. 1814, op. 9, d. 2768, l. 10; d. 1, l. 1; d. 1533, ll. 18–19; d. 2768, l. 15.
34. RGALI, f. 1814, op. 9, d. 1, l. 3.
35. RGALI, f. 1814, op. 9, d. 1533, l. 19.
36. N. Ivanova, 'Konstantin Simonov "Glazami cheloveka moego pokoleniia"', *Znamia*, 1997, no. 7; RGALI, f. 1814, op. 10, d. 339, l. 8; interview with Aleksei Simonov, London, May 2004; interview with Marina Babak, Moscow, November 2003.
37. RGALI, f. 1814, op. 6, d. 170, l. 17; interview with Aleksei Simonov, Moscow, September 2003; Lazarev, *Shestoi etazh*, p. 213.
38. Karaganov, *Konstantin Simonov*, pp. 9–10; A. Simonov, *Chastnaia kollektsiia* (Nizhny Novgorod, 1999), pp. 22–4; SLFA, Zhenia Laskina to Vladimir Lugovskoi, 28 August 1943; Sonia Laskina to Vladimir Lugovskoi, 21 August 1943; interview with Lazar Lazarev, Moscow, November 2003; RGALI, f. 1814, op. 9, d. 1812, ll. 1–2.
39. RGALI, f. 1814, op. 10, d. 339, l. 20; K. Simonov, *Segodnia i davno* (Moscow, 1978), p. 321; E. Dolmatovskii, *Bylo: zapiski poeta* (Moscow, 1982), p. 58 (also RGALI, f. 1814, op. 6, d. 170, l. 2).
40. *Krasnaia zvezda*, 28 August 1941, p. 1; 7 November 1941, p. 4; RGALI, f. 1814, op. 1, d. 993, l. 37; K. Simonov, *Glazami cheloveka moego pokoleniia* (Moscow, 1990), p. 87.
41. Simonov, *100 sutok voiny*, pp. 550–51.
42. Ibid., pp. 17–21.
43. Merridale, *Ivan's War*, pp. 134–8.
44. R. McNeal, *Stalin: Man and Ruler* (London, 1988), p. 241; R. Parker, *Moscow Correspondent* (London, 1949), pp. 21–2.
45. Pushkarev, *Po dorogam voiny*, p. 60; E. Seniavskaia, *Chelovek na voine. Istoriko-psikhologicheskie ocherki* (Moscow, 1997), pp. 47–8; Lazarev, *Konstantin Simonov*, p. 68; Karaganov, *Konstantin Simonov*, p. 68; Simonov, *Sobranie sochinenii*, vol. 1, pp. 105–7; A. Werth, *Russia at War 1941–1945* (London, 1964), p. 412. Werth is mistaken about the play's final words. The phrase he quotes appears earlier in the play.
46. K. Simonov, *Pis'ma o voine, 1943–1979* (Moscow, 1990), p. 110.
47. D. Samoilov, *Podennye zapisi*, 2 vols. (Moscow, 2002), vol. 1, p. 140; 'Zaveshchanie zhivym (pis'ma s fronta)', *Sovetskaia Rossiia*, 9 May 1991.
48. Seniavskaia, 'Dukhovnyi oblik', p. 49; V. Kondrat'ev, 'Ne tol'ko o svoem pokolenii. Zametki pisatelia', *Kommunist*, 1997, no. 7, p. 122.
49. S. Conze and B. Fieseler, 'Soviet Women as Comrades-in-Arms: A Blind Spot in Soviet History', in *The People's War*, p. 212.
50. Interviews with Rebekka (Rita) Kogan, St Petersburg, June, November 2003.
51. A. Chuyanov, *Stalingradskii dnevnik, 1941–1943* (Volgograd, 1968), p. 209; *Konstantin Simonov rasskazyvaet* (Moscow, 1981), p. 106.
52. RGASPI, f. 17, op. 125, d. 190, l. 16.

53. D. Glantz, *The Siege of Leningrad, 1941–1944: 900 Days of Terror* (London, 2001), pp. 75–6.

54. The classic statement of this influential theory is E. Shils and M. Janowitz, 'Cohesion and Disintegration in the Wehrmacht in World War II', *Public Opinion Quarterly*, 1948, no. 12, pp. 280–315.

55. E. Seniavskaia, *Frontovoe pokolenie 1941–1945: istoriko-psikhologicheskoe issledovanie* (Moscow, 1995), p. 86; same author, 'Dukhovnyi oblik', pp. 46–7; C. Merridale, *Night of Stone: Death and Memory in Russia* (London, 2000), p. 279.

56. R. Overy, *Russia's War* (London, 1998), p. 197.

57. J. Erickson, *The Road to Berlin* (London, 1983), p. 40.

58. V. Zemskov, 'Ukaz ot 26 Iunia 1940 g. (Eshche odna kruglaia data)', *Raduga*, 1990, no. 6, p. 47.

59. MP, f. 4, op. 15, d. 2, ll. 7–9; d. 3, l. 2.

60. MP, f. 4, op. 11, d. 2, ll. 26–8.

61. E. Bacon, *The Gulag at War: Stalin's Forced Labour System in the Light of the Archives* (London, 1994), p. 144; L. Borodkin and S. Ertz, 'Coercion versus Motivation: Forced Labor in Norilsk', in Paul Gregory and Valery Lazarev (eds.), *The Economics of Forced Labor: The Soviet Gulag* (Stanford, 2003), p. 78.

62. S. Ertz, 'Building Norilsk', in *The Economics of Forced Labor*, pp. 127–50; *O vremeni, o Noril'ske, o sebe . . . Vospominaniia*, 5 vols. (Moscow, 2001–6), vol. 3, p. 12; Borodkin and Ertz, 'Coercion versus Motivation', pp. 77, 86–8.

63. MM, f. 12, op. 18, d. 2, l. 27.

64. Interviews with Vasilina Dmitruk, Vera Pristupa, Maria Treimanis (née Fishchuk), Norilsk, July 2004.

65. Interview with Anna Darvina, Norilsk, July 2004.

66. Interview with Semyon Golovko, Norilsk, July 2004.

67. MM, f. 2, op. 5 ('Khranit' vechno!', ms.).

68. RGALI, f. 3084, op. 1, d. 1390, ll. 1, 13; MSP, f. 3, op. 22, d. 2, ll. 19–21, 36–7; d. 4, ll. 15–16; interviews with Natalia Babailova, Severodvinsk, March and November 2005; interview with Nina Sazhnova, Saratov, November 2004; interview with Nina Levina, Krasnoiarsk, August 2005.

69. N. Mandelstam, *Hope Abandoned* (London, 1989), p. 252; B. Pasternak, *Doctor Zhivago* (London, 1958), p. 453; O. Ivinskaia, *V plenu vremeni: gody c B. Pasternakom* (Moscow, 1972), p. 96.

70. Kondrat'ev, 'Ne tol'ko o svoem pokolenii', p. 224.

71. M. Gefter, 'Stalin umer vchera . . .', in *Inogo ne dano* (Moscow, 1988), p. 305; VFA, A. Levidova, 'Vospominaniia', ms., p. 118.

72. H. Smith, *The Russians* (London, 1976), p. 369; V. Kondrat'ev, 'Paradoks frontovoi nostal'gii', *Literaturnaia gazeta*, 9 May 1990, p. 9.

73. Interview with Lazar Lazarev, Moscow, November 2003.

74. P. Blake and M. Hayward (eds.), *Dissonant Voices in Soviet Literature* (New York, 1962), pp. 164–7 (translated by Walter Vickery).

75. On the collapse of the Party's ideological training centres in the war see R. Brody, *Ideology and Political Mobilization: The Soviet Home Front During World War II* (Pittsburgh, 1994), pp. 24–6.

76. Merridale, *Ivan's War*, p. 141; Werth, *Russia at War*, p. 943; *Pravda*, 24 June 1944, p. 2; interview with Lazar Lazarev, Moscow, November 2003; MSP, f. 3, op. 30, d. 2, l. 23.

77. Smith, *The Russians*, p. 370.

78. MM, f. 12, op. 25, d. 2.

79. MSP, f. 3, op. 14, d. 2, ll. 46–53, 87–90; d. 3, ll. 27–33.

80. MP, f. 4, op. 11, d. 2, ll. 10, 34–7.

81. V. Pirozhkova, *Poteriannoe pokolenie* (St Petersburg, 1998), p. 154.

82. TsAODM, f. 1870, op. 3, d. 1, ll. 15–17; d. 3, ll. 33–4.

83. MM, f. 12, op. 21, d. 2, ll. 31–2.

84. E. Zubkova, *Russia After the War: Hopes, Illusions and Disappointments, 1945–1957* (London, 1998), p. 17; 'Voina, kotoruiu ne znali: iz dnevnika, prokommentirovannogo samym avtorom 45 let spustia', *Sovetskaia kul'tura*, 5 May 1990, p. 4; interview with Lazar Lazarev, Moscow, November 2003.

85. M. Prishvin, *Sobranie sochinenii*, 8 vols. (Moscow, 1986), vol. 8, pp. 392, 435–6; VFA, A. Levidova, 'Vospominaniia', ms., p. 119; S. Gus'kov, *Esli ostanus' zhiv* (Moscow, 1989), p. 215; interview with Lazar Lazarev, Moscow, November 2003.

86. GARF, f. 9041, op. 2, d. 202, l. 8; RGASPI, f. 558, op. 11, d. 868, l. 56; f. 17, op. 122, d. 122, ll. 27–30; *Pravda*, 11 September 1989.

87. GARF, f. 7253, op. 16, d. 79, l. 173; Merridale, *Ivan's War*, pp. 292–3.

88. Seniavskaia, 'Dukhovnyi oblik', pp. 49–50.

89. T. Dunmore, *Soviet Politics 1945–53* (London, 1984), p. 129; Zubkova, *Russia After the War*, p. 94; Bordiugov, 'The Popular Mood', pp. 66, 68.

90. MSP, f. 3, op. 4, d. 2, ll. 41–2, 46, 57–8.

91. MSP, f. 3, op. 16, d. 2, ll. 30–34, 74–8, 98.

92. Simonov, *Sobranie sochinenii*, vol. 9. p. 639.

93. SLFA, M. Laskin, 'Vospominaniia', ms., p. 72.

94. *Pravda*, 27 June 1945.

95. *Chelovek v istorii. Rossiia – XX vek: sbornik rabot pobeditelei* (Moscow, 2002), p. 293.

96. See Merridale, *Ivan's War*, pp. 232–4.

97. Kondrat'ev, 'Ne tol'ko o svoem pokolenii', pp. 112–16; same author, 'Paradoks frontovoi nostal'gii'.

98. MSP, f. 3, op. 29, d. 2, ll. 5–6.

99. MM, f. 1, op. 1, d. 1942; d. 1944; f. 12, op. 16, d. 2, ll. 12–15, 68–9.

100. MM, f. 1, op. 1, d. 1944.

101. MM, f. 1, op. 1, d. 1944; f. 12, op. 16, d. 2, ll. 27, 29, 69.

102. MM, f. 12, op. 16, d. 2, ll. 32–3.

103. MM, f. 12, op. 16, d. 2, ll. 34, 71–2, 85.

7: Ordinary Stalinists (1945–53)

1. MP, f. 4, op. 2, d. 2, ll. 64–89.

2. E. Zubkova, *Russia After the War: Hopes, Illusions and Disappointments, 1945–1957* (London, 1998), pp. 20–21, 38; *Liudskie poteri SSSR v period vtoroi mirovoi voiny: sbornik statei* (St Petersburg, 2005), p. 130.

3. M. Heller and A. Nekrich, *Utopia in Power: The History of the Soviet Union from 1917 to the Present* (London, 1986), pp. 472–3; RGALI, f. 1814, op. 10, d. 387, l. 4; d. 389, l. 10.

4. Zubkova, *Russia After the War*, pp. 11, 40. A lower rate of mortality (1.5 million deaths) is given by M. Ellman, 'The 1947 Soviet Famine and the Entitlement Approach to Famines', *Cambridge Journal of Economics*, 24 (September 2000), p. 615.

5. MP, f. 4, op. 2, d. 2, ll. 13, 19–20, 24–6, 76–9.

6. RGASPI, f. 17, op. 117, d. 530, ll. 37–8.

7. 'Iz suzhdenii sovetskikh liudei o poslevoennykh problemakh i o zhizni v SSSR', *Istoriia otechestva v dokumentakh, 1945–1993* (Moscow, 1995), p. 17.

8. I. Ehrenburg, *The War, 1941–45* (London, 1964), p. 124; R. Service, *A History of Twentieth-Century Russia* (London, 1997), p. 299 (quotation altered for clarity); A. Mikoian, *Tak bylo: razmyshleniia o minuvshem* (Moscow, 1999), pp. 513–14.

9. Interview with Marianna Gordon, St Petersburg, October 2003.

10. Interview with Valentina Aleksandrova, St Petersburg, December 2003.

11. RGASPI, f. 17, op. 125, d. 424, ll. 58–71. On these groups see J. Fürst, 'Prisoners of the Self? Political Opposition Groups in Late Stalinism', *Europe-Asia Studies*, vol. 54, no. 3 (2002), pp. 353–75; H. Kuromiya, ' "Political Youth Opposition in Late Stalinism": Evidence and Conjecture', *Europe-Asia Studies*, vol. 55, no. 4 (2003), pp. 631–8.

12. MSP, f. 3, op. 20, d. 2, ll. 53, 59.

13. MSP, f. 3, op. 47, d. 2, ll. 21, 31, 35, 38, 55.

14. See N. Tumarkin, *The Living and the Dead: The Rise and Fall of the Cult of World War II in Russia* (New York, 1994), p. 104; L. Lazarev, *Pamiat' trudnoi godiny. Velikaia otechestvennaia voina v russkoi literature* (Moscow, 2000), pp. 61–3.

15. *Pravda*, 10 February 1946; A. Applebaum, *Gulag: A History of the Soviet Camps* (London, 2003), p. 415.

16. R. Overy, *Russia's War* (London, 1997), pp. 304–7.

17. A. Danilov and A. Pyzhikov, *Rozhdenie sverkhderzhavy: SSSR v pervye poslevoennye gody* (Moscow, 2001), p. 108.

18. GARF, f. 9401, op. 2, d. 234, ll. 148, 153; d. 199, l. 392; S. Fitzpatrick, 'Postwar Soviet Society: The "Return to Normalcy", 1945–1953', in S. Linz (ed.), *The Impact of World War II on the Soviet Union* (Totowa, 1985), pp. 143–5.

19. P. Gregory, 'An Introduction to the Economics of the Gulag', in P. Gregory and V. Lazarev (eds.), *The Economics of Forced Labor: The Soviet Gulag* (Stanford, 2003), pp. 14, 16; G. Alexopoulos, 'Amnesty 1945: The Revolving Door of Stalin's Gulag', *Slavic Review*, vol. 64, no. 2 (Summer 2005), p. 274; Y. Gorlizki and O. Khlevniuk, *Cold Peace: Stalin and the Soviet Ruling Circle, 1945–1953* (Oxford, 2004), pp. 130–31, 268–71.

20. For a good example of a family reunited in Norilsk see the Kuznetsova-Babailova archive in MSP, f. 3, op. 22, dd. 2–5.

21. MM, f. 12, op. 20, d. 2.

22. MSP, f. 3, op. 8, d. 2.

23. L. Borodkin and S. Ertz, 'Coercion versus Motivation: Forced Labor in Norilsk', in Gregory and Lazarev (eds.), *The Economics of Forced Labor*, pp. 102–3.

24. V. Dunham, *In Stalin's Time: Middle-Class Values in Soviet Fiction* (New York, 1976).

25. N. DeWitt, *Education and Professional Employment in the USSR* (Washington, 1961), pp. 606–7, 638–9.

26. A. Inkeles and R. Bauer, *The Soviet Citizen: Daily Life in a Totalitarian Society* (Cambridge, Mass. 1959), pp. 289, 326–7.

27. C. Miłosz, *The Captive Mind* (London, 1953), pp. 55, 57.

28. Interviews with Irina Aleksandrova, St Petersburg, May, November 2003.

29. MSP, f. 3, op. 37, d. 2, ll. 44–5.

30. MFA, L. Makhnach, 'Oskolki bylogo s vysoty nastoiashchego', ms., p. 76.

31. MSP, f. 3, op. 34, d. 2, l. 4. See also MM, f. 12, op. 32, d. 2, ll. 77–8.

32. MP, f. 4, op. 2, d. 2, ll. 32–3.

33. MP, f. 4, op. 13, d. 2, ll. 37–8, 39, 42–3, 56.

34. Interviews with Iurii Streletsky, St Petersburg, May 2003, February 2004.

35. PFA, 'Vospominaniia', ms., pp. 17, 22–4; interviews with Tatiana Elagina, Moscow, May, October 2003 (name changed on the request of the informant).

36. MP, f. 4, op. 7, d. 2, ll. 3, 7, 11–12, 26, 28, 39–40.

37. RGALI, f. 1814, op. 10, d. 360, l. 45; K. Simonov, *Glazami cheloveka moego pokoleniia* (Moscow, 1990), p. 82; A. Karaganov, *Konstantin Simonov vblizi i na rasstoianii* (Moscow 1987), p. 103.

38. RGALI, f. 1814, op. 10, d. 346.

39. K. Simonov, *Segodnia i davno* (Moscow, 1978), pp. 143–4; N. Pushnova, *Valentina Serova* (Moscow, 2003), pp. 215–16.

40. K. Chukovskii, *Dnevnik, 1901–1969*, 2 vols. (Moscow, 2003), vol. 2, p. 210; RGALI, f. 631, op. 15, d. 1004, l. 150; Simonov, *Glazami cheloveka moego pokoleniia*, p. 116.

41. Interview with Aleksei Simonov, Moscow, November 2003; interview with Marina Babak, Moscow, November 2003.

42. RGALI, f. 1814, op. 10, d. 343, l. 1; N. Bianki, *K. Simonov i A. Tvardovskii v 'Novom mire'* (Moscow, 1999), p. 7; L. Fink, *Konstantin Simonov* (Moscow, 1979), pp. 220, 235, 251, 274.

43. L. Chukovskaia, *Sochineniia v 2 tomakh* (Moscow, 2000), vol. 2, pp. 182, 186, 216. Simonov was accused of a similarly dictatorial manner as the editor of *Literaturnaia gazeta* (see RGASPI, f. 558, op. 11, d. 878, l. 55).

44. RGALI, f. 1814, op. 9, d. 229, ll. 16, 20; Bianki, *K. Simonov i A. Tvardovskii v 'Novom Mire'*, p. 16; B. Pankin, *Chetyre Ia Konstantina Simonova* (Moscow, 1999), pp. 19, 23, 35–5; interview with Aleksei Simonov, Moscow, November 2003; interview with Marina Babak, Moscow, November 2003.

45. RGALI, f. 1814, op. 9, d. 2590, ll. 1, 2. On Portugalov in Kolyma see the touching reminiscences about him by Varlam Shalamov in RGALI, f. 2596, op. 2, d. 133, ll. 1–10.

46. Karaganov, *Konstantin Simonov*, p. 136. On Smeliakov: *Sluzhili dva tovarishcha: kniga o zhizni kinodramaturgov Dunskogo i Frida* (Moscow, 2002), pp. 592–5.

47. RGALI, f. 1814, op. 1, d. 454, ll. 43, 45; d. 643, ll. 1–2; op. 9, d. 1812, l. 4.

48. I. Berlin, 'Meetings with Russian Writers in 1945 and 1956', in *Personal Impressions* (Oxford, 1982), pp. 160–61; N. Mandelstam, *Hope Abandoned* (London, 1989), p. 375.

49. G. Carleton, *The Politics of Reception: Critical Constructions of Mikhail Zoshchenko* (Evanston, 1998), pp. 231–2.

50. 'Doklad t. Zhdanova o zhurnalakh *Zvezda i Leningrad*', *Novyi mir*, 1946, no. 9, pp. iv–xix.

51. Simonov, *Glazami cheloveka moego pokoleniia*, pp. 104–7; RGASPI, f. 17, op. 132, d. 229, l. 21.

52. Simonov, *Segodnia i davno*, pp. 337–8; A. Borshchagovskii, *Zapiski balovnia sud'by* (Moscow, 1991), p. 235.

53. RGALI, f. 1814, op. 9, d. 331, ll. 1–2; Simonov, *Glazami cheloveka moego pokoleniia*, pp. 118–20, 137, 141; interview with Lazar Lazarev, Moscow, November 2003.

54. SLFA, 'K.M.', two-part film on DVD, comments by Benedikt Sarnov in Part 1, at twenty-six minutes; interview with Lazar Lazarev, Moscow, November 2003.

55. B. Schwarz, *Music and Musical Life in Soviet Russia, 1917–1970* (London, 1972), pp. 208, 218; Gorlizki and Khlevniuk, *Cold Peace*, pp. 35–8; Zubkova, *Russia After the War*, pp. 119–23.

56. H. Salisbury, *American in Russia* (New York, 1955), pp. 16–20, 38; G. Ivanova, 'Poslevoennye repressii i Gulag', in *Stalin i kholodnaia voina* (Moscow, 1998), p. 255.

57. J. Brent and V. Naukov, *Stalin's Last Crime: The Doctors' Plot* (London, 2003), p. 96.

58. 'Evreiskii antifashistskii komitet', *Izvestiia TsK KPSS*, 1989, no. 12, p. 40; *Reabilitatsiia: politicheskie protsessy 30–50-kh godov* (Moscow, 1991), p. 326.

59. Cited in A. Weiner, *Making Sense of War: The Second World War and the Fate of the Bolshevik Revolution* (Princeton, 2001), p. 195.

60. RGALI, f. 1814, op. 9, d. 2645, ll. 3–4, 9, 18; Borshchagovskii, *Zapiski balovnia sud'by*, pp. 3, 77, 94; G. Kostyrchenko, *Tainaia politika Stalina. Vlast' i antisemitizm* (Moscow, 2001), pp. 319ff.

61. A. Gerasimov, 'Za sovetskii patriotism v iskusstve', *Pravda*, 10 February 1949; N. Gribachev, 'Protiv kosmopolitizma i formalizma v poezii', *Pravda*, 16 February 1949; T. Khrennikov, 'Burzhuaznye kosmopolity v muzykal'noi kritike', *Kul'tura i zhizn'*, 20 February 1949; 'Do kontsa razoblachit' kosmopolitov-antipatriotov', *Pravda*, 26–27 February 1949; L. Bol'shakov, 'Razgromit' burzhuaznyi kosmopolitizm v kinoiskusstve', *Pravda*, 3 March 1949; etc.

62. Kostyrchenko, *Tainaia politika Stalina*, pp. 334–5; Borshchagovskii, *Zapiski balovnia sud'by*, pp. 185, 188–91; RGASPI, f. 83, op. 1, d. 5, ll. 92–5.

63. RGASPI, f. 17, op. 132, d. 237, ll. 13–15. See also RGASPI, f. 77, op. 4, d. 73, ll. 7–11; Bianki, *K. Simonov i A. Tvardovskii v 'Novom Mire'*, p. 19.

64. RGASPI, f. 17, op. 118, d. 229, l. 17.

65. N. Tipot (Sokolova), 'Dnevnik', private archive. On Sofronov and Simonov as rivals to succeed Fadeyev see the thoughts of Borshchagovsky in A. Borshchagovskii, *Pustotelyi monolit* (Moscow, 2002), pp. 133–4.

66. RGALI, f. 1814, op. 9, d. 19 ('Vospominaniia o kampanii po bor'be s kosmopolitiz-mom', ts., 1976); Borshchagovskii, *Zapiski balovnia sud'by*, p. 214.

67. See e.g. K. Simonov, 'Zadachi sovetskoi dramaturgii i teatral'naia kritika', *Pravda*,

27–8 February 1949 (where the Sartre and Miller quotation comes from); same author, 'Zadachi sovetskoi dramaturgii i teatral'naia kritika', *Literaturnaia gazeta*, 5 March 1949.

68. RGASPI, f. 17, op. 132, d. 226, ll. 1–6; d. 229, l. 30; Kostyrchenko, *Tainaia politika Stalina*, pp. 339–40.

69. Borshchagovskii, *Zapiski balovnia sud'by*, pp. 19, 35–6, 49, 187, 200, 204, 215, 223, 272, 278–9; interview with Aleksandr Borshchagovsky, Moscow, November 2003.

70. Borschagovskii, *Zapiski balovnia sud'by*, pp. 266, 279; interview with Aleksandr Borshchagovsky, Moscow, November 2003; RGALI, f. 1814, op. 9, d. 4, l. 4.

71. Interview with Aleksandr Borshchagovsky, Moscow, November 2003; Borshchagovskii, *Zapiski balovnia sud'by*, pp. 4, 240.

72. Ibid., pp. 261–2.

73. See A. Kozhevnikov, 'President of Stalin's Academy: The Mask and Responsibility of Sergei Vavilov', *Isis*, vol. 87, no. 1 (March 1996), pp. 18–50; N. Tolstoi (ed.), *Brat'ia Nikolai i Sergei Vavilovy* (Moscow, 1991); M. Popovsky, *The Vavilov Affair* (Hamden, 1984); S. Ivanovich *Vavilov: ocherki i vospominaniia* (Moscow, 1991). Vavilov acted surreptitiously against official decisions and his opposition went unnoticed for many years – perhaps one reason why he was maligned as a 'lackey president of the Academy of Sciences' by Solzhenitsyn: A. Solzhenitsyn, *The Gulag Archipelago 1918–1956: An Experiment in Literary Investigation*, 3 vols. (London, 1974–8), vol. 2, p. 638.

74. RGASPI, f. 17, op. 132, d. 237, ll. 14–15; RGALI, f. 1814, op. 9, d. 1365, l. 1; f. 2203, op. 1, d. 333, l. 1; f. 631, op. 16, d. 90; f. 2203, op. 1, d. 333, l. 5; d. 336, l. 11; interview with Nina Arkhipova, Moscow, November 2003; Borshchagovskii, *Zapiski balovnia sud'by*, p. 321.

75. RGALI, f. 1814, op. 6, dd. 70, 173; d. 170, l. 17; interview with Lazar Lazarev, Moscow, November 2003; interview with Aleksei Simonov, Moscow, July 2004.

76. RGALI, f. 1814, op. 1, d. 500.

77. Simonov, *Glazami cheloveka moego pokoleniia*, pp. 126–8; Fink, *Konstantin Simonov*, p. 229.

78. RGALI, f. 1814, op. 1, d. 563; op. 4, d. 10; op. 9, d. 5, ll. 69–70; RGASPI, f. 82, op. 2, d. 1458, l. 49; f. 558, op. 11, d. 806, l. 164; Simonov, *Glazami cheloveka moego pokoleniia*, pp. 128–31.

79. Ibid., pp. 135–7.

80. RGALI, f. 1814, op. 9, d. 809, ll. 1–6; Karaganov, *Konstantin Simonov*, pp. 88–9; Simonov, *Segodnia i davno*, pp. 609–10.

81. K. Simonov, *Sobranie sochinenii*, 12 vols. (Moscow, 1979–87), vol. 12, p. 41.

82. Interview with Aleksei Simonov, Moscow, November 2003; RGALI, f. 1814, op. 1, d. 454, ll. 28–41.

83. Simonov, *Glazami cheloveka moego pokoleniia*, pp. 185–9.

84. See *Gosudarstvennyi antisemitizm v SSSR: ot nachala do kul'minatsii, 1938–1953* (Moscow, 2005), pp. 27–61.

85. Borshchagovskii, *Zapiski balovnia sud'by*, p. 267.

86. MSP, f. 3, op. 37, d. 2, ll. 13, 52; I. Shikheeva-Gaister, *Semeinaia khronika vremen kul'ta lichnosti: 1925–1953* (Moscow, 1998), pp. 72–3, 78–9, 257.

87. MM, f. 2, op. 5, d. 3; f. 12, op. 30, d. 2, l. 27.

88. Interviews with Mark Epshtein, St Petersburg, June and October 2003.

89. SLFA, various documents; interview with Fania Laskina, Moscow, June 2003; interview with Aleksei Simonov, Moscow, November 2003; RGALI, f. 1814, op. 9, d. 1533; RGASPI, f. 495, op. 199, d. 207 (Zaidler).

90. A. Simonov, *Chastnaia kollektsiia* (Nizhny Novgorod 1999), p. 61.

91. RGALI, f. 1814, op. 9, d. 1541, l. 36; d. 1770, l. 2.

92. Simonov, *Chastnaia kollektsiia*, pp. 59–61.

93. RGALI, f. 1814, op. 9, d. 2581.

94. Kostyrchenko, *Tainaia politika Stalina*, pp. 619–26.

95. Interviews with Fania Laskina, Moscow, June 2003, July 2004; interviews with Aleksei

Simonov, Moscow, November 2003; SLFA, Iakov Kharon to Sonia Laskina, 8 March 1954; Yevgeniia to Sonia Laskina, 28 May 1954.

96. RGALI, f. 1814, op. 1, d. 454, l. 32; op. 10, d. 92, l. 37; RGASPI, f. 17, op. 133, d. 390, ll. 81-4; d. 389, ll. 158-63; interview with Lazar Lazarev, Moscow, November 2003. For evidence of Simonov's authorship of the letter of 24 March see *Nash sovremennik*, 1999, no. 1, p. 206.

97. Simonov, *Glazami cheloveka moego pokoleniia*, pp. 189-204.

98. RGALI, f. 1814, op. 1, d. 802, l. 95.

99. RGASPI, f. 17, op. 119, d. 452, ll. 4-6; Simonov, *Glazami cheloveka moego pokoleniia*, pp. 220-22; Fink, *Konstantin Simonov*, p. 112.

100. Brent and Naukov, *Stalin's Last Crime*, pp. 9, 129, 176, 184; SLFA, M. Laskin, 'Vospominaniia', ms., p. 86; Zubkova, *Russia After the War*, p. 137.

101. S. Sebag Montefiore, *Stalin: The Court of the Red Tsar* (London, 2003), p. 568.

102. Simonov, *Glazami cheloveka moego pokoleniia*, pp. 223-7.

103. Ibid., p. 229.

104. RGALI, f, 1814, op. 4, d. 10, l. 5.

105. SLFA, M. Laskin, 'Vospominaniia', ms., pp. 87-8.

106. MP, f. 4, op. 2, d. 2, ll. 13, 30.

107. MP, f. 4, op. 23, d. 2, l. 15.

108. Mandelstam, *Hope Abandoned*, p. 385.

109. MM, f. 12, op. 9, d. 2, l. 67.

110. MP, f. 4, op. 11, d. 2, l. 46; op. 5, d. 2, l. 12.

111. MSP, f. 3, op. 4, d. 2, l. 31.

112. A. Knight, *Beria: Stalin's First Lieutenant* (Princeton, 1993), p. 185; A. Lokshin, ' "Delo vrachei": "Otkliki trudiashchikhsia" ', *Vestnik evreiskogo universiteta v Moskve*, 1994, no. 1, pp. 52-62.

113. MSP, f. 3, op. 4, d. 2, ll. 43-4.

114. Interview with Zinaida Belikova, St Petersburg, May 2003.

115. Shikheeva-Gaister, *Semeinaia khronika*, p. 175.

116. *Sluzhili dva tovarishcha*, p. 357; MM, f. 12, op. 30, d. 2, l. 22; O. Adamova-Sliuzberg, *Put'* (Moscow, 2002), p. 201.

117. See Applebaum, *Gulag*, pp. 435-53.

118. A. Makarova, 'Noril'skoe vosstanie. Mai-avgust 1953 goda', ms.; Applebaum, *Gulag*, pp. 437, 440; MM, f. 12, op. 20, d. 2, ll. 74-5, 89, 91.

119. MM, f. 12, op. 20, d. 2, ll. 34, 48; f. 1, op. 1, d. 1925, ll. 11-30.

120. MM, f. 12, op. 20, d. 2, l. 92; MSP, f. 3, op. 8, d. 2, l. 18; d. 3, ll. 20-22; interview with Vasilina Dmitruk, Norilsk, July 2004.

121. On the similarly moderate demands of the uprising in the Kengir division of the Steplag special camp in Kazakhstan in May–June 1954 see S. Barnes, ' "In a Manner Befitting Soviet Citizens": An Uprising in the Post-Stalin Gulag', *Slavic Review*, vol. 64, no. 4 (Winter 2005), pp. 823-50.

122. MM, f. 12, op. 20, d. 2, ll. 98, 101.

123. *Istoriia stalinskogo gulaga: konets 1920-kh – pervaia polovina 1950-kh godov. Sobranie dokumentov v semi tomakh*, vol. 6, *Vosstaniia, bunty i zabastovski zakliuchennykh* (Moscow, 2004), pp. 320-413; Applebaum, *Gulag*, pp. 441-2; interview with Semyon Golovko, Norilsk, July 2004.

8: Return (1953-6)

1. SLFA, Spravka MVD, 11 November 1955; Yevgeniia to Sonia Laskina, 8 September 1955, 5 October 1955; interview with Fania Laskina, September 2003; interview with Aleksei Simonov, November 2003.

2. *Reabilitatsiia: kak eto bylo. Dokumenty prezidiuma TsKPSS i drugie materialy: mart 1953-fevral' 1956* (Moscow, 2000), p. 213.

3. SLFA, Sonia Laskina to Dmitry Shepilov, 4 June 1955; V. Frid, *58½: zapiski lagernogo pridurka* (Moscow, 1996), pp. 358–9.

4. Y. Gorlizki and O. Khlevniuk, *Cold Peace: Stalin and the Soviet Ruling Circle, 1945–1953* (Oxford, 2004), p. 131; D. Shepilov, *Neprimknuvshii* (Moscow, 2001), p. 267; A. Knight, *Beria: Stalin's First Lieutenant* (Princeton, 1993), pp. 209–10; K. Simonov, *Glazami cheloveka moego pokoleniia* (Moscow, 1990), pp. 246–7.

5. V. Naumov, 'Repression and Rehabilitation', in W. Taubman, S. Khrushchev and A. Gleason (eds.), *Nikita Khrushchev* (New Haven, 2000), pp. 90–91; SLFA, Sonia Laskina to Dmitry Shepilov, 4 June 1955; Konstantin Simonov to Yevgeniia Laskina, 24 September 1955.

6. N. Khrushchev, *Khrushchev Remembers: The Last Testament*, translated and edited by S. Talbott (Boston, 1974), p. 79; A. Hochschild, *The Unquiet Ghost: Russians Remember Stalin* (London, 1994), p. 223; N. Adler, *Beyond the Soviet System: The Gulag Survivor* (New Brunswick, 2002), pp. 90–93.

7. SLFA, Yevgeniia to Sonia Laskina, 16 September 1955; Vladimir Lugovskoi to Yevgeniia Laskina, 20 July 1956; Maia Bykova to Yevgeniia Laskina, 25 December 1974; interview with Aleksei Simonov, Moscow, June 2003.

8. E. Bonner, *Mothers and Daughters* (London, 1992), pp. 89–90, 328, 330–31; interview with Elena Bonner, Boston, November 2006.

9. Compare this with the memoirs of the dissident Liudmila Alekseyeva, who recalls that her moral distancing from the Soviet regime was similarly influenced by her reading of Herzen and by the example of the Decembrists: L. Alexeyeva and P. Goldberg, *The Thaw Generation: Coming of Age in the Post-Stalin Era* (Boston, 1990), pp. 34–5.

10. MSP, f. 3, op. 33, d. 2, ll. 33, 39.

11. MSP, f. 3, op. 45, d. 2, l. 47.

12. MSP, f. 3, op. 45, d. 2, ll. 132, 166.

13. MSP, f. 3, op. 45, d. 2, ll. 26–7, 89–90, 134.

14. MSP, f. 3, op. 24, d. 2, l. 38.

15. MSP, f. 3, op. 35, d. 2, ll. 40–54.

16. MSP, f. 3, op. 39, d. 2, ll. 27, 29.

17. MSP, f. 3, op. 39, d. 3, ll. 1–5.

18. MSP, f. 3, op. 39, d. 2, ll. 31.

19. MSP, f. 3, op. 39, d. 2, ll. 36, 47, 52, 54.

20. B. Okudzhava, 'Devushka moei mechty', in *Izbrannye proizvedeniia v dvukh tomakh* (Moscow, 1989), vol. 2, pp. 283–94.

21. MP, f. 4, op. 10, d. 2, ll. 9, 28.

22. MSP, f. 3, op. 38, d. 2, ll. 19, 36.

23. MM, f. 12, op. 29, d. 2, l. 20.

24. SFA, I. Slavina, 'Tonen'kii nerv istorii', ms., p. 17; interview with Ida Slavina, Cologne, June 2003.

25. MP, f. 4, op. 2, d. 2, ll. 23–4, 43–5.

26. GFA, letter from Anatoly to Liuba Golovnia, 5 December 1940; O. Golovnia, 'Predislovie k pis'mam', ms., p. 70; L. Golovnia-Babitskaia, 'Predsmertnye zapiski', ms., p. 4; A. Bachinskii, 'Zhizn', liubov' i smert' Anatoliia Golovni', *Stolitsa S*, 17 January 1997; interview with Yevgeniia Golovnia, Moscow, July 2004.

27. MSP, f. 3, op. 46, d. 3, l. 43; MM, f. 12, op. 29, d. 2, ll. 34–5.

28. M. Nikolaev, *Detdom* (New York, 1985), p. 96; interviews with Viktoriia Shweitser, Moscow, July 2004; Amherst, November 2006.

29. O. Adamova-Sliuzberg, *Put'* (Moscow, 2002), p. 153.

30. Ibid., pp. 154–5.

31. On this see D. Field, 'Communist Morality and Meanings of Private Life in Post-Stalinist Russia, 1953–64' (Ph.D. dissertation, University of Michigan, 1996). On youth culture: J. Fürst, 'The Importance of Being Stylish: Youth, Culture and Identity in Late Stalinism', in same author (ed.), *Late Stalinist Russia: Society between Reconstruction and Reinvention* (London, 2006), pp. 209–30.

32. MM, f. 12, op. 16, d. 2, ll. 78, 79–80, 85, 97.
33. MFA, L. Makhnach, 'Otets', ms., pp. 3–8; interview with Leonid Makhnach, Moscow, July 2004.
34. MSP, f. 3, op. 8, d. 2, l. 24.
35. L. El'iashova, ' "Kak zhit"? O zhizni Sof'i Mikhailovny Firsovoi', *Sankt-Peterburgskii Universitet*, no. 22 (3489), 20 October 1998, p. 24; Frid, *58½*, p. 389; *Sluzhili dva tovarishcha: kniga o zhizni kinodramaturgov Dunskogo i Frida* (Moscow, 2002), p. 146.
36. MM, f. 12, op. 18, d. 2, ll. 12–14, 17–19.
37. MSP, f. 3, op. 41, d. 2, ll. 37–41, 83–6; d. 3, l. 2.
38. MP, f. 4, op. 22, d. 2, ll. 16, 29, 35, 50, 53, 59.
39. MM, f. 1, op. 1, dd. 841, 2676; f. 12, op. 4, d. 2, ll. 59–80.
40. GFA, N. Iznar, 'Avtobiografiia'; Natalia Iznar to Elena Abezgauz, undated.
41. RGALI, f. 1814, op. 9, d. 2581, ll. 28–36.
42. RGALI, f. 1814, op. 9, d. 229, ll. 15, 17, 18, 21, 32, 47, 48.
43. MM, f. 2, op. 1, d. 45, l. 1105; A. Solzhenitsyn, *The Gulag Archipelago 1918–1956: An Experiment in Literary Investigation*, 3 vols. (London, 1974–8), vol. 3, p. 455.
44. A. Applebaum, 'After the Gulag', *New York Review of Books*, vol. 49, no. 16 (24 October 2002), p. 41.
45. MP, f. 4, op. 10, d. 2, ll. 10–13.
46. Adler, *Beyond the Soviet System*, pp. 30–31; A. Applebaum, *Gulag: A History of the Soviet Camps* (London, 2003), p. 460; C. Hooper, 'Terror from Within: Participation and Coercion in Soviet Power, 1924–64' (Ph.D. dissertation, Princeton University, 2003), p. 377.
47. Solzhenitsyn, *The Gulag Archipelago*, vol. 3, p. 451.
48. RGASPI, f. 560, op. 1, d. 37, l. 487.
49. MM, f. 2, op. 1, d. 29 (Anatolii Brat [Zhukov], 'Zhutkie gody').
50. MSP, f. 3, op. 8, d. 2, l. 28.
51. MP, f. 4, op. 6, d. 2, ll. 28–30, 39–40.
52. MM, f. 12, op. 20, d. 2, l. 124.
53. MP, f. 4, op. 6, d. 2, l. 29.
54. MP, f. 4, op. 2, d. 2, l. 26.
55. Adamova-Sliuzberg, *Put'*, pp. 207–8.
56. MP, f. 4, op. 2, d. 2, l. 46.
57. MP, f. 4, op. 43, d. 2, l. 2.
58. MSP, f. 3, op. 46, d. 2, ll. 51–4; d. 3, ll. 49–50.
59. TsAFSB, Arkhivno-sledstvennoe delo I. V. Slavina (P-51969); 'Delo reabilitatsii' (N4N-012826/55); SFA, I. Slavina, 'Put'' na plakhu', ms., pp. 3–6, 103; interview with Ida Slavina, Cologne, June 2003.
60. MSP, f. 3, op. 10, d. 2, ll. 15, 30–31; d. 3, ll. 34–5. See also MSP, f. 3, op. 38, d. 2, ll. 23–6; MM, f. 12, op. 2, d. 2, ll. 28–30.
61. L. Chukovskaia, *Zapiski ob Anne Akhmatovoi*, 3 vols. (Paris, 1980), vol. 2, p. 137.
62. MSP, f. 3, op. 12, d. 2, ll. 60–67, 131–3.
63. MSP, f. 2, op. 51, d. 2, ll. 3–7.
64. MM, f. 12, op. 10, d. 2, ll. 18–23.
65. MSP, f. 3, op. 14, d. 2, ll. 66–8; d. 3, ll. 54–5.
66. I. Sherbakova, 'The Gulag in Memory', in L. Passerini (ed.), *International Yearbook of Oral History and Life Stories*, vol. 1: *Memory and Totalitarianism* (Oxford, 1992), p. 114 (translation slightly altered for clarity).
67. See A. Inkeles and R. Bauer, *The Soviet Citizen: Daily Life in a Totalitarian Society* (Cambridge, Mass., 1959).
68. N. Mandelstam, *Hope Against Hope* (London, 1989), p. 48.
69. Ibid., p. 49.
70. *Vokrug Fadeeva: neizvestnye pis'ma, zametki i dokumenty* (Moscow, 1996), pp. 12, 122; RGALI, f. 1814, op. 9, d. 5, l. 30; V. Kaverin, *Epilog: memuary* (Moscow, 2002), pp. 313–24.

71. *Izvestiia TsK KPSS*, 1990, no. 10, p. 147.
72. On Fadeyev's kindness see K. Chukovskii, *Dnevnik, 1901–69*, 2 vols. (Moscow, 2003), vol. 2, pp. 282–3; A. Borshchagovskii, *Zapiski balovnia sud'by* (Moscow, 1991), p. 21; and the letter by Akhmatova to Fadeyev on 10 March 1956 in which she thanked him for his efforts to release her son Lev Gumilyov from a Siberian labour camp ('You have been more kind and sympathetic than anybody in these frightful years') in *Vokrug Fadeeva*, p. 161.
73. RGALI, f. 618, op. 16, d. 88, l. 16.
74. *Literaturnaia gazeta*, 17 July 1954, pp. 2–3; 20 July 1954, pp. 2–3.
75. Simonov, *Glazami cheloveka moego pokoleniia*, pp. 248–53; interview with Lazar Lazarev, Moscow, November 2003.
76. *Pravda*, 4 July 1954, p. 3.
77. RGALI, f. 1814, op. 9, d. 1770, ll. 21–2. On the public response to the novel see D. Kozlov, 'Naming the Social Evil: The Readers of *Novyi mir* and Vladimir Dudintsev's *Not by Bread Alone*, 1956–1959', in P. Jones (ed.), *The Dilemmas of De-Stalinization: A Social and Cultural History of Reform in the Khrushchev Era* (London, 2005), pp. 80–98.
78. RGALI, f. 1814, op. 9, d. 1770, l. 15; K. Simonov, *Segodnia i davno* (Moscow, 1978), p. 78; *A za mnoiu shum pogoni: Boris Pasternak i vlast'. Dokumenty 1956–72* (Moscow, 2001), pp. 89–90.
79. L. Lazarev, *Shestoi etazh: kniga vospominaniia* (Moscow, 1999), p. 201.
80. *Reabilitatsiia: kak eto bylo*, pp. 349–51; W. Taubman, *Khrushchev: The Man and His Era* (London, 2003), pp. 270, 272, 274, 278.
81. *Reabilitatsiia: kak eto bylo*, pp. 5–6; Taubman, *Khrushchev*, pp. 273–4.

9: Memory (1956–2006)

1. W. Taubman, *Khrushchev: The Man and His Era* (London, 2003), pp. 282–3.
2. P. Jones, 'From the Secret Speech to the Burial of Stalin: Real and Ideal Responses to De-Stalinization', in same author (ed.), *The Dilemmas of De-Stalinization: A Social and Cultural History of Reform in the Khrushchev Era* (London, 2005), p. 47.
3. L. Alexeyeva and P. Goldberg, *The Thaw Generation: Coming of Age in the Post-Stalin Era* (Boston, 1990), p. 4.
4. MM, f. 12, op. 4, d. 2, ll. 47, 78.
5. MSP, f. 3, op. 18, d. 2, ll. 21–2.
6. MP, f. 4, op. 26, d. 2, ll. 12–14.
7. MP, f. 4, op. 22, d. 2, ll. 14, 62–4.
8. MP, f. 4, op. 2, d. 2, ll. 36–41.
9. MSP, f. 3, op. 19, d. 2, ll. 5, 24–33.
10. MP, f. 4, op. 19, d. 2, ll. 26–7, 41–5; d. 3, l. 1; d. 4, ll. 1–3.
11. I. Shikheeva-Gaister, *Semeinaia khronika vremen kul'ta lichnosti: 1925–1953* (Moscow, 1998), pp. 266–7; MSP, f. 3, op. 37, d. 2, ll. 31–2, 76.
12. MSP, f. 3, op. 8, d. 2, l. 25; MP, f. 4, op. 2, d. 2, l. 23; MM, f. 12, op. 30, d. 2, ll. 36–8.
13. V. Shalamov, 'Dry Rations', in *Kolyma Tales* (London, 1994), p. 43; MSP, f. 3, op. 37, d. 2, l. 45. See also: op. 1, d. 2, ll. 33–4; op. 36, d. 2, ll. 7–9.
14. C. Merridale, *Night of Stone: Death and Memory in Russia* (London, 2000), p. 21.
15. C. Garland (ed.), *Understanding Trauma: A Psychoanalytical Approach* (London, 1998), pp. 4–5; D. Laub, 'Truth and Testimony: The Process and the Struggle', in C. Caruth (ed.), *Trauma: Explorations in Memory* (Baltimore, 1995), pp. 61–75.
16. MSP, f. 3, op. 15, d. 3, l. 1.
17. Interview with Aleksei Simonov, Moscow, November 2003; interview with Marina Babak, Moscow, November 2003; interview with Nina Arkhipova, Moscow, November 2003.

18. RGALI, f. 1814, op. 9, d. 1538; V. Pushnova, *Valentina Serova* (Moscow, 2003), pp. 258–84; interview with Maria Simonova, Moscow, March 2004.

19. Pushnova, *Valentina Serova*, p. 322; RGALI, f. 1814, op. 9, d. 775, l. 1.

20. Interview with Maria Simonova, Moscow, March 2004; RGALI, f. 1814, op. 9, d. 775, l. 1.

21. RGALI, f. 1814, op. 9, d. 1770, l. 18; interview with Aleksei Simonov, Moscow, September 2003.

22. SLFA, Yevgeniia Laskina to Aleksei Simonov, 28 August 1957; Mark Laskin, 'Vospominaniia', ts., p. 15; RGALI, f. 1814, op. 10. d. 342, l. 20; interview with Fania Laskina, Moscow, July 2004; A. Simonov, *Chastnaia kollektsiia* (Nizhny Novgorod, 1999), pp. 42, 44–5, 148.

23. RGALI, f. 1814, op. 9, d. 2199, l. 2.

24. SLFA, Aleksei Simonov to Yevgeniia Laskina, 19 August 1956; Aleksei Simonov to Konstantin Simonov, 24 October 1956; Konstantin to Aleksei Simonov, 31 August 1956.

25. SLFA, Yevgeniia Laskina to Aleksei Simonov, 26 September 1956; Simonov, *Chastnaia kollektsiia*, p. 67; Aleksei to Konstantin Simonov, 7 February 1957.

26. Interview with Aleksei Simonov, Moscow, November 2003; SLFA, Aleksei Simonov, Diary, 23 December 1956; Aleksei Simonov to Vladimir Dudintsev, 13 December 1956; RGALI, f. 1814, op. 9, d. 1770, ll. 15–17, 22.

27. K. Simonov, *Glazami cheloveka moego pokoleniia* (Moscow, 1990), p. 12; interview with Lazar Lazarev, Moscow, November 2003; RGALI, f. 1814, op. 2, d. 127, ll. 2–3, 8.

28. RGALI, f. 1814, op. 9, d. 1770, l. 12.

29. RGALI, f. 1814, op. 9, d. 1770, l. 13.

30. RGALI, f. 1814, op. 6, d. 170, l. 17.

31. V. Kondrat'ev, 'Ne tol'ko o svoem pokolenii. Zametki pisatelia', *Kommunist*, 1997, no. 7, p. 122.

32. Interview with Marina Babak, Moscow, November 2003.

33. K. Simonov, *Sto sutok voiny* (Smolensk, 1999); same author, *Raznye dni voiny: dnevnik pisatelia*, 2 vols. (Moscow, 1977–8).

34. RGALI, f. 1814, op. 9, d. 11, ll. 1–21; op. 8, d. 58, l. 98.

35. RGALI, f. 1814, op. 9, dd. 2590, 681, 1857.

36. Simonov, *Chastnaia kollektsiia*, pp. 147–55. The cuts, which amounted to sixty typed pages, immediately appeared in samizdat, and were included in foreign editions of the novel from 1969. The complete version of the novel first came out in the Soviet Union in 1973. See R. Pevear's 'Introduction', and his notes on the text in his translation of M. Bulgakov, *The Master and Margarita* (London, 1997), pp. vii–xix.

37. Interviews with Aleksei Simonov, Moscow, September, November 2003, February 2004.

38. RGALI, f. 1814, op. 10, d. 376, ll. 20–21; *Konstantin Simonov v vospominaniiakh sovremennikov* (Moscow, 1984), p. 291; N. Bianki, *K. Simonov i A. Tvardovskii v 'Novom Mire'* (Moscow, 1999), pp. 32–3.

39. L. Lazarev, *Shestoi etazh: kniga vospominaniia* (Moscow, 1999), pp. 208, 210; interview with Lazar Lazarev, Moscow, November 2003; Simonov, *Sto sutok voiny*, pp. 550–54; RGALI, f. 1814, op. 9, d. 5, l. 63; op. 9, d. 19 ('Vospominaniia o kampanii po bor'be s kosmopolitizmom', ts., 1976).

40. K. Simonov and I. Ehrenburg, *V odnoi gazete: reportazhi i stati 1941–1945* (Moscow, 1979); Lazarev, *Shestoi etazh*, pp. 201–2.

41. A. Solzhenitsyn, *The Oak and the Calf: Sketches of Literary Life in the Soviet Union* (London, 1980), p. 299.

42. Interview with Viktor Erofeev, Moscow, November 2003; interview with Andrei Erofeev, Moscow, April 2004; interview with Nina Arkhipova, Moscow, November 2003; D. Gillespie, 'Metropol' ', *The Literary Encyclopedia*, 19 November 2005.

43. Simonov, *Glazami cheloveka moego pokoleniia*, pp. 7–8.

44. Ibid. Fragments of the memoirs were first published in the journal *Znamia* in 1988, no. 3, pp. 3–66; no. 4, pp. 49–121; no. 5, pp. 69–96.

45. See e.g. A. Mikoian, *Tak bylo: razmyshleniia o minuvshem* (Moscow, 1999), p. 589 ('Of course we bear a great responsibility. But we must understand the circumstances in which we worked. There was a lot we did not know, we believed, but in any case there was simply nothing we could change.')
46. Lev Razgon, *True Stories* (London, 1997), pp. 21-34.
47. Interview with Ivan Korchagin, Akmolinsk, September 1988.
48. IFA, 'Kommentarii k pis'mam', ts., 1988; Mikhail Iusipenko to M. Zelder, 29 December 1988; Mikhail Iusipenko to Sergei Barinov, 18 August 1988; interview with Oksana Kozmina, Moscow, 1988.
49. MM, f. 1, op. 2; f. 2, op. 5; f. 12, op. 9, dd. 2, 3.
50. On the relationship between memory and narrative see V. Skultans, *The Testimony of Lives: Narrative and Memory in Post-Soviet Latvia* (London, 1998).
51. *Alexander Dolgun's Story: An American in the Gulag* (New York, 1975), p. 4.
52. I. Sherbakova, 'The Gulag in Memory', in L. Passerini (ed.), *International Yearbook of Oral History and Life Stories*, vol. 1: *Memory and Totalitarianism* (Oxford, 1992), pp. 112-13 (translation slightly altered for clarity).
53. See e.g. MSP, f. 3, op. 42, d. 3, ll. 1-24.
54. M. McAuley, *Soviet Politics 1917-1991* (Oxford, 1992), pp. 56-7.
55. On the Gulag memoir as a literary genre see Leona Toker, *Return from the Archipelago: Narratives of Gulag Survivors* (Bloomington, 2000).
56. E. Ginzburg, *Into the Whirlwind* (London, 1968); *Within the Whirlwind* (London, 1981).
57. C. Merridale, *Ivan's War: The Red Army 1939-1945* (London, 2005), p. 334; A. Applebaum, 'The Real Patriotic War', *New York Review of Books*, vol. 53, no. 6 (6 April 2006), pp. 16, 18.
58. Ginzburg, *Within the Whirlwind*, p. 201.
59. *O vremeni, o Noril'ske, o sebe: vospominaniia*, 5 vols. (Moscow, 2001-4); A. Macqueen, 'Survivors', *Granta*, 64 (Winter 1998), p. 39.
60. Interview with Vasily Romashkin, Norilsk, July 2004.
61. Interview with Olga Iaskina, Norilsk, July 2004. This paragraph is based on interviews with over fifty people in Norilsk during July 2004. See the List of Interviews in Sources.
62. *Moscow News*, 4 March 2005.
63. Mikhail Baitalsky, *Notebooks for the Grandchildren: Recollections of a Trotskyist Who Survived the Stalin Terror* (New Jersey, 1995), pp. 97-8.
64. MP, f. 4, op. 13, d. 2, l. 18.
65. MP, f. 4, op. 24, d. 2, ll. 64-7.
66. MP, f. 4, op. 22, d. 2, ll. 67-71.
67. On this phenomenon in general see H. Krystal, *Massive Psychic Trauma* (New York, 1968); D. Wardl, *Memorial Candles: Children of the Holocaust*, London, 1992; N. Burchardt, 'Transgenerational Transmission in the Families of Holocaust Survivors in England', in D. Bertaux and P. Thompson (eds.), *International Yearbook of Oral History and Life Stories*, vol. 2: *Between Generations: Family Models, Myths and Memories* (Oxford, 1993), pp. 121-37. For details of an interesting pilot study of these issues carried out by the psychologist Marina Gulina among children brought up by survivors of the siege of Leningrad, see 'Malen'kii prints v blokadnom Leningrade: psikhoanaliticheskoe issledovanie', *Sankt-Peterburgskii Universitet*, no. 9 (3698), 5 May 2005, pp. 32-5.
68. MSP, f. 3, op. 11, d. 1, ll. 1-2; d. 2, ll. 53-60, 74-84.
69. MSP, f. 3, op. 37, d. 2, l. 63; interview with Vladimir Korsakov, St Petersburg, May, October 2003.
70. Interviews with Aleksei Iurasovsky, Moscow, July 2004, October 2005.
71. MP, f. 4, op. 24, d. 2, ll. 36-7, 44-7; MSP, f. 3, op. 16, d. 2, l. 91.
72. MP, f. 4, op. 26, d. 2, ll. 6-8; op. 3, d. 2, l. 37.
73. MP, f. 12, op. 4, d. 2, ll. 75-6.
74. MP, f. 12, op. 16, d. 2, l. 23; op. 17, d. 2, l. 52.

75. MP, f. 12, op. 17, d. 2, ll. 52–3.

76. B. Slutskii, *Sud'ba. Stikhi raznykh let* (Moscow, 1990), p. 40.

77. See e.g. MP, f. 4, op. 5, d. 2, l. 20; op. 24, d. 2, ll. 70–73. Some oral historians have argued that under Vladimir Putin's authoritarian government, after 2000, the Russians became 'socialized into reticence', as they had been in the Soviet period, and that, compared to the early 1990s, they were 'reluctant to give candid interviews' (D. Bertaux, P. Thompson and A. Rotkirch (eds.), *On Living Through Soviet Russia* (London, 2004), pp. 8–9).

78. MSP, f. 3, op. 14, d. 3, ll. 52–4.

79. MSP, f. 3, op. 14, d. 2, ll. 41–5, 59–64, 76, 85–9, 93, 119; d. 3, ll. 34, 39–40, 45–6. Antonia died in December 2006.

Sources

Archives

Public archives

AFSBTO	Archive of the Federal Security Service of Tambov Oblast, Tambov
AFSBVO	Archive of the Federal Security Service of Vologda Oblast, Vologda
AMILO	Archive of the Moscow Historical-Literary Society ('Vozvrashchenie')
ARAN	Archive of the Russian Academy of Sciences, Moscow
GAOO	State Archive of Orel Oblast, Orel
GAPO	State Archive of Perm Oblast, Perm
GARF	State Archive of the Russian Federation, Moscow
GARK	State Archive of the Komi Republic, Syktyvkar
GASO	State Archive of Sverdlovsk Oblast, Yekaterinburg
GAVO	State Archive of Vologda Oblast, Vologda
GMPIR	State Museum of Political History of Russia, St Petersburg
GOPAPO	State Socio-Political Archive of Perm Oblast, Perm
HP	Harvard Project ('Project on the Soviet Social System'), Harvard University, USA
IISH	International Institute of Social History, Amsterdam
IRL RAN	Institute of Russian Literature, Russian Academy of Sciences ('Pushkin House'), St Petersburg
MM*	Archive of the Memorial Society, Moscow
MP*	Archive of the Memorial Society, Perm
MSP*	Archive of the Memorial Society, St Petersburg
OR RNB	Manuscripts Department, Russian National Library, St Petersburg
RGAE	Russian State Archive of the Economy, Moscow
RGAKFD	Russian State Archive of Documentary Films and Photographs, Krasnogorsk
RGALI	Russian State Archive of Literature and Art, Moscow
RGASPI	Russian State Archive of Social and Political History, Moscow
SPbF ARAN	St Petersburg Filial of the Archive of the Russian Academy of Sciences
SSEES	School of Slavonic and East European Studies, University of London
TsAFSB	Central Archive of the Federal Security Service, Moscow
TsAODM	Central Archive of Social Movements of Moscow
TsDNA	Centre of Documents, 'the People's Archive', Moscow
TsGAIPD	Central State Archive of Historical Political Documents, Moscow

*All the materials cited from the archives of Memorial were collected and organized by the research project connected to this book. Most of them are available online at http://www.orlandofiges.com, where further details of the project can be found.

TsGASP   Central State Archive of St Petersburg
TsIAM   Central Historical Archive of Moscow
TsKhDMO   Centre for the Preservation of Documents of Youth Organizations, Moscow
TsMAMLS   Central Moscow Archive-Museum of Personal Collections

Private archives

AFA   Alekseyeva Family Archive, Moscow
GFA   Golovnia Family Archive, Moscow
IFA   Iusipenko Family Archive, Akmolinsk, Kazakhstan
LFA   Levitina Family Archive, St Petersburg
MFA   Makhnach Family Archive, Moscow
MIFA   Mikheladze Family Archive, Tbilisi, Georgia
MUFA   Muratov Family Archive, Moscow
PFA   Pavlukhina Family Archive, St Petersburg
RFA   Ramensky Family Archive, Strugi Krasnye
SFA   Slavin Family Archive, Cologne, Germany
SLFA   Simonov-Laskin Family Archive, Moscow
VFA   Vittenburg Family Archive, St Petersburg
VOFA   Voitinsky Family Archive, St Petersburg

List of Interviews

Adasinskaia, Galina Antonovna (St Petersburg)
Akkuratnova, Maia Pavlovna (Moscow)
Aksyonova, Iraida Petrovna (Usole)
Aleksandrova, Irina Mikhailovna (St Petersburg)
Aleksandrova, Valentina Lvovna (St Petersburg)
Aliavdina, Veronika Anatolevna (St Petersburg)
Alkaeva, Raifa Izmagilovna (Krasnokamsk)
Anastaseva, Margarita Viktorovna (Moscow)
Andreyev, Oleg Grigorevich (St Petersburg)
Arapov, Aleksandr Pavlovich (St Petersburg)
Arkhipova, Nina Nikolaeva (Moscow)
Atapov, Sergei Mikhailovich (Tambov)
Avdasheva, Ninel Nikolaevna (St Petersburg)
Babaeva, Klavdiia Mikhailovna (Moscow)
Babailova, Natalia Borisovna (Severodvinsk)
Babak, Marina Mikhailovna (Moscow)
Babikova, Yevgeniia Spiridonovna (Norilsk)
Babina, Rada Lvovna (Moscow)
Babitskaia, Vlada Alekseyevna (Moscow)
Babushkina, Lydia Vasilevna (Perm)
Badaeva, Valentina Fyodorovna (Perm)
Badiaeva, Galina Ivanovna (Perm)
Baigulova, Elena Alekseyevna (Moscow)
Balandin, Grigorii Pavlovich (Perm)
Baranenko, Nadezhda Pavlovna (Perm)
Barinov, Sergei Mikhailovich (Akmolinsk)
Barkovskaia, Marianna Iosifovna (Izobilnoe, Stavropol district)
Batin, Pyotr Yefimovich (Usole)
Batishcheva, Maria Karlovna (Norilsk)
Batrakova, Nina Dmitrevna (Perm)
Bazilevskaia, Valentina Borisovna (Voronezh)
Bazilevskaia, Vladilena Borisovna (Moscow)

Bekker, Valentin Vladimirovich (St Petersburg)
Belikova, Zinaida Vasilevna (St Petersburg)
Beloborodov, Nikolai Nikolaevich (Perm)
Belousov, Arkadii Sergeyevich (Penza)
Belova, Anna Pavlovna (Krasnokamsk)
Beneta, Svetlana Anatolevna (Norilsk)
Blagoveshchensky, Andrei Borisovich (Moscow)
Bletsko, Tatiana Nikolaevna (St Petersburg)
Blium, Arlen Viktorovich (St Petersburg)
Blium, Igor Vsevolodovich (St Petersburg)
Bogdanov, Sergei Nikolaevich (St Petersburg)
Bogdanova, Natalia Borisovna (Moscow)
Bolchis, Tatiana Vasilevna (St Petersburg)
Bonner, Elena Georgievna (Boston, USA)
Borodina, Valentina Semyonovna (Norilsk)
Borozna, Mikhail Danilovich (Orel)
Borshchagovsky, Aleksandr Mikhailovich (Moscow)
Bronshtein, Svetlana Aleksandrovna (Moscow)
Bronshtein, Yekaterina Mikhailovna (St Petersburg)
Budkevich, Maria Stanislavovna (St Petersburg)
Bulat, Inessa Pavlovna (St Petersburg)
Burylovna, Zoia Pavlovna (Perm)
Bushueva, Angelina Vladimirovna (Perm)
Chechik, Elizaveta Natanovna (Moscow)
Cherepanova, Praskovia Iakimovna (Perm)
Cherkasova, Karina Leonidovna (Moscow)
Cherkasskaia, Bella Martynovna (St Petersburg)
Cherkesov, Oleg Vsevolodovich (St Petersburg)
Cherkesova, Svetlana Vsevolodovna (St Petersburg)
Cherniaev, Boris Dmitrievich (Tambov)
Cherniaeva, Dalita Artyomovna (Krasnokamsk)
Chesnokov, Vladimir Ivanovich (St Petersburg)
Chulkova, Antonina Alekseyevna (Perm)
Chuprun, Gerta Yevgenevna (Moscow)
Dadzis, Lydia Ianovna (St Petersburg)
Danilenko, Irina Aleksandrovna (Norilsk)
Danilov, Viktor Petrovich (Moscow)
Danilova, Natalia Stepanovna (Moscow)
Danilovich, Liia Iakovlevna (Perm)
Darvina, Anna Andreyevna (Norilsk)
Davydova, Inna Pavlovna (Voronezh)
Delibash, Elizaveta Aleksandrovna (St Petersburg)
Dmitrenko, Irina Aleksandrovna (Norilsk)
Dmitruk, Stepan Kuzmich (Norilsk)
Dmitruk, Vasilina Korneyevna (Norilsk)
Dobrovolskaia, Ella Dmitrievna (Moscow)
Dombrovskaia, Elena Petrovna (Moscow)
Drozdov, Boris Pavlovich (Moscow)
Dudareva, Galina Vasilevna (St Petersburg)
Eisenberg, Vera Ignatevna (Kolpino)
Eliashova, Liudmila Leonidovna (St Petersburg)
Eliashova, Marksena Leonidovna (St Petersburg)
Ender, Zoia Borisovna (Rome, Italy)
Epshtein, Mark Borisovich (St Petersburg)

Erofeev, Andrei Vladimirovich (Moscow)
Erofeev, Viktor Vladimirovich (Moscow)
Feofilaktova, Nina Ivanovna (St Petersburg)
Filimonova, Larisa Fyodorovna (St Petersburg)
Filippova, Kira Ivanovna (St Petersburg)
Fomin, Vladimir Leonidovich (St Petersburg)
Fursei, Georgii Nikolaevich (St Petersburg)
Gabaeva, Natalia Sergeyevna (St Petersburg)
Galchinskaia, Liudmila Mikhailovna (St Petersburg)
Galitsky, Pavel Kalinikovich (St Petersburg)
Garmash, Larisa Danilovna (Moscow)
Garmash, Vitalii Ivanovich (Moscow)
Gavrilov, Boris Nikolaevich (St Petersburg)
Genishta, Vladimir Sergeyevich (Novosibirsk)
Genishta, Yevgeny Sergeyevich (Moscow)
Gernet, Galina Yevgenevna (St Petersburg)
Glazova, Margarita Nikolaevna (St Petersburg)
Godes, Anri Mikhailovich (St Petersburg)
Goldevskaia, Yekaterina Ivanovna (St Petersburg)
Goldobin, Andrei Borisovich (St Petersburg)
Golovanova, Genrietta Ivanovna (Severodvinsk)
Golovko, Semyon Georgievich (Norilsk)
Golovnia, Oksana Anatolevna (Moscow)
Golovnia, Yevgeniia Viktorovna (Moscow)
Golubiatnikova, Natalia Nikolaevna (Norilsk)
Goncharov, Yevgeny Yefimovich (Norilsk)
Goncharova, Klavdiia (Moscow)
Gorbach, Larisa Fyodorovna (Perm)
Gordon, Marianna Lvovna (St Petersburg)
Gorshkova, Tamara Filippovna (Perm)
Gotman, Rudolf Gotlibovich (Perm)
Gremiakina, Antonina Dmitrevna (Krasnokamsk)
Gribelnaia, Nina Andreyevna (St Petersburg)
Grigoreva, Natalia Vasilevna (Moscow)
Gukovsky, Maksim Stepanovich (Voronezh)
Gurevich, Sergei Grigorevich (St Petersburg)
Gurova, Irina Gavrilovna (Moscow)
Iablokov, Iurii Yevgenevich (Moscow)
Iakovlev, Gennady Ilarionovich (Usole)
Iakovlev, Mikhail Ivanovich (St Petersburg)
Iakovleva, Lelita Andreyevna (Adler, Krasnodar region)
Iakovleva, Nina Andreyevna (St Petersburg)
Iakubovich, Vladimir Andreyevich (St Petersburg)
Ianchevskaia, Maria Leopoldovna (St Petersburg)
Ianin, Vladimir Andreyevich (Moscow)
Ianovich, Elena Petrovna (St Petersburg)
Iashkov, Anatoly Vasilevich (St Petersburg)
Iaskina, Olga Ivanovna (Norilsk)
Iazykov, Vladimir Aleksandrovich (Moscow)
Ibragim-Zade, Dilara Ibragimovna (Moscow)
Ilina, Inna Vasilevna (Moscow)
Ilina, Liana Lvovna (St Petersburg)
Iodis, Praskovia Andreyevna (Norilsk)
Iurasovsky, Aleksei Mikhailovich (Moscow)

Iushkevich, Mikhail Ivanovich (St Petersburg)
Iusipenko, Mikhail Terentevich (Akmolinsk)
Iusopova, Antonina Samsonovna (Krasnokamsk)
Ivanishcheva, Sofia Nikolaevna (Krasnokamsk)
Ivanov, Aleksei Petrovich (Voronezh)
Ivanov, Sergei Borisovich (Tambov)
Ivanova, Margarita Fyodorovna (Krasnokamsk)
Ivanova, Marina Nikolaevna (St Petersburg)
Ivanova, Olga Stepanovna (St Petersburg)
Ivanova, Tatiana Ivanovna (St Petersburg)
Kagner, Irina Borisovna (Moscow)
Kalnina, Maia Konstantinovna (St Petersburg)
Kanepei, Elena Vasilevna (Yeisk, Krasnodar region)
Kasatkina, Lydia Dmitrevna (Perm)
Kashin, Boris Romanovich (Perm)
Kashtanov, Aleksei Mikhailovich (Penza)
Kasimova, Sanie Isliamovna (Berezniki)
Katseilidi, Vera Dmitrevna (Krasnokamsk)
Katseilidi, Yekaterina Dmitrevna (Krasnokamsk)
Kavelina, Olga Aleksandrovna (Moscow)
Kazakova, Zoia Pavlovna (Perm)
Kem, Vilgelmina Ivanovna (Usole)
Kharitonova, Ella Ilinichna (St Petersburg)
Khlystova, Svetlana Veniaminovna (Perm)
Kiselyova, Yevgeniia Konstantinovna (Moscow)
Kleimenova, Zoia Izrailevna (Moscow)
Kofman, Maia Lazarevna (Moscow)
Kogan, Rebekka (Rita) Samoilovna (St Petersburg)
Kolla, Galina Nikolaevna (Perm)
Kollakova, Julia Vasilevna (Moscow)
Kollang, Rene Almarovich (St Petersburg)
Kolobkov, Viacheslav Petrovich (St Petersburg)
Koltsova, Laura Vladimirovna (St Petersburg)
Kondratenko, Dina Vladimirovna (St Petersburg)
Kondrateva, Adalina Veniaminovna (Moscow)
Konstantinova, Elena Aleksandrovna (Petrozavodsk)
Konstantinova, Natalia Aleksandrovna (St Petersburg)
Korchagin, Ivan Petrovich (Karaganda)
Korsakov, Vladimir Georgievich (St Petersburg)
Kosaryov, Vladimir Valentinovich (St Petersburg)
Kosheleva, Galina Andreyevna (St Petersburg)
Kovach, Nikolai Ivanovich (Yeisk, Krasnodar region)
Kozhin, Viktor Aleksandrovich (St Petersburg)
Kozmina, Oksana Yevdokimovna (Moscow)
Kozyrev, Aleksandr Nikolaevich (St Petersburg)
Kraeva, Klara Maksimovna (Perm)
Kraevsky, Karl Borisovich (Moscow)
Krasilnikov, Grigorii Pavlovich (Krasnokamsk)
Krasnova, Elena Iosifovna (St Petersburg)
Krasnova, Elena Ivanovna (St Petersburg)
Krasovitov, Mikhail Gavrilovich (Krasnokamsk)
Krauze, Elena Fridrikhovna (Moscow)
Kreines, Natalia Mikhailovna (Moscow)
Krivulina, Julia Aleksandrovna (Ufa)

Kropotina, Valentina Andreyevna (Perm)
Kruglova, Tatiana Sergeyevna (Moscow)
Krutilova, Larisa Solomonovna (St Petersburg)
Krylov, Nikolai Arkhipovich (Perm)
Krylova, Irma Adolfovna (St Petersburg)
Krylova, Valentina Ivanovna (Perm)
Kulak, Lydia Fyodorovna (Krasnokamsk)
Kurko, Nadezhda Adolfovna (St Petersburg)
Kurochkina, Olga Aleksandrovna (Perm)
Kuznetsov, Anatoly Pavlovich (Perm)
Kuznetsova, Julia Nikolaevna (Perm)
Kuznetsova, Maria Ilinichna (Moscow)
Kuznetsova, Tatiana Borisovna (St Petersburg)
Lapchev, Vasily Stepanovich (Perm)
Lapko, Laris Ivanovich (Gaiva)
Lapko, Rem Ivanovich (Yekaterinburg)
Lapko, Stanislav Ivanovich (Krasnokamsk)
Lapko, Stanislav Ivanovich (Perm)
Larionov, Maksim Mikhailovich (St Petersburg)
Larkov, Sergei Alekseyevich (Moscow)
Laskina, Fania Samoilovna (Moscow)
Lazarev, Lazar Ilich (Moscow)
Lazareva, Valentina Grigorevna (Krasnokamsk)
Lazareva, Zoia Grigorevna (Krasnokamsk)
Lebedeva, Nadezhda Mikhailovna (St Petersburg)
Lebedeva-Epshtein, Tatiana Valerevna (Moscow)
Leshchukova, Maria Ivanovna (Usole)
Leven, Leonid Petrovich (St Petersburg)
Levidova, Ada Lvovna (St Petersburg)
Levin, Valerii Pavlovich (Moscow)
Levina, Nina Pavlovna (Krasnoiarsk)
Levitina, Bella Iosifovna (St Petersburg)
Liberman, Irina Solomonovna (St Petersburg)
Likhachyov, Sergei Ivanovich (Penza)
Lileyev, Nikolai Ivanovich (St Petersburg)
Liubavskaia, Mella Pavlovna (St Petersburg)
Liubich, Olga Aleksandrovna (Moscow)
Liverovskaia, Olga Alekseyevna (St Petersburg)
Lobachev, Vladimir Mikhailovich (Moscow)
Lomakin, Iurii Mikhailovich (Tambov)
Lopatin, Roman Aleksandrovich (Stavropol)
Lorentsson, Lilia Vikinitevna (Perm)
Loshkareva, Taisia Grigorevna (Romanovo, Usole district)
Loviagina, Polina Nikiforovna (Perm)
Lukomsky, Georgii Vladimirovich (St Petersburg)
Makhnach, Leonid Vladimirovich (Moscow)
Makridin, Vasily Platonovich (St Petersburg)
Maksimov, Vladimir Ivanovich (St Petersburg)
Malakhovskaia, Terezia Valerianovna (St Petersburg)
Malanichev, Nikolai Ivanovich (Krasnokamsk)
Margulin, Valentin Mikhailovich (St Petersburg)
Markelova, Galina Georgievna (St Petersburg)
Martinelli, Elena Arvidovna (St Petersburg)
Medvedeva, Marina Sergeyevna (Moscow)

Melnikova, Tsetsiliia Vladimirovna (Cologne, Germany)
Meshalkin, Nikolai Ivanovich (Perm)
Meshalkina, Elfrida Gotlibovna (Perm)
Mezentseva, Klara Isaakovna (St Petersburg)
Miftakhov, Tolgat Latfyllinoch (Krasnokamsk)
Miftakhova, Asia Sadykova (Krasnokamsk)
Mikhailov, Valentin Mikhailovich (Tambov)
Mikhailova, Nadezhda Nikolaeva (Moscow)
Mikheladze, Vakhtang Yevgenevich (Moscow)
Mikova, Nina Grigorevna (Usole)
Mikueva, Irina Ilinichna (Perm)
Mikueva, Tamara Nikolaevna (Stavropol)
Mikuevich, Anatoly Pavlovich (Voronezh)
Mileiko, Vitalii Bronislavovich (St Petersburg)
Milkevich, Vladimir Vilkentivich (Berezniki)
Minusova, Vera Viktorovna (Perm)
Mitina, Valentina Nazarovna (Moscow)
Moiseyenko, Yevgeniia Mitrofanovna (Moscow)
Moiseyeva, Antonina Mikhailovna (Perm)
Molotkov, Lev Vladimirovich (St Petersburg)
Monko, Ianina Davydovna (Moscow)
Morozov, Nikita Fyodorovich (St Petersburg)
Mukhina, Nina Nikolaeva (Perm)
Muravnik, Leonid Iakovlevich (Moscow)
Muravsky, Valentin Tikhonovich (St Petersburg)
Muravsky, Vladimir Valentinovich (St Petersburg)
Nardina, Zoia Iakovlevna (Norilsk)
Nemishchenko, Galina Parfenevna (Moscow)
Netto, Lev Aleksandrovich (Moscow)
Neverova, Nina Vasilevna (Usole)
Nevskaia, Veronika Aleksandrovna (St Petersburg)
Nikiforova, Marksena Mikhailovna (St Petersburg)
Norkina, Maia Nikolaevna (Moscow)
Noskova, Tatiana Aleksandrovna (Perm)
Novikova, Minora Zinovevna (Moscow)
Novoseltseva, Roza Aleksandrovna (Moscow)
Obst, Elizaveta Iosifovna (Norilsk)
Orlova, Yekaterina Aleksandrovna (St Petersburg)
Osipov, Pavel Aleksandrovich (Orel, Usole district)
Ostasheva, Larisa Sergeyevna (Moscow)
Ovchinnikova, Nadezhda Ignatevna (St Petersburg)
Ozemblovskaia, Sofia Aleksandrovna (Perm)
Paches, Nikolai Ivanovich (Perm)
Paduchikh, Lydia Andreyeva (Orel, Usole district)
Panova, Nonna Vladimirovna (St Petersburg)
Paramonova, Margarita Ivanovna (St Petersburg)
Paramonova, Nina Pavlovna (St Petersburg)
Pavlovich, Aleksandr Georgievich (Moscow)
Perepechenko, Elizaveta Dmitrievna (Moscow)
Petrova, Galina Ivanovna (Strugi Krasnye)
Petrovich, Valentina Iakovlevna (Perm)
Piatnitsky, Vladimir Iosifovich (St Petersburg)
Pikulova, Anastasia Nikolaevna (Perm)
Pishchalnikova, Aleksandra Gavrilovna (Moscow)

Pleskina, Anastasia Gavrilovna (Krasnokamsk)
Poloz, Rada Mikhailovna (Moscow)
Ponomaryov, Nikolai Iakovlevich (Usole)
Popkova, Linda Emmanuilova (Usole)
Potapova, Nona Petrovna (Perm)
Potapova, Olga Mikhailovna (Petrozavodsk)
Potter, Nadezhda Nikolaevna (St Petersburg)
Pristupa, Vera Ignatevna (Norilsk)
Proskurina, Marina Semyonovna (Krasnokamsk)
Pukhova, Lydia Aleksandrovna (St Petersburg)
Radzevsky, Nikolai Semyonovich (Krasnokamsk)
Ragozina, Nadezhda Nikolaeva (Perm)
Ramenskaia, Olga Ivanovna (Strugi Krasnye)
Reifshneider, Ninel Kirillovna (Moscow)
Remchuk, Olga Grigorevna (Norilsk)
Riabova, Tamara Nikolaevna (Perm)
Riabtseva, Tatiana Yevgenevna (St Petersburg)
Riabushinsky, Mikhail Petrovich (Stavropol)
Rimm, Eduard Robertovich (Perm)
Rodak, Maia Isaakovna (Moscow)
Roginsky, Martyn Aleksandrovich (St Petersburg)
Romanov, Sergei Dmitrievich (Krasnokamsk)
Romanova, Natalia Ivanova (Krasnokamsk)
Romashkin, Mstislav Antonovich (Penza)
Romashkin, Vasily Feoktistovich (Norilsk)
Rozonovskaia, Svetlana Leonidovna (St Petersburg)
Sakulina, Ella Iakovlevna (Perm)
Saltykov, Leonid Konstantinovich (Perm)
Samieva, Inessa Petrovna (Pushkino)
Samsonov, Gennady Mikhailovich (Stavropol)
Sazhnov, Igor Natanovich (Norilsk)
Sazhnova, Nina Petrova (Saratov)
Sedukhina, Inessa Mikhailovna (Perm)
Selezneva, Vera Petrovna (Krasnokamsk)
Serbin, Semyon Semyonovich (Usole)
Serpokril, Nina Vasilevna (St Petersburg)
Shabrova, Iia Ivanovna (Moscow)
Shangina, Tatiana Mstislavovna (St Petersburg)
Shchegoleva, Yevgeniia Sergeyevna (Usole)
Shcherbakova, Emiliia Aleksandrovna (Perm)
Shchukina, Klavdiia Pavlovna (Perm)
Shchurenkova, Vera Anatolevna (Moscow)
Shenshina, Inna Yevgenevna (Perm)
Shikheyeva, Inna Aronovna (Moscow)
Shirkunova, Aleksandra Romanovna (Krasnokamsk)
Shirokikh, Pyotr Grigorevich (Perm)
Shishkina, Emma Ivanovna (Usole)
Shliapnikova, Klara Konstantinova (Krasnokamsk)
Shmelyov, Boris Vasilevich (St Petersburg)
Shtakelberg, Iurii Ivanovich (St Petersburg)
Shtein, Galina Aleksandrovna (Kirishi, Leningrad district)
Shumatov, Aleksandr Petrovich (Perm)
Shumilo, Vera Ivanovna (Norilsk)
Shumovsky, Teodor Abramovich (St Petersburg)

Shuvalova, Elena Vladimirovna (St Petersburg)
Shvartsvald-Khmyznikova, Elena Pavlovna (St Petersburg)
Shvartsvald-Khmyznikova, Konstantin Pavlovich (St Petersburg)
Shweitser, Viktoriia (Moscow)
Simonov, Aleksei Kirillovich (Moscow)
Simonova, Anna Iosifovna (St Petersburg)
Simonova, Maria Kirillovna (Moscow)
Simonova, Tatiana Petrovna (Krasnokamsk)
Sirman, Anzhelika Alekseyevna (St Petersburg)
Siuz-sin-Nian, Boris Ivanovich (Moscow)
Skachkova, Aleksandra Petrovna (Moscow)
Skachkova, Varvara Petrovna (St Petersburg)
Skanchenko, Nadezhda Ivanovna (Moscow)
Skorobogatov, Mikhail Mikhailovich (Perm)
Skripnik, Marta Ivanovna (Moscow)
Slanskaia, Veronika Petrovna (St Petersburg)
Slavina, Ida Ilinichna (Cologne, Germany)
Smelskaia, Valentina Stepanovna (St Petersburg)
Smirnova, Yevgeniia Vladimirovna (Moscow)
Soboleva, Nina Aleksandrovna (Perm)
Sorokina, Yekaterina Nikolaevna (Usole)
Stepanova, Antonina Fyodorovna (Perm)
Stepantseva, Natalia Ilinichna (Perm)
Stogova, Alla Aleksandrovna (Moscow)
Stogova, Liubov Ivanovna (Moscow)
Streletsky, Dmitry Nikolaevich (Perm)
Streletsky, Iurii Sergeyevich (St Petersburg)
Striapunin, Vasily Nikolaevich (Krasnokamsk)
Sukhobaevsky, Igor Iurevich (Norilsk)
Sushentseva, Liudmila Vasilevna (Perm)
Suutarinen, Khugo Ivanovich (Shemeinyi, Usole district)
Suvorov, Artur Mikhailovich (Moscow)
Suvorova, Diana Mikhailovna (Moscow)
Suvorova, Elizaveta Petrovna (Usole)
Svetlov, Iurii Valentinovich (Moscow)
Taisina, Rezeda Shamsuvalievna (Perm)
Tamanov, Boris Borisovich (Voronezh)
Tarasova, Nina Fyodorovna (Krasnokamsk)
Tell, Vilgelm Tosifovich (Moscow)
Tetiueva, Liubov Aleksandrovna (Perm)
Tikhanova, Valentina Aleksandrovna (Moscow)
Tikhantovskaia, Margarita Vasilevna (Perm)
Tikhomirov, Sergei Aleksandrovich (St Petersburg)
Tikhomirova, Elvina Georgievna (Perm)
Timofeyeva, Zoia Andreyevna (St Petersburg)
Titorenko, Nikita Stepanovich (Voronezh)
Tokmacheva, Yevgeniia Ivanovna (St Petersburg)
Torchinskaia, Elga Grigorevna (St Petersburg)
Treimanis, Maria Aleksandrovna (Norilsk)
Trofimova, Galina Yevgenevna (St Petersburg)
Tronina, Anna Ivanovna (Perm)
Tropina, Sofia Mikhailovna (Kolpino)
Trubina, Tamara Konstantinovna (Perm)
Turkina, Vera Aleksandrovna (Perm)

Uglitskikh, Ivan Ivanovich (Krasnokamsk)
Usanina, Valeriia Viktorovna (Perm)
Vangengeim, Eleonora Alekseyevna (Moscow)
Vasileva, Tatiana Pavlovna (St Petersburg)
Vasileva, Yevgeniia Pavlovna (St Petersburg)
Vasileva-Ruzova, Tatiana Sergeyevna (St Petersburg)
Vasiltseva, Vera Ivanovna (Perm)
Veber, Nina Vasilevna (Moscow)
Veksler, Arkadii Favishevich (St Petersburg)
Verzakova, Liudmila Nikolaevna (Krasnokamsk)
Vikhrova, Aleksandra Antonovna (Norilsk)
Vilensky, Nikolai Alekseyevich (Moscow)
Vinogradov, Iurii Abramovich (St Petersburg)
Violina, Lydia Mikhailovna (Moscow)
Vishniakova, Angelina Dmitrevna (Perm)
Vitkevich, Maria Ivanovna (St Petersburg)
Vittenburg, Yevgeniia Pavlovna (St Petersburg)
Vlasov, Vladimir Aleksandrovich (St Petersburg)
Volkonskaia, Elena (Cettona, Italy)
Volkov, Sergei Aleksandrovich (St Petersburg)
Volkova, Julia Mikhailovna (Moscow)
Volynets, Viktor Flegontovich (St Petersburg)
Vorobyov, Aleksei Mikhailovich (Moscow)
Vorovsky, Semyon Leonidovich (Moscow)
Yefremova, Nina Aleksandrovna (Perm)
Yegorovna, Vera Nikolaevna (Usole)
Yelsukova, Liudmila Anatolevna (Perm)
Yevangulova, Yevgeniia Pavlovna (St Petersburg)
Yevgenova, Irina Nikolaevna (St Petersburg)
Zagurskaia, Lilia Grigorevna (Moscow)
Zagurskaia, Tamara Grigorevna (Moscow)
Zaletaeva, Avgusta Pavlovna (Krasnokamsk)
Zavadskaia, Olga Sergeyevna (Irkutsk)
Zelenina, Nina Ignatevna (Perm)
Zelenina, Valentina Abramovna (Romanovo, Usole district)
Zeziulina, Anna Leonidovna (Perm)
Zhuravleva, Margarita Udovna (St Petersburg)
Zimniaia, Irina Nikolaevna (Moscow)
Znamenskaia, Antonina Nikolaevna (St Petersburg)
Zorin, Ilia Mikhailovich (Romanovo, Usole district)

Index

italic page numbers refer to illustrations